PETRE ŢUŢEA

Petre Ţuţea (1902–91) was one of the outstanding Christian dissident intellectuals of the Communist era in Eastern Europe. Revered as a saint by some, he spent thirteen years as a prisoner of conscience and twenty-eight years under house arrest at the hands of the *Securitate*. This book explores his unique response to the horrors of torture and 're-education' and reveals the experience of a whole generation detained in the political prisons. Ţuţea's understanding of human needs and how they can be fulfilled even amidst extreme adversity not only reflects huge learning and great brilliance of mind, but also offers a spiritual vision grounded in personal experience of the Romanian Gulag. Following the fall of the Ceauşescus, he has begun to emerge as a significant contributor to ecumenical Christian discourse and to understanding of wider issues of truth and reconciliation in the contemporary world.

As Ţuţea's pupil and scribe for twelve years, as a psychiatrist, and as a theologian, Alexandru Popescu is uniquely placed to present the work of this twentieth-century Confessor of the faith. Drawing on bibliographical sources which include unpublished or censored manuscripts and personal conversations with Ţuţea and with other prisoners of conscience in Romania, Popescu presents extensive translations of Ţuţea, which make his thought accessible to the English-speaking reader for the first time.

Through his stature as a human being and his authority as a thinker, Petre Ţuţea challenges us to question many of our assumptions. The choice he presents between 'sacrifice' and 'moral suicide' focuses us on the very essence of religion and human personhood. Resisting any ultimate separation of theology and spirituality, his work affirms hope and love as the sole ground upon which truth can be based. At the same time, hope and love are not mere ideal emotions, but are known and lived in engagement with the real world – in politics, economics, science, ecology, and the arts, and in participation in the Divine Liturgy that is at once the traditional offering of the Church and the cosmic drama of the incarnate Word.

It is splendid that this work is being published. It presents an enormous contribution to East–West understanding: the Romanian perspective has a specially important part to play. A very admirable work.
The Most Revd Dr Rowan Williams, Archbishop of Canterbury

Ţuţea ranks alongside Bonhoeffer in articulating the philosophy of Christian endurance. I have cherished the hope that an English publisher may publish this work.
The Revd Canon Oliver O'Donovan, Regius Professor of Moral and Pastoral Theology, Christ Church, Oxford

This pioneering work in a new interdisciplinary field – the psychology of religion – is of profound importance, not only to those concerned with Eastern European Orthodoxy during the late twentieth century, but to a much wider public who are interested in the relationship between theology, psychology of religion, and the political sciences.
The Right Revd Dr Kallistos Ware, Bishop of Diokleia, Spalding Lecturer in Eastern Orthodox Studies, University of Oxford

Popescu offers a comprehensive understanding and a thorough mastery of Ţuţea's writings, as well as of the context – political, philosophical, and personal – of their production. This excellent account of many of Ţuţea's most important preoccupations (his theological anthropology and his understanding of spirituality, his critiques of Soviet-style political life, his experiences as a political prisoner, and his metaphysics of differentiation and understanding of creation) will serve as a bench-mark for future interpretation. The author's unique knowledge of Ţuţea has been put to very good use.
The Revd Canon John Webster, Lady Margaret Professor of Divinity, Christ Church, Oxford

A truly epoch-making book. I don't recollect ever having recommended a book more strongly for publication. Popescu puts the Romanian Orthodox Church centre stage and brings an element into focus which is hardly known to anyone outside his own country. Ţuţea is a figure of seminal importance, and one of the great figures of the universal Church of the twentieth century. This book provides a perspective on the history of the traumatic Ceauşescu years. Popescu and Ţuţea between them provide a philosophical and Christian basis for placing the disaster of Communism in its proper perspective and offer pointers to the future. It is not just a study of Islam which challenges the Christian world today.
The Revd Canon Michael Bourdeaux, DD, Founder of Keston Institute, Oxford

This work on Ţuţea has opened my eyes to important aspects of recent church history, particularly the revival of an ascetic theology in the Orthodox tradition. This book presents a real contribution to the history of theology and reflects Popescu's intellectual ability both as a theologian and as a psychiatrist.
The Revd Dr Christopher Rowland, Dean Ireland's Professor of Holy Scripture, Queen's College, Oxford

Petre Țuțea
Between Sacrifice and Suicide

ALEXANDRU POPESCU
Balliol College, University of Oxford
Fellow of the George Bell Institute, UK

ASHGATE

Published by
Ashgate Publishing Limited
Gower House
Croft Road
Aldershot
Hants GU11 3HR
England

Ashgate Publishing Company
Suite 420
101 Cherry Street
Burlington
VT 05401–4405
USA

Ashgate website: http://www.ashgate.com

British Library Cataloguing in Publication Data
Popescu, Alexandru
    Petre Ţuţea : between sacrifice and suicide
    1.Ţuţea, Petre 2.Christians – Romania – Biography
    3.Theologians – Romania – Biography 4.Political prisoners –
    Romania – Biography
    I.Title
    281.9'498'092

US Library of Congress Cataloging-in-Publication Data
Popescu, Alexandru D. (Alexandru Daniel), 1960–
    Petre Ţuţea : between sacrifice and suicide / Alexandru Popescu.
        p. cm.
    Includes bibliographical references and index.
    ISBN 0-7546-3550-3 (alk. paper) – ISBN 0-7546-5006-5 (pbk. : alk. paper)
        1. Ţuţea, Petre. I. Title.

    B4825.T874P66 2003
    230'.19'092—dc22

                                                                2003057841

ISBN 0 7546 3550 3 (Hbk)
ISBN 0 7546 5006 5 (Pbk)

Printed on acid-free paper.

Typeset in Times New Roman by N^{2}productions.
Printed and bound in Great Britain by MPG Books Ltd, Bodmin, Cornwall.

This book is dedicated with much love and gratitude to
Eufrosina Costea-Yanchenko (1907–2000), my grandmother,
whose family endured the Gulag. From her I gained
the strength to complete this work.

We have all emerged from Țuțea's overcoat, just as the great Russian writers came out of Gogol's *Overcoat*.

Mircea Eliade[1]

Țuțea was not a man, he was a universe... One had to recognise that his ego was a sort of absolute, and accept that this led him to speak as if he had just been elected head of state or head of the entire universe.

Emil Cioran[2]

To my master and brother Petre Țuțea, the most authentic Orthodox thinker in Romania, in homage and profound admiration.

Fr Dumitru Stăniloae[3]

1   Reported to the author in separate interviews by Christinel Eliade and Ioan Alexandru. See Bibliography.
2   Gabriel Liiceanu, *Itinéraires d'une vie: E.M. Cioran, suivi de Les Continents de l'insomnie, entretien avec E.M. Cioran*, French trans. Alexandra Laignel-Lavastine (Paris: Michalon, 1995), pp. 98–9.
3   Inscribed on the front page of Țuțea's copy of Stăniloae's book, *Spiritualitate și Comuniune în Liturghia Ortodoxă*, Bucharest, 9 May 1990. [*Spirituality and Communion in the Orthodox Liturgy.*]

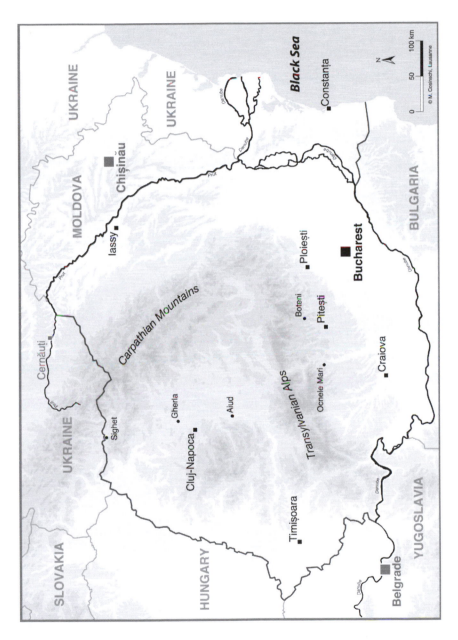

Map of Present-Day Romania

Contents

List of Plates

Foreword

What matters most about human nature will often appear only when humanity is most severely under attack, when the human face is most obscured by violence and evil. Some have written of the twentieth century as the age of the 'death-cell philosopher' – a phrase used by the late Margaret Masterman, a distinguished philosopher of science and expert in communications theory; there are things about human nature which are discovered only in the extreme places of experience, in the camps and the Gulag. Here, it is not only a matter of facing death – we must all do that – it is facing the systematic denial of freedom, truth and hope, and so facing death in its most acutely meaningless shape.

This book is the record of a death-cell philosopher. His history is in miniature the history of a great swathe of the European experience in the modern age: living through the dissolution of traditional social forms, the rise of Fascism, that seductive and deceptive response to modernity's challenges, the removal of literal as well as moral landmarks in the wake of the Second World War and the advent of what we see more and more as a sustained attempt to reinvent humanity in the imposition of Communist tyranny. Some of the most unforgettable pages of this remarkable book are those where we read about how the reinvention of humanity in the horrific re-education programmes of the Romanian prison camps prompted the reinvention in another sense of the Christian Church. The solidarity in profound prayer, patient suffering, and eager learning that emerged around figures like Țuțea shows dramatically what the Church most seriously and deeply is: an alternative human community whose indestructible strength rests upon the fact that it works with the creator's purpose for humanity. The disfigured face of humanity revealed in the workings of the camps is *transfigured* by the presence and witness of those who reflect in their own faces the reality of Christ.

Petre Țuțea comes before us here in all his human and intellectual complexity; he is not a two-dimensional saint or hero, he arrives at his transfiguring faith after false starts and a good deal of flailing around in the ferment of pre-war Romania (and what a world that was, still looking for a chronicler who can do justice to the years when Bucharest was one of the most intellectually exciting cities in Europe). But the person who emerges into the light in the post-war years of persecution and humiliation is a truly extraordinary man. One element that stands out most clearly in this portrait is the discovery of a *priestly* calling and identity that is much larger and deeper than any ecclesiastical office. Looking at the theology of Țuțea's friend and fellow sufferer, Fr Dumitru Stăniloae, one of the foremost Orthodox theologians of the century, we can see something of a common vision when Stăniloae writes of the essence of priesthood as giving a voice to the prayer, the need and the love of the Body of Christ.

xi

Ţuţea did not think of his rôle as 'priestly' because he was a counsellor or a problem solver or a provider of religious comfort, but because he had been given the grace of providing a voice for the vision of humanity made in God's image and called to the common service of worship – liturgy in its widest sense. He does not always quote the familiar theological texts; he does not offer systematic theological analyses of the doctrinal heritage of his church. But, as Dr Popescu shows, his vision is again and again shaped by the most significant currents of Eastern Christian thinking; you can hear very plainly the voice of Maximus the Confessor and Gregory Palamas in his meditations, and he demonstrates what many Orthodox writers of the past century have claimed, that the great themes of this theology have more pertinence than ever in an age when the human face is so disfigured by cruelty and ignorance.

Ţuţea is strikingly free, however, from the almost routine criticisms of Western religious thought that are common in Orthodox writers, and, while his loyalties and priorities are not in doubt, he is able to use elements of medieval and modern Western thinking to fill out his picture. In this, he is reminiscent of some of the Russian thinkers of the pre-Revolutionary period who were eager to reclaim Orthodox theology as the key to a proper response to modern fragmentation and confusion, but were not therefore disposed to ignore the reflections of the same Christian wisdom in the Western Christian world. So Ţuţea would, I think, have appreciated being linked with one particular Roman Catholic writer of recent decades, Donald Nicholl (another lay theologian whose charisms would have been described by many as 'priestly' in much the same sense as Ţuţea's). Nicholl wrote a short essay in 1969[*] on what he called the 'biological mutation' in humanity represented by Stalinist and post-Stalinist practice, and pointed to the way in which the ancient tradition of being a fool for Christ's sake had come to life again in this environment. In an environment where the inhuman is taken for granted as normal, the calling to holiness can become a calling to ask the unimaginable, the ludicrous question. What Ţuţea has to say about the *homo stultus* of the Communist regimes is very close to this, and his own witness has about it some of that *yurodstvo*, that holy folly, which Nicholl identifies.

Dr Popescu is uniquely qualified to write such a study as this. Equipped both in psychological and in theological skills to a rare degree, he has an almost unparalleled personal knowledge of Ţuţea – and he knows from within the pressures and the costs of living in the middle of the 'biological mutation' that was nurtured in the days of Ceauşescu. This is a book about a spiritual giant from a world little known to the English-speaking reader, but it will undoubtedly stir the desire to know more of that world and of its spiritual resources – the revival of monastic spirituality in the midst of the modern urban setting, the rediscovery of classical theology as liberation and enlargement represented by so many modern Romanian writers like Stăniloae. Dr Popescu does not force the point; but, as we read, we may well recognise that there are

---

[*]   Donald Nicholl, 'Stalinensis/*yurodivi*', reprinted in his *The Beatitude of Truth, Reflections of a Lifetime*, ed. Adrian Hastings (London: Darton, Longman and Todd, 1997), pp. 114–21.

tyrannies other than those of a totalitarian state. The human can be disfigured in other ways, the 'biological mutation' can be cultivated in other laboratories even if they are labelled 'free' and 'democratic'. If this book is read merely as a record of heroic resistance against a tyranny somewhere over there, supported by an impressive but rather exotic religious system, it will have failed. Dr Popescu has written a tract for our times, that should be pertinent to the whole of the 'new world order' that we inhabit but are only just beginning to understand. Christian witness and reflection need to engage in this task of understanding with all the resources they can; but we shall do well to remember that Marx was right at least in saying that the task was transformation, not just understanding. Țuțea's life and work are a record of transformation, and they should stir us to the same hope.

The Most Revd Dr Rowan Williams, Archbishop of Canterbury

Preface

As a first-year medical student, Alexandru Popescu found himself quite by chance at the bedside in a Bucharest hospital of Petre Țuțea, an aged Christian visionary and philosopher. Even though the older man's ideas were strange to the young Alex, who had recently completed a Marxist–Leninist education, the two established an immediate bond. The patient was soon to become the doctor's mentor; the doctor, his student.

These were dangerous times in Romania. Nicolae Ceaușescu was in his heyday, his 'tolerant' and non-conformist image, well polished for foreign consumption, being the exact opposite of the reality of his savage domestic policies. Thus, when Alex became Țuțea's disciple, he was risking his career, possibly even his liberty. Nevertheless, the relationship lasted for twelve years, right up to Țuțea's death in 1991. *Between Sacrifice and Suicide* is therefore, in a sense, autobiographical, while at the same time being a remarkable study of an outstanding Christian of the second half of the twentieth century.

At the heart of this book is the conflict between atheist materialism and Christian belief. This was the religious battlefield of the twentieth century and one of the most unyielding of all time. It continues even today in some parts of the world and the fall-out from it affects religious life in many post-Soviet States. It is, therefore, remarkable that not more attention has been paid to it by scholars, particularly to its philosophical aspect. Possibly this lacuna may be explained by the fact that it was the Orthodox Church which bore the brunt of the assault. This, whether in its Russian, Romanian, Bulgarian or even Greek forms, remains too little known outside the territories where Orthodoxy predominates.

The siege of the citadel of Catholicism at the Reformation has stimulated a bibliography of tens of thousands of titles. The siege of the Orthodox Church by Communist atheism was an attack not just on a religious system, but on the very roots of a Faith that had lasted for almost a millennium. This was a seismic upheaval in history, comparable in scale – however different in its substance – to the Reformation itself. The survival, and now the revival, not only of the Orthodox Church, but also of other main streams of the Faith was the major event in world religion in the last century. Neither East nor West shows an inclination to devote any significant resources to the study of this massive although failed experiment in human engineering; yet this work must be done in the greatest detail if future tragedies are to be avoided. This alone is reason enough to welcome Popescu's outstanding work. There are only a few in-depth studies of the Church under Communism, however, and those which exist concentrate mainly on the Catholic Church. George Weigel's ground-breaking study of the influence of Pope John Paul II on the democratic process in Poland, *The Final Revolution: the Resistance Church and the Collapse of Communism*, provides a marker for future work. Regarding the Orthodox Church, there is nothing to compare with the late Jane Ellis's book, *The Russian Orthodox Church: A Contemporary History*, published as long ago as 1985.

Petre Țuțea remained almost unknown during his lifetime, even in Romania (the only exception being those in his immediate circle, especially his fellow prisoners, who shared with him years of imprisonment and torture). Popescu not only reveals his stature as a Christian lay leader, but also represents him as one of the great figures of the universal Church of the twentieth century, a man of exceptional physical endurance and philosophical depth, who both exhibited and inspired moral resilience and excellence. To the Romanian people, this book will reveal a new area of understanding of their immediate past (if a Romanian version can be published); to the English-speaking world, it will make known Petre Țuțea's name and his system of belief, forged as it was under prison conditions of extreme brutality. Popescu describes this torture and the coinciding evolution of the Christian answer to it in a fascinating and masterly way (Chapter 4 being unlike anything else which exists even in the extensive literature on the Soviet Gulag). The Russian word for the kind of Christian heroism described here, untranslatable into English, is *podvig*. Only when the concept behind this word becomes well known will the world at large understand why the Orthodox faith finally overcame the State-imposed system which tried systematically to eliminate it. This book makes possible the knowledge of Petre Țuțea's *podvig* and will help humanity avoid the repeat of such a tragedy.

Alex Popescu himself experienced the journey to the Faith, largely under the influence of the subject of his biographical study. It happened that these years, 1980–91, also encompassed the pomp and the fall of the tyrant Ceaușescu himself. Therefore the narrative of Țuțea's life and the analysis of his philosophy is played out against a dramatic political backdrop. The author and his subject provide a Christian basis for placing the disaster of Communism in its proper perspective and, at the same time, give direction to the future.

I have known Alex for ten years now, since he came to England under the Oxford Theological Exchange Programme. This book is the culmination of that decade of work, for which he has already received his doctorate. Even after spending a lifetime studying the Church under Communism, I had never heard of Petre Țuțea until I reviewed Alex's application to come to Oxford. Țuțea's name will be unknown to most English-speaking people who encounter this book; but it is written so clearly and beautifully that it should not be difficult for the careful reader to absorb Țuțea's life story or to apprehend his fascinating and individual philosophy. It is truly a privilege – one of my most valued in recent years – to be asked to write a preface for this book, and I do not recollect ever having recommended a work more strongly.

The Revd Canon Michael Bourdeaux

Acknowledgements

The original impetus for this book came from a song which my late grandmother sang to me after 1989. It was a song from the Soviet Gulag, which she had learnt from her brother who himself had died in the Gulag. The song begins:

I know I shall die,
but my song will live on
for my song is the beating
of your heart, little girl…

God's grace working through innumerable channels has made this book possible. In acknowledging my thanks to the many people who have helped me, I do not mention their titles, distinguished as these often are. Recalling the central experience of Țuțea's theology, that of divine encounter in recognition of God's image in the human person, I simply thank people by name. I record my indebtedness to the hundreds of Țuțea's fellow prisoners whose names we shall never know, and whose witness, ideas, and prayers enriched his *oeuvre*.

I am grateful for the assistance given to me by many people. I would particularly like to acknowledge the help received from my doctoral supervisor Kallistos Ware, whose original idea it was to write this book, for his inspiration, love, and scholarly guidance. I am also grateful to Hugh Wybrew, my co-supervisor, who for six years generously collaborated with me on the first English translation of some of Petre Țuțea's writings. A person who encouraged me to start this thesis was Baruch Blumberg. I shall never forget our providential meeting in Balliol College Hall when he helped me to see that it was my vocation to conduct this interdisciplinary research on the psychology and spirituality of political prisoners under Communism. Creative and sacrificial help with my translations came from Isabel Mary, Edna Monica, and the late Eileen Mary, from whom I learnt my knowledge of theology and deepened my love for the English language. I am profoundly indebted to Rowan Williams for his unfailing encouragement and care. Basil Osborne has supported me unconditionally in this work.

I would also like to thank: John Webster, Christopher Rowland, Oliver O'Donovan, John Macquarrie, Richard Swinburne, Thomas Torrance, John McGuckin, and the late Hugh Trevor-Roper, for their kind advice and suggestions throughout my years of research in Britain; Michael Bourdeaux, Margaret Yee, James Brock, Mark Chapman, Charles Miller, David Moss, Catherine Atherton, Caroline Humfress, Mark Edwards, and John Nandriş, for their lasting friendship and stimulating criticism; Douglas Dupree and John Jones, for having made possible my research in

Oxford; the late Elizabeth Leyland whose home in Old Headington provided such a good atmosphere for writing a D.Phil.; the Community of the Resurrection (Mirfield), the Community of the Sisters of the Love of God (Oxford), Church Mission Society, the George Bell Institute, Daphne Worraker, and Şerban Cantacuzino, who offered me their friendship, fellowship, and financial support during my period of full-time research; Jonathan Greener and James Neal, whose help in revising an early version of this book was invaluable. Xenia Dennen gave me enormous support by proof-reading the typescript and compiling the index. Cristina Neagu advised me on the bibliography. Micheline Cosinschi provided the map of Romania. I am greatly indebted to Jan Ross for her editorial suggestions and constructive criticism.

My thanks are also due to: Nicolae Chirilă and Marcel Petrişor for allowing me access to Ţuţea's unpublished manuscripts and photographs; Ileana Tilea for making letters available to me from the archive of her father, the diplomat V.V. Tilea; the late Emil Cioran and Simone Boué who spoke to me in Paris about Cioran's deep friendship with Ţuţea; the late Christinel Eliade who talked to me in Chicago in 1993 about the bonds of affection between Eliade and Ţuţea; Nicolaus Sombart for his hospitality during my stay in Berlin; the family in Bonn of the late Ioan Alexandru, poet of Transylvania and disciple of Ţuţea; Ioana Pavelescu who gave me permission to quote from her MA thesis; Gabriela Dumitrescu of the Romanian Academy Library who provided me with material from the library's collections of Romanian periodicals; Mircea Coloşenco who shared with me his research on Ţuţea; Marius Şopterean who assisted me in tracking down archival material.

I am grateful to Constantin Dimoftache-Zeletin, for his inspiring friendship and erudition. I also extend thanks to Virgil Cândea, Mihai Cârciog, Alexandru Dragomir, Andrei Pleşu, Emilian Popescu, and Mihail Şora, for their advice and encouragement. Maria Neagu gave me access to her private library.

I am very grateful to the holders of the following archives for allowing me to use various documents: Arhiva Ministerului Afacerilor Externe al României, Bucharest; Arhivele Naţionale ale României, Direcţia Arhivelor Centrale, Bucharest; Direcţia Judeţeană Argeş and Direcţia Judeţeană Cluj; Biblioteca Academiei Române; Geheimes Staatsarchiv Preußischer Kulturbesitz, Berlin-Dahlem; Institutul Român – Biblioteca Română, Freiburg im Breisgau; Universitätsarchiv, Humboldt University, Berlin; Arhiva Stării Civile, Primăria Comunei Boteni, Argeş; private archives: Vasile Arimia, Ion-Octavian Bănică, Corina Constantinescu, Camelia Cristian, Mihai Neagu, Nicolae Tatu, Viorel Ţuţea. Sorin Ilieşiu provided videographic images of Ţuţea.

Survivors of political prisons have provided me with vital information about their years of imprisonment. I am profoundly grateful to the following: the late Sofian Boghiu, Dumitru Bordeianu, Adelina Busuiocescu-Călin, Nectarie Ciolacu, Petre Ercuţă, Paul Gălăşanu, Simion Ghinea, Nicolae Grebenea, Virgil Mateiaş, Gheorghe Măruţă, Nicu Naum, Horia Stanca, and Vasile Vasilachi; Bartolomeu Anania, Demostene Andronescu, Grigore Băbuş, Olimpiu Borzea, Roman Braga, Ion Cazacu, Cornel Deneşeanu, Felix Dubneac, Gabriel Dumitrescu, Ion Gavrilă-Ogoranu, Ion Halmaghi, Aristide Ionescu, Ioan Iovan, Radu Mărculescu, Iuliana Mihail, Ioan Negruţiu, Mircea Nicolau, Nicolae Nicolau, Aspazia Oţel Petrescu, Zahu Pană,

Arsenie Papacioc, Justin Pârvu, Traian Popescu, Eugen Raţiu, Tache Rodas, Corneliu Ursu, Raul Volcinschi; Alexandr Ogorodnikov, Irina Ratushinskaya, Vladimir Shchelkashchyov, and the late Kenneth McAll.

The book could not have been completed without the help, wit, and devotion of James Ramsay. I treasure his friendship as a gift from the Holy Spirit. Finally, I am most grateful to my family in Romania, Russia, and England, for their loving support and encouragement.

Ad majorem Dei gloriam.

A Note on Țuțea's Use of Language

Petre Țuțea[1] at times expresses himself in a way that some (especially Western) readers may find narrowly focused on the priestly ritual and liturgy of the Christian Church. There are two points to be made here. First, Țuțea did not consider it ultimately possible to separate liturgical categories of experience from the process of intellectual enquiry and analysis. This affects the way he uses language. The Romanian literary critic Ștefan Lavu, writing in 1968, described Țuțea as having a *hieratism intelectual impunător*, literally an 'impressive intellectual hieratism'.[2] The word *hieratism* is a highly unusual word in Romanian, and captures not only the idiosyncratic nature of Țuțea's style, but also his understanding of intellectual activity as having a hieratic, priestly character. The second point, that will help the reader engage with Țuțea, concerns his understanding of the Church and liturgy.

For Țuțea, the worship of God is, so to speak, the iconic form of humanity. Far from being confined to church ritual, true worship is the sacrificial offering of each person's whole life and being to God through Christ. Liturgical celebration in church is definitive of the full offering of this sacrifice. At the same time, to participate liturgically without active discipleship in love and service to God and one's neighbour, in every aspect and moment of life, is not a full celebration of the Liturgy.

Țuțea sees 'Church' as defined by the visible Tradition, yet this includes God's personal calling of every individual, and can never be confined to the ecclesiological self-definitions of an institution. The Church in Țuțea's own life and religious practice was the Romanian Orthodox Church. However, it is striking in his writing how rarely he refers to Orthodoxy as such. He almost invariably spoke of Christianity or the Church without denominational reference. Perhaps the fact that he was not a priest, monk, or formally trained theologian makes him all the more difficult to place in a systematic 'classification' of denominational identity. Of course, his theological understanding was also enriched by what he learnt from Greek and Roman Catholics, Protestants, Jews, Muslims, and agnostics in the 'Great University' of political prison.

Rooted in Orthodox practice and tradition, he nevertheless consistently went against the grain of his fellow Orthodox thinkers by using terms of Latin rather than Slav origin, closer to the Greek-Catholic tradition. For example, *sacru* ('sacred') rather than *sfânt*; *spirit* ('spirit') rather than *duh*; *damnațiune* ('damnation') rather than *pedeapsă*.[3] He uses the Greek word *mister* ('mystery') rather than the Slavonic

---

1   Pronounced 'tzutzea'.
2   Ștefan Lavu, 'Confuzie', *Familia*, Oradea, December 1968, p. 23.
3   See, for example, Petre Țuțea, 'Oaspete la Petre Țuțea', interview by Theodor Redlow, *Alternative*, Bucharest, June 1990, p. 1. ['A Visit to Țuțea'.]

taină. He quoted Thomas à Kempis's *Imitatio Christi* in preference to Nicholas Cabasilas's discourses concerning *The Life in Christ*, although he had both on his shelves. As I will show, he would refer to Aquinas freely, but would only refer to a pre-schismatic theologian such as Dionysius the Pseudo-Areopagite in his criticisms of the *Summa Theologiae*.

His extensive knowledge of the Western tradition and formulation of profoundly Orthodox theology in such uncompromisingly Western terms have meant that his Orthodox 'credentials' are sometimes questioned by those who, perhaps understandably, but nevertheless superficially, have a distrust of everything Western. It is precisely this cross-cultural dynamic that makes him significant to contemporary ecumenical discussion. His Christian identity is neither 'other-worldly' nor, on the other hand, 'above transcendence'.

In seeking to express this vision, it is hardly surprising that Ţuţea used language in a way that at times stretches the very fabric of conventional grammar and vocabulary. In this prefatory note I have tried to alert the reader to a particular aspect of this, in relation to his use of the terms 'Church' and 'Liturgy'. However, his writing as a whole raises constant questions of translation, since it has a peculiarly personal, often oral, stylistic 'content'. On the whole, in trying to render Ţuţea into English, I have sought to achieve a natural idiomatic style of English and, thus, have been quite free on occasions with the sentence structure and idioms of the original (as tends to be required anyway in moving from any Romance language to Anglo-Saxon). However, where the original is particularly idiosyncratic, I have tried to suggest something of the same style. This is especially the case in Ţuţea's use of certain words, like 'theandry', 'objecticity', and 'suprahistory'. Where Ţuţea uses *omul* as a matter of course to mean 'mankind' I prefer to say 'the human being' or, occasionally, 'humanity' rather than 'man'.

Unless otherwise specified, all biblical passages in this book are from *The Orthodox Study Bible, New Testament and Psalms* (Nashville, TN: Thomas Nelson, 1993).

Chronological Table

Year	Historical Context	Petre Țuțea
1858		Birth of Țuțea's father, Petre Bădescu (d. 1925).
1859	The Southern and Eastern provinces of modern Romania (the Kingdoms of Wallachia and Moldavia) are united.	
1881	Wallachia and Moldavia become a single Kingdom under Carol I.	
1885		Birth of Țuțea's mother, Ana Simon Oprea Țuțea (d. 1960).
6 October 1902		Birth of Petre Țuțea, in Boteni, Muscel.
1909–14		Primary School in Boteni.
1914–18	First World War. German occupation of Romania.	Secondary School (Gymnasium Dinicu Golescu) in Câmpulung.
1917	Russian Revolution.	
1918	Formation of the modern Romanian State, Greater Romania, by the union of Transylvania with the Kingdom of Wallachia and Moldavia.	
1918–20		Studies interrupted due to post-war circumstances.
1920–23		State scholar at Lyceum George Barițiu in Cluj-Napoca.
1921	Romanian Communist Party founded.	

Year	Historical Context	Petre Țuțea
1922	Mussolini's dictatorship established in Italy.	
October 1924 – January 1928		Master's degree in Law at King Ferdinand I University in Cluj-Napoca.
1927	*Legiunea Arhanghelului Mihail* (Legion of the Archangel Michael) founded – renamed *Garda de Fier* (Iron Guard) in 1931.	
1928–29		Begins to publish articles in *Patria* and *Chemarea Tinerimei Române* (newspapers of the National Peasant Party in Cluj-Napoca).
1928	The Ukrainian Vitaly Kholostenko becomes General Secretary of the Romanian Communist Party.	
June 1929		Doctorate in Administrative Law.
1929–32		Works at the magistrates' court in Pui, Transylvania.
November 1932		Co-founds the Marxist journal *Stânga*, in Bucharest.
1933	Hitler becomes Chancellor of the German Third Reich.	Head of Department in the Ministry of Trade and Industry.
1933–34		'Țuțea studies in Berlin and expects, with unrealistic hopes, democratic reform in Romania' (Emil Cioran, letter from Berlin).
1935		Co-authors *Manifestul Revoluției Naționale* (*The National Revolution Manifesto*).

Year	Historical Context	Petre Ţuţea
1936–39		Director in the Ministry of Trade and Industry (renamed Ministry of National Economy in April 1938), in charge of the Office of Economic Publications and Propaganda.
1938	King Carol II establishes royal dictatorship in Romania.	Contributes articles to Nae Ionescu's *Cuvântul* (*The Word*).
1939–45	Second World War. Romania is initially neutral, but later becomes a German ally.	
1940	King Carol II abdicates, following the annexation of Bessarabia by the USSR, and of Transylvania by Hungary (Vienna Diktat). Mihai I becomes king.	Director of the Research Office in the new Ministry of Foreign Trade.
13 September 1940	Romania is declared a National Legionary State.	
November 1940– February 1941		Travels to Moscow as a member of the Romanian economic delegation.
21 January 1941	'Legionary Rebellion'.	
27 January 1941	The National Legionary State is abolished.	
1941	Stalin has tens of thousands of Romanians deported to Siberia.	
22 June 1941	Marshall Ion Antonescu becomes dictator and declares war on USSR.	Asks to be sent to the front line (USSR), but the Ministry of External Affairs refuses.
1941–44		Director in the Ministry of War Economy.
23 August 1944	Romania changes allegiance to the Allies. Antonescu is arrested.	Director of Studies in the Ministry of National Economy.

Year	Historical Context	Petre Țuțea
30 December 1947	Under pressure from the USSR, King Mihai I abdicates. Romania is proclaimed a People's Republic. Russification begins.	
11 June 1948	Communism is officially established in Romania under Soviet control.	
1948–53		Arrested and imprisoned without trial in various political prisons. Accused of being 'Anglo-American spy', and undergoes the first phase of re-education in Ocnele Mari.
1949–52	Re-education experiment starts in Romania.	
1953	Death of Stalin. Russification continues. The spelling of the country's name is changed from Românía to Romînía (to obscure the Romance etymology).	
May 1953		Released from prison.
May 1953– December 1956		Unable to find work; lives with friends.
October 1956	Soviet forces suppress the Hungarian uprising and install a new pro-USSR government in Budapest.	
December 1956– August 1964		Imprisoned again without trial.
1958	The Red Army withdraws from Romania.	
1960–64		In Aiud prison, where he is subjected to the second phase of re-education.
1961	Foundation of Amnesty International.	

Year	Historical Context	Petre Ţuţea
1962	Collectivisation of agriculture is completed.	
August 1964	General amnesty of political prisoners.	Released from Aiud.
August 1964 onwards		Unemployed. Known as the 'street philosopher' of Bucharest.
August 1964– December 1989		Under *Securitate* surveillance.
1965	Nicolae Ceauşescu becomes leader of the Romanian Communist Party. American troops arrive in Vietnam.	Produces a treatise on the principles of co-operation, which he passes to the Communist Party Central Committee. No answer received.
1968	Ceauşescu refuses to assist Soviet 'intervention' in Czechoslovakia, marking a cooling of relations between Romania and the USSR.	Publishes for the first time fragments of his dialogues (*Bios* and *Eros*) and of his play (*Everyday Happenings*).
1969		Finishes writing *The Philosophy of Nuances*.
1971	Ceauşescu visits North Korea and China.	
1974	Ceauşescu becomes President of Romania.	
1977	Devastating earthquake in Bucharest.	Begins to write his *Religious Reflections on Human Knowledge*.
1978	Queen Elizabeth II makes Ceauşescu Knight Grand Cross, Order of the Bath (knighthood withdrawn after his execution in 1989).	
1982	According to Ceauşescu, Romanians are eating too much. The Rational Eating Programme is introduced.	

Year	Historical Context	Petre Țuțea
1983	Decree no. 98/1983: possession of typewriter requires police authorisation.	
July 1983		Dictates *A Meeting with Brâncuşi*.
1984 onwards		Works on his *Treatise on Christian Anthropology* (never completed). Friends and disciples are interrogated by *Securitate*.
1985	*Perestroika* is launched by Gorbachev in the USSR. Decree no. 410/1985: abortion is legal if the woman has delivered five children and has them under her care. Culture of *nici o ovulaţie fără fecundaţie* (no ovulation without fecundity) begins.	
1987	Demonstrations by workers in Braşov calling for reform. They are brutally suppressed by the army and *Securitate*.	*A Meeting with Brâncuşi* (1st published 1985) is republished under Țuțea's own name.
1988	Rural systematisation programme introduced.	
1989	Public uprising against the government.	Begins to dictate *Dogmas*, the final part of his *Christian Anthropology*.
25 December 1989	Nicolae and Elena Ceauşescu executed following mock trial.	
1 January 1990		Visits Dumitru Mazilu, Vice-President of the new National Salvation Front.

Year	Historical Context	Petre Țuțea
22 April–13 June 1990	Prolonged occupation of University Square in Bucharest by anti-Communist students and intellectuals. Miners are drafted in to disperse them. Numerous casualties, including people not involved in the demonstration.	Becomes a public figure following a national television interview. Becomes a member of the National Liberal Party. To show his support, Lech Walesa sends personal greetings via a Polish journalist.
20 May 1990	Communist leader Ion Iliescu becomes President of Romania.	
1991	Gulf War. Boris Yeltsin becomes President of Russia.	Admitted to Christiana Orthodox Hospital in Bucharest.
3 December 1991		Dies at Christiana Orthodox Hospital. Later buried at Boteni. English-language obituaries appear in the *Independent*, the *Guardian*, and on BBC Radio.
1992	The Yugoslav Federation disintegrates.	
1992 onwards		More than ten books by Țuțea are published with national sales and international interest.
1993		Țuțea's *Bios* and *Eros* are staged in front of the Egyptian pyramids, in the open air.

List of Abbreviations[1]

APHORISMS	*321 Aphorisms of Petre Țuțea* (1st edn 1993)
BGMP	*Between God and My People* (1992)
DAYS	*Days with Petre Țuțea* (1st edn 1992)
DIALOGUES	*Last Dialogues with Petre Țuțea* (2000)
DOGMAS	*Treatise on Christian Anthropology. Dogmas* (2000)
ELIADE	*Mircea Eliade. An Essay* (1992)
INTERVIEW	'Interview on the Operating Table' (*Viața Medicală*, 1990)
MANIFESTO	*National Revolution Manifesto* (1st edn 1935)
NUANCES	*Philosophy of Nuances* (1995)
OLD AGE	*Old Age and Other Philosophical Texts* (1992)
ON ART	'On the Power and Limits of Art' (*Sourozh*, 1997)
PROBLEMS	*Treatise on Christian Anthropology. Problems* (1992)
PROJECT	*Project for a Treatise. Eros* (1992)
REFLECTIONS	*Religious Reflections on Human Knowledge* (part I, 1992; part II, 1977, unpublished manuscript)
RESTORATION	'The Restoration of the Natural Order' (*Timpul*, 1990)
SOPHISTRY	'The Apparent Triumph of Sophistry in the Modern World, or the Utilitarian Caricature of the Real' (undated typescript)
STYLES	*Treatise on Christian Anthropology. Styles* (parts I and II, 1988, typescript)
SYSTEMS	*Treatise on Christian Anthropology. Systems* (1993)
THEATRE	*The World as Theatre. Theatre as Seminar* (1993)

---

1   Abbreviations of titles of works by Petre Țuțea frequently referred to in the text. See Bibliography for full titles and publication details.

Chapter 1

Introduction

In a life that spanned almost the entire twentieth century, Petre Țuțea experienced the formation of the modern Romanian State in 1918, both World Wars, the traumatic decades of the Communist 'experiment', and the 'Stolen Revolution'[1] of 1989. For much of his adult life he was in political prisons or under city arrest. His influence in post-revolutionary Romania has been considerable. His works are widely published, and his sayings quoted. His experience of prison and torture stands as a paradigm of the experiences endured by hundreds of thousands of people of many different faiths and world views. His death in 1991 was national news. The BBC Romanian Section broadcast a special programme in his memory, and the English papers the *Independent* and the *Guardian* published obituaries.[2] All this despite the fact that his books were published posthumously, and until now there has been no detailed study, either in Romania or abroad, of his life and thought.

The sources for this present study include, as well as his published works, his unpublished and censored manuscripts (for example the third volume of his five-volume *Treatise on Christian Anthropology* and the second volume of *Religious Reflections on Human Knowledge*), cassettes, and notes from my personal conversations with him and with people who knew him. In this way I hope to offer a substantial exposition of his thinking.

Țuțea's works have, implicitly and often explicitly, a polemical character engendered by the political circumstances of his life. He is one of those thinkers whose *oeuvre* is to be read not only in his writings, but also in the unwritten suffering and oppression which he, with so many, courageously endured. Thus it is helpful to refer to wider unpublished material and conversations both with members of Țuțea's circle and with others who experienced political imprisonment. As general background I have particularly used material about the experiment of re-education in Stalinist Romania (see the 'Interviews' section of the Bibliography).

This book is the first attempt at an analytical examination of Țuțea's life and work as a whole, and seeks to establish his significance both to Romania and to the wider world of faith and intellectual development in 'post-Communist' society. I believe that his witness as a confessor of the Christian faith – in the traditional sense of

---

1   See Dumitru Mazilu, *Revoluția Furată, Memoriu pentru Țara mea* (Bucharest: Cozia, 1991).

2   See 'Petre Țuțea: Obituary', *Independent*, London, 20 December 1991, p. 27; 'Petre Țuțea: Romania's White Monk, Symbol of Resistance and Renaissance', *Guardian*, London, 31 December 1991, p. 17.

'confessor' as one who testifies to Christ through a martyrdom of sacrificial living – can contribute to ecumenical dialogue and reconciliation.

Specifically, in ecumenical terms, he can bring new insight and inspiration to the discussion of the place of Orthodox Christianity within Europe. Brought up 'living and breathing' traditional Orthodoxy, he also came to be able to express those ideas in the terms of the Western philosophical tradition and of Latin Christian culture. This, together with his ability to integrate personal experience with informed intellectual argument, represents an important contribution to Orthodoxy's 'Tradition' of living Christian faith.

In this respect he offers Orthodoxy a new path by which it may broaden and deepen its own self-understanding. His writings, interviews, and personal stature as a man of courage, humour, compassion, and integrity also have a crucial message for Romania as a nation. They show that honest and loving acknowledgement of even the most terrible experiences of the twentieth century can be redemptive.

At the same time, through his exceptional understanding of Western culture and his confidence in using its language to reflect on his own culture, he has much to say both to Europe as a continent in process of redefinition, and to Churches throughout the world struggling, in cross-cultural engagement with 'the West', to obey the Gospel imperative for Christian unity. Equally important, he also challenges 'the West' to engage in this cross-cultural obedience to the Gospel.

Ţuţea as a Teacher

Ţuţea's style is at once laconic, controversial, eclectic, apologetic, and subversive. He was the product of the age of *samizdat*, and lived much of his life outside the academic establishment. Some of his work has been published, although unsatisfactorily edited; much is in the form of interviews, or left only as notes; much remains unpublished. In the circumstances his phenomenal memory was the arena in which he developed his ideas. His was a compelling intellect, at once irritating and stimulating. He gave interviews, but disliked being 'intelligent to order'. His intellectual methodology was largely oral and dialogic, and in this sense Socratic. This was not just the result of political circumstances. It also, in a specific way, expressed what he was trying to do – namely to bring a less rigidly systematic approach into contemporary academic life.

I first met Ţuţea in 1980 at the Bucharest Municipal Hospital, when he was a patient and I a first-year medical student. He had been allocated to my care by the professor, who had mistaken me for a more senior student. So off I went proudly to see 'my' patient. At first, the *Securitate* minder by Ţuţea's bed would not allow me to talk to him. Eventually, out of curiosity, I went to see him during a night shift, when there was no guard and I was able to speak to him. At first I thought he was slightly deranged: he talked relentlessly about philosophers and famous names known to me from my school studies, as though they were his own relatives or contemporaries. He would talk of Kant or Aristotle just as I would talk about my mates in the volleyball team. Gradually, however, I realised he was not simply fantasising about these people.

I once lent him, for less than a day, a newly published book written in French (a 'decadent' book about Teilhard de Chardin's *Le Milieu Divin* which, as a young Romanian in the 1980s, I was very proud to possess). By the time he returned it to me he had not only learnt it by heart, but was also able to explain the difficulties which I had encountered in it. I realised at this point that, far from being someone who needed my psychiatric interest, he was in all respects my master. His mind was literally full of books and ideas, and he had an extraordinary gift as a teacher, able to convey complex arguments clearly and simply.

It will thus be clear that my relationship with Țuțea was very personal. In this book I have worked in the tradition of the disciple who seeks to record both the master's teaching and his life. I could have given the raw text of Țuțea's writings without contextual evidence and personal interpretation, leaving readers to make their own assessment. However, the more personal approach which I have adopted is itself inspired by Țuțea's maieutic[3] intellectual method and anagogic purpose.[4]

Țuțea's Theology of Experience

'If you are a theologian, you will pray truly. And if you pray truly, you are a theologian.'[5] The life and work of Petre Țuțea gives a thoroughly contemporary interpretation of this famous epigram of Evagrios of Pontos (disciple of the Cappadocians and of the Desert Fathers, d. AD 399). To Țuțea, as to the Church Fathers, theology means more than a systematic exposition and development of Christian doctrine through God-given reason. It involves – indeed in a sense it *is* – a Trinitarian vision of God, experienced not through the reasoning mind alone, but through the wholeness of 'human being'. Theology is a gate to an eschatological, salvific reality: 'The experience of truth as mystery is redemptive.'[6] It is a revealed 'science of Transcendence' (*știință a Transcendenței*), which 'receives and communicates God as unique Truth'; it is handed on by 'sacred history and tradition', and is experienced during liturgical ritual, in prayer, and through evangelical

---

3　Socrates professed maieutics, the art of the spiritual 'midwife', helping deliver a person's latent ideas into clear consciousness. See the trans. of *Theaetetus* (150) by M.J. Levett, rev. by Myles Burnyeat, in Myles Burnyeat, *The Theaetetus of Plato* (Cambridge: Hackett, 1990), pp. 269–70.

4　In the sense of ἀναγωγή, literally a lifting up – a spiritually inspiring, 'uplifting' vision, which looks prophetically into and beyond history, thus providing a foretaste of the world to come.

5　*The Philokalia. The Complete Text Compiled by St Nikodimos of the Holy Mountain and St Makarios of Corinth*, trans. G.E.H. Palmer, Philip Sherrard, and Kallistos Ware, 4 vols (London: Faber and Faber, 1979–95), I (1979), p. 62.

6　Petre Țuțea, *Omul, Tratat de Antropologie Creștină, vol. 1, Problemele sau Cartea Întrebărilor*, afterword and ed. Cassian Maria Spiridon (Iassy: Timpul, 1992), p. 44. [*The Human Being, Treatise on Christian Anthropology, vol. 1, Problems, or the Book of Questions* = PROBLEMS.]

catechesis; it is also, crucially, experienced in theophany and ecstasy, for God's manifestation of Himself 'can be revealed to the (chosen) saints at any time and in any place'.[7]

A focus on 'transcendence' perhaps inevitably risks leading to either fundamentalism or abstracted formalism. Țuțea's originality is in the way in which he restates transcendence in contemporary language, shying away from neither the intense personal claim of the mystic nor the intellectual complexities of systematics. His life led him to an understanding of the Gospel which cuts across the common dividing lines of theological and denominational differences. He does not provide 'a theology of this' or 'a theology of that'. Rather, as I said above, quoting Evagrios of Pontos, he provides 'theology'.

While in prison, he rediscovered his Christian faith. This became the focus of his whole being, underpinning his actual physical survival no less than his intellectual and spiritual consciousness. In the Communist world, where Christian confession sometimes became attenuated through compromise, his integrity made him a 'fool for Christ's sake' (1 Cor. 4:10). Yet the 'folly' of his sacrificial witness to Christ reveals the wisdom of God, and the example he offers inspires others.

In this inspiring *martyrion* of faithful discipleship, testifying to transcendent grace against the extreme brutality of materialism, three key concepts may be identified: revelation, *anamnesis*, and *theosis*. Let us briefly examine each of these, to help chart the way in understanding this particular life of 'folly'.

Revelation

Under Communism, Christian belief was dismissed as superstition. The Christian lived in a world that proclaimed the 'self-evident' superiority of matter over spirit, based on 'new' (secular) values constructed in an atmosphere of revolutionary excitement. Țuțea had lived in the Western world in which this secular creed had taken shape. Indeed, in his youth he had doubted the value of his own Christian culture. He had later, however, after a period of study in Berlin, become disillusioned by Communism, which he finally rejected after his visit to Moscow in 1940.[8] Then, in prison, he saw the Communist system for what it was, inhuman and manifestly untrue – revolution did not bring about a new humanity. Through his experiences in prison he came to a very particular understanding of Christian revelation: 'Dogma is mystery revealed.'[9] The real revolution is that of repentance, *metanoia*, that 'change of mind' without which 'there can be no new life, no salvation, no entry into

7   PROBLEMS, pp. 50–51.
8   Oxford–Madrid telephone interview on 1 September 2001 with Mrs Chiriachița Popescu (1908–2002), friend of Țuțea and wife of Traian Popescu (1910–2002) – former commercial attaché at the Romanian Legation in Istanbul in the early 1940s.
9   Petre Țuțea, 'Intra-viu pe masa de operație', introd. by Alexandru Prahovara [Popescu], *Viața Medicală*, Bucharest, 6 April 1990, p. 3. ['Interview on the Operating Table' = INTERVIEW.] See also note 16 in Chapter 6.

the kingdom'.[10] Repentance, at the very heart of the Christian *kerygma* – the self-revelation of God's Word in the person of Jesus – enables martyrs[11] to experience Christ as divine strength in their human weakness: 'My grace is sufficient for you, for My strength is made perfect in weakness' (2 Cor. 12:9).

Anamnesis

This was a unifying principle in Țuțea's life and theological thought – not in its Platonic sense, that is, the recollection (ἀνάμνησις) of a previous acquaintance with the Forms or Ideas,[12] but in its traditional theological meaning of making Christ's sacrifice on the Cross, as it relates to human suffering, present in the world. The liturgical *anamnesis* of the Eucharist is the efficacious sacrament of divine truth. Țuțea came to a very personal understanding of how Christ's call for people to take up their Cross daily (Luke 9:23) is to be fulfilled in the individual life of every disciple. All are called to bear witness to the way of the Cross, entering into Christ's self-offering for all through Eucharistic remembrance. This is the way of Resurrection.

Anamnesis also has a clinical meaning: the patient's account to a doctor of their medical history – their *personal recollection of symptoms*. For Țuțea the politician and economist, this process was needed by the consciousness of a society or nation. Perhaps we may see in the life of this honest physician of the human condition a martyr's account of the sufferings inflicted upon an entire nation between 1940 and 1990. In a 'post-Communist' Romania that still refuses to put the crimes perpetrated by Communists on trial, Țuțea's life and works could contribute towards a much needed national *anamnesis* that would have international relevance. Ultimately such secular *anamnesis* receives its value from its sacred paradigm. Without repentance for, and understanding of, individual history and experience, both corporate and personal, humanity is condemned to moral chaos.

Theosis

Orthodox tradition and ritual are sometimes regarded as irrational or superstitious by Westerners. Yet they are a sign of the limited ability of human language to express the nature of Christian mystery. Although language and reason are among the highest attributes of humanity, they often prevent the realisation that the truth of Christianity is not imposed from above or deduced from below, but rather is discovered through a

---

10   Kallistos Ware, 'The Orthodox Experience of Repentance', *Sobornost* 2:1, 1980, p. 18.
11   I speak here not only of martyrs in the outward and literal sense, as those who died for Christ under persecution, but also of those 'whose martyrdom is inner and hidden. This is inevitable, for martyrdom is an all-inclusive category, a universal vocation': Kallistos Ware, *The Inner Kingdom* (Crestwood, NY: St Vladimir's Seminary Press, 2000), p. 121.
12   See *Meno* (81c–86b), in Plato, *Protagoras and Meno*, trans. W.K.C. Guthrie (London: Penguin, 1956), pp. 129–39.

life of discipleship, our way to union with God in Christ – the way of 'deification', or *theosis*.[13]

Petre Țuțea rediscovered, by the grace of Baptism and his personal living out of faith, what it means to say that human beings are created in the image and likeness of God. Through his personal martyrdom, as a confessor of faith who willingly accepted suffering for God's sake, he discovered the power of God's Holy Spirit. And in the light of this intensely felt Christian understanding he warns the secular world that, for those who do not live in accord with the Holy Spirit, the Spirit of joy and fullness of Life, there is only mere self, cut off from creative relationships in a condition of 'spiritual autism'.[14] While the joyful self-giving of the martyr leads to deification, 'spiritual autism' represents isolation and an absence of inter-personal communication, which leads to annihilation. Martyrdom is where we learn most about faith, as Țuțea was to discover in Aiud prison. Selfishness is where we embrace nothingness.

In his torrential, incantatory style resembling that of liturgical prayer, mantras, or perpetual stage rehearsals, Țuțea taught me – often with prophetic solemnity, sometimes with mischievous humour, even through gross exaggeration, which was intended to shake my unacknowledged prejudices – that the most important choice that has to be made in life is between spiritual self-sacrifice and moral suicide. In our long 'conversations' I seldom had a chance to ask questions about how this might apply in my own life. How do martyrdom and self-sacrifice apply in situations where circumstances do not force us into this clear way of *theosis*? How do they apply to the Christian believer in the affluent world today? Writing this book has helped me to formulate certain questions that I had neither the time nor the maturity to pose during my encounter with Țuțea in the flesh. The answers have still to be worked out. Yet the encounter – relationship, conversation, love – continues beyond physical death.

> *And what the dead had no speech for, when living,*
> *They can tell you, being dead: the communication*
> *Of the dead is tongued with fire beyond the language of the living.*[15]

The answer is that to which each human being shall be called at the coming again of Christ, at that Day of the Kingdom for which the Lord instructs his disciples to pray.

---

13   My doctoral research on Țuțea entailed interviewing former prisoners of conscience who were tortured in the Romanian and Soviet gulags. Paradoxically the attempt to force them to renounce their faith and national identity had the effect of deepening their awareness of God. The system that sought to eradicate their sense of divine mystery became the arena of a martyrdom in which human beings were transfigured in *deification*: a condition of mystical union with that love that is God's very being.

14   See Kevin Vanhoozer, 'Human being, individual and social', in Colin Gunton (ed.), *The Cambridge Companion to Christian Doctrine* (Cambridge: Cambridge University Press, 1997), p. 177.

15   T.S. Eliot, 'Little Gidding', in Helen Gardner (ed.), *The New Oxford Book of English Verse, 1250–1950* (Oxford: Oxford University Press, 1972), p. 892.

Chapter 2

Biography and Intellectual Formation

An outline of Țuțea's biography, with an account of the main stages in his intellectual and political development, will help the reader to understand how his influence came to extend from the realm of politics, economics, and philosophy to that of political theology.

Early Years

Petre Țuțea was born in the ancient village of Boteni, in Muscel county, on 6 October 1902. His father Petre Bădescu (1858–1925), and his grandfather before him, had been the Romanian Orthodox parish priests of the village. His mother Ana Simon Oprea Țuțea (1885–1960) was of peasant[1] stock, and Țuțea proudly referred to her as *țăranca din Boteni*, 'the peasant woman from Boteni'. His birth certificate gives only his mother, aged sixteen, as a parent. His place of birth is recorded as the house of Fr Petre Bădescu, parish priest of Boteni, who signed the certificate as a witness. In 1906 Bădescu made a deed act granting all his possessions and finances to Ana. He died in 1925, survived by Ana, Petre their eldest son, and another seven children. That Bădescu signed the birth certificate as a witness rather than as the father theoretically opens the possibility that someone else could be Petre Țuțea's father; but it should be remembered that, as a widowed Orthodox priest (according to local sources his wife Efrosina, b. 1862, 'died of typhoid fever before 1900' leaving a daughter, Filofteia), Bădescu was forbidden to remarry.[2]

The eldest of four brothers and four sisters, Petre was brought up in the traditional rural way of life, ruled by the seasons rather than the clock. He had an exceptional memory. As a child he did not speak until the age of four, when he composed a nursery

---

1   The connotations of the English word 'peasant' are probably misleading for a Western reader. The Romanian word *țăran*, feminine *țărancă* (deriving from *țară*, 'land' – Latin *terra*) generally meant an independent smallhold farmer. *Țărani* still represented a significant percentage of the population at the time that Țuțea was writing (about 30 per cent in 1981), and continue to be an important element of contemporary Romanian society. See Vlad Georgescu, *The Romanians: A History* (Columbus: Ohio State University Press, 1991), p. 261.
2   Presumably, however, the bishop sanctioned Petre Bădescu's relationship with Ana, since he continued as a parish priest while he lived with her. The relevant diocesan archive was apparently destroyed in the First World War. See Arhiva Primăriei Boteni, Argeș, Registrul Stării Civile 1/1902, Nașteri, nr. 72.

rhyme. Indeed he was known as *Mutu Popii*, 'the Priest's Mute-boy'. In an interview
with me, his younger brother Victor recalled how from an early age their mother
would consult Petre over the house-keeping. As a teenager in the First World War,
when the German army arrived in his village, it was Petre who quickly mastered
German and conducted negotiations with the occupying force.

The spiritual dimension of Ţuţea's upbringing was defined by Orthodox tradition.
Another inevitable influence was the dominant concern of nineteenth-century
Romania, national identity, which was attained when the country became a national
unitary State in 1918 (see Appendix I). Ţuţea as an intellectually lively teenager
shared in the experience of national fervour during these formative years of
Romanian independence. In 1920, when he was nearly eighteen, he moved to
Cluj-Napoca, the capital of Transylvania, to attend the Lyceum *George Bariţiu*, the
best-known high school in the principality. To finance this he tutored his host
and benefactor, Captain Sevastian M. Ciupagea (1890–1923) of the 31st artillery
regiment in Cluj-Napoca, who felt that a wider grounding in the humanities would
improve his prospects of promotion.[3]

After a century of Austro-Hungarian rule and a thousand years of Hungarian
oppression of the majority Romanian population of Transylvania, these Romanians
spoke an ancient dialect that preserved more Latin elements than contemporary
standard Romanian.[4] School colleagues from Cluj-Napoca were to remember Ţuţea –
newly arrived from the old kingdom of Wallachia and Moldavia – not only as an
exceptionally gifted student, but also as a model of eloquence, with a mastery of the
Romanian official language admired by all.[5]

In January 1928 Ţuţea graduated in administrative law at King Ferdinand I
University in Cluj-Napoca.[6] He went on to study for a doctorate in the same field at
the same university, completing his thesis in 1929. In his final year at Cluj-Napoca
Ţuţea contributed numerous articles to *Patria*, a newspaper of the National Peasant
Party. He showed a great interest in promoting the values of public education,
democracy, and co-operation in his essays 'On the Problem of University Education',
'The Baccalaureate', 'Democracy and Force', and 'National Peasant Democracy'.

---

3   See Mircea Coloşenco's foreword to Petre Ţuţea, *Lumea ca Teatru. Teatrul Seminar*
     (Bucharest: Vestala and Alutus, 1993), p. x. [*The World as Theatre. Theatre as Seminar* =
     THEATRE.]
4   Genealogically, 'Romanian is what remains of the vulgar Latin spoken in the province of
     Dacia, in the Balkan mountains, and along the Black Sea coast. In the earliest stage it
     included elements of the Thracian idiom spoken by the local population (a language of
     which linguists believe they can identify between 80 and 110 words), and later it was
     subjected to a heavy Slavic influence. But the Latin grammatical structure has remained
     virtually unchanged. The Slavic impact was primarily lexical: recent research has
     calculated that from 16 to 20 per cent of the words in the basic vocabulary are of Slavic
     origin': Georgescu, *Romanians*, p. 13.
5   Horia Stanca, interview, Bucharest, 3 September 1997.
6   Before beginning his law studies Ţuţea studied medicine for a few months, hoping to
     become a doctor. However, his inability to 'draw an egg', as he himself put it, made it
     impossible for him to pass the necessary anatomy exams.

Agrarian Socialist Orientation

Țuțea had already become a member of the National Peasant Party[7] while working on his doctoral thesis. In 1930 he moved from his intellectual university world to a place where socialist principles could be applied directly to everyday life. Completing his doctorate 'Magna cum laude' on 29 June 1929, he settled in Pui, not far from the remains of what had been the most significant Roman colony in Transylvania. He was at this time a militant member of the youth wing of the National Peasant Party, *Chemarea Tinerimii Române din Transilvania* (*Call to the Romanian Youth of Transylvania*). Between 1929 and 1932 he published about forty articles in *Chemarea*, the party's magazine.[8] In Pui he worked for more than a year at the magistrate's courts.[9] There he must have seen for himself the harsh life of the workers in the timber industry, and of the local peasants and miners at a time of worldwide financial depression.

Chemarea had come into being after the resignation of the liberal Prime Minister Ion I.C. Brătianu, who was replaced by General Alexandru Averescu, leader of the People's Party. Averescu had led the harsh military reprisal against the peasants' uprising of 1907. He had only five supporters in Parliament. His installation as Prime Minister had angered the younger generation in the Romanian National Party of Transylvania and galvanised them into making an open appeal – in *Chemarea* – to the Romanian youth of Transylvania.[10] *Chemarea* soon had more than 50 per cent of the vote in eighteen counties of Transylvania. 'This wonderful result' was taken to justify 'the call to fight against corruption in politics' and 'abuses in the administration, and for a free political life with free elections'.[11] Țuțea's caustic words published while still at Cluj-Napoca describe his attitude to these events:

---

7   See Appendix I.

8   *Chemarea Tinerimii Române* (1929–32) in Cluj-Napoca, abbreviated as *Chemarea*.

9   In a letter of 26 November 1929 from Pui to his friend and benefactor V.V. Tilea, Țuțea writes: 'I am so completely paralysed by useless bureaucratic work, that I cannot do any more than a dim-witted clerk!' In two of his sarcastic pamphlets – 'Judecătoria din Pui sau grajdul d-lui jude Bogdan', *Chemarea*, 24 November 1929, p. 3 ['Pui Court or Judge Bogdan's Pigsty'], and 'Câinele bătrân nu piere', *Chemarea*, 15 December 1929, p. 4 ['The Old Dog Never Dies'] – Țuțea condemns the idiocy of a fossilised judge and the judicial masquerade in the court of law at Pui. In the same letter to Tilea, Țuțea explains his initial failure to establish a branch of *Chemarea* in Pui as he and Tilea had hoped.

10   Averescu unsuccessfully sued *Chemarea* for defamation. Basil Gruia (1909–96), a lawyer who represented *Chemarea*, remained Țuțea's lifelong friend and, when he died in Cluj-Napoca, the papers found on his desk on which he had been working were an index of Țuțea's work. He had been intending to produce a complete edition of Țuțea's *oeuvre* from his earliest writings to his last posthumously published volumes. Copies of these papers are now in my own archive, courtesy of Ms Camelia Cristian.

11   Ileana Tilea (ed.), *Envoy Extraordinary, Memoirs of a Romanian Diplomat: Viorel Virgil Tilea* (London: Haggerston, 1998), pp. 95–6.

General Averescu, with his tired withered face, demonstrated bitter hatred against *Chemarea* of Transylvania, because the emergence of this vibrant political organisation was a challenge to 'Averescism' which had its final fling in 1926, when he was Prime Minister. Happy to murder peasants during their uprising in 1907, the general has always sought to satisfy the blind interests of the corrupt and incompetent ruling class. Due to his complete lack of political sense, he ended up a willing puppet of oligarchic cliques.[12]

In 1929 he wrote a critical analysis of the causes leading to the miners' strike at Lupeni, not far from Pui,[13] which he included in a report for *Chemarea*. Moving to Bucharest around 1932, Ţuţea co-founded the political weekly *Stânga* (*The Left*), for which he wrote articles and editorials from November 1932 to March 1933. On the first page of the first issue, his editorial, 'The Rules of the Democratic Game', advocated Communist principles such as the abolition of private property by a working-class revolution and the institution of a planned economy:

> On the question that continues to occupy our generation: 'Left or Right?', we respond categorically: 'Left.' This choice is made for us by the needs of the starving and of the exploited, those who have come to see that their misery does not have to last for ever, and that unemployment has easily recognisable origins. They are not the will of a capricious God.[14]

In the late 1930s, while working for the Ministry of Trade and Industry (renamed the Ministry of the National Economy in April 1938), Ţuţea suggested that the Romanian economy should be centralised and population growth encouraged to achieve '60 million inhabitants by the end of the twentieth century'. He promoted agrarian democracy in Romania, but thought it necessary to limit land ownership, thus preventing the formation of great estates:

> *Latifundia perdiderunt Italiam…* The great estates were the undoing of Italy. Looking at different kinds of ownership, what should not be tolerated is the formation of great country estates. And in the city a person must be free. Industrial property should remain unlimited. Land ownership has to be limited. For if Romania consisted of great estates it would have a small population, and with a small population you cannot create a culture.[15]

---

12   Petre Ţuţea, 'Procesul Chemării: Un proces politic sau lupta între două lumi', *Chemarea*, 2 November 1930, p. 1. ['The Trial of "Chemarea": A Political Trial or the Conflict between Two Worlds'.]

13   Petre Ţuţea, '"Cocoşii" consiliilor de administraţie de pe Valea Jiului', *Chemarea*, 11 August 1929, p. 1. ['The Administrative "Turkeys" of the Jiu Valley'.]

14   Petre Ţuţea, 'Regulile jocului democratic', *Stânga* (1932–33), Bucharest, 13 November 1932, p. 1. ['The Rules of the Democratic Game'.]

15   Petre Ţuţea, *Între Dumnezeu şi Neamul Meu*, ed. Gabriel Klimowicz, foreword and afterword by Marian Munteanu (Bucharest: Anastasia, Arta Grafică, 1992), p. 358. [*Between God and My People* = BGMP.]

The Berlin Period

In 1933–34, through the support of Prime Minister Alexandru Vaida-Voievod, Țuțea had the opportunity of pursuing post-doctoral studies in political science at Friedrich-Wilhelm University, while working as a commercial attaché at the Romanian Legation in Berlin.[16] He became acquainted, during this period, with the thinking of two economists, Werner Sombart (1863–1941) and Othmar Spann (1878–1950), and the Roman Catholic thinker and jurist Carl Schmitt (1888–1985), all of whom were to influence his own thinking. At the end of the nineteenth century Werner Sombart had introduced the thought of Karl Marx and Friedrich Engels to the German academic world[17] and was influential in winning supporters for Marxism all over the world, including Russia.[18] Sombart's *Deutscher Sozialismus* (1934) challenged Marx's view that the working-class revolution could be triggered simultaneously in all countries where the proletariat was ready to overthrow capitalism. Although he put strong emphasis on the national character of any socialist revolution, he was not a member of the National Socialist Party. He died in 1941, out of favour with the Nazis.

Țuțea met Sombart through the latter's Romanian wife Corina (1893–c. 1971), daughter of Niculai Leon, Rector of Iassy University. Corina's salon, one of the most cultivated in Berlin,[19] saw the launch of many intellectuals in Germany including,

---

16   Arhivele Naționale ale României, Direcția Arhivelor Centrale, Bucharest, Ministerul Industriei și Comerțului, Direcțiunea Comerțului Interior, Dosar 130/1933, f. 15; Dosar 131/1933, f. 276.

17   See Werner Sombart, *Das Lebenswerk von Karl Marx* (Jena: Gustav Fischer, 1909). For Sombart's discussion on the economic thought of Marx and Engels, see Michael Appel, *Werner Sombart: Theoretiker und Historiker des modernen Kapitalismus* (Marburg: Metropolis, 1992), pp. 29–31, 48. Sombart rejected Marxist economic theory and economic theories in general. His 'realist method' was based on economic empirical facts. He described each period of economic history in terms of a particular 'style' corresponding to 'eine gestaltende Funktion': Barbu Solacolu, *Sombart, în marginea omului și a operei* (Bucharest: Analele Economice și Statistice, 1930), p. 44. Engels himself praised Sombart's correct interpretation of Marx's *Capital*: Herman Lebovics, *Social Conservatism and the Middle Class Germany, 1914–1933* (Princeton, NJ: Princeton University Press, 1969), p. 58.

18   Sergii Bulgakov (1871–1944), before his transition from Marxism to Orthodoxy, corresponded with Sombart. At a meeting of the Law Society in Moscow he lectured on Sombart's assessment of Marx's theories of value and surplus value. See Bulgakov's letter of 6/18 April 1896 to Sombart, Geheimes Staatsarchiv Preußischer Kulturbesitz, Berlin-Dahlem, I. HA, Rep. 92 Sombart, Nr. 10a, Bd. 1, fol. 182.

19   Carl Schmitt was a central figure among Corina's guests: Dr Nicolaus Sombart, interview, Berlin, 20 September 1996. See also Nicolaus Sombart, *Jugend in Berlin, 1933–1943. Ein Bericht* (Frankfurt am Main: Fischer Taschenbuch, 1994), pp. 57–68, 291–5; Friedrich Lenger, *Werner Sombart, 1863–1941, Eine Biographie* (München: C.H. Beck, 1994), pp. 278–81. Cf. Elsa Lüder, 'Corina Leon Sombart (Iași-Berlin-Heidelberg)', *Dacia Literară*, 5:13, nr. 2, Iassy, 1994, pp. 29–30. There is a discrepancy over Corina's year of death. Lüder gives it as 1967, whereas Nicolaus Sombart gives the later year of 1971.

for instance, Ţuţea's friend Emil Cioran, who studied philosophy at Berlin in 1934–35[20] before becoming established in Paris. As the newly appointed economic advisor to the Ministry of the National Economy in Bucharest, Ţuţea was interested in the anthropological approach to economics which Sombart developed in his last important work, *Vom Menschen. Versuch einer geisteswissenschaftlichen Anthropologie* (*Of the Human Being. Towards a Humanist Anthropology*). Ţuţea endorsed Sombart's theory that commerce is the historical dimension of human consciousness, seeing all human ways of life as dependent on a particular economic system rooted in the national psychology of various peoples.[21] People are 'political animals' that trade in accordance with their national character:

> Although human beings – as creatures of nature – are the object of anthropology conceived as a natural science, they are also the fruit of historical developments [that is, socio-economic evolution]. In the latter case, they are the research object of an anthropology whose criteria are ethno-political. Take away this historical dimension of anthropology and you can define humanity any way you like, regardless of reality.[22]

Regarded today as 'the most important theorist of the corporate state in Central Europe',[23] Othmar Spann was a Roman Catholic anti-Socialist of Austrian origin whose thinking was built on the idealist writings of the German Romantics. Ţuţea critically developed Spann's discussion of society as 'whole' or 'totality' (*Ganzheit*) and came to feel that Spann did not take sufficient account of transcendence as the unifying principle in his political theory. By the end of his time in Berlin Ţuţea had come to view autonomous political systems as inconclusive, explaining nothing. It was probably during the mid-1930s that he started to return to a belief in God, though perhaps still at rather an intellectual level.

True 'explanation' has a mystical character, according to Ţuţea, for both explanation and reason are ultimately rooted in a unique transcendent cause. The

---

20   Humboldt-Universitätsarchiv, Berlin, Rektorat 125 (18.10.1934–7.6.1935), matriculation nr. 2044.

21   In his *Die Juden und das Wirtschaftsleben* (Leipzig: Duncker & Humblot, 1920) Sombart expressed respect for the Jews. As Lebovics wrote: the Jews 'had contributed greatly to the evolution of the modern spirit of capitalism in general and to the spirit of rationality in particular. Their religious beliefs, their intellectualism, and their long history as wanderers has implanted within them character traits which permitted them to develop the "idea" of capitalism to its highest level': Lebovics, *Social Conservatism*, p. 56. Cf. Werner Sombart, *Le Bourgeois, Contribution à l'histoire morale et intellectuelle de l'homme économique moderne*, trans. Dr S. Jankélévitch (Paris: Payot, 1926), pp. 431–3.

22   Petre Ţuţea, *Proiectul de Tratat. Eros*, ed. and foreword by Aurel Ion Brumaru (Braşov and Chişinău: Pronto and Editura Uniunii Scriitorilor, 1992), p. 103. [*Project for a Treatise. Eros* = PROJECT.] Apart from a letter to V.V. Tilea and a couple of letters to his friend, Prof. Nicolae Tatu, I have no writings by Ţuţea from his time in Berlin. The reflections quoted in this section are all later, dating from the 1970s.

23   John J. Haag, 'Othmar Spann and the Politics of "Totality", Corporatism in Theory and Practice' (unpublished D.Phil. thesis, Rice University, Houston, Texas: May 1969), p. 1.

Aristotelian principle that the whole precedes its parts – adopted by Spann as the premise for his theory of the true State (*Der wahre Staat*)[24] – was inconclusive, since it eluded the absolute, creative unity that is prior to both the whole and its parts. In Aristotelian logic, totality and generality are mutually opposed. Spann could not therefore logically make a totality out of the sum of generalities. To Țuțea something was required beyond this, a dimension of transcendence and revelation. After the Second World War he expressed it thus:

> In the mystical vision, the created whole can be known by revelation; it contains no 'mystery' [is not unfathomable], since it can be known in its entirety. For 'mysteries' are extra-mundane unities (like Platonic Ideas), and have their place in the great mystery of Godhead.[25]

Carl Schmitt was 'undoubtedly the most controversial German legal and political thinker of the twentieth century',[26] who predicted the demise of liberalism and is probably its most profound critic.[27] However, 'if liberalism were to restrict its apoliticism to the sphere of civil society, and acknowledge the necessity of a sovereign state that retained the monopoly of the political, Schmitt would not object to conservative or authoritarian liberalism'.[28]

Țuțea attended some of Schmitt's lectures and seminars on political theory and international law in 1933–34 and read, annotated, and referred to the 1932 edition of his *Der Begriff des Politischen* (*The Concept of the Political*). He seldom employed Schmitt's concept of political theology as such, but this heavily annotated work remained on his bookshelves even when, after his release from prison (when no Communist employer would give him a job), he had to sell most of his valuable books.

---

24   See Othmar Spann, *Der wahre Staat, Vorlesungen über Abbruch und Neubau der Gesellschaft*, rev. edn (Leipzig: Quelle & Meyer, 1923; 1st edn 1921).

25   THEATRE, p. 499. For the late Țuțea, it is God who creates and 'includes all things' in Himself, although 'He cannot be confused with them' ('Totul este în Dumnezeu, fără contopirea Lui cu acest tot'), THEATRE, p. 491. In his universalistic 'theory of categories' Spann stressed that *die Ganzheit* ('the whole') is both prior to its members and more than the sum of its parts. See Othmar Spann, *Kategorienlehre* (Jena: Gustav Fischer, 1924), pp. 54ff. For an introduction to Spann's writings, see J. Hanns Pichler (ed.), *Othmar Spann, oder: Die Welt als Ganzes* (Vienna: Böhlau, c. 1988).

26   See George Schwab's introduction to Carl Schmitt, *Political Theology, Four Chapters on the Concept of Sovereignty*, trans. George Schwab (Cambridge, MA: MIT Press, 1985), p. xi.

27   Paul Piccone, 'Ostracizing Carl Schmitt: Letters to "The New York Review of Books"', *Telos*, nr. 109, Fall 1996, p. 87. See also chapter 'Staatsrechtliche Dekonstruktion der Verfassung der Moderne', in Reinhard Mehring, *Carl Schmitt zur Einführung* (Hamburg: Junius, 2000), pp. 69–100.

28   Renato Cristi, *Carl Schmitt and Authoritarian Liberalism: Strong State, Free Economy* (Cardiff: University of Wales Press, 1998), p. 6.

Fundamental to Schmitt's thinking was the idea that right 'preceded the state, and the purpose of the latter was to realise the former; the proper order of things was right, state, individual'.[29] Ṭuṭea agreed, but also spoke explicitly, in his *Treatise on Christian Anthropology*, of 'divine right'. For him the universal spiritual values expressed in the Christian Church determine what is right.

Schmitt considered politics to be a secularised version of theology. In general, he regarded the modern concept of *national sovereignty* as an attribute of a profane deity in secular mode, replacing the omnipotence of God and the divine right of kings. For Ṭuṭea too, national sovereign authority could not be equated with political legislation. As products of human reason, laws are always relative, transcended by mystical dogmas which belong to what Ṭuṭea commonly referred to as 'the realm of certainty'. For him sovereignty alone, understood as a given 'principle' unbounded by space and time, had absolute authority in international relations:

> I emphasise most vigorously the *principle* of national sovereignty expressed by the national state. The liberty, dignity, prosperity, and happiness of the Romanian people depend on the application of this principle.[30]

Schmitt challenged the idea that the State can be defined merely in terms of legal order. He attempted to demonstrate that, since 'the exception is that which cannot be subsumed', one should liberate the concept of sovereign power from the so-called scientific system of norms. For Schmitt, national sovereign authority not only guaranteed the normally valid legal order, it also transcended it:

> The core of this authority is its exclusive possession of the right of, or its monopoly of, political decision making. Thus Schmitt's definition: 'Sovereign is he who decides on exception'.[31]

Ṭuṭea was to extend the discussion on the ultimately transcendent essence of any sovereign power to a metaphysical and mystical understanding of miracle. He believed that 'miracle is the expression of the power of the Absolute conceived on a human scale'.[32] For him, only the divine or divine inspiration can, in history, achieve the 'impossible' (that is, a miracle or an exception). However, he could not deny that humanity craves miracles. Miracles give humanity the illusion of escape from impossible situations, yet also threaten to overwhelm the world, replacing order with chaos. Prayer is the means of mediating between order and exception: 'Prayer is

---

29   Schwab, introduction to Schmitt, *Political Theology*, p. xii.
30   Ṭuṭea's conversation with Prof. Dumitru Mazilu, Palatul Victoria, Bucharest, 1 January 1990. For Ṭuṭea 'principle' has the sanction of Almighty God. Cf. PROJECT, pp. 46, 85, 103. See also Vadim Borisov, 'Personality and National Awareness', in *From under the Rubble*, ed. Alexander Solzhenitsyn, et al., and trans. Michael Scammell (London: Fontana, 1975), pp. 194–228.
31   Schwab, introduction to Schmitt, *Political Theology*, p. xviii.
32   THEATRE, p. 144.

meant to alleviate the human situation, subject as it is to the harshness of nature's laws.'[33]

Țuțea's analysis of the Romanian political scene was also influenced by Schmitt's idea that politics exercises control over the disciplines of the human mind. Țuțea believed, like Schmitt, that politics is ultimately independent of any secular determinant, which gives it a transcendent dimension similar to the authority of the Church. Țuțea thus deplored the French Revolution, which led to the separation of Church and State in Europe (destroying the symbiosis between Christianity and the political authority). In this context he acknowledged 'the polemical character of political concepts', which is why Schmitt constructed 'a table representing a radical opposition between the liberal-democratic and the feudal worlds'.[34] However, Țuțea came later to accept that, despite this separation, Christianity and the liberal political order are compatible.

He saw more hope in what Schmitt termed authoritarian liberalism, which guarantees individual freedom but also requires restraint between individuals, preferably by consensus. Here Țuțea saw a parallel between authoritarian liberalism and the Christian 'programme' of the Sermon on the Mount. However, the ultimate principle of love comes from the transcendent God and leads to the unifying concept of love for one's neighbour (friend *and* enemy) – rather than Schmitt's radical separation: friend *or* enemy.[35] Țuțea never fell into the trap of seeing human rights as mere privileges but considered them to be a balance of privilege and responsibility entrusted to human beings as the pinnacle of God's creation. God alone is beyond all that exists. Only God can give to human society the equality which political theory tries to formulate.

The National Revolution Manifesto

Țuțea always aspired to be a man of integrity. In his early thirties, while still working in Berlin, he admits his spiritual struggle in an unpublished letter of 28 October 1934 from Berlin to Viorel V. Tilea:

> Like traces in the sand of an apparently chaotic life, my moral development can be viewed in terms of geological eras. It took me thirty-one years of inner exploration to discover the negative aspect of my life, and get rid of what was worthless in myself ... Whenever I aspire to holiness, I feel the ground slipping away under my feet.

---

33   THEATRE, p. 111.
34   THEATRE, p. 306.
35   Țuțea notes that, for Schmitt, the ultimate distinction to which political actions and motives can be reduced is that of friend or enemy – that is, the friend–enemy antithesis is not derived from external criteria in the way that other antitheses can be: THEATRE, p. 307. For Țuțea's discussion of Schmitt's *Feind–Freundgruppierung*, see also PROJECT, p. 76.

During his time in Germany he never lost his idealist sense of Romania's identity and future. The emphasis of Sombart, Spann, and Schmitt on national character in political theory had significantly influenced him. Many years later these influences were to bear fruit, when he came to stress the mystical nature of diversity in Christ[36] and warned against supranational uniformity. Already at this point he was beginning to develop a vision in which every nation has its equal and non-negotiable place at the Heavenly Banquet (Rev. 21:24). He saw that political theory divorced from God would lead to the exaltation of power as the only truth. Although his thinking in the 1930s was still at a formative stage in terms of his ultimate vision, he perhaps already sensed the tragic polarity which was to become so stark: on the one hand, National Socialism, a corporate all-inclusive State without God; and, on the other hand, Communist internationalism in which revolution was the inevitable conclusion of a historical process without God (history seen in terms of Schmitt's 'friend–enemy' dichotomy).

Disillusioned by developments in his own country in 1935 (see Appendix I), however, he collaborated with two distinguished Romanian philosophers, Sorin Pavel (1903–57) and Nicolae Tatu (1910–97), to produce *The National Revolution Manifesto*.[37] Pavel and Tatu also had a deep first-hand knowledge of German culture.[38] The *Manifesto* reveals Țuțea's shift toward a right-wing ideology, in which the Orthodox identity of the Romanian people was proposed as the basis for a national policy to be adopted by a dominant (if not sole) party and guaranteed by an authoritarian monarch. At this stage he (with his co-authors) believed in the divine right of kings. The *Manifesto* defines the National Revolution as a divinely inspired struggle for the restoration of divine order:

> The transition from constitutional monarchy to absolute monarchy – the only truly constitutional principle – takes the form of a national revolution, in an age of relentless unrest when the neo-liberal state is being abolished. The parliament of this state was created by a deliberate mystification of the whole concept of national sovereignty. The introduction of proportional representation has led to the betrayal of our nation as a whole. Sovereignty is

---

36   In Borisov's words, 'Christianity introduced to the world the concept of the *plurality of personalities of a single mankind*'. See Borisov, 'Personality and National Awareness' in *From under the Rubble*, p. 209.

37   Petre Țuțea, et al., *Manifestul Revoluției Naționale* (Sighișoara: Tipografia Miron Neagu, 1935). [*The National Revolution Manifesto* = MANIFESTO.] The MANIFESTO credited three other authors, Gheorghe Tite (former Romanian ambassador in Budapest), Petre Ercuță (economist, Werner Sombart's last doctoral student before his death in 1941), Ioan Crăciunel (priest, co-sponsor of the MANIFESTO). According to Prof. Tatu, however, they were not involved in its formulation.

38   Prof. Tatu told me that he and Pavel wrote most of the first section of the MANIFESTO, 'Critical Introduction to Historical Politics', and contributed to the second section, 'The Romanian State Today', while Țuțea was mainly responsible for the third section, 'The Nation' (with five subsections: a. The National State; b. The Economy; c. The Family; d. The Church; and e. War and Peace). Interview, Bucharest, 16 March 1994.

being forfeited, because the nation has no way in which it can directly express its opinion on vital problems, except through referendum. [During the National Revolution] egalitarian democracy and liberalism will be replaced by a democracy based on a direct vote of the whole electorate.[39]

The *Manifesto* presents the country as being in a sorry spiritual state, while reflecting the common prejudices of the inter-war period, particularly anti-Semitism; in that respect, it all too worryingly conforms to 'the principalities and powers' of the very society it wished to cure:[40]

> The state of the Romanian Orthodox Church, of Christ and His teaching, in our country, has for a century been dire. In the Romanian countryside sects multiply and superstition flourishes. In the towns there is indifference and blasphemy. Free thought, popular philosophical materialism, illuminist masonry, historical materialism, the irreconcilable hostility of Judaism towards the Crucified Christ, and the cultural mania of those who still maintain we would have been more cultivated had we been Catholic rather than Orthodox – all these have broken the fusion between Orthodoxy and the Romanian nation.[41]

The *Manifesto* nevertheless contains ideas that merit attention. The real 'enemy' is identified as those who undermine the Church 'by turning it into an ethical institution', who seek to destroy its place in the heart of the people 'by pointing to the gulf between the ideal and the reality, between the mission of the priests and their behaviour'.[42] Here was the heart of the crisis:

> The flaw in the atheist arguments against the Church is that it ignores the rôle of the priest as physician of the soul and replaces it with that of lay moraliser. When the priest is turned into a social functionary, it is easier to discredit him.[43]

The clergy themselves, however, were often the worst culprits, becoming servants of the State instead of the Church:

---

39   MANIFESTO, p. 42.
40   A central point of this book is that Țuțea's own participation in the sufferings of twentieth-century Europe took him through the 'refiner's fire' to a deeper level of insight and understanding. The distortions of his 'human mask' (see Chapter 9) were transformed during this vocational process. It is by God's grace, he would say, that he has the authority to reflect – not backwards, but forwards in the light of his experience – and to offer his message. There are those on the political right in Romania today who on the strength of the MANIFESTO seek to claim Țuțea as a thinker of the extreme right. The MANIFESTO now, however, is important in supplying historical evidence of the development of a thinker whose significance transcends party claims. In 1990 Țuțea pointedly joined the National Liberal Party.
41   MANIFESTO, p. 84.
42   MANIFESTO, p. 85.
43   MANIFESTO, p. 85.

The servants of the Orthodox altar have become the most ridiculous State 'functionaries'. Around the Church has gathered an atmosphere of suspicion and mockery, which not only alienates people from the Church, but discourages vocations to the priesthood ... A few of our clergy can wear the sacred vestments in good faith. The rest are stuffed cassocks. It is difficult for good priests to do their work when hampered by incompetent colleagues. Surrounded by ridicule and hate, it is hard for them to rebuild a community that will draw people to the source of eternal life, witnessing to Jesus as the Truth and the Life.[44]

Although Ţuţea's theology later came to express a more integrated vision of virtue and divinity, in 1935 he was clearly convinced that nothing less than a National Revolution could stop the progressive corruption of Romanian traditional values:

The National Revolution will halt this process of alienation of the country from the Church's teachings. It will compel the wicked to hold their tongue and give back to the Church the respect in which this nation has always held it. Only when the best and finest of our young people take on the Christian task, rather than pursuing worldly careers – which, though useful, are insignificant in comparison with the service of the sanctuary – only then will the Romanian Church come alive in our souls and the work of national integration become possible.[45]

This nationalist idealism (it should be remembered that 'Greater Romania' had existed as a State for only just over twenty years), with its vision of a Christian Church at the centre of a corporate State, was what led Ţuţea to support the Legionary Movement. The young Marxist had swung to the other end of the ideological scale.[46]

---

44   MANIFESTO, p. 86.
45   MANIFESTO, p. 86.
46   Underlying this swing to right-wing ideology, however, was Ţuţea's 'thirst for moral perfection' which motivated him throughout his life. In a letter written later to his friend V.V. Tilea, Ţuţea looked back on his years as an activist in the *Chemarea* movement and as co-author of the MANIFESTO:
      'I look back on the past with a strange mixture of regret and irony... Our irreproachably moral rebellion petered out and today seems pointless. At the present moment, I am wrestling to comprehend "the space beyond the heavens", as Plato says. I am struggling with pure ideas, because wisdom gives you unexpected things, especially when the demands of contemporary political society and of the flesh incline you to sarcasm and indifference'. Letter of 7 November 1939 from Bucharest to Tilea in London.
      V.V. Tilea was appointed Minister Plenipotentiary to London in the last days of 1938 – a year that saw the accession of King Carol II to the throne of Romania and the start of a calamitous royal dictatorship, controlled from behind the scenes by Carol II's mistress Madame Lupescu and her cosmopolitan camarilla.

Țuțea's Relationship with the Legionary Movement[47]

From January to April 1938 Țuțea contributed articles on political economy to *Cuvântul* (*The Word*), edited by Nae Ionescu (1890–1940),[48] a charismatic right-wing university lecturer whose vision had deeply influenced young Romanian intellectuals. Ionescu's *trăirism* (literally, 'living-ism') stressed the realism of the 'inner spiritual life' and gave a boost to Romanian Orthodoxy. Moving on from the ideas of the *Manifesto*, these articles in *Cuvântul* aimed to promote traditional Romanian values. They built on the 1921 Agrarian Law, which had abolished the great estates and made Romania a nation of small landowners. Țuțea supported so-called 'anarchic liberalism'[49] (with free competition) at the level of small communities, and 'authoritarian liberalism' (a strong State to guarantee local freedom of competition) at the national level. The radical anti-liberal views expressed in the *Manifesto* had thus changed to something resembling Adam Smith's 'free hand', promoting free trade and privatisation.

However, when he examined the reality of Romanian political life he had to admit that the hopes he had placed in an authoritarian monarchy, as the guarantor of a liberal system, were dashed by the corruption that had infiltrated the royal household. In an unpublished letter of 7 November 1939 to his friend Viorel V. Tilea, Țuțea looks back and senses prophetically the tragedy which would soon face Romania:

> Senile and dishonest democrats became ministers in the authoritarian monarchy I had envisaged. There was a time when our distinguished sovereign was troubled and distracted, when he and true and genuine royalists should have united against the Jacobin worm that had burrowed under the royal mantle.

Like many distinguished Romanian intellectuals of his time, Țuțea was in sympathy with the nationalist and Christian aspects of Legionary ideology, which had interested

---

47   The Legionary Movement remains one of the 'hot potatoes' of Romania's modern history and will continue to remain so as long as KGB and other secret archives from outside Romania, as well as the archives of the Romanian Communist Party, remain inaccessible to researchers. Information is transmitted in a fragmentary, doctored, indeed myth-ologised form. Even in the 2000 general election *Legionarism* was used as a form of vilification by ultra-nationalist Communists.

      Presented by many historians today as a straightforward Nazi or Fascist organisation, it was clearly within that extremist spectrum, and was involved in retaliatory and 'punitive' acts, yet it is significant that the Nuremberg Tribunal did not proceed against the Legion, while they condemned as criminal other organisations: Prof. Hugh Trevor-Roper, interview, Didcot, 19 March 2002. See also Louis L. Snyder, *Encyclopedia of the Third Reich* (Ware, Hertfordshire: Wordsworth, 1998), p. 256. Iron Guard leaders found themselves imprisoned in Nazi camps such as Rostock and Buchenwald. Perhaps these details can serve as a caution to approach this period of history with care.

48   Professor of Logic and Metaphysics at the University of Bucharest.

49   Petre Țuțea, 'Ieftinirea vieții: ix. Economie înapoiată', *Cuvântul*, Bucharest, 27 February 1938, p. 8. ['Reducing the Price of Human Subsistence: ix. Underdeveloped Economy'.]

him as early as 1938. The Legionary Movement, an extreme nationalist organisation, better known by the title of its paramilitary wing, the Iron Guard, was founded in Romania in 1927, under the leadership of Corneliu Zelea Codreanu (see Appendix I). According to *declarații silite* ('forced declarations') from recently published *Securitate* files,[50] Țuțea became a member of the Iron Guard in 1940. In his re-educative 'memoirs' written in Aiud prison, Petre Pandrea showed that in 1933 at the Hotel Adlon in Berlin Țuțea met Nae Ionescu, the ideologue (though never a member) of the Legionary Movement. In 1936 Ionescu seems to have persuaded Țuțea to serve the Legionary cause.[51] In his later years Țuțea himself denied ever having been a member, and, indeed, as a civil servant he was not allowed to belong to any political party.[52] Nevertheless, on 12 April 1948 he was arrested and charged with 'Legionary activity'.[53]

The late Mihai Cârciog, Romania's commercial attaché in Rome and then Belgrade in the early 1940s, was Țuțea's colleague in the Ministry of Foreign Trade (set up by Decree no. 465 of 16 February 1940). He confirmed to me that after the 1941 'Legionary Rebellion' neither of them was forced to resign, unlike their director, Georgel Demetrescu, in charge of the Service for International Trade Agreements, who was accused of Legionary activity by Ion Antonescu's security forces and had to flee Romania. Demetrescu (and others of his staff who were similarly accused) found refuge in Spain where he died, while Țuțea remained at the same Ministry where he was promoted.[54]

I possess files, based on prison 'interviews', in which Țuțea acknowledged that he was a member of the Iron Guard in 1940. Such files,[55] however, are unreliable since they were based on information extracted under torture and, furthermore, were often doctored. It remains true, nevertheless, that during the four months of the National Legionary State he did publish articles in pro-Legionary papers such as *Cuvântul*.[56]

---

50   See Ioan Opriș, *Cercuri Culturale Disidente* (Bucharest: Univers Enciclopedic, 2001), pp. 287–300.
51   See Petre Pandrea, *Garda de Fier. Jurnal de filosofie politică. Memorii penitenciare*, ed. Nadia Marcu-Pandrea (Bucharest: Vremea, 2001), p. 419. Cf. Demostene Andronescu, 'Avocatul Diavolului: Petre Pandrea, "Garda de Fier. Jurnal de filosofie politică. Memorii penitenciare"', *Puncte Cardinale*, Sibiu, March 2002, p. 6.
52   'Înalt Decret Regal', nr. 870/1938, *Monitorul Oficial*, nr. 39, 17 February 1938. See also Ion Papuc, in Gabriel Stănescu (ed.), *Ultimile Dialoguri cu Petre Țuțea* (Norcross, GA: Criterion Publishing, 2000), p. 73. [*Last Dialogues with Petre Țuțea* = DIALOGUES.]
53   Ministerul de Interne, Direcția Secretariat, letter to Petre Țuțea, nr. 77011, 10.05.1991.
54   Interviews with Mihai Cârciog, London, 19 July 1999 and 8 April 2001. Cf. Stelian Neagoe, *Istoria Guvernelor României, de la începuturi – 1859 până în zilele noastre – 1995* (Bucharest: Machiavelli, 1995), p. 132.
55   See Plate 10. In Țuțea's *Securitate* file, 1937 is mentioned as the year when he joined the Legionary Movement. In the same 'Proces-verbal de Interogator' Țuțea says: 'The truth is that officially I became a member of the Legionary organisation immediately after 6 September 1940', Arhivele Sistemului Român de Informații, Dosar Fond penal nr. 25375, vol. 23, f. 296.
56   See Bibliography.

During the 1937 election the Legionaries gained a substantial share of the vote. In February 1938, however, its influence was radically curbed by the establishment of Carol II's royal dictatorship, which adopted a corporatist Constitution and abolished the independent judiciary as well as all political parties. In April Codreanu and other prominent Iron Guard leaders were arrested, then executed in November. A reign of terror ensued: the Iron Guard responded by assassinating Prime Minister Armand Călinescu, the king's main ally. In August 1939, with the Ribbentrop–Molotov agreement, Romania's fate was decided: in 1940 the country was divided up between Germany and the Soviet Union. Faced with general opposition and a nascent Legionary uprising, Carol II was forced to abdicate and flee the country, but not before granting General Ion Antonescu dictatorial powers as chief of State and president of the council of ministers. Carol II's son Mihai I, now aged nineteen, formally became king. The Iron Guard were given positions of power when the National Legionary State was established under Antonescu's leadership.

This co-operation was short-lived: by January 1941 the Legionaries and Antonescu found themselves in open conflict (described in Appendix I). The everyday government of the country had continued to need administration, and Țuțea's skills were in demand as a technocrat in the Ministry of National Economy. From February 1940 he worked as Director of the Research Office within the Ministry of Foreign Trade.[57]

In November 1940 Țuțea had been sent to Moscow with the Romanian economic delegation led by the former Foreign Secretary, Grigore Gafencu,[58] with the near impossible task of negotiating economic terms to 'normalise' Romania's relationship with the Soviet Union (an aggressor State which, in June 1940, had occupied Bessarabia and northern Bukovina).[59] On 23 January 1941, when the *Rebeliunea Legionară* ('Legionary Rebellion') was crushed in Bucharest, Țuțea was still in Moscow.[60] He recalled reading about Antonescu's 'successful military coup' in the

---

57   See Arhivele Naționale ale României, Direcția Arhivelor Centrale, Bucharest, Ministerul Economiei Naționale, Oficiul de Studii, Dosar 3/1943, f. 32. In the *Almanach de Gotha, Annuaire Généalogique, Diplomatique et Statistique 1944* (Gotha: Justus Perthes, 1944), p. 1081, Țuțea is listed among the directors of the Romanian Ministry of National Economy. He kept this position for almost four years, even after the Soviet takeover in August 1944.

58   Gafencu was aligned with the National Peasant Party (opposed to the Legionary Movement) and described Țuțea as a 'Guardist super-intellectual', yet the two were able to work as colleagues. Perhaps this gives an indication of the nature of the diplomatic milieu in which Țuțea moved. See Grigore Gafencu, 'Jurnal (1 Iunie – 13 Decembrie 1940)', typescript ed. and annotated by Ion Ardeleanu and Vasile Arimia, Bucharest, p. 445.

59   Grigore Gafencu, *The Last Days of Europe* (London: F. Muller, 1947), p. 10. Cf. Appendix I.

60   The Romanian delegation returned on 27 February 1941. See Arhiva Ministerului Afacerilor Externe, Bucharest: Telegram of 13 November 1940, Fond 71, 1920–1944, URSS, Telegrame Moscova 1940, vol. 3, MAE; Telegram of 28 February 1941, Fond 71, 1920–1944, URSS, Telegrame Moscova 1941–1944, vol. 4, MAE.

Soviet press.[61] When, on 22 June 1941, Hitler forced Antonescu to take the Romanian army across the Soviet border, Țuțea asked to join the front line, along with Legionaries who had been sent there as punishment for this 'Rebellion'. This favour was refused by the Minister for External Affairs, Mihai Antonescu[62] (no relation of the dictator), who told Țuțea that he could not be spared simply to serve as cannon fodder.

Throughout these years, during which his political thinking continued to evolve, Țuțea was a practising Christian of a conventional kind, perhaps taking Holy Communion at Christmas and Easter. Unlike Sergii Bulgakov, who moved to the Church from a position of religious scepticism, his religious journey might best be described as a reorientation toward the deeper truths of the faith in which he had been brought up. Perhaps it was this sense of spiritual reorientation that led him to remain in Romania, even though tempted to pursue an academic career abroad, at a time when many of those who had taken a traditionalist, anti-Western position on the political right, were leaving the country.[63]

Prison and Christian Illumination

In 1944 the Red Army imposed an oppressive Communist régime on a country where a Communist Party barely existed. The Red Army's presence in Romania was to continue until 1958. After King Mihai's abdication in 1947, the 'people's tribunals', created in 1944 to try war criminals, became convenient instruments for the disposal of opponents. From 12 April 1948 to 29 May 1953 Țuțea was detained in various political prisons including Ocnele Mari. It is difficult to determine his religious position at this time.[64] On 22 December 1956, after the Hungarian

---

61   Petre Țuțea, personal conversation at Municipal Hospital, Bucharest, 21 November 1980.
62   Simion Ghinea, interview, Bucharest, 29 August 1994.
63   Among these were: Eugène Ionesco (1912–94), 'the playwright of the absurd' who was to become a member of the French Academy; Emil Cioran (1911–95), Țuțea's friend, who was later recognised as one of France's leading philosophers; and Mircea Eliade (1907–86), who became internationally famous as a professor of the history of religions at the University of Chicago.
64   See Petre Pandrea, *Crugul Mandarinului, Jurnal intim (1952–1958)*, ed. Nadia Marcu-Pandrea, preface by Ștefan Dimitriu (Bucharest: Vremea, 2001), p. 228. Pandrea gives an enigmatic account of anti-religious comments spoken loudly by Țuțea in the street in December 1954, whilst walking with his friend the actress Corina Constantinescu. He goes on to describe the comments as 'butade ieftine și iresponsabile' (*cheap, irresponsible jokes*). Țuțea's heart is nevertheless 'mai curată decât a porumbelului' (*purer than a dove's*). It is clear that all three (Corina, Țuțea, and Pandrea) were followed by the *Securitate* in the street. In two interviews with me, Corina has denied that Țuțea was agnostic or atheistic after his first period of imprisonment. It will take a skilled biographer to do justice to this period of Țuțea's development. See also Corina Constantinescu, interview, Bucharest, 20 April 1999.

Revolution, he was again imprisoned for 'conspiring to overthrow the social order'.[65] On 1 August 1964 he was released from Aiud, where he had spent the last four years.

Aiud aimed specifically at destroying its inmates' Christian faith. In Țuțea's case, it achieved the opposite effect. The eldest son of an Orthodox priest, who according to custom would have inherited the parish from his father, he turned decisively to his roots. In solitary confinement he used the pipes in his cell to tap out prayers, messages, and Bible lessons in Morse code to other inmates. Sharing a dormitory with fellow Romanian academics, he was able to deepen his knowledge of Latin, and biblical Greek and Hebrew. These political prisoners, including priests and laymen, came to see themselves as living manuscripts, regarding prison as the Great University. Some of the anecdotes from these prison years are strikingly similar to the sayings of the Desert Fathers recorded in the *Apophthegmata Patrum*. Indeed they referred to their daily records of prison life as *Apophthegmata Patrum Rediviva*.

The Experience of Re-education

In 1949, at the Ocnele Mari labour camp and salt mine, Țuțea was included in the 'preparatory psychology' group of political prisoners who were to be re-educated through torture. The aim of this euphemistically named process of re-education was to replace the victims' identities with those of their executioners. 'New men' (re-educated fellow prisoners) became their *torționari* (torturers); they were subjected to mental 'torsion' until they confessed to, and repented of, crimes they had never committed – crimes to which in fact they themselves were being subjected. The process displayed a sadistic ability on the part of the *torționari* to induce psychopathology in their most courageous opponents.

Amid so much suffering, Țuțea discovered that he had a God-given ability to offer encouragement and inspiration in the most terrible circumstances. With his fellow prisoners dying, morally and physically, around him, it was in Ocnele Mari that Țuțea embarked on that struggle with the divine which is essential to any human being's spiritual growth. In the Old Testament, Jacob, having wrestled all night with the angel, acquires the name 'Israel', meaning 'may God shew his strength' or popularly, 'strong against God' (Gen. 32:28). Similarly perhaps, through the experience of Ocnele Mari and its aftermath, Țuțea wrestled – against the divinely testing lures of dejection, despair, belief in the absence, illusoriness, or negligibility of God – towards that power of faith, beyond mere intellectual apprehension or emotional conviction, which is life-sustaining and life-transforming. No longer merely the spectacular 'oral genius' of the coffee bars of Bucharest, as Mircea Eliade had described him,[66] he

---

65   Ministerul de Interne, Direcția Secretariat, letter to Petre Țuțea, nr. 77011, 10.05.1991.
66   Later, in 1967, in a discussion in Paris with the Romanian poet Ioan Alexandru, Eliade gave a more reverential account of Țuțea, paraphrasing Dostoyevsky's homage to Gogol: 'We have all come from Țuțea's overcoat.' Interview with Ioan Alexandru, Bonn, 6 September 1996. See also Nicolae Manolescu's articles: 'Mircea Eliade', *România*

encouraged his fellow prisoners to regard their deprivation as voluntary fasting, and to declare a hunger strike in protest against re-education. Amid the régime of torture he would give lectures on subjects which related theology and faith to culture and philosophy. His favourite theme was 'suicide and sacrifice in the Bible' (I Samuel 31:1–13; II Samuel 17:23; II Maccabees 14:37–46). He did not regard accounts of suicide in the Hebrew scriptures as models for pious imitation. Suicide was a violation of the inherent sanctity and wholeness of the human body. However, he discerned a possible sacrificial dimension to suicide – thus when political prisoners threatened the prison authority with collective suicide by a general hunger strike, an inherently selfish and godless act became sacrifice for the community.[67]

It was at Aiud prison in the early 1960s that Țuțea lived the *martyrion* that has so profoundly moved and influenced me and many others. Those who underwent 're-education' were required to make a public confession of their past errors. Țuțea's 're-education confession' was a three-hour speech on the subject 'Plato, the greatest among philosophers, as a modest precursor of Christ the Saviour'. The prison governor apparently asked Țuțea to re-dictate the speech for his own private records. Unfortunately, I have not managed to obtain a transcript of this speech. It is said that the priests in detention, who listened to Țuțea's confession, proposed to elect him Metropolitan Archbishop of Aiud prison without ordination.[68] Țuțea declined any such recognition. From then on, however, fellow prisoners and even guards would ask to see him for personal confession and spiritual guidance, while continuing to respect him as a philosopher.

Prison and Prayer

Țuțea's original approach to pre-Christian and secular philosophy led him to convert many people to the Christian faith and made him a target in the Communist purge of intellectuals. Yet he survived prison; something beyond intellectual power supported him and enabled him to take the spiritual way of perfection (Matt. 19:21) – that is, humble identification with Christ's suffering and the life of prayer.[69]

Prison became for Țuțea a 'university open to God' where he sought to break down the walls separating the Church and the world. It was here that he met the theologians Nichifor Crainic (1889–1972) and Fr Dumitru Stăniloae (1903–93). Crainic had been editor-in-chief of the traditionalist magazine *Gândirea* (*Thought*), 1926–44, and professor of Contemporary Religious Literature and Orthodox Mysticism and Doctrine (teaching a course on Mystical Theology[70] at the University of Bucharest).

    Literară, Bucharest, 19–25 March 1997, p. 1; and 'Declarație', *România Literară*, Bucharest, 11–17 November 1998, p. 1.

67   Dr Virgil Mateiaș, interview, Washington, DC, 12 August 1990.

68   See Chapter 4, section 'Metropolitan Archbishop of Aiud Prison?'.

69   See INTERVIEW, p. 3: 'Suffering in silence is the soul's sublime way to redemption.'

70   See the focus on the Prayer of the Heart in Nichifor Crainic, *Sfințenia – Împlinirea Umanului, Curs de Teologie Mistică (1935–1936)*, ed. Hierodeacon Teodosie Paraschiv

Stăniloae had been a professor at the Theology Faculty of Sibiu and the Theological Institute of Bucharest, and by 1948 had translated the first four volumes of the Romanian version of the *Philokalia* (see Appendix II). They had in common a high level of both education and reverence for what they had learned from traditional village life. Together with Stăniloae and Crainic, Țuțea the philosophical thinker discovered that life for political prisoners could be experienced as the desert where the Hesychast could attain a life of prayer focused enough to resist and overcome the principalities, powers, and rulers of the darkness of this age (Eph. 6:12).

After Prison, 1964–89

Țuțea was released from prison at a time when the hitherto Stalinist régime of Gheorghe Gheorghiu-Dej was distancing itself from Moscow and promising Romania greater autonomy. Gheorghiu-Dej died suddenly in March 1965, having designated the young Nicolae Ceaușescu as the next Communist Party leader. Ceaușescu would continue to develop Gheorghiu-Dej's independent foreign policy, also showing, at first, signs of liberalisation in domestic policy.

Although released from prison in August 1964, at a time of an apparent political 'thaw', Țuțea had to live either under house arrest in a small eighth-floor room with microphones behind the walls, or confined to Bucharest and monitored by *Securitate* officers day and night. This continued for almost thirty years until December 1989. During this period he would walk in Cișmigiu Park and other public places in the centre of Bucharest and simply speak philosophy and preach the Gospel to all and sundry. Another regular venue was the restaurant of the Romanian Writers' Union where, as well as his inevitable *Securitate* 'audience', he would attract writers, artists, university teachers, and students.

Țuțea as a 'Writer'

Although on his release from prison Țuțea had longed to work as an economist, he was obliged to subsist on a nominal pension from the Ministry of Health and Social Security. In July 1968, the Romanian Writers' Union granted him a pensionary writer status, although he had never published a book, which shows the extent of his influence in intellectual circles. He himself used to joke that his 'books' had been recorded on tape by *Securitate* agents and that he was therefore *de jure* a member of

---

(Iassy: Editura Mitropoliei Moldovei și Bucovinei, 1993), Chapters 14–17, pp. 127–66. The spiritual heritage of St Paisy Velichkovsky (see Appendix II) is also discussed in Nichifor Crainic, *Ortodoxie și Etnocrație, cu anexa: Programul Statului Etnocratic*, introd., notes, and ed. Constantin Schifirneț (Bucharest: Albatros, 1997), pp. 124–5. See also Nichifor Crainic, *Dostoievski și Creștinismul Rus*, foreword by Archbishop Bartolomeu Anania, afterword by Răzvan Codrescu (Cluj-Napoca, Bucharest: Arhidiecezana Cluj, Anastasia, 1998).

the Writers' Union. One of those agents (who also interrogated me in the mid-1980s) came to see Țuțea after the 1989 Revolution to tell him that he had been converted to Christianity while listening to his secretly recorded tapes. Many young intellectuals made the pilgrimage to the revered dissident's 'cell'. It may well be that his amazing courage, as well as his hilarious 'prayers for the sick' of the Ceaușescu dynasty,[71] contributed through these visitors to the dramatic events of December 1989.

Before 1989 Țuțea's published works appeared for the most part under the pseudonym Petre Boteanu, a necessary device to avoid suppression by the State. The last of his essays to be published during the Communist era was a memorandum about a meeting with the Romanian sculptor Constantin Brâncuși in 1938. He dictated this piece to me in 1983, but a censored version was published under his real name only in 1987 in *Arta*, the magazine of the Romanian Fine Arts Union. The text is significant not only because it develops a synthesis of pre-Christian and Orthodox elements in the light of Brâncuși's thinking, but also because it sets forth Țuțea's aesthetic and religious credo. It is a dialogue[72] about spiritual light, present from the origin of the world and fully revealed in Christ.

After 1989

Țuțea stressed 'the liberating rôle of prayer', as 'one of a series of paradoxes in religious thought'.[73] He suggested towards the end of his life that if the whole nation were to focus on a particular issue about the quintessential nature of the Romanian people, this would concentrate everybody's secret will into a collective petition in defiance of all expectations. Something of this nature occurred on 21 December 1989 when Ceaușescu appeared on the balcony of his Communist Party headquarters:

> What is the significance of the jeers that greeted the tyrant Ceaușescu, before his fall? The people were demanding the restoration of the natural order which had been trampled underfoot by the Stalinist tyrant, whom the crowd now refused to trust. When the crowd rejects a despot, he steps into the void.[74]

---

71   With the *Securitate* listening through their bugging devices, Țuțea would use caustic Rabelaisian language to pray for the paranoid presidential couple who were inflicting such atrocities upon the country.

72   Alexandru Popescu (ed.), 'Constantin Brâncuși and Petre Țuțea: On the Power and Limits of Art', *Sourozh*, nr. 69, Oxford, August 1997, pp. 8–16. [= ON ART.] In his monograph, *Brâncuși, Amintiri și Exegeze* (Bucharest: Meridiane, 1976), pp. 96–7, Petre Pandrea traces the Hesychast sources of Brâncuși's art.

73   THEATRE, p. 111.

74   Petre Țuțea, 'Restaurarea ordinei naturale, De vorbă cu Petre Țuțea', interview by Ion Coriolan Malița and Alexandru Prahovara [Popescu], *Timpul*, Iassy, 17 March 1990, p. 4. ['The Restoration of the Natural Order, Conversation with Petre Țuțea' = RESTORATION.]

Țuțea was able to convey the theology implicit in his spirituality through everyday language because of his great talent for conversation and his love of 'table talk' in the manner of Luther. He had a great gift for 'preaching' during meals or in café bars, to any audience and in the most unpromising circumstances. In 1990, while undergoing abdominal surgery on the operating table with local anaesthetic, he delivered an *ex tempore* lecture on the works of the seventeenth-century French writers Jacques-Bénigne Bossuet and Blaise Pascal, as compared with the sayings of early Christian monks.

Between 1989 and 1991 interviews with and essays by Țuțea were published in major Romanian newspapers.[75] He appeared on national television and spoke on the radio. On 1 January 1990 Prof. Dumitru Mazilu, Vice-President of the newly established Provisional Council of the National Salvation Front, asked to meet Țuțea for spiritual counsel.[76] On 21 January 1990 Andrei Pleșu, the Minister of Culture, wrote in the newspaper *România Liberă* an essay-portrait dedicated to Țuțea. The essay was entitled 'Petre Țuțea – un țăran imperial', ('Petre Țuțea – A Kingly Peasant').[77] In April 1990 he was awarded honorary membership of the newly established Association of Romanian Writers (which had replaced the pre-1989 Romanian Writers' Union). Some of his manuscripts, confiscated by the *Securitate*, were returned to his disciples, who began to publish them.[78] In the Spring of 1990, the highly respected writer Gabriel Liiceanu initiated a dialogue, recorded on film, between Țuțea in Bucharest and his old friend Emil Cioran in Paris. As it was being made, this East–West dialogue began to generate great interest and, although it was only finally shown on television a week after Țuțea's death, its impact was considerable.[79] Țuțea's 'Mircea Eliade' was serialised in the prestigious monthly magazine *Familia* in 1990.[80] Romanians in exile began to organise lectures on Țuțea. I remember Țuțea's responding to his sudden fame with a quote from the French diplomat, Talleyrand: 'Exaggeration is the hallmark of the insignificant.'

---

75 Some interviews, essays, and letters were posthumously collected and published in BGMP.

76 Țuțea's conversation with Prof. Dumitru Mazilu, Bucharest, 1 January 1990. I was the intermediary for this meeting, and I treasure the record of their conversation taken in short-hand, which is in my possession.

77 See Andrei Pleșu, 'Petre Țuțea – un țăran imperial', in *Chipuri și măști ale tranziției* (Bucharest: Humanitas, 1996), p. 323. In translating *imperial* as 'kingly' rather than 'imperial' it should be noted that, due to the Byzantine background of Romanian Orthodox experience, kingship was understood in terms of the Imperial Court of Byzantium. Thus, for instance, in the Lord's Prayer, 'For Thine is the Kingdom' translates as *Că a Ta este Împărăția*.

78 From March to May 1990 Țuțea's essay 'Filosofia Nuanțelor' ('Philosophy of Nuances'), for example, was serialised in the weekly newspaper *Baricada*. See Bibliography.

79 See Liana Ionescu, 'Ultimul Socrate și scepticul de serviciu', *România Liberă*, Bucharest, 18 December 1991, p. 4. See also Gabriel Liiceanu, 'Prefață la un film despre Cioran', in *Apel către Lichele* (Bucharest: Humanitas, 1992), pp. 52–60.

80 See Bibliography.

Nevertheless, his influence was significant. For instance, anti-Communist students and intellectuals demonstrated in Bucharest between 22 April and 13 June 1990, the longest demonstration in Romanian history. The protesters were brutally suppressed when President Ion Iliescu brought in miners to disperse the crowds. Ţuţea had provided inspiration for this remarkable protest:

> It has been said that the demonstration in University Square in Bucharest, led by my disciple Marian Munteanu, was due to me. It gave me pleasure. To mobilise students is not at all the same thing as bringing miners from the valley of the river Jiu to smash heads.[81]

During the year before his death (3 December 1991) Ţuţea was cared for in the Christiana Orthodox Hospital in Bucharest.

Ţuţea's Posthumous Reputation

Revered by some as a saint, and dismissed by others as prolix, obscure, and idiosyncratic, some seek to use Ţuţea as an icon for the 'new right'. Ţuţea the politician was, however, rehabilitated by the Supreme Court of Justice in 1997.[82] Since his death, his works have been widely published, mainly in highly inaccurate editions. The most reliable is Mircea Coloşenco's *Lumea ca Teatru. Teatrul Seminar*. Coloşenco's foreword combines biographical and historiographical accuracy with informed scholarship in the relevant areas, as well as perceptive general interpretation. There are also a few sketchy but useful introductions to some of Ţuţea's writings.

A somewhat unreliable presentation of Ţuţea is Radu Sorescu's 'unauthorised biography'.[83] In the first chapter, 'Petre Ţuţea's Life', Sorescu makes extensive use of Mircea Coloşenco's foreword, but neglects to acknowledge this. On biographical matters he claims that Ana Ţuţea had affairs which led to other children (who would thus be Ţuţea's step-brothers and -sisters), and that his father Petre Bădescu was

---

81   Petre Ţuţea, 'Omul este un animal care poate fi mişcat din loc de iluzie', interview by Marius Costineanu, *Tinerama*, 16–23 November 1990, p. 16. ['Man is an Animal Who Can Be Swayed by Illusion'.]

82   George Roncea, 'Petre Ţuţea a fost reabilitat de Curtea Supremă de Justiţie', *Ziua*, Bucharest, 21 October 1997, p. 12. Writing in prison in 1963, the left-wing writer and lawyer Petre Pandrea included Ţuţea among the *scriitori antifascişti* ('anti-Fascist writers'). See Pandrea, *Garda de Fier*, p. 307.

83   Radu Sorescu, *Viaţa şi Opera lui Petre Ţuţea* (Bucharest: Scripta Press, 1999), with a bibliography (pp. 120–32) and an appendix (pp. 133–41). The book has caused distress to Ţuţea's family. In an e-mail to me, Andrea Chirilă, a graduate in philosophy (grand-daughter of Ţuţea's younger sister, Angela), told me that she found the book extremely offensive. Răzvan Codrescu, *În căutarea Legiunii pierdute* (Bucharest: Vremea, 2001), p. 133, describes Sorescu's monograph as combining 'dubious sensationalism with a second-rate intellectual exercise'.

violent, but he produces the flimsiest of evidence.[84] There is nothing either in Ţuţea's own work or recorded conversations, or in my interviews with his younger brothers, sisters, and relatives to substantiate such claims.

Sorescu meanwhile demonstrates remarkable ignorance about much of the theology that was so central to Ţuţea both as a man and as a thinker. Undeterred by his ignorance, however, he proceeds to deny Ţuţea's spiritual authenticity, dismissing his mysticism as 'formal, assumed only at the level of language'.[85] While he quotes from Ţuţea's published books, these quotations are not identified.

Finally, Sorescu demonstrates an inadequate reading even of Ţuţea's published work. For instance his third chapter ('The lure of philosophy. Escape from the system', only ten pages) does not even refer to the second volume of Ţuţea's *Christian Anthropology*.[86] Indeed this major five-volume work receives only one mention in Sorescu's book, where he simply quotes two of Ţuţea's definitions of theology.[87] It is in part to redress this and other false assessments of Ţuţea's character and achievements that the present book has been written.

Overview of Ţuţea's Political and Religious Thought

Ţuţea addressed the issues of his day with a passionate concern for first principles. Although not directly concerned with the questions of pluralism and sustainable global development that perhaps represent the most urgent dilemmas of the twenty-first century, his very personal 'voice', bringing together the universal and the particular with analytical acuteness, at once challenges our assumptions and stimulates our own capacity to recognise first principles and to think from them for ourselves.

In this final section of the present chapter – before exploring in more detail the philosophical and theological ideas that mark Ţuţea as a true theologian ('the one who prays') – I will look briefly at Ţuţea's thinking on a number of broad issues: nationalism and the Romanian *ţăran* (peasant), freedom, the co-operative principle, and liberalism.

---

84 Sorescu's information appears to be based on antipathetic village gossip and an interview with Cornel Tican who was born only in 1940. On 23 August 2000, Cornel (the son of Ţuţea's sister Maria) told me in a conversation in Boteni that he was drunk at the time of his interview with Sorescu, whose claims he denied.

85 Sorescu, *Viaţa şi Opera*, p. 118.

86 See Petre Ţuţea, *Omul, Tratat de Antropologie Creştină, vol. 2, Sistemele sau Cartea Întregurilor Logice, Autonom-Matematice, Paralele cu Întregurile Ontice*, afterword and ed. Cassan Maria Spiridon (Iassy: Timpul, 1993). [*The Human Being, Treatise on Christian Anthropology, vol. 2, Systems, or the Book of Logical Wholes, Mathematically Autonomous, Parallel to Ontic Wholes* = SYSTEMS.]

87 Sorescu, *Viaţa şi Opera*, p. 51; see also Chapter 4, 'Gândirea Religioasă', written by Sorescu on Ţuţea's religious thought, pp. 51–61.

Ţuţea's Nationalism

Între Dumnezeu şi Neamul Meu (*Between God and My People*), a book containing interviews with and essays by Ţuţea, was published in 1992. This title epitomises his later political vision, which came to be dominated by two apparently contradictory ideas: on the one hand, nationalism (the nation as a means of salvation) and on the other hand, liberalism (though only as understood in the light of the Christian Gospel). In their *Concise Theological Dictionary*, Karl Rahner and Herbert Vorgrimler present nationalism alongside Marxism as a substitute religion of the nineteenth century, a 'wilful abandonment of religion' following the Enlightenment:

> It was Europe's great temptation to interpret God's revelation as the self-revelation of man, redemption by the Son as man's self-redemption, and thus to fall into diabolic pride – a temptation to which it largely succumbed. Yet even here, even in its atheism, Europe followed Christianity (completely misunderstood, of course).[88]

Ţuţea would partially agree with this. However, he produced no systematic work on nationalism. What follows in this section has been assembled from references to the subject scattered throughout his writings and interviews.

The modern Romanian State was constitutionally established in two stages: first, with the unification of the principalities of Wallachia and Moldavia in 1859; secondly, with the formation of the Romanian unitary State including Transylvania in 1918 (see Appendix I). The outstanding representative figure of this period was Mihai Eminescu (1850–89). As the leading political theorist of the nation-State and 'national poet' of Romania, he wrote:

> The fundamental principle is nationality within the boundaries of truth: the untrue does not become true, the ugly does not become beautiful, evil does not become good merely because it is a national characteristic.[89]

In 1939, when Romania was on the verge of disintegration, Dumitru Stăniloae expressed the difference between true and false national values in his classic *Ortodoxie şi Românism* (*Orthodoxy and the Romanian Spirit*):

> There are various kinds of nationalism. One kind can be a fall into sinfulness – and this is very often what happens; yet anti-nationalism is a more serious fall into sin, being contrary not only to the Christian way of community life, but also to nature... Like anything genuine, salvific belief in the nation as opposed to nationalism need not lead to our destruction if developed in accord with faith. Though not in itself redemptive, it is not destructive. What saves us is faith, the Christian spirit we infuse into national aspiration. Nationalism of

88   Karl Rahner and Herbert Vorgrimler, *Concise Theological Dictionary*, ed. Cornelius Ernst OP, trans. Richard Strachan (London: Burns & Oates, 1968), p. 401.
89   Mihai Eminescu, 'Naţionalii şi Cosmopoliţii', in *Opere Politice*, 3 vols (Iassy: Timpul, 1997–99), II (1998), pp. 614–15. Cf. Ion Papuc, in DIALOGUES, p. 71.

itself can neither save nor destroy. But in practice all nationalism is either redemptive or destructive, according to whether or not it is animated by Christian faith.[90]

Țuțea's views on nationalism continued in the tradition established by Eminescu and further articulated by Stăniloae. In 1964 – after his release from prison, but long before he was able to join the National Liberal Party (abolished in 1947 and restored after 1989) – Țuțea formulated his concept of the nation-State afresh, deriving it from the principle of equality among nations. He related this concept to global development:

> Although the nation should not be identified with the human race as a whole, it should behave concretely and spiritually as if it were. The idea of equality applied to the community of peoples confers on every people the right to comprehensive development on both levels. Every nation within its own borders aspires to develop as a whole, with all its material resources, and tends to reflect in its essential being the characteristics of the universal order...

> Economic power can be acquired peacefully at a global level, on the basis of the principle of economic competition, when the equality of all peoples is respected. [But] the autocratic tendencies of the great powers transform spheres of economic dominance violently or imperceptibly into *Lebensraum* for themselves.[91]

Țuțea believed that Romania's national character, reflected in its way of life, can legitimately take the form of national struggle:

> Any powerful nation weaves its history from its own substance, as the spider weaves its web. The history of our nation reveals wonderful patterns of pure spirit and unostentatious heroism. Our physical and psychological make-up compels us to sacrifice everything for the preservation of our national being.[92]

Elsewhere he called the Romanian people a 'community of destiny'.[93] In the first volume of his *Christian Anthropology* he insists that their national consciousness had been nurtured and inspired by participation in the sanctity that God has allowed the Romanian people to attain throughout history, as a nation and through representative individuals ('iconic figures'):

> I belong to the Romanian people, to its time and space, and participate in the eternity of the Christian order lived out by that people, with all the vigour of its Latin spirit. And because my people *is*, therefore I am. The soul of the whole human race [as incarnate in the Saviour] is experienced by every Romanian who is aware of existing, both spiritually

---

90   Dumitru Stăniloae, *Ortodoxie și Românism* (Sibiu: Tiparul Tipografiei Arhidiecezane, 1939), p. 104.
91   PROJECT, pp. 103, 105.
92   THEATRE, p. 273.
93   THEATRE, p. 134.

and iconographically, in a way specific to our nation. *Valorile neautohtonizate* ['non-autochthonous values'] are fictions.[94]

Țuțea stressed that what ultimately defines Romanian identity is the visible Latin and Christian elements which the Dacians[95] assimilated from Roman legions and Christian missionaries both before and after the Roman conquest in AD 106.[96] He associated the 'Latin spirit' with the idea of civilisation transmitted by the Roman Empire, with its legislative genius, its emphasis on order and discipline, its civic planning and the 'confidently assumed right to dominate others'[97] through its institutions, and its political and economic power. He also emphasised the gradual process of osmosis by which Christianity spread, after the Roman invasion in the first century AD, throughout the territories now inhabited by the Romanian people. He noted that, unlike the Russians (who celebrate the anniversary of the 'Baptism of the Rus' in AD 988) and the Germans (converted to Christianity under Charlemagne in AD 800), the conversion of proto-Romanians cannot be assigned to a specific date.[98]

---

94   PROBLEMS, p. 63 (italics added). For Țuțea, 'one cannot establish the spiritual profile of Romanian people outside of the Christian Church': see his *Mircea Eliade (eseu).* foreword by Crăciun Bejan, afterword and interview by Dumitru Chirilă, ed. Ioan Moldovan (Oradea: Biblioteca Revistei Familia, 1992), p. 57. [*Mircea Eliade. An Essay* = ELIADE.]
95   Native 'barbarians' of Thracian origin called *Getae* in Greek sources – the Romans later called them *Dacii* (Dacians). See Georgescu, *Romanians*, p. 3. Cf. Emilian Popescu, *Christianitas Daco-Romana* (Bucharest: Editura Academiei Române, 1994), pp. 30–43.
96   Țuțea is aware of the difficulties encountered by historians in their efforts to elucidate the enigma of the Dacian language, of which only few words survived. But, strictly speaking, although the Romanian people are thought to derive from a 'Dacian-Roman synthesis', in the light of modern Romanian culture and history, the Romanian spirit and language are in fact seen to be 'predominantly Latin'. See Petre Țuțea, 'Stilurile, sau Cartea Unităților Cultural Istorice și a Modalităților Estetice ale Artelor, sau Omul Estetic', 2 vols (Bucharest: December, 1988), II, p. 242. ['Styles, or the Book of Historical Cultural Unities and of the Aesthetic Forms of the Arts, or Aesthetic Humanity', I and II (typescript) = STYLES, I and II.] For a discussion of Țuțea's view of the Dacian and Latin elements of Romanian psychology, see also Alexandru Popescu, '"The Peasant Chats over the Fence with God": A Christian Sense of the Land with Reference to the Thought of the Romanian Dissident Petre Țuțea', *Humanitas*, 4:1, Birmingham, 2002, pp. 63–6.
97   Alex Scobie, *Hitler's State Architecture, The Impact of Classical Antiquity* (London: Pennsylvania State University Press, 1990), p. 136. Scobie quotes from Virgil's *Aeneid* 6.851–3: 'Remember, Roman, to exercise dominion over nations. These will be your skills: to impose culture on peace, to spare the conquered, and to war down the proud', a passage often quoted by Țuțea in conversation.
98   STYLES, II, p. 242. The 'folk Christianity' of proto-Romanians combined common sense, religious discipline, and local superstitions. The neo-Latins living between the Carpathians and the Danube had developed an understanding of the sacraments, observed periods of fasting, celebrated Christian festivals, believed in wonders as signs of divine intervention, honoured the saints and venerated their relics. See Nelu Zugravu, *Geneza*

But the essence of 'Romanian-ness' remains elusive, a 'complex synthesis'[99] of an infinite range of nuances of history and pre-history – a potent reality, actively felt and experienced, that can never be entirely comprehended within definitions of State and factual historiography, but which may, in its 'not of this world' power, beauty, and mystery, point to that Kingdom into which only the village carpenter's son from Nazareth can receive us.

For Țuțea, 'values which are not embodied in a people are fictions', while all national cultures are – by their values, artefacts, and civilising institutions – 'sources of spiritual nourishment'.[100] He maintains that national identity earths a person and gives him his language, thus profoundly determining self-identity:

> If one morning I woke up without being aware of myself as a Romanian, and speaking an unknown language, I would be like a drunk man, unable to find my way home.[101]

Individual human identity is thus neither abstract nor temporary. Rather, it is definitive and inseparable from the economy of the Incarnation. The same holds true at the level of ethnic and national identity, which are related to the geographical territory within which particular languages, cultures, and customs have developed. In the late 1960s, at a time when Ceaușescu's Communist nationalism was trying to counteract Soviet hegemonic internationalism, Țuțea stressed the importance of a rational understanding of nation and ethnicity:

> To believe that nations eventually disappear shows either irresponsibility or weariness, or alternatively sheer selfishness and greed. The desire of certain nations for expansion and dominance cannot be satisfied without the destruction of others. Realisation of the individual and of the corporate must begin from the present, historically determined state of things. Ethnicity constitutes the premise of any human activity.[102]

In his *Project for a Treatise*, reflecting on what could be called tribal consciousness, Țuțea quotes the Romanian historian Vasile Pârvan (1882–1927), who maintained that 'ethnicity is a point of departure and not of arrival' in the development of humanity.[103] Ethnicity refers to racial groupings, many of which can be included in a single nation, and thus it should not be confused with national identity. Ethnic identification is, for Țuțea, a primitive stage of social evolution. National identity expresses a more advanced level of human development. Nevertheless, he insists that:

Creștinismului Popular al Românilor (Bucharest: Ministerul Educației, Institutul Român de Tracologie, Bibliotheca Thracologica, XVIII, 1997), pp. 543–4.

99   Lucian Boia, *Istorie și Mit in Conștiința Românească*, 2nd edn (Bucharest: Humanitas, 1997), p. 136.
100 PROBLEMS, p. 63.
101 THEATRE, p. 273.
102 Petre Țuțea, *Philosophia Perennis*, ed. Horia Niculescu, afterword by Matei Albastru (Bucharest: Icar and Horia Niculescu, 1992), p. 187.
103 PROJECT, p. 83.

no one can affirm with certainty that the nation is the final stage in universal evolution. In our present state of development, however, the nation is a reality dominated by the constant tendency to absorb the material and spiritual values of humanity and fully realise its potential, reckoning that it has a duty to give expression to humanity.[104]

More than ethnicity, nationhood thus constitutes a precious reality, which gives people the foundation from which to grow and be transformed by human culture. At the same time human beings are called beyond this to realise their adoption as co-heirs with Christ, by means of *theosis* – a process requiring and implying continuous personal and collective change. As a Christian, Țuțea had a vision of the heavenly city in which race, ethnicity, nationality, and gender, while remaining eternally recognisable, are not the ultimate defining factors of personhood. He respected the logical impossibility of directly identifying the 'mythic' time of the first Adam and the return in glory of 'the last Adam' (1 Cor. 15:45) with chronological time (with its boundaries of State, language, culture, and customs). He undoubtedly had a high view of nationhood: 'when nations disappear we enter the Tower of Babel'.[105] Yet he understood, too, the Gospel imperative for change and development through *metanoia* (repentance), and conformity to the commandments of Christ.

Individuals do not exist separately from the people of whom they are part. The very nature of the Incarnation involves particularity of time, place, and physical existence. Like Stăniloae, Țuțea understands that national and ethnic identity are essential vehicles for personal perfection in Christ. Christ Himself was a Jew, and this was essential to God's redemptive work. 'The Way, the Truth, and the Life' (John 14:6) embraces ethnic identity, but also transcends it. Where nationalism becomes irrational – fuelling pride, greed, aggression, and intolerance – it negates its own meaning and destroys its own beauty, becoming an instrument of evil and respecting no boundaries: 'Excessive nationalism is chauvinism. It is an exaggeration and as such intolerable.' However, 'while chauvinism is intolerable because it exaggerates, so also is radical democracy' (for example, the mob rule imposed by the Bolsheviks), 'because it too exaggerates'.[106]

Thus, Țuțea observed in 1964 that Soviet Russia was ostensibly a democracy (according to its Constitution). Yet, he would say later, the Russian people enjoyed more true freedom during the tsarist period than under Gorbachev: 'You respected the Tsar, and his law and authority; then you did what you wanted. A Tolstoy was possible.'[107] Tsarism was part of the Russian people's identity, while the Communist

---

104 PROJECT, p. 83.
105 BGMP, p. 99.
106 Țuțea, 'Omul este un animal', p. 16. While speaking of democracy as 'the only system compatible with human dignity and freedom', Țuțea reminds us that – whether in antiquity or in the present time – it has no criteria for selecting values other than the rule of the majority: see RESTORATION, p. 4.
107 Țuțea, 'Omul este un animal', p. 16. Just as the Augustinian is exhorted to 'Do anything in the name of love' ('Dilige et quod vis fac', *In Epistolam Joannis ad Parthos*, tractatus 7, sec. 8), so the true democrat needs a basis of belief (organically linked with a loving,

system was an artificial and illegitimate construct based on a utopian concept of 'proletarian internationalism':

> Those who operate within a supranational structure are therefore working against nature. Those who aspire to the unity of the human species deny the principle of competition among peoples. They deny the very principle of modern civilisation, which had to fight its way into existence.[108]

His belief in the salvation of his nation led Țuțea to an optimistic view of Romania, despite the increasing secularisation of the Balkan States:

> When I think as a Romanian among Romanians, I am full of hope for the future. One day a Greek said to me: 'We Greeks no longer exist, but you Romanians, you have a future.' When they read their ancient history, contemporary Greeks are faced with a sense of futility and decadence, they must sometimes feel like committing suicide. They are Greeks in a geographical sense, but that's it! With us Romanians it is very different.[109]

Țuțea extends his Christian hope for the future to all nations that survived the Soviet catastrophe in Eastern and Central Europe. In 1990, he wrote:

> Not only the Russian people, but all the peoples of Eastern and Central Europe are now experiencing a Christian renaissance. It is obvious that the current process of ethical and social purification is taking place under the guidance of the Holy Spirit. Christian virtue and religion are vastly superior to the hypocritical code of conduct (*science des moeurs*) imposed in such a repugnant way by the atheist Stalinist régime. In Romania this was endured and eventually overthrown by the Christian spirit of the people.[110]

The victory of the Romanian people to which Țuțea refers (and in which he participated) was one of obedience to the divine command, 'Be wise as serpents and harmless as doves' (Matt. 10:16). The grace of divine love casts out the fear and self-interest that generate cynicism and servility.[111] Political prisoners in Romania had borne witness to that within the human spirit which is of God, which will always defy brutalisation: the divine indwelling revealed in the Resurrection and glorification of Christ. Through their discipleship of self-denial, their identity – personal and therefore cultural and national – was preserved and extended. Țuțea's

---

purposeful intuition of creative power) rather than ideology (a mechanistic conceptual construct of power and creativity). See Angela Partington, *The Oxford Dictionary of Quotations*, 4th edn (London: Oxford University Press, 1992), p. 37.

108 BGMP, p. 299. Țuțea's warnings proved to be all too well founded during the conflicts of the 1990s in former Yugoslavia and Chechnya.

109 Petre Țuțea, *321 de vorbe memorabile ale lui Petre Țuțea*, 1st edn, foreword and ed. Gabriel Liiceanu (Bucharest: Humanitas, 1993), p. 88. [*321 Aphorisms of Peter Țuțea* = APHORISMS.]

110 RESTORATION, p. 4.

111 PROBLEMS, p. 171.

own thinking about nationhood was, in this process, also extended. In 1986 he wrote that individual and social identity at every level, within its evolutionary economy, is taken up in that all-embracing love and 'perfection of which the Saviour speaks in the Sermon on the Mount'[112] and which He enjoins upon His disciples.

On the Romanian Țăran

Although for a time in the late 1920s and early 1930s Țuțea was a Marxist activist,[113] he always maintained a 'mystical link' with the countryside where he was born: he wished to be buried in his so-called 'native land',[114] which, for him, was integrated with the ancient culture of the Romanian peasantry.[115] The theological understanding which he developed during his period of political imprisonment led him to discover an eschatological dimension to the agrarian socialist ideas of his youth. He came to recognise the inherent limitations of the idealistic programme for social and national justice which he had promoted during his early Marxist period. His vision of a *țăran* as the archetypal husbandman – light years away from the depersonalised ruthlessness of modern global agribusiness – points to principles of social and international practice that derive from a primordial sense of justice imprinted on the human soul at creation. An urban 'hermit' who remained spiritually close to the

---

112   See PROBLEMS, pp. 116–17.
113   According to Cioran, who was introduced to Țuțea by Corina Sombart in Berlin, 'Il était marxiste à l'époque; un marxiste enthousiaste, mystique': Liiceanu, *Itinéraires d'une vie: E.M. Cioran*, p. 30. Cf. Emil Cioran, interview, Paris, 17 August 1992.
114   Țuțea's letter of 26 January 1970 to the late Fr Stanca Sisoe, parish priest (courtesy of Fr Dumitru Prunoiu, parish priest, St Paraschiva Church, Boteni, Argeș, see Arhiva Parohiei). Cf. Țuțea's letter of 20 March 1991 to the parish council, Arhiva Parohiei.
115   The traditional *țăran* culture and way of life are still a living reality: their buildings and clothes include a great variety of styles. Architecture varies according to the geography, and includes stylised carvings and combinations of colours which decorate arches, fences, gates, and doors. Each region has its own traditional costume for men, women, and children, intricately embroidered in a multiplicity of colours and designs inspired by the flowers, fauna, and landscape of the region. In what they create, the *țărani* seem to capture a sense of cosmic beauty and design, enfolding themselves in nature through the patterns on their clothes and in the way they decorate their houses. Even their names are connected to their environment: girls are called by names of flowers and plants like *Florica* ('Little Flower'), *Viorica*, *Violeta*, *Crenguța* ('Little Branch'); and boys by the names of trees and rivers, such as *Brăduț* ('Little Fir Tree'), *Alun* ('Hazelnut Tree'), and *Olt* (the largest inland river in Romania).

     Their connection with nature is also expressed in their relationship with animals, which they treat almost as their children by singing to them, petting them, and dedicating poems to them. Nevertheless, these animals are their livelihood, and if the *țăran* is to survive, the beast must be slaughtered. They have a highly developed sense of food, wine, and cuisine. People are expected to savour their food, and visitors are entertained lavishly. The best room in many old Romanian houses is kept specially for guests, who are treated as if they were Christ Himself.

village of his birth, where his father had served as a priest, Țuțea devoted the later decades of his life to prayer and winning souls in the city. Towards the end of his life he would contrast town and village thus:

> You cannot say that in a village all people think as one... Human beings do not think as a group. *Țăran* culture is built on the individual personality of every peasant. *Țărani* have an apparently anonymous personality, very different from townsfolk who leave their mark everywhere, on paper and in graffiti... In the countryside truths spring up naturally, like fir trees or beech trees. There is no such thing as initiative or, as Blaga[116] calls it, 'the creative tendency of the village'... *Țărani* form a community, townsfolk form a society. In the countryside, society is organic in nature, while urban society is artificially constructed. Townsfolk are bundled together like potatoes in a sack, while *țărani* live together in a village, following rules of behaviour that ensure the healthy balance of the environment. *Țăran* community creates only rural customs; it does not set normative principles for living in a modern society.[117]

Like Marx, Țuțea saw traditional rural life and modern city life as sharply opposed. He did not, however, consider them antagonistic, since both are inhabited by human beings in different forms of social organisation.

For Țuțea the concept of the *țăran* is primarily neither ethical, nor social. It is an ontological concept, illuminating the very nature of humanity. There is something of the *țăran* in every human being: everyone needs their 'feet on the ground', no-one can defy gravity for long, all are ultimately dependent on the fruits of the earth, which is the point of reference for humanity's basic sense of stability, distance, and depth. In the end, the earth is also the element to which everyone physically returns. We are all *țărani* in the sense that, whether we like it or not, and whether we are aware of it or not, we have this dependency upon the soil. In the spiritual domain, awareness of this dependency and a humility toward the mystery of being, in this earthbound creaturely order, are essential to human knowledge of God.

> When the last *țăran* disappears from the world – that is, from all nations – the last member of the human species will disappear. And then we shall have apes in human clothing.[118]

According to Țuțea human beings cannot be considered separately from their relationship to both the environment and God. In Genesis, man's relationship with the earth was radically changed by the choice made by Adam and Eve to disobey the divine command. After the Fall, instead of tending the land as a divine gift, Adam had to work it by the sweat of his brow (Gen. 3:17–19). No longer pure blessing, the link with the land took on an aspect of curse.[119] Within the dispensation of wrath

---

116 Lucian Blaga (1895–1961), Romanian philosopher, poet, and diplomat; friend of Țuțea. See I. Oprișan, *Lucian Blaga printre Contemporani, Dialoguri adnotate* (Bucharest: Minerva, 1987), p. 21.
117 BGMP, p. 358. Cf. APHORISMS, pp. 99–100.
118 APHORISMS, p. 105.
119 See PROBLEMS, p. 312.

(Eph. 2:3), however, there is still what might be called a natural relationship with the divine. For all the 'animality', the superstition, and fearfulness of fallen creatures, we nevertheless have a sense of natural beauty and, in modern terms, environmental awareness and a sense of responsibility for the planet. The Darwinian subhumanity envisaged by Țuțea has lost this.[120]

Țuțea ascribed to the *țărani* an archetypal significance, as stewards of creation. He related their culture and way of life to the Adam of the biblical story, *omul absolut*[121] ('the absolute man') invested with responsibility for tending the earth. Thus, though confronting the elements and having to cope with the harshness of working the land, oppressed and exploited by the sinful callousness of human society, the *țăran* nevertheless fulfils the crucial rôle of producing the essentials for the whole of humankind, and offers through the traditional customs and lore of rural life a glimpse of an original good. In a society affected in every aspect by Marxist–Leninist materialism, Țuțea persisted in affirming that the human race will destroy itself if it continues to live 'by bread alone' rather than 'by every word that proceeds from the mouth of God' (Matt. 4:3). The 'solutions' he points to, both in his life and in his writing, lie in the realm not of economics and politics, but of the spirit.

Freedom and Political Theology

After sixty years of wrestling with his ideas Țuțea embarked upon his *Christian Anthropology*. In the introduction, written in 1984, he describes in Augustinian terms the human journey from *civitas terrena sive diaboli* to *civitas Dei*.[122] For him, everything is part of God, but God is more than the sum of everything.[123] The earthly world is governed from above, although we fail to recognise this, and is purged of its imperfections at that 'truly purifying, liturgical' moment, when 'transcendent heaven veils the physical heaven, while earth laments its imperfections and disharmony'[124] with heaven's divinely created order; this is the experience of those who are divinely inspired, whose spiritual *charisms* can 'enlighten both the seeker' (who does not fully know) 'and the benighted' (who is simply ignorant):

> Everything is to be seen from above, sustained by inspiration and faith, not sought for either deductively or inductively, since there is no rational way to the Absolute. This transcendent

---

120   See section 'Animalism și Hominism', in PROBLEMS, pp. 285–90.
121   APHORISMS, p. 105.
122   PROBLEMS, p. 7.
123   See THEATRE, p. 490.
124   THEATRE, p. 390. Țuțea refers here to the 'cosmic liturgy', what Lars Thunberg, following Maximus the Confessor, calls the mediation between heaven and earth, effected by Christ in that 'he *ascended into heaven* with his earthly body, consubstantial with ours, and thereby demonstrating *the unity of sensible nature* through the elimination of the particularity of its separating division'; see Lars Thunberg, *Microcosm and Mediator, The Theological Anthropology of Maximus the Confessor*, 2nd edn, foreword by A.M. Allchin (Chicago: Open Court, 1995), p. 391 (Thunberg's italics).

heaven is sovereign over earth, it does not merge with it, but descends to it and redeems it and judges it.[125]

According to Ţuţea, any strictly political definition of freedom is at best ambiguous because it lacks a transcendental dimension:

> Freedom means independence from external conditioning... I connect the idea of happiness with the idea of freedom, even if freedom is deceptive and implies uncertainty, as Faust says. The slave cannot be happy. Inner freedom must be completed by external freedom, otherwise it is only an illusion. When the powerful theorise about freedom, it becomes a cunning form of domination. Talleyrand's attitude is more honest when he says: 'Solidarity between governor and governed resembles the solidarity between the horse and its rider'. Cynics are closer to nature.[126]

I have shown that for Ţuţea God's love for all creation transcends the friend–enemy distinction. This crucial truth is articulated in the Sermon on the Mount, which Ţuţea believed to be the quintessential Christian message. Jesus's soteriological programme includes and goes beyond the Ten Commandments precisely because it requires us to love our enemies.

Ţuţea's fundamental understanding of freedom is in terms of unconditional Christian love, which is not subject to the limitations of human emotions or political control. Although both love and hate are transcendent, he contrasts the supra-personal nature of hate with the personal nature of love, which therefore has the power to 'unite and create', rather than 'divide and destroy':

> If we want to see why individuals and peoples disintegrate and why ethical political values decay, we must look to the realm of the emotions, for their corruption is reflected in the forms and practices of government... Two social classes, in a revolution, or two nations at war, embody this paradox: they hate each other objectively. Their hate is not the sum of individual hates, but has a supra-personal reality.[127]

In the late 1930s in Berlin, asked by his mentor, Nae Ionescu, what 'the characteristics of a true Romanian should be', Ţuţea had responded in wider human terms. Individuals owe their identity to their specific ethno-political context, but at the same time true freedom can be discovered only in self-giving love as taught by Christianity. The true Romanian should therefore 'be a Christian, since religious consciousness is what defines a human being; and be ready to give his life for Romania without regret'.[128]

---

125 THEATRE, p. 390.
126 THEATRE, p. 307. Charles Maurice Talleyrand-Périgord (1754–1838), French states-man (1797–1807); Foreign Minister (1814–1815). From 1808 he secretly negotiated with the Allies against Napoleon I.
127 THEATRE, p. 307.
128 Epigraph to PROBLEMS, p. 5.

Christians may be instructed to render unto Caesar what is Caesar's and to God what is God's (Matt. 22:21), but where and how is the line drawn? Țuțea seems to suggest that, in the earthly city, membership of a nation demands that a person be ready to die for that nation. Similarly, citizenship of heaven demands sacrifice. Țuțea would later define human freedom in terms of a voluntary decision to live according to the fundamental tenets of Christianity, which are grounded in Christ's supreme command to love: 'Christian love can reconcile the dual principles of authority and freedom, and make the exercise of political power tolerable for the Christian citizen'.[129]

On the Co-operative Principle

Although he was widely known as the Romanian Socrates, Țuțea never had the freedom to employ the Socratic methods of self-discovery and education. Instead, his rôle was necessarily to challenge and shock the younger generation into awareness of a reality – a reality other than that of dialectical materialism – which existed and could be pursued even in a police State. Unlike the Communist system which imposed a single line of thought, Țuțea, in true Socratic fashion, invited even his ideological opponents to engage with him in a dialogue about the future of Romania, which, rather than polarising positions, encouraged united action. On his release from prison, he wrote *Project for a Treatise*, a history of the co-operative principle, which he offered to the authorities in a sincere attempt to be of service to his country:

> To look for and find solutions to major national problems at a given historical moment requires, not a policy of compromise, but an attempt at grand syntheses through the application of ideas to concrete reality.[130]

Written in 1965, the year Ceaușescu came to power, Țuțea's treatise assessed the Communist project in Romania in the light of his experience as a national economic advisor. His astonishing attempt to contribute to the economic development of the Communist State was of course not deemed worthy of official acknowledgement. Parts of his treatise were, however, incorporated word for word in what would later become the platform of Ceaușescu's foreign policy:

> ... national sovereignty and independence, equal rights with other nations, non-interference with the country's internal affairs, mutual benefit, peaceful and multilateral co-operation with all other nations irrespective of their social or state system of organisation.[131]

---

129   Petre Țuțea, *Bătrânețea și Alte Texte Filosofice*, afterword by Ion Popescu (Bucharest: Viitorul Românesc, 1992), p. 130. [*Old Age and Other Philosophical Texts* = OLD AGE.]

130   PROJECT, p. 83. See also Țuțea's covering letter to Ceaușescu, in Petre Țuțea, in collaboration with Sorin Pavel, et al., *Reformă Națională și Cooperare*, texts established and preface by Mircea Coloșenco, afterword by Mihail Șora (Bucharest: Elion, 2001), pp. 235–40. [*National Reform and Cooperation*.]

131   PROJECT, p. 46. For a discussion on Țuțea's tactful rather than naive attempts to initiate

In relation to Romanian internal affairs, Ceaușescu's version could not admit the concept of 'our spiritual sovereignty and autonomy' as Țuțea stated in the following passage:

> Peoples are huge collective forces, national entities, not a simple arithmetical sum of individual energies... The main object of government is to husband the biological force of the nation. From this human substance there springs naturally national culture, which in this sense is derivative... In a way, what determines the internal and foreign policy of Romania is the spirit of the age. But this *Zeitgeist* cannot simply swallow us up. Our spiritual sovereignty and autonomy allow us to choose, to incorporate and assimilate all that is of universal worth and, at the same time, compatible with our nature and essential interests.[132]

Agricultural co-operatives of production were imposed over the whole of Romania during the period leading up to 1962. Țuțea considered these to be unworkable, having had the opportunity in prison to discuss the issues with agricultural workers who had refused to accept the new legislation. He nevertheless firmly believed in the co-operative principle at every level, and sought to explain the basis for his approach. In his view at the economic level the principle was based on the concept of synergy. At the religious level the co-operative principle resembles Orthodox *koinonia* (communion, communal sharing) – a resemblance which, to oblige the censors, he did not point out:

> I have said that the universal and national economic order can be seen also in terms of a co-operatist state. I had in mind co-operation as an economic system, as we find it throughout the history of ideas, institutions and economic facts... There is, however, another understanding of co-operation called 'synergism'... According to Lester Ward, the synergetic process begins with collision, conflict, antagonism, and opposition. However, because no movement can be lost, this movement is transformed. There come into being less antagonistic states of opposed terms, rivalries and mutual influences. At first these take the form of a reciprocal *modus vivendi* or compromise, but they end up working together, co-operating with each other.
>
> Müller-Lyer transfers the principle of synergy from the sphere of knowledge to that of the will. Once the synergetic process and its importance for the good of humanity have reached the level of consciousness, they become an ethical social obligation. The supreme ideal of 'euphoric philosophy' [of Marxism-Leninism] can only be attained by social synergy, by 'the co-operation of all, based on the principle of decision in the labour forces. In the broader application of the principle of cosmic synergy, there is required a co-ordinated co-operation of humanity and nature – it is a question of cosmic harmony' (H. Schmidt).

---

dialogue with Ceaușescu in the mid-1960s, when the latter was seeking to make Romania autonomous from the Soviet Union, see Mihail Șora's afterword to Petre Țuțea, et al., *Reformă Națională și Cooperare*, pp. 250–53.

132 PROJECT, p. 97.

The economic concept of co-operation, as it has evolved historically, is vital to the solution of the problems of the Romanian economy at its present stage of development. However, while the concept of co-operation is too restricted for the development of a Romanian system of political economy, the concept of synergy, with its cosmic dimensions, is too broad. Its application goes beyond the limits of economic science, for which it is simply a framework. History shows that certain politico-economic problems can be solved through economic co-operation, while theoretical problems can be solved by a concept of synergy.[133]

Țuțea extended his discussion of synergetic models of political economy (and by implication, the *koinonia* principle of mutual sharing) to the level of international relations. Thus his argument implicitly favours the idea of a European, even a global, community which, however, required a spiritual common denominator. This he saw as lying in the Christian heritage of Europe. To Țuțea tolerance was the key spiritual principle in this context – it inspired every true 'gladiator for Christ's sake'[134] – and the Sermon on the Mount was a manifesto of such tolerance in its ultimate, liberating sense.

Liberal Orthodoxy

It is significant that Țuțea joined the National Liberal Party in 1990. He condemned both Communist and Legionary extremism, and died a member of the National Liberal Party.[135] He saw liberalism neither as democracy, nor as the rule of the majority, nor, again, as tyranny, but as a historically-evolved approach to life, like Christianity. However, whereas Christian principles are already 'perfect', exemplified in Christ's life and work, liberal principles have still to be perfected, and can be developed, but only in accordance with Christian values. Above all they should reflect love and tolerance for others, including agnostics and atheists, as well as people of different faiths. Compassionate love is characterised by:

> the humane treatment of those who are disadvantaged, disabled, mentally handicapped, morally depraved or who manifest deviant forms of life, because it abhors the concept of 'bio-social waste'. It awakens us to see how limited is the theoretical, technical, and practical awareness of the world of enquiry and investigation, of false mental certainty.[136]

For Țuțea, then, love is everything. Apart from love, 'it is obvious that truth, being in essence transcendent, cannot be found either in humanity or in the world'.[137] However, rather than advocating a non-democratic form of polity, Țuțea's Christian understanding of liberalism stressed constitutional tolerance and freedom as its

---

133   PROJECT, pp. 83–4. Lester Frank Ward (1841–1913), American sociologist, founder of a psychological evolutionism. Franz Müller-Lyer (1857–1916), German sociologist.
134   THEATRE, p. 512.
135   See BGMP, pp. 289, 367.
136   OLD AGE, pp. 130–31.
137   OLD AGE, p. 131.

definitive elements.[138] He was convinced that Romania's dominant Church could help develop a national sense of personal freedom within community. The self-transcendence that made solidarity possible even in prison led Țuțea to maintain that individuals are equal only in the sight of God.[139] A Christian community, where individuals are equal within a divine order subordinate to God, is essentially free. Social by nature, the individual can most effectively secure his private interests by transcending himself within a spiritual community where, Țuțea explains, the self finds its eternal significance:

> Christianity appeared in history, yet is eternal. Eternity descended in time and space... Although historical, liberalism is constant in universal history. One cannot go beyond liberalism because this would mean a collective sterilisation of the human personality.[140]

The sense of ownership is associated with possessing property. Although the Communist system abolished private ownership, the desire for personal property, far from being destroyed, was intensified. Understanding that personal ownership is fundamental to human nature, Țuțea advocated a liberal political and economic system after the collapse of Communism:

> It was said of Adam Smith's *Wealth of Nations* that it was the only weapon against the Napoleonic campaigns, which were based on expansion, violence, and force. In addition, Adam Smith also wrote a study of morality, *The Theory of Moral Sentiments*. Liberalism is essentially moral and is alone compatible with the eternal Christian order.[141]

---

138 In my conversations with Țuțea he mentioned Guido de Ruggiero's *The History of European Liberalism* as a reference book. In his preface, R.G. Collingwood, the English translator of this book (Boston: Beacon Press, 1959), pp. vii–viii, wrote:

> Liberalism, as Professor De Ruggiero understands it, begins with the recognition that men, do what we will, are free; that a man's acts are his own, spring from his own personality, and cannot be coerced. But this freedom is not possessed at birth; it is acquired by degrees as a man enters into the self-conscious possession of his personality through a life of discipline and moral progress. The aim of Liberalism is to assist the individual to discipline himself and achieve his own moral progress; renouncing the two opposite errors of forcing upon him a development for which he is inwardly unprepared, and leaving him alone, depriving him of that aid to progress which a political system, wisely designed and wisely administered, can give. These principles lead in practice to a policy that may be called, in the sense above defined, Liberal; a policy which regards the State, not as a vehicle of a superhuman wisdom or a superhuman power, but as the organ by which a people expresses whatever of political ability it can find and breed and train within itself. This is not democracy, or the rule of mere majority; nor is it authoritarianism, or the irresponsible rule of those who, for whatever reason, hold power at a given moment. It is something between the two. Democratic in its respect for human liberty, it is authoritarian in the importance it attaches to the necessity for skilful and practised government.

139 APHORISMS, p. 45.
140 INTERVIEW, p. 3.
141 Unpublished interview with Țuțea, Bucharest, 3 June 1990.

In contrast to liberalism, democracy is in the last analysis dominated by number, by earthly power rather than by the paradoxical and 'nuanced' values taught by Christ: 'Blessed are the meek, for they shall inherit the earth' (Matt. 5:5). Carl Schmitt's distinction between democracy and liberalism influenced Țuțea, who came to see the Soviet Union as perhaps the best example of 'democracy' as Schmitt conceived it. For Schmitt democracy implied equality, and the supreme expression of political equality was surely what Karl Kautsky[142] called, as quoted by Țuțea in conversation, the ideal of Communism as 'ultimate anarchy' and permanent revolution.[143]

Țuțea also opposes the aristocratic components of liberalism to those features of democracy that stress quantity at the expense of quality. He rejects the social uniformity that results from the triumph of collectivist principles over the individual. He speaks approvingly of the entrepreneur as the founder of modern civilisation, while criticising contemporary liberal systems for their inability to prevent capitalist competition, with its materialistic emphasis, from creating a socially underprivileged class.[144] His view that Christianity and liberalism are historically compatible reflects his belief that the sacred expresses itself through the political. For example, he saw the jeering crowd, which led to Ceaușescu's downfall, as somehow inspired.

Acknowledging that Christianity and extreme nationalism cannot be ultimately reconciled, he would nevertheless insist: 'I am a Christian and a Romanian nationalist, because that is what I want.'[145] Here is a challenge both to theocracy with its imperialistic claims upon the created order, and to ultra-nationalism with its claims to divine sanction over and above the universal significance of Christ's humanity.

Liberalism is authoritarian in that it seeks to develop the skills of the legitimate governing authority. Țuțea notes that the extremes, left and right, have never been at ease with Christianity, whereas for liberalism Christianity is ultimately fundamental. This gives him a critical perspective. In his view, American liberalism, for instance, is concerned with social and civil order here on earth. He places society and the State within the world of norms, which are human rational constructs.[146] But the Christian faith requires that the order of norms should be congruent with truth revealed in Scripture: 'If it ignores Christian teaching, liberalism loses direction and becomes ineffective.'[147] After the Romanian Revolution of 1989, he spoke of 'restoring the natural order, rather than revolution':

---

142   Karl Kautsky (1854–1938), Austrian politician. He was Engels's secretary (1881) and published the third volume of Marx's *Capital*.

143   BGMP, pp. 30, 62, 276. In a Communist society, where all are equal and there is no God, all may take what they wish, for wish and need are one and the same. Friedrich Engels claimed that the ultimate political aim of Communism was 'to overcome the state as such, and hence also democracy as one form of the state': see Tom Bottomore, et al. (eds), *A Dictionary of Marxist Thought* (Oxford: Blackwell, 1983), p. 443.

144   RESTORATION, p. 4.

145   Petre Țuțea, 'Convorbire cu Petre Țuțea', interview, in Dorin Popa, *Convorbiri Euharistice* (Iassy: Institutul European, 1992), p. 15. ['Conversations with Petre Țuțea'.]

146   BGMP, p. 282.

147   BGMP, p. 282.

It has been said that there is no such thing in history as revolution, only insurrectionary techniques in the struggle for power. De Tocqueville called the French Revolution 'the new *ancien régime*'... It is encouraging to discover a high degree of political consciousness in the Romanian people when, at a given moment, they embody the tradition and history of their country. What began as a revolution in December 1989 quickly became a [neo-Communist] restoration and a new struggle for political power. That is perfectly natural, since the struggle for power is inherent in a multi-party system, even when rival political groups exist in conditions of freedom and equality.[148]

Țuțea criticises the utopian values of the French Revolution which, despite their inherent contradictions, have affected the whole of European history:

What wonderful massacres have been carried out in the name of freedom! Lafargue spoke of the three ideas of the French Revolution as 'the three metaphysical whores'. If you put liberty into practice, then equality is impossible. If you put equality into practice, then liberty is impossible. If we are all brothers, the genius becomes first cousin to the fool. When, in fact, as Eminescu says, 'the world is as it is, and as the world is, so are we all'.[149]

Despite having embraced the values of the French Revolution, the old National Liberal Party still has, Țuțea believes, the right to govern in post-Communist Romania. It was, after all, the creator of the modern Romanian State:

Liberals led the struggle for the formation of Greater Romania in the war of Independence in 1877. For me, Greater Romania is the work [not of sober conservatives but] of the liberals who, in the last century, were demagogues. They became more refined, having been educated in the conservative world of the *Junimea* ('Youth') cultural movement [influenced more directly by German rather than French culture]. The liberals are the creators of the modern Romanian State and society, while the conservatives are the creators of modern Romanian culture, of the temple of high culture.[150]

As ever, even in old age, his thinking identifies tensions and tries to synthesise and express them in an illuminating and stimulating way. The 'answer' he offers is simple yet radical – nothing less than reorientation to the simple truth of Christ's teaching. The true vocation of the nation is to be a 'community of love',[151] served alike by the dominant culture and the ethnic minorities who share the same homeland. International and inter-ethnic relations cannot be entirely legislated. Human identity at every level and in every aspect can only be perfected through obedience to Christ's commandment to 'love your neighbour as yourself' (Matt. 19:19). In Țuțea's view,

---

148 RESTORATION, p. 4.
149 Țuțea, 'Omul este un animal', p. 16.
150 Personal conversation, Emergency Hospital Bucharest, 26 April 1990. Cf. Petre Țuțea, 'Eu sunt un om neîmplinit', fragments of interviews by Liliana Stoicescu and Delia Verdeș, *România Liberă*, Bucharest, 7–8 December 1991, p. 2. ['I am an unfulfilled man'.]
151 THEATRE, p. 134.

true Christian tolerance guarantees liberal pluralism, which extends to all people, of any faith or of none.

Chapter 3

From Philosophy
to Christian Commitment

As a man of broad cultural and intellectual curiosity, Țuțea was formatively influenced by art, literature, and music (particular influences are identified in Chapter 10). However, like the influences of personal friendships and the ordinary events of life, cultural influences are more properly explored in a biography. In this chapter I shall concentrate on two major intellectual and spiritual influences that shaped Țuțea's intellectual development.

Țuțea had been profoundly influenced in his formative years (including his Berlin period and while he was working in the Ministry of Trade and Industry) by Plato and Kant. It was in prison, however, that he was led to integrate their philosophy with his Christian faith. Plato's world of Ideas helped Țuțea to perceive the divine origin of the world, while Kant's system of categories showed him the limits of rational and logical knowledge. Plato's ontology and Kant's epistemology prepared him for St Paul's doctrine of creation as a hierarchy of two worlds, the transient and the eternal (2 Cor. 4:18), and gave him an optimistic view of the world.[1]

Founded on Christian revelation, Țuțea's optimism, however, did not exclude a tragic vision of the human condition – rather, his vision transcended and redeemed it. He emphasised that divine revelation and inspiration are the means by which humanity acquires knowledge of the Pauline 'two worlds'. His lifelong study of Plato and Kant, interpreted in the light of his experience and rediscovery of Christian faith, enabled him to discern the divinely inspired principles which underlie the workings of the world as we perceive it. His self-discipline in the application of philosophical methods and his rigorous use of scientific enquiry gave him a language rooted purely in human knowledge. His experience as both a scholar and a prisoner led him to speak of a knowledge which cannot be acquired through sheer personal effort but comes 'from above', for it belongs to the realm of God's self-communication. This vision was enriched and elaborated by his reading of St Augustine and Pascal (in particular Augustine's *The City of God* and Pascal's *Pensées*).

Țuțea never excludes empirical knowledge and natural sciences from his interpretation of creation and its Creator. For him scientific enquiry and the progress of science, or the exploration of truth 'from below', establishes a frame of reference, which enables people to orientate themselves in their environment and to talk about

---

1   PROBLEMS, p. 189.

their spiritual and historical place in the universe. Without science, such human orientation within the universe is blind or random:

> Science is human experience formulated in ever more precise concepts and judgements, even though human judgements about reality are always approximate. We can never do without hypotheses, opinions, and beliefs. For theoretically human expansion in the cosmos seems to have no limits. Philosophical and scientific knowledge regulates every kind of human activity: science, art, technology.[2]

Philosophy works alongside science. Theoretically the world can be understood in terms of philosophical categories and scientific systems. In Țuțea's essays he employs what he calls *stilul categorial*,[3] a style suited to reflection on humanity and nature. He added to the philosophical categories of Aristotle, Descartes, and Spinoza, Kant's category of interaction (*die Kategorie der Wechselwirkung*)[4] which is essential for understanding logical wholes and the empirical world.[5] Țuțea develops his 'categorial style' by employing Platonic–Socratic dialogue while critically assimilating and building on Kant's 'table of categories' and methodology. By 'style' he understands 'method of enquiry', which employs both rational and imaginative skills:

> So far as style is concerned I add a few things concerning the place of passive or active human beings, dependent upon whether reason or imagination is in charge. In other words: are we calligraphers of laws that transcend us; or are we creators of endless imaginary worlds?[6]

Kant defines 'transcendental' ('formal' or 'critical') idealism as the doctrine of a priori knowledge of 'appearances' only, and not of 'things as they are in themselves'.[7] Țuțea describes his own methodology as a delicate fabric of 'categories, notions,

---

2   THEATRE, p. 106.
3   THEATRE, p. 106.
4   Țuțea quotes Kant's definition of this category from Heinrich Schmidt, *Philosophisches Wörterbuch*, 9th edn (Leipzig: Alfred Kröner, 1934), p. 453: '*Alle Substanzen, sofern sie im Raume als zugleich wahrgenommen werden können, sind in durchgängiger Wechselwirkung*' ('All substances, insofar as they *are simultaneous*, stand in thorough-going community', that is, interaction with one another). See the unified edition of Immanuel Kant, *Critique of Pure Reason*, trans. Werner S. Pluhar, introd. by Patricia W. Kitcher (Cambridge: Hackett, 1996), p. 276. Pluhar translates *Wechselwirkung* as 'interaction', 'reciprocal action', or 'reciprocal causation'.
5   THEATRE, p. 107.
6   THEATRE, p. 107.
7   Roger Scruton, *Kant* (Oxford: Oxford University Press, 1996), p. 42. 'Idealism proper always has a mystical tendency, and can have no other; but mine is solely designed for the purpose of comprehending the possibility of our *a priori* cognition of objects of experience': Immanuel Kant, *Prolegomena to Any Future Metaphysics, That Will Be Able To Come Forward As Science*, the Paul Carus trans., newly revised by J.W. Ellington (Cambridge: Hackett, 1974), p. 114.

judgements, laws, norms, systems, disciplines, methods, research techniques, obser-
vations, experiments, reasoning, wholes, parts, structures, functions, circumstances,
chaos, order and so on'.[8] This combines Plato's realism about universals[9] and Kant's
theory of knowledge to illustrate (not analyse) reality and awaken (not explain) the
human sense of mystery.

Although science and philosophy are useful attempts to explain the world
rationally by reducing it to a set of answerable questions, Țuțea believes that ultimate
explanations belong to the realm of religious dogma, which delineates divine
mysteries but can never exhaust them. He distinguishes between objectivity and
obiecticitate ('objecticity'). *Obiectic* denotes that which exists independently of
our conceptual powers and cannot be achieved through human values alone.
'Objecticity', by contrast to objectivity (which is just another degree of subjectivity),
'incorporates mystically the empirical and the rational, matter and order' in a unity
governed by God, a hierarchical unity wherein humanity has been entrusted with
dominion over nature.[10] Only thus can Țuțea speak of objective laws of nature, or
purely and simply of laws. In his view the laws of nature are ambigous terms because
they 'confuse objectivity with "objecticity" – that is to say, the active consciousness
(which prevails in virtue of the brilliance and precision of its points of view) with
consciousness as a mirror' which, because inspired, reflects the Kingdom of God.[11]

In this sense, distinguishing between the different levels at which human
knowledge is acquired, Țuțea sees inspiration as 'obiectic', independent of human
searching. Reception of truth is at a different level from the intellectual search
for truth.[12] Transcending both objectivity and subjectivity, the 'obiectic' exists
beyond human understanding, and is defined as the transcendence of the object
contemplated.[13] Objectivity and subjectivity are determined by particular points of
view, while 'objecticity' is an inspired glimpse into the realm of absolute truth, a
realm revealed to the enlightened. 'Obiectic' vision is the result of a state of
watchfulness in accordance with God's grace:

---

8   THEATRE, p. 107.
9   Țuțea views Plato and Socrates as fundamentally mystical thinkers. For him the certainty
     Plato seeks is not that of 'the truths of mathematics' (that is, of axiomatic conventions),
     but rather, that of real truth, of vision and recognition deriving from knowledge of the
     actually existent Ideas. Cf. R.M. Hare, *Plato* (Oxford: Oxford University Press, 1982),
     p. 33: 'Plato hankered, in his search for real knowledge, after the kind of certainty which
     the truths of mathematics have; but because he was after things and not truths, the things
     had to be necessarily existing things.'
10   THEATRE, p. 358. For a discussion on Țuțea's 'objecticity', see also Chapter 8, notes 55
     and 58.
11   THEATRE, pp. 107–8.
12   THEATRE, p. 358.
13   Petre Țuțea, *Filosofia Nuanțelor* (*Eseuri. Profiluri. Corespondență*) anthology, preface,
     and notes by Mircea Coloșenco, ed. Sergiu Coloșenco (Iassy: Timpul, 1995), p. 110.
     [*Philosophy of Nuances* (*Essays. Portraits. Letters*) = NUANCES.]

The truth hidden in things can only be reached by hard work. Although the world is not opaque, i.e. we can understand it, it must be questioned and sometimes compelled to reply. To maintain a state of watchfulness is tiring and often fruitless when the methodology of observation is used. Scientific experiment is necessary too. But no one whose life is shaped by religious dogma will let himself be led off course by interminable testing of experience. The constraints to which the religious human being is subject have a pacific effect... The anxiety of choosing between two worlds, the closed world of Ideas and the open world of experience, dominated Joseph de Maistre[14] too when he formulated *Les soirées de Saint-Pétersbourg*. He chose the style of the Platonic dialogue,[15] although sometimes he was content to be carried along by facts which he believed to be revelatory. Every part of his moral universe is shaped by a monumental system of rigorous ideas. This is a fundamental way of seeing life and the world, a product of the need for certainty.[16]

Ţuţea insisted that scientific enquiry leads to relative knowledge, while religious experience takes us into the realm of absolute certainty.

As I now turn to look in more detail at Ţuţea's use of Plato and Kant, it will become clearer that his 'mysticism' was not intellectually escapist, but a genuine integration of intellect, heart, and will achieved through a lifetime of struggle. His achievement is directly relevant to a world in which the quest for spiritual truth, the claims of national, ethnic, and religious identity, the horrors and tests of conflict and peace-making remain inextricably intertwined.

Plato

Ţuţea was aware that Platonism – with its concept of this world as a shadow of the world of Ideas – lacks a dynamic, soteriological understanding of history. Yet to Ţuţea, Plato is a mystical thinker who perceived in the universe a spiritual dimension and a divine cause, which, in essence, transcends human reason.

What is Platonism? It is the world of Ideas. We cannot speak of a doctrine or theory of Ideas. Nor, in the light of the archetypes, can we speak of Plato's system, just as we cannot speak of a religious system, because the world of ideas is mystical not dialectical. Socrates, in Plato's *Republic*, distinguishes two kinds of knowledge: knowledge of the real (i.e. knowledge of the Ideas), and aleatory knowledge in this world (i.e. knowledge of concepts).[17]

---

14   Count Joseph-Marie de Maistre (1753–1821), French writer and diplomat.
15   See Joseph de Maistre, *Les soirées de Saint-Pétersbourg, ou entretiens sur le gouvernement temporel de la Providence*, introd. by L. Arnould de Grémilly, notes by Pierre Mariel (Paris: La Colombe, 1960), pp. 25–32.
16   THEATRE, p. 107.
17   Petre Ţuţea, MS 1983 (Bucharest: 1983), dictated manuscript, p. 113. For Plato's distinction between intelligence (*noesis*) and mathematical reasoning (*dianoia*) – that is, between 'full understanding, culminating in the vision of ultimate truth' and 'the procedure of mathematics, purely deductive and uncritical of its assumptions' – see Plato, *The Republic* (509d–511e), 2nd edn, trans. and introd. by Desmond Lee (London: Penguin, 1987), pp. 309–12.

Țuțea regards the theory of Ideas as rooted in 'Platonic mysticism'.[18] He is primarily interested in 'mystical knowledge' (*gnosis*) or 'mystical contemplation' (*theoria*) that is, knowledge or contemplation of the mystery.[19] Ideas cannot be reduced to immanence. They are not representations received from objects in the sensible world, but are 'living, eternal essences beyond time and space'.[20] Human beings participate through their vocation in this world or, still following a vocational call, they contemplate these essences in the other world, in the realm of truth, in close proximity to the gods. Țuțea maintains that, although Plato's theory of being includes neither theophany (as the visible manifestation of God) nor the definitive elements of Christian mystery (the Incarnation and Trinitarian Godhead), by its reference to the 'supreme good' it can prepare us to understand the world in a Christian way.[21] Plato distinguished human enquiry in this world from the certainty of the transcendent world of Ideas:

> For him perishable existence cannot be equated with essence. He did not confuse the idea of human being with the actual human being. He considered that what is good, true, and beautiful in human artefacts are only imperfect manifestations of the good, the true, and

---

18 'Mysticism' in its Christian sense is the study of God as mystery. The terms 'the mystic', 'mysticism', and 'mysticality' are defined by Fr Gilbert Shaw in 'Recovery', an unpublished address to the Community of the Sisters of the Love of God, Oxford, 1962:

> *The mystic* is one who knows what he is doing in the disciplined ascent to union with God. He does not seek his own end, but to find his true completion and what that means in positive relationship with the creation of which he is a part.
>
> *Mysticism* is a study of the records of the mystics and of the phenomena associated with them. It is of course a proper study as a discipline of the intellect, but a general interest particularly in the accidental phenomena is no substitute for the discipline of self and the practice of religion.
>
> *Mysticality*. There is mysticality and it is nonsense. In it the soul through techniques seeks and attains that which is beyond its normal sensible experience, and through it develops powers which it would not otherwise possess and which it uses for its own ends.

In Țuțea's understanding too, a real mystic proceeds through degrees of love, knowledge, and prayer towards a state of union with God. Christian mysticism certainly has antecedents in Platonic mysticism which has, however, to be sharply distinguished from false mysticism, 'mysticality', or 'techniques of existence' (that is, the attempt to gain knowledge of the spiritual world for the increase of individual 'power' which often leads people to become absorbed in magic or to behave with oppressive authoritarianism).

19 Cf. Henri Crouzel, 'The Doctrine of Knowledge', in *Origen*, trans. A.S. Worall (Edinburgh: T. & T. Clark, 1989), pp. 9–119.

20 PROBLEMS, p. 184.

21 Țuțea was thoroughly familiar with the thought of neo-Platonist Renaissance humanism and had a high regard for the *Quatrocento* and 'the theistic refinement of Florence': THEATRE, p. 464. Following the latter, he spoke of Socrates and Plato as 'brilliant pre-Christians': THEATRE, p. 414.

the beautiful in themselves. Plato's mystical concept of the Absolute brings him close to Christianity, from an epistemological point of view.[22]

Platonism 'awakens' the Christian sense of *eterna ordine vie de sus* (the 'living and eternal order from above').[23] The sacred transcends history even as it permeates and sanctifies space and time. For Țuțea, therefore, the Christian anthropologist studies not merely a humanity describable through sensory perception and intellect, but a humanity endowed with the potential for sanctification, having its *telos*, or end, in God. Platonic idealism does not deny scientific progress, nor does it rule out the possibility of developing a method whereby Socratic principles might be used to stimulate reflection on the transcendent or even on the 'thirst for the Absolute', as it might be experienced under a totalitarian régime:

> So-called *scientific truth* – which has the force of prejudice – is necessary though inadequate, while absolute truth is the goal of the religious or metaphysical consciousness. Where does this thirst for the Absolute come from? From the presence of three fundamental terms of knowledge: God, man and nature. That is how we can understand Plato's theory of Ideas and Socratic mysticism, which he never abandoned but only deepened, thus managing to transcend nature, society, and earthly human experience with its imperfect language, symbolism, and predication... Pedagogy? Yes. Scientific progress? Yes. The true, the good, and the beautiful, however, are things in themselves, ideals for the enlightened.[24]

In prison Țuțea came to experience the full power of the reality of these Ideas. Both during his internment and after his release, he used the maieutic method of Socrates to expound his belief in the reality of spiritual virtues and the truth of personal vocation and freedom, in the face of a system that denied these things:

> Social life is dominated by certain fundamental virtues that are the property of any normal human being. Anyone can grasp this simple maxim: do whatever suits your vocation and training. As in the past, human beings today are incapable of applying natural skills in an egalitarian direction. Ruler and ruled, conqueror and conquered alike, should be governed by the principle of justice, that is to say by an understanding of the limits of human power. Since truth is outside us, there is only one way by which we can know it: inspiration, i.e. the grace of God, the only ruler. This is Plato's message in the brilliant letter to the people of Syracuse (*Letter VII*). If we share Plato's thinking about morality, the so-called 'new man' of our time fills us with disgust.[25]

---

22   Petre Țuțea, *Reflecții Religioase asupra Cunoașterii*, part I, introd. and afterword by Ion Aurel Brumaru (Bucharest: Nemira, 1992), pp. 118–19. [*Religious Reflections on Human Knowledge* = REFLECTIONS, I.]
23   THEATRE, p. 436.
24   Petre Țuțea, *Reflecții Religioase asupra Cunoașterii*, part II (Bucharest: 1977), p. 285. ['Religious Reflections on Human Knowledge' (manuscript) = REFLECTIONS, II.]
25   REFLECTIONS, I, p. 125. While recognising scholarly discussion on the authenticity of *The Seventh Letter*, Țuțea stressed the testamentary character of this Platonic work. He points to the fact that by intervening in Sicilian affairs following the murder of his pupil, Dion of Syracuse, the philosopher does not hesitate to put his own life at risk.

Ţuţea's rejection of the Communist political system and Ceauşescu's tyranny was undisguised. Plato's model of free education for all was necessary as an ethical, political, and anti-tyrannical model.[26] Ţuţea compared Platonic *paideia* ($\pi\alpha\iota\delta\varepsilon\acute{\iota}\alpha$)[27] with Christian catechism and suggested that both were based on a mystical certainty about the eternal world. The divine inspiration behind Plato's vision of the transcendent world of Ideas challenged the dialectical and historical materialism imposed on schools and society by the Communist State:

> As archetypes, Platonic Ideas belong to divine wisdom and transcend the time and space in which Plato received them. The human being, seen in the light of Platonic Ideas, is a limited and imperfect creature, who can through faith and grace participate in the world of Ideas. Of course, as Christians we cannot accept that these originate in a supreme Good (resembling a deity). Nor can we accept the [Platonic doctrine of] transmigration of souls. Yet, the world of Ideas cannot be grasped by means of dialectic, because in dialectical terms they remain, as Aristotle – in his criticism of Plato – defined them, hypostasized concepts.[28]

At the level of logic, we speak of fact, deed, name, concept, definition and system, objects and products of method employed without the aid of divine grace. In its ancient meaning, dialectics is principally a method that employs dialogue:

> Socrates worked with this method, convinced that knowledge cannot be taught, that is to say, is not passed on by one spirit to another, but is discovered by each individual within himself; knowledge cannot be written down and contained in books, it is something active and alive, expressible only in dialogue.[29]

Platonic philosophy is fully engaged in the problems of the city (326a–b) and has at the same time a mystical character. The leaders of the city should combine leadership skills and philosophical wisdom (rather than mere epistemological knowledge), like the philosopher-kings in the *Republic*. In a way, Ţuţea himself embodied some of these qualities in the totalitarian city. See Plato, *Phaedrus and Letters VII and VIII*, trans. Walter Hamilton (London: Penguin, 1973), pp. 114–16. For Ţuţea's theological interpretation of the Platonic digression on 'knowledge of essential being' in *Letter VII* (342–3): see SYSTEMS, p. 233.

26   REFLECTIONS, II, pp. 284–5.
27   Ţuţea refers in detail to Julius Stenzel's classic *Platon der Erzieher*, introd. by Konrad Gaiser (Hamburg: Felix Meiner, 1928; repr. 1961). See: Chapter III, 'Der "Staat". Erziehung zur Gemeinschaft', and especially, Chapter VII, 'Der siebente Brief. Das Wesenhafte im einzelnen Gegenstande', pp. 302–24.
28   Ţuţea, MS 1983, pp. 113–14. Ţuţea is aware that Socrates 'seems to be the one Athenian assigned with the task of exhorting others to philosophise, even at the risk of death... [T]he practice of philosophy enjoined on us is connected with the improvement of what Socrates continually refers to as "the soul"', in the words of Mark L. McPherran, *The Religion of Socrates* (University Park, PA: Pennsylvania University Press, 1996), p. 246; see also McPherran's chapter on 'Socratic Reason and Socratic Revelation', pp. 174–246, to which Ţuţea would have perhaps subscribed.
29   Ţuţea, MS 1983, pp. 111–12.

Ţuţea stresses the importance of Platonism in helping to prepare young people in a
Communist society to understand the Pauline distinction between what is heavenly
and what is earthly, yet he is also aware of fundamental differences between
Platonism and Christianity. Thus in Plato's *Republic* (508e) the supreme archetype is
the Idea of the Good, the principle beyond all other Ideas, while the Platonic god
is only a demiurge[30] bringing order into pre-existent chaos but not creating the world
ex nihilo as the Deity of the Abrahamic religions does. The Christian Trinitarian God
is the principle beyond all categories, yet all things are held in being by God. His
essence is incomprehensible, yet He can be known through the Incarnate Logos.

   Also, Ţuţea distinguishes between generality (a logical inductive process of
generalisation) and totality (ascribable to God alone as the uncreated source of
everything, the 'Whole' beyond logical categories). '*The* totality is the goal and not
the object of enquiry.'[31] Dialectical method on its own confines the inapprehensible
archetypes to a logical system which can only distort them:

> Dialectical method and logical generalisation cannot lead to a genuine and comprehensive
> mystical knowledge... Dialectical method reduces Platonic Ideas to logic. But Ideas cannot
> be sought or found by generalisation. They can only be experienced and recollected by the
> inspired psyche that has contemplated them in another existence, in close proximity to the
> gods. Ideas cannot otherwise be considered eternal models of the sensible world.[32]

Ţuţea's reading of Plato is thus very different from the official Communist
interpretation that sees Plato merely as a dialectical idealist – an interpretation also
common in the West. Against such Western opinions Catherine Pickstock develops
the thesis that Plato's philosophy 'did not assume, as has been thought, a primacy
of metaphysical presence, but rather a primacy of liturgical theory and practice',
which was developed in medieval Christendom.[33] Her reading of Plato supports
Ţuţea's interpretation of Platonic *paideia* as preparation for the human encounter
with God:

> The dialogues represent the dissemination of 'theology' in a fragmented society, as intended
> to lead therapeutically towards the doxological life, not only through their content, but also
> their structure, for the dialogic form dislodges an empiricist epistemology which seeks
> discrete manoeuvres at a remove from an embedded ethical existence. The Platonic
> dialogue is therefore a kind of writing free from the dangers of writing, resisting singular

---

30   That is, 'a supreme artist', 'not a creator': THEATRE, p. 212.
31   SYSTEMS, p. 82 (italics added).
32   Ţuţea, MS 1983, p. 113. Plato often refers to philosophy as dialectic, 'a term whose
      modern associations are quite misleading in interpreting the *Republic*, but which, with
      that caution, remains a convenient translation', according to Desmond Lee, in a note to
      Plato, *The Republic*, p. 311.
33   Catherine Pickstock, *After Writing, On the Liturgical Consummation of Philosophy*
      (Oxford: Blackwell, 1998), p. xii. Of course, Ţuţea's 'Orthodoxy' is very different from
      Pickstock's 'radical Orthodoxy', which enshrines the medieval Western liturgy.

attribution of author, genre, and medium. Is it Socrates or isn't it? Is it a tractate or a drama? Is it a text or not? Its resistance to any foundation reveals it to possess the flexibility of orality, together with its form as a 'literary', or theological, rather than straightforwardly doxological, prayer.[34]

Pickstock's questions and her concluding phrase above would be appropriate tools for the exploration and assessment of Țuțea's own written 'style' and oral 'genius'. I will show in Chapter 8 that, like Socrates, Țuțea used dialogue (and *teatrul seminar*) as a liturgical means of education and as a way of being in the totalitarian city.

Kant

In Țuțea's view, 'the only thing certain' in Kant's theory of ideas is that 'they are fictions empty of content'.[35] Țuțea contrasts them with Platonic Ideas which are 'real – archetypes, the eternal models of sensible things'. In the end, he concludes, empirical criticism is the rational position of the 'self-styled autonomous individual' incapable of going beyond the 'limits' of nature: this so-called autonomy is 'an epistemological interplay of intellect and experience' serving an illusion of 'normative authority within the moral order'.[36]

Țuțea insists that exactness is the prerogative of God, and its application will be revealed at the Last Judgement. Divine exactness is both transcendent and salvific. It cannot be deduced from enquiry and is incompatible with any purely human process of becoming. Self-commitment to God's eschatological rigour is the prerequisite of real freedom. The proud man's mind, as Țuțea frequently puts it, is opaque to divine light. Although Kant argues for the inseparability of reason and freedom on almost every page of his *Critique of Practical Reason*,[37] to Țuțea it is precisely that systematic opaqueness which makes Kant's humanist approach incapable of apprehending that which appears to be without content, the transcendent realm of freedom, immortality of the soul, and divine existence. The 'triangle of God, immortality, and freedom' must be conceived in a mystical, biblical way, 'not fictionally as in Kant, for whom these three sides of the triangle are only *als ob wäre*'.[38]

For Țuțea earthly order is the imperfect reflection of heavenly order. But he finds that Kant speaks of God 'in an ambiguous way', as a 'transcendental idea' derived from the logical functions of reason. Unlike understanding (*Verstand*), however, Kantian reason (*Vernunft*) is not tied to the conditions of 'a possible experience':

---

34   Pickstock, *After Writing*, pp. 42–3.

35   SYSTEMS, p. 104.

36   SYSTEMS, p. 103.

37   Howard Caygill, *A Kant Dictionary* (Oxford: Blackwell, 1995), p. 349.

38   That is, 'as if they existed': PROBLEMS, p. 186.

In freeing itself from the limitations of experience, [reason] is driven to regard objects such as the soul, the world as a whole, and God as if they were objects of a possible experience. This leads reason in a tangle of paralogism, antinomy and constitutive ideals.[39]

Kant's assertion that 'transcendent ideas are subjectively deduced' from the character of reason is criticised by Ţuţea precisely because 'such deduction is not objective'.[40] 'This deductive, subjective character of transcendent ideas' shows that 'real entities and the Absolute' are absent from Kant's 'pure logic':[41]

Is there any Truth in Kant? The answer is: no! If Divinity, freedom and immortality are metaphysical ideas, or tasks of pure reason, then one cannot speak of Truth in Kant's work. The rational logical level and the ontic level – existence in general and in particular, as possible experience – do not relate to the Truth that is linked with God, freedom and immortality. The way from these ideas to reality is through revelation rather than quest. As logical fruits of the intellect and sensible intuition, Kantian concepts denote the limits of his apriorism.[42]

Ţuţea shows that Kant reduces the 'triangle' God–humanity–nature to a straight 'line', humanity–nature. Kant's awareness of the 'moral law within' (which in his view is universal) excludes everything except human reason from the conduct of life in the world. Ţuţea believes this to be a false autonomy: humans have no title to it, since they are created beings and recipients of everything that they are and have. The epistemological and ethical aspects of the autonomy of pure reason imply an inconsistency, 'unless they merge into a fictional combination':[43]

According to Kant, the human being is unreal, and moves between sensory receptivity and so-called spontaneous thought. The Kantian human being resembles the Aristotelian, poised on two terms: *nous poietikos* and *nous pathetikos*.[44] In Kant, as in Aristotle, science is the work of the active intellect. Kant claims there is no such thing as philosophy,

---

39   Caygill, *A Kant Dictionary*, p. 349.
40   For Ţuţea's view on Kant's treatment of 'the transcendental and yet natural illusion in the paralogisms of pure reason', see SYSTEMS, pp. 102–3. Cf. part II, Chapter 1 of Kant, *Critique of Pure Reason*, pp. 418–19.
41   SYSTEMS, p. 103.
42   SYSTEMS, pp. 144–5. See Kant's discussion on 'The existence of God as something postulated by pure practical reason', in his *Critique of Practical Reason*, trans. H.W. Cassirer, ed. G. Heath King and R. Weitzman, introd. by D.M. MacKinnon (Milwaukee: Marquette University Press, 1998), pp. 156–66.
43   SYSTEMS, p. 160. See also Scruton, *Kant*, p. 77: 'Pure reason falls over itself in the attempt to prove the existence of God and the immortality of the soul.'
44   Both the Aristotelian term *nous poietikos* (*intellectus agens*) and the post-Aristotelian *nous pathetikos* (*intellectus passibilis*) are fundamental cognitive terms on which scientific and discursive knowledge is based. See H.J. Blumenthal, '*Nous Pathêtikos* in Later Greek Philosophy', *Oxford Studies in Ancient Philosophy*, supplement, 1991, pp. 191–206. Cf. SYSTEMS, pp. 168–70.

but philosophers deserve the title if they are original. I cannot detect anything original in Kant.[45]

Systematic exposition cannot include what is originally inexpressible, but, nevertheless, human beings have constructed systems in which useful forms of thought can be found. Whereas the modern world prides itself on 'a triumph of logic in its explanation of the ontic', in fact, Țuțea believes, this is 'a triumph of sophism'.[46] One cannot speak about a real God in Kant's empirical critical terms. According to Țuțea, the critical spirit in general cannot comprehend God as reality, it can only conceive of the divine in terms of religious dogma:

> There is no such thing as secular dogma, either philosophical or scientific. Dogma is a theological way of thinking that imparts essentially transcendent truth. Human reason, restricted by the use of indemonstrable axiom, reveals the limitations of human capacity for knowledge.[47]

Reduced to the human level, reason cannot be a vehicle for truth, for 'human beings and nature are not sources of truth'.[48] Kant's categorical imperative of a universal moral law 'within' humanity is purely self-referential. Human morality must be grounded in the ultimate source of being, namely God.

The Heart

Divine knowledge is for Țuțea a matter of the heart, which for those who are enlightened becomes the seat of divine presence, grace, and knowledge. Those who fail to perceive this creative dependency are captive to 'illusory autonomy',[49] their 'hardened' hearts (Mark 6:52) devoid of mystery. In his teaching both within prison and after his release, Țuțea uses Platonism and Kantianism in a way that resembles Pascal's mystical approach – the 'reason of the heart' representing 'the reason of the spirit'.[50] The heart represents a faculty of enquiry. This exemplifies Țuțea's belief

---

45 SYSTEMS, p. 160. It should be remembered that Țuțea had a high regard for Kant and a somewhat particular view of originality: 'Only God and idiots are original.' This paradox was frequently used by Țuțea in conversations.
46 SYSTEMS, p. 105.
47 SYSTEMS, pp. 103–4.
48 SYSTEMS, p. 104.
49 'The illusory autonomy of the self considers *die Weltbildung als Weltordnung*': PROBLEMS, p. 148.
50 THEATRE, p. 314. Țuțea is aware of Kant's antipathy to the notion of grace: 'One penetrates by means of grace through to the world of mysteries, but grace is entirely absent from Kant's system', SYSTEMS, p. 143. For Kant, 'to expect an effect of grace means... that the good (the morally good) is not of our doing, but that of another being – that we, therefore, can only *come by* it by *doing nothing*'. See Immanuel Kant,

that enlightenment and scientific discovery are ultimately gifts from above rather than products of human intuition and effort. In his dialogue *Eros*, published as part of *Teatrul Seminar*, he quotes Mihai Eminescu on Kant's *Transcendental Aesthetics* to illustrate his own spiritual view of the heart:

> Every generous thought, every great discovery, proceeds from the heart and appeals to the heart. It is extraordinary, when somebody understands Kant and adopts his point of view, a point of view so alien to this world and its ephemeral desires: the mind becomes simply a window through which a new kind of sun penetrates the heart. Time disappears[51] and the grave face of eternity gazes upon you from all things. It is as if you had awoken in a world where all beauty is frozen. In this state, birth and death seem mere appearances. In this state the heart is no longer capable of rapture. It vibrates slowly from top to bottom like an Eolian harp. The heart is the only thing to move in this eternal world; it is its glory.[52]

Țuțea employs Eminescu's 'cardiotics',[53] an affective concept of knowledge, using Plato to interpret Kant. Țuțea notes that according to Kant 'intuitive certainty', that is to say, what is evident, 'can never come from a priori concepts'.[54] He concludes that 'the irrationality of sensibility proves Eminescu right about Kant. Platonic Ideas must be understood similarly.'[55] Platonic Ideas are 'forms of divine thought reflected in the human mind as logical concepts, the only way to conceive rationally of truth'.[56] Ideas both embrace and transcend thought and feeling. Although there is a long patristic tradition influenced by Platonism, the Christian goes beyond Plato's mystical realm of Ideas: in the Incarnation, thought and feeling are raised into a new dimension through the redemptive embrace of flesh in spiritual grace, action, attitudes, and virtuous living.

To Țuțea this fullness of incarnational living is centred in the heart (in the discussion of 'cardiotics' mentioned above, he uses the phrase 'intimate consciousness'). The life of a Christian requires uncompromising commitment to the impossible, called perfection, and here Țuțea refers particularly to Thomas à

Religion and Rational Theology, trans. and ed. Allen W. Wood and George di Giovanni (Cambridge: Cambridge University Press, 1996), p. 97.

51   Cf. Kant's description of time and space as 'pure forms of sensibility before all perception of experience': Kant, *Prolegomena to Any Future Metaphysics*, p. 114.

52   Mihai Eminescu, *Lecturi Kantiene, Traduceri din Critica Rațiunii Pure*, ed. C. Noica and A. Surdu with two fragments trans. Titu Maiorescu (Bucharest: Univers, 1975), pp. vii–viii. For Țuțea's quotation and comments on this fragment, see THEATRE, pp. 314–15.

53   I remember Țuțea telling me that he coined the word 'cardiotics' in a discussion with Cioran in Berlin in the 1930s. The concept is mentioned in THEATRE, p. 315.

54   THEATRE, p. 315.

55   THEATRE, p. 315.

56   PROBLEMS, p. 160. Cf. PROBLEMS, p. 302.

Kempis's *Imitatio Christi*.[57] He personally embraced this 'impossibility' through the discipline of his prison experience. Sentiment in this context takes the form of unchangeable attitudes without which there can be no contact with the eternal world. The Christian life involves always choosing perfection (trusting that indeed 'with God all things are possible') as the way to communion with God. In the end, through the experience of unjust imprisonment, terror, and suffering, Țuțea knew that philosophy was not enough. And it was at this point of need that certain fellow prisoners of conscience opened up to him the spiritual power of the invocation of the Name of Jesus.

The *Philokalia* had been studied in the infernal 'cell' where Țuțea found himself in the early 1950s and 1960s. The books had by then been destroyed, but the prisoners themselves had become the books, generating a spiritual power impervious to torture and death[58] – a power and grace often expressed in music, art, and poetry, as well as through the simple miracle of survival. One political prisoner testifies in his published memoirs to this 'mystery of salvation through poetry':

> The assertion that poetry – culture in general – is a privilege of the elect cannot be accepted. On the contrary, the status of poetry is ontological. The proof is the extent of the poetic phenomenon in political prisons [where poetry was written with a needle on soap, on cloth, and transmitted in Morse code, or orally from person to person]. By these means hundreds of my verses reached other comrades. With every verse learned by heart by my fellow prisoners, my fears gradually subsided, like wax melting in fire. So I became human once again, capable of joy and offering joy to the others, though taking many risks in doing so...

> More significant than the poem itself was the fact that I 'wrote' poetry, not with a pencil (which was strictly forbidden), but in my memory and in our collective memory. This is an irreducible mystery, for the *raison d'être* of poetry in the prison world does not reside in its object, but in the creative act of its conception. A poem can be confiscated, treasured, or burnt. But that which has been conceived in the sacrificial act of writing (for Christ's glory, in solidarity of suffering with other inmates, with the joy of self-recovery) cannot be destroyed. In the prisons of Romania, poetry was miraculously transformed into bread and wine, sacred body and blood, as Hölderlin sought to achieve in his famous poem 'Wine and Bread'.[59]

---

57   As Țuțea was dying he kept repeating the words *scoate-mă* ('take me out'). People were puzzled. In fact he was quoting from Thomas à Kempis's *Imitatio Christi*. Țuțea had written years before, that in the *Imitatio Christi* freedom is presented thus: 'Take me by Your power, Lord, out of my limitation and cosmic enchainment', PROBLEMS, p. 318. I have not been able to identify the source of this quotation. Țuțea might have slightly misquoted from memory.

58   See Fr Constantin Voicescu, 'Cuvânt la slujba de înmormântare a martirilor de la Târgu Ocna', *Din Documentele Rezistenței*, nr. 5, Arhiva Asociației Foștilor Deținuți Politici din România, Bucharest, 1992, pp. 269–83 (sermon given in 1990 at the funeral service of the political prisoners who died in the 'Penitentiary Sanatorium' at Târgu Ocna and were buried in Communist common graves).

59   Summarised after Viorel Gheorghiță, *Et Ego: Sărata-Pitești-Gherla-Aiud, Scurtă istorie a devenirii mele* (Timișoara: Marineasa, 1994), pp. 214–16.

The vision, thinking, and writing of Petre Țuțea were nourished by this Eucharistic mystery, in which the gifts of culture and sacrifice, joy and miracle, become the realisation of Truth.

Chapter 4

Re-education and Unmasking

Petre Ţuţea, who endured so great an ordeal during his political detention at Aiud prison that I wonder how such a man could possibly survive to the age of ninety, is an abiding genius of Orthodoxy and of the Romanian people. For during his imprisonment he was always on strike, engaged in a permanent struggle with the whole administration and staff of that Communist prison. This man was called by God to embody and express all that is most valuable and pure in our spiritual and moral life. Ţuţea is more than a political party. He is more than a saint.[1]

Ţuţea was imprisoned in Communist labour camps as were many hundreds of thousands of other Romanians. He was always reluctant to speak about the 're-education' experience which he underwent in prison, and which he regarded as 'a blot on the conscience of the Romanian nation'.[2] Rather than write of his time in prison, he turned his observation of human nature to account in a creative direction. His experience profoundly influenced his ethical thinking and informed his theology,

---

1   Archimandrite Iustin Pârvu (b. 10 February 1916), *starets* of Petru Vodă Monastery near Neamţ, Moldavia, political prisoner 1948–64, one of the great spiritual fathers of Romania. In the early 1960s he was imprisoned at Aiud where he met Ţuţea. The above epigraph is a recorded interview, not a written appreciation. His observation 'more than a saint' thus conveys the feelings and respect inspired by one who renews one's own sense of what sainthood is: interview, 2 September 2000. See also Camelia Corban, 'Părintele Iustin Pârvu – isvor al demnităţii româneşti', *Permanenţe*, Bucharest, March 2001, pp. 3–4.

2   The re-education programme is concisely described by Dennis Deletant in his useful book, *Ceauşescu and the Securitate, Coercion and Dissent in Romania, 1965–1989* (London: Hurst, 1995), pp. 13–43. Deletant's main sources are archive material and a work by Dumitru Bacu, a former political prisoner who was not subjected to re-education himself, but who compiled 'some of this fragmented history' in 1963. See Dumitru Bacu, *Piteşti, Centru de Reeducare Studenţească*, 2nd edn (Bucharest: Atlantida, 1991), with a foreword by Fr Gheorghe Calciu, a survivor of Piteşti prison, who has given me invaluable data (an English translation of Bacu's book, *The Anti-Humans*, was published in 1971). For my book I have interviewed other survivors of the re-education programme (such as the late Dumitru Bordeianu, Gheorghe Măruţă, and Octavian Voinea, as well as Aristide Ionescu and Traian Popescu) and referred to books written out of personal experience of re-education (see Bibliography). I also interviewed the late Colonel Gheorghe Crăciun, the former governor of Aiud prison, and Lieutenant-Colonel Aurel Lungu who worked as a 're-educator' and undercover *Securitate* officer while Ţuţea was imprisoned at Aiud.

so that he was able to offer a powerful personal contribution to the classical Orthodox theology of deification, which will be considered in the next chapter.

It is important to understand what 're-education' in Communist Romania involved; it is, therefore, necessary in this chapter to quote at some length from first-hand accounts, as well as to discuss Țuțea's own writings in relation to this issue. English translations of these testimonies and assessments have not been recorded elsewhere and some are little known even in Romania.[3] I believe it is important for them to be preserved in print.[4]

Stalinist Re-education in Romania[5]

Stalinist 're-education' methods were first tried out on Romanian soldiers and officers imprisoned in Soviet concentration camps during the Second World War, and then brought to Romania when military prisoners were repatriated at the end of the war. In the memoirs of his imprisonment in the 'Corrective Labour Camp' at Oranki (between Moscow and Novgorod), Artillery Lieutenant Radu Mărculescu describes the experiences of the first victims in the Soviet camps.[6] He records that the Red Army had *carte blanche* to suppress and destroy all resistance to the establishment of Communism in occupied territories:

---

3   Dennis Deletant, *România sub Regimul Comunist* (Bucharest: Fundația Academia Civică, 1997), pp. 87–8. Cf. Fr George Calciu, *Christ Is Calling You! A Course in Catacomb Pastorship* (Platina, CA: St Herman of Alaska Brotherhood, St Paisius Missionary School, 1997), pp. 96–7, 115–21, 131–48.

4   In her doctoral thesis in clinical psychology and psychopathology, *Terreur communiste et résistance culturelle: Les arracheurs de masques* (Paris: Presses Universitaires de France, 2000), Dr Iréna Talaban examines psychoanalytically the experience of re-education among survivors of Pitești. The original title of this thesis was *Le Christ s'est arrêté a Pitesti, Psychologie et psychopathologie du traumatisme individuel et collectif dans une société totalitaire communiste, La Roumanie communiste, 1945–1989*. Talaban's clinically based analysis is independent from, although very encouraging to, my own research carried out in the field of pastoral psychiatry and political theology.

5   The translations of Aleksandr Solzhenitsyn's works into English had a crucial rôle in raising awareness in the West about the atrocities of the Gulag. See Aleksandr I. Solzhenitsyn, *The Gulag Archipelago, 1918–1956, An Experiment in Literary Investigation, I–II*, trans. Th.P. Whitney (London: Harper & Row, 1974).

6   See Alexandru Popescu, 'Tradition as the Transfigured Cross', *Fairacres Chronicle*, 34:1, Oxford, Spring 2001, pp. 14–22. In connection with the Sovietisation of other peoples, see Anița Nandriș-Cudla's *Twenty Years in Siberia*, trans. from the Romanian by Mabel Nandriș, afterword by Gheorghe Nandriș (Bucharest: Editura Fundației Culturale Române, 1998), an English translation of a remarkable book by a peasant woman born of a Romanian family in northern Bukovina who (in July 1941 together with 13 000 other Romanians) experienced the terror of Soviet deportation beyond the Arctic Circle. Indeed, the aim of such deportations was to exterminate rather than re-educate peoples under the Red Army's occupation.

Immediately after the Second World War, the Romanian officers held as prisoners of war in Soviet concentration camps were subjected to merciless pressure to become Communist collaborators in Romania, with the alternative of being morally and even physically neutralised.

Never was forced labour harder, food more wretched, the behaviour of guards more brutal, the lock-ups more densely crammed, informers more assiduous, and blackmail for our repatriation more openly rife than in the aftermath of the war, especially after the meeting at Yalta between Roosevelt, Churchill and Stalin. The Western powers, although they knew perfectly well what was happening, dared not lift a finger against the Soviet Union.[7]

This persecution, however, had the reverse effect on many Christians re-educated in the labour camps who were in fact transformed, not by their physical torments, but by the discovery of an indestructible love which sustained them in the midst of extreme adversity. At the beginning of his memoirs Mărculescu writes:

The decisive battles at the end of this millennium were not those fought on the battlefield. The human heart is the Armageddon of this aeon, and there too the final battle will take place. What is at stake in this confrontation is the divine spark within the human heart. This is where, until the end of time, the powers bent on fragmenting and enslaving the soul confront the heavenly powers which protect it in its struggle for perfection and freedom. This battle was fought in us throughout the years of imprisonment in the Soviet Gulag and thereafter in Romania. It was a battle for our souls, which our captors wanted to destroy and replace with a subhuman product: 'the new man', an automaton that would function in a world from which moral values had been eliminated.

The desperate effort to preserve our ontological identity, the image and likeness in which God made us, gave shape and substance to our resistance to these infernal forces bent on annexing our inner freedom... It was there that human dignity and even human holiness were revealed to us in all their transfiguring power... This is what we 'confess', this desperate and tragic battle to remain human beings to the very end.[8]

---

7   Radu Mărculescu, *Pătimiri şi Iluminări din Captivitatea Sovietică* (Bucharest: Albatros, 2000), pp. 243–4. Radu Mărculescu was born in 1915 in Bucharest. In 1938 he graduated in philosophy at the University of Bucharest and then taught Romanian in high schools in the capital. Following the 1940 Soviet annexation of the Romanian territories of Bessarabia (which later became the Soviet Socialist Republics of Moldova and Ukraine), he fought in the Romanian Royal Army as a 2nd Lieutenant. In November 1942, during the battle for Stalingrad, he was taken prisoner near the river Don and detained in the Soviet Gulag until 1951 when he returned to Romania. Having written three subversive poems, he was imprisoned between 1959 and 1964 as an 'enemy of the Romanian working class'. Cf. Nicholas Bethell, *The Last Secret, Forcible Repatriation to Russia: 1944–1947*, introd. by Hugh Trevor-Roper (London: Penguin, 1995).

8   Mărculescu, *Pătimiri*, pp. 17–19.

Comintern[9] agents recruited in Romania were specially trained in the Soviet Union to create a military force of two divisions. Named after heroes of the Romanian struggle for national freedom during the eighteenth and nineteenth centuries ('Horia, Cloșca, and Crișan' and 'Tudor Vladimirescu'), they were used in the Soviet 'liberation' of Romania, Hungary, Czechoslovakia, and Austria, and subsequently in the imposition of a pro-Soviet government in post-war Romania. The mission of these supposedly 'voluntary divisions' of Romanian prisoners was to set up an apparatus of repression and to maintain through terror 'the abnormality of a system which – left to its own resources – could not have survived for a single day'.[10]

So while the 'repatriated' prisoners had expected to find freedom on their return home to Romania from the Soviet Gulag, they found the same system installed there as well.[11] This was Mărculescu's experience on his arrival in Aiud, the prison for those accused of military and Legionary membership, whose nationalism epitomised opposition to pan-Sovietism and Marxist–Leninist utopia.

Following an election rigged by Moscow, in November 1946, the new pro-Bolshevik government of Romania forced King Mihai I to abdicate and leave the country in 1947, and set up a programme of de-Christianisation and de-nationalisation of the opposition.

Rooted in Marx's atheist materialism, Communism rejected all religions as illusion;[12] dialectical materialism – a compulsory subject in all schools and universities under Communism – saw material existence as determining human consciousness. Lenin[13] and Stalin put into practice 'the classic Marxian formula

---

9   *Comintern* or *Komintern*: short for Communist International; an international Communist organisation founded by Lenin in Moscow in 1919 and dissolved in 1943; it degenerated under Stalin into an instrument of Soviet politics. Ana Pauker (née Rabinsohn, 1893–1960) was a Moscow Comintern agent, who became Romania's Minister of the Interior after the Second World War.
     'In September 1947 the Communist Information Bureau (Cominform) was set up in Poland. Unlike the Comintern, the Cominform was not a world organisation, but limited to the Communist parties of the USSR, of the countries of Eastern and Central Europe which fell within the Soviet sphere, and, significantly, of France and Italy.' See Leonard Schapiro, *The Communist Party of the Soviet Union* (London: Methuen, 1963), pp. 540–41.
10   Mărculescu, *Pătimiri*, p. 10.
11   Cf. Fr Ioan Iovan, *Memorialul durerii* (Tg. Mureș: Recea Monastery, no date), p. 8: Romanian prisoners of war (released under a Soviet 'amnesty') were met by the *Securitate* at the Soviet–Romanian border to be re-imprisoned as 'war criminals' in places like Gherla penitentiary.
12   As the 'opium of the people', religion is for Marx at best a palliative of mythological superstitions: see his introduction to the 'Contribution to the Critique of Hegel's Philosophy of Right' (1844), in Robert C. Tucker (ed.), *The Marx–Engels Reader*, 2nd edn (London: Norton, 1978), pp. 53–65.
13   For Lenin's repudiation of God and the Bolshevik programme and tactics on religion see Bohdan R. Bociurkiw, 'Lenin and Religion', in Leonard Schapiro and Peter Reddaway (eds), *Lenin: The Man, the Theorist, the Leader* (London: Pall Mall Press, 1967), pp. 107–34.

deriving religious alienation from the more basic economic and social alienation and, consequently, transforming the struggle against religion into a struggle against the social system which creates the need for religious illusion'.[14] The paradox of Christ's commandment to love was subjected to the test of Communist desecration of the divine image in human beings.

A Soviet-inspired programme of 're-education and unmasking', based on physical and mental torture and brainwashing, was undertaken between 1949 and 1952 (beginning at Suceava, then in prisons at Pitești, Ocnele Mari, Târgșor, Gherla, Târgu Ocna), and between 1960 and 1964 (at Aiud, Gherla, and Botoșani). The experiment was also carried out on the canal built by political prisoners, linking the Danube with the Black Sea, and in the sanatorium of Târgu Ocna where gravely ill prisoners were held. Almost entirely ignored by the Western media,[15] this programme was supervised from Moscow by Stalin's Minister for Internal Affairs, Lavrenti Beria (1899–1953), and even by Stalin himself.[16]

Applying the theories of Marxist atheism, Pavlovian reflexology, and Freudian psychoanalysis, the architects of re-education aimed to eliminate religion, particularly Christianity, and traditional Romanian culture, especially among the younger generation. National consciousness was to be subordinated to Communist ideology. The psychological engineering practised in political prisons was intended to destroy that which Christians proclaim as the image and likeness of God within the human person. The brainwashing process started with individuals in prison but was later extended across the whole of society, as those people de-personalised by prison experience acted as ideological contaminants in the more general programme. Some people were subjected to re-education because of their political views (for example, former members of political parties before the Soviet takeover in Romania), others because they were *kulaks* (that is, 'reactionary' peasants who owned their own farms

---

14 Bociurkiw, 'Lenin and Religion', p. 109.
15 I happen to know that first-hand information about re-education got to the West in the early 1950s through the wife of a medical doctor and political prisoner killed by the guards on the canal. It should be remembered in this context that the Soviet invasion of Hungary in 1956 was officially accepted by the Western leaders as an 'internal affair' of the Soviet Union. However, private citizens were deeply indignant. I know from the late Mrs Wendy Noica-Muston, wife of the Romanian philosopher and prisoner of conscience Constantin Noica (a friend of Țuțea's), that her husband's case led to the formation of a lobbying group which contributed to the foundation of Amnesty International in 1961. Cf. Roland Barthes, 'Un raport secret', *Memoria*, 34, January 2001, pp. 82–6: Barthes was the French cultural attaché in Romania, before being expelled by the Stalinist authorities. In a secret report to his government dated 21 July 1949, he exposed and analysed Soviet techniques of censorship and indoctrination applied to members of the Romanian Academy and the universities.
16 This process was outlined in Deletant, *Ceaușescu and the Securitate*, p. 30. Deletant's scholarly contributions focus on the history of the Romanian Communist Party. Although relying also on memoirs published after 1989, they inevitably emphasise historical facts and archive material relevant to his theme rather than the personal spiritual journey of Christians under Communism.

and opposed collectivisation), and some for their religious beliefs. I focus here on Christian and nationalist[17] victims, while recognising that there were numerous other groups who suffered for their faith or ideological 'errors'. Many of those imprisoned in Romanian political prisons were detained on charges which, whether fabricated or not, remained unknown to them. Țuțea himself was initially detained without trial and apparently on 'preventive' grounds at Ocnele Mari. Țuțea used to say: 'If I knew why I was imprisoned, I would be awarded a Nobel prize for science.'[18]

The torturer-in-chief at Pitești, was a former Legionary, Eugen Țurcanu (b. 1925). Although a prisoner himself, he had close contact with the Ministry of the Interior and clearly could not have acted without the knowledge and co-operation of the administration. His behaviour may be explained by his hostility towards those Legionaries who, unlike himself, had remained faithful to their ideals. He may well have hoped for eventual reward, and of course he knew that he had the Soviet system behind him. Although he was in fact manipulated and did not personally initiate the atrocities, he nevertheless bore responsibility for what happened. He had, after all, been put in charge of the re-education programme in Pitești, been instructed in torture, and told what to do when victims died. Finally when the re-education experiment ended in 1952, he made a convenient scapegoat.[19]

Nicolae Călinescu, another former Legionary and political prisoner, gave a systematic account of Pitești where he too underwent re-education. At a psychological level, the process had deliberately destructive aims:

1   physical abuse, repeated shocks, constraint and terror were meant to weaken the victim's ego or even cause it to disintegrate;

---

17   By 'nationalist' here I mean opposed to the imposition of a Soviet system on Romania.
18   Because of his 'rotten bourgeois ideology', as the standard propagandistic rhetoric of the era would have it, he 'endangered' the newly established Soviet system. In some of Țuțea's files in the *Securitate* archives he is charged with subversive Legionary activity intended to overthrow the régime of the People's Republic of Romania (see Plate 10).
19   The date of Țurcanu's death remains uncertain. Officially he was executed on 17 December 1954 following a show trial in 1953 to prove that re-education was strictly an ad interim matter of Legionaries detained at Pitești, who would have initiated the experiment without prior permission from the prison governor. This claim is grotesque, as proved by a great number of documents, memories, and interviews published after 1989 (and confirmed to me by the late Gheorghe Măruță in an unpublished interview, Bucharest-Tg. Jiu, 24–25 August 2000). Some of the victims of Pitești, however, believe that he was released in secret (and perhaps still lives in the Soviet Union): Doina Jela, *Lexiconul Negru, Unelte ale represiunii comuniste* (Bucharest: Humanitas, 2001), p. 291. For the official interpretation of re-education, see Nicolae Henegaru and Silvia Colfescu (eds), *Memorialul Ororii, Documente ale Procesului Reeducării din închisorile Pitești, Gherla* (Bucharest: Vremea, 1995), pp. 697ff.; and also Richard Wurmbrand, *In God's Underground*, ed. Charles Foley (London: W.H. Allen, 1968), p. 90. Cf. Mihail Giuran, 'Crimele lui Andrei Coler', *Buletin de Informații al Românilor din Exil* (*BIRE*), nr. 775, Paris, 16 May 1983, pp. 7–8.

2   periodical 'unmasking of hidden thoughts' was to bring about radical 'purification' by destroying the old set of perceptions, values, and moral norms of the world that had shaped the individual's personal development; any reference for orientation in this inter-personal chaos was abolished;
3   the terrified victim would acquire a guilt complex; in time this became rationally justified; self-esteem was destroyed by humiliation (insults, defamation, obligation to eat faeces);
4   having experienced loss of personal integrity, the victim would be compelled to construct a new self-image;
5   the semantic reference was changed; old concepts preserved in the victim's consciousness were emptied of content and invested with different meaning; identification of the victim with the aggressor was gradually induced through disintegration of the personality.

Călinescu described how the slightest divergence from the Marxist official line was treated as a criminal offence. In this 'academy' of terror, victims became torturers. Suicide was excluded by an ever vigilant system. The slightest resentful thought had to be confessed and registered as a cause for concern, as a sign of progress in the re-education 'course'. 'Sincerity' was assessed according to the victim's readiness to denounce parents, friends, and close collaborators.[20]

According to Călinescu, other irreversible psychological changes were brought about by: deprivation of food, light, air, and sleep (leading in many cases to death); endless interrogations involving the unmasking of one's own and others' personal thoughts; continuous scrutiny of the victim's memory and consciousness to expose hostility towards Marxist ideology; 'sincerity' imposed through shock tactics; submission imposed through electric shocks; continuous correction of personal ideological 'position'; obligation to examine minutely personal unconscious experience, from childhood to the present time, and to disclose one's hostile thoughts towards the system and 'ideological trespasses' noticed or suspected in others.

---

20   Summarised after Nicolae Călinescu, 'Procesele de Brainwashing', *Permanenţe*, Bucharest, February 1998, pp. 12–13. Other forms of re-education used forced labour:
> Another efficient method created a split between intellectuals on the one hand, and peasants and workers on the other. In all labour camps special brigades were formed: some included only intellectuals, others only peasants and workers... Competition [for example, production quotas] between class-defined brigades was used to 'demonstrate' that intellectuals were workshy. In reality intellectuals (unused to hard physical labour, and many of them old or ill) were almost always unable to compete in terms of physical strength.

See Dumitru Văcariu, 'Aspecte ale "educării" şi "reeducării" în închisorile comuniste şi lagărele de muncă forţată', in Romulus Rusan, *Analele Sighet 9, Anii 1961–1972: Ţările Europei de Est, între speranţele reformei şi realitatea stagnării* (Bucharest: Fundaţia Academia Civică, 2001), pp. 356–7. Marx's theory of class conflict was thus 'proved': as educated representatives of the propertied classes under capitalism, intellectuals remained a 'reactionary' obstacle to the working-class revolution even under Communism. They were 'enemies of the people'.

The victim's change of attitude and newly acquired convictions were continuously tested. Torturers would apply the 'treatment' to correct 'infidelity to the working class'. Inflexibility, especially resistance to Communism, was carefully diagnosed and 'treated' with narcotics, electric shocks, or brain surgery. When the will was entirely annihilated, the victim was forced to perform shameful acts. Personal guilt would prevent return to a normal life. 'Re-educated' people would be rejected by prisoners who had refused to compromise.[21] This was the case at Pitești and Ocnele Mari.

We know, however, from Țuțea's fellow prisoners that he did not become a torturer. On the contrary, he used his spiritual authority to unite political prisoners at Ocnele Mari against the prison administration by threatening mass suicide if the re-education experiment was not stopped.[22]

Methods of Re-education

In the 1920s the Soviet educationalist Anton Makarenko (1888–1939) devised a method for the re-education of young criminals and thieves (though not of political detainees) through violence and intimidation inflicted by fellow prisoners specially trained to create a régime of terror.[23] It is not known how far this sadistic experiment was taken in the Soviet Union, but there can be no doubt that a group of prisoners authorised to create terror could achieve truly horrific results.[24] In Romania it

---

21   Călinescu, 'Procesele de Brainwashing', p. 12.
22   See Virgil Mateiaș, 'Anii de groază din România Comunistă', printed typescript, Făgăraș, 21 March 1991, pp. 4, 52.
23   See Anton S. Makarenko, *The Road to Life (An Epic of Education)*, *Book One*, trans. from Russian by Ivy and Tatiana Litvinov (Moscow: Progress Publishers, 1973). Makarenko's re-educational programme, perfected at Pitești, was initially applied to political dissidents detained at the Solovki Monastery on the Solovetsky Islands in the White Sea: Dumitru Bacu, 'Cred în destinul acestui neam', interview by Marcel Petrișor, *Puncte Cardinale*, Sibiu, December 1991, p. 8. Described by Solzhenitsyn in *The Gulag Archipelago*, this monastery 'had been the site of a notorious labour camp from 1920–36 and among the thousands who died there of exhaustion and torture were many priests and 26 bishops': Jane Ellis, *The Russian Orthodox Church: Triumphalism and Defensiveness* (London: Macmillan in assoc. with St Antony's College, Oxford, 1996), p. 61.
24   In 1965, four of Makarenko's 'Lectures' were translated into English and published in Moscow in typical propagandistic style. The table of contents is significant in itself. It reads: 'A.S. Makarenko – an Outstanding Soviet Educator; *Lecture One*. Methods of Upbringing; *Lecture Two*. Discipline, Regimen, Punishment and Reward; *Lecture Three*. Methods of Individual Approach; *Lecture Four*. Work Training, Relations, Style and Tone'. In the introduction, Anton Makarenko, 'this remarkable man' and 'Soviet educator, theoretician and writer' is compared with John Locke, Jean Jacques Rousseau and Johann Pestalozzi. See Anton S. Makarenko, *Problems of Soviet School Education*, compiled by Candidates of Pedagogical Science V. Aransky and A. Piskunov, trans. O. Shartse (Moscow: Progress Publishers, 1965), p. 5.

was mostly students and intellectuals who were *satanizaţi* ('satanised')[25] through re-education (that is, given a diabolical change of identity by passing through an 'eternity of hell'[26]) where fellow prisoners – indeed prisoners who had been particular friends – inflicted sustained physical and psychological torture on each other. An individual was transformed into a robot of the Communist system, an informer, a torturer, a madman, or a mere corpse for secret disposal. This terrifying process is described by Grigore Dumitrescu:

> Everything takes place in a perfect, automaton manner. The robots, i.e. re-educated torturers, are like machines, with total brutality, showing the extent to which they have lost their human character... Here at Piteşti you need to lie to save your life. If, rather than lie, you tell the truth, this will inform the robots that your conscience is so 'rotten' that re-education is not effective in your case... The robots claimed that, even if we were released from the political prison without being re-educated, the working class would anyway kill us. So, to kill us while we were still in prison was actually our torturers' duty.[27]

The re-education experiment originated in the 1930s, when Soviet society was systematically subjected to Stalin's personality cult. After 1941 Romanian military prisoners in the Soviet Gulag were exposed to this ideology and 'persuaded' to accept it. People also had to accept the assertion of Soviet 'superiority' over Western capitalism, and the idea that every member of the Soviet working class could and should become a model of Soviet humanity and culture.[28]

The experiment of re-education in Romania took place in two phases: the first, between 1949 and 1952, when tens of thousands of young people who refused to submit to the Soviet occupation and ideology were imprisoned;[29] the second, between 1960 and 1964 (when a general amnesty was granted to political dissidents), following the Red Army's withdrawal in 1958.

---

25 'Satanic', 'satanism', and so on, with reference to contemporary Western black magic, bears little (though perhaps not absolutely *no*) similarity to the complete negation of God implied by Romanian writers in this context.

26 See Petre Grigore C. Anastasis (Puiu Năstase), *Înfruntarea: Reeducările de la Gherla* (Bucharest: Ramida, 1997), pp. 48–51.

27 See Grigore Dumitrescu, *Demascarea* (Bucharest: Jon Dumitru & Mediana, 1996), pp. 100, 145.

28 On the Sovietisation of Romania see: Florica Dobre and Alesandru Duţu, *Distrugerea Elitei Militare sub Regimul Ocupaţiei Sovietice în România, vol. I, 1944–1946* (Bucharest: Academia Română, Institutul Naţional pentru Studiul Totalitarismului, 2000); Flori Stănescu and Dragoş Zamfirescu, *Ocupaţia Sovietică în România, Documente 1944–1946* (Bucharest: Vremea, 1998); Constantin Rădulescu-Motru, *Revizuiri şi Adăugiri, vol. 6, 1948*, ed. Rodica Bichis (Bucharest: Floarea Darurilor Press, 2000).

29 Organised military anti-Communist resistance continued in the mountains for more than a decade. See Ion Gavrilă-Ogoranu, *Brazii se frâng, dar nu se îndoiesc*, 2 vols (Timişoara: Marineasa, 1993; 1995).

These two phases differed in at least two respects; the first phase aimed to re-educate the younger generation (mainly students and school pupils accused either of belonging to anti-Communist and pro-monarchist organisations, or of being 'enemies of the working class' – that is, members of the 'rotten' and 'corrupt' bourgeoisie) and to bring them into the Communist fold. The second phase was aimed at mature people who had usually experienced at least a decade of political imprisonment, and had survived the extermination régime of the first phase and even earlier forms of oppression (members of the Iron Guard had been imprisoned under Marshal Antonescu as early as 1941). Victims of the second phase were no longer to be brainwashed (like the youngsters tortured during the first phase), but 'persuaded' by more subtle methods to co-operate with the now firmly established Communist State. These methods, however, still involved confinement in filthy conditions and deprivation of the basic necessities of life together with reportedly deliberate poisoning and infection with tuberculosis.[30]

The First Phase: Re-education and Unmasking at Piteşti

Anyone who ended up in prison was seen as evil and despicable, concealing their wickedness behind a mask of religion, honour, and duty, for the purpose of leading others astray. Torture and terror were used to remove this 'mask', to expose 'the beast within' – the person's alleged real identity. Hence the mechanical slogan shouted at the victims: 'Wake the beast inside you!' Torture was not publicly acknowledged as part of the system. 'Piteşti begins where inter-personal relationships end and human beings lose trust in each other, where all are suspect and everyone is an enemy.'[31] The re-education process had five stages, which Puiu Năstase summarised.[32]

After a preliminary interrogation upon arrest, the first stage involved gaining the victim's confidence. An informer posing as a fellow prisoner would follow up the *Securitate* inquiry without the victim's knowledge, to find out as much as possible about anti-Communist activity not disclosed at the inquiry, and to construct a psychological profile. This profile would establish how religious the victim was, what ethnic and cultural values were most cherished, what political views were held, and which members of the family they were most fond of. The profile applied particularly to young prisoners, whose views on religion, nationalism, politics, and civil society were still at a formative stage.

The second stage involved sudden infliction of torture, which began without warning with a terrible beating intended utterly to confuse the victim. This was accompanied by psychological terrorisation – such as swearing, insults, and repeated

---

30   Mircea Nicolau, interview, Bucharest, 4 September 2000. See also Nicolae Mărgineanu, *Amfiteatre şi Închisori (Mărturii asupra unui veac zbuciumat)*, ed. and introd. by Voicu Lăscuş (Cluj-Napoca: Dacia, 1991), p. 257.

31   Nicolae Călinescu, *Sisteme şi Procese de Brainwashing în România Comunistă* (Bucharest: Gama, 1998), p. 60. Cf. Mihai Timaru, 'Mecanismele terorii', *Memoria*, 33, April 2000, pp. 102–7.

32   See Puiu Năstase, *Înfruntarea*, pp. 45–6. Năstase himself underwent re-education.

use of the word *bandit*[33] – by a group of torturers imprisoned in the same cell as the victim. Often they were informers or even officials disguised as fellow prisoners to whom the victim would previously have confessed their innermost thoughts. All this would induce obsessive 'guilt' feelings in the victim.

The third stage of re-education, called 'private unmasking', entailed an initial 'external unmasking', by applying continuous physical torture to compel the victim to confess any public activities. This meant confessing all activities against the Communist régime and denouncing anyone (including members of their own family) who had ever done, said, or even thought anything against it. This was followed by an 'internal unmasking' or denouncing of fellow prisoners who had shown 'hostility to Communism'. It made the prisoner de facto a *Securitate* collaborator, and potentially a useful witness in other trials. Those who had been reduced to making such denunciations (often of invented crimes) could be used to testify against anyone else the 'Red Investigator' chose to pursue.

There followed a substage of 'meditation', in which victims had to sit silently in a fixed position, hands on knees, while their faces were scrutinised for signs of 'sincerity'. The victim might have to adopt different wax-like postures (for example, standing on one foot with hands up) for hours, becoming reduced to what would later be described as a state resembling rigid catalepsy (frequently observed in catatonic schizophrenia). Physical exhaustion was intended to elicit 'passive' non-verbal confessions. The victim's face became a virtual mirror of inner thoughts. The aim was to induce a hypnotic state in which the torturer could read the victim's mind.

Eventually, the victim would be forced to blaspheme against God, curse admired public figures, then curse and denounce family members, whom they would vilify and accuse of the worst sins, such as incest, or adultery. This 'private unmasking' concluded with personal self-criticism in the presence of torturers (fellow prisoners, or prison officials, or both) and led to the fourth stage of re-education, 'public unmasking', as the victim grew to believe in his own guilt and confessed to other prisoners. The long sessions of unmasking were broken up periodically by short intervals, used for so-called meals and medical assistance.[34]

During the fifth stage there was a moral pseudo-rehabilitation by a change of identity from uninitiated victim to experienced torturer. Victims would finally acknowledge publicly and in writing that, with their background, and being inevitably worthless and vicious criminals who deserved torture and humiliation, their partial rehabilitation could be achieved on joining the torturers and the *Securitate*. At Piteşti the choice was either to become a torturer or die. Some accepted the system only for the duration of their imprisonment. Those who continued to be informers or who 'co-operated' with the system after their release from prison did so by secretly signing an agreement which, if broken, could be held against them.

At Ocnele Mari, where Ţuţea was detained, methods similar to those of Piteşti were employed:

---

33   In Romanian, this was a deeply hurtful and insulting word.
34   Călinescu, *Sisteme şi Procese*, pp. 42ff.

At Ocnele Mari the political prisoners were forced to drink urine and to eat faeces for theoretical reasons relating to their anti-Communist views. It was necessary to inflict a psychological shock, a radical internal transformation, as a result of which the student or intellectual prisoner (re-education was carried out for preference on these categories) suddenly and usually became the very best Marxist–Leninist, having been opposed to the Bolshevik system introduced into Romania by the Soviets.[35]

The Second Phase: Re-education and Unmasking at Aiud

For reasons still not publicly disclosed, the re-education experiment at Piteşti ended in 1952. Aiud was the flagship prison of the second phase of re-education. The leaders of the Romanian Communist Party closely followed the progress of this second phase. On 21 October 1963, Alexandru Drăghici, then Vice-President of the Council of Ministers, and Minister of Internal Affairs, attended a secret meeting on re-education. On this occasion the Communist leaders decided to continue the process 'of misleading and demoralising political prisoners in order to break down their unity and compromise their leaders who were still active both in Aiud prison and abroad'. This process had been secretly sanctioned as early as June 1959.[36]

Between 1960 and 1964, however, the experiment was resumed in an even more insidious form at Aiud in the heart of Transylvania, using less physical violence and more psychological pressure. In her *Lexiconul Negru, Unelte ale represiunii comuniste* (*Black Lexicon, Tools of Communist Repression*), Doina Jela describes the whole process, from its beginning in the late 1940s to its end in 1964, as 'perverse re-education whose aim was to annihilate completely the personality of those who had opposed' Communism.[37] The former governor of Aiud, the late Colonel Crăciun,

---

35   Petre Pandrea, *Reeducarea de la Aiud*, ed. Nadia Marcu Pandrea (Bucharest: Vremea, 2000), p. 90. Petre Pandrea was in Ocnele Mari with Ţuţea. On Pandrea, see note 54 in this chapter.

36   Constantin Aioanei and Cristian Troncotă, 'Modelul reeducării prin autoanaliză: Aiud şi Gherla 1960–1964', *Arhivele Totalitarismului*, 2:1–2, Bucharest, 1994, pp. 60f. Cf. Demostene Andronescu, 'Reeducarea de la Aiud', I, *Puncte Cardinale*, Sibiu, August–September 1993, p. 6.

37   Jela, *Lexiconul Negru*, p. 87. The termination of re-education at Aiud 'was not an act of humanitarian good will, but the result of international pressure from the West. We know today that the Romanian Prime-Minister Ion Gheorghe Maurer was due to make an official visit to France, but General de Gaulle made it a condition that first all political prisoners had to be released': Dragomir Manta, 'Graţierile politice din anii 1963 şi 1964', in Rusan (ed.), *Analele Sighet 9, Anii 1961–1972*, p. 359. Maurer visited France between 27 July and 3 August 1964, see Constantin G. Giurescu, et al. (eds), *Chronological History of Romania* (Bucharest: Editura Enciclopedică Română, 1972), p. 377. Ţuţea was released from Aiud on 1 August 1964. He describes his years of isolation at Aiud, in DIALOGUES, pp. 37–8. Cf. Octavian Voinea, *Masacrarea Studenţimii Române în închisorile de la Piteşti, Gherla şi Aiud, Mărturii*, ed. Ggeorghe Andreica (Bucharest: Majadahonda, 1996), p. 198.

tried to claim that the second phase of the re-education experiment was more humane. Unlike Țurcanu before him, Crăciun's aim was not the re-education of younger generations but that of mature political prisoners – already physically and psychologically weak from years of detention – into collaborators by 'personal conviction'.[38] However, in Aiud torture, terror, and forced labour were replaced with a régime of isolation, starvation, exposure to the cold and psychosomatic exhaustion (through lack of sleep and confinement in unventilated cells without access to basic medical remedies). It is estimated that hundreds of prisoners died at Aiud.

Alongside the brainwashing, victims were bribed into adopting Marxist–Stalinist slogans and committing themselves to the programme[39] (for example, the governor promised 'co-operative' prisoners the chance of a new life by allowing them to return to their families from whom they had been separated for years). In the early years of the Soviet era many still hoped that America would intervene. Now, after so many years, the argument went, 'Come on, you can see the capitalist system is collapsing, you'd better join us'. Even natural altruism was manipulated and abused: 'your fellow prisoners will all be freed if *you* stop being stubborn and accept us'.

In so-called 're-education clubs', previously re-educated prisoners had to discuss newspaper articles and Soviet propaganda films and attend lectures on ideology. Some victims were driven around the country in police vans, to see for themselves 'the glorious achievements' of Communism so that they might report back to

---

38   Interview with Colonel Gheorghe Crăciun, Bucharest, 16 October 1999. Cf. Virgil Maxim, *Imn pentru Crucea Purtată*, 2 vols (Timișoara: Gordian, 1997), II, pp. 175ff.

39   Youthful aspirations and intimate beliefs had to be abjured in such a way that any idea opposed to Communism would be literally erased from the former dissident's consciousness. Fear of the totalitarian system, displaced into the unconscious, had to be transformed into attachment to Communist 'ideals', in a process of unconditional identification with them. 'Idealists' deceived in their innocence by 'reactionary' leaders of pre-Stalinist Romania, the 'enemies of the people', now would wish to deny their past by serving the Communist cause. Dr Alexandru Popovici, a prisoner at Aiud, wrote in his *auto-critica* ('self-analysis') as a 're-educated' man:

> We were honest in our fight for our credo. But we were led astray by people in whom we trusted. All of us were suffering from that morbid mass psychosis, mainly due to our unhealthy emotional attachment [to religious and national feelings]. This corrupted our logic and common sense. Let us knock these myths off the pedestal we stuck them on. It is the only way to clear our minds!

See Aioanei and Troncotă, 'Modelul reeducării', p. 61. Cf. Ilie Bădescu and Dan Dungaciu, 'Experimente totalitare. Modelul reeducării: Pitești, Gherla, Canal, 1949–1952', *Arhivele Totalitarismului*, 2:3, Bucharest, 1994, pp. 7–16.

Another former political prisoner who interviewed 're-educated' victims claims that when the experiment was successful, 'it was enough for the torturer simply to refer to his methods of torture, for the victim's psyche to become "anaesthetised" so that he would behave according to the will of his tormentor': Mihai Rădulescu, *Casa Lacrimilor Neplânse: Martor al Acuzării în Procesul 'Reeducatorilor'* (Bucharest: Ramida, 1993), pp. 75–9.

'unreformed' fellow prisoners. Ţuţea, when asked after one such trip what had most impressed him, replied: 'A willow tree.'[40]

Re-education in Society at Large

By means of aggressive propaganda and indoctrination in schools and universities, the re-education programme finally turned the whole country into a quasi-prison. The two main goals of this long process were robotisation and suppression of the past.

The systematic process of robotisation and collaboration, whereby young people were forced to identify with the Soviet 'revolutionary proletarian', spread like an epidemic, initially throughout the prison communities, then across the country to the capital, Bucharest. Networks of *Securitate* informers, created first of all in the prisons, would later proliferate throughout society. Meanwhile, the headquarters of the Romanian Communist Party under Soviet control continued their propaganda in the press and on the radio. In 1965 when Ceauşescu came to power and Russian influence diminished, the indoctrination continued, but retained a strong nationalist flavour which eventually degenerated into a Ceauşescu personality cult.

What was it like to live in such a society? Even in the late 1980s there was no room for 'ordinary' life in Communist Romania. Everyone, from the poorest citizens to prominent Communist Party members and apparatchiks, lived in competition with the bourgeois enemies in the capitalist 'rotten' world. They had to achieve higher yields of crops, higher industrial production, and better results than their competitors (for example, in military, scientific, cultural, and sporting events). 'Duty' required them to overcome what the rhetoric of the time habitually denounced as under-development inherited from the bourgeois era, and to prove the superiority of Communism. This constant need to demonstrate superiority affected everything. All 'decadence' had to be purged – thus, toilet paper was a luxury, often absent from shops, and chicken claws were a feast. Most horrific of all, human beings themselves became products of this competitive ideology. I will not go into the details here of Ceauşescu's infamous policy of birth control.[41] However, the imposition of police surveillance over one of the most intimate, essential, and mysterious aspects of human life, namely procreation, induced a brutalised psychological state of mind in the re-educated society. By such means the universal practice of duplicity and complicity (ranging from the endemic black economy to prostitution of artistic talent in the service of the Ceauşescu cult) became the almost institutional norm of civic and social life.

The suppression of history became a significant part of the re-education of society. The personal Christian faith of public figures along with their identity was to be

---

40   Personal conversation, Ţuţea's flat, Bucharest, 1 March 1990. In his memoirs, *La capăt de drum* (Iassy: Institutul European, 1997), p. 199, the writer Marcel Petrişor attributes a similar reply to another political prisoner. Cf. Viktor E. Frankl, *Man's Search for Meaning* (New York: Washington Square Press, 1985), p. 90.

41   See Gail Kligman, *The Politics of Duplicity, Controlling Reproduction in Ceauşescu's Romania* (Los Angeles: University of California Press, 1998).

erased from history, since victims were required to proclaim publicly their new ideological convictions. The capacity of atheist Communism to create the 'new man', *homo Sovieticus*, was demonstrated at Aiud when some of the staunchest defenders of Christian and national identity in Romania were broken under the strain. And yet, many survivors of political imprisonment were, like Țuțea, granted an extraordinary revelation of mystical truth through their living martyrdom. What Fr Nicolae Steinhardt called 'the mystical solution of faith', which transcends both ideology and psychopathology, is the only basis for a true account of human history and identity. His assessment of the capacity for moral survival in a re-educated society should now be more closely examined.

The Testimony of Fr Nicolae Steinhardt

Fr Nicolae Steinhardt (1912–89) was a Jew, converted to Christianity while imprisoned at Gherla in Transylvania.[42] Significantly entitled *Jurnalul Fericirii* (*The Diary of Happiness*), his book begins with a 'Political Testament' in which he analyses the totalitarian experience in Communist Romania. Fr Nicolae writes that, in order to survive when the whole universe has become a concentration camp (he is concerned here not just with prison existence but with all social manifestations of totalitarianism), there are three solutions dependent on human resources and thus open to everyone. There is also a fourth, which is from God.[43]

The first solution is that of Alexander Solzhenitsyn. Fr Nicolae writes: 'When somebody crosses the threshold of the *Securitate* or any similar coercive institution, he has to say: "At this very moment, I am dead." If he can think of himself as dead, he is saved, for he can no longer be threatened, blackmailed, or fooled.' Once hope is extinguished, virtual suicide brings escape from this world. But, Fr Nicolae insists, it must be a firm belief in death, all hope must be abandoned.

The second solution is exemplified by Alexander Zinoviev's 'Tramp', who has no permanent residence, no identity card, and no place of work.[44] For him, the solution is to refuse to adapt to the system. 'He eats here and there, he lives from day to day. Once in a while, he lands in prison or is interned in a labour camp, but he obstinately refuses to live by the system. He will not accept any job which would imply acknowledgement of it.' He is a misfit living on the margins of a society to which he

---

42   Steinhardt's Baptism on 15 March 1964 is described in his *Jurnalul Fericirii* (Cluj-Napoca: Dacia, 1991), pp. 84–6. He was baptised by Fr Mina Dobzeu, an Orthodox priest and fellow prisoner at Jilava. See George Ardeleanu, *Nicolae Steinhardt, Monografie* (Brașov: Aula, 2000), p. 89.

43   The following is a summary from Nicolae Steinhardt, *Jurnalul Fericirii*, pp. 6–9, an account of his years in prison.

44   Alexander Zinoviev (b. 1922), Russian logician and political dissident. Steinhardt refers to his novel *The Yawning Heights*, a burlesque autopsy of totalitarianism (published in 1976, it led to Zinoviev's defection to West Germany).

is impervious. He is a fool for the sake of freedom. Poverty becomes his credo. He is King Lear's jester.

The third solution is that of Winston Churchill, and also of Vladimir Bukovsky.[45] If people find themselves up against an evil tyranny, they simply do not give in. On the contrary, they make it a reason for living and fighting to the death, according to Fr Nicolae. He quotes Churchill's words to Princess Martha Bibescu from Romania: 'War is coming. Britain will be reduced to rubble. Death is hard on our heels. But I can feel myself getting twenty years younger'. Then Fr Nicolae quotes Bukovsky, whose patience was stretched to the limit on the night when he was first summoned to the KGB headquarters: 'I was awake all night, because I could not wait for morning to come; to confront them, tell them just what I thought of them, and to go at them like a tank. Nothing would have given me greater pleasure.'

Finally the fourth solution in *Jurnalul Fericirii* is 'the mystical solution of faith'. That is 'not of this world' but a grace, granted by God to whom He pleases. Totalitarianism is above all 'an expression of the death-wish', although it may look like any other economic, biological or social theory. For Fr Nicolae, each person is free to choose in this situation whether to consent to death, to make light of it, or go out to meet it. Only God provides the ultimate solution, beyond any form of human 'consent'. The secret of those who cannot be held down by death is simple: they love life, not death. And 'who', asks Fr Nicolae at the end of his 'Political Testament', 'is the One who has overcome death? The One who trampled down death by death.'

Some Glimpses of Ţuţea at Aiud

Having examined the re-education process, I will now look at three testimonies from Aiud which may afford an insight into Ţuţea's experience. For him Fr Nicolae's 'fourth solution' was constant. But because he preferred not to speak about prison life as such, we do not know how his choice was worked out in the details of everyday life throughout those months and years. In an age which consumes journalistic stories of inhumanity and horror with such appetite, it is perhaps worth reflecting on Ţuţea's silence.

Metropolitan Archbishop of Aiud Prison?

First, there is an anecdote which I heard one day from both Ţuţea and Fr Stăniloae. As we were walking together in Cişmigiu Park, they recalled, half jokingly, a proposal to make Ţuţea Metropolitan Archbishop of Aiud prison.

---

45   Vladimir Bukovsky (b. 1943), Russian prisoner of conscience in the 1960s and 1970s. His expulsion from the Soviet Union to Switzerland in 1976 was in fact an exchange for the Chilean Communist leader Luis Corvalan. His book *To Build a Castle, My Life as a Dissenter* (London: André Deutsch, 1978) is a major document in the literature of human rights.

It appears that certain Orthodox priests and others imprisoned with Ţuţea had asked him to be their Metropolitan Archbishop – an invitation he declined. These priests had no official function and, in the prison where no Orthodox bishops were detained, they were without an ecclesiastical superior. Actual consecration would have been impossible in the circumstances.

What then did the proposal mean? Was it simply a way of acknowledging that, in virtue of his exceptional gifts and spiritual wisdom, Ţuţea was already fulfilling the rôle of a bishop, and was in a sense already their spiritual father?[46] Certainly his spiritual authority was recognised even by interrogators such as Crăciun.[47] Whatever truth there may be in the story,[48] it points clearly to Ţuţea's moral and spiritual stature. The same is true of the dedication inscribed by Fr Stăniloae in one of his books, presented to Ţuţea in 1990: 'To my master and brother, Petre Ţuţea, the most authentic Orthodox thinker in Romania.'[49] From Stăniloae, who rarely used superlatives even when talking of the saints, this is praise indeed.

The following exchange (already published) between the two men[50] reinforces the impression that, apart from sacramental ordination, Ţuţea had, to all intents and purposes, the authority of a priest:

– Mr Ţuţea, you know that in Bucharest they call you the Romanian Socrates.
– Nothing of the sort, Fr Dumitru, I consider myself simply a priest.
– But where is your parish?
– I haven't got one, I just hear confessions where I can.[51]

---

46 Cf. Ion Coja, 'Petre Ţuţea era un reper moral', in *Ultimul Socrate: Petre Ţuţea, Încercare de portret*, Festschrift in honour of Petre Ţuţea (Bucharest: Academia Universitară Athenaeum, 1992), p. 13. See also Petrişor, *La capăt de drum*, p. 186. Cf. Radu Preda (ed.), *Jurnal cu Petre Ţuţea*, with commentary by Radu Preda and preface by Gabriel Liiceanu (Bucharest: Humanitas, 1992), p. 46. [*Days with Petre Ţuţea* = DAYS.]

47 There is another testimony about a torturer who, in order to intimidate one of those who bravely resisted re-education, told him: 'I was the one who interrogated Ţuţea and you think you can fool me?' See Andrei Pleşu's essay 'Petre Ţuţea – un ţăran imperial' (on the victory of the victim who gains his torturer's respect), in his *Chipuri şi măşti ale tranziţiei*, p. 323. In 1958, while detained at Jilava prison (in transit for Aiud), Ţuţea suffered from temporary amnesia following torture. See Corneliu Coposu, *Confesiuni, Dialoguri cu Doina Alexandru* (Bucharest: Anastasia, 1996), p. 145.

48 Secret ordinations did take place in Russia, but there was always a bishop present for the consecration of a new bishop. For Catholic ordinations in Russian prison camps see *Témoin de Dieu chez les sans-Dieu: Journal de prison de Mgr. Boleslas Sloskans* (Paris: Aide à l'Eglise en Détresse, 1986), pp. 84–5; Irina Osipova, *Se il mondo vi odia...: Martiri per la fede nel regime sovietico* (Milano: R.C. Edizioni La Casa di Matriona, 1987), pp. 265–6; Paul Mailleux, *Exarch Leonid Feodorov: Bridgebuilder between Moscow and Rome* (New York: P.J. Kennedy and Sons, 1964), pp. 200–201.

49 Stăniloae's autograph inscription is included at the start of the present book.

50 This was confirmed to me by Ţuţea.

51 BGMP, p. 18.

In his letter *On Confession*, St Symeon the New Theologian seems to imply that the authority to hear confessions is granted by the Holy Spirit, regardless of whether the one hearing confession is ordained or not.[52] It was certainly Țuțea's conviction, and one to which he held with the utmost seriousness, that a man is ordained priest or consecrated bishop in response to a divine initiative rather than to a decision of the ecclesiastical hierarchy. He believed firmly in the vocation of all believers to the 'royal priesthood' (1 Pet. 2:9), and saw his own 'priesthood' in terms of a quasi-monastic calling and an apostolate of encouragement:

> I am in a dilemma as to the monk's relationship with the world. By living virtuously, the monk strives to bring to God the offering of a life made perfect through self-denial. It is not his task to propagate the species, but to personify its essence, in eternity. I have been a kind of monk without a monastery. Mission is the dogmatic expression of vocation. My vocation has been that of legislator, not preacher, nevertheless I have spread faith as the wind scatters microbes. In prison I enabled my comrades in suffering to see faith because only by means of their faith could they be saved from the huge temptation of the political prison where at every step you have an opportunity to betray faith and principles for a bowl of food.[53]

Petre Pandrea

Petre Pandrea[54] was a Marxist who in the early 1930s had edited *Stânga* with Țuțea. They remained lifelong friends, despite Țuțea's change of political orientation. The words which follow are from his *auto-demascare* ('self-unmasking') discovered in the files of the *Securitate* and published in 2000.[55] An example of re-educative

52   St Symeon's teaching on spiritual fatherhood was (and is) controversial. For a full discussion of his argument, see the foreword by Kallistos Ware to Irénée Hausherr, *Spiritual Direction in the Early Christian East*, trans. Anthony P. Gythiel (Kalamazoo, MI: Cistercian Publications, 1990), pp. xxi–xxvii. For an alternative view see 'Appendix: Letter on Confession', in St Symeon the New Theologian, *On the Mystical Life, The Ethical Discourses*, trans. Alexander Golitzin, 3 vols (Crestwood, NY: St Vladimir's Seminary Press, 1995–97), III: *Life, Times and Theology*, (1997), pp. 185–203.
53   DAYS, p. 46. See also Țuțea's letter of 7 July 1974 to Emil Cioran, in DIALOGUES, p. 39.
54   Petre Pandrea (1904–68), doctor in Law, eminent lawyer, jurist, writer, and polyglot. Studied in Berlin, Heidelberg, Munich, Paris, Rome, Vienna, Prague, and Budapest. Jurisconsult attaché to the Romanian Legation in Berlin (1928–32). Consultant lawyer in Vienna, Barcelona, Athens, Rotterdam, New York, and Philadelphia (1932–48). Author of the classic *Beiträge zu Montesquieus deutschen Rechtsquellen, Eine Untersuchung der hinterlassenen Manuskripte* (Bucharest: Cartea Românească, 1934). Political prisoner under Communism (1948–52 and 1958–64).
55   Pandrea, *Reeducarea*. For a valuable assessment of the re-educational method employed in the writing of this book (at Aiud in the early 1960s) and the tendentious nature of the published version of Pandrea's 'self-analysis', see Mircea Stănescu, 'Istorie, memorie și practică în editarea lui Petre Pandrea', *Memoria*, 34, January 2001, pp. 106–20.

auto-critica,[56] Pandrea's words show the workings of a mind caught between the pressure of a totalitarian system and the will to be a free person. It is important to understand that this book is Pandrea's official, written 'self-accusation' or 'unmasking'. It has caused controversy in Romania because, to those who do not appreciate the circumstances under which it was written (a barbaric prison régime in which hundreds of people died), it seems to give a favourable picture of the second phase of re-education at Aiud. But Pandrea speaks here under duress with bitter irony. The message intended by the *Securitate* was that the first (Russian-led) programme, which was indeed horrific, had been replaced by a civilised (Romanian-controlled) régime. In order to understand its real implications, however, it should be read as a document written under inhuman pressure:

> What characterises the Aiud type of re-education, as against that at Piteşti, Gherla and Ocnele Mari? *Hic jacet lepus.* There is a radical difference: here, at Aiud, books, newspapers, magazines... are provided... People speak to prisoners in a normal way without shouting. The old Romanian kindness is making a tentative come-back.[57]

We also learn from Pandrea that there was a vigorous prayer life as well as an active intellectual life at Aiud:

> Once the university pattern of lectures had been introduced at Aiud, rhythm and movement began, life returned. Yogic and Athonite contemplation gave way to an active life. The power of contemplation (*vis contemplativa*) was replaced by an active power (*vis activa*).[58]

This fails to do justice to the extraordinary spirituality which I know developed at Aiud, and nurtured a form of prayer described elsewhere in Pandrea's account:

> The political prisoners at Aiud looked like monks. I saw 300 of them in the cinema of the 're-education club' in the prison at Aiud. The arrival of the colonel-commandant of the prison was awaited as though he were a Metropolitan, rather than a soldier. The prisoners were monks with striking facial expressions, locked in spiritual combat, living in chastity, fasting and prayer. I suddenly had the impression that I was waiting for the Athonite abbot Glicherie, in the refectory of the Old Calendar monastery at Slătioara... I was also reminded of the highly educated monks of Kloster-Andechs, whose hospitality I enjoyed as a student for three days, at Munich, a Catholic monastery near Amersee.[59]

---

56 In practice, the prison administration manipulated prisoners by playing on their weaknesses, for they had reached a stage very close to the limits of human endurance. At the top of Dr Petre Pandrea's handwritten 'self-analysis', Colonel Crăciun, the prison governor, concluded: 'Pandrea needs to value his gifts as a lawyer since, according to him, he can make people believe whatever he tells them. If he wants, and he *must* want this, then he should reduce Ilie Niculescu, the Jesuit, to a disgusting rag whom even his most fanatical supporters would disown.' See Aioanei and Troncotă, 'Modelul reeducării', p. 62.

57 Pandrea, *Reeducarea*, p. 89.

58 Pandrea, *Reeducarea*, p. 92.

59 Pandrea, *Reeducarea*, p. 88; see also pp. 141–2, 228.

There were men who said hundreds of prayers every day. People practised constant prayer, until they went to sleep and began again when they woke up. There were people who prayed fervently 14 hours a day. I am not mistaken in stating that 95% of the prisoners at Aiud prayed every day. Those who were weakest at prayer prayed in the morning, at night, at the third, sixth and ninth hours at least, five times a day. The hermits at Aiud reached a level of prayer not beneath that of the yogi and lamas, their brothers in the Himalayas and Tibet.[60]

While it would be wrong to claim this as evidence of the Hesychast life of the prisoners, there is, nevertheless, a certain spiritual dimension to the picture presented which appears to confirm what is already known about how the Prayer of the Heart was practised in that prison (see Appendix II).

Another aspect of life in a political prison in the early 1960s was its intellectual vigour. Like the 'Underground Academy' at Ocnele Mari in the early 1950s,[61] Aiud was *Marea Universitate*, the Great University where, amid the horrific squalor, violence and abuse of principle and trust, there nevertheless flourished an extraordinary intellectual vitality that sustained truth and freedom in the face of brutality and manipulative coercion:

Here in Aiud prison, Țuțea acts as a catalyst for community through his irrepressible verbal fluency, the versatility of his mind, his boundless delight in intellectual debate, his unprecedented talent as a lecturer... his contagious morning laughter, and his encyclopaedic knowledge unequalled by any in our generation.

I tried to waken Savel Rădulescu, an eminent Doctor of Law at the Sorbonne, to some awareness of the suffering of 1200 brothers, by introducing him to the economist Petre Țuțea, the lion of our prison menagerie. Țuțea takes Savel, the elegant intellectual, between the jaws of his ferocious encyclopaedism, knocks him about with Carl Schmitt's doctrine of international law, and then grabs his respect with a highly original exposition in his, Savel's, own field of expertise. For fifteen years in fact, Țuțea has been extending his knowledge by patient daily research. We, his friends, can testify to the scale of his achievement, and [its significance] for our national history.[62]

---

60   Pandrea, *Reeducarea*, pp. 92–3. Parts of this description may make many readers uneasy – as if Pandrea was not quite in his right mind when he wrote this *sui generis* 'un-masking' declaration. It reads as if the political prisoners' practice of constant prayer, like un-masking re-education, was the consequence of brainwashing. Pandrea was of course at that time under constant surveillance and would have written his account of the re-education clubs under extreme pressure.

61   For details about the inmates' 'Mastermind' competition final won by Țuțea against the former Minister of External Affairs, Mihail Manoilescu, see my interview with Cornel Deneșeanu, Țuțea's fellow prisoner at Ocnele Mari (Sâmbăta de Sus, Sibiu, 23 July 2000). The story was also confirmed in an interview which I have on tape between myself and the son-in-law of one of the guards (name withheld in order to protect anonymity).

62   Pandrea, *Reeducarea*, pp. 356–7.

Ion Halmaghi

In August 2000 I interviewed Ion Halmaghi,[63] an American-born Romanian, who was also a prisoner of conscience alongside Țuțea. He had previously been a student of philosophy. Here he recalls his first encounter with Țuțea (some twenty years his senior), and speaks of the process of re-education as practised at Aiud. The passage illustrates the subtlety of Țuțea's resistance to re-education. The prisoner could choose to die, or to collaborate. Țuțea, however, used apparent collaboration to subvert the system, to develop his understanding of divine mask and human vocation, and to follow his personal calling as an educator and teacher of Christian truth to others:

A Moment with Petre Țuțea at Aiud Prison

In the spring of 1964, a few months before our release from prison, re-education was in full swing at Aiud. The warders moved us from one cell to another, mixing the prisoners in the most illogical combinations, without our understanding their real objective. I was put into a larger cell with narrow wooden bunks one on top of the other. Later, Petre Țuțea arrived too. I had not known him before, except through mutual friends. I was very upset because, although I knew nothing for certain, a rumour was circulating in the prison that he had made certain concessions during a re-education session.

Later I tried to draw Țuțea into friendly conversations. He, however, was rather anxious and wanted to know whether I knew anything about what he had been doing most recently. I told him that I did not know very much. He explained to me that he was giving a course on philosophy which was meant to be Marxist philosophy for those who were being re-educated. He told me why he had agreed to give this course. For a long time he had resisted the temptation to take part in re-education. Eventually, Colonel Crăciun, the prison governor, came to him and asked him plainly: 'Why do you think, Mr Țuțea, that the prisoners refuse to come to the re-education clubs and to read the literature which is provided for them there? And particularly why do they reject Marxism?'

Țuțea gave him a detailed answer: The prisoners had tried for years to get books to read and had always been refused. The reluctance of the prisoners now to read books in the club was due to the constant refusal of their earlier requests. A second reason was that they rejected Marxism because they did not understand it.

Colonel Crăciun then drew up a project with which he came back to Țuțea and asked him whether he might be willing to give a series of talks, or an introductory course on Marxism. Țuțea refused. He was ill, weak, and did not have the necessary energy. Crăciun persisted in asking and offered Țuțea different prison conditions, because he wanted 'to help him and the others'.

Țuțea then proposed a more difficult condition. Such an introductory course could not be given hastily, since Marxism itself as a doctrine did not appear spontaneously, and to understand it one had to begin with Antiquity, and in particular with Aristotle, who was the fountain head of philosophy and sociology. And that demanded time and preparation for the one giving the course. Eventually, the two of them agreed that the planned course should begin. At this point in his explanation, Țuțea showed me part of his course, some notebooks

---

63   Ion Halmaghi, b. 20 December 1918, Ohio.

which he had written. He asked me to look through them and to tell him if what he had done was all right.

I did not want to commit myself in any way that could give even a small opening for inviting me to the re-education club. So, I replied: 'Mr Ţuţea, my opinion is of no importance whatsoever. I would like to have a look at some of your notebooks, just to kill time, for I am sure that they will make instructive reading.' About three days later, Ţuţea asked for my opinion on what I had read, but he insisted I express it 'in straightforward terms, rather than in metaphors'. 'I will do that, dear Mr Ţuţea, in a few years time, after you have finished the course, if you ever have time to finish it.' He gave me a great hug and said that he was very glad that I had understood *everything*.[64]

This story shows both the subtlety of the re-education process at Aiud, and the way in which Ţuţea succeeded in deflecting it to the advantage of those supposedly being re-educated. For an exhausted prisoner, to continue to refuse dialogue with a system that had now been in place for twenty years would serve no useful purpose. Better, he realised, to negotiate with those responsible, and find a way forward that was acceptable to both sides. And so it was that he found himself as a political prisoner inside a Communist prison teaching pre-Socratic philosophy, able to function as a philosopher and spiritual guide in a notoriously evil place.

By this means Ţuţea achieved a new power of dissent and a deeper understanding of *martyrion*. He draws a distinction between 'suicide' – when prisoners allowed the system to kill them, morally and intellectually, through their collaboration with that system – and 'sacrifice' through an appearance of collaboration that might actually be more effective against the régime.[65] Later on, he developed the idea of sacrifice in his writings on the 'pious lie' that deftly concealed overt resistance:

> *Pia Fraus.* 'Be wise as serpents, and harmless as doves' (Matt. 10:16). Sacrifice for a moral, national, social, scientific, or artistic cause is called heroism and its result is always limited in time. Sacrifice for the truths of faith is called martyrdom, by which one goes beyond time. A Christian believer lives between silence and martyrdom. The pious lie is justified, for it is morally permissible in the battle for the triumph of these truths under tyranny. The Christian warrior defends 'existence as it should be' over against 'existence as it is'. The Christian is not immersed in this world.[66]

---

64 Trans. from Ion Halmaghi, 'Un moment cu Petre Ţuţea la Aiud', *Permanenţe*, Bucharest, 3 March 1998, p. 15. Cf. Ion Papuc, in DIALOGUES, p. 78. See also Voinea, *Masacrarea Studenţimii Române*, pp. 198–9. According to Voinea, a collective 'Black Book of the Legion' was written under extreme pressure by political prisoners at Aiud, in which 'Legionary history was falsified'. Ţuţea was forced to write a review at the end of this book, but he was 'careful not to denigrate either the Legion or its members': Voinea, *Masacrarea Studenţimii Româna*, pp. 192–3.

65 There is a connection here with G.K. Chesterton's 'Paradoxes of Christianity', which Ţuţea liked to quote. Christianity marks the spiritual distance between 'the awful graves of the suicide and the hero, showing the distance between him who dies for the sake of living and him who dies for the sake of dying': G.K. Chesterton, *Orthodoxy*, foreword by Philip Yancey (London: Hodder & Stoughton, 1996), p. 300.

66 THEATRE, p. 342. See also PROBLEMS, p. 171.

Țuțea's Christian Confession in Prison

Despite the silence Țuțea maintained about his prison experiences, they nevertheless shaped his thinking and writing in a number of ways. One of these is the theology of confession. Again, although this is a crucial concept for Țuțea, it is one about which he speaks through silence.

To know Christ is to be unmasked in the true sense. Confession of faith is the confession of the divine truth of our being. In the re-education process Țuțea experienced the diabolical reversal of this. Yet paradoxically that very experience constituted a martyrdom that was to provide him with the basis for a highly original theological and intellectual doxology. In this section I shall explore the nature of confession and repentance in both the genuine creative (Christian) sense and in the vicious (idolatrous) sense of ideological persuasion. The Christian is first and foremost called to a change of heart (*metanoia*), to reject ideological tenets, and to put on Christ (Gal. 3:27) – to embrace theological certainty in the revelation of divine love, in the precepts of the new Covenant, in mystical union with God. This is the mystery, power, and wonder of conversion, through which, ultimately, evil itself is unmasked.

Prison excluded Christ, and the life and worship of the Church were forbidden; but, paradoxically, it also became a place of Christian formation, through which the presence of Christ was experienced. This is where mystical experience and Orthodox tradition begin to come to the fore. In the following pages I will describe something of this process, contrasting Aiud's bestial re-education with divine 're-education', the very process of salvation.

I will contrast sacramental confession (or, in the absence of a priest, confession to a fellow Christian, or in the heart to God), with the dehumanising practice of denunciation and pseudo-confession; Christian freedom, a theme beloved by the prisoner St Paul (Rom. 6:22), with the prison cell and Communist society in general; and the unhealthy 'unmasking', which robs a man of his individuality, with the unmasking of evil through which a man is truly set free.

Țuțea saw his vocation to teach, as a way to exorcise the experience of the Romanian people under atheist totalitarianism. He began to find his true voice as he developed his theology of theatre, which was to become central to his life's work. This will be taken up fully in Chapter 8. Like a classical teacher surrounded by his pupils, Țuțea tried to teach using his experience of the tortuous complexity of prison life. His clear aim was to unite individual experience with the definitive pattern of life revealed in the humanity of Christ. Deification itself (*theosis*) is nothing less than a lifetime's work. Evil must be counteracted by a life of true 'unmasking', lived in thankful and repentant discovery of God's faithfulness.

Confession of Faith

Confession reconciles one's inner and outer being, unites body and soul in the grace of Christ. While in prison Țuțea rejected the pseudo-confession extracted under torture, preserving his national and religious identity at huge personal cost. This brought him joy for he could identify, even if only in part, with Christ's suffering on the Cross. He thus refused even the compromise of feigning madness in an environment where mental illness, like death, was a blessing. At the end of his 'unmasking' declaration at Aiud, addressing several hundred political prisoners gathered in an enclosed courtyard and watched by the prison governor, Ţuţea declared:

> My brothers, if we all die here wearing striped clothing and in chains, it is not we who honour the Romanian people by dying for them, but they who do us the honour of letting us die for them. Colonel Crăciun, please tell the Minister of the Interior, Drăghici,[67] that in my view the Romanian people is one of God's wonders revealing His glory on earth. And you Communists will never be revolutionaries until you follow the example of the most generous deity the world has ever known, Jesus Christ. In the parable of the lost sheep, a shepherd leaves the whole flock to look for one sheep. Because in Christ's universe, a single cell which still lives in a dying person is more precious than all possible galaxies.[68]

For Ţuţea, locked in a political prison, Christ's presence, even without the structures of the institutional Church, was a 'gate to salvation'. This anticipated the fulfilment of the world to come, granting mystical freedom through union with God. It defied both the loss of civil liberty and those spurious forms of freedom which derive from mankind's supposed autonomy:

> There are two positions with regard to freedom: one Christian, the other philosophical. Christian freedom is real freedom, which in this world is experienced in the liturgical framework of the Church, and in the other world is absolute. In Christian teaching, I refer to the understanding of freedom as *imitatio Christi*: 'Make me your slave, Lord, that I may be free!'[69]

---

67   Alexandru Drăghici, the most powerful Minister of the Interior (1952–65) under Communism. In 1991 he fled as a political refugee to Hungary, where he died in 1993.

68   Conversation with Prof. Dumitru Mazilu, Vice-President of the National Salvation Front, Bucharest, 1 January 1990. Cf. APHORISMS, p. 95.

69   RESTORATION, p. 4. According to Prof. Victor Iliescu, one of Ţuţea's friends:
> We put too much emphasis on the fact that free will cannot function without restriction. We make the mistake of reducing freedom to the level of our free will, by washing our hands like Pilate. For even under the most terrifying tyranny, freedom is not limited to free will. If you always give with the same heart with which you receive – irrespective of whether you are rich or poor, at the top or at the bottom of the social hierarchy, under a tyrant or in a democracy – then you are free.

   In Iliescu's terms, to have the same heart is called *isosthenia*, that is to say, to have the same power of the Spirit irrespective of circumstances. See Victor Iliescu, *Cele Trei Alibiuri şi Condiţia Noastră Umană Posttotalitară* (Bucharest: Vitruviu, 1999), p. 235. See also Victor Iliescu, *Fenomenologia Diabolicului* (Bucharest: Eminescu, 1995). Although concerned with the Romanian experience of Communism, Iliescu makes a most profound theological analysis of totalitarianism. It is deeply regrettable that his books, more or less ignored in Romania, were not translated into other languages before his death. Cf. Leonard Schapiro, *Totalitarianism* (London: Pall Mall, 1972).

Sacramental Confession

According to Orthodox tradition, a person is cleansed when sins are entrusted to God in the sacramental act of confession.[70] Purification starts in the conscience as awareness of the need for personal change. This compunction (*penthos*, grief for sin) continues with a personal resolve to change (*metanoia*). To grow in holiness and virtue according to God's will for human perfection, it is then necessary to co-operate with grace and to follow the way of Christ as expressed in the Sermon on the Mount. *Penthos*, *metanoia*, and *theosis* are present whenever a confession is made.[71] The human aspect of purification is completed in communion with God. In Țuțea's view, individuals freely long for this communion, accepting it during the liturgy, when 'embraced together with the priest' in the mystery of the Eucharist:

> Truth is transcendent in essence, and is received through grace by the Christian priest. He then communicates it to the believers who, like him, experience sacramental truth in the liberating form of ritual. Truth resides neither in the speculative mind, nor in a laboratory, nor in observation, but in the Church.[72]

Pseudo-Confession

The re-education programme in Romania sought to change people's Christian and national sense of identity by means of what survivors called 'demonic confession'. This was a perversion of Christian confession, described above. For the Orthodox, repentance is a state of grace initiated by an inner experience marking, in earthly terms, the beginning of salvation (Matt. 3:2, 4:17; Jer. 2:23), 'the starting point of the Good News'.[73]

---

70   Cf. St Symeon the New Theologian, *On the Mystical Life*, III, p. 192: 'Let us run instead directly to the spiritual physician and vomit up the venom of sin through confession and spit out its poison.'

71   Rooted in spiritual discrimination (*diakriseis pneumaton*) between virtue and vice, good and evil, they influence peoples' decisions for the future as they 'advance' unceasingly and make 'perpetual progress through the infinite ages of eternity'. Cf. Kallistos Ware's introduction to St John Climacus, *Ladder of Divine Ascent*, trans. Colm Luibheid and Norman Russell, notes by Norman Russell, preface by Colm Luibheid (London: SPCK, 1982), p. 57.

72   Petre Țuțea, *Omul, Tratat de Antropologie Creștină (ultima parte), Dogmele sau Primirea Certitudinii*, foreword by Cassian Maria Spiridon (Iassy: Timpul, 2000), p. 104. [*The Human Being, Treatise on Christian Anthropology (final part), Dogmas, or the Reception of Certainty* = DOGMAS.] Cf. PROBLEMS, p. 315.

73   Ware, 'The Orthodox Experience of Repentance', pp. 18f. See also, St Symeon the New Theologian, *On the Mystical Life*, III, p. 67: 'Repentance is nothing less than renewal of baptismal grace from which all have fallen away since infancy. It is accompanied – rather, signalled – by a piercing of the heart in which grief for sins is combined with the fire of longing' for God.

'Self-unmasking' was a pseudo-repentance, elicited or rather extorted by terror and brutality, that caused victims to pretend to externalise feelings they did not possess. Christian repentance implies feelings of guilt and sorrow, 'a sense of grief and horror at the wounds we have inflicted on others and on ourselves',[74] leading to *metanoia*, a decisive transformation of outlook which in turn changes a person's behaviour and leads them to see themselves in a new light – the light of the transfigured Christ.

Repentance brings about a metamorphosis of the self, as the values of the Kingdom of God become the focus of the penitent's entire being. This brings us to Țuțea's theology of masks explored in Chapter 9. The 'divine mask' (a person's likeness to God) is restored through a right wearing of the 'human mask' (a person's unique personal vocation). Pseudo-repentance destroys the 'divine mask', and Țuțea calls this 'spiritual death'. It excludes any sense of the forgiveness of sins, for sin itself – in the form of a false confession – is what the torturer requires of his victim in order to effect a 'conversion'.

Christian penitence anticipates and indeed necessitates confession; it is not a product of confession. The confession of the re-educated person desecrates him, for 'conversion' from faith to ideology – from life to death – desecrates the humanity of beings created in the image and likeness of God.[75]

Resistance to Re-education

Unmasking of the System

Țuțea's resistance to re-education, his attempt to retain his humanity in the face of systematic torture, became for him an 'unmasking of evil'. He preferred sacrifice to capitulation. So long as he could hold on to his identity as God's creature, he was able to see re-education as something wholly destructive of humanity. The very term 're-education' was blasphemous.

Even when he apparently agreed to be part of the re-education system, it was not because, like others, he had lost his identity. Instead he used the power of his spirit and vocation as a teacher to undermine the goals of his torturers. Required to teach Marxism in the re-education clubs at Aiud, what he actually taught was classical philosophy in relation to the Gospel.

---

74   Ware, 'The Orthodox Experience of Repentance', p. 19.

75   Such desecration was not merely a feature of life in Communist Romania; it may be seen to permeate the consumer–materialist culture of the contemporary world. 'Secular liberals may dislike the idea of confession because it smacks of secrecy and autocracy, but they may also dislike it because quaintly old-fashioned words like repentance are not part of their lexicon. They smack instead of some bone-headed Evangelicalism': Terry Eagleton, 'Qui s'accuse, s'excuse', *London Review of Books*, London, 1 June 2000, pp. 34–5.

Țuțea opposed with his whole being a régime supported by a nationwide apparatus of terror. Rather than adopt a Manichean view of evildoers as people possessed by their own evil – the view adopted in Romanian *proletcult* literature of the 1950s, designed to reflect a 'purely proletarian' ethos – he perhaps believed, with the Russian dissident Alexander Solzhenitsyn, that 'to do evil a human being must first of all believe that what he is doing is good'.[76] Ideology justified an evil which was 'on a scale calculated in millions'.[77] This view made Țuțea, like Solzhenitsyn, 'an implacable anti-Communist or, more correctly, an anti-ideologist'.[78] For it was not the communitarian aspect of Communism to which such dissidents primarily objected, but 'the radical dissociation of Communism from any sense of right and wrong. That is the feature it shares with all ideological systems.'[79]

Against Marxist Reductionism

In his youth Țuțea acquired a thorough knowledge of Marxist theory,[80] and even in his later years was not opposed to all aspects of it. Although he exposed the shortcomings of Marxism, he was aware of the gap between Marxist theory and the Soviet application of Communism. In the 1980s he said in conversation with a close friend, Dr Horia Stanca:

> Can't you see to what our working-class leaders have reduced us? They reason simplistically and understand Socialism at a low intellectual level. As things are now, Socialism is nothing but systematic organisation of all that is inconvenient. You join a queue, I come from a queue, and both are pointless. What we seek we do not find, what we find we do not need.[81]

---

76   Alexander I. Solzhenitsyn, *The Gulag Archipelago, I–II*, p. 173. See also the introductory chapter, 'The Crimes of Communism', in Stéphane Courtois, et al. (eds), *Le Livre Noir du Communisme, Crimes, terreur et répression* (Paris: Robert Laffont, 1997).

77   Solzhenitsyn, *The Gulag Archipelago, I–II*, p. 174.

78   David Walsh, *After Ideology: Recovering the Spiritual Foundations of Freedom* (New York: HarperCollins, 1990), p. 74.

79   Walsh, *After Ideology*, p. 74.

80   Țuțea's knowledge of Marx's writings was mainly based on his reading during his left-wing period which was coming to its end in the mid-1930s. I know from our conversations that in the late 1920s and early 1930s he studied Marx's critique of capitalism in *Capital*, the *Theses on Feuerbach*, and the revolutionary programme of the *Communist Manifesto*. After his visit to Moscow in 1940, when he saw the results of Marxist–Leninist ideology, he finally rejected Marxism. It is likely that he did not read, for instance, the *Grundrisse* published by the Institute of Marx–Engels–Lenin in Moscow, 1939–41. Also, he was perhaps not familiar with Marx's early manuscripts published in the 1930s and described by Tucker as 'a pivotal event in the history of Marxism and of scholarship about Marxism': Tucker (ed.), *The Marx–Engels Reader*, p. xix.

81   Horia Stanca, *Așa a fost să fie* (Cluj-Napoca: Dacia, 1994), p. 288.

However, Țuțea particularly disagreed with the Marxist view of the labour theory of value, the concept of co-operation, and the validity of religious experience. I will look at these three points in turn. He first challenged Marx's view of human labour as the only source of value.[82] In his essay on Mircea Eliade, Țuțea expresses the view that alienation from the means of capitalist production ultimately reflects the human condition and state of the cosmos after the Fall: 'labour is an existential technique' and nothing more. Even human labour, however sophisticated, 'is not axiological', that is, it does not bestow value; inspired creativity gives value; everything else 'can be carried out by animals and machines'.[83]

Every element of skill and intuition (including the training and management of animals and the use of technology) derives, in Țuțea's view, from God. 'Perfection *exists*. It cannot be achieved by effort – it is not an expression of "human enthusiasm", of "formative striving"... An aesthetics founded on labour is legitimate',[84] if the sensory aspect of aesthetics (from αἴσθησις, sensation) is taken into account – the artist, like the scientist, remains captive to the senses. Truth cannot be attained by searching, it can only be 'dis-covered'.

In general Țuțea argued against 'the absurd cult of labour' characteristic of Marxist societies. 'The biblical understanding of "work as punishment" is a constant in human history'.[85] True value is not located simply in what Marx calls 'labour power', it transcends production and distribution, both in society at large and in labour camps. Țuțea would not countenance the rhetoric and hypocrisy of forced labour as a means of 'corrective education': 'Bio-social experiments are modern forms of slavery in proletarian tyrannical societies.'[86] The same criticism might extend, *mutatis mutandis*, to the work ethic that drives capitalist citizenship in the contemporary world. What Țuțea calls the 'labour cult' is 'symbolised by the robot, this existence emptied of truth and degraded in the darkness of matter'.[87]

---

82   According to Marx a thing 'has value only because human labour in the abstract has been embodied or materialised in it'. 'Lastly nothing can have value without being an object of utility'. Things such as 'air, virgin soil, natural meadows, etc.' have no value since their utility 'is not due to labour'. See Marx's *Capital*, vol. 1, I:1, in Tucker (ed.), *The Marx–Engels Reader*, pp. 305–8. Marx seems never to have given an account of why human labour in itself gives a thing 'value'. For a discussion of the 'massive contradiction' between Marx's theories of value and the actual facts of capitalist life, see Daniel L. Pals, *Seven Theories of Religion* (Oxford: Oxford University Press, 1996), pp. 150–52. Cf. Gary North, *Marx's Religion of Revolution, Regeneration Through Chaos* (Fort Worth, TX: Institute for Christian Economics, 1989), pp. 39–43.

83   ELIADE, p. 68.

84   See ELIADE, pp. 68–9. For Marx, sense-perception 'must be the basis of all science', that is, of '*true* science': Tucker (ed.), *The Marx–Engels Reader*, p. 90.

85   ELIADE, p. 68. Before the Fall, Adam's rôle in tending the garden of Eden is expressed in terms of dominion, gift, and commission, rather than pain and effort (Gen. 1:28–30, 2:8–15).

86   PROBLEMS, p. 264. Cf. REFLECTIONS, I, p. 126: 'labour is a modern form of slavery'.

87   PROBLEMS, p. 167. Whilst in this context the reference to matter may smack somewhat

The second point on which Țuțea takes issue with Marx is the concept of co-operation. As I have shown, Țuțea agreed with the principle of co-operative association.[88] However, he strongly opposed the destruction of the Romanian peasantry as a class and its transformation into an agricultural proletariat under the collective system. He argued for the preservation of the freedom and creativity of the property-owning peasantry through the development of their traditional sense of community – a living social organism imbued with the values and rituals of the Orthodox Church, reflecting even in this fallen world the universal *koinonia* of the Kingdom of God.

At the level of social human ordinance, Țuțea regarded as criminal the Communist expropriation of land, animals, and agricultural tools that led to poverty and dependence on the State.[89] He also rejected a centralised planned economy that would abolish private property, individual initiative, and commercial enterprise. Such policies created artificial communities. He advocated instead a form of economic liberalism that combined the 'authoritarian liberalism' of Carl Schmitt with that of the 'free market'. He considered agricultural and industrial entrepreneurs to be the key players in the economy.

Finally, Țuțea disagreed with Marx over the validity of religious experience. He was critical of Marx's thesis of class struggle, focusing particularly on the atheist foundation of the Communist social programme. He criticised Marx's reductionist approach to religion and asserted the reality of religious experience and the right to freedom of religious belief and practice. In his view, psychological, political, social, economic, and other factors inevitably influence religious experience, and indeed are comprehended and sanctified within the economy of the Incarnation. Under secular totalitarianism, however, they become the be all and end all, thus denying the divine origin and destiny of humanity. Țuțea, therefore, was not so much merely an anti-Marxist, but rather someone who in all things – philosophy, economics, politics, and aesthetics – affirmed and celebrated the redemptive work of Christ.

Conclusion

Without minimising the importance of the Marxist critique of the autonomy of consciousness, it must also be recognised that in the New Testament there is deep

---

of Manichean or gnostic rejection of matter, it should be remembered that Țuțea saw the soul in terms of materiality. His dismissal of secular ideological materialism was not a rejection of matter in the gnostic sense.

88   The concept of co-operation was considered by Marx in the general perspective of working-class emancipation. After Marx's death, it was developed by Friedrich Engels and adopted by Marxism–Leninism. See Marx's *Critique of the Gotha Programme*, part III, and *Capital I*, Chapter XIII, in Tucker (ed.), *The Marx–Engels Reader*, pp. 536 and 384f. Cf. Gromoslav Mladenatz, *Socialismul și Cooperația* (Bucharest: Independența Economică, 1946), pp. 40–51.

89   RESTORATION, p. 4.

suspicion of conscience as a safe space where God can speak to humanity: conscience is fallible, indeed corruptible (Tit. 1:15), and it is not the only way in which God makes his will known to a person. Under Communist persecution, it was above all a new experience of their materiality (as people whose bodies were tortured) which brought martyrs to prayer, *koinonia* in suffering, and life-giving knowledge of God. Their faith was deepened, not by catechetical teaching or theological enquiry, but by wounds inflicted on their own flesh and psyche by their fellow men.

The Communists tried to achieve irreversible discontinuity between the inner and the outer person, by attacking the latter and by denying existence to the former. The prison system was one aspect of a principle that enslaved the whole nation; the postulation of a 'new man' who would be the obedient creature of re-education, conformed to ideological formulae rather than to the living truth. This principle required the exclusion of God from every aspect of anthropology.

In the following chapters we shall see how Țuțea developed a highly personal yet deeply traditional way of speaking about God, and an intellectual affirmation of the human experience of God's all-transforming power of Love even in a world of atheist tyranny.[90]

---

90   In trying to come to terms with the re-education experiment, it may be helpful to apply the words of Ulrich Simon in his *A Theology of Auschwitz* (London: SPCK, 1978), p. 47, to the Romanian trauma:

A theology of Auschwitz cannot be written unless its findings issue in prayer, for we can face the horror only by coming to terms with it liturgically. Thus we are bidden to re-enact the arrest of the innocent. This prayer is an existentialist decision for the faith which links freedom with God. It releases in us the spirit which yearns to crown innocence with freedom. It articulates the need for an eternal reality of freedom and acknowledges God as the champion on the way to, and as the goal of, freedom.

Chapter 5

Anagogic Typology

In this chapter I will show how Țuțea's typology[1] reflects his belief that human fulfilment is attained through the grace of God's self-revelation in Christ, the Word made flesh. Thus, typology became an eschatologically oriented interpretation of both Scripture[2] and personal mystical experiences, an *anagogy* (from ἀνάγω, to lift up). This anagogic typology does not so much reflect the totalitarian topos as invite its audience to embark on a spiritual journey wherein the soul is lifted towards union with God. It should be remembered that references to Țuțea's 'typology' assume this anagogic dimension.

In defining his 'types of men' Țuțea draws, characteristically, on both German philosophy and his personal experience of Marxist ideology and Freudian psychoanalysis as applied in political prisons as a means of achieving universal 'happiness' and 'mental health'. In practice, in Țuțea's experience, these means could be applied only through oppressive methods such as re-education – a travesty of the Christian discipleship which is most fully expressed in the saint. Above all, his view of deification was influenced (albeit implicitly rather than explicitly) by the living martyrdom of political prisoners under Communism, and by Orthodox tradition as expressed, for example, in St John Climacus's *Ladder of Divine Ascent*.[3]

Over and against atheistic Marxist–Leninist materialism, the relativism of Kantian 'theoretic morality',[4] and neo-Kantian logical formalism, and based on Țuțea's personal 'ladder of divine ascent' from re-education to sanctification, I present here his classification of human vocational types in terms of a vertical typology that culminates in Christ and proclaims a mystical identification with God's saving love.

---

1   The concept of typology was assimilated by Țuțea from the neo-Kantians during his Berlin period. In time his understanding of typology became more dynamic and more spiritual. It was perhaps in prison that his view underwent a process of what he called *deparazitare* (literally, de-parasitization), 'detoxification' from its philosophical connotations: BGMP, pp. 94–5.

2   DOGMAS, p. 53.

3   For centuries, 'The Ladder' has been the Romanian Orthodox priest's handbook of spirituality. Although he did not refer to it in writing, Țuțea told me that as a boy, reading his father's books, he had absorbed 'the Ladder'.

4   'The illusory autonomy of Kant's reason turns him into his own law-giver and ruler', PROBLEMS, p. 206. Cf. PROBLEMS, p. 209.

From German Philosophy to Prison Experience

The Genius and the Hero

Ţuţea's moral thinking assimilated critically Kant's examination of the nature of reason and moral action, but he was troubled by Hegel's understanding of the Incarnation, Schopenhauer's pessimistic reflections on the fearsome depths of the human will, and Nietzsche's ideal of the *Übermensch* with its emphasis on the unconscious and self-destructive sides of human nature. At the University of Berlin in the 1930s, Ţuţea studied neo-Kantian sociology, in particular Max Weber's *The Protestant Ethic and the Spirit of Capitalism*, Eduard Spranger's *Types of Men*, and Max Scheler's *Formalism in Ethics and Non-Formal Ethics of Values*.[5]

Ţuţea argued against the pantheism of Hegel's philosophy, suggesting that in triadic terms Hegel broadly identifies God with logic, the Incarnation with the philosophy of nature, and the Holy Spirit with the philosophy of mind. He saw Hegel as equating 'aesthetic sentiments' with theological virtues, thus confusing human ideals with divine truth. In particular he criticised the concepts of honour and love in Hegel's *Aesthetics*.[6] According to Ţuţea, Hegel's introduction to the 'sentiment of honour' highlights the worldly nature of honour, which relates to proud humanity, for 'the way to the divine Absolute is that of humility and self-denial, which liberate human beings from their ridiculous pride. It is because of persistent pride that humanity continues to be punished by the principle of death.'[7] Challenging Hegel's idealist and somewhat romantic view of *imitatio Christi*, Ţuţea views martyrdom, when it is a true offering of love, as a gift of the Incarnation. For Hegel, union with God is actually mediated by repentance and martyrdom. In Ţuţea's view it can be mediated only by Christ; active self-offering in love (as opposed to the 'accidental' situation of being a victim) is a supra-human gift, inspired and granted by grace, not the result of human initiative and ascetic effort. Martyrdom requires genuine commitment to God, and any clinging to this world will nullify redemption. Yet, in the end, the initiative is God's:

> Hegel gives an obscure account of the Theandric mystery.[8] It is not repentance and martyrdom that lead to union with God. Reconciliation between humanity and God is exclusively the work of the Incarnate Christ: the human being separated from God cannot become redemptive. It is Christ who is the Redeemer. But, if repentance and martyrdom

---

5   The impact of German sources on Ţuţea's own exploration of human values is important and deserves a separate study.

6   G.W.F. Hegel, *Aesthetics, Lectures on Fine Art*, trans. T.M. Knox, 2 vols (Oxford: Clarendon Press, 1975), I, pp. 557–8.

7   STYLES, I, p. 97.

8   That is, the Incarnation. See 'The Redemptive History of Christ', in Hegel, *Aesthetics*, section III: 'The Romantic Form of Art', Chapter 1: 'The Religious Domain of Romantic Art', p. 534.

cannot lead to our union with God, nor can our human love of God lead to reconciliation with Him.[9]

Țuțea's typology adapted the 'types' of the Romantic genius and the neo-Classical hero from Schopenhauer's *The World as Will and Representation*[10] and particularly Nietzsche's *The Birth of Tragedy*.[11] In Țuțea's view, the genius is 'the supreme example of one spiritually endowed with unusual intuition, able to see inter-connections and to acquire intellectual knowledge'.[12] However, the genius is not 'one of nature's favourites' (as Kant thought), but, viewed from a Christian perspective, one endowed by God with extraordinary gifts. For Țuțea an encounter with an intelligent man (in person or through his written works) is the antithesis of the brainwashing experience. Human creativity in the history of ideas is the result of intellectual labour in which reason is both a divine gift and a vehicle for ultimate truth:

> A genius appears only through the heavenly hierarchy of our human species... The appearance of a great thinker is to the human brain what a bath is for one who has worked hard, sweated, and got dirty. Thought is a 'washing' of the brain. Sometimes this makes me think that thought is not produced by the brain, and that the human brain is not the seat of consciousness. Because not all people with brains produce it.[13]

According to Țuțea, Christians gifted with exceptional abilities experience God's grace with humility and submissiveness, without the conceit of claiming to be original. While geniuses may have exceptional personal qualities, heroes may achieve exceptional things in relation to the community.

Țuțea notes two meanings of 'the hero'. In the classical sense, the hero is a name given in Antiquity to a son born of a god and a mortal, or of a goddess and a mortal. Also, the hero is someone distinguished by extraordinary qualities or brilliant victories in battle. According to Bossuet, quoted by Țuțea, 'heroes who lack humanity are alien to us.'[14] In the modern sense, a hero is anyone who is distinguished by strength of character and personality and by a high degree of virtue. In this way, from

---

9   STYLES, I, p. 101. Cf. 'The Crisis of Hegelianism and Post-Hegelian Thought', in Emil L. Fackenheim, *The Religious Dimension in Hegel's Thought* (Chicago: University of Chicago Press, 1967), pp. 235–42.

10 See 'On Genius', in Arthur Schopenhauer, *Philosophical Writings*, ed. Wolfgang Schirmacher, trans. E.F.J. Paine (New York: Continuum, 1998), pp. 83–97. Țuțea's concept of genius is also shaped by the Romanian poet Mihai Eminescu who, in the nineteenth century, was influenced by Schopenhauer's Romantic pessimism.

11 See Friedrich Nietzsche, *The Birth of Tragedy and the Case of Wagner*, trans. and commentary by Walter Kaufmann (New York: Vintage Books, 1967), pp. 56–60. Cf. the position of the genius on Țuțea's scale of human values: OLD AGE, p. 129.

12 OLD AGE, p. 127: Țuțea quotes here the entry on 'Genie' in Schmidt, *Philosophisches Wörterbuch*, pp. 146–7.

13 BGMP, pp. 332–3.

14 OLD AGE, p. 128.

an ethical and social point of view, 'the hero is distinguished by love, self-giving and brotherhood'.[15]

Țuțea's understanding of the hero draws on Nietzsche's theories about the origins of classical Greek tragedy.[16] According to Nietzsche, tragic poets combine the myths of rational Apollo and irrational Dionysus as paradigmatic types.[17] Țuțea starts building a scale of human values based on Apollonian and Dionysian heroes. For him, however, heroes exist for the glory of God, rather than the glory of an individual person. He wished to replace all forms of artistic vocation attributed to the Muses, 'those mythological fabrications',[18] with Christian vocation.

Review of Neo-Kantian Humanism

Drawing not only on Nietzsche's Apollonian–Dionysian mythological types, but also on neo-Kantian sources, Țuțea set up a ladder of human values at the top of which stands the saint, the follower of the Incarnate God. In general terms Țuțea distinguishes '*the religious man*' from both '*the atheist*' (including secular metaphysicians, scientists, artists, and technologists, who are all 'religiously unaware') and '*the indifferent*' or the Pyrrhonian sceptic who believes in 'suspending judgement' in order to attain imperturbable peace of mind (*ataraxia*).[19]

In order to understand Țuțea's types it may be helpful to think of two intersecting axes of classification. At the top of the vertical axis in union with Christ stands the saint, while *homo stultus* (who systematically denies God) stands at the bottom. What Țuțea called his 'scale of human types' is, so to speak, a horizontal classification of vocation and includes, for instance, the hero, the genius, the ordinary person, the gifted, and the handicapped. In different contexts Țuțea gave a different list, and the reader should always bear in mind that his thinking was essentially non-systematic.[20]

---

15   OLD AGE, p. 128.
16   OLD AGE, p. 128.
17   Cf. Schmidt, *Philosophisches Wörterbuch*, pp. 24–5. In contrast to the Apollonian type, Nietzsche's heroic superman is Dionysian. Impassioned, living a tragic life and motivated by the will to power, he strives to transcend the transitory nature of all human experience by insisting seductively on the brevity and frailty of life.
18   OLD AGE, p.129. Țuțea dismisses Nietzsche's view that: 'The God on the cross is a curse on life, a pointer to seek redemption from it; Dionysus cut to pieces is a promise of life: it is eternally reborn and comes back from destruction'. See Notes (1888) [1052] in Walter Kaufmann (ed.), *The Portable Nietzsche*, trans. Walter Kaufmann (New York: Penguin, 1954), p. 459. When employing the Nietzschean contrast, 'Dionysus versus "the Crucified One"', Țuțea stresses the eschatological dimension of Christian heroism and martyrdom: PROBLEMS, pp. 201–2, 335; cf. BGMP, p. 21.
19   PROBLEMS, pp. 65–6.
20   This schematic presentation in terms of vertical and horizontal axes is not Țuțea's own, although for the purposes of illuminating his thought it is perhaps helpful. To do justice to the complexity and subtlety of his vision, however, it is also important to return to the less systematic, sometimes apparently self-contradictory, material of his own creative dynamic 'style', and not to disregard that which cannot entirely be comprehended

The vertical axis, what may be called Ţuţea's 'ladder of divine ascent', in a sense corresponds to the 'divine mask' to be discussed in Chapter 9. Each type listed[21] on the horizontal scale of vocations exists within time and space but all may move up the vertical ladder. Ultimately all are called to sanctification in whatever may be their God-given vocation. At different points he also includes other types, such as the priest, the prophet, and the political leader. Every individual has a particular vocation (their 'human mask'), and Ţuţea emphasises the vocational element of the Christian life. In living out this vocation, in accord with their 'type', each individual is called to sainthood.

Ţuţea saw human values as ontologically defined, rooted in the Creator's love for creation. This challenges secular, pragmatic interpretations of humanity. For example, he rejected Vilfredo Pareto's quasi-Fascist[22] hypothesis of *homo oeconomicus* (a humanity defined by economic effectiveness) which puts no value on those who are mentally or physically impaired. Pareto's definition would exclude such people not only from society but also from God's salvific plan for humanity. Ţuţea stresses that all human beings are created in the image and likeness of God. Moreover, since all humans have a particular vocation received as a gift from above, each person is called to grow by fulfilling this vocation in Christ. According to Ţuţea, God's ultimate judgement remains a further mystery:

> Handicapped people can in no sense be described in Vilfredo Pareto's terms as 'bio-social waste', because in Christianity they are saved by virtue of their existence as human beings created in the image and likeness of God. The Saviour came for the salvation of all, and in particular for the disadvantaged, who are in the world of His will.[23]

Weber's Rational Asceticism, Charisma, and Ideal Types

Ţuţea examines Max Weber's distinction between mystical 'religiosity' and the 'rational economy'[24] built up by the work ethic of Protestant 'worldly asceticism'.[25] Weber 'solves' the paradox that 'rational asceticism itself has created the very wealth

---

systematically. Thus, although the saint is at the top of the vertical axis, and therefore is not a 'vocation' on the horizontal scale, sanctification radically transforms the vocational type of the one who has achieved such spiritual enlightenment, and the saint therefore does become a new vocational type, liberated from mere historical determination.

21 For example, '*homo religiosus, homo sapiens, zoon politikon, homo ludens, homo oeconomicus, homo faber, homo stultus*': PROBLEMS, p. 246.
22 '*Subjectivement parlant, Pareto n'est pas l'apôtre du fascisme, mais il en a été le prophète*': G.H. Bousquet, *Vilfredo Pareto: Sa Vie at Son Oeuvre* (Paris: Payot, 1928), p. 190.
23 OLD AGE, p. 127.
24 H.H. Gerth and C. Wright Mills (eds), *From Max Weber: Essays in Sociology*, trans. and introd. by H.H. Gerth and C. Wright Mills (London: Routledge, 1991), p. 332.
25 Max Weber, *The Protestant Ethic and the Spirit of Capitalism*, trans. Talcott Parsons, introd. by Anthony Giddens (London: Routledge, 1996), p. 143.

it rejected', by what he calls the Puritan ethic of 'vocation'. As a religion for an élite of virtuosi, 'Puritanism renounced the universalism of love' and on a rational basis 'routinized all work in this world into serving God's will and testing one's state of grace'.[26] For Weber, the incomprehensibility of God's discrimination between the damned and the elect was made even more obscure by the requirement imposed upon the faithful to fulfil their duty to God in the formal ascetic practices of Catholic tradition. In reaction, the Reformation developed the 'Protestant work ethic', the basis of modern capitalism.

Țuțea rejects this 'solution' and Puritanism itself, with its judgemental attitude, which in his view is connected with Kant's 'rational construction of concepts'[27] and moralism. Drawing on Weber's analysis of active versus contemplative asceticism, he distinguishes the 'culture of leisure' (*civilizația răgazului*) with its 'meaningless pleasures' and 'labour as a curse' (*munca-blestem*), from the 'purifying recollection' (*reculegerea purificatoare*) in prayer during 'festive ritual' (*ritualul sărbătoresc*) which bears witness to God and provides personal meaning and legitimisation.[28]

Weber's 'charisma' refers to 'extraordinary' powers inherent in or acquired by certain objects, actions, or persons, regardless of whether these exceptional qualities convey something 'actual, alleged or presumed'.[29] He also employs 'certain elements of reality' to create mental constructs or 'ideal types' which can be integrated 'into a logically precise conception'[30] of humanity bearing no direct relation to real life.

By contrast, Țuțea sees vocation not in narrow terms as a single calling, but as a plurality of divine gifts, deriving from God's unconditional love for humanity. He criticises Weber's immanentist description of 'charismatic authority'.[31] His own

---

26   Gerth and Wright Mills (eds), *Weber: Essays in Sociology*, p. 332. 'Weber acknowledges the psychological insecurity that the doctrine of predestination induced in those who accepted it and was explicit in emphasising that hard work in the pursuit of one's calling was the way Calvinistic Protestant preachers recommended for the removal of that anxiety and for attaining some reassurance of salvation': Malcolm Hamilton, *The Sociology of Religion, Theoretical and Comparative Perspectives* (London: Routledge, 1995), p. 155.

27   PROBLEMS, p. 43.

28   Petre Țuțea, MS 1982 (Bucharest: 1982), dictated manuscript, p. 29.

29   Gerth and Wright Mills (eds), *Weber: Essays in Sociology*, p. 295. Charisma transcends established ideas and the established order. It tends to be radical and revolutionary and opposed to tradition. The prophet is the agent of religious change and of the development of new and more complete solutions to the problem of salvation. In contrast to the prophet the priest stands for tradition, established authority and conservatism: Hamilton, *The Sociology of Religion*, p. 142.

30   Gerth and Wright Mills (eds), *Weber: Essays in Sociology*, p. 59. The ideal type, as Weber sees it, entails abstraction from certain aspects of reality as well as a selection among them: Richard Swedberg, *Max Weber and the Idea of Economic Sociology* (Princeton, NJ: Princeton University Press, 1998), p. 193. Țuțea suggests that by using ideal types one removes factors not strictly relevant to a hypothesis which cannot then be validated empirically.

31   PROBLEMS, p. 336.

'scale of human values' is inspired by St Paul's understanding of the 'gifts' of the Holy Spirit (χαρίσματα). He suggests that Weber's 'ideal types' are not actual, recognisable human types but formal methodological tools for understanding reality 'from below'. They do not imply or require any ethic of imitation.[32] Although 'ideal' – that is, beyond what exists in reality – they are, so to speak, borderline cases valuable for analysis, because 'historical realities, which almost always appear in mixed forms... still move between such pure types'.[33]

Spranger's Typology

For Ţuţea, ideals – whether ideal types or human types (*Lebensformen*)[34] categorised according to a formally arbitrary system – are irrelevant to Truth.[35] For 'the religious spirit is at home not in the human ideal, in the pleasing representations of art or in scientific symbolism, but in the world of Christian dogma, where thought is theological, not philosophical'.[36] He regards Spranger's ideal types of human individuality (theoretic, economic, aesthetic, social, political, and religious) as 'psychosomatic models of the complete human being'.[37] Every human being has a vocation to one or other of these types which, however, exist in various combinations determined by the social division of labour.

In volume three of his *Christian Anthropology* Ţuţea describes how, in a 'modern society' (one which considers only 'the efficiency of human actions'), vocation extends over all professions. All people live 'in relationship with God, community, and themselves', they ask questions which arise from these relationships, but no answer is purely theoretical, aesthetic, or political:

> The theoretic human type is precise, and differs both from the political type who is dominated by thirst for power, and from the aesthetic who is governed by aesthetic norms. The theoretic type seeks out the laws of nature so as to turn them into absolutes... For the religious type, who experiences dogma as a vehicle for essentially transcendent Truth, questions have a random, peripheral character, because Truth is revealed therein [in dogma] and does not have to be sought.
>
> Each human type has the same psychological faculties: imagination, intellect, and intuition. And although the soul is a real entity that exists as wholeness, every human type is characterised by a dominant faculty. The autonomous theoretic type is characterised by

---

32 Gordon Marshall (ed.), *The Concise Oxford Dictionary of Sociology* (Oxford: Oxford University Press, 1994), p. 230.
33 Gerth and Wright Mills (eds), *Weber: Essays in Sociology*, p. 244.
34 See Eduard Spranger, *Lebensformen, Geisteswissenschaftliche Psychologie und Ethik der Persönlichkeit*, 5th edn (Halle: Max Niemeyer, 1925); English trans. Paul J.W. Pigors: *Types of Men, The Psychology and Ethics of Personality* (Halle: Max Niemeyer, 1928). In the early 1930s Spranger was Ţuţea's professor at the University of Berlin.
35 For Ţuţea's discussion on 'types' summarised here, see STYLES, I, pp. 58–9, 78–84.
36 STYLES, II, p. 226.
37 STYLES, I, p. 58.

intellect, the aesthetic by imagination, the political by will to power, and the social by a sympathetic desire to mirror the self in the other, finding identity in the neighbour.[38]

From a Christian perspective these types of humanity are merely relative concepts which do not describe the universal vocation to deification of each individual human being. Țuțea adds 'the ordinary person who has no special vocation' to Spranger's 'types':

> How does he [the ordinary person] behave in the relationships mentioned above? Where piety is the dominant element in his life, leading him to faith in the divine Absolute, the ordinary person encompasses – by virtue of this Absolute – all the theoretical and aesthetic aspects of the universe, human community and the human self, since God embraces all.
>
> I emphasise the superiority of piety over vocation. This emphasis testifies, from a Christian point of view, to the only real equality which exists among human beings, since all are equally God's creatures. From a purely philosophical, scientific or artistic point of view, equality and liberty are alike sheer fiction, as the spectacle of daily life demonstrates.[39]

Țuțea believes that 'our spiritual faculties (imagination, intellect, intuition, affectivity) taken together' still do not enable a human being to achieve self-knowledge and self-control, nor knowledge and control of nature. Proceeding merely from 'the subjective moment in the process of knowing', epistemology, ethics, and aesthetics cannot lead to real knowledge, for truth is not derived from humanity and nature:

> Type is a concept, i.e. a logical form of thought reached by means of observation, experiment, reasoning, and historical information. That which is supra-individual, i.e. the human type, cannot be perceived by intuition in the features of an individual. The individual can in appearance express the human species, but not the human type, which is methodologically split off from the human being as a psycho-somatic whole...
>
> The ideal type as a notion is human in its very essence, socially utilitarian, and specific in the exploration of a humanity compartmentalised according to certain methodological criteria. In a non-rational and vast world of appearances, our best aesthetic, ethical, and epistemological acts reflect our own finitude.[40]

Țuțea's Response to Scheler's Non-Formal Ethics

Țuțea starts where Max Scheler's 'theory of all types of the value-person'[41] ends. Scheler's unexpected death prevented him from fulfilling the task which he sets himself at the end of his monumental *Formalism in Ethics and Non-Formal Ethics*

---

38   STYLES, I, pp. 58–9.
39   STYLES, I, pp. 94–5.
40   STYLES, I, pp. 83–4.
41   See Max Scheler, *Der Formalismus in der Ethik und die materiale Wertethik*, 5th edn, ed. Maria Scheler (Bern: Francke, 1966).

of Values.[42] Țuțea's contribution to 'non-formal ethics' (as Scheler's *materiale Wertethik* is translated)[43] is important in that, albeit from an Orthodox standpoint, he develops Scheler's phenomenological critique of Kant's *Critique of Practical Reason.*[44]

Along with Scheler, Țuțea believes that the paradigm of Christian discipleship is the Incarnate Logos. However, Scheler's model is based on moral actions designated as 'acts of value-cognition',[45] contrasted with acts of the will and 'acts of deed or expression, or voluntary or involuntary acts of imitating deeds and expressions'.[46] Through the concept of an objective, absolute good 'for one's own self'[47] Scheler tries to define his model in ontic terms. He discusses the ways in which, by faithfulness to the moral model, a person can be morally transformed:

> This transformation is neither obedience, nor imitation. It is, rather, the growth of the being of the person and the growth of the moral tenor according to the traits and the structure of the model: growth encompassed by an attitude of devotion to the exemplary model.[48]

There are three forms in which a model can be passed from generation to generation: cultural–scientific knowledge, tradition, and hereditary transmission. Scheler analyses these phenomenologically and eventually comes to a characterisation of his types as related to the idea of God.[49] Against this background he describes what he calls 'the essential tragic' characteristic of all finite personal being and its '(essential) moral imperfection'.[50] Scheler designates as,

> (pure) 'formal' a priori interconnections all those that are independent of the types and qualities of values, as well as of the idea of a 'bearer of values', and all those that have their foundation in the essence of values as values. They represent a pure axiology which in a certain sense corresponds to logic.[51]

---

42 I use here the English trans. of Max Scheler, *Formalism in Ethics and Non-Formal Ethics of Values, A New Attempt toward the Foundation of an Ethical Personalism*, trans. Manfred S. Frings and Roger L. Funck (Evanston, IL: Northwestern University Press, 1973). No manuscripts on 'Types of the Value-Person and the Sociology of Human Occupations' were found among Scheler's papers (see translators' note 324, Scheler, *Formalism*, p. 595).

43 See the translators' foreword in Scheler, *Formalism*, p. xv. Țuțea translates Scheler's phrase as 'material axiological ethics' ('*etica material-axiologică*'), PROBLEMS, p. 28.

44 Scheler, *Formalism*, foreword, p. xiii.

45 Scheler, *Formalism*, p. 577.

46 Scheler, *Formalism*, p. 577.

47 Scheler, *Formalism*, preface, xxviii.

48 Scheler, *Formalism*, p. 580.

49 Scheler, *Formalism*, p. 588.

50 Scheler, *Formalism*, p. 590.

51 Scheler, *Formalism*, p. 81.

Ţuţea's approach to the human person goes beyond mythology and axiology. He suggests that heroism, artistic and scientific vocation, as well as holiness, also give another dimension to life and express the mystery of God. This approach is against Scheler's claim that only a 'universal ethics' derived from the pure types of 'value-person' can delineate universally valid 'value-persons'.[52] Scheler insists that the hero is one who corresponds (more or less adequately) to the type of the 'value-person', 'not one who has some nameable properties in common with other empirical men'.[53] Types of the 'value-person' must not be 'hypostatized' in historically factual persons in such a way that 'they are confused with mere exemplars'.[54]

Emphasis on the Incarnation

Where Scheler speaks of human types at a phenomenological level ending in morality, Ţuţea's types are divinely given as part of the image and likeness of God in which every person is made.[55] In Ţuţea's view Scheler's formal ethics is concerned with a God who, although all-loving and all-sanctifying,[56] seems to belong more to the Old Testament than to the New Testament, and more to history than to the world to come. By contrast Ţuţea's idea of the saint is essentially incarnational. The supreme 'saint' whom all are called to follow is the Son of Man, who embraces and redeems the tragic, since he is also Son of God and Saviour of the whole created order. The transcendent value of tragic destiny (εἱμαρμένη) is thus implicitly exceeded by Ţuţea's model of the saint. Ţuţea's saint is not a tragic, but a happy figure, in the holy sense of 'happy' – that is, a blessed one following the blessed One. In Scheler's assessment the saint, the genius and the hero are 'the highest types of all positive and

---

52   Scheler, *Formalism*, p. 584. In Scheler's understanding of typology, 'there are good and bad statesmen, generals, but not good and bad heroes, saints'. For the unity of the 'person-type' itself is constituted by a 'positive value': Scheler, *Formalism*, p. 585.

53   Scheler, *Formalism*, pp. 585–6.

54   Scheler, *Formalism*, p. 586. In *Formalism*, p. 589, Scheler also writes of 'counter-types' formed in reaction to prevailing ideas of the divine, 'which in extreme cases are called in relation to this idea, atheism'. Such counter-types remain entirely dependent on the prevailing idea of God. For their mere denial does not change the inner 'value-structure' (and the content, that is, *materialer Wert*) of the idea of God which they deny. For an exploration of 'moral types' see chapter 12, 'The Structure of Values and Their Historical Variations', in Max Scheler, *On Feeling, Knowing, and Valuing,* ed. and introd. by Harold J. Bershady (Chicago: Chicago University Press, 1992), pp. 253–9.

55   It should not, however, be thought that relations between human beings made in the divine image and likeness are 'imitations of the form of true unity' in the Holy Trinity (whose mystery is ultimately 'incomprehensible and unknowable'). Ţuţea's 'types' are rather within the vein of the 'antitypes' of Cyril of Alexandria. See Metropolitan Hierotheos of Nafpaktos, *The Person in the Orthodox Tradition*, trans. Esther Williams (Levadia-Hellas: Birth of the Theotokos Monastery, 1998), pp. 222–3, who examines St Cyril of Alexandria's *Commentary on John 11*, PG 74, pp. 556f.

56   Scheler, *Formalism*, p. 588, note 306.

good models'.[57] In contrast, Ţuţea makes a sharp distinction between the saint and any other human type: the saint receives the deifying grace of the Holy Spirit, which is beyond mental or physical qualities, however exceptional.

Ţuţea dismisses Scheler's non-formal ethics – whose ultimate values are those of a *Gottsucher* (God-seeker) – since 'true, biblical religion is revealed religion, not religion which is sought'.[58] For him, the ultimate values are those which reflect the Ten Commandments and the Sermon on the Mount. These are God-given, while the 'autonomous' human being's definition of morality is relative. Thus for Ţuţea murderers can never be heroes, not even immoral ones, for they break God's commandment. In defining 'the saint', Ţuţea goes beyond 'non-formal ethics' to suggest a phenomenology of evil: vices have the purpose of 'awakening' the inclination to virtue.[59]

The Saint as Normal Christian

The saint is for Ţuţea the ultimately normal (in the sense of normative) human being, rather than pure (that is, logically 'formal') super-being:

> The saint is the one who is rooted in eternity, who sacrifices himself and becomes a martyr through his sacrifice. He is distinct from the genius, from the talented and from the ordinary human being, all of whom are dominated by time. In this distinction, pure [that is, as opposed to logically formal] truth is opposed to what is temporal. Professional vocation applies to the whole scale of values from the genius to the artisan, but the saint's calling places him outside time and beyond history. Lack of vocation in the natural realm – where equality between individuals does not exist – is irrelevant to our truth before Christ.[60]

While 'the genius is historical, the saint is eternal',[61] for his holiness is the result of a change rooted in the Incarnation. The creaturely Son of Man is one with the only begotten Son of God. In this sense Jesus Christ is what Ţuţea frequently calls humanity's gate to the divine Absolute. Ţuţea's understanding of the concept of the saint was transformed by his prison experience and encounter with 'new martyrs'.[62] He came to see the saint no longer as a subject of academic enquiry, but as the exemplar of what is truly real. Political prisoners were severely punished for praying or taking communion, yet liturgical life miraculously continued in Romanian Communist prisons. This perhaps explains why he never separates the Christian saint

---

57   Scheler, *Formalism*, p. 585.
58   PROBLEMS, p. 338.
59   PROBLEMS, p. 336. According to Philokalic tradition, constant watchfulness against evil spirits helps in the practice of 'stillness' or *hesychia* on the ladder of virtues. Cf. *The Philokalia*, I (1979), p. 367.
60   Personal conversation with Ţuţea, Cişmigiu Park, Bucharest, 10 June 1985. Cf. OLD AGE, pp. 129–30; PROBLEMS, pp. 202–3.
61   PROBLEMS, p. 335.
62   See Nicolae Trifoiu (ed.), *Studentul Valeriu Gafencu, Sfântul închisorilor din România* (Cluj-Napoca: Napoca Star, 1998).

from the ecclesial and Eucharistic context which grants him access to the sacred. Țuțea understands ecclesial sanctity thus:

> The Christian is the eternal human being. There is no such thing as an eternal religious person separate from the one who takes part in the Christian ritual. Without Christian ritual and the Eucharist there is no holiness.[63]

Iconic Ontology

The Greek theologian Panayiotis Nellas writes in *Deification in Christ* about 'iconic ontology',[64] a profound engagement with the philosophical implications of proclaiming a concept of being in terms of 'image and likeness' rather than either empirically deducible or ultimately illusory substance. Țuțea affirms this against Kant's 'autonomy'. In Nellas's words:

> the ontological truth of man does not lie in himself conceived as an autonomous being – in his natural characteristics, as materialist theories maintain... Since man is an image, his real *being* is not defined by the created element with which the image is constructed, in spite of the iconic character which the created 'matter' itself possesses, but by his uncreated Archetype. The category of biological existence does not exhaust man.[65]

For Țuțea, as for Nellas, the anthropological meaning of deification is Christification. This rejects the neo-Kantian concept of Christ implied by Scheler's 'phenomenology of the idea of God'.[66] While Scheler shows that the 'a priori value-idea of the divine has *no* foundation in the existence of a world and an ego',[67] Țuțea affirms the theandric revelation of God in the Word made flesh. This is the ground of hope, and of the triumphantly paradoxical proclamation – against all forms of idealism – of the resurrection of the body.

Prison Experience

In discussing the totalitarian régime of Communist Romania, the focus in this book is obviously on the persecution of Christians. But it should never be forgotten that, alongside those imprisoned for their Christian beliefs, many people were imprisoned for other 'crimes' of belief or allegiance.

---

63   PROBLEMS, p. 337. On Țuțea's understanding of Church and liturgy, see also A Note on Țuțea's Use of Language. He does not advocate a purely 'formal' ritualism.
64   Panayiotis Nellas, *Deification in Christ, Orthodox Perspectives on the Nature of the Human Person*, trans. Norman Russell (Crestwood, NY: St Vladimir's Seminary Press, 1987), p. 34.
65   See Nellas, *Deification*, p. 33.
66   Scheler, *Formalism*, p. 295.
67   Scheler, *Formalism*, p. 293. See p. 294, for Scheler's disagreement with 'all forms of ontologism'.

Heroes, whether pagan or of no religion, are endowed with a gift of abnegation which leads them to lay down their lives for their cause. This may be a noble and uplifting and profoundly moving act which can give another dimension to life and express the Mystery of God. Yet in Ţuţea's view, neither the genius nor the hero can be wholly equated with the martyr saint, whose inspiration is God alone and whose reward is with the Lord. The saint is inspired by faith in eternal life, the hero is dominated by illusory 'aesthetic glory': the real meaning of history can be understood only in the 'supra-historic terms' of the Incarnation, and not in terms of human values, however fine.[68]

Whereas 'typology can be constructed starting from myths'[69] (that is, from models external to real human beings) and 'there cannot exist a correlation between creation and the Creator',[70] Ţuţea, through his prison experience, came to understand how the divine and creaturely worlds interact through the mediating mystery of the Incarnate Logos.[71] The human tension of living in both of these worlds simultaneously (Phil. 1:21–6) is expressed in his view of Christian sacrifice as the redemptive paradigm of martyrdom.[72] The martyr bears witness to the inner likeness of God, externalised by grace in his life. As a type of humanity the martyr is a living reminder that, in Ţuţea's words, Christians are allowed 'access to the Absolute by means of faith'.[73]

For the materialist it is folly to embrace martyrdom (though a materialist may indeed give up life heroically for some cause). Yet it is in accepting God's all-embracing love that the saint manifests what it is to be truly human – that is, one with God – through the *martyrion* of vocation, which includes both literal, outward, 'red' martyrdom of blood in times of persecution, and secret, inward, 'white' martyrdom of the conscience.[74] The human being's likeness to God is revealed when creatures return in love the supreme gift of life to the living God, their loving Maker. As I have shown, Ţuţea proposes a ladder of human 'normality', with Christ at the summit where the martyr saint (who of course may be of *any* vocational type) is received

---

68   See THEATRE, pp. 137, 428.
69   THEATRE, p. 244.
70   PROBLEMS, p. 99.
71   For Ţuţea the unceasing love of the Incarnate Logos for His creation distinguishes Christianity both from Platonism and from Judaism: PROBLEMS, p. 327. This view should be distinguished from the Judaic concept of *tzimtzum* – that is, God's withdrawal from the world. See Gershom Scholem, *On the Kabbalah and Its Symbolism* trans. Ralph Manheim, foreword by Bernard McGinn (New York: Schocken Books, 1996), pp. 110–11. Also, Ţuţea disagrees with deism, reflected in the concept of *deus otiosus* who leaves His creation without apparent influence on it. See Mircea Eliade, *Patterns in Comparative Religion*, trans. Rosemary Sheed, introd. by John Clifford Holt (London: University of Nebraska Press, 1996), pp. 46–50.
72   THEATRE, p. 342. Cf. PROBLEMS, p. 65: 'Holiness is related to martyrdom'.
73   THEATRE, p. 515.
74   On the distinction made by St Cyprian of Carthage (d. AD 258) between 'red' and 'white' martyrdom, see Ware, *The Inner Kingdom*, pp. 121–2.

into the divine glory. True freedom is to be found through a life in imitation of Christ: 'Transcending nature in religious practice, submission to God's will defines human freedom.'[75]

Critique of Secular Anthropology

Re-education assumed the two basic theories of Marx's critique of religion as 'the opium of the people' and the sentimentality of a 'heartless world'; and Freud's 'pansexual' understanding of libido[76] as the primordial energy projected into, and activating, religious, spiritual, and artistic activities.[77] Just as Țuțea contrasted confession as preparation for the Eucharist with pseudo-confessions made either under physical torture or in psychoanalytical processes of free association, so he developed a critique of secularised humanity by contrasting the norm of the saint with Marxist ideology and Freudian psychoanalysis. Inevitably, he suggests, such anthropocentric systems end up reducing humanity to its animal elements, subservient to manipulation by ideologues.

Basic to Țuțea's Christian anthropological view is the relationship between Creator and created, which he explored in his concepts of mask, rôle, and 'theatre as seminar'. He criticises both Marx's quest for universal human emancipation through the 'revolution of the proletariat' and Freud's understanding of neurosis as a form of sexual and social maladaptation present in varying degrees in every individual and remediable by psychoanalytical 'free association' or 'talkative cure'.[78]

These two approaches to 'salvation' exclude God's original and eternal love as the First Cause of all creation, and exemplify revolt against God. By denying original sin, they compound that sin and hence the fragmentation of human existence. In neither has suffering any significant function. Marxist orthodoxy saw human mind, consciousness, and ideas as having no independent existence apart from material productive activities.[79] Freudian inner life amounted to no more than an insatiable quest for pleasure, avoidance of pain, and fear of death. Following his imprisonment, Țuțea saw ideological movements such as Marxism–Leninism and psychoanalysis as perversions of the Judaeo-Christian eschatological hope. He dismissed as hubris the idea that the fundamental crisis of the contemporary world might be resolved through correct political theory and dynamic popular leadership.

---

75   THEATRE, p. 440.
76   SYSTEMS, p. 195.
77   THEATRE, p. 332.
78   J.A.C. Brown, *Freud and the Post-Freudians* (London: Penguin, 1961), p. 219.
79   Tucker (ed.), *The Marx–Engels Reader*, p. 489.

Marxist and Darwinian 'Pseudo-Ontology'

Țuțea links Darwin's evolutionary 'struggle for life' with Marx's 'class struggle'.[80] Marx describes human history as a series of 'progressive epochs in the economic formation of society'.[81] For him the development of society's 'material productive forces' determined the relations and 'mode of production' of each epoch, which are 'the basis of all history'.[82] However, the bestiality of the Romanian Communist prison régime which Țuțea experienced disproved Marx's view of revolution as 'the driving force' of historical progress. In rejecting the 'Promethean analysis' of Marx, Țuțea adopts a Christian ontology:

> Since Truth is transcendent, it belongs neither to autonomous consciousness nor, more specifically, to reason (which can be a vehicle for it), nor to nature as such.[83] Of course, for a Christian, nature is not illusory – as in Plato's cave – because it is the work of God. But when culture is 'the work of humanity subjected to nature', sinful humanity falls into the illusion of being a demiurge and sees itself as the creator of history.[84]

In support of his argument Țuțea quotes from Alfred Russel Wallace (1823–1913), an English naturalist who, independently of Darwin, identified the principle of natural selection. Although an advocate of evolutionary theory, Wallace, according to J.H. Brooke, 'caused Darwin anxiety by suggesting that certain mental qualities – a pronounced aesthetic sense, mathematical skill, or musical appreciation – were beyond the power of natural selection to explain'.[85] In general, Țuțea rejected the evolutionary 'genealogy of autonomous human beings who experience the illusion of self-redemption and the "chimera of progress"'.[86] Țuțea criticises Wallace for creating a picture of humans as essentially domesticated animals, rather than creatures placed by God at the summit of the natural hierarchy – the crowning glory of

---

80 PROBLEMS, pp. 69–70. See also Marx's 'Contribution to The Critique of Hegel's Philosophy of Right', in Tucker (ed.) *The Marx–Engels Reader*, pp. 53–4 .

81 Tom Bottomore, et al. (eds), *A Dictionary of Marxist Thought*, p. 398.

82 Tucker (ed.), *The Marx–Engels Reader*, p. 164.

83 That is, matter or existence in general as defined by dialectical and historical materialism. According to a Romanian philosophical dictionary published before 1989, matter is 'an objective reality, uncreated and indestructible, infinite, in constant movement and development, governed by its own laws': Pavel Apostol, et al. (eds), *Dicționar de Filozofie* (Bucharest: Editura Politică, 1978), pp. 447–8.

84 Petre Țuțea, MS O (Bucharest: undated), typescript, p. 33.

85 John Hedley Brooke, *Science and Religion: Some Historical Perspectives* (Cambridge: Cambridge University Press, 1998), p. 294.

86 PROBLEMS, p. 314. Țuțea resembles Orthodox thinkers in the West, such as Philip Sherrard, for whom evolution can be understood only 'from above, downwards' (rather than 'from below, upwards'), and who understand the lower beings through the higher, not vice versa. This is compatible with the view in Genesis that human beings are stewards of the whole creation. See Kallistos Ware's forword to Philip Sherrard, *Christianity: Lineaments of a Sacred Tradition* (Edinburgh: T. & T. Clark, 1998), p. xxxv.

creation, not simply the end of the process of evolution. What matters to Țuțea is God's plan of creation from 'above', with no evolution beyond man. Human beings are 'tamers of nature through culture', and are in turn 'tamed' by God:

> Since self-taming is a non-sense, we have to elevate the taming of human nature to the mystical sphere and to believe in original sin. We must then admit that, through sin, the human being has torn himself from the bosom of nature. We need to recognise in original sin the fact of rupture with God.[87]

Freudian 'Pseudo-Confession'

Psychology and psychoanalysis are alike, in Țuțea's view, based on a concept whose object of study, the human psyche, is imprecise and without objective content. The psyche can be conceived only as part of the undivided psychosomatic entity, which is 'the whole human being created in the image and likeness of God'.[88] For Țuțea, the human psyche has no independent existence and can be understood only in terms of relationship with God:

> The psyche in itself is not an object of scientific investigation. Psychology studies the empirical data of consciousness and of the self, and the laws that govern them... Rational psychology claims that, through consciousness, we can know more than empirical data, and can, of ourselves, grasp reality in its proper nature and essence... [Such claims are based on] two kinds of elements: empirical data (the material of knowledge), and a priori forms (which, however, no experiment has been able to reproduce).[89]

Rather than arguing within the 'box' which psychoanalysis creates for itself, Țuțea takes issue with fundamental assumptions of psychoanalysis about the nature of the psyche.[90] Freud showed that neurosis 'is not an illness in the classical sense but

---

87 PROBLEMS, p. 277.
88 SYSTEMS, p. 203. In this section where Țuțea uses the word *suflet* ('soul') I have chosen to use 'psyche', emphasising etymologically the psyche as the object of study in 'psychology' and 'psychoanalysis'.
89 SYSTEMS, p. 201. Țuțea discusses psychoanalysis in two sections of SYSTEMS, pp. 181–95. Although in these discussions he is principally thinking of Freud and to a lesser extent of Jung, he does not engage in a detailed critical account of these thinkers. Indeed, he only occasionally mentions them. In his judgements about psychoanalysis he assumes rather than demonstrates knowledge of the subject. This is in some respects a weakness and leaves him potentially open to criticism. Also, Țuțea, imprisoned at the time, was unaware that Jung and others were trying to awaken the contemporary individual both to the danger of nuclear destruction and to 'the spiritual and moral darkness of State absolutism' behind the Iron Curtain. See C.G. Jung, *The Undiscovered Self*, trans. R.F.C. Hull (London: Routledge & Kegan Paul, 1958), pp. 3–4, completed in the aftermath of the 1956 Hungarian uprising.
90 It is significant that in SYSTEMS, he quotes long passages from the *Phaedo* (78c–79a, b, d), the Platonic dialogue in which Socrates spends his last hours arguing for the immortality of the soul: SYSTEMS, pp. 153–4. See also SYSTEMS, pp. 90, 156, 164, 182, 184.

a form of social maladaptation' that is neither entirely present nor absent in a given individual, but 'present in varying degrees'.[91] Țuțea agrees with Freud that the psyche, as such, 'cannot be ill'.[92] For him, however, the psyche is 'an object of mystical knowledge',[93] and social maladjustment ultimately reflects sin and the nature of the fallen world.

Țuțea insists on, and develops, Aristotle's argument that the human psyche has a capacity for reasoning. Neither 'the materiality of the psyche (i.e. its reality) nor the materiality of reason (i.e. its reality) come into the purview of the senses', since the senses are incapable of thought. The materiality of the human psyche is 'of a different nature'[94] from that accessible to the senses. Having said this, it needs to be remembered that the senses are of course integral to the full humanity of Christ, in whom is the fulfilment of creaturely wholeness. This, however, relates to the further discussion of the unity of body and soul.

Human beings are, in Țuțea's view, caught in the interplay between existence and essence, to use the terminology of Greek and Western European philosophy. Indeed, once they distance themselves from the created materiality of life and of the world, they are at the mercy of existence in its nakedness. However, every person who experiences even a glimpse of the vision of God can experience also the uncreated divine energies. Țuțea comments on the mystical vision of the unity of creation, which led the Scottish pastor Thomas Reid (1710–96) not only to affirm the existence of God, but also to suppose, against 'the common sense of mankind', that the human psyche itself must exist in a somewhat material form:

> Immaterial things do not exist within the Christian universal order. If the psyche is not material, or of a materiality which cannot be accounted for by the human mind (Thomas Reid), it disappears under the form of psychological facts (as incorporated in the working hypotheses of experimental psychology).[95]

---

91 J.A.C. Brown, *Freud and the Post-Freudians*, p. 219. Cf. Sigmund Freud, *Art and Literature: Jensen's Gradiva, Leonardo da Vinci and other works*, trans. under the general editorship of James Strachey, ed. Albert Dickson (London: Penguin, 1985), pp. 224, 299.

92 SYSTEMS, p. 194. Manifestly people do have mental illnesses. However, Țuțea suggests that the higher part of the human psyche remains beyond the reach of psychopathological distortions, though it can be obscured by sin. He was aware of Aristotle's use of the term *nous* (or intellective capacity) in *De Anima* II.2 (413b) and Aquinas's distinction between *synderesis* (the infallible ability to distinguish good from evil) and fallible *conscientia* in *Quaestiones disputatae de veritate* 16.2, 16.3, 17.1, 17.2. See, respectively, Aristotle, *De Anima (On the Soul)*, trans. with introd. and notes by Hugh Lawson-Tancred (London: Penguin, 1986), pp. 158–61, and the extracts from Aquinas's *Quaestiones disputatae*, in Timothy C. Potts, *Conscience in Medieval Philosophy* (Cambridge: Cambridge University Press, 1980), pp. 122–33.

93 SYSTEMS, p. 202.

94 SYSTEMS, p. 168.

95 PROBLEMS, p. 321. Cf. MS Chirilă, p. 88. See also: Thomas Reid, *An Inquiry into the Human Mind*, ed. and introd. by Timothy Duggan (Chicago: University of Chicago Press,

Ţuţea implies that the human psyche gives unity to the human person and mediates it within the seamless coherence of the human and the divine in Christ. He rejects psychoanalytical methods because they treat neuroses through conscious assimilation of unconscious memories. Freud's 'talking cure' employed to attain 'health' and 'freedom' relies exclusively on nature and humanity to explain not only material but also spiritual causality.[96] Ţuţea sees psychoanalysis as an attempt to replace religion with 'magical para-psychology' or 'techniques of the self'. But the self 'is incapable of self-knowledge' if reduced to reasoning.[97] He describes psychoanalysis as 'pseudo-confession', a travesty of the Christian sacrament, conveying a spiritually sterile view of human nature. It ignores the healing power of confession as a means whereby humanity, society, and environment can be brought into reconciliation with their Creator. It deprives humanity of any sense of the mystery of creation:

> Psychoanalysis constructs a symbolism that skates over the surface of pathological actions and aspects of the human body while claiming to explain them. Freud's psychopathology is not a new psychology, nor is it a safe therapy.[98]

Ţuţea would maintain that without a sacramental context there is no redemptive healing. In his view, psychoanalysts interpret only certain fragments of human life, 'phantasmal' psychosomatic unities.[99] True human wholeness is possible only within the relationship between creature and Creator:

> the lack of a real psyche – as an intelligent, affective, and volitional substance, and as *a real unity* of the psychosomatic human being and society – confronts us with a para-psychology. The essential flaw in Freud's thinking is his atheism, while scientific prejudice restricts his field of investigation.[100]

1970), pp. 268–9: 'When a man suffers himself to be reasoned out of the principles of common sense, by metaphysical arguments, we may call this *metaphysical lunacy*'; and especially, p. 261: 'by just reasoning upon the Cartesian principles, matter was stripped of all its qualities; the new system, by a kind of metaphysical sublimation, converted all the qualities of matter into sensations, and spiritualised body, as the old had materialised spirit. The way to avoid both these extremes is to admit the existence of what we see and feel as a first principle, as well as the existence of things whereof we are conscious'.

96   Cf. discussion on 'The Precipitating Cause of the Illness' of the 'Rat Man', in Sigmund Freud, *Case Histories II, The 'Rat Man', Schreber, The 'Wolf Man', A Case of Female Homosexuality*, trans. under the general editorship of James Strachey, compiled and ed. Angela Richards (London: Penguin, 1979), pp. 75–80.

97   SYSTEMS, p. 195.

98   SYSTEMS, p. 195.

99   Ţuţea, MS O, p. 34. Cf. SYSTEMS, pp. 186–7.

100 SYSTEMS, p. 195 (italics added). Ţuţea's view of the psyche itself being this 'real unity' of the psychosomatic human being accords with his use of the word 'Trinity' in place of the Holy Spirit (discussed in Chapter 6) – it is psychologically consistent with Ţuţea's *opus*.

Țuțea maintains that scientists who reject religion reduce divine mystery to the level of human problems, and can provide only approximate answers: they find the right solution only by chance, within the confines of a 'doctrine of absolute death'.[101] He distinguishes between theology as 'revealed science' and psychoanalysis as 'occult science'. If the reality of psyche can only be known through mystical knowledge, any attempt to restore psychic balance by non-mystical means entails 'the suppression of the religious sense'.[102] He stresses, and this is one of Țuțea's most important phrases, that 'modern man's healing from his disturbing denial of transcendence' must be in 'religious' terms,[103] because 'Healing comes through Confession, not through its secular surrogate, the reductionist psychoanalysis of the atheist Freud, who debased what he had built up.'[104]

For Țuțea, Freud is 'one of those pseudo-scientists who confuse the apparent with the Real'.[105] Psychoanalysts work in a self-referential system, using arbitrary symbols[106] 'derived from the world of the senses'.[107] Thus 'Freudian pseudo-confession'[108] cannot gain insight into 'the transcendent world of mysteries'.[109] The psychoanalytical approach denies the rôle of the Holy Spirit as the giver of life, and substitutes a system of para-psychology akin to occultism, representing as it does '*das Nebelreich der Psychologie* ("the foggy realm of psychology") as Henning[110] calls occultism'.[111]

At the same time Țuțea believes that Freudian psychoanalysis, in attributing the origin of psychic activity to the sexual instinct, turned the useful therapeutic concept of *libido* into a voracious abuser, pan-sexualism. He takes a theological view of the harmony between body and soul, a mystical unity (given by 'the Power from Above')[112] which cannot be restored 'from below' by psychoanalysis. He rejects the indiscriminate application of psychoanalytical techniques and Freud's suggestion that all human beings to some degree require psychoanalysis: 'Psychoanalytic techniques for restoring psychic equilibrium using the psychogenetic interpretation of dreams represent psycho-synthesis in a vacuum.'[113]

---

101 SYSTEMS, p. 195

102 Țuțea, MS O, p. 34. See also SYSTEMS, p. 192.

103 SYSTEMS, p. 192.

104 Țuțea, MS O, p. 34. Cf. REFLECTIONS, I, p. 46.

105 Țuțea, MS O, p. 34.

106 SYSTEMS, p. 195.

107 Țuțea, MS O, p. 34.

108 PROBLEMS, p. 315. Cf. THEATRE, p. 488: psychoanalysis is a 'disfigurement of sacramental confession'.

109 SYSTEMS, p. 175.

110 Hans Henning (1885–1946), German psychologist. Cf. Schmidt, *Philosophisches Wörterbuch*, p. 312.

111 Țuțea, MS. O, p. 34. See also SYSTEMS, p. 174.

112 SYSTEMS, p. 176. For Țuțea's view of the psychosomatic unity, see SYSTEMS, p. 175.

113 Conversation with Țuțea, Bucharest, 26 April 1990. Cf. Țuțea, MS O, p. 34.

He also notes that Jung denies Freudian pan-sexualism, and that 'Freud himself transfers the erotic into the realm of mythology' when he opposes Eros (standing for the life instinct) to Thanatos (a term used by Freud, in conversation but not actually in writing, for the death instinct).[114] In a significant passage he suggests that psychoanalysis reduces humanity to the bestial, by ignoring that original likeness of human beings to their Creator which constitutes the divine mask: 'When the human person – defined as a psycho-somatic whole – ceases to look like a being created in God's image and likeness, that falling away of the divine mask debases him to the level of animals.'[115]

This debasement was manifest in Communist Romania. It was manifest, however, not in the prisoners who suffered the re-education process that was intended to destroy their definitive 'primordial mask' (the image of God, in which humans are made),[116] but in those responsible for this bestial experiment who, through the abuse of their human vocation in becoming torturers, 'stripped away' their own divine mask, to put on an *ersatz* humanity, the mask of the ideologue.

From Re-education to Deification

In relation to learning, Țuțea prefers to speak of *initiation* rather than education, although he makes it clear that without inspiration neither can lead to truth. He contrasts ascetic life (presented as 'vocation to deification')[117] with the dialectical method[118] which totalitarian systems pervert to re-educate humanity into what he calls 'demonised man'.[119]

He places initiation between the two extremes of the vocational spectrum, *imitatio Christi* and Communist typology: the one leading toward humanity's restoration in the image and likeness of God (deification), the other to an increase of secular knowledge that can only descend to subhumanity. Using a term borrowed from

---

114 SYSTEMS, pp. 194–5. Cf. SYSTEMS, p. 189. For Țuțea's assessment of Freud's concept of the *libido* see also THEATRE, p. 332. Cf. entry on 'Thanatos', in Jean Laplanche and J.-B. Pontalis, *Vocabulaire de la Psychanalyse* (Paris: Presses Universitaires de France, 1990).

115 SYSTEMS, p. 203. Țuțea's 'divine masks' are discussed in Chapter 9.

116 See Chapter 9.

117 THEATRE, p. 507.

118 Țuțea's criticism is directed at dialectic used in the secular context of Communist atheism, not in the Socratic and Platonic sense which assumes divine and mystical reality. He maintains that 'the dialectical table of pairs of opposites is marked by what is rational and magical, mythical and mystical, sacred and satanic': PROBLEMS, p. 245. Thus one ends up with a human being who spins like a 'top' (PROBLEMS, p. 246), or is blown about like a 'weathercock' (SYSTEMS, p. 256).

119 THEATRE, p. 507. Even 'seeking and systematic thought are forms of demonic seduction': PROBLEMS, p. 300.

Sombart to characterise the Faustian[120] spirit of modern times, Țuțea calls that descent spiritual 'animalism'.[121] It is embodied in *homo stultus*, whose nature I will explore later in this chapter. Re-education is for Țuțea a sort of taming, or brutalisation, that denies the divine origin of humanity. Such a process cannot lead to wisdom or knowledge of the Real, which is a gift of the Holy Spirit and can only be attained on the 'ladder of divine ascent'.

Initiation

In Țuțea's view both pagan and secular initiation lack divine inspiration. Uninspired initiation can take two forms: first, '*esoteric*' *private initiation*, that is, pagan 'communication of special knowledge to which ordinary people have no access'; and second, '*exoteric*' *public initiation*, that is, a secular pedagogical 'introduction to a problem, system, or discipline'. According to Țuțea, 'neither kind of initiation leads to moral truth, but only to concepts, systems, and norms'.[122]

Pagan mystagogy is a 'pseudo-science' based on 'the mythological world of false interpretations of the inner and outer worlds'.[123] In Țuțea's view, the pagan priest is a mystagogue who initiates into 'mythical pseudo-mysteries' ('false secrets without content'), while the Christian priest is 'a theologian who initiates into mysteries beyond the reach of human enquiry'.[124] Mystagogues, pagan or secular, 'cannot penetrate mysteries': these are 'received and communicated' through ritual by the Christian priest.[125] On the other hand, although truth is transcendent in essence, it can be known through divine revelation and inspiration.[126] Those who are inspired, who 'reflect' truth, are contrasted by Țuțea with those who are merely seekers of God and who can still 'go astray'. The atheist seeker is not in touch with God and therefore thinks 'he is his own creator'; or else he mindlessly imitates nature, 'absurdly content to be submerged in it'.[127]

Anthropocentric initiation then is mimetic, confined within secular understanding

---

120 PROBLEMS, p. 245. Țuțea opposes 'Faustian seeking' to divine grace: PROBLEMS, p. 44. In Țuțea's view, '*la déesse raison* conceived the illusion of man as a ruler': PROBLEMS, p. 36.

121 Țuțea notes that, according to Sombart, animalism begins with the crumbling of the two 'pillars' that had sustained the health of the Catholic Church: the idea of the cosmos (which was also the premise of the *Divine Comedy*) and the idea of human beings made in the image and likeness of God, and called to share in eternal life: THEATRE, p. 203.

122 Țuțea, MS 1983, p. 308.

123 STYLES, II, p. 143. Țuțea also suggests, however, that inspiration is a universal gift: 'Greek mystagogy was an initiation which acquired an explanatory character when the priest was inspired', THEATRE, p. 501. He does not explore the universalist implications of this and other similar passages in his work. Nevertheless, he clearly would not accept any non-mystical, spiritually utilitarian claim concerning the exclusiveness of Christ.

124 STYLES, II, p. 143. See also PROBLEMS, p. 318.

125 PROBLEMS, p. 134.

126 PROBLEMS, p. 140.

127 PROBLEMS, p. 138.

of humanity and nature. Even if scientific knowledge can lead to a full understanding of the created world, it proves only that the world and humanity are exhaustible 'pseudo-mysteries' (that is, 'problems' that can be rationally elucidated). For to claim to elucidate mysteries is 'to degrade them to the level of problems which require solutions'.[128] Education is the playground for the discovery of solutions to the world of scientific enquiry. Ţuţea follows Gabriel Marcel's classic distinction between mystery (which is inexhaustible) and problem (which is solvable and 'places the enquiring spirit in the realm of questions'):

> A genuine problem is subject to an appropriate technique by the exercise of which it is defined, whereas a mystery, by definition, transcends every conceivable technique. It is, no doubt, always possible (logically and psychologically) to degrade a mystery so as to turn it into a problem.[129]

The real and ultimate mystery is the uncreated God, the Creator. When approached from below, the divine mystery is inaccessible to initiation, inquiry or analogical language. Knowledge of divine mystery is ultimately subject to God's grace, accessible to humanity through the Incarnate Logos and the inspiration of the Holy Spirit.[130]

Mimesis

There is, nevertheless, a preliminary level at which information is acquired and a sense of vocation is 'awakened' by inspired 'participation in the Real'.[131] As I will show in the following chapters, Ţuţea regards 'the awakening function' of dialogue and 'the cathartic function' of theatre as the educational means necessary, although not sufficient, to prepare human beings for their encounter with the divine. He quite deliberately links the concept of initiation to classical Greek notions such as the Platonic concept of truth as correspondence and identity,[132] and the Aristotelian idea

---

128   STYLES, II, p. 143.
129   Gabriel Marcel, *The Mystery of Being*, trans. René Hague, 2 vols (London: Harvill Press, 1951), II: *Faith and Reality*, pp. 211–12. For a description of mystery as 'something which is revealed for our understanding', but 'which we can never understand exhaustively', see also Illtyd Trethowan, *Mysticism and Theology, An Essay in Christian Metaphysics* (London: Geoffrey Chapman, 1975), p. 65. Cf. PROBLEMS, p. 16.
130   However, as mentioned before, Ţuţea stresses that believers are called to work in synergy with Christ, thus participating in their own salvation.
131   Petre Ţuţea, 'Triumful Aparent al Sofisticii în Lumea Modernă, sau Caricatura Utilă a Realului' (Bucharest: undated), pp. 172, 174. ['The Apparent Triumph of Sophistry in the Modern World, or the Utilitarian Caricature of the Real' (typescript) = SOPHISTRY.] See also THEATRE, p. 409; PROBLEMS, p. 300.
132   According to Plato, the being that exists in reality has a mimetic relation to the idea of which it is, within the limitations of space and time, an imperfect reflection: Samuel Ijsseling, *Mimesis: On Appearing and Being*, trans. Hester Ijsseling and Jeffrey Bloechl (GA Kampen: Pharos, 1997), pp. 16–17.

of *mimesis tes physeos*, or human art as an imitation of nature perfected in the craftsman's act of creation.[133]

However, without divine inspiration, any act of human initiation has for Țuțea the connotation of a stage performance from which the leading actor is absent: mere 'knowledge of nature does not lead to human deification'.[134] Such 'purely human' experience is unreal, unoriginal, and a counterfeit of true Christian discipleship. Țuțea's view of human initiation as flawed *mimesis* of divine initiative affords an insight into his understanding of *imitatio Christi*.

Țuțea's 'Ladder of Divine Ascent'

The Imitation of Christ

'*Imitatio Christi* contradicts intentional, tangible purpose.'[135] The imitation of Christ is for Țuțea a gift of grace rather than an acquisition, since Christ cannot be imitated by creatures. To ape Christ would be to reduce Him to a figment of imagination rather than to climb 'the ladder of divine ascent' in response to the call to deification. Nor can individuals imitate even 'the first man Adam' (1 Cor. 15:45) in his original purity: 'In sacred history there is no place for nostalgia for Paradise and Origen's *apokatastasis*, since Christians look always ahead of their time.'[136] Human beings are initiated by Baptism into Christ's divine life:[137] 'Only once has history been punctuated by a new Adam, when the old Adam was purified by Baptism into the sacrifice of the Saviour.'[138] From thenceforth the human vocation is to develop and grow in the likeness of Christ by all the means of grace, sacramental and otherwise, available to them in His Church, the 'mystical Body', manifest, though not confined to, the visible, organisational, and sacramental structures. However, because they have fallen away from their vocation so drastically in their secular history, Țuțea suggests, human beings today find themselves reduced to a state lower than that of Adam.[139]

---

133 In Aristotle's *Poetics* mimesis, usually translated as 'representation', has the function of allowing reality to appear (in a new way). The work of art, that is to say the image or the poem, can show what is essential and necessary 'in the accidental and the transitory. In a certain respect it is therefore higher than reality': Ijsseling, *Mimesis*, p. 17.

134 THEATRE, p. 245.

135 PROBLEMS, p. 156.

136 PROBLEMS, p. 335. Țuțea rejected Origen's idea of *apokatastasis*, at least as it was understood in the West following the circulation of Rufinus of Aquileia's translation of Origen's *De Principiis*, 'that ultimately all, including the devil and his angels, will be saved'. See W.J. Collinge, in Augustine, *Four Anti-Pelagian Writings*, trans. John A. Mourant and William J. Collinge, introd. and notes by W.J. Collinge (Washington, DC: The Catholic University of America Press, 1992), p. 119.

137 For 'the last Adam' is 'a life-giving spirit' (1 Cor. 15:45).

138 DOGMAS, p. 161.

139 DOGMAS, p. 161.

Limitations inherent in human existence prevent a full understanding of the relationship between this world and the world to come. As created beings, even the saints have only glimpses of the Kingdom of God. Yet their conduct is in harmony with their faith, their soul penetrated by the Holy Spirit, they experience mystical union with God. It needs to be said at this point, however, that Țuțea is keen to recognise that any talk of 'correspondence' or 'analogy' between Christology and anthropology should not neglect the ontological distinction between Christ and the Christian.[140] Christian faith must be expressed within the limits of temporal and physical existence in a life that demonstrates and enacts, at whatever cost, the content and substance of theological virtues: 'In Christianity it is essential to be really honest in one's attitudes. Faith must find expression within the limits of ordinary earthly human capacity.'[141] Although Țuțea lays great emphasis on the need to escape forgetfulness, to wake up to the mystery of the existence of all in God, this awakening is related to St Paul's Christian 'faith working through love' ($\pi i \sigma \tau \iota \varsigma$ $\delta \iota$ $\dot{\alpha} \gamma \dot{\alpha} \pi \eta \varsigma$ $\dot{\epsilon} \nu \epsilon \varrho \gamma o \nu \mu \dot{\epsilon} \nu \eta$, Gal. 5:6) and clearly precludes any kind of mysticality[142] or Hegelian immanentism. For Țuțea, as for King Solomon:

> fear of God is the beginning of wisdom. The lack of fear of God conditions the shamelessness with which people in our time torment themselves and their neighbours, whether from lust for power or from thirst for illusory innovation, ignoring the fact that human beings are always pre-determined.[143]

According to Țuțea the human condition is 'pre-determined' in the sense that created beings can never be equal to the One who creates *ex nihilo*, the Giver of life and free will. Nevertheless, this does not limit our freedom to respond to God's call to perfection according to personal vocation. Thus, in Țuțea's view, the desire to be masters of the universe and the 'unshakeable will to know the causes or the unique cause of all things' are 'legitimate'[144] as long as creation is approached in the fear of God: 'Creatures are not the Creator, although they are vocationally pre-determined from the beginning of time.'[145]

---

140 For the relationship of Jesus Christ to human morality, see John B. Webster, 'The Imitation of Christ', *The Tyndale Biblical Theological Lecture*, 1985, pp. 95–120.
141 OLD AGE, p. 127.
142 See Chapter 3, note 18. Țuțea's *Treatise on Christian Anthropology* is different from those 'works that represent the Gnosticism of Valentinus and his followers, especially the famous *Gospel of Truth*, a sermon of salvation by gnosis which many think actually comes from Valentinus'. 'They have little emphasis on the fall and ascent of the soul, but rather present a kind of mysticism of immanence in which the major themes are containment and awakening. The gospel that Jesus brings reveals the mystery of the uncontained Father, who contains all things in himself', Bernard McGinn, *The Foundations of Mysticism, Origins of the Fifth Century* (London: SCM Press, 1992), p. 93.
143 DOGMAS, p. 161.
144 NUANCES, p. 24.
145 PROBLEMS, p. 340.

The Deified Christian

In his works Țuțea does not use the Greek word *theosis* (which has only relatively recently come into common use),[146] nor does he refer to the Palamite teaching on the vision of the uncreated light. However, he does employ the Latinate terms: deification, divinisation, perfection, and the Romanian *sfinţenie* (from *sanctus*). His strong and constant emphasis on the notion of deification, as the ultimate goal of human existence,[147] points to a deep convergence of his experiential theology with the tradition of the Greek Fathers. Kallistos Ware's definition of deification perhaps best summarises Țuțea's understanding of *imitatio Christi*:

> In the Orthodox understanding Christianity signifies not merely an adherence to certain dogmas, not merely an exterior imitation of Christ through moral effort, but direct union with the living God, the total transformation of the human person by divine grace and glory – what the Greek Fathers termed 'deification' or 'divinization' (*theosis, theopoiesis*).[148]

For Țuțea holiness is always given by God as human perfection and recognised by those who are open to God's grace. Perfection therefore 'cannot be found among the qualities of body and soul, if it is conceived as *imitatio Dei*. Moreover, one cannot find a perfect model within humanity – with its achievements – and nature'.[149]

'On the human level, purity is called holiness'[150] and is manifest in the saint, who accepts deification as the goal of human life, while preparing himself through

---

146 The emphasis on *theosis* is part of what the Greek theologian Georgios I. Mantzaridis describes as the 'Palamite renaissance' of the twentieth century. *Theosis* has been rediscovered to some extent by Orthodox theologians in relation to St Gregory Palamas (through the pioneering works of a then Russian monk on Mount Athos, Fr Basil Krivocheine, and the Romanian scholar, Fr Dumitru Stăniloae). As a far wider theme than Palamism, deification in itself was also approached by Julius Gross, a Roman Catholic theologian. Krivocheine, Stăniloae, and Gross all published important studies in the same year, 1938. See Georgios I. Mantzaridis, *The Deification of Man: St Gregory Palamas and the Orthodox Tradition*, trans. Liadain Sherrard, foreword by Kallistos Ware (Crestwood, NY: St Vladimir's Seminary Press, 1984), pp. 8, 13, 132–3.

147 Mantzaridis, *Deification*, p. 13.

148 Kallistos Ware, in his foreword to Mantzaridis, *Deification*, p. 7. Cf. note 12, Chapter 9.

149 PROBLEMS, p. 46. Cf. STYLES, II, p. 219; PROBLEMS, p. 134. Adam, as a representative of the original perfection of creaturely nature, is merely 'a type of Him who was to come' (Rom. 5:14). Thus, when Țuțea speaks of humans being made in the image and likeness of God, it is important to bear in mind the eschatological tension between type and the fulfilment which it prefigures (1 Cor. 15:45, 15:47). Țuțea's incorporation of the anagogic tradition of theological typology into secularised classificatory typology of the neo-Kantian tradition is not purely a linguistic artifice, although probably it is the sort of intellectual device that makes him obscure to many readers. To address the inadequacies of the neo-Kantian tradition, without recourse to merely historicist theology, is in fact a fundamental challenge.

150 PROBLEMS, p. 137.

ascetic effort in response to Christ's initiative, for 'the saint shows forth the pure form of religious expression, at the very peak of human values'.[151] It is as if the saint were bathing in the light of Christ on Mount Tabor. Christ is the living icon and transfiguring presence for all human beings. Țuțea never specifically discusses Transfiguration despite the importance of the Transfiguration in Orthodox theology.[152] Nevertheless, he refers indirectly to the saint as partaking of the light of Transfiguration, in his repeated depiction of the saint as transcending historical space and time.

As I have shown, ordinary people have no special vocational gifts, but lead their life either well or badly in the rôle that befalls them. They represent Everyman, *Biedermann, l'homme moyen sensuel*. In temperament there are *the curious*, who remain somehow unengaged, going through life, as it were, in neutral; *the doers*, 'absorbed in completeness', that is, living 'with the grain' of the natural world of multiplicity; and *the seekers*, 'absorbed in immanent truth', that is, those with a pantheistic sense of personal fulfilment.[153]

It is important to remember that the ordinary person, of whatever temperament, can become a saint. This is crucial to Țuțea's typology. Faithful, humble, and virtuous bearing of the human mask, whatever it may be, is pleasing to God and conforms each person to the divine in a way that 'the world' may not necessarily ever appreciate. This sanctity of the ordinary person is, nevertheless, charged with all the fullness of the creative and living power of God. The ordinary saint is thus more extraordinary than the Nietzschean superman who merely embodies the 'all-too-human'. The ordinary saint represents God's inexhaustible generosity of vision and creativity, in a way that transcends even the Kantian moral law.

Human qualities and virtues express a spiritual meaning originating in God. Just as the genius who has received grace must be creative within the limits of Christian ethics, so must the ordinary person who has received grace be open to transcending the human limitations of 'ordinariness'. All types are raised out of the fallen state of their particularity, but only the mystically enlightened transcend the supra-history within which all human types are contained.[154] For Țuțea, Christian mystics 'bring the impossible into actuality by living out belief in what is unbelievable, hope in what is hopeless, and love for what is unlovable'.[155]

A symptom of humanity's fallen state is its instinctual negative attitude towards the handicapped or disabled, its tendency to see them as people who deserve their condition, are stupid, unlucky, even downright evil – or, in certain cases divinely

---

151   OLD AGE, p. 127.
152   Likewise Țuțea only once explicitly discusses the Trinity, although his theology is profoundly imbued with Trinitarian insight, as I will show in analysing his use of the word 'Trinity' for the third hypostasis of the Triune One. See Chapter 6.
153   Petre Țuțea, 'Firimituri de la un festin interzis', interview by M. Bădițescu, *Altfel, Curier Literar de Târgoviște*, Târgoviște, February 1990, p. 4. ['Crumbs from a Forbidden Banquet'.]
154   OLD AGE, p. 129.
155   THEATRE, p. 377.

(prophetically) stricken. To the natural, unredeemed psyche, they are *anathemata*, untouchable, cursed, subject to the violence of the sacred described in chapter 7. Fascism, Nazism, and the Romanian Communist régime legitimised this prejudice philosophically and politically by ruthless means. It was against such attitudes in particular that Țuțea stressed the vocation of the disabled, and their capacity for deification along with the genius and the hero. In the Christian universal order, natural fallen prejudices that create cardboard cut-out saints and repulsive 'inadequates' vanish 'philosophically, by sympathy, and religiously, by love'.[156]

Very different, however, is the case of those who are spiritually disordered, including the ignorant or the wilfully stupid and morally corrupt.[157] These constitute *homo stultus* (see next section) and are responsible precisely for those societies and communities that 'demonise' and destroy the saints. Only in the Church can humanity find its real definition:

> Do you know where you can find a definition of humanity? In a church. In the Church. There you can match yourself against God, because you express His image and likeness. If the Church were to disappear from history, history would no longer know humanity. Humanity would disappear too.[158]

Homo Religiosus versus Homo Sovieticus

In this section I look at Țuțea's analysis of *homo religiosus* in contrast to *homo Sovieticus*. These two types represent the two extremes on his 'ladder of divine ascent' – and it is this sense of universality that he brings to his understanding of Christ's salvific love for the world. Țuțea frequently uses the phrase *homo religiosus* and in practice, within his own context, he speaks of Christianity. However, his use of the word *religiosus* rather than *Christianus* reflects his sense of a universal conflict between religious faith and militant atheism.

'The Christian' defines health in terms of spiritual, metaphysical, and physical harmony. In Țuțea's view Christian catechisation and liturgical participation in the Eucharist (even when restricted, as under Communism) are intrinsic to human normality. While still in prison he developed a mystical view of martyrdom, at both the individual and the national level, which I shall describe as redemptive 'sacrificial normality'. For all its imperfections, human life is fulfilled in martyrs, through their unconditional love for 'the Giver of Life'.

By implication, those who feign mental illness (to try to avoid martyrdom) may suffer from a sort of 'egotistical abnormality' which has moral rather than psychological connotations. Țuțea would never have pretended to be mad in order to

---

156 OLD AGE, pp. 129–30. Cf. Scheler's analysis of 'sympathy' and 'love' in his *On Feeling*, pp. 69–115.

157 In Țuțea's view 'the stupid are guilty' insofar as they refuse knowledge, enlightenment, or the opportunity of learning from experience. In this they indulge their sinful state. See interview, Bucharest, 28 January 1990.

158 BGMP, p. 337.

escape re-education and the political prison, he would never deny his moral convictions – embodied in his identity as a Romanian Christian – for the sake of external freedom. He believed that there is a wholeness to any human being, expressed in a harmony of morality and normality, a coincidence between moral integrity and mental health, which he would never violate:

> I have a consolation and please believe this: within the historical greatness of the Romanian people I am a tiny cog, invisible, but I am. For all that I have suffered I ought to be inconsolable, and I would have been inconsolable during my imprisonment, if I had not lived with the firm conviction that a great people, pregnant with history and with its brilliant future, was giving me the honour of suffering. That preserved me from madness. Otherwise, I should have to call the press here and issue a denial of my past, confess that I have been mistaken, in such a scholarly way that my 'confession' would be front page news. And I do have the mental ability to make a fool of myself. My moral conscience, however, stands in the way.[159]

The torturers, nevertheless, found the faith of their victims mysterious and threatening. The mutual solidarity among prisoners, and their sense of solidarity with previous Christian martyrs, as well as political pressure from the West, led to the end of the re-education experiment in 1964. Those responsible for the experiment finally had to recognise that the spiritual principle is not negotiable. Ţuţea stands as an exemplar of the experience of a whole people, acquiring, through suffering and weakness, an ever firmer grasp of that principle.[160]

In the description of Aiud, I mentioned *homo Sovieticus* as the Communist manifestation of *homo stultus*, the universal type at the bottom of the ladder.[161] (I will look in more detail at *homo stultus* later in this chapter.) *Homo religiosus* describes humanity as God intends humanity to be. *Homo Sovieticus* describes an attempt at

---

159 BGMP, p. 341.
160 The immovable spiritual principle can be contrasted with one of the tortures used in the 'unmasking', which required the victim to maintain a literally 'fixed position' for long periods of time. The result of this torture is described by its victim in terms which resemble schizophrenic catatonia, 'consisting of gross purposeless excitement and agitation, or withdrawal and elective mutism, rigidity, negativistic resistance to all attempts to remove the patient, or bizarre posturing': Steven L. Dubovsky, *Clinical Psychiatry* (Washington, DC: American Psychiatric Press, 1988), p. 168 (in other words, in terms which describe total ill health or the denial of what it means to be truly human). Remaining steadily fixed upon the spiritual principle has exactly the reverse effect, bringing a new revelation of freedom and human potential. See also Chapter 4.
161 Literally, 'stultified' or 'stupid' man – proud, self-destructive and sinful, under the sway of demonic forces, and under the illusion of being entirely self-sufficient. Ţuţea's concept of *homo stultus* was perhaps inspired by his reading of Erasmus of Rotterdam's Μωρίας Ἐγκώμιον, seu Laus Stultitiae (1509) trans. Betty Radice as *Praise of Folly and Letter to Maarten Van Dorp*, introd. and notes by A.H.T. Levi (London: Penguin, 1993). Erasmus's presentation of *stultitia* in the normal, unpraiseworthy, sense is brought into clearer focus by the Renaissance discussion of godly 'folly' (which may itself be compared with the tradition of the 'holy fool' in Orthodoxy).

self-creation. A particular feature of Soviet ideology was its preoccupation with the destruction of *homo religiosus*, spiritual wise men, who were replaced by *homo stultus* and debased to the level of animalism. 'The ignorant fool, *homo stultus*, suffers from the anxiety produced by the reduction of humanity to sub-humanity. He remains limited within dialectical pairs of opposites: value and equality, authority and freedom, truth and error, life and death.'[162] Characteristic of *homo Sovieticus* was his attack on the national identity of countries 'liberated' by the Red Army:

> Russian Bolsheviks used Orthodoxy for their selfish ends. This is why the Chinese saw those people in the Kremlin as 'red tsars'. However, Bolshevik insolence and cynicism stemmed from bourgeois rather than Christian values. This favoured elemental attitudes which, on behalf of so-called universal peace, led to Soviet expansion.[163]

> The Marxist–Leninist utopia is a cloak for Russian expansion. Russian nationalism takes two forms: Soviet patriotism, which disguises the process of Russification of the peoples inside the Soviet Union; and proletarian internationalism whereby class war (which for Communists is the sole content of history) is used to justify expansion and to destroy the national identity of subject peoples.[164]

Homo Sovieticus is obsessed with *homo religiosus* because the latter is loyal to God over and above the dictates of the State. To some extent, this makes *homo religiosus* immune to the sickness of the Communist system which Țuțea lampoons in terms of physical illness and spiritual 'animalism':

> Communism is a social cancer or 'leprosy'.
> A Communist believes that he is a rational animal who will die. But, in that case, there is no difference between a Communist and a skunk.[165]

Incapable of the sacrificial normality of *homo religiosus*, ruled by *spiritual stupidity*, and exposed to *metaphysical autism*, *homo Sovieticus* is terminally dysfunctional.

Spiritual Stupidity

For Țuțea *homo stultus* or the atheist is a ubiquitous human type who perennially denies the existence of God and, 'in his spiritual stupidity, applies the logic of facts'[166] to the domain of mystery, remaining captive to this world in which he acts mechanically, like a 'spinning top'.[167] For those 'blundering about in this world', in Țuțea's words, the world below becomes a substitute for the world above in which

---

162 PROBLEMS, pp. 191–2.
163 PROBLEMS, p. 192.
164 PROBLEMS, p. 284.
165 APHORISMS, pp. 30–31.
166 SYSTEMS, p. 192. For a succinct definition see PROBLEMS, p. 213: 'The anti-religious man? *Homo stultus.*'
167 SYSTEMS, p. 193.

everything is revealed.[168] The Communist torturer who believes that he acts rightly is *homo stultus* manifested as *homo Sovieticus*. The Christian victim who under torture abjures his faith, at least for a time, becomes *homo Sovieticus*. In general, however, while interviewing 're-educated' people I realised that the denial of their Christian faith was, almost without exception, a temporary lapse and had in fact led them to a stronger belief in the all-comprehending, all-forgiving, saving presence of Christ.

In general Țuțea describes atheists as distant, 'aloof people' who 'lack grace' and 'seek without finding the truth'.[169] Their 'spiritual stupidity', however, can be overcome by God's other gifts to them. Țuțea affirms unequivocally that Christians are ruled by the principle: 'judge not, that you be not judged' (Matt. 7:1).[170] Christians are required to exercise discernment rather than judgement.[171] They must, most importantly, distinguish between the 'evil' atheist (*homo stultus*)[172] – who is, so to speak, actively indifferent ('spiritually dead') and could not care less whether God exists or not – and the 'good' atheist – who, despite his metaphysical denial of God, lives and acts according to the light of his conscience, ultimately reflecting, as the believer would assert, 'the true Light which gives light to every man coming into the world' (John 1:9). The useful but ambivalent distinction between agnostics and atheists is not one which Țuțea explores: 'A Christian classifies people according to religious criteria. The indifferent are spiritually[173] dead, atheists are struggling and still alive, and believers are permanently alive.'[174]

---

168   SYSTEMS, p. 193.
169   PROBLEMS, p. 203.
170   PROBLEMS, p. 202.
171   Interview with Țuțea, Bucharest, 28 January 1990. I will show in Chapter 8 that, as a 'new Socrates', Țuțea did not suffer fools gladly. As an elderly man he acknowledged also a 'Homeric' impatience with his own physical disability. It is perhaps his recognition of his own limitation that prevents his view of *homo stultus* from becoming simply the inversion of Nietzsche's *Übermensch*. At all levels of society and in all areas (including the Church) *homo stultus* can be found. Moreover, all individuals have elements of *homo stultus* within themselves. Only the saint achieves that liberation from stultified being that is God's desire for everyone.
172   There is a fine line between psychopathology and demonology, which is intuited by Țuțea in his reflections on spiritual stupidity. The spiritual dimension of psychiatry has to develop towards or be completed by the spiritual knowledge of pastoral theology. 'God's decisions are mysterious: in the Christian world they are revealed to the enlightened and communicated to the unenlightened who can either accept or, through idiocy or satanisation, reject them': PROBLEMS, p. 117.
173   In the original this is *sufletește morți*. *Suflet* is the word for 'soul', but it would be incorrect here to translate 'psychologically dead', and absurd to say 'soulfully dead'. Cf. Bruno Bettelheim, *Freud and Man's Soul* (London: Hogarth Press, 1983), pp. 70–78. Bettelheim demonstrates that the standard English mistranslations of central concepts of psychoanalysis (in particular the systematic rendering of *die Seele* as 'mind', not 'soul', thus losing the crucial distinction in Freud between 'Geist' and 'Seele') obscures Freud's ultimate meaning.
174   Țuțea, *Philosophia Perennis*, p. 134.

Metaphysical Autism

The more the victims of torture gave in to re-education, the more they suffered in reality, because they entered a personal hell. In the light of Ţuţea's analysis, it is possible to draw a parallel between the psychological features of Soviet man and the description generally used in psychopathology to identify pervasive developmental disorders, particularly autism. (It goes without saying that the causes of actual autism and the causes of the 'metaphysical autism' of *homo Sovieticus* are entirely different.)

The features of autism as defined in the 'Diagnostic Criteria' from the *Diagnostic and Statistical Manual of Mental Disorders* are:

1. Qualitative impairment in social interaction;
2. Qualitative impairments in communication (i.e. stereotyped or repetitive use of language, elective mutism, inability to initiate or sustain a conversation);
3. Repetitive and stereotypical patterns of behaviour, interests, and activities.[175]

The causes of conditions such as clinical autism are at least partially organic or genetic in origin, rather than acquired (or imposed as in the case of *homo Sovieticus*). Ţuţea perceives the incongruity between the spiritual gifts bestowed on humanity and humanity's refusal or inability to accept these as mediating their sacred origin – that is, as communicating ultimate truth and wholeness. This inability leads me to use the phrase 'metaphysical autism'. Following the Swiss psychiatrist Eugen Bleuler (1857–1939), Ţuţea himself refers to autism, specifically in its original and now outmoded psychiatric sense, as a symptom of schizophrenia. He uses Heinrich Schmidt's *Philosophisches Wörterbuch*[176] to define autism as 'a pathological state characterised by lack of affective empathy with the external world and by erratic, impulsive, suspicious thinking'.[177]

Ţuţea implies that spiritual 'aloofness' leads to atheism and nihilism. By losing his likeness to the Creator (although never his essence as the image of God, the primordial mask), 'the human person becomes sub-human'; 'if the subject to whom truth is offered cannot communicate his spiritual state, what is the point of dialogue and discourse?'[178] According to Ţuţea, communication through dialogue has two pedagogical, illuminative[179] functions: to awaken the memory or awareness of the

---

175   *Quick reference to Diagnostic Criteria from DSM-IV*[TM] (Washington, DC: American Psychiatric Association, 1994), pp. 57–9. Abridged by this author, who is by professional training a medical doctor with expertise in the field of autism.
176   The 9th edn of Schmidt's dictionary used by Ţuţea was published in 1934, nine years before Leo Kanner first defined the new psychiatric entity of autism. See also Eugen Bleuler, *Dementia Praecox or the Group of Schizophrenias*, English trans. Joseph Zinkin (New York: International Universities Press, 1950; 1st German edn 1911).
177   THEATRE, p. 183; Schmidt, *Philosophisches Wörterbuch*, pp. 42–3.
178   THEATRE, p. 447. See the discussion of 'image' vis-à-vis 'likeness' in chapter 9.
179   Ţuţea's writings, like the visions of early Christian martyrs such as Polycarp, Perpetua, and Felicitas, are – to use McGinn's words – 'directed to strengthening and/or

limits of human knowledge[180] in this world (for which, according to Plato, divine revelation is necessary); and to maintain in a state of watchfulness those ordinary faithful Christians who lack inspiration but obediently participate in the life of the Church.[181]

For Țuțea, revelation and faith are the only means whereby the spirit can penetrate the opacity of our worldly existence. However, those gifted with revelation and faith do not necessarily conform to the world's view of 'ordinary humanity' – they may, by the standards of that 'stultified' view, be judged as eccentric or even mad.

Metaphysical autism is a general description and an academic theory which I propound on the basis of Țuțea's intuitions and deduce from my investigations in the world of re-education. One particular manifestation of metaphysical autism – the case study that Țuțea identified from his experience – was *homo Sovieticus*. This Soviet brand of *homo stultus* included Țuțea's torturers. Victims of re-education were forced into metaphysical autism but, Țuțea points out, the victim, by and large, whilst rendered metaphysically autistic, did not become stupid – that is, did not reject God at the fundamental spiritual level. There was a way back to health as soon as re-education ceased. For most of the torturers, however, the situation even today remains unresolved. They believe that Communism may still 'work'. They remain in the grip of what Țuțea calls 'stupidity' – out of touch with the divine:

> *Homo stultus* has lost, through pride, the likeness he received from God, becoming submerged in complacency and things, renouncing the assistance of the Divine Guide.[182]

Madness: Diabolical, Pathological, and Divine

Țuțea stresses that the religious aspects of life which are 'consoling and salvific' are situated above science and art which are 'all too human'. He makes a sharp distinction between a religious person and a person stultified by atheism:

> Religious mysteries liberate us from anxieties caused by our own limitations, by our cosmic captivity, and by the very fact that mysteries cannot be elucidated. The stupid man (*homo*

---

illuminating the individual believer for some task', dignified resistance as a Christian confessor under Communism, in Țuțea's case. Even when they teach or illuminate, they too 'do so not by conveying some new and deeper message but by confirming the meaning of the tradition of the church': McGinn, *The Foundations of Mysticism*, p. 97.

180 Țuțea is aware that we should use human reason as far as we can. In the concluding paragraph of PROBLEMS, p. 341, he writes: 'Of course, one cannot do theology without reason but, in doing theology, reason becomes a vehicle of transcendence, a tool which bears dogmatically the revealed truth, preserved by sacred history and tradition.'

181 See THEATRE, p. 447. The link between Țuțea's epistemology and the patristic concept of νῆψις (watchfulness) is obvious. See note 124 in Chapter 7.

182 PROBLEMS, p. 8.

stultus) wishes to end his life in this world. He is the only creature that is worn out by his own doubt because he does not see God and his prayers do not lead to miracles.[183]

Under Communism, *homo stultus* starts as a dogmatic[184] atheist who plans to change the world through permanent Soviet revolution. Atheist stultification becomes a cloning process. Young people are brainwashed and re-educated to produce *homo Sovieticus* – an appropriate term for an artificially planned and brutally delivered by-product of Soviet culture and propaganda. In general, by rejecting God, *homo stultus* refuses personal vocation in the divine drama of salvation. Having rejected love, the highest virtue because it is nearest to God, *homo stultus* becomes spiritually dead in the rôle of an automaton on the stage of totalitarian society:

> No other virtue equals love because love reflects the divine nature. Love concerns the whole human person in relationship with self, neighbour, the cosmos, and God. It is the affective way of seeking the Great Union [of humanity with God] and no pedagogical system, no method of education or instruction, can achieve positive results without the experience of love in all its aspects. The will to procreate and perfect life, joy in living, and creative desire are closely linked with love. Neglect or denial of feelings (i.e. of living spiritual forms) causes a human being to dry up and become indifferent to himself and everything. A human being seen only in terms of the degree of his intellectual knowledge, devoid of spiritual capacity, is simply [another kind of] machine.[185]

These automaton-like beings 'communicate' through logical conventions and mental stereotypes of scientific language, replacing absolute, sacred truth with the relative findings of secular human reason. They can no longer converse with the divine Word. They remain in a state of cosmic aloofness, a metaphysical autism. This 'desacralised mind' ruled by ignorance defines *homo stultus*.

Psychiatric Illness and Spiritual Foolishness

Homo stultus chooses 'not to be open to revelation'.[186] Țuțea sees in this attitude a 'crass stupidity' – the refusal to keep mind and heart open to divine revelation and inspiration – rather than guilt in the legal sense of a fault condemned by God. He suggests (with his friend, the Romanian philosopher Constantin Noica) that illnesses of the spirit, such as the condition of *homo stultus*, are different from those of the psyche.[187] Țuțea distinguishes between psychopathology (of mentally ill people),

---

183 STYLES, II, p. 168.
184 I use the word 'dogmatic' here in the common pejorative sense, to reinforce the contrast between this debased concept of dogma (part of a distorted 'divine mask') and the high mystical view of dogma proposed by Țuțea (as essential to the form of the 'divine mask').
185 THEATRE, p. 334.
186 DAYS, p. 79.
187 Noica even calls them 'maladies of the contemporary spirit': Constantin Noica, *Șase Maladii ale Spiritului Contemporan* (Bucharest: Humanitas, 1997).

lack of divine inspiration (as in *homo stultus*), and the Pauline 'foolishness of God' which is 'wiser than men' (1 Cor. 1:25):[188]

> *The inspired* is chosen. Mental illness is a pathological condition. We speak of 'the foolishness of the Cross' as an exaltation of the Cross, that is, an overwhelming experience of it. But this shows that the word madness can be used not only in a pathological sense, but also metaphorically. However, one cannot speak of Jesus Christ's madness.[189]

Although some people do speak of Christ as 'the divine fool'[190] and on more than one occasion Jesus was judged to be mad by some of his contemporaries (Mark 3:21; John 10:19), the following questions arise: could God act through a person's unchosen madness; and could a person be mentally ill and yet spiritually well? While Țuțea seems to suggest, in the passage quoted above, that between mental illness and divine inspiration there is an unbridgeable gulf[191] (although he would always recognise that God can bring good out of evil), his view nevertheless implies that people who sustain psychosomatic disablement retain their gifts. God-given, these are never withdrawn. Țuțea in no way suggests that the mentally ill cannot be vehicles of God's grace. Indeed, as I have shown, in his rejection of the notion of 'bio-social waste', he considered that those afflicted with a handicap are particularly precious to God.

Mystical Definition of Health

For Țuțea, medicine, or more specifically psychiatric medicine, could be regarded as the supreme science, requiring not just knowledge of particular conditions, but also wisdom to discern the border between psychopathology and the health (or otherwise) of the spirit. True medicine is 'the art of healing, which theoretically has no limits'.[192]

---

188 Țuțea himself was named 'God's fool' by many of his prison mates, although he does not use the phrase 'fool in Christ'. For this 'paradoxical figure' of the Christian East see Kallistos Ware, 'The Fool in Christ as Prophet and Apostle', in *The Inner Kingdom*, pp. 153–80.

189 DAYS, p. 79.

190 Cf. Ware, 'Imitators of the Divine Fool', in *The Inner Kingdom*, pp. 171–2.

191 Very talented people (such as the 'idiot savant', or, in clinical terms, the high-functioning autistic) are often reckoned to be 'mad' because they do not resemble *ordinary people*. But geniuses, although different from ordinary people, 'are not insane: they are exceptionally gifted, which is a different matter'. On the other hand, Țuțea suggests, insanity is a fallen aspect of the human spirit. Thus, 'logic is absent from a psychiatric hospital.' Or, if it appears from time to time, it is as a paradox, 'a small oasis of lucidity'. This is why 'a visit to a psychiatric ward is much more dramatic than a visit to a cancer ward'. See DAYS, p. 80.

192 Personal conversation with Țuțea, Bucharest, 10 June 1985. Cf. DAYS, p. 80. See also Jean-Claude Larchet, 'Connaissance de Dieu et santé spirituelle', *Thérapeutique des maladies spirituelles. Une introduction à la tradition ascétique de l'Église orthodoxe*, 3rd rev. edn (Paris: Éd. du Cerf, 1997), pp. 811–15.

Even if spiritually it has no limits, however, medicine works within the bounds of verifiable treatment. If, for instance, somebody is given grace and heals you with holy water this can easily be acknowledged scientifically. Yet the limits of scientific verifiability can be terrifyingly stretched:

> Any medical doctor, whether he likes it or not, has to know everything. For how can a doctor give me a true diagnosis if I act like a lunatic just to fool him? I am quite a clever man, and unless that doctor is cleverer than me, he can label me a dangerous psychopath.[193]

Țuțea affirms the absolute uniqueness of human beings in their psychosomatic, moral, and spiritual integrity. This implies a mystical definition of health[194] and normality based on the individual's call to deification in union with God rather than any purely human 'wholeness'. Following Maximus the Confessor, Țuțea stresses again that man's real illness is his ignorance of God (the clouding of his *nous* which confines humanity to 'a trap of hell and a pit of darkness').[195]

What of mental illness? Although a scholar who is mentally ill and talks nonsense is different from an 'ordinary person' suffering from the same illness, the psychiatric significance of his speech is similar. For Țuțea, mental illness is a great 'equaliser' since people with the same psychiatric diagnosis can appear 'uniform'.[196] However, if the *nous* in the mentally ill is not clouded through denial of transcendence, those suffering from mental illnes could still be capable of apprehending the divine and thus of being spiritually healthy. Is mental disorder a consequence of the original split between humanity and God? At the spiritual level, Țuțea seems to suggest that atheism in effect leads its adherents to an equality of ignorance – that is, an indulged

---

193 DAYS, p. 80. See THEATRE, p. 229, for Țuțea's comments on one of Leonid Andreev's characters, a doctor who 'puts on the mask of a psychopath' to escape punishment for the murder he has committed (following Raskolnikov's 'experimental' dilemma in Dostoyevsky's *Crime and Punishment*). See note 49 in Chapter 7.

194 Cf. the World Health Organisation's necessarily secular definition of health: 'Health is a state of *complete* physical, mental and social well-being and not merely the absence of disease or infirmity' (italics added). By reducing 'soul' to 'mind', the concept of *mental* illness is equally unsatisfactory. See World Health Organisation, 'Constitution of the World Health Organisation', *Official Record of the World Health Organisation*, nr. 2, 1946, p. 100.

195 See 'Orthodoxy according to the Holy Fathers', in Metropolitan Hierotheos of Nafpaktos, *The Mind of the Orthodox Church*, trans. Esther Williams (Levadia-Hellas: Birth of the Theotokos Monastery, 1998), p. 79; also the definition of *nous* in Metropolitan Hierotheos of Nafpaktos, *The Person in the Orthodox Tradition*, p. 28.

196 DAYS, p. 80. It must be remembered that 'the concepts of mental normality and normal behaviour are both conditional. In the absence of a scientifically based definition of normal behaviour, what generally passes for the norm is no more than a projection of the accepted norms of the social group, level, or class to which the person called upon to evaluate behaviour and divide it into normal or deviant, belongs': Dr Semyon Gluzman, *On Soviet Totalitarian Psychiatry* (Amsterdam: International Association on the Political Use of Psychiatry, 1989), p. 26.

maladjustment vis-à-vis ultimate personhood, which might be a definition of Hell. The opposite is equality of wisdom in Christ.

In identifying the condition I have called metaphysical autism and its behavioural and attitudinal manifestation in *homo stultus*, we must therefore differentiate between three entities, or forms of 'madness': spiritual 'madness'; psychiatric 'madness'; and divine 'madness'. Metaphysical autism is spiritual 'madness'. In its rejection of God it differs from psychiatric 'madness', which is a pathological condition of the psyche. There is then the 'madness' we describe as divine, that action of God which supersedes human understanding. Spiritual 'madness' rejects the 'madness' of God and seeks to define the believer as 'mad' in a psychiatric sense (corresponding to delusion, or psychotic belief).[197] The results of this point of view are the totalitarian experiments and experiences of the Gulag and the treatment of those with religious principles as psychiatric cases.[198] In the last analysis secular medicine is not a self-defining science, for it cannot transcend its relativist definitions of normality. Truly to understand another person requires the 'discerning of spirits' (1 Cor. 12:10).

Mental illness is one of the consequences of the Fall. It is not a spiritual illness, for the mentally impaired may still be open to God's grace – they too are made in the image of God. The stupid or stultified are, by contrast, *spiritually* sick and creep into their shell of metaphysical aloofness. The wise (sometimes considered to be mad) find meaning in the creation of a loving Creator and in relationship to Him – that is, in the fulfilment of who they are rather than of what they know.

At the spiritual level, pathological insanity is no barrier to the workings of God's grace. The person who is mentally ill (however severely) invariably manifests, in Țuțea's words, 'small oases of lucidity',[199] where free will can be exercised. It is in these 'oases' that the person is open to God's grace and can be the sphere of God's action, either by direct inspiration or through the sacramental channels of the whole

---

197   On ethical difficulties in translating the psychiatric term 'delusion' from English into Romanian (a language in which this term does not exist as such and, following the underdevelopment of Romanian psychiatry under Communism, is still imperfectly rendered by *credința psihotică*, meaning 'psychotic belief'), see note 13 of Alexandru Popescu's translation of Prof. William Fulford's 'The Concept of Disease', in Sidney Bloch and Paul Chodoff (eds), *Etică Psihiatrică*, trans. R. Țuculescu, A. Popescu, N. Bizamcer, and L. Cosma (Bucharest: The Association of Romanian Free Psychiatrists, Geneva Initiative on Psychiatry, 2000), pp. 108–9. Țuțea's frequent use of the phrase 'going astray' with reference to *homo stultus* is related to πλάνη, a technical word in Greek ascetic theology, meaning literally deflection from the right path. Cf. the literal sense of sin ἁμαρτία as 'missing the mark'. See *The Philokalia*, II (1981), pp. 384, 386.

198   See Alexandru Popescu, 'Psychiatric Abuse in Romania Today', communication to Jubilee Campaign/Parliamentary Human Rights Group, Parliamentary Briefing Session: *Romania's Psychiatric Prison Hospitals* (London: The House of Commons, 7 November 1991). Cf. C. Thau and A. Popescu, 'Romanian Psychiatry in Turmoil', *Bulletin of Medical Ethics*, 78, May 1992, pp. 13–19.

199   DAYS, p. 80.

body of the Church.[200] Problems arise when people use the term 'insane' to describe their neighbours. The 'enemies' of *homo Sovieticus* were declared mad and in need of treatment, whereas, according to Țuțea's mystical definition of health, the only real disorder was to reject God and refuse divine love. In this sense, *homo stultus* has, from the beginning of time, been radically disordered. In the twentieth century, in the form of *homo Sovieticus*, *homo stultus* regarded Christians as 'out of order' ('mad' and requiring treatment).

An Ontology of Christian Order

Christian Love

Țuțea's anagogic typology is undergirded by an ontology of Christian order. In everything there is an 'ontic triangle' made up of God, humanity, and nature. God remains ultimately a mystery. Everyone has a vocation to grow in this mystery, extending humanity by a common 'priestly' holiness,[201] and discovering the divine givenness of nature in right stewardship of creation. Where mystery is excluded (as in dialectical materialism) there can be no truth. God's all-embracing love is the definitive element of the created order. As far as veracity is concerned:

> it is obvious that truth, being transcendent in essence, cannot be found either in humanity or in the world. Christian harmony is incompatible with an order that rests on Joseph de Maistre's 'three pillars': the priest, the landlord, and the executioner. There is no place for the Christian priest [as Țuțea understands the universal vocation to priesthood] alongside the landlord and the executioner.[202]

Țuțea looks beyond mere criticism of the 'modern age' and the Communist era, where atheism and materialism were based on apparently noble humanitarian principles. The Communist project to humanise, falsify, or merely ignore the divine resulted in a destructive confusion of values. In Christ, love reconciles authority and freedom, and makes political power compatible with divine humility. Țuțea's incarnational view of the human being embraces and goes beyond the theoretical level of the theological virtues. Above all, Christian love opens to everyone the door to the Kingdom of God, which Țuțea calls 'the realm of certainty'.

---

200 The Romanian word for 'madman' is *nebun*, literally 'not good', or possessed by 'evil'. *Nebunia* ('madness') has the connotation of an intermittent crisis rather than of a permanent state. Țuțea saw as significant the fact that in the Middle Ages mentally ill people were cared for in *bolnițe* (from *boală*, disease), infirmaries attached to a monastery – that is, to the Eucharistic centre of a community.

201 Cf. the New Testament image of the 'royal priesthood' of believers (I Peter 2:9). Țuțea sees all Christians as having in this sense a priestly vocation. This is perhaps another aspect of his 'Reformed' outlook, although he would of course not agree with Protestant objections to sacramentally ordained priesthood.

202 OLD AGE, p. 131.

Sanctification as Gift

Țuțea uses the term 'person' to refer to those on their way to deification by grace. As I will show, in his theology of 'mask' he, in a certain sense, re-works the classical distinction between divine 'image' and 'likeness'.[203] Just as 'the image' is potentially likeness and 'the likeness' is actually image, so also the human person is potentially 'human' in the fullest sense, while 'the human' is actually personal.[204] Deification requires asceticism. In Țuțea's view human holiness is conditioned, although not ultimately determined, by individual understanding of the world as a sacred gift. He believed that freedom can be defined only with reference to the ontic relationship between humanity and God.

The mutual relationship between the natural and the supernatural points to the divine origin of humankind. Natural knowledge, based as it is on sense-perception, inevitably leads to an imperfect and partial understanding of the world. A full understanding of humanity, as the crowning glory of God in creation, implies both communion between creature and Creator and actual participation in the 'purifying, illuminating and deifying energy of God'.[205]

Thus, only in God can life have ultimate meaning. Only in God's love can people find what Țuțea calls real freedom. The ultimate human calling is to the condition of 'the saint', who, through union with Christ, experiences this freedom:

> In terms both of nature and of culture a human being can seem to be free, while remaining in reality a slave to sin. Only the religious human being is free in a real sense. The absolute form of freedom is holiness. The saint is free in reality, because he is not overwhelmed either by the sufferings of this world, or by fear of death.[206]

Țuțea adds that philosophy, science, art, and the techniques of existence cannot lead to consolation or salvation. The supreme vocation of humanity, real freedom, is to be stewards of the order of the new Creation redeemed by 'the last Adam'.[207] Through obedience to God – who is eternally present to them in the 'High Priest', Jesus Christ – individual believers, as members of the 'royal priesthood' (I Peter 2:9), ascend the 'ladder' to sanctification. Only thus, in the sacrificial Body of Christ, the ultimate form of human perfection and divine self-realisation, is humanity's original vocation to personhood in the image and likeness of God fulfilled.

---

203 In this, Țuțea follows Origen, *On First principles*, being Koetschau's text of the *De Principiis*, Book III, Chapter VI, 1, trans. and ed. George W. Butterworth (London: SPCK, 1936), p. 245. See note 31, Chapter 9.

204 See also, Metropolitan Hierotheos, *The Person in the Orthodox Tradition*, p. 79.

205 Metropolitan Hierotheos, *The Person in the Orthodox Tradition*, p. 79.

206 STYLES, II, p. 151.

207 Like Fr Stăniloae, Țuțea regards creation as the primordial gift of God. See 'The World as a Gift', in Charles Miller, *The Gift of the World, An Introduction to the Theology of Dumitru Stăniloae* (Edinburgh: T. & T. Clark, 2000), pp. 58–60. Cf. Kallistos Ware's foreword to Sherrard, *Christianity, Lineaments of a Sacred Tradition*, pp. xxviii, xlii.

Chapter 6

Christian Anthropology

In the last decade of his life Țuțea suffered from an increasingly severe form of intention tremor, which made it difficult for him to write.[1] He had to dictate or re-dictate many pages when his handwriting was too shaky. Despite this he managed to complete a substantial part of his five-volume *Omul, Tratat de Antropologie Creștină* (*The Human Being, Treatise on Christian Anthropology*). Țuțea's anthropology is very different from anthropology in the sense in which it is normally understood, as a discipline of the social sciences. His subject is defined not by sociological, cultural, and ethnographic behaviour, but by the essentially spiritual givenness of human existence. Secular anthropologies conceive of existence as an experience of transition from birth to death. Christian anthropology understands existence in terms of eternal life in God.

Three of the five volumes of his *Christian Anthropology* have now been published. Despite many printing errors and poor editing, they have attracted much interest among Romanian theologians. The first volume, *Problemele sau Cartea Întrebărilor* (*Problems, or the Book of Questions*) was written in the mid-1980s. The original manuscript of this volume was confiscated from Țuțea's flat by *Securitate* agents, but copies had been entrusted to his friends and scribes. Immediately after the Revolution of December 1989, the architect Ion Doja-Fodoreanu courageously rescued the manuscript from the *Securitate*. Thus it started to appear in the literary magazine *Timpul* (*The Times*) in Iassy, January 1990. Timpul Press published *Problems, or the Book of Questions* posthumously in 1992, which was followed in the same year by the second volume of *Christian Anthropology*, *Sistemele sau Cartea Întregurilor Logice, Autonom-Matematice, Paralele cu Întregurile Ontice* (*Systems, or the Book of Logical Wholes, Mathematically Autonomous, Parallel to Ontic Wholes*). The manuscript of this second volume had been finished and revised by Țuțea in 1988.[2]

---

1   Dr Mihai Neagu, 'Amurgul lui Petre Țuțea', *Vatra*, 44:194, Freiburg im Breisgau, June 1994, p. 6. According to Țuțea's family his neurological tremor was acquired in prison. Interviews: Victor Țuțea (Țuțea's brother), Boteni, Muscel, 12 April 1999, and Angela Chirilă (Țuțea's sister), Bucharest, 19 April 1999. A medical certificate (no. 73 of 26 March 1957) reads: 'A specialist medical commission examined Petre Țuțea and found no psychiatric disturbances which would render him irresponsible. The neurological examination showed that he presented functional disturbances'. These functional disturbances probably indicated intention tremor, diagnosed in the late 1960s by Dr Neagu who was Țuțea's personal doctor for more than twenty years. Arhiva Sistemului Român de Informații (Archives of the Romanian Security Service): Dosar nr. 105531/6, fol. 91.

2   The original manuscripts of the first two volumes of his *Christian Anthropology*

The writing and dictating of the last three volumes of *Christian Anthropology*, achieved in the face of severe intention tremor, were, in a sense, another aspect of Țuțea's martyrdom. The third volume is entitled 'Stilurile, sau Cartea Unităților Cultural Istorice și a Modalităților Estetice ale Artelor, sau Omul Estetic' ('Styles, or the Book of Historical Cultural Unities and of the Aesthetic Forms of the Arts, or Aesthetic Humanity'). The final two volumes are: *Științele sau Disciplinele Minții Omenești* (*Sciences, or the Disciplines of the Human Mind*) and *Dogmele sau Situarea Spiritului în Imperiul Certitudinii* (*Dogmas, or the Location of the Spirit in the Realm of Certainty*).[3]

Țuțea's unpublished manuscripts perhaps deserve a separate study. Some of their central ideas are formulated or anticipated in the first two volumes of his *Christian Anthropology*, as well as in his late interviews, and in some of the ten books which have been published since his death. All these are non-systematic works. In this book I have referred to them alongside the more methodical (although still often aphoristic and elliptical) *Christian Anthropology*.

Țuțea's 'Method' and 'Style'

Although Țuțea approaches fundamental themes of anthropology such as creation, the Fall, the image of God, human nature, society, death, and life after death, it is his approach which is unsystematic. Perhaps it would be more accurate to say that his 'system' is not that of verifiable connections, proofs, and syntheses. His repetition of ideas gives his work an oral flow, and becomes a prayer-like refrain running through the five volumes of the *Christian Anthropology*. His writings, thus, have a performative character, in the spirit of the Orthodox liturgy, and their length and complexity require both dedication and discernment on the part of the reader.

Eclectic Synthesis

As an example of Țuțea's mode of thinking, I will look at how he treats the theme of 'Creation *ex nihilo*' in his *Christian Anthropology, Problems*.[4] The six-page section

---

(PROBLEMS and SYSTEMS) are in my personal archive, courtesy of Prof. Marcel Petrișor, Țuțea's lifelong friend, fellow prisoner, and scribe. I have referred to them throughout, correcting the published editions where necessary.

3   I also possess a handwritten dictated version of the third volume, STYLES, I–II, along with a typed version which contains typing and editing errors. In my translation from this unpublished third volume I used both versions. The fourth volume exists in a fragmented state as reflections and aphorisms on scientific enquiry. The fifth volume, DOGMAS, is unfinished and similarly exists in both a handwritten dictated version and a typed version. The typed version was published under an abbreviated title: *Dogmele sau Primirea Certitudinii* (Iassy: Timpul, 2000). These manuscripts were also entrusted to me by Prof. Petrișor.

4   PROBLEMS, pp. 93–9.

starts with the Prologue of St John's Gospel, followed by Țuțea's translation of Question 45, on 'the mode of emanation of things from the first principle which is called creation', of Aquinas's *Summa Theologiae* (Ia. 45). Țuțea then comments on this passage in two short notes. In the first he relates Aquinas's vision of creation *ex nihilo* to Plato's view of the Demiurge in *Timaeus*, making the distinction between the Christian God who creates out of nothing and the Greek god who brings order from pre-existing chaos. In the second, he distinguishes between God's original creativity and human creativity. In his view the latter is erroneously so named since it always has its source in a gift from God. In five paragraphs he then discusses the following:

1   the unique and unknowable character of God as First Cause;
2   the origin of life and the distinction between organic and inorganic elements;
3   the theories of Louis Pasteur (1822–95) and Ernst Haeckel (1834–1919) on biological causality;
4   pre-Socratic cosmology;
5   scientific hypotheses about the fundamental constituents of matter from atomism to quantum theory.

He then devotes a paragraph to 'Natural Order' (in which there is no moral sense) versus 'Divine Order' (in which morality is given), listing the 'seven enigmas of the world' identified by Emil du Bois-Reymond,[5] after which he moves on to naturalism, evolutionism, and creationism, illustrated with quotations from Claude Bernard, Lavoisier, Laplace, Napoleon, and Cuvier. Thereafter he devotes eight lines to the German biologist Ludwig Rhumbler (1864–1939) whose *Das Protoplasma als physikalisches System* (1914) raises objections to evolutionary naturalism.

To conclude, Țuțea points to theism as the only rational answer to all questions regarding the origin of the universe, life, and humankind, and in a final paragraph affirms his belief in a single Creator, supporting his affirmation with quotations from the Catholic theologian A.D. Sertillanges (*Dieu ou rien?*) and St Paul (II Cor. 4:18; I Cor. 13:12). He then offers a brief Credo:

> Through His coming, as the Incarnate Word, Christ the Saviour offered us the joy of the Great Mystery of Theandry [the coinherence of divinity and humanity] and through His life, death, and Resurrection created, according to St Paul, the New Adam restored by Baptism.[6]

Finally he refers to Origen's idea of *apokatastasis* in *De Principiis*, and concludes that, 'irrespective of his spiritual understanding, a believer experiences the two worlds', regarding 'this world as an antechamber of the world above'.[7]

This vertiginous tour of European intellectual history may give some sense of the virtuosity of Țuțea's 'method', which in certain respects, in terms of strict academic discourse, is clearly also its weakness. As an Orthodox thinker wishing to express

---

5   Emil du Bois-Reymond (1818–96), German biologist, Professor of Physiology in Berlin.
6   PROBLEMS, p. 99.
7   PROBLEMS, p. 99.

his belief in the incarnational and Trinitarian foundations of the world as creation *ex nihilo*, Țuțea is perhaps unique in his ability and willingness to employ so much 'non-Orthodox' scholarship.

The Experience of Țuțea's 'Style'

Like the author of the Pseudo-Areopagitic corpus, Țuțea often employs what Bernard McGinn describes as 'dialectical combinations of contrary and even contradictory predicates in relation to God', using language 'to subvert the claims of language'.[8] Combining an extraordinary intellectual endowment with a high degree of spiritual sensitivity, tested for many years in the furnace of intense suffering and cruelty, Țuțea would employ all his resources to raise the consciousness of his readers and hearers in an anagogical Christian anthropology.

It is important to explore the apparent 'oddity' of Țuțea's style of thinking. His thought processes are pyrotechnic, advancing in dramatic spurts rather than logical progression. He is capable of a kind of intellectual osmosis, in which the reader participates. His writing is like a coral reef containing a myriad constructs of experience and thought. It has the simultaneous versatility and precision of liquid crystals.

In analysing the actual content of his thought, we of course need to be systematic. It should be borne in mind, however, that from the point of view of his overall achievement as an exponent of Christian truth, any systematisation of his intellectual and theological vision will inevitably be somewhat arbitrary. The corpus of a thinker of this kind remains ultimately proclamatory rather than analytical in character.

Sequential Theology

Țuțea took care over both the order and the details of the five volumes of *Omul*. He hesitated between two alternative orders: the first being *Problems*, *Systems*, *Styles*, *Disciplines*, and *Dogmas*; the second being *Problems*, *Systems*, *Styles*, *Dogmas*, and *Disciplines*. For the purposes of this book, I have adopted the first order. This moves from a human perspective towards revealed dogmas, indicating a spiritual journey from secular knowledge to the mystery of deification in Christ, which can be stated but never expressed.[9] Christian dogmas represent 'the realm of certainty'. Yet, even for the greatest saint, let alone for the institutional Church as a collective whole, certainty is a divine gift rather than something arrived at by human effort and reason. Reception of this gift entails alertness, compassion, and spiritual combat. Discipline of reason, discernment, and practical virtue are required if a person is to return to God. This is the *martyrion* to which all are called through their various

---

8   McGinn, *The Foundations of Mysticism*, p. 176.
9   A year before Țuțea died, he wrote a letter to Cioran using the first order, BGMP, pp. 12–13; see also PROBLEMS, p. 341; elsewhere he used the second: see title page of Petre Țuțea, 'Omul, IV, Dogmele sau Primirea Certitudinii', typescript (Bucharest: 15 May 1989). In the end he expressed no definitive decision on the matter.

1 Petre Bădescu, Țuțea's father (before 1910)

2   Dr Petre Țuțea (1929)

3 Ana Ţuţea with two of her sons: Ion (magistrate) and Petre (economist, left)
(1935)

4 Petre Țuțea (right) at a wedding ceremony on 15 January 1948, three
   months before his imprisonment

5   Boyhood friends at Boteni, Muscel: Petre Țuțea (right) and Ion Chelcea
    (Professor of Ethnography at Iassy University) in the 1980s

6   Petre Țuțea (left) and the author in the surgical ward of the Emergency
    Hospital, Bucharest, 26 April 1990

7 First page of Fr Petre Bădescu's deed of gift by which he transferred his entire estate to Ana Țuțea (1906)

8 'Whenever I aspire to holiness, I feel the ground slipping away under my feet': second page of Țuțea's letter of 28 October 1934 from Berlin to his friend Viorel V. Tilea, later to be appointed Romanian Minister Plenipotentiary to London

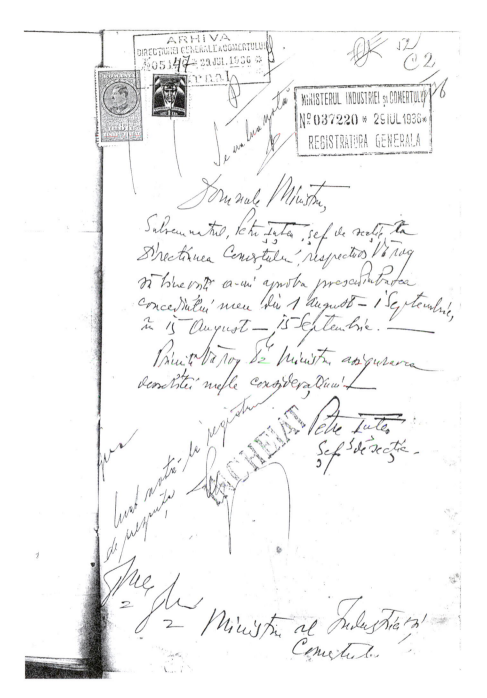

9 In a letter to the Minister of Trade and Industry Ţuţea asks for his one-month leave to be granted two weeks earlier than initially requested (1936)

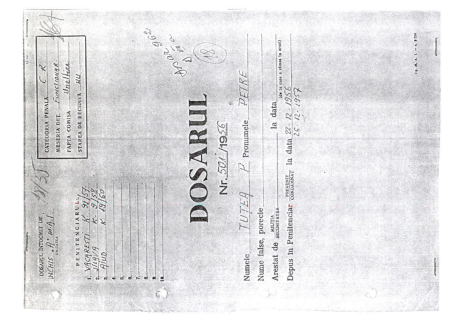

10   Personal file: Petre Ţuţea in the top security prison, Bucharest (1957)

11   Page of Țuțea's handwriting in the late 1980s, showing the effects of intention tremor acquired in prison

1 iunie 1991. La spitalul „Christiana" Petre Țuțea levitează între viață și moarte. Este unul dintre acei mai-mult-ca-oameni (Noica, Steinhardt, Anton Dumitriu, Nichita) de care m-am apropiat întotdeauna timorată fie și cu gândul numai. La insistențele domnului Gabriel Gheorghe îndrăznesc să-l tulbur în singurătatea desprinderii sale de lume. Timp de 13 ani, cât Magistrul a stat la închisoare, o mare parte a manuscriselor sale au fost ascunse acasă la Gabriel Gheorghe. Câțiva ani, cei doi au stat împreună la pușcărie. Acum, în libertate, sunt nedespărțiți.

Bărbatul falnic care fusese Petre Țuțea este acum o făptură transparentă din care spiritul s-a zburătăcit și mai revine arar, ca printr-un miracol. Este o zi de vară astăzi, când am norocul să asist la unul din aceste miracole. Tocmai am reușit să public în ziarul la care lucrez, câteva din scrierile lui Petre Țuțea. Aflând că opera sa vede lumina tiparului și că valoarea sa este recunoscută (era în 1991) Petre Țuțea se deșteaptă parcă din somn și ne vorbește. Gabriel Gheorghe îmi sugerează să deschid reportofonul. Pe bandă vor rămâne imortalizate sunetele ce vin dinspre minitelevizorul care îi ține de urât bolnavului, foșnetul copacilor, ploaia de afară și grindina de mărgăritare cu care Petre Țuțea ne înrourează sufletul pentru ultima oară. Iată acea parte a convorbirii care a rămas înregistrată pe bandă:

„Poporul român este una din minunile lui Dumnezeu"

P.Ț.: Filosofia nuanțelor este un joc dominant psihologic.
G.H.: Pictorii încearcă și ei să demonstreze asta.

38

P.Ț: Nu e un joc logic ci psihologic. A apărut ceva?
G.G.: „Filosofia nuanțelor" v-a apărut în întregime. În patru numere, câte o pagină tipărită cu caracter mic.
P.Ț.: Păi, e o broșură!
G.G.: Mi-ați zis că v-au plătit bine.
P.Ț.: 5.000 de tot. Știu și eu cât face?
G.H.: Ați dori să transmiteți ceva cititorilor dumneavoastră?
P.Ț.: Mă cheamă Petre Țuțea. Omagiile mele pentru interesul arătat personalității mele.
G.H.: Un interes cam târziu... Alți oameni importanți de cultură n-au rezistat presiunilor și au plecat în alte țări. Dumneavoastră de ce n-ați plecat?
P.Ț.: N-am plecat pentru că sunt român.

G.G.: Un om cu adevărat mare nu-și părăsește niciodată țara. Nici Noica n-a plecat deși a fost de mai multe ori în străinătate. Nici Anton Dumitriu n-a plecat deși ar fi avut destule posibilități s-o facă.
P.Ț. Și eu am fost în străinătate și n-am rămas. Puteam să rămân.
G.G.: Mi-ați spus odată că v-ați întâlnit cu Pătrășcanu după 23 august și l-ați invitat la dumneavoastră acasă când stăteați în Știrbei Vodă 164. V-a propus să mergeți alături de ei, de comuniști. Vă amintiți ce i-ați răspuns?
P.Ț.: Da, așa i-am spus: Dumneavoastră intrați slugoi la ruși pentru salvarea neamului iar noi murim pentru panașul lui. Vorba lui Clemenceau: „cine până la vârsta de 30 de ani nu e «progresist», adică de stânga, n-are inimă, dar

dacă peste 30 de ani nu e conservator, e cretin. (Prin fereastra întredeschisă se vede ruperea de

vocations. The emphasis on the importance of reason is especially important when considering a thinker whose critique of conventional intellectual method can appear to support irrationalism. For Țuțea 'the ontic' is 'given', and also 'preliminary to the logical'.[10] In principle, he rejects any schematic split between ontology and epistemology, although for methodological reasons he uses these two terms. 'Knowledge' ('wisdom') is always dependent on 'being' and both are givens.

The titles of the five volumes of Țuțea's *Christian Anthropology* trace his own spiritual and epistemological journey. Starting as an enquirer, seeking to resolve the problems of philosophy and science in order to make sense of the world, Țuțea then comes to distinguish between divine mysteries (which, being uncreated, cannot be exhausted or fully explained without reference to God as *causa prima*) and human problems (which can be elucidated by rational enquiry). To solve human problems the enquirer employs reason and tries a variety of approaches: logical systems, cultural styles, scientific disciplines. Secular philosophy, art, and science employ human reason, which is a gift from God, but as such cannot lead to God. The 'ontic triangle' God–humanity–nature is incomplete without the 'epistemological triangle' God–freedom–immortality.[11] Both these triangles characterise the human being as a discrete whole defined by the relationship between creature, creation, and Creator. Logical systems presuppose (but exist separately in parallel with) 'ontic wholes', which belong to the divine and are not reducible to the level of human reason. Cultural and aesthetic styles are similarly not absolutely autonomous.

Exactitude and Precision

Țuțea distinguishes between divine exactitude and human precision. Individuals become at best more and more precise within their given limitations in the created world. Only God is exact in His transcendence. Human precision cannot attain to the divine exactitude, which is received as mystery. This mystery is revealed gradually and (in human terms) incompletely through grace, which always transcends human reason.

Between the divine and the human is a dimension of silence which, for the faithful person, waiting upon God's Word in prayer, can bear 'much fruit' (John 15:5). By contrast the cosmic silence (Țuțea also uses the term 'opaqueness') of the materialist and atheist mind leads to fear, decay, and annihilation. For, 'if anyone does not abide in Me, he is cast out as a branch and is withered' (John 15:6). Divine silence leads to

---

10   PROBLEMS, p. 50.
11   The elements of Țuțea's 'epistemological triangle' are taken from Kant's preface to his *Kritik der praktischen Vernunft* (Riga: Johann Friedric Hartknoch, 1788). There is a Romanian trans. of this edn of the *Critique of Practical Reason*, used and annotated by Țuțea (now in my personal archive). He knew by heart the German text of Kant's preface. See Immanuel Kant, *Critica rațiunii practice*, trans. Cristian Amzăr and Raul Vișan, with two introductions by C. Rădulescu-Motru and Nae Ionescu (Bucharest: Editura Institutului Social Român, no date), p. 5. See also section on 'Mystical Triangles' in this chapter.

revelation, which in human terms takes the form of religious dogmas. These, unlike philosophical problems, logical systems, cultural styles, and scientific disciplines, open into the realm of divine certainty and exactitude. God is always exact in His unknowable essence.

'Exactitude, which should not be confused with precision', belongs to the transcendent nature of dogmas 'where language does not interpose itself disturbingly between subject and object. Mystical evidence is beyond reason and intuition.'[12] Divine love is the perfect exactitude of the omniscient, omnipotent Creator, which inexhaustibly completes and subsumes the precision of the illuminated mind of the creature. Being made in the image and likeness of God, human beings are thus capable of enlightenment by the original light of the Creator Himself.

Țuțea also distinguishes between *simțul comun* ('common sense') and *bunul simț* ('good sense'). The latter 'alone is capable' of bringing persons 'in touch with revealed truth',[13] which leads to enlightenment. As Țuțea writes in *Bios*, one of the essays contained in *Teatrul Seminar*, although enlightenment comes through divine intervention, the mystics nevertheless 'decide their position in the world', because they thirst for the exactness of God even within the mere precision of temporal existence; while human decision alone cannot determine reality, and 'human beings of themselves cannot rise above their limited perspective, just as they cannot rise above their own shadow', yet even under these conditions, truth can be mediated through the mystic's thirst for the Absolute.[14] Moreover, human beings can discern the lack of realism in their decisions, even if their forms of thought and feeling cannot embrace reality as a whole. The mystic is 'awakened', through enlightenment, abandoning himself to the will of God and discovering himself in the embrace of God. The image and likeness of God in which humanity is originally created are restored in the arms of the Incarnate Logos to the very glory of God. In human experience this includes knowledge of divine Judgement: mystics can reflect the sinless and eternal glory of the world to come by being, so to speak, transparent to God's redemptive love.

This notion of awakening enabled Țuțea not just to assert abstract theological principles, but to articulate his faith as one who combined scholarly training with a deep personal experience of Christ, which was tested under exceptional circumstances. His view does not deny the creative element of secular scientific, artistic, and philosophical inspiration. He stresses that ultimately these are part of divine revelation, simply the fruit of talents which are in themselves God-given. In Christ 'are hidden all the treasures of wisdom and knowledge' (Col. 2:3).

Scientific discoveries may in theory lead to complete knowledge of this world, but they can never lead to knowledge of God, which is only accessible to a dimension of the human spirit beyond the striving intellect. For Țuțea the supreme exemplar of the scientist who understands the rôle of inspiration in scientific discovery is Newton,

---

12   THEATRE, p. 379.
13   THEATRE, p. 108.
14   THEATRE, p. 108.

whose description of the physical universe draws 'on the discovery of order and not on its violation'.[15] Authentic knowledge is given freely by grace and, as an experience of God, shows that human beings are members of His Kingdom.

Mystery versus System – Țuțea's Approach to the Real

Inherent in Țuțea is the tension and dynamic between, on the one hand, affirmation of the Real as essentially unknowable and, on the other, affirmation of the Real as wholly revealed in Jesus Christ. He does not apply the terms apophatic or cataphatic to this, but where he talks about *unio mystica* and ecstasy, it may be helpful to use the negative and the positive ways. Perhaps his choice of language stresses not so much the process of understanding actual experience of God as the mystery of understanding to which it leads.

The Real as Essentially Unknowable

Țuțea's description of Christian dogma as 'revealed mystery'[16] is paradoxical: how can something 'revealed' be 'mystery'? He identifies a number of steps in the apophatic revelation of mysteries. Although the Word of God is fully revealed in the mystery of the Incarnation, there are many things which are not yet understood about the incarnate Christ. Dogma cannot be understood through philosophical enquiry and discursive intellectual thinking – it needs to be experienced through total surrender to the divine mystery. We are constrained to speak of divine mystery – and indeed about many of the world's secrets such as subatomic particles – in symbol, image, analogy, and an infinitely nuanced medium of signs.[17]

Țuțea describes the attempt to comprehend ontic wholes through logic as inadequate. Logic can only achieve, so to speak, asymptotic approaches to the Real. The supreme ontic whole (the Real, God) is logically unknowable. Only at the level of revelation and dogma can human beings have knowledge of ontic wholes, which are 'whole' by being participant in God, the uncreated source of all creation. Like

---

15 PROJECT, p. 138. Cf. SOPHISTRY, p. 172: 'There is no such thing as invention, but only inspired discovery, the elect show us.' Țuțea stressed that Newton in a literal sense 'dis-covered' what was already given. In the General Scholium written for the conclusion of the third book of his masterpiece, *Philosophiae Naturalis Principia Mathematica*, 2nd edn, 1713, Newton had said unequivocally that he feigned no hypotheses: *Hypotheses non fingo*. See also THEATRE, p. 204.

16 INTERVIEW, p. 3. Țuțea paraphrases Lalande's definition of Christian 'mystery' as 'revealed dogma': '*Mystère. Dans la théologie chrétienne, dogmes révélés que le fidèle doit croire, mais qu'il ne peut comprendre.*' See André Lalande, *Vocabulaire technique et critique de la philosophie*, 6th edn, 2 vols (Paris: Presses Universitaires de France, 1988), I, p. 661.

17 Cf. Kallistos Ware, 'The Debate about Palamism', *Eastern Churches Review*, 9:1–2, 1977, p. 53. See also ON ART, notes 14 and 18, pp. 15–16.

Platonic eternal archetypes, ontic wholes are reflected by human consciousness. However, knowledge of them implies more than a static mirroring of the eternal archetype in the mind of the contemplator. In Țuțea's view, human 'reflection is determined'.[18] In other words, Platonic reflection is limited by the relationship between created subjects and the ideal object of their knowledge. Knowledge of ontic wholes is real and dynamic, uniting the subject's human mind with the divine object of knowledge. This leads to an awareness of human createdness and implies experience of God as Creator. Only by divine inspiration (working through scientific, philosophical, and artistic vocation as well as through religious 'virtues') can the human mind 'discover' the real world, the Kingdom of God.

Țuțea insists that Christian realism preserves 'the mystery of vocation, inspiration, and revelation, that is, the active presence of Divinity in all acts of knowledge'.[19] Formulation of a whole or *the* ontic whole requires paradoxical statements – that is, affirmations which not only stand in opposition to each other but which are also true. Conceptually elaborated systems can only reflect ontic wholes in the human mind, they can never contain the fullness of revelation.

Țuțea's view of ontic wholes resembles the apophatic approach of the Cappadocian Fathers. Maximus the Confessor and Gregory Palamas also emphasise the limitations of human discursive thought and language, and the incomprehensibility of God, while striving to give coherent expression to their theological convictions.[20] *Apophasis* or *via negativa* denotes continuous progress in mystical knowledge entailing, at the logical level, contradictory and negative statements about God. Implicit in Țuțea's thinking is the distinction between *dianoia* (discursive reason; medieval Western *ratio*), and *nous* (spiritual understanding; Latin Western *intellectus*). This distinction is clarified by Kallistos Ware:

> The *ratio* or *dianoia* operates by means of dissection and analysis; it derives its information from objects external to itself, and by a process of abstraction from these objects it formulates certain general ideas or concepts. The *nous* or spiritual intellect, on the other hand, knows things through knowing their inner *logoi*, that is, through participating in the divine energies which bring all things into existence and maintain them in being. Thus the spiritual intellect operates through direct experience and intuition, not through abstract concepts and discursive reasoning; it does not derive knowledge from matter which is external to itself, but receives it through an inward union with the divine Logos himself.[21]

---

18   SYSTEMS, p. 18.
19   SYSTEMS, p. 18.
20   It is interesting to explore the link between Țuțea's theology of the ontic whole and Maximus the Confessor's 'essentially dynamic doctrine of salvation'. According to Maximus, the ultimate aim of the divine plan is human deification: 'the whole people might participate in the whole God' (*theos holos holis metekhomenos*). See John Meyendorff, *Christ in Eastern Christian Thought* (Crestwood, NY: St Vladimir's Seminary Press, 1975), p. 143.
21   Ware, 'The Debate about Palamism', p. 50.

Țuțea uses *dianoia* to mean 'accomplished reason'.[22] However, as has been indicated, intuition and reason cannot lead to knowledge of the Real. Only revelation opens up the world of revealed mysteries, or dogmas. Supposedly autonomous humanity, in captivity to the senses, 'has at its disposal method, contemplation, and speculation; but the Lord has revelation at His disposal'.[23] In the world of dogmas the Real – that is, God – is experienced through faith, not discursive reason.

The Concept of 'The Whole'

According to Țuțea the significance of history cannot be grasped within the spatial and temporal limits of history itself, but only in the light of eternal truth. He regarded rational ('normative') human constructs as 'unstable' and subject to the process of becoming.[24] He rejected the use of logical systems in theological argument as merely parallel to 'ontic', 'real' wholes. He saw information acquired 'without the fear of the Lord' as relative, having no bearing on the theophanic, theandric and Trinitarian object of theology, or on Christian wisdom:[25]

> We are in a world beset by problems, and endless questions are raised by need, wonder, curiosity, and ever-deceiving causality. In this world we can describe, by simplification, two fundamental human types: the believer, who by personal experience accepts the impossible in the very depths of his soul, and the seeker, the inquiring type who questions himself and others, muddying the waters of both the inner and the outer world, increasingly absorbed in endless experimentation, under the dialectical sign of non-fulfilment.[26]

Țuțea frequently accuses secular epistemology of 'non-fulfilment', 'failure' or 'going astray'. This is what the Fathers of the *Philokalia* meant by ἁμαρτία, 'failure to achieve the purpose for which one is created', that is to say, sin 'viewed not primarily in juridical terms, as the transgression of a moral code, but rather in an existential perspective, as the failure to be one's real self. Sin as a lack of true humanness', brought about by loss of relationship with God.[27]

In contrast to mystical knowledge, which is theocentric and relational, Țuțea sees *systematic knowledge* (through philosophy, science, art, and techniques of existence such as psychoanalysis) as anthropocentric, non-relational, and merely acquired. It is the labour of humanity banished from paradise. Ignoring God through reliance upon systems, people stray ever further from the divine, arrogating to themselves

---

22   REFLECTIONS, I, p. 105.
23   DOGMAS, p. 104.
24   Țuțea, 'Eu sunt un om neîmplinit', p. 1.
25   THEATRE, p. 342.
26   PROBLEMS, p. 340.
27   Kallistos Ware, 'The Understanding of Salvation in the Orthodox Tradition', in *For Us and Our Salvation: Seven Perspectives on Christian Soteriology*, ed. Rienk Lanooy (Utrecht-Leiden: Interuniversitair Instituut voor Missiologie en Oecumenica, 1994), p. 109.

the authority of the Creator. This is the attitude of the demiurge, which leads to metaphysical anxiety, fear of death, lack of hope, and nihilism.

The Real (always equated by Ţuţea with God) is not composed of the sum of different systems, as logic assumes it to be. The Real is the source of all-embracing unity. Creation is *ab origine* a sacred ontic whole. Yet that wholeness has been shattered by original sin. Human experience of ultimate wholeness and unity in this fallen world is at best a union juxtaposing the world's various sacred and desacralised elements. God's continual disclosure of His transfiguring glory grants even in this present age signs of the Kingdom in which His original intention is restored and brought to fulfilment.

Ţuţea questions the way in which different scientific disciplines establish the parameters within which they try to find answers about reality as a whole:

Systematic exposition cannot include the inexpressible, but nevertheless human beings have constructed systems in which useful forms of thought can be found. Man's daring attempt to comprehend everything is noble and defines the human spirit which seeks to construct the universe... If we are not to wear the mask of Sisyphus,[28] we must avoid two assumptions: autonomous construction and infinite progress, whose usefulness has nothing in common with truth, just as nature too has nothing in common with it.[29]

He doubts whether the concept of 'the whole' plays a significant, if indeed any, rôle in the human sciences. Personal wholeness is to be found in the individual's relationship with God. It is the Incarnation that enables humanity to participate in the whole, the totality that is God entering into finite human experience, bringing finite humanity into the totality. Philosophy does not lead to salvation. However, for Ţuţea, systematic philosophy is a mental tool for investigating the world of time and space, and guiding the conduct of human relations. A 'Real system' is inconceivable, Ţuţea constantly argues. The Real by definition transcends autonomous human reason, which fumbles between 'natural law' and empirical observation. Entirely deductive systems of propositions about the Real reduce it to the level of logic, says Ţuţea, citing Hegelian pantheism as an example:

Wholes, their parts, and the relationships between them escape the cognitive capacity of isolated human beings. Analysis of wholes and synthesis of the resulting parts does not lead to the Real, only to appearances. Analysis and synthesis, like evolution, are working hypotheses of only relative use. The benefits of investigating life and the world do not remove the human being from the 'horizon of mystery' (Blaga). No one has so far discovered the real unity between self and non-self. Where the unity of self and non-self is assumed we find ourselves in 'the world of fictions' (Vaihinger).[30]

---

28   The concept of mask is fundamental to Ţuţea's understanding of humanity and will be explored in detail in Chapter 9.
29   REFLECTIONS, II, pp. 285–6.
30   SYSTEMS, pp. 82–3. Hans Vaihinger (1852–1933), German Professor of Philosophy at Halle University, author of *Die Philosophie des Als Ob* (1911). This study on Kant's

This reductionist assumption (that is, of the unity of self and non-self) leads, in the field of experimental psychology, to 'psychologism'. Since 'the soul and its actions are transcendent in essence, they can be known only by revelation'.[31] Thus psychology, assuming the psyche to be complete in itself, is incapable of explaining the object of its research. Țuțea emphasises that the psyche does not exist as a whole, since it is conceived and defined according to its manifestations from moment to moment, in experimental psychology. As unifying syntheses, 'psychological laws or rather constants are *a posteriori*' and cannot define the soul as a created whole.[32]

The psyche is definable only in relation to the Real. A human being is ultimately and mysteriously interrelated with the Creator and the rest of creation. Țuțea finds secular holistic philosophy wanting, in relation both to the human self and to the world outside the self. He speaks of 'the incapacity of the human spirit, with its three faculties of imagination, intellect, and intuition, to arrive at structures which express wholes'; for him structuralist thought is merely formal: 'there can be no question of reconstructing a divided whole from its parts, because the concepts resulting from inquiry themselves have a formal character', that is to say, they are themselves products of synthesis and juxtaposition.[33] Soul and body are 'real', inaccessible to any non-mystical form of psychotherapy. In the end the true therapist is 'the whole spiritual man',[34] Jesus Christ.

Mystical Triangles

Fundamental constructs of Țuțea's methodology are his ontic and epistemological 'triangles'. For him there is no ultimate separation between the being of God as divinely revealed and theological interpretation of God's redemptive work. Epistemology cannot ultimately be separated from ontology. Individuals become real human persons insofar as they grow in mystical knowledge[35] of the all-embracing Holy One. He affirms 'the Christian triangle: God is, the two worlds are, the human being is' (*triunghiul creștin: Dumnezeu este, cele două lumi sunt, omul este*).[36]

Let us take a closer look, then, at Țuțea's 'mystical triangles'. His *Christian Anthropology* addresses the inter-relationship of nature, human identity, and the divine. Hence the 'ontic triangle' of God, humanity, nature (or God–the human

---

theory of fictions is quoted by Țuțea. See also note 43 in this chapter. For Blaga, see Chapter 2, note 116.

31 SYSTEMS, p. 202.
32 SYSTEMS, p. 82.
33 SYSTEMS, p. 82.
34 SYSTEMS, p. 186.
35 See PROBLEMS, p. 26.
36 PROBLEMS, p. 37. Cf. SYSTEMS, p. 19. For Țuțea's discussion of 'the two worlds', with specific reference to 2 Cor. 4:18, see PROBLEMS, p. 305. Cf. ON ART, note 17, p. 16. But elsewhere he would strongly reject human 'perspectivism' – that is, distancing from God through an interpretative point of view, however inspired. See also note 22 in the following chapter.

being–the world) to which he so frequently refers.[37] He contrasts false knowledge, the sterile outcome of chance and inquiry 'overwhelmed by appearances and unjustifiable extrapolation'[38] from the profane to the transcendent, with true knowledge, the fruit either of revelation or of inspiration.

Within the ontic triangle he speaks of spiritual freedom and interaction. Remove God from the equation, however, and sacred and profane become indistinguishable. The world according to the findings of secular enquiry, or matter regarded as primordial and non-derivative (as in Marx), are 'appearances coming out of nowhere within fictitious space'.[39] Metaphysical principles concerning the relationship of human beings with the Divinity, the cosmos, society, and other human beings are, in Ţuţea's view, illegitimate, 'all too human' speculations, particularly when logic is applied to the realm of mystery. Christian anthropology differs from other forms of anthropology in recognising that humanity and nature are inconceivable without God:

> The heteronomous nature of Christian dogma shows us the meaning of life and real freedom, as suprahistoric forms. Christian anthropology has as its object the real human being. Other anthropologies show us the historical forms of the apparent human being... a number in an endless series without purpose and subject to the law of entropy.[40]

Theological study of the human person as an independent entity is a recent phenomenon. Ţuţea contrasts secular Christian anthropology with Patristic Christology, in which Christ represents the union of divine and human nature. Like his Patristic predecessors Ţuţea did not make an absolute distinction between anthropology and Christology. Indeed, he was critical of purely sociological approaches such as that in Werner Sombart's *Vom Menschen*.[41] He lists these anthropologies of 'the apparent human being' according to Sombart's categories :

- *anthropology as a natural science*
- *ethno-historical anthropology*
- *philosophical anthropology*
- *aesthetic anthropology*
- *anthropology as science of the spirit*
- *technical anthropology*
- *typological anthropology*.[42]

---

37   For *triunghiul Dumnezeu–om–natură*, see PROBLEMS, p. 308. For *triunghiul Dumnezeu–om–lume*, see PROBLEMS, p. 328.
38   PROBLEMS, p. 313.
39   PROBLEMS, p. 313.
40   PROBLEMS, pp. 313–14.
41   See Werner Sombart, *Vom Menschen. Versuch einer geisteswissenschaftlichen Anthropologie*, 2nd edn (Berlin: Duncker & Humblot, 1956; 1st edn 1938).
42   PROBLEMS, p. 314. See also PROBLEMS, pp. 260–313.

All these anthropologies may, in Țuțea's view, be useful at a functional level, but none of them helps human beings to understand the real 'point' of humanity. He criticises secular anthropologies as dealing purely with externals. For atheist anthropologists the only way to understand this world is through the senses. True anthropology, on the other hand, as I have shown in the previous chapter, starts with the assumption that the human person is made in the image and likeness of God. It interprets human life in terms of 'suprahistory', that is, history redeemed through God's loving purpose in the Incarnation.

Having established that humanity is not self-sufficient, Țuțea identifies a second (Kantian) triangle, that of God, immortality, and freedom. Non-Christian anthropologies see the human being in purely historical, sociological, and biological terms. Lacking any conception of the transcendent, they deprive humanity of its distinctive destiny – eternal life. Only at the level of 'suprahistory' can a human individual be a whole, having access through Christ to immortality and freedom.

The terms used to describe the 'epistemological triangle' (God, immortality, freedom) may have come from Kant, yet the historical conditions under which Țuțea lived and wrote gave them an incisive reality: they did not simply remain *als ob* ('as if'),[43] in the realm of postulates. The 'epistemological triangle' cannot be entirely separated from the 'ontic'. Rather they exist in symbiotic relationship: 'Revelation, the two worlds, immortality, freedom, ultimate finality, real freedom, and salvation have their place within the triangle God–the world–the human being. The awakening principle of these *realia* is God, as unique truth'.[44]

Revelation and Inspiration

Țuțea used precise theological formulations in order to avoid anthropomorphic ideas of God. Generally speaking, in his view there are two kinds of work which God initiates and performs in human history: *revelation*, as 'the active presence of divinity'; and *inspiration*, as a 'divine breathing' and 'a favour' granted by God and mediated through the Holy Spirit[45] to people who receive God's truth under divine

---

43   In the Kantian sense, 'the expression, "I believe in God", means simply that "I act *as if* a God really existed... In this sense the atheist who acts morally also believes practically in God and immortality, since he acts *as if* God and immortality existed': Hans Vaihinger, *The Philosophy of 'As if', A System of the Theoretical, Practical and Religious Fictions of Mankind*, 6th edn, trans. C.K. Ogden (London: Kegan Paul, 1924), pp. 315–17.

44   '*În triunghiul Dumnezeu, lumea și omul au sediul: revelația, adevărul, cele două lumi, nemurirea, finalitatea reală și mântuirea. Principiul trezitor al acestor realia este Dumnezeu, ca adevăr unic*': PROBLEMS, p. 318. *Principiul trezitor* ('the awakening principle'), found in Țuțea's manuscript, is erroneously transcribed as *principalul trezitor* (literally, 'the principal awaker') in the printed edition.

45   PROBLEMS, p. 309. Țuțea follows the distinction made between inspiration and revelation by the Romanian Greek-Catholic Archbishop Traian Crișan (1918–90), former Secretary to the Vatican Commission for Beatification. Crișan's pamphlet *Despre Inspirația Biblică* (*On Biblical Inspiration*), from which Țuțea frequently quotes, was published independently and circulated in dissident circles before 1989.

impulse. He postulates an epistemological polarity between, on the one hand, the transparency of the created human mind to the uncreated light of God in those who are 'divinely inspired' and, on the other, the opacity of the created world to the 'uninspired' enquiry of the fallen human mind. Without divine intervention the natural light of reason cannot of itself heal 'the psychological cripple',[46] which is Ţuţea's description of fallen man reduced to himself and to the natural order by his separation from God. He maintains a Pauline distinction between the visible and the invisible in creation (2 Cor. 4:18). The unseen world may be approximately described but not precisely interpreted, although Paul himself speaks of a hierarchy of 'rulers of the darkness of this world' (Eph. 6:12). In Ţuţea's view, the rational knowledge of the enquiring mind is always incomplete, limited to the 'seen', in contrast to the integral knowledge of the 'human being enwrapped in mystery and ruled by faith'.[47]

Supernatural revelation is mediated to the faithful by means of Scripture and in the Eucharist, or to those 'chosen by God to be inspired' through the created order. Implicit in Ţuţea's understanding of the divine light is the distinction drawn by Gregory Palamas between the uncreated divine essence and the uncreated divine energies. Divine revelation is like a light piercing and dispersing the 'opaqueness' of the fallen world and of the mind closed to God in consequence of original sin. Not only the human mind, but the whole created universe has become 'opaque' and 'silent'. Only when inspired by the Holy Spirit do Christians become transparent and resonant, able to perceive the divine light and hear the Word of God.

Living close to Christ and witnessing His miracles, the disciples saw God and their own humanity as in a perfecting mirror. With the revelation of divine light in the Transfiguration,[48] that mirror became a window onto 'the Real'. The Transfiguration is that moment in historical time when divine revelation becomes human realisation. Ţuţea uses Heinrich Rickert's word *übergeschichtlich*[49] to convey the unity of 'supra-historic nature' and 'historic nature' in Christ. According to Ţuţea, 'the

---

46   THEATRE, p. 393.

47   THEATRE, p. 352.

48   It is remarkable in an *oeuvre* so permeated by the theology of deification that Ţuţea, who often speaks significantly of divine enlightenment or illumination, seems to make no explicit reference to the Transfiguration. Perhaps this is in line with the stylistic allusiveness of his thought, which for instance almost never refers directly to the Trinity in the proper sense (yet is deeply Trinitarian) or to Orthodoxy (although it is quintessentially Orthodox).

49   PROBLEMS, p. 264. The notion of supra-history (*Übergeschichte*) is employed by Heinrich Rickert (1863–1936), Professor of Philosophy at Freiburg and Heidelberg, whose neo-Kantian theory of concept formation in the sciences is described in his *Die Gegenstand der Erkenntnis*, 6th edn (Tübingen: Mohr, 1928; 1st edn 1892) and in his *Die Grenzen der naturwissenschaftlichen Begriffsbildung: Eine logische Einleitung in die historischen Wissenschaften*, 4th edn (Tübingen: Mohr, 1921; 1st edn 1902). See also Heinrich Rickert *Science and History: A Critique of Positivist Epistemology*, trans. George Reisman, ed. Arthur Goddard (London: D. Van Nostrand, 1962). Cf. THEATRE, p. 393.

supra-historical is sacred punctuation of time and space, not the result of enquiring humanity's tendency to acquire knowledge and value'.[50]

What Ţuţea calls 'the inspired human mind' is like a 'prism' breaking up the mystery of uncreated 'light of divine revelation'[51] into an intelligible spectrum of created realities which provide evidence of God and make 'known unto us the mystery of his will' (Eph. 1:9–10). For Ţuţea, then, the perception of God is not something natural to human beings. God chooses to make Himself known. Similarly, since the Fall, immortality and freedom are no longer integral to human nature. They can be received only as gifts from God. Although they are objects of the perennial human quest, for Ţuţea this quest is doomed to fail unless it is pursued within the order of Christian revelation.

Non-Christian anthropology, which understands humanity in exclusively human terms, can lead, in Ţuţea's understanding, only to death. Only when a person is given some apprehension of transcendence can they begin to conceive of any life beyond the grave. A corollary of this understanding of eternal life is judgement before the throne of Almighty God. For immortality is a gift that brings responsibilities; it requires dedicated fulfilment of the human vocation to be stewards of creation. Thus, in order to understand properly Ţuţea's Christian anthropology we need also to consider the nature and context of his theology.

Mystical Knowledge

Ţuţea's theology was worked out against the materialistic culture of Communism. He presents Christian faith as belief in a God whose power and initiative remain effective, although denied by Soviet ideology. He attempts to reassert the recognition of God as the source of life and knowledge and, in so doing, to emphasise the importance of human response to God's initiative. In opposing Marxist ideology, he himself can at times seem narrowly dogmatic. His theology must be understood not simply as a reaction to atheism and dialectical materialism, but as a way of life. He did not just release people from ideology but confronted Communist ideology on his terms, according to human beings' real significance and dignity. To the 'obligatory' Communist view, Ţuţea opposed St Paul's concept of 'the new man, created according to God, in true righteousness and holiness' (Eph. 4:24).

At the same time, Ţuţea was always suspicious of 'scientific' scholastic theology that claimed to be able to prove systematically the doctrines of Christian faith. For him religion is primarily a matter of experience, not of assent to an abstract system. Proof of God is not the outcome of an argument, nor a syllogistic formula, but a certainty communicated through direct personal encounter.

In the realm of theology, therefore, Ţuţea gives priority to mystical knowledge expressed through paradox and antinomy. In this way the limitations of the reasoning brain are transcended. Syllogisms and systematic argument grant no access to

---

50   PROBLEMS, p. 297.
51   STYLES, II, p. 135. Cf. PROBLEMS, p. 313.

transcendent truth, whereas paradox can help human reason to break through the constraints of dialectic. Freedom is gained when the mind goes beyond what it understands:

> The Orthodox and Catholic Churches, despite their ecclesiastical authority, do not impound the free will of believers. The believer's choice to say either 'Yes' or 'No' carries a risk. There are numerous pairs of opposites – sacred and satanic, good and evil, truth and error, right and wrong, just and unjust, order and anarchy, faith and unbelief etc. – between which the Christian is free to choose, although the positive realm of existence (i.e. the truth of faith) signifies redemption, and the opposite means damnation. In essence, the freedom of the Christian believer is like a rope by which one may descend into darkness. But a believer's decisions have neither a conventional character since 'strait is the way that leads to Salvation', nor a dialectic character, i.e. as unities of contraries resolvable through Hegelian triads. Their character is dogmatic. For the unbeliever, it is a paradox to consider dogma – this 'revealed mystery' – as a form of real freedom, because in this world it takes the form of hope, and [only] in the world above of real freedom ...
>
> Understood dialectically, 'Yes or No' does not conform with Christian dogma, which is neither discursive nor critical. The dialectical, critical, conventional spirit places the seeker between contraries: when he does not go astray, he moves conveniently or usefully, but not truly. The notion of alternatives does not work in Christianity, since it is foreign to its spirit ... One cannot construct a human being out of contraries and argument, by means of 'Yes or No'. In the world of dogma, the Real (God) is experienced and thus received non-discursively through faith.[52]

So, it begins to become clear that Christian discipleship depends upon a positive response to the invitation of God, who calls us into a relationship with Him that is our eternal salvation. Philosophy may offer a dialectic in which there is freedom to choose between 'yes' and 'no', whereas Christian faith affirms 'yes', 'amen', the fulfilment of God's promises in Christ (II Cor. 1:18–20). Christian freedom thus paradoxically (as rational argument would see it) only comes through free submission of the human will to that of God. Holding on to the option 'yes' or 'no' ultimately brings not freedom, but imprisonment in the material world. Thus, while Țuțea's life raises the key question of how to survive morally under Communism, his mystical theology addresses a set of fundamental questions in dogmatic theology: how do we understand religious truth? What kind of truth is religious truth? What kind of proof or verification do we require from an experience of God?

Theology as Divine Revelation

From an anthropological point of view theology has various functions which will be explored in Chapter 10, when I look at Țuțea's important concept of nuance. It is sufficient at this point to say that in the context of his life and work theology not only

---

52   DOGMAS, pp. 130–33.

provided an experiential dimension in the sphere of his thinking about fundamental reality, but also helped a prophetic dissenting voice to articulate its message within a totalitarian society. In consequence it also played an exorcising and redemptive rôle. How did Ţuţea himself understand the nature of theology? He opens his five-volume *Christian Anthropology* with a brief but significant definition: 'Theology is knowledge of the Real, of divinity manifest in theophany, theandry, and trinity, transmitted through sacred history and sacred tradition.'[53]

His terms 'theophany', 'theandry', and 'trinity' have startling implications. Where he says 'theophany' he is referring to the first person of the Trinity, God the Father. Theandry refers to the second person, the Incarnate Christ. One would then expect a reference to the Holy Spirit, the third person of the Trinity, in some equivalent to the allusive terms used for the Father and the Son. However, what he gives is the very word 'trinity'. This is obviously deliberate and needs investigation. Ţuţea never himself directly elucidates this issue.

A good starting point is the Nicene-Constantinopolitan Creed, which definitively sets out the Orthodox understanding of Trinity as Father, Son, and Holy Spirit. This begins with declaratory affirmations of faith – in one God, the Father Almighty, and in the Son – doctrinal statements leading on to the narrative of Jesus Christ's life and proclamation of the Kingdom of God. And then the Holy Spirit: doctrinal definition (as the Lord, the giver of life) leads directly to *koinonia*, in a sense an equivalent of the Christological narrative, but proclamatory and embracing past and future – the Holy Spirit is the sustaining, guiding, informing *dynamis* of the holy Catholic apostolic Church, and inspires the tradition and teaching of the church, which is precisely Trinitarian.

Ţuţea's proclamation of 'trinity' in place of the Holy Spirit is a kind of prophetic slap in the face: Wake up! Don't turn Father–Son–Holy Spirit into a conceptual idol. It is a typically Ţuţean abridgement of ideas, an attempt to safeguard the Triune mystery by pointing to the danger of unconsciously adding Trinitarian Oneness as a fourth hypostasis to Father, Son, and Holy Spirit.[54]

---

53   PROBLEMS, p. 7. See PROBLEMS, p. 52, for Ţuţea's discussion on revealed theology as 'based on the Word of God preserved in Holy Scripture'. Cf. also Lalande, *Vocabulaire*, II, p. 1125. For the discussion of trinity that follows, I am indebted to James Ramsay, the Anglican Chaplain in Bucharest.

54   This is particularly relevant in the context of Jung's advocacy of 'Christian' quaternity rather than Trinity in his 'A Psychological Approach to the Trinity' (1942/1948). That the Blessed Virgin Mary, having completed her earthly life, was in body and soul assumed into heaven was proclaimed as a dogma of the Catholic faith by Pope Pius XII in 1950. Symbolically, this added a fourth, and a feminine principle to what Jung saw as the essentially masculine Trinity, converting it into a quaternity: Andrew Samuels, Bani Shorter, and Fred Plaut, *A Critical Dictionary of Jungian Analysis* (London: Routledge, 1991), pp. 29–30. As a verbal tactic, Ţuţea's concision resembles that which I explored in Chapter 5 when he describes the psyche as the 'real unity' of the 'psychosomatic' human being. Cf. C.G. Jung, *Jung: Selected Writings*, select. and introd. by Anthony Storr (London: Fontana, 1983), p. 321.

As I will show later, Țuțea describes the Trinity as 'a truth on which no one can lay profane hands. Even in prison it cannot be touched'.[55] But what precisely is this 'truth'? What is it that cannot be touched? Let us turn to the Gospel narrative, where Jesus the Word, on the Cross, has exhausted all rational human utterance – 'It is accomplished', 'Father, forgive them...' What happens next? In the synoptic Gospels, he gives a loud cry. In St John's Gospel he bows his head and renders up his spirit. At the point at which all human powers of recognition, conceptualisation, and memorialisation – *anamnesis* itself – have been destroyed, what then is the ultimate gift of the Holy Spirit to humanity? What could not be taken away even in the dereliction of prison? It is this great cry. Simple being, in its naked finitude which relates directly to the Nativity. What do we need from a baby to show there is life? That little cry, which can be heard throughout the house. This is what we hear from the Word on the Cross, the cry of the birth of the new creation.

Here, then, is Trinity, the one thing that 'cannot be touched'. Individual holding of credal truth (in human *anamnesis* of Jesus of Nazareth as the Christ, and all that follows from this) can be broken and destroyed – and this happened to many in the re-education prisons when, proposition by proposition, credal truth was demolished at the level of human reason. What cannot be destroyed is the divine image within the simple givenness of being. This image is permanent, whether a person believes in the existence of God or not. Paradoxically, in prison even those who lost their faith revealed by their sacrifice – their Christ-like cry of dereliction – the sacrificial nature of God fully shown forth in Christ crucified. For although *anamnesis* is quite properly the loving remembrance of God's faithfulness toward humanity, ultimately humanity is sustained by God's constant loving remembrance of each and every human person. Thus, Trinity in Țuțea's sense is knowledge, rather than conceptual acceptance, of the fact that human self-giving – even in the form of heightened spiritual awareness and practice of virtue – is simply in the end the offering of naked dependency, desire, and creaturely finitude.

Țuțea perhaps wants to convey – through that deliberate distortion of the normal Trinitarian formula (a distortion paradoxically affirming trinity as an idea) – the rôle played by grace in ultimate human awareness. This is crucial to dogmatic formulation of the Great Mystery, as Țuțea understands it. It is a question of style. The mystery of the proclamation Father, Son, and Holy Spirit itself requires the defeat of the logic that sustains the proclamation.[56] It is as though the sheen of perfection of well articulated theology needs to be shown up for what it is: the gilded picture frame needs to be 'distressed'. The potential glibness of Trinitarian formulae is interrupted by an immediacy of the spirit, breaking through into the human formula with the very term of the dogma that is the divine self-giving. In the end, Țuțea is certainly warning

---

55   DAYS, p. 175.

56   'St John Damascene said "the Son is the image of the Father, and the Spirit is the image
      of the Son". It follows that the third Hypostasis of the Trinity is the only one not having
      His image in another Person. The Holy Spirit, as person, remains unmanifested, hidden,
      concealing Himself in His very appearing': Vladimir Lossky, *The Mystical Theology of
      the Eastern Church* (Cambridge: James Clarke, 1973), p. 160.

us against striving for a 'God's eye view'[57] of the Real. The Real remains ultimately mysterious and transcendent. Mystical knowledge (knowledge of the Real) is acquired through various forms, or, rather, moments of revelation, within which God communicates Himself to humanity and humanity joyfully responds.

Let us now examine in turn each of the persons of the Trinity, as Ţuţea presents them in his definition of theology at the start of the *Christian Anthropology*, and then conclude with his final two concepts of 'sacred history' and sacred tradition.

Theophany as Unmediated Divine Self-Revelation

This is the supreme level (in terms of human knowledge) of the mystery of God's unaccountable self-communication to humanity. Perhaps the revelation to Moses of the 'non-attributive' divine name 'I Am Who I Am' (Exodus 3:13–15) is the formative account of this. It cannot be defined since it is only identifiable with itself.[58] Theophany as a supra-natural phenomenon mediating knowledge of the one transcendent God is inexpressible within the normal rules of language. Ever aware of this mystery, Ţuţea uses substantivisation rather than predication[59] – that is, nouns without verbal predicates. His lists of 'mystical terms'[60] and antinomic pairs of nouns[61] are an attempt to make language function as a 'vehicle of transcendence'.[62] They release 'the tension from pairs of opposites'[63] since, 'soluble or insoluble, contradictions define the historical human being'.[64] Frequently he resorts to exclamations, in an attempt to get beyond language, wanting to attain reflective 'silence'. In his approach to theophany, Ţuţea's emphasis is on the movement from God to humanity. He rejects any natural theology that seeks to prove the existence of God on the basis simply of accepted human concepts.

Theandry as God Incarnate

Ţuţea sees the New Testament as reflecting divine self-revelation through the mystery of Incarnation, *theandric* revelation in the Word made Flesh, divinity encountered in the humanity of Jesus, and confessed as such by historical human beings, like the Apostle Thomas in the words 'My Lord and my God' (John 20:28). Theandry is for Ţuţea the 'act of God who loves humankind, who reveals himself and redeems'.[65]

---

57   See Hilary Putnam's critique of metaphysical realism in *Reason, Truth, and History* (Cambridge: Cambridge University Press, 1981), pp. 49–74.
58   PROBLEMS, p. 52.
59   See 'Language', in PROBLEMS, pp. 328–34. Cf. PROBLEMS, pp. 53–9, 179.
60   PROBLEMS, p. 313.
61   He stresses that 'substantivisation has an aporetic character', PROBLEMS, p. 107. For a 'substantivising' list of terms, see PROBLEMS, pp. 152–3.
62   PROBLEMS, p. 53.
63   PROBLEMS, p. 315.
64   PROBLEMS, p. 169.
65   REFLECTIONS, I, p. 28.

What was Țuțea's own personal experience of Christ? The answer is not simple. He spoke implicitly about it, rather than in terms of illumination or *epiphany* as such. Nevertheless his theology is based on the revelation of Christ as *his* personal Saviour, and in some of his last interviews he mentions this explicitly. Clearly, he himself felt that through more than a decade of imprisonment divine Providence had sustained him. God could be rationally inferred as the agent of Țuțea's miraculous survival. God's Word and Spirit had transformed people who had been subjected to physical torture and psychological annihilation. Something of Christ's *holiness* was revealed to the world through those who had been sanctified by the experience of political prison and martyrdom:

> If anyone had said to me during my thirteen years in prison that I would be on television, I would have laughed. While I was there I expected to die in the normal way: to be taken in the prison rubbish cart and thrown into a common grave. When I escaped from what I escaped, there could be no question of destiny. I have no destiny. God protected me. Destiny has no relevance to me. Events overwhelmed me but did not succeed in destroying me. That led me in my thinking to God who is above the events of my life. And He led me.[66]

Only the presence of the living Christ (the community of prayer, the mutual encouragement of prisoners who communicated through messages tapped on the walls, and the occasional kindly act of a warder) enabled Țuțea to endure imprisonment.

The Trinity as Relational and Actualised Divine Presence

Țuțea's offering of himself as a vehicle of transcendent truth in no way points to a subjective view of the revelation of God as Trinity. His is not a merely individual, therefore relative or subjective, theology. On the contrary, Trinitarian truth is for Țuțea a matter of inter-personal communion, objectified and re-discovered historically within the Church, in Liturgy and Scripture and daily discipleship, as an actualisation of the 'believer's participation in his or her personal redemption'.[67] He eschews the technicalities of Trinitarian debate, rejecting what he calls 'the luxury' of modern theodicies with their 'purely theoretical concerns'. His experiential theology starts where the Trinitarian God of genuine hope opposes the 'non-essential' evils of suffering and injustice. He believes that evil is foreign to created nature, since nothing is in itself evil. At the Baptism of Jesus (Luke 3:21–2), the Trinitarian unity of love is historically made manifest (in his conversations Țuțea referred to Epiphany as 'Trinitarian punctuation of history'). This indestructible divine unity translates into Christian virtues that are human means of overcoming evil and suffering in the contemporary world:

---

66   Petre Țuțea, 'Petre Țuțea', television interviews, in Vartan Arachelian, *Cuvântul care Zidește* (Bucharest: Roza Vânturilor, 1993), pp. 71–2.
67   PROBLEMS, p. 258.

The theologians and historians of the tradition, not looking to an imaginary original purity irreversibly corrupted by sin, admit the existence of evil as a result of original sin, but also affirm the Saviour's Redemption, 'the purifying Baptism of the New Adam' (St Paul) and the participation of the faithful in their own redemption. Within the Trinity God is omnipotent, good and forgiving, since in Christianity evil is not essential but historical.[68]

Țuțea rediscovers tradition at a personal experiential level. The light of the Trinity brings the enjoyment of freedom. Trinitarian relational truth is the paradigm of an ontology of loving communication derived from the very being of God, present both at the Eucharist and in the reading of the Gospel. Inspiring the solidarity of prisoners of conscience, Trinitarian unity broke down the quasi-autistic absence of communication that resulted from political and ideological coercion. It filled the vacuum of atheist relativism and dehumanisation with Christian love:

> Can you imagine what the dogma of the Holy Trinity means for someone in prison? It is a truth on which no one can lay profane hands. Even in prison it cannot be touched. This is the greatness and the freedom of dogma.[69]

In prison Țuțea found the strength to resist attacks on his faith. This strength he believed was God-given. Clearly nothing can ultimately prove the 'authenticity' of his experience, yet something enabled him to remain more inspiringly human than his warders. In all he said and wrote about this period in his life, Țuțea bore witness to the sustaining presence of the living Christ. On a number of occasions, he recounted that the appeal to divine grace left both him and others with a sense of total assurance. It is at this point that we can no longer engage philosophically or theoretically with his writings. His understanding of faith, like his understanding of God, is rooted wholly in the conscious reception of grace, which mediates divine revelation and love. He did not descend into irrationality, however, but ascended into that supra-rationalism which can talk of God from direct, personal knowledge of divinity. Țuțea knew God, he did not just know about Him intellectually. Open to accusations of fantasy or delusion, his position is nevertheless vindicated both by the many others who shared his experiences and faith, and by the 'fruits' of his own experience. His warmth, friendliness, and lack of bitterness toward his persecutors were legendary.

The authority of revelation does not, for Țuțea, depend on the authority of personal experience, although it is substantiated thereby. To deny Trinitarian existence is definitive human self-denial. It is 'folly' (Ps. 14:1, 53:1). The dogma of the Holy Trinity points towards the mystery of humanity's ultimate relation to the Real, in which individuals participate not only by direct encounter with God, like Moses, but also through their sharing in the 'ordinary' Eucharist:

---

68   PROBLEMS, p. 258. See BGMP, p. 38, for Țuțea's reference to Jesus's Baptism as a manifestation or epiphany of the Holy Trinity.

69   DAYS, p. 175.

Theological thought occurs in the realm of the Real, which is not subject to questions and polysemy, since the Real-divine is not to be sought, demonstrated or illustrated, but is received through revelation, as in the case of Moses, by means of theophany, and through liturgical worship.[70]

Sacred Tradition as Continuing Revelation

Ţuţea's Christian realism concentrates on experiential rather than symbolic validation of the revelatory truth of *sacred history* and *sacred tradition*. *Sacred history* is the continuous narrative of salvation, made up of individual revelatory events in history including God's manifestations of Himself, the Incarnation and the procession of the Holy Spirit. It is transmitted down the generations as sacred scripture in the Old and New Testaments, written at the inspiration of the Holy Spirit by prophets, apostles, and those associated with them. In an extended sense, it becomes 'supra-history' – that is, historical communication of eternal revelation to God's chosen ones.[71] *Sacred tradition* is faithful to, and dependent upon, sacred history. It develops orally or in written form through those entrusted with apostolic authority as hierarchs of the Church and by those, like the saints, to whom divinity 'may show and reveal itself at any time and in any place'.[72] I will explore seven aspects of tradition.

Tradition between Sacred and Profane History

Ţuţea's ontology establishes a polarity between Creation as a complete 'manifestation of divine wisdom' providing 'the real and only explanatory principle of appearance as existence',[73] and history which, emptied of sacred meaning in the 'autonomous' human mind, can only be 'open to the grave'.[74] He sees 'the historical human being' as trapped in 'cycles' of profane history by sin, error, ignorance, or utilitarianism, while 'the eternal human being' has, through the Incarnation, the option of living in 'supra-history', liberated from cosmic (spatio-temporal) captivity:

> Sacred and profane history coexist, the truth of the former being unaffected by the dialectical illusions of the latter, since from the sin of Adam to our own day God has not forbidden the devil to operate at His side, that human beings might be put to greater moral and religious test.[75]

For Ţuţea 'the suprahistorical is the sacred punctuating space and time'.[76] 'Supra-history' comprises events, facts, discoveries, and achievements marked by, or

---

70   DOGMAS, p. 54.
71   See PROBLEMS, pp. 49–51.
72   PROBLEMS, p. 51.
73   PROBLEMS, p. 82.
74   BGMP, p. 40.
75   THEATRE, p. 412.
76   PROBLEMS, p. 185.

resulting from, the decisive work of grace. Everything in history that relates to the economy of salvation is supra-historical. The historical Christ and the Holy Spirit co-operate in every age and in every community – whether it be a community of political prisoners or a whole nation united against tyranny.

Christ is the effective manifestation of 'supra-history'. Țuțea also used the term to refer to what remains unaffected by original sin within creation. His thinking was perhaps influenced by Nicolas Berdyaev's discussion of the tension between 'the doctrine of progress and the goal of history'. Berdyaev, too, 'strengthens the hope and expectation that the tragedy of history will be ultimately resolved on the plane and in the perspective of eternity, of eternal reality'.[77] Țuțea holds the optimistic belief that personal limitation and selfishness can be transcended historically and theologically by those who are 'perfect in Christ' (Col. 1:28):

> I believe that the only science which includes everything is theology. That science which has as its object divinity and everything created thereby is the only science which embraces everything since, from a Christian point of view, the Creator animates creation from its very origins, despite its corruption by sin, to its ultimate end, the Saviour bringing the whole universe to perfection.[78]

Tradition as Liturgical Memory

Tradition for Țuțea, as for Dumitru Stăniloae, only really exists within an eschatological context. It is the living manifestation of a 'pneumatological understanding of the Bible'.[79] This has 'the theological merit of providing a basis at once rational and dogmatic'[80] for revealed truth. It is a dynamic synthesis, part of divine revelation, living unity and harmony, encompassing creation in the will of the self-giving Creator.[81] Orthodox tradition is rooted in the Saviour's presence, realised in the individual through the act of remembrance (*anamnesis*). As opposed to the 'natural', 'fallen', 'corruptible', or 'virtual storage' memory, with its stereotypical repetition of the external gestures of Christ, this *liturgical memory*, vitally active in eternal presence at the Eucharist, is joyous recognition and inner discovery of the One who was raised from death:

---

77   Nikolai Berdyaev, *The Meaning of History*, trans. George Reavey (London: Centenary Press, 1936), p. 206; see especially 'The Doctrine of Progress and the Goal of History', pp. 186–206.

78   DOGMAS, pp. 33–4.

79   Dumitru Stăniloae, *Iisus Hristos sau Restaurarea Omului* (Craiova: Omniscop, 1993), p. 386.

80   THEATRE, p. 367.

81   See Dumitru Stăniloae, 'The Orthodox Conception of Tradition and the Development of Doctrine', *Sobornost*, 5:9, Summer 1969, pp. 653–4; Kallistos Ware, 'Tradition and Personal Experience in Later Byzantine Theology', *Eastern Church Review*, 3:2, Autumn 1970, pp. 131–41. Cf. Țuțea's discussion on 'Patristic Tradition' in THEATRE, pp. 367–70.

In the religious view of the Bible the two worlds [the temporal and the timeless] *are*. From a biblical point of view they are granted by grace to those who are inspired by God, and by faith to those who are not – to them they are communicated by means of ritual.[82]

Tradition as Evangelism

Integral to tradition, Ţuţea suggests, is inspired biblical exegesis. This is evangelistic. It empowers, nurtures, and develops the Christian community. Biblical interpreters address the issues of their day and offer a response, and their responses over time form the basis for the further development of tradition, ensuring creative integrity between the past and the new evangelised community. New interpretations are tested against the traditional canons, developing from them rather than denying them. Evangelistic and doctrinal development is not dialectical but, like the growth of a tree, a process of organic transformation.[83]

For Ţuţea, as for Stăniloae, tradition is thus to be seen as a practical application and a continuous and deepening understanding of the content of Scripture.[84] It is contextual exegesis and therapeutic interpretation (in the original senses of θεραπεύω, to minister and serve, to nurse and heal). Ţuţea's theology proceeds from God as divinely revealed truth – that is, from beyond human free will. He is not concerned to demonstrate or logically explain this 'unique' and 'absolute' truth, but desires to share it with those in despair and difficulty, and with those who have less sense of, or belief in, the redemptive existence of God:

> A human being without revelation cannot say much... Explanation is bound up with transcendence. Where there is no revelation – that is to say where God does not grant you the grace [*favoare*] of knowing who you are, why you are, and to what end you are – there can never be an answer.[85]

Prophetic Tradition

The God of whom Ţuţea writes in his *Christian Anthropology* is the One revealed to the 'religious human being' in Scripture, namely the God of the prophets and of eschatology, rather than the god of philosophical ontology.[86] He stresses that the religious human being, one of the constituents of the 'ontic triangle', is 'the human being as a whole, eschatologically immortal'.[87] By contrast the 'estranged human

---

82   PROBLEMS, p. 83.
83   See PROBLEMS, pp. 317–18.
84   Dumitru Stăniloae, *The Experience of God* (Brookline: Holy Cross, 1994), p. 45.
85   Ţuţea, 'Petre Ţuţea', in Arachelian, *Cuvântul care Zideşte*, p. 74.
86   See also the *actualisation* of the divine in relation to the historical actions of prophecy, covenant, and salvation, as explored in Richard Kearney, *Heidegger's Three Gods, with a response by Martin Warner* (University of Warwick: Centre for Research in Philosophy and Literature, 1992), p. 26.
87   PROBLEMS, p. 220.

being' is an individualist demiurge, who 'has fallen into time'[88] and is captive to a world of illusions, fictions, and anxieties aroused by earthly limitation.[89] Țuțea distinguishes 'the apparent', as a manifestation of the Real, from 'the illusory or the fictitious' encountered by the enquiring mind.[90]

Although 'no prophet is accepted in his own country' (Luke 4:24), Țuțea encouraged his fellow Romanians by the prophetic authority with which he spoke of God's plan of salvation. This was still inexorably at work despite all political and ideological appearances. He insisted that 'the principal function of authentic religions is to give hope, meaning and purpose in our life'.[91]

Tradition as Liberating Dogma

In his written works Țuțea does not try to relate divine revelation, as witnessed by Scripture, with theories of human rationality. Grace cannot be sought. Rather, it is received as a gift from above. In the same way, Christian freedom is the actualisation of the potential for salvation. The Incarnation is the embodiment of this truth, giving 'dogmatic' meaning to the human person and to the world. Christian dogma and individual freedom can be harmonised, Țuțea argues, through the dynamic transformation brought about by personal response to Jesus's call to discipleship (Matt. 5:48). Dogma, he maintains, 'frees one from the anxieties of personal limitation, from cosmic and social restriction, from the *Angst* aroused by the prospect of the infinite and of death'.[92]

He deplores the condition of the 'isolated, anxious man of modern times', obsessed with 'the ways of man' and ignoring 'the ways of God',[93] searching in vain for happiness in a secular society which excludes human freedom and where decisions about what should be thought and believed are taken by a handful of politicians. He affirms the need for moral choice and, in his use of Scripture, refers to themes that underline humanity's creaturely dependence on God: for example, creation, original sin, and the Sermon on the Mount. He also quotes the parables (whose earthly reference points are universal). He does not get drawn into doctrinal issues or issues about the historical Jesus, although he reminds his fellow Romanians that, 'Jesus was born in Bethlehem, not in Fălticeni, Moldavia'.[94]

For Țuțea, dogma is living reality: that which is revealed by the living God. It is to be distinguished from myth, which is humanity's way of speaking about God.

---

88   PROBLEMS, p. 330. See also: E.M. Cioran, *La Chute dans le Temps*, in E.M. Cioran, *Oeuvres* (Paris: Gallimard, 1995), pp. 1071–112.
89   PROBLEMS, p. 293.
90   PROBLEMS, p. 60.
91   APHORISMS, p. 92.
92   Țuțea, 'Petre Țuțea', in Arachelian, *Cuvântul care Zidește*, p. 72.
93   PROBLEMS, p. 323.
94   APHORISMS, p. 22.

Nevertheless, myth – defined by Mircea Eliade as 'an account of a "creation"',[95] of how things came into being – can be transformed into dogma through ritual and exegesis (that is, it can give to the Christian community a living perception of the nature of God). For Țuțea, while myth can allow a glimpse of the living God, dogma is 'mystery revealed'. Jesus Christ's original message is thus continually rediscovered and re-authenticated from a contemporary perspective. Dogma is 'heteronomous' in this sense, being the result of God's will, a fruit of inspiration, rather than resulting from 'the mythological quest' of 'pagan interpreters, mystagogical priests who initiate into pseudo-mysteries':[96]

> Dogma is mystery revealed. Germans call it *Zwangsidee*, the idea of constraint. I regard freedom as dogmatically having two bases: one here, in the Christian temple, where the Trinity, through the liturgy, envelops the priest as consecrator of the Eucharist... the other beyond, in the invisible world referred to by St Paul, where freedom is absolute.[97]

Țuțea uses the word *mystery* here[98] in a biblical and apostolic sense – that is, as the 'mystery of God' whose revelation is gradually and unceasingly made perceptible to our senses. In strictly theological terms, this mystery denotes revelation through which the inaccessible is made accessible to human understanding as manifestation of divine transcendence extending beyond our comprehension. It also has the New Testament revelatory sense of Incarnation: the divine encounters the human in the theandric ontology of the person of Jesus. This occurs in a mysterious way beyond human understanding which yet, through faith, can release us from the bondage of the mythical, the magical, and the rational:

> If a human being has a religious consciousness, not only is he not troubled by mystery, but he sees it as a gateway to the Absolute, a force which releases him from cosmic and social bondage. Through mystery the human being exchanges illusory autonomy for real peace.[99]

Țuțea's theological understanding is influenced by his political and economic background and environment. Some of his apparently rigid definitions perhaps reflect the totalitarian milieu of his time, albeit in a creative, often paradoxical, way. While adopting the Pauline view expressed in the Letter to the Galatians, that Christ sets us free from the Law, Țuțea defines freedom as unconditional, sacrificial

---

95   David Cave, *Mircea Eliade's Vision for a New Humanism* (Oxford: Oxford University Press, 1993), p. 67.
96   PROBLEMS, p. 75.
97   INTERVIEW, p. 3.
98   From the Greek noun *mysterion*, deriving from the verb *muo*, meaning 'to close', particularly 'to close the eyes': Louis Bouyer, '"Mysticism": An Essay on the History of a Word', in *Mystery and Mysticism*, ed. A. Plé and Louis Bouyer, et al. (New York: The Philosophical Library, 1956), p. 121. See also Bouyer's 'Mysterion', in *Mystery and Mysticism*, pp. 18–32.
99   PROBLEMS, p. 58.

'submission to mystical dogma'.[100] This is only apparently self-contradictory: secular legal freedom and God-given freedom are not the same. In the secular realm, unrestrained freedom is impossible. For a Christian the Law is not an imposition, but an expression of loving relationships based on tolerance, acceptance, and mutual respect for the other, a gift of the Holy Spirit (Gal. 5:18).

Tradition as History of Charisma

Accepting in theory Max Weber's typology of forms of authority,[101] Țuțea nonetheless believes in the power of the 'charismatic elect' who, under the inspiration of the Holy Spirit and through their endeavours, either in monastic solitude or in professional communities, contribute to the development not only of Christian doctrine but also of science, art, and philosophy. Since God is a unique 'object' of study different from those explored by the natural sciences, however, theological inquiry cannot be fully accommodated in empirical or cognitive methods, whose domain of definition is ultimately transcended and decisively inter-penetrated by the all-encompassing light of God:

> Without grace things are silent; they speak only when the Creator commands... Without grace, things cannot answer the enquirer's questions. In history those who discover natural laws and those who wisely expound laws are by nature charismatic (E. Troeltsch,[102] M. Weber). I do not extrapolate from charisma to immanence, because I understand charisma mystically, as an awakening somewhere between virtue and vice... Throughout secular history religious truth has had this awakening rôle, leading to illumination.[103]

The word 'elect' should not be understood as in Calvinism where only certain people are predestined to be saved. Țuțea's Orthodox approach implies firstly that although God calls all to salvation, only some respond; secondly, that these have access to true knowledge, albeit only by grace; and thirdly, that 'the Real is not to be sought, it is revealed' to those inspired by God,[104] or received in the Church at the Eucharist by those who, though not inspired, can 'experience through love' the New Law inaugurated in Christ's first commandment.[105] Having granted free will to His people, therefore, God invites all but compels none, while desiring 'that all men should find salvation and come to know the truth' (1 Tim. 2:4). In terms of human order,

---

100 INTERVIEW, p. 3.
101 Gerth and Wright Mills (eds), *Weber: Essays in Sociology*, pp. 295ff. See also Marshall (ed.), *The Concise Oxford Dictionary of Sociology*, p. 50. Cf. Hartmut Lehmann, *Max Webers 'Protestantische Ethik'* (Goetingen: Vandenhoeck & Ruprecht, 1996), pp. 113f.
102 Ernst Troeltsch (1865–1923), German philosopher and theologian, contemporary and close friend of Max Weber, who also made a major contribution to the sociology of religion.
103 PROBLEMS, p. 336.
104 PROBLEMS, p. 75.
105 PROBLEMS, p. 143.

the debate between centrally planned and free-market economies, for instance, will in Țuțea's view remain arbitrary and inconclusive if universal justice (derived from Christian virtues and especially from Christian charity) is not the ultimate goal.

Tradition as Participation in Salvation

'Salvation comes through participation in the truth, damnation through non-participation therein'.[106] Țuțea's understanding of 'participation in God' is linked to the vital Patristic concept of μετοχή ('sharing', 'partnership'). Human beings can find freedom by choosing to affirm Christian dogma, thus participating in their own salvation.

Țuțea's thinking here is close to the Palamite epistemology with which he had become familiar in 1938 when Dumitru Stăniloae published his classic work, *Viața și Învățătura Sfântului Grigorie Palama* (*The Life and Teaching of St Gregory Palamas*). Humanity cannot participate in the divine simply through intentional acts. Union with God through logically and deliberately prepared experience is inconceivable. It is God who takes the initiative, through grace, to make possible at the divine level what at the human level is actually impossible, namely *theosis* (or deification), whereby human beings participate in the divine energies (albeit not in the divine essence, which remains eternally transcendent). Secular history is the consequence of humanity's succumbing to the temptation to play God, and as such represents culpable and absurd separation from absolute heaven:

> Original temptation is man's quest for divinisation through knowledge and curiosity: pride urges us on to achieve equality with God. In humanism this perfection-seeking pride takes another form: replacement of God by perfectible humanity.[107]

However, 'we know, fundamentally, through revelation; enquiry and speculation are not fundamental, since essences are not engaged in questioning.'[108] Dogma is thus for Țuțea a 'theological form' through which theological thinking can convey the invisible and ultimately incomprehensible transcendent into the supra-rational doctrine of the Church.[109] It has an antinomic character.[110] This doctrine is mystical knowledge, implying God's intervention from above. 'The praying, awaiting, and receiving believer' is inspired, but his inspiration 'is no dianoetic virtue'[111] (inspiration cannot be reduced merely to discursive reason). Theology is exploration of the transcendent dimension of a given, universal reality, rather than retrospective 'creation' of God in its own image and likeness.

---

106   ELIADE, pp. 77–8.
107   PROBLEMS, p. 144.
108   PROBLEMS, p. 162. See also DOGMAS, p. 58: 'It is not within humanity's power to know the essence of God'.
109   SYSTEMS, p. 192.
110   Ware, 'The Debate about Palamism', p. 49.
111   THEATRE, p. 342.

Ţuţea's Christian Anthropology: An Overview

Ţuţea's work resists systematisation and affirms the priority of experience (as it were, lived theology) over systematic discourse. This arises naturally from his opposition to Communism's systematic imposition of a political ideology and denial of freedom of conscience. He is critical not only of political and economic systems, but also of philosophical systems, and of any attempt to define the truth exclusively through abstract reason, logical methodologies, and 'techniques of existence'. It is therefore somewhat 'non-Ţuţean' to try, as I seek to do in this book, to systematise his work. While this section aims to shed light on Ţuţea's inner motivation and vast knowledge, it should be borne in mind that his thought is essentially mercurial, dialogic, and apodictic rather than explanatory.

Petre Ţuţea was part of the religious revival which took place in Romania during the last decade of the twentieth century.[112] His work, like that of the Fathers, represents a synthesis of philosophical, scientific, and cultural knowledge with theology. He is able to use secular language to articulate his Christian convictions. Even when critical, his writings and interviews express freshness and hope. While disapproving of anthropocentric Renaissance humanism, he nevertheless proposes a new Christian humanism, which is rooted in the conviction that people need to be guided both by the Church[113] in its worship, centred on the mystery of the Eucharist, and by 'charismatic' holy individuals, particularly by those who in his own time had withstood Communist ideology and seemed chosen to spread the Word of God. Such defenders of the faith, whether or not representatives of the institutional Church,[114] were living proof of continuity with traditional Orthodoxy.

There is an inherent optimism in Ţuţea's thought, even though his view of philosophy, science, technology, and art as no more than practical means for explaining human existence in this world, may superficially seem pessimistic. His life and work reveal how vital spiritual life continued throughout a century riven with collective traumas and in a culture often thought to be spiritually impoverished. His ability to communicate the Christian *kerygma* powerfully in a contemporary context shows how the Christian religion can speak to human beings in the language of their own age. Although Ţuţea was virtually helpless, he showed great skill in negotiating with his Communist 're-educators'. He was able to inspire and nurture spiritual growth and genuine education through his interpretation of his prison experience.

Christ's life and message are presented as a transcendent paradigm of human life, while emphasising Christ's call to perfection (Matt. 19:21). Although this call may appear opposed to the world, it in fact proclaims the divinisation of humanity through

---

112   Already developing 'underground' in the aftermath of the Second World War, this phenomenon only became evident following the collapse of Communism.

113   See 'A Note on Ţuţea's Use of Language', p. xix.

114   Ţuţea describes *biserica* ('the Church') as 'a permanent form of the relationship between humanity and God, since outside the spirit of the community of faith there is no such thing as salvation; separated from this community, the individual falls into heresy or dies spiritually': REFLECTIONS, I, p. 24.

Incarnation, as Christ enters into the very core of human life in order to restore its purpose and significance. The imitation of Christ is the human way to perfection. Țuțea's synthesis of experience and theology is that of a highly gifted man who himself strove for that perfection which can be known only through grace, personal discipleship, and faithful perseverance in the communion of the Church.

Chapter 7

Sensing the Mystery

Țuțea's Approach to the Sacred

Țuțea's life and work are permeated by a sense of the sacred. Perhaps the goal of all his writing was to fuse the achievements of the post-Hellenistic intellectual culture, of which he was a part, and 'the sacred dimension of existence' which he recognised as imperfectly, yet powerfully, communicated in pre-Socratic philosophy and the primordial peasant culture of his childhood:

> Archaic cultures include the mythical and the magical, while modern Christian post-Hellenistic cultures include everything – although their emphasis on the rational renders them unable to absorb the sacred dimension of existence.[1]

> I understand the mystical as a limit of the mythical.[2]

At the outset it is important to clarify how Țuțea uses the word 'sacred'. At times he uses it in the normal sense of 'holy', that which is of God, mysterious, unapproachable, powerful, and dangerous. At other times, he uses it as a synonym for God. Of course, it is precisely this ambivalence which indicates that mystery which Țuțea seeks to illuminate. A divine message 'must not be reduced to the human scale, to the interplay between interpretation of signs and silence. Communication is clothed, in pseudo-explanatory guise, in the imperfect forms of language'.[3]

Influences

The formative context for Țuțea's understanding of the sacred included both his extensive knowledge of Scripture, Patristic literature[4] (in particular the *Philokalia*, see Appendix II), and philosophy, and his own personal experience of grace. He

---

1 ELIADE, p. 11. It is evident from the books found in his library after his death, and from his own comments, that Țuțea was interested in other faiths such as Judaism and Islam, and that he wrote about Buddhism. See the published bibliographies of what remained of his library: THEATRE, pp. 523–30; NUANCES, pp. 323–32.
2 ELIADE, p. 34.
3 ELIADE, p. 10.
4 The word 'Patristic' is used here in its broad Orthodox sense which includes the Fathers who continued to develop the tradition in the spirit of the early 'Patristic Age' of the first to the eighth century.

explored the ideas of his friend, the Romanian historian of religions Mircea Eliade, who was concerned not with the relation between the rational and non-rational elements of religion, but with the sacred in its entirety. According to Eliade, 'the first possible definition of the sacred is that it is the opposite of the profane'.[5] Yet Ţuţea insisted that in order to understand the sacred it is necessary to go beyond the dialectic of sacred and profane as a pair of opposites. Also, one cannot 'discover' the sacred from below, through a hermeneutics of, in Eliade's terms, 'ascensional hierophanies'. For Ţuţea such an approach amounts effectively to a mythical point of view reducible to the psychology of human experience and natural religion. In his understanding, revelation through theophany as well as Eucharistic mystery alone imparts knowledge of God:

> Human beings are not capable of describing God but only of sensing His presence as the Great Mystery, the source of all mysteries that free us from our cosmic, social, or individual bondage.[6]

Ţuţea's monograph *Mircea Eliade, An Essay* (1992) examines Eliade's interpretation of *homo religiosus* existing on the boundary between the sacred and the profane. The sacred is for Eliade related to primitive peoples' spiritual experience of some power which appears to be beyond the individual self and from which they can receive grace in their everyday lives. Moreover, Eliade emphasises the private and emotional aspects of religion, thereby making plain that, in Russell McCutcheon's words, 'the scholar of religion should be truly religious. He should avoid studying what Schleiermacher had earlier characterised as the mere externals of religion, for these are dead forms without the immediate experience of religious feelings'.[7]

In his work on Eliade, Ţuţea makes an important reference to *The Divine Names* of Dionysius the Pseudo-Areopagite (as quoted by Aquinas in the *Summa Theologiae*)[8] in relation to the being and attributes of God.[9] From the Pseudo-Areopagitic writings[10] Ţuţea would have developed his strong sense of the apophatic approach in theology. It is characteristic of Ţuţea to use modern philosophical language to

---

5   Mircea Eliade, *The Sacred and the Profane, The Nature of Religion*, trans. from French by Willard R. Trask (London: Harcourt Brace, 1987), p. 10.

6   DOGMAS, p. 69 (italics added). Elsewhere Ţuţea writes: 'God, truth, and salvation are experienced by religious human beings in ritual: pure joy is experienced by them when enveloped in the Great Mystery.' See Petre Ţuţea, *Omul, Tratat de Antropologie Creştină, Addenda: Filosofie şi Teologie*, foreword and ed. Cassian Maria Spiridon (Iassy: Timpul, 2001), p. 71. [*The Human Being, Treatise on Christian Anthropology, Addenda: Philosophy and Theology.*]

7   See Russel T. McCutcheon, 'The Autonomy of Religious Experience', in Russel T. McCutcheon (ed.), *The Insider/Outsider Problem in the Study of Religion, A Reader* (London: Cassell, 1999), p. 69.

8   See Question 13, in Anton C. Pegis (ed.), *The Basic Writings of Saint Thomas Aquinas*, introd. and notes by Anton C. Pegis, 2 vols (Cambridge: Hackett, 1997), I, pp. 112–34.

9   See DOGMAS, pp. 46, 68, 76, 78–80.

10   See DOGMAS, p. 81.

convey a theology wholly compatible with Maximus the Confessor's 'transcendental apophaticism' (as Dumitru Stăniloae calls it)[11] and Gregory Palamas's distinction between divine essence and divine energies.

Ţuţea never explicitly refers to Stăniloae's *Viaţa şi Învăţătura Sfântului Grigorie Palama* (*The Life and Teaching of St Gregory Palamas*), but I can say with confidence that he was familiar with the first ten volumes of the *Philokalia* (translated and annotated between 1946 and 1981), Stăniloae's translation of Maximus the Confessor's *Ambigua*, and his *Teologia Dogmatică Ortodoxă* (*Orthodox Dogmatic Theology*), published in 1978. I know from personal talks with Ţuţea that he had read these books, which reflect Stăniloae's mature views, and was planning to discuss them in the (unfinished) fifth volume of the *Treatise on Christian Anthropology, Dogmas, or the Place of the Spirit in the Realm of Certainty*.

From philosophy Ţuţea's view of the sacred drew primarily on Platonism and German thought. He discussed the contrast in Platonism between eternal Ideas (or Forms) and transient forms accessible to the senses, and commented on Plato's theories about recollection of Ideas (*anamnesis*) and the Good as the supreme Form.[12] German philosophy and anthropology helped Ţuţea to develop, alongside his ontological view of the sacred, an original and dynamic understanding of the traditional doctrine of human deification. Nietzsche's poetic and aphoristic rejection of God in *Thus Spoke Zarathustra* and *Human, All Too Human* was, not surprisingly, regarded by Ţuţea as symptomatic of the modern world's secularism. Reflecting on the modern world's gradual loss of a sense of the sacred, Ţuţea also made critical reference to the concepts of nature, culture, and humanity as presented in Sombart's last major work, *Vom Menschen. Versuch einer geisteswissenschaftlichen Anthropologie*.

Ţuţea's vast reading converged with his personal experience to create a solid sense of the sacred, which developed during his detention and through the worship of the Church. In his own life the sacred signified, simply, the presence of God. In Philip Sherrard's words, God is 'the initial and ultimately unique presupposition of the sacred, for the simple reason that without that presence there is no sacredness anywhere'.[13]

Apostolic Discipleship

It is the symbiosis of wide-ranging interdisciplinary erudition with direct personal experience of life as a dissident in Communist Romania that distinguishes Ţuţea's work and gives it authority. Intellectual ability, moral resilience, and spiritual insight combine in his treatment of the sacred to express a unique personal vision. The existence of God, he maintained, can never be disproved even in the most fiercely

---

11   See Stăniloae's note 6, in Maximus the Confessor, *Ambigua*, trans., introd., and notes by Dumitru Stăniloae (Bucharest: Editura Institutului Biblic şi de Misiune al Bisericii Ortodoxe Române, 1983), p. 11.

12   See, for example, ELIADE, pp. 19ff; and REFLECTIONS, I, pp. 31ff.

13   Philip Sherrard, *The Sacred in Life and Art* (Ipswich: Golgonooza, 1990), p. 1.

atheist environment. His very life demonstrated that the materialism, 'dialectical' or otherwise, created by propagandists on both sides of the Cold War was powerless to abolish Christian belief in the existence of God. Again and again he insists that logical argument can neither prove nor disprove the existence of God.

The rôle of the practising Christian theologian is to be steadfast in affirming the existence of God even in the midst of adversity, interpreting contemporary experience 'in the fear of the Lord', in the light of Judgement, for the benefit of fellow Christians. The virtue of perseverance (what Țuțea calls 'the thirst for the sacred') is expressed through personal and collective sacrifice, as well as through the ability to live positively and to hope, despite the loss of what is most precious in terms of values and material benefits. This stimulates a re-discovery of the relationship between humanity and God.

The call to live by the virtues of apostolic discipleship was a principle which he deduced from his own experience. Believers must embrace the Cross and Resurrection, and a life of ascetic effort in the broadest sense, through prayer, fasting, almsgiving, and participation in a Eucharistic community. For Țuțea, the Ten Commandments and the Sermon on the Mount together, as the teaching of God Incarnate, encompass the meaning of the Christian way of life.[14]

Țuțea criticised socialist humanism, which sees a fundamental opposition between civilisation, defined by Marxists as 'the totality of human spiritual achievements',[15] and nature, understood by them as impersonal and primordial.[16] When, in the Incarnate Logos, humanity and nature are seen in their due relationship to God, then human lordship over nature – intended by the Creator from the beginning – is restored. Humanity and nature are reconciled in Christ. A complete vision of the human person is possible only within the 'ontic triangle' in which there is no opposition between culture and nature. For through *sacra Redempțiune* (divine Redemption)[17] humans recover their authority over nature. Only when civilisation has God for its goal and end, will humanity cease to abuse and exploit the divine gift of dominion over created nature:

> When the human being breaks the triangle God–nature–humanity, he remains epistemologically and ethically alone, a rational animal in the world of the senses, questioning, erring, sick and dying, coming from nowhere, going nowhere, moving without understanding between the beginning and end of this world (which are beyond his powers of knowledge) and a world of assumptions.[18]

---

14   See PROBLEMS, pp. 160, 189.
15   PROBLEMS, p. 281.
16   A similar opposition (though a reverse image of it) may be discerned in the Enlighten-
      ment ideal of the 'noble savage' and in the Western Romantic sensibility, which tended to
      see in nature a reflection of the divine. Țuțea's analysis is thus also directly relevant to
      cultures that have not experienced the dominance of socialist humanism.
17   PROBLEMS, p. 288.
18   Țuțea, MS 1982, p. 27.

The Incarnation, the Cross, and Resurrection open historical experience to eternal life, in what Țuțea, as I have shown, called 'supra-history' or history 'punctuated' by the presence of God. Societies under Communist rule were forced to reject the Incarnation, and hence also the redemptive work of Christ. The human vocation to express in action the 'ontological reciprocity'[19] proper to beings made in the image and likeness of God was thus stifled. In a totalitarian State, human beings turn their backs on God and imagine it is possible for them to work out their own salvation. Philosophy as ideology, and the fruitless battle between idealism and materialism (two systems which in Țuțea's view are equally removed from truth), both alike bring disaster, since they are opposed to the Christian vision of life and the world.[20]

If the opposition between Christianity and dialectical materialism is self-evident, that between Christianity and philosophical idealism is no less evident in the light of the Incarnation. Christianity insists on the importance of both body and soul as God's creation. For Țuțea the attempt to conceive of culture as Nietzsche did in terms of the superman – whose thoughts, words, and deeds are inwardly motivated by a 'feeling of distance'[21] with respect to others – comes from the spirit of the demiurge. Țuțea viewed secular 'perspectivism'[22] as no more Christian than materialism, since it attributes reality only to a particular perspective, denying the reality and sacredness of the whole human being. By excluding the Creator as the sustaining cause of the Universe, Marx's materialist concept of the 'new man' and Nietzsche's ideal of the 'superman' both fail to define 'the religious man who bears within himself both God and the human species, and is confirmed by the Church'.[23] In line with Pascal, Țuțea believed that ultimate definitions (in the sense of explanatory identification) can only be made with reference to the Creator. Nevertheless, he observes, not without irony, that pseudo-definitions of the human being exist, and refers to Sombart, who claimed that definitions of what a human being is are either partial or false. In Sombart's view, Țuțea notes, the only two definitions worth considering are: 'Man is a biped without feathers' (Țuțea believes this appealed to the Prussian economist because Frederick II, in his 'boundless contempt for humanity', had liked it) and 'Man is a creature who gets bored.'[24]

By ruling out their sacred origin, dialectical materialism can only define human beings inadequately, in terms of their component parts.[25] Products of human enquiry, logically describable wholes are (as discussed in the previous chapter) merely

---

19   See Lars Thunberg, *Man and the Cosmos, The Vision of St Maximus the Confessor* (Crestwood, NY: St Vladimir's Seminary Press, 1985), p. 55.

20   OLD AGE, p. 130. Cf. PROBLEMS, p. 289.

21   THEATRE, p. 208.

22   'Perspectivism' is the claim that all knowledge is relative, 'perspectival' – that is, it reflects different points of view. Cf. Chapter 5, 'Perspectivism', in Maudemarie Clark, *Nietzsche on Truth and Philosophy* (Cambridge: Cambridge University Press, 1995), pp. 127–58. See also PROBLEMS, p. 158.

23   THEATRE, p. 505.

24   SYSTEMS, p. 250.

25   SYSTEMS, p. 251.

'parallel' to ontic, given wholes. For Ţuţea only a theological approach can truly define humanity:

> Human beings of themselves cannot know themselves, nor are they capable of knowing life and the world as these truly are. As Socrates suggests in Plato's dialogue *Charmides*, in order that they may define themselves and discover what wisdom is, they need the presence of a God who reveals.[26]

An Attempt to Define the Sacred

In his struggle to speak of God, Ţuţea's considerable powers of language were stretched to the limit. He used various terms to refer to God: 'the Sacred, that is to say, the all-embracing Real, the unique cause of all things',[27] 'the Absolute', 'the Unity of all unities', and 'the Great Mystery'. However, the sacred (as the Real) can never be adequately defined: 'Apart from the Real and dogma, which is a revealed form of the divine mystery, all other terms can be defined.'[28] Dogma is by no means the dry cerebral statement or concept it is often thought to be:

> Human beings cannot think in dogmas, they cannot dogmatise, because dogma is not a human rational construct. Dogma is revealed and therefore transcendent, like the truth (conceived as mystery) which it conveys. So-called philosophical, scientific, or social political dogmatism does not exist and cannot be opposed to freedom. Although it is apparently static, dogma is the living form of real freedom... To ordinary understanding, dogma as a form of freedom is paradoxical... Thus human beings cannot dogmatise, they absolutise, that is to say, they exaggerate, because of the attitude which their theoretical consciousness takes at any given moment towards concrete real objects.[29]

Ţuţea sees the philosophical distinction between nominal definition (words conveying concepts) and real definition (relationship to ultimate causes) as nonsense. This is because, in his terms, causes can only be described, not defined. Actual definition of things cannot ignore the ultimate mystery of being. For Ţuţea the sacred is transcendent. The essence of the uncreated God is beyond human knowledge and language. Indeed even sacred texts are beyond purely secular hermeneutics. He begins *Dogmas* by commenting on the chapters about the existence of God and 'What God Is Not' in Aquinas's *Summa Theologiae*. This is Ţuţea's commentary:

> The quest for God leads only to a form of words. Thomas Aquinas, who investigates and seeks this name of God, finds it neither in nature nor in his own consciousness. In the end,

---

26   PROBLEMS, p. 102.
27   ELIADE, p. 83.
28   PROBLEMS, 59. As noted in the introduction to this chapter, Ţuţea understands the sacred in an ambivalent way: in one sense as a term that 'can be defined', and in another sense as 'the Real' itself.
29   DOGMAS, pp. 89–90.

like Dionysius the Areopagite, he concludes that human beings cannot approach the essence of God through investigation and inquiry nor have any conception thereof. As far as things sacred, and in particular God, are concerned, inquiry and investigation lead to a solution, not to very God. We cannot be certain that inquiry, investigation and solution (forms of human reflection) are predetermined. Scripture says: 'Seek and you will find, knock and it will be opened to you.' It is thus difficult to apply hermeneutics to sacred texts.[30]

Țuțea's affirmations are often negatively expressed: God is in essence unknowable. Dionysius the Areopagite, frequently referred to nowadays as Pseudo-Dionysius, speaks of a 'hierarchy' established *ab origine* between the uncreated Creator and creation. The curiosity of the first couple in the Garden of Eden is symptomatic of a demiurgic lust to level this God-given hierarchy and be equal with the supreme and unique Creator of all things. Țuțea sees this impulse as lying at the root of a distorting self-image which cuts individuals off from their true nature and vocation,[31] namely to be in the image and likeness of God. The original distinction between Creator and creature which God saw as 'very good' (Gen. 1:31) thus becomes a terrible separation. In the lostness of this separation from God, apophatic language – which avoids the danger of proclaiming a merely human perspective – has the capacity to reflect at least in part the all-healing vision of God. However, it is the incarnate and resurrected Jesus alone who fully mediates the grace which penetrates human being and restores 'religious dignity'[32] – that is, who restores the hierarchy of creation and thus fulfils God's plan. Like Pseudo-Dionysius, Țuțea is aware that the transcendence of God is beyond all language, even the apophatic. He nevertheless often speaks of God in what he calls a non-attributive way:

> Dionysius the [Pseudo-]Areopagite maintained, as Thomas Aquinas would later do, that God has no name and no impression can be formed of Him... Limited and sinful after the Fall, mankind has sought to formulate concepts to explain God's essence, thus reducing the Great Mystery... to the level of logic. According to Dionysius, mankind is thus left with Moses's vision of Divinity without attributes; to him God replied that *I Am Who I Am*. Humanly speaking, in order not to be led astray by reasoning in relation to the name and the essence of God, we must think of Him without attributes. And I repeat, any attempt to discover a name of God that expresses His essence is doomed to failure. This is the flaw of all enquiry geared to finding solutions. Solutions have no doctrinal theological meaning.[33]

A God defined by his attributes is far from the perfection that is called simplicity. The tension between apophatic and cataphatic attempts to designate what God is, and what He is not, follows logically from the imperfection of human seeking.[34]

---

30   DOGMAS, pp. 81–2.
31   See PROBLEMS, p. 340.
32   THEATRE, p. 440.
33   DOGMAS, pp. 79–80.
34   'Human seeking' is based on 'hope for what is already seen' and on ignorance of spiritual needs: for 'we do not know what we should pray for as we ought' (see Rom. 8:24–6).

Țuțea uses Nicholas of Cusa's paradoxical descriptions of human knowledge as *docta ignorantia* and human language about God as *coincidentia oppositorum*. The sacred eludes reason. Thus, rational discourse about God leads to either theological delusion or a logical dead end (*aporia*). Țuțea considers that all questions concerning God 'reduce Him to the level of a problem and, as such, throw up debate and solutions that render communication of the sacred by means of theological doctrine impossible'.[35] Thus the being of God is not just a hypothesis awaiting scientific confirmation, but the only framework of reality in which valid theology and honest science are possible:

> To communicate the existence of God as He reveals Himself, in theophany and theandry, this is theology. It is not mystagogy [that is, initiation into mysteries by the passing on of received wisdom]. To establish God's existence in the forms in which He reveals Himself does not imply a seeking and understanding of His essence, for it is beyond human power to know this. The Great Mystery *purely and simply is*.[36]

Țuțea's belief in the impossibility of knowing and saying anything about the uncreated essence of God is a direct reflection of the doctrine of creation *ex nihilo*, which he accepts as an article of faith. He acknowledges a tension between the imperfections of language and the perfection of the Creator. Faith, however, embodies a resolution of this tension. In his *Celestial Hierarchies* Pseudo-Dionysius presents a scale of degrees of creaturely existence. Because all creatures are equally dependent on God for their existence, all are equally close to Him.[37] Starting from the Pseudo-Dionysian image of divine hierarchy, Țuțea reflects on Aquinas's attempt to define the divine essence by means of analogy:

> Our view is that Aquinas's argument, combining analogical images with the creative power of the intellect as a means whereby the human mind can gain knowledge of God, is a futile and inconclusive exercise. All the more so since, as Aquinas admits, the images of things are not things in themselves. St Anselm of Canterbury wonders: *Cur Deus homo?* (Why did God become a human being?). But the human mind cannot answer this question, since it cannot elucidate the mystery of the Incarnation, by which God manifests Himself through His Son.[38]

Țuțea holds that the coming of the Saviour and the story of His life are perceived through images. Believers 'accept the theandric mystery' and thus find themselves in the presence of:

---

35   DOGMAS, p. 63.
36   DOGMAS, p. 58 (Țuțea's italics).
37   Denys Turner writes that there can be no 'degree of distance between creatures and God': Denys Turner, *The Darkness of God, Negativity in Christian Mysticism* (Cambridge: Cambridge University Press, 1998), p. 31.
38   DOGMAS, p. 77.

a miraculous drama that outstrips the enquiring intellect. Yet the truths of faith need expression in dogmatic theological terms. Unique Truth, transcendent in essence, is the sole principle of all things. Their laws emanate from God, not from themselves.[39]

The sacred (in its attributive sense) is not absolutely coterminous with God. For this reason even rational proofs for the existence of God that use the terminology of the sacred can reduce the Great Mystery of God to an argument at the service of believer and atheist alike.[40]

The Sacred as the Absolute

Ţuţea considered himself a plain active Christian, that is, simply one whose life is centred on the Eucharist in the fellowship of the Church. The practising Christian moves between the visible world and the invisible, having access to the Absolute through a personal faith that enables him to transcend any doubt concerning the existence of these two worlds. This Pauline view of two distinct worlds relates to the doctrine of creation *ex nihilo*, rejection of which, according to Ţuţea, leads to the despair and 'fear of death' experienced by existentialists and nihilists.[41]

Ţuţea distinguishes between the Absolute and the infinite, often quoting William Hamilton[42] for whom all human knowledge implies limitation. Hamilton defines the Absolute paradoxically as 'the limited unconditioned', while the infinite is 'the unlimited unconditioned'.[43] Ţuţea suggests that this paradox expresses the very mystery of the Incarnation: as Logos Incarnate, Christ is 'the limited unconditioned' in the sense that, although unconditioned by His divine nature, He limits Himself by becoming human.

On the other hand, the infinite is merely an attribute of chaos or 'the originating mass of the universe' in its pre-Socratic sense of ἄπειρος ('unlimited'): 'in the beginning, before the cosmogonic moment, there was a mass of quality-less stuff, unlimited in extent and infinitely old'.[44] So, for Ţuţea the unconditioned belongs

---

39 DOGMAS, p. 77.

40 See DOGMAS, p. 78.

41 Kierkegaard's *Angst*, Cioran's *le néant*, and Kant's *Leere* (void space) all reflect this 'modern' state.

42 I was personally pleased, while working on my doctoral thesis as a Balliol graduate, to discover that the Scottish philosopher Sir William Hamilton (1788–1856), for whom Ţuţea had such regard, was a Balliol man.

43 '[T]he unconditional negation of limitation gives one unconditioned, the Infinite; as the unconditional affirmation of limitation affords another, the Absolute': William Hamilton, 'Philosophy of the Unconditioned', in *Discussions on Philosophy and Literature, Education and University Reform*, 3rd edn (London: Blackwood, 1866), p. 28.

44 Jonathan Barnes, *The Presocratic Philosophers* (London: Routledge & Kegan Paul, 1982), p. 29. On p. 36, according to Barnes: 'A powerful chorus of scholars propose a new etymology for *apeiros*: it is formed not from alpha privative and the root of

to 'the realm of the unintelligible (for to think means to condition)'.[45] He insists that:

> God is the Absolute. He is *not* an infinite substance... Since the Creator is ubiquitous and extramundane, His position in relation to humanity and the world is beyond our human capacity to understand, for human understanding does not extend to the world of mysteries.[46]

Ţuţea thus confronts a problem encountered by the Pre-Socratics,[47] who considered the infinite to be irrational and unpredictable, having no limits, boundaries, or shape. The universe is all that is not God. It is 'privatively infinite' rather than 'negatively infinite' according to Nicholas of Cusa; the universe is infinite not because it has no end but because its end is unlimited: 'For nothing actually greater than it, in relation to which it would be limited, can be given.'[48] Hence Ţuţea's observation that the infinite is incomprehensible because it is formless. The infinite, he suggests, reflects sub-reason (similar to primordial chaos), while the Absolute transcends the human mind and is rational. In a commentary on *After the Resurrection of Lazarus*, a short story by Leonid Andreyev,[49] Ţuţea describes the author's view of the infinite:

> He conceives of the infinite as 'emptiness and darkness'. The characters in his short story, *After the Resurrection of Lazarus*, are in the grip of fear and despair when confronted by the great emptiness. Those who have seen Lazarus raised from the dead felt like this:
>
> > 'Everything which the eye saw and the hands touched seemed empty, weightless, transparent, as luminous shadows in the darkness of the night. For the great darkness which enshrouded creation was not dispersed either by the sun, or by the moon, or by the stars; it covered the earth like an infinite black veil, it enfolded it like a mother's arms...'
>
> Miracle is the expression of the power of the Absolute conceived on a human scale. Things emerge from emptiness and vanish into emptiness when the Absolute is replaced or is confronted by the infinite. The dizzying whirlpool of the emergence of things from emptiness and their disappearance into emptiness presents us with a shattering spectacle.
>
> The infinite considered as emptiness and darkness is a tragic concept. It resembles the idea of the sublime as a transcendent power that overwhelms limited and powerless human beings. The miracle of the raising of Lazarus, linked with the infinite, fills those who

---

peras ("limit"), but from alpha privative and the stem of *peraô* ("traverse"); and the etymological meaning of the word is thus "untraversable".'

45   THEATRE, p. 139.
46   PROBLEMS, p. 50 (italics added).
47   See Gregory Vlastos's chapter on Anaxagoras, in Alexander P. D. Mourelatos (ed.), *The Pre-Socratics, A Collection of Critical Essays* (Princeton, NJ: Princeton University Press, 1993), p. 470.
48   Nicholas of Cusa, *Selected Spiritual Writings*, trans. and introd. by H. Lawrence Bond, preface by Morimichi Watanabe (New York: Paulist Press, 1997), pp. 130–31.
49   Leonid Andreyev (1871–1919), Russian playwright and dissident writer who opposed Lenin, Trotsky, and Bolshevism.

witness it with terror, since he is alien because of his silence concerning things seen and unseen in the world beyond... The world is not created from nothing in the sense of emptiness, but from God who does not represent emptiness, but who overflows from His own abundant fullness. The matter and patterns of creation are contained within the Absolute.

Christian substantialism is incompatible with the idea of emptiness. In this sense, it has been said that the creation of the world is not a miracle, but sprang necessarily from the omnipotence of God. In any case, it is easier to understand God through the natural order than through events which we call miracles, which conceal Him still further from our sight.[50]

Miracles confront humanity with God's infinite power to break the laws of the finite. To creaturely human finitude, without the support of faith, the experience of miracles and the temptation to try to provoke them are characterised (and driven) by a certain terror. The divine and human levels cannot be reconciled logically, but are united in the mystery of the Incarnation wherein God's omnipotence co-exists with the loving self-imposed limitations of the Logos Incarnate.[51] I will show in the next section that, for Țuțea, the philosophical confusion between the Absolute and the infinite originates in what Hegel calls 'the One as unique and infinite substance'.[52] By contrast, for Plato, and for Christians:

the human being – awakened by the sensible world and governed by the idea of participation – seeks the Real conceived as the Absolute. The Absolute can be linked with eternity, which is not to be confused with the infinite as understood in the logic of extension. According to Kant, extension in its quantitative sense is incompatible with perfection. In order to understand absolute beauty in Plato (more particularly having seen how the sublime is linked to an idea of infinity confused with the Absolute), we must distinguish between the Absolute and the infinite, as Hamilton rightly does.[53]

This distinction is only fully made in the Word made flesh. As Țuțea has suggested, the 'limited unconditioned' is precisely the condition of the Incarnation. Only in this light can humanity bear God and transcend the infinite which, for unbelievers, is the unlimited unconditionality of what Țuțea calls 'absolute death'. This is not to say that death ceases to be a painful and terrifying experience for Christians (death is still the fruit of original sin, Rev. 6:16, 21:23). It is, however, to affirm that the mystery of death is contained within a greater mystery, namely the absolute purpose of God's love in creation. For God made Christ 'who knew no sin to be sin for us, that we might become the righteousness of God in Him' (2 Cor. 5:21).

---

50   THEATRE, pp. 143–4. Țuțea quotes from 'După învierea lui Lazăr', in Leonid Andreyev, *Juda Iscarioth și alte povestiri*, trans. George B. Rareș (Bucharest: Editura Traducătorului, 1925), pp. 79–100.

51   Origen also sees the divine power as self-limited because, if it were infinite, it would be irrational (which would contradict the fact that God is order and true meaning, and therefore rational). See Origen, *On First Principles*, Book II, Chapter IX, 1, p. 129.

52   THEATRE, p. 150.

53   THEATRE, p. 151.

The Sacred beyond the Sublime and the Beautiful

In Țuțea's view Lazarus's miraculous encounter with Jesus in this world, following his experience of death and the other world, is a paradigm of the human condition placed at the intersection between the sacred and the profane. Although we live in a created material world whose infinity is sublime in its enchanting or terrifying character, we are also granted access to uncreated beauty. In his dialogue *Bios*, explored in the next chapter, Țuțea's discussion of the sublime vis-à-vis the beautiful starts by quoting Hegel's critique of Kant's distinction[54] between the two:

> Kant's view is that 'the sublime, in the strict sense of the word, cannot be contained in any sensuous form but concerns only Ideas of Reason which, although no adequate representation of them is possible, may be aroused and called to our mind [soul] precisely by this inadequacy which does admit of sensuous representation' (*Critique of Judgement*, 1799, p. 77, [§ 23]).

> The sublime in general is the attempt to express the infinite, without finding in the sphere of phenomena an object which proves adequate for this representation. Precisely because the infinite is set apart from the entire complex of objectivity as explicitly an invisible meaning devoid of shape and is made inner, it remains, in accordance with its infinity, unutterable and sublime above any expression through the infinite.[55]

Țuțea continues by observing that Kant demonstrates a certain hubris of 'pure subjectivism and anthropocentrism'.[56] He situates Kant's method of 'critique' between rationalism and empiricism, and views Kant's sublime as a 'gratuitous enchantment of our mind reflected in itself'.[57] He points to a sort of empirical, critical narcissism underlying Kant's subjectivism. This he sees as deriving from what Hegel calls the 'prolixity' of Kant's discussion on the sublime (with its 'premissed reduction of all categories to something subjective, to the powers of mind, imagination, reason').[58] In the same essay, Țuțea quotes Edmond Goblot's description of the sublime based on Kant's distinction between the sublime and the beautiful:

> The sublime is not a species of beauty. It is of a different nature from beauty. Beauty is orderly and proportioned. It satisfies us. The sublime is immeasurable in both scope and power. It confounds and crushes us. Sometimes it terrifies us.[59]

This terrifying view of the sublime is hardly adequate as an ideal for human nature. Țuțea believes that Kant's sublime can be conceived as 'the infinite' or as

---

54   See 'Symbolism of the Sublime', in Hegel, *Aesthetics*, I, pp. 362–77.
55   Hegel, *Aesthetics*, I, pp. 362–3.
56   THEATRE, p. 142.
57   THEATRE, p. 142.
58   Hegel, *Aesthetics*, I, p. 362.
59   Edmond Goblot, *Vocabulaire philosophique* (Paris: Armand Colin, 1938), p. 87, quoted by Țuțea in THEATRE, p. 142.

'an immense disorder extended to cosmic chaos'; at the same time, however, the transcendent, ineffable nature of this sublime 'cannot comfort human consciousness which tries to grasp it'; nor can it satisfy the human appetite for sacred beauty, which on the whole responds to 'subtle harmonies' (*acorduri mărunte*).[60] In Ţuţea's view the infinite is held in being, within the dispensation of the Incarnation, by the Absolute who is Love, and to this extent cannot be entirely ineffable. By contrast, the ineffable for Kant is the objective source of awareness of human superiority to nature. As has been shown in the previous chapter, following Hans Vaihinger's *Philosophie des Als Ob* (*The Philosophy of 'As If'*), Ţuţea regards Kant's ideas of God, freedom, immortality, soul, and infinity as fictions, since they are purely *als ob* ('as if' truly existent). Such ideas are 'called up to ennoble the mask of that finite creature, the human being. Debased to the level of pure subjectivity', by existing simply *als ob*, they are 'emptied of content' and serve merely as 'instruments of theoretical consciousness (their worth demonstrated by their efficacy)'; in Ţuţea's words, 'constructivism replaces their *objecticity*'.[61] In Kant the sublime is a construct of the human mind: any reality beyond subjectivity and objectivity is denied. *Als ob* fictions preclude the existence of a trans-personal order of things. For Ţuţea logic and art are incompatible insofar as 'the logician looks for essences in the interplay of appearances, seeking the nature of things, while the artist scans the deceptive brilliance of this interplay'.[62] He reacts against both Kant's subjective view of the sublime and Hegel's logical view. Hegel, in his discussion on the symbolism of the sublime, suggests a pantheist understanding of 'the All', that is:

> of the one substance which indeed is immanent in individuals, but is abstracted from individuality and its empirical reality, so that what is emphasised and meant is not the individual as such but the universal soul, or, in more popular terms, truth and excellence which also have their presence in this individual being.[63]

According to Hegel, this 'unity' is 'afforded in general by mysticism, developed as it has been in this more subjective way within Christianity too'.[64] In *Bios* Ţuţea points to the aporia of Hegel's absolute idealism, which is perhaps at the root of his mistaken assessment of Christian mysticism as 'pantheistic unity, emphasised in relation to the subject who feels himself in this unity with God and senses God as this presence in subjective consciousness'.[65] Ţuţea's position is intuitively consistent with Gregory Palamas's distinction between the uncreated and inaccessible essence of God and the uncreated yet accessible divine energies, although he does not refer directly to this Church Father. Palamas's understanding of the uncreated light of

---

60   THEATRE, p. 143.

61   THEATRE, p. 143. For Ţuţea's understanding of *obiecticitate* see also Chapter 8, notes 55 and 58.

62   THEATRE, p. 143.

63   Hegel, *Aesthetics*, I, p. 365.

64   Hegel, *Aesthetics*, I, p. 371.

65   Hegel, *Aesthetics*, I, p. 371.

Mount Tabor[66] is in no sense one of 'pantheistic unity' between the transcendent and the immanent. Rather, it is the mystical union,[67] mediated by, through, and in the Logos Incarnate, between God and humanity. God who is essentially unknowable cannot be identified with creation in a pantheistic manner. Nevertheless, the human mind can be enlightened and brought into union with God by uncreated grace.

Ţuţea's experiential and intellectual Christian journey brought him to an understanding very similar to that of Palamas. Christian vision is not pantheistically confined to either nature or humanity, Ţuţea believed, nor does it exclude these, because 'everything partakes of God, but He is never confused with anything'.[68] Christianity is, rather, a vision[69] of human life lived in its integrity in this world within the triangle God–humanity–nature. In this triangle, it is God who harmonises 'spirit and matter, which are not contradictory'[70] but which find their fulfilment in the eternal world.

Ţuţea claims that Hegel's 'art of the sublime' is 'sacred art'.[71] He sees Hegel as wishing to unify 'the religious with the aesthetic, the individual with the universal, the general with the particular, the finite with the infinite, the transitory with the eternal'.[72] But this dialectical definition of sacred art by means of pairs of opposites conveys Hegel's pantheism. For, 'if existence is confused with essence, things merge into their accidental aspects'.[73] Although Hegel speaks of 'human unworthiness in the presence of God',[74] Ţuţea observes that this 'does not prevent the human being from bearing God within himself, just as he bears the infinite'.[75]

The Sacred as Revelation and Inspiration

For Ţuţea, the defining characteristic of the sacred is that it is a gift of divine revelation, 'a gate to the Absolute',[76] 'opened by grace'.[77] Knowledge of the sacred cannot be acquired solely on the basis of human experience, nor can its reality be demonstrated by a process of reasoning. It can lead neither to certainty nor to faith. For amid the flux of experience and demonstration that constitutes the world, the

---

66   Kallistos Ware, 'The Hesychasts: Gregory of Sinai, Gregory Palamas, Nicolas Cabasilas', in Cheslyn Jones, Geoffrey Wainwright, and Edward Yarnold SJ (eds), *The Study of Spirituality* (London: SPCK, 1986), pp. 244–8.
67   See section 'Theological Science and Mystical Union' in this chapter.
68   THEATRE, p. 491.
69   Vision here is dynamic and effective, rather than an aloof spiritual empiricism.
70   THEATRE, p. 491.
71   See THEATRE, pp. 145, 147.
72   THEATRE, p. 147.
73   THEATRE, p. 149.
74   Hegel, *Aesthetics*, I, p. 376.
75   THEATRE, p. 150.
76   ELIADE, p. 37.
77   ELIADE, p. 70. Cf. BGMP, p. 202.

Absolute can never be grasped. Only through inspiration, a view 'of the world and life from Above',[78] can the truth of any religion be received.

Țuțea seems to suggest that revelation, as the self-disclosure of God, has a universal quality accessible to all: 'Truth in the Socratic-Christian sense is transcendent in essence.'[79] All religious systems are an attempt to approach this transcendent sacred truth, and all fall short in different respects, including merely systematised Christianity. Jesus Christ is the Name above all names, Lord of lords, *Pantokrator*. All natural psyche, human experience, and religious understanding is redeemed in the One who came not to judge the world but to be its Light. Christ breathes upon the disciples the Holy Spirit, 'who will guide into all truth' (John 16:13).[80] Țuțea seems open to the absolute unbounded power of the Holy Spirit to work even through non-Christians, to bring forth the creaturely fullness and glory of the revelation of Christ. Revelation can penetrate and enfold systems. Țuțea refers to the Indian mystic Sankara – for whom the Vedic revelation, formulated as 'sacred knowledge' of the Hindus, is 'the unique mode of access to truth' – and concludes:

> In historical-philosophical and historical-religious terms, myths, religious beliefs, legends, feats of magic, redemption, immortality, freedom, the sense of imprisonment in matter represent a perpetual interplay between the sacred and the profane.[81]

Țuțea's openness derives from his view of the Sermon on the Mount as a radical document of tolerance, which differs from syncretism in that it affirms the uniqueness of the Incarnate Word precisely as the empowering Lord of that tolerance.

Objective and Subjective Views of the Sacred

The Absolute is, for Țuțea, something received by faith; it does not need to be ascertained. Orpheus looked back at Eurydice to convince himself of her existence, but the sacred forbids such looking back. To reduce the sacred to contingency is to forfeit it. Thus Țuțea, with Eliade, points to Orpheus's lack of faith – 'the sin of Orpheus'[82] – which denotes a human inability to accept the given limitations of creaturely existence. Eliade's notion of the sacred as a 'centre' linked to experience of the Real highlights 'the dependence of order on the Absolute'. I noted that Hamilton defined the Absolute as 'the limited unconditional' regarded as an object of knowledge. However, for Țuțea the sources of truth are situated in the realm of mystery, not metaphysical and logical-mathematical speculation. Truth has to be

---

78 BGMP, p. 198.
79 ELIADE, p. 77.
80 The tendency of Christians to pre-empt this work of the Holy Spirit by assuming that their own historically articulated Church 'tradition' already constitutes all the truth, is a natural psychic corruption of authentic 'Tradition', which continues to speak eschatologically and to pray, *Maranatha*, 'Come Lord Jesus!'.
81 ELIADE, p. 14.
82 See Crăciun Bejan's essay, 'The Actuality of the Sacred', in ELIADE, p. 14.

conceived in the religious terms of salvation and eschatology. Metaphysics and logic remain with what is useful, convenient, and pleasant. In Țuțea's terms, existentialism and the aesthetics of the absurd 'sink' in the river of 'historical meandering'; these meanderings cannot lead to the mystical 'centre' of the human being, without which we are simply captives of an infinite 'circle whose centre is everywhere and whose limits are nowhere':[83]

> None of these states and processes lead to truth. Knowledge without faith confines humanity and nature within an illusory autonomy. Subjectivity and objectivity are equally distant from truth. *Objecticity* belongs to the mysticism of the ideal which cannot be attained by searching, but is revealed.[84]

The Sacred as Eucharistic Liturgy

Human interpretation of the Real reduces it to 'mere phenomenism', since communication naturally occurs within the forms of the language available to it. The practising Christian can experience the sacred dynamically in 'the necessary act of participation in truth', through liturgical worship in the Christian temple, where 'the mystery of the Trinity envelops both priest and people'.[85] Țuțea makes a clear distinction between discursive initiation and mystical participation in the Christian mysteries, that is, between pre-Christian mystagogy as a pagan hermeneutic art, and the inherently communicative nature of the Christian Eucharist:

> To show that God exists, with or without attributes, is to disregard the fact that He has communicated to us His existence through theophany and Incarnation. The quest for the existence of God is called mystagogy, that is, 'a manner of interpreting mysteries – an explanation of mysteries employed in polytheism' (Littré). In Christianity, mysteries are not explained. They are communicated through ritual by the priest and, as such, are the only means of human liberation from cosmic, social, and personal captivity. The priest does not have an explanatory rôle since he, like the believer, is enveloped in the mysteries.[86]

While for Țuțea the Christian priest is a communicator rather than an interpreter of mysteries, the biblical exegete and the historian of religions occupy the rôle of the commentator who 'deciphers signs and mysteries' without ever escaping 'the flux of contingency'; nevertheless, through the sacred (divine inspiration or participation in the liturgical rite) the Christian community is released from the state of an interpreter decoding symbols.[87]

---

83   This description of the nature of God has been attributed to Empedocles and is quoted by St Bonaventure in *Itinerarius Mentis in Deum*, Chapter 5 *ad fin*. See Partington (ed.), *The Oxford Dictionary of Quotations*, p. 16.

84   ELIADE, p. 77 (italics added). For the terminology used in this quotation, see Chapter 8, note 55.

85   ELIADE, p. 20.

86   DOGMAS, p. 62. The bracketed reference is to the classic French *Dictionnaire* Littré.

87   See ELIADE, pp. 13–14. Here the sacred is a function of the Other.

The Sacred in the Trinity and Platonic Ontology

Those inspired by grace receive Trinitarian truth 'through the sacerdotal ministry of communion. Christian mysteries within ritual are not "remembered", but experienced in an immediate way as pure actuality'.[88] Țuțea's view of the sacred is intrinsically Trinitarian (within his hermeneutic 'trinity' denoting the third person of the Holy Trinity). Let us briefly recall his characteristic articulation of the mystery of the Three in One:

- theophany (the revelation of God the Father, Creator of all things);
- theandry (revelation through Incarnation, the Son of God become truly human, with bodily and cognitive limitations, to redeem the whole human race, mediating God's desire to cancel the distance between Himself and humanity resulting from original sin);
- trinity (revelation of the eternal immediacy of God's power, the Holy Spirit of God present in every believer in Baptism).

While Țuțea does not seem to speak directly of the Holy Spirit in the sense of the bond of love between Father and Son, his use of the word 'Trinity' to denote the third person of the Trinity indicates an essentially relational understanding of spirit. The salvific economy of the Triune God is not susceptible to:

> opinion, problem, search, solution, axiom, demonstration, or method. As the science of receiving and conveying ultimate truth, theology finds its place not in the world of ideas as archetypes, but in the transcendent world of ultimate truth where the Lord creates life and orders it in ways past human understanding. The God who alone is truth is not a demiurge, like Plato's deity, but a God who creates *ex nihilo*. Human beings cannot conceive, intuit or imagine creation and its goal, that is to say, they cannot link beginning and end. Thus Alcmaeon of Croton distinguished mortal humans from God.[89]

Țuțea makes a clear distinction between Christian dogmas and canonical tradition, based on revelation, and Platonism, which is closer to mythology:

> The form of revealed truth is Christian dogma. In the sacred language of Christian sacerdotalism the canons of the Church exclude Platonic Ideas considered as archetypes.[90]

Understood in secular terms, archetypes do not lead to religious knowledge of essentially transcendent truth. Țuțea believes that in this world, truth can be approached only in mystical terms, through Christian dogma. Platonic mysticism is a philosophical and mythological cul-de-sac:

---

88   ELIADE, p. 26.
89   PROBLEMS, p. 51. Cf. Barnes, *The Presocratic Philosophers*, p. 115.
90   PROBLEMS, p. 316.

Platonic Ideas are fabrications of philosophical imagination revealing nothing, while revelation comes from Above in theophanic, theandric, and trinitarian forms. Platonic ideas were correctly likened to myths.[91]

Myths, in Ţuţea's view, are human intimations of something unattainable by the human mind. Imprisoned in human imagination, anchored as that is in anthropomorphism, myths often provide an inchoate interpretation of the individual's inner and outer worlds. Ţuţea accepts Mircea Eliade's mystical interpretation of the sacred, but insists that the sacred cannot be experienced merely individualistically: there must be active participation in the Divine Liturgy[92] – that is, the liturgical celebration as well as the cosmic reality. Eliade understands the sacred as 'an element in the structure of consciousness and not a stage in the history of consciousness',[93] and therefore establishes what he calls a morphology of the sacred. This vision of both Eliade and Ţuţea contrasts with that of Roger Caillois, for example, who describes the sacred as 'a category of sensibility' which 'cannot be approached unless we die', and which, paradoxically, we have to respect and celebrate if we want to avoid sacrificial 'contamination of the profane by the sacred'.[94] Following Plato, both Eliade and Ţuţea would agree that, as a manifestation of sacred reality, hierophany is also 'ontophany',[95] that is, an awakening – within the created order – to the Divine, a manifestation of true being. There is nevertheless a fundamental difference in their respective views of the sacred, in both conceptual and methodological terms. For Eliade the sacred is fundamentally a qualitative and limiting distinction from the profane. According to David Cave, 'though Eliade assumes the irreducibility of the sacred, the sacred is not dualistically separable from the profane, for the sacred is contained in and qualifies the profane'.[96] Methodologically, Eliade believes it is possible to decipher the sacred. He asserts the possibility of having access to the sacred through a sort of hierophany initiated from below ('progressional view of hierophanies'),[97] in order to de-camouflage the sacred by means of a so-called 'creative imagination'.[98] In Ţuţea's view, Eliade's hermeneutics moves 'between legend and myth', establishing a polarity between two methods of enquiry: epic folklore and personal imagination. Neither of these leads to truth. For, according to Ţuţea, in folklore the mythic and the magical combine in an epic manner, while 'the indistinct belongs to the world of fantasy which, through the force of imagination,

---

91   PROBLEMS, p. 316.
92   See PROBLEMS, p. 337 and ELIADE, p. 83.
93   Mircea Eliade, *A History of Religious Ideas*, trans. Willard R. Trusk, 3 vols (London: Chicago University Press, 1978–85), I (1978), p. xiii.
94   Roger Caillois, *Omul şi Sacrul*, trans. Dan Petrescu (Bucharest: Nemira, 1997), p. 20.
95   Cave, *Mircea Eliade's Vision*, p. 36.
96   Cave, *Mircea Eliade's Vision*, p. 37.
97   See Cave, *Mircea Eliade's Vision*, p. 39.
98   Bryan S. Rennie, *Reconstructing Eliade, Making Sense of Religion*, foreword by Mac Linscott Rickets (New York: State University of New York Press, 1996), pp. 223–5.

attracts the concrete, the fabulous and the mystical. For, the human being – not God – stands at the centre of magic fabrications and of modern natural science.'[99]

Also, Eliade orders hierophanies in a sort of ascending sequence ending in the Incarnation as the supreme hierophany. Țuțea finds Eliade's position limited by subjective, psychological, social, and historical factors:

> We should not confuse Christian living... with the religious experience of which Mircea Eliade speaks. The latter is subjective, has its source within the human being, and is open, while in Christian experience the Divine Absolute is incorporated in a human being, and embraces continuously [through participation] all those who believe. [Christianity] is mystical living in the world of dogma. Mircea Eliade's religious experience can be located in the ante-chamber of knowledge of religious truth. The historical symbolism it carries, with the variability implied in it, cannot go beyond the psychological and social – notwithstanding Eliade's anti-historicism – since intentionality of the phenomenological kind (Husserl) is not constitutive of meaning and therefore of sacrality... No matter how much the historian of religions would like to detach himself from the profane, he is unable to do so, so long as he remains a historian.[100]

In the end, Țuțea adopts a mystical Trinitarian position, in contrast to Eliade's scholarly dialectics and language of 'progressively ascending hierophanies':

> Only Trinitarian Unity can enter the blind process of becoming without its uniqueness being affected. In other words, seen in a biblical light, Divinity is self-revealing in immanence, yet without compromise of its purity. It is revealed in Its entirety, since Christian symbolism is not influenced by the variability of historical forms. Mircea Eliade's sacred is similarly unaffected by the profane in history, but is conceived from the point of view of human intentionality and thus, being something other than Divinity, cannot constitute the content of religion. It is identical with the holy of Rudolf Otto.[101]
>
> From a Christian point of view history is described as it truly is in the two opposed 'cities' of St Augustine: *Civitas Dei* and *Civitas terrena sive diaboli*. Sacred language is dogmatic, its sacred content unchanging. It must always therefore be distinguished from profane language. Eliade describes the sacred in terms of the profane language of progressively ascending hierophanies.
>
> Christian norms are not characterised by that historical incompleteness in which, as Mircea Eliade puts it, the 'irreducible, eternal, real and infinite sacred is revealed paradoxically'.[102]

---

99   ELIADE, p. 14.

100 PROBLEMS, pp. 316–17. The phenomenological method of enquiry developed by the German philosopher Edmund Husserl (1859–1938) greatly influenced Eliade.

101 Rudolf Otto (1869–1937), German theologian whose celebrated book *Das Heilige* (*The Idea of the Holy*, 1917) is an inquiry into the relationship between rational and non-rational aspects of religious experience. Țuțea also read Otto's comparative analysis of the nature of mysticism, *West–Östliche Mystik* (*Mysticism East and West*, 1926), which compares the German mystic Meister Eckhart (thirteenth–fourteenth century) and the Hindu thinker Sankara (eighth century AD), who commented on the Upanishads and Bhagavad Gita.

102 PROBLEMS, p. 317.

In distinguishing between sacred and profane language Țuțea is warning us that any attempt to interpret the sacred risks reducing God to the realm of mythology, magic, or rationalism. Nevertheless, 'the Great Mystery' is known ritually in the Eucharist.[103] And Țuțea emphasises the unity between creation and the uncreated God effected by the indwelling, within the human heart, of the Holy Spirit, the seal of the One in whose image and likeness humanity is made. Within the triangle God–nature–humanity, the relationship between the human spirit and natural things is assured by 'the triangle's actual existence originating in, and being governed by, the sacred'.[104]

The Reality of the Sacred in a Secular World

Theological Science and Mystical Union

Țuțea considers Christian theology to be 'a science of transcendence'[105] based on faith in God as unique, transcendent Truth revealed in Jesus Christ and communicated through sacred tradition and sacred history. He uses the word 'science' here in its Latin sense of *scientia*,[106] knowledge, deliberately resisting its reductionist application simply to the material, physical sciences. While 'the pure Christian science'[107] has the immediate precision of any human science, it also has mediated exactness, because it is rooted in dogma. For Țuțea, the theologian is not a scientist, but one who is enlightened: 'Mystical theological knowledge is mediated knowledge, since it comes from without, from the Transcendent. Immediate philosophical knowledge is accessible to all, but is relative rather than real, a useful speculative way of relating to things.'[108]

Țuțea concurs with Augustine's view of the revealed truth of faith as redemptive, and with Aquinas's demonstration of theology's 'superiority over other disciplines, a superiority derived from its sublime object, the one sole, salvific Truth'.[109] Theology provides true knowledge, Țuțea believes, since it reflects the truth of the whole human being in relation to God. It is 'true science' for it relates to God and immortality.[110] The science of theology is *scientia cordis*. This distinguishes theology from other disciplines of the human mind, making it, as the medievals held, 'queen of the sciences':

---

103 PROBLEMS, p. 318. This should not be understood in a narrow 'churchy' sense. See
      'A Note on Țuțea's Use of Language', p. xix.
104 ELIADE, p. 62.
105 PROBLEMS, p. 51.
106 See also Constantin Noica, *Mathesis sau Bucuriile Simple* (Bucharest: Humanitas, 1992),
      pp. 53f.
107 THEATRE, p. 516.
108 DAYS, p. 132.
109 DOGMAS, p. 24.
110 SYSTEMS, p. 115.

From Aristotle to the present day, philosophy has failed to be *scientia scientiarum* because it lacks that single principle which gives theology unifying power. From the perspective of truth philosophy remains *ancilla theologiae* (the handmaid of theology).[111]

Theology is also a 'fundamental domain of culture',[112] in which faith is expressed in different cultural contexts. This does not affect the 'scientific' integrity of theological truth. But, Ţuţea warns, 'one should not forget the terms *theophany* and *ecstasy*, the epistemological content of which is transmitted by language' and therefore is subject to varied interpretations.[113] Theophany, the self-manifestation of very God, is fundamental to knowledge of the divine which, 'along with ecstasy, renders all argument for the existence of God – ontological, cosmological, noetic, historical, or teleological – redundant'.[114]

Here Ţuţea may seem to deny reason any rôle in leading to knowledge of God. In fact he is, albeit in characteristically provocative style, merely asserting the limits of reason in the human quest for God. He would not deny that arguments for the existence of God retain whatever validity they have in the realm of scientific enquiry, but in terms of *scientia cordis*, the precondition, so to speak, of enquiry is simply the radical initiative of God that shapes and sustains reason itself within the creaturely constraints of freedom. As ever, he reminds the reader of the absolute primacy of God's initiative and self-revelation:

God cannot be conceived or seen from below, but only in divine self-revelation: theophany, theandry, and trinity. Christian moments: creation *ex nihilo*, original sin, baptism... Last Judgement, damnation, and salvation. Not thirst for origins, nor human ascent, but eschatological correction.[115]

In other words, those who search for meaning and truth solely through the self-sufficient intellect, epistemologically detached from mystery and the liturgy, from living discipleship in the Body of the Church, condemn themselves to illusion. Reason may attain heroic detachment from the world, but such detachment is in itself a mere worldly *askesis*.[116] True detachment from the world can been attained only through Love:

For Christians, the unifying principle is love, which is identified with the Godhead... Love opens a window onto the Absolute and does not stop at its threshold as immanentist approaches do. Therein are united both worlds, this world and the world to come, the

---

111 DOGMAS, p. 34.
112 PROBLEMS, p. 49.
113 PROBLEMS, p. 50.
114 PROBLEMS, p. 50.
115 PROBLEMS, p. 321. Ţuţea's refusal to follow normal grammar (in this instance, omitting verbs, subject, and object) makes reading laborious sometimes. It can, however, add an exhilarating momentum and open up new possibilities of meaning. His style implicitly protests against ever taking structure for granted, an intellectual tactic to re-sensitise those whom he addresses to the value and mystery of meaning.
116 See PROBLEMS, p. 150.

perishable and the imperishable. Through this miraculous union, the believer escapes the jaws of absolute death [which is itself but the form of the atheist's mind].[117]

The science of the transcendent is based on knowledge of divine truth. Union with God requires in the first place detachment from the sensible world and from every kind of knowledge acquired through the senses. Illumination is, for Ţuţea, 'the extraordinary light with which God sometimes suffuses our soul'.[118]

Mystical knowledge[119] cannot be acquired by autonomous enquiry, just as it cannot be acquired either by physical and mental techniques. Nor can ecstasy be merely induced by initiation into 'techniques of existence', although encounter with the divine does require rational preparation and a discipline of alertness (staying 'awake'). 'Mystical ecstasy, as a way of knowledge and decision, belongs to holiness.'[120]

Unio mystica, as Ţuţea understands it in the work of the neo-Platonist philosopher Plotinus, differs fundamentally from the Christian incarnational vision of relationship and union between God and humanity. Although his view of Plotinus is not shared by all modern interpreters, it is perhaps illuminating for a personal understanding of Ţuţea to see how he views Plotinus's theory of emanations. Ţuţea saw these means, whereby the mystic can return to 'the One' or 'the Good', as expressing 'shame' towards the body in its fallen state. Rather than a rational detachment of the self from the physical world, emanations as understood by Ţuţea arise from spiritualised intellectual self-distancing from the body.[121] Understanding the mystical essentially in terms of revelation, 'the only means of awakening and gaining access to truth',[122] Ţuţea sees Plotinus's position on ecstasy as metaphysical rather than mystical.[123] Knowledge of mystical truth presupposes watchfulness and humility,[124] while 'a metaphysician is one who has not yet awoken to religion'.[125]

---

117 PROJECT, p. 186.
118 See Ţuţea, in Cornel Ciomâzgă, 'O, genii întristate care mor...', *Tinerama*, Bucharest, 6–12 December 1991, p. 16.
119 See note 18, Chapter 3.
120 Ţuţea, in Ciomâzgă, 'O, genii întristate care mor...', p. 16. See also the final section of this chapter, on human deification as continuous revelation of the sacred.
121 PROBLEMS, p. 150. For a similar, though more detailed, conclusion on Plotinus's ascetic view of the physical body see Peter Brown, *The Body and Society: Men, Women, and Sexual Renunciation in Early Christianity* (New York: Columbia University Press, 1988), pp. 178–80.
122 ELIADE, p. 31.
123 PROBLEMS, p. 150.
124 The virtue of watchfulness or circumspection, often emphasised by Ţuţea in conversation, can be likened to the spiritual vigilance needed for practising all Christian virtues. His understanding resembles the broad Hesychast definition of νῆψις given by Hesychios the Priest in his work 'On Watchfulness and Holiness', see *The Philokalia*, I (1979), pp. 162–98. The original complete title of the Greek *Philokalia* can be translated as *The Philokalia of the Neptic Fathers*, that is, of 'the fathers who practised and inculcated the virtue of watchfulness': *The Philokalia*, IV (1995), p. 437.
125 PROBLEMS, p. 32.

According to Ţuţea's reading, Plotinus's understanding of thought is that it moves out of the body 'which he is ashamed to possess' and out of the world of the senses, 'but not out of the original One'[126] or 'the Good'. This movement out of the self, a refined self-distancing from the world, differs from Christian mysticism in that Christian revelation comes from above, from outside the self, and cannot be comprehended by human consciousness, which labours to achieve ecstasy in terms of this world. For Ţuţea 'Christian truth is received'.[127] And this reception of Christian truth ultimately partakes of the relational nature of Love.

Thus it is in human community, in one form or another, that a person experiences the fullness of divine truth that is communion in and with God. At the level of personal self-giving to this *dynamis* of union, believers are called to a life of discipleship and discipline. Whether as anchorites or 'ordinary' members of local churches, all belong to one another, as 'members incorporate in the mystical Body'. Human existence is a waiting upon God, undertaken corporately through 'a state of watchfulness'[128] and humility. This actively receptive corporate mystery is the only true mysticism. It is not philosophy, but rather the work of divine grace in the Body of Christ. Thus, 'there is no such thing as mystical philosophy'.[129] Although Ţuţea would disagree, therefore, that in Plotinus 'we find the supreme exponent of an abiding element in what we might call "mystical philosophy"',[130] he would perhaps agree with Andrew Louth's conclusions on Plotinus:

> The One has no concern for the soul that seeks him; nor has the soul more than a passing concern for others engaged on the same quest: it has no companions. Solitariness, isolation; the implications of this undermine any possibility of a doctrine of grace – the One is unaware of those who seek it, and so cannot turn towards them – or any positive understanding of the co-inherence of man with man. These limitations... disclose a radical opposition between the Platonic vision and Christian mystical theology.[131]

---

126 PROBLEMS, p. 150.
127 PROBLEMS, p. 320.
128 PROBLEMS, p. 320.
129 PROBLEMS, p. 320.
130 Andrew Louth, *The Origins of the Christian Mystical Tradition* (Oxford: Clarendon Press, 1981), p. 36.
131 Louth, *Origins*, p. 51. Cf. J.M. Rist, *Plotinus, The Road to Reality* (Cambridge: Cambridge University Press, 1967), Chapter 16, 'Mysticism', pp. 213–30. Rist places Plotinus within the framework of four types of mysticism, defined as pantheistic, ascetic, monistic, and theistic by Robert C. Zaehner in *Mysticism: Sacred and Profane* (Oxford: Clarendon Press, 1957). Rist regards Plotinus's thought as 'theistic mysticism, where the isolated soul attains to union and is "oned" with a transcendent God, though *a fortiori* it is not itself identical with that God': Rist, *Plotinus*, p. 214. Rist concludes that Plotinus is 'the most metaphysical of all philosophers', 'a prince among metaphysicians': Rist, *Plotinus*, p. 247. Ţuţea considers mysticism and philosophy as mutually exclusive: philosophers are by definition 'metaphysicians' (that is, foreign to any form of mysticism), while theologians are by definition 'mystics'.

Țuțea's view of the sacred is similar to that of Rudolf Otto in that he emphasises the inherent limitations of human reason and emotions. These point to the illusory character of human 'autonomy'. Although the sacred can be discerned through mystical experience, it cannot be quantified or explained, but only presented (for example, as paradox). Only by suspending their critical faculty and accepting through faith the possibility of human communion with ultimate reality can individuals open themselves to that reality. When humans search for their origin without God they become trapped in a labyrinth. The only exit is through inspiration or ecstasy:

> When we are driven by a passion for truth as religious paradox, then we understand its source and the simple usefulness of human seeking and measuring. Ariadne's thread symbolises the limits of the autonomous human being in his eternal seeking. The inspired or ecstatic – detached from self and from the world by true Christian love – being the object of God's favour, can live out the Platonic idea of human being.[132] But seeking it, observing it, reflecting it through a whole life-time or series of life-times, leads merely to a vast accumulation of signs, without knowledge.[133]

Țuțea thus re-asserts the status of theology as a science. For real mystical knowledge comes from Above through Christian dogmas:

> In other words, can there be a science of the transcendent? If truth is one, and if this is received by revelation and communicated, not sought, as sacred history and sacred tradition make clear, then a science of the transcendent can exist, a science through which God is communicated to us, as the name of this branch of knowledge, theology, literally suggests.[134]

Sacred Space and Time

According to Țuțea the Church bears responsibility for the sacredness of the space it inherits. Christians should be involved in continuous worship, fulfilled in *anamnesis*, remembrance of God. Through the sacredness of liturgical time, the believer's 'participation through the ritual' of the Church[135] in the mysterious presence of Christ, in every aspect of life in the community, is guaranteed. Sacrality, therefore, is mutual rather than unilateral. God communicates through the sacred liturgy, while people offer themselves to God in their whole life. Space and time, the Divine Liturgy in the temple of the Church, and our lived discipleship in the place and age in which

---

132   For Țuțea, as for Maximus the Confessor, there is between God the Creator and created humanity the fundamental reciprocity that exists 'between an archetype and its image. It should become manifest on the *existential* level through a double movement: God's movement towards man in the Incarnation (or in different incarnations or embodiments) and man's movement toward God in the imitative process of deification': Thunberg, *Man and the Cosmos*, p. 62.

133   ELIADE, pp. 73–4.

134   PROBLEMS, pp. 49–50.

135   See 'A Note on Țuțea's Use of Language', p. xix.

human beings are called to show forth the divine Image in the world, are both alike creatures of the Holy:

> The Real is to be found in the sacred space of the Church and in the sacred time of the religious festivals which enable humans to escape the emptiness of the infinite.[136]

The experience of truth as mystery leads to salvation.[137] Like Alexander Schmemann in his book *For the Life of the World*, Ţuţea stresses the cognitive and participatory connotations of sacramental symbolism, whose theological 'semantics' has meaning only 'within a wider theological and spiritual context'.[138] Sacraments are integral to, not independent of, liturgy, because 'the ritual content of divine worship is Truth':[139]

> Sacred space – the Church – and sacred time – Christian festivals – are defined by the presence of Deity. The symbols of mystical thought are manifestations of the Real, and their form and content coincide; this is not the case with profane dialectic or aporetic symbolism which only indicate what is accidentally useful, conveniently formal or pleasing... The presence of God through revelation or priestly mediation in liturgical celebration goes beyond the predication and intuition of supposedly autonomous humanity; this real heteronomy includes everything: subject, object and symbol.[140]

Sacred time and space envelop and nurture the faithful who, anchored within the Eucharistic community, are taken up into the great company of heaven:

> Religion is like a harbour where ships take shelter during a storm. Religious thought alone can identify completeness with perfection – in the supreme Being, revealed in this world to the elect who have understood the coming of the Saviour, and contemplated in the next by the redeemed: under the dome of the Church, that sacred space in which is celebrated the festive ritual of sacred time, whose Lord is the Absolute.[141]

The Sacred and Theodicy

Ţuţea contrasts *the mystic*, as the recipient of revelation, with *the magician*, who is on the side of the deceiver and so never escapes bondage to this world. For the mystic, 'there is nothing conventional in biblical symbolism, since religion is the realm of the Real'.[142] Meanwhile, the scientist relies on his own knowledge to produce apparently magic results which, however, can never explain all that is. The artist too, like Faust, is tempted to strive for the ultimate with his own resources, and to think his talent is

---

136 ELIADE, p. 32.
137 PROBLEMS, p. 44.
138 Alexander Schmemann, *For the Life of the World, Sacraments and Orthodoxy* (Crestwood, NY: St Vladimir's Seminary Press, 1968), pp. 146–7.
139 PROBLEMS, p. 87.
140 ELIADE, p. 79.
141 ELIADE, p. 9.
142 PROBLEMS, p. 178.

the source of knowledge and beauty. For Țuțea this is demonic self-deception, evidence of evil in the created universe. 'A realist demonology is necessary, since evil is present in this world.'[143] He sees sacred tradition and profane 'originality', sacred history and profane history, as co-existent, although 'the dialectical illusions' of the latter in each case do not compromise the truth of the former because, from Eden itself until now, 'God has not forbidden the devil to operate at His side',[144] so that the freedom of human beings might be exposed to the risks incurred in moral and religious testing. Despite the presence of evil and the consequences of original sin, human beings still have access to the sacred, thanks to the love of God in the Incarnation of the Logos. In Țuțea's thinking, the possibility of true knowledge arises out of the very nature of God which guarantees room for human responsibility and choice. Exercising their free will, the faithful can thus participate in their own redemption: 'Within the Trinity, God is omnipotent, good and forgiving, since in Christianity evil has an historic rather than an essential character.'[145]

Sacred Language as Mystery

For Țuțea, the very 'nature of language is a mystery'.[146] 'Mysteries are communicated through language'.[147] Language can only be received and deciphered as a 'divine favour'.[148] The study of language in itself is a useful, but not revelatory, spiritual exercise: 'Mysteries are not to be found by seeking. As Goethe says in *Faust*, they are not located in darkness, but in that world whose light compelled Dante to keep silence.'[149]

Perhaps following Gregory Palamas's comment on a passage from the Pseudo-Areopagitic corpus,[150] Țuțea suggests here that human organs of sense-perception will experience the world of mysteries as darkness unless grace is active in them. Only the immediacy of inspiration can open our 'eyes' to the transcendent light of God, but this is so far beyond our ability to comprehend that the revelation confounds all human distinctions of vision, bringing us to an experience beyond vision, to the pure darkness of ineffable light. Although language is a mystery, it is used both by

---

143   PROBLEMS, p. 178.
144   THEATRE, p. 412.
145   PROBLEMS, p. 258.
146   THEATRE, p. 496.
147   PROBLEMS, p. 255.
148   THEATRE, p. 447.
149   THEATRE, p. 496.
150   Taking up the statement of Dionysius the Pseudo-Areopagite, 'The divine darkness is the unapproachable light in which God is said to dwell' (*Letter 5: Patrologia Graeca* 3.1073A), 'Palamas says that "in the strict sense it is light", for it is a supremely positive reality; but, "by virtue of its transcendence", it is experienced by us as "darkness" (*Triads*, II, iii, 51)': Kallistos Ware, 'The Hesychasts: Gregory of Sinai, Gregory Palamas, Nicolas Cabasilas', in Cheslyn Jones, et al. (eds), *The Study of Spirituality* (London: SPCK, 1986), pp. 252–3.

theists and atheists alike. Țuțea reminds us that, when used as 'the vehicle of human inquiry', language cannot escape plurality of meaning, being external to the object and meaning it represents. It can transmit false reasoning and specious argument.[151] In his view, word, image, sound, sign, event, indeed all forms of communication, 'convey (of course by grace) part of the whole, in this world where everything is seen through a glass, darkly (1 Cor. 13)'.[152] The human tongue is inadequate to describe supernatural mystery, not because there is anything vague about the mystery, nor because of any obscurity within the mystery, but because of the limitations of human understanding expressed in language.

Țuțea considers that language conveys truth at the level of the sacred. In Rudolf Otto's terms, the *mysterium tremendum et fascinans* is at once attractive and fearsome. This mystery 'is found in Scripture and made manifest in ritual'.[153] Țuțea's theological anthropology tries to avoid anthropomorphic induction, deduction or retroduction of God from a description of humanity since:

> language is not rooted in individual human beings who cannot define themselves, nor in blind nature. At these levels everything moves in silence. Who holds together the visible and the invisible, this world and the world to come? God, who inspires charismatic people and manifests Himself in history. What do human beings do with language as mystery? When they are not inspired, they use it in ways which are useful, convenient, groundless or erroneous.[154]

Mystery can be communicated through language, but never totally revealed. Even theological language, which necessarily employs philosophical terminology, is, as Țuțea frequently asserts, only 'a vehicle for grace'. (It should of course be borne in mind that he does not dismiss 'vehicle' from ultimate Reality – he affirms the resurrection of the body.) Talk of grace is not simply a truer way of talking about nature, nor is it abandonment of the natural world. In Țuțea's view, the transcendent dimension of grace is definitive. This can raise awareness of God, for real knowledge of humanity is revealed only from above:

> It is not possible to define the human being outside the realm of grace and revelation. Philosophy and science operate in utilitarian, aporetic, or false ways external to human

---

151 Lucifer is, of course, the angel of light, that is, there can be pseudo-clarity in spiritual matters – a spurious 'illumination' that in fact is the darkness of diabolical arrogance. 'Sometimes writers, such as Gregory of Nyssa, have used the metaphor of darkness to state that human concepts are inadequate to express God's nature, for God is "separated on all sides by incomprehensibility as by a darkness" (life of Moses)', Cheslyn Jones, 'Liturgy and Personal Devotion', in Jones, et al. (eds), *The Study of Spirituality*, p. 16.

152 Țuțea, MS 1982, p. 24.

153 Țuțea, MS 1982, p. 24. See also, Rudolph Otto, *The Idea of the Holy, An Inquiry into the non-rational factor in the idea of the divine and its relation to the rational*, 2nd edn, English trans. John W. Harvey (Oxford: Oxford University Press, 1950), pp. 13–40.

154 Țuțea, MS 1982, p. 25.

nature. Without grace and revelation philosophers and scientists just potter about. Pascal, the scientist, was inspired when he found peace and certitude in the biblical God.[155]

When we forget that 'sacred language belongs to theology'[156] and, as such, is ultimately a divine gift granted to humanity as a means of communication with the Divine, then language fails to fulfil its function as a 'vehicle' for transcendent grace. Ţuţea believes that the relative inarticulateness of creatures in their relationship to the divine affects the very content of revelation as made accessible to them. Also, in order to distinguish between inspiration ('divine breath')[157] and inquiry, it is necessary 'to eliminate polysemy' (the faculty of some words to have more than one meaning) and to maintain through faith the divine meaning – that is, that which is ultimately significant – of inspiration.

Reason between Science and Revelation

In Ţuţea's view, there are two levels at which human reason may function: that of *inquiring reason*, in which the search for scientific knowledge is initiated by the human mind (when not aware of its limitations, this form of reason may be governed by evil); and that of *acquiring reason*, in which theological knowledge is communicated by grace to the inspired (who become 'vehicles of divine truth'). Reason has also the function of safeguarding sacred history and sacred tradition: 'Truth is received from Above, not from below', by those whose 'praying, patient, and receptive spirit' is 'sustained by sacred history and sacred tradition'.[158]

According to Ţuţea, the distinction between scientific discovery of universal laws of nature and personal revealed truth is one of degree. The findings of discursive reason are conditioned by grace, since 'no human path leads to the centre, and so to truth', without the help of the Deity.[159] Even when he distinguishes between methodologies employed by exact sciences and humanities, Ţuţea stresses that scientists and humanists alike need the prevenient assistance of grace:

> Philosophers and artists, unlike scientists, technocrats and artisans, operate either efficiently through intellectual, moral or aesthetic values or suggestively, transforming the human soul for better or for worse. Without the presence of Divinity, self-knowledge can lead to the true, the good, and the beautiful only by chance; and even so, these are relative compared to 'things in themselves', no more spiritually meaningful than a child playing in the sand or wondering at his own face in the mirror.[160]

---

155   PROBLEMS, p. 116.
156   PROBLEMS, p. 332.
157   PROBLEMS, p. 179.
158   PROBLEMS, p. 323.
159   ELIADE, p. 82.
160   THEATRE, p. 358.

Țuțea uses the word 'desacralised'[161] where one might normally refer to 'secular' to describe society or mind. This is a challenge to any view of the secular as the 'normal' state of being, with religious faith as somehow additional to this 'normality'. It suggests the radical importance of faith as essential to genuine normality. In fact, Țuțea often uses the much stronger epithets 'satanic/satanised' and 'demonic/demonised' (for example, 'seeking and systematic thought are forms of demonic seduction').[162] Rather than the antithesis 'sacred/profane' adopted by Eliade, he frequently uses 'sacred/satanic'.[163] The violence of these words is intended to remind us of the genuinely horrific nature of sin, and thus of the moral and spiritual fragility of the natural, secular order. We must bear in mind, therefore, as we explore Țuțea's ideas about 'desacralised' mind, that he is talking about life and death issues which we would by nature wish to avoid at all costs.

The logical conventions of scientific language replace absolute truth with the relative, ultimately unverifiable findings of secular human reason. Mind is thus 'desacralised' (though of course the constructs of desacralised mind may be very beautiful and moving – and may thus be worthily offered up to God) and remains in a state of cosmic isolation resembling autism, incapable of communication with the divine mind. Țuțea emphasises that the desacralised mind is actually the victim of ignorance and belongs to *homo stultus*, who is self-destructive and sinful, controlled by demonic forces, and under the illusion that there is no God.

I have shown that in observing this mismatch between humanity's spiritual gifts and its refusal to acknowledge its sacred origins, Țuțea referred to autism in the original – and inaccurate – definition given in Heinrich Schmidt's philosophical dictionary of 1934, nine years before Leo Kanner described it for the first time as a psychiatric phenomenon in itself. In Țuțea's theological use of this term, metaphysical 'autism' leads to atheism and nihilism, while ontologically humanity becomes sub-humanity, for it loses its resemblance to its Creator. But 'if the spiritual state of the subject who receives truth cannot be communicated, what are dialogue and discourse?'[164] This is Țuțea's answer:

> The purpose [of dialogue and communication] is to awaken our memory or awareness of the limits of human knowledge in this world (whose origin cannot be explained without a revelatory god, as in Plato), and to maintain in a state of watchfulness those uninspired faithful Christians who obediently participate [in the mystery of the Eucharist]. Revelation and faith are the only forms through which the spirit can penetrate what Heidegger called the opaque limits of existence.[165]

Țuțea shows that the epistemological gap between the sacred and the profane reflects a division between love and knowledge in the human being, as a consequence of our

---

161 Țuțea, MS O, p. 33. See also REFLECTIONS, I, p. 41.
162 PROBLEMS, p. 300.
163 ELIADE, p. 21.
164 THEATRE, p. 447.
165 THEATRE, p. 447.

estrangement from God. In the nineteenth century, the historically unprecedented progress of technology led to a crisis in human knowledge exemplified by Marx's repudiation of religion and Nietzsche's celebrated 'death of God'. Although in his analysis of the development of contemporary secularism Ţuţea would recognise that some of the impetus for secular, scientific, and philosophical progress came precisely through opposition to established Christianity in its politically abusive, morally decadent, and spiritually vapid aspects, the tendency of his whole argument is to affirm human dependence on God.

With God written out of history, there was nothing (other than an all-too-human belief in decency and 'civilisation') to stop the growth of ideologies like Communism and Fascism, which set about destroying Christian belief. Such ideologies (to which church communities were not immune) cultivate the spirit of bourgeois *ressentiment*.[166]

Reduced to the level of secular morality, forgiveness and reconciliation can no longer sustain Christian trust in the redemptive grace of God, with its mysterious power to transfigure humanity and the world. Yet Ţuţea believes that truth in itself is unaffected by individual ability or inability to grasp it. God's love is for human beings as they are, and is not dependent upon their realisation of the gifts bestowed on them by divine love. It is absolute. By contrast, Nietzsche exulted in the ultimately aloof 'superman'. Ţuţea frequently speaks of what he calls the Nietzschean 'pathos of distance' which, he believes, has no substance. It is remedied at the religious level:

> by love as defined in the Sermon on the Mount and at the Last Supper. *Ressentiment*, rational democratic sterilisation of feelings, have given rise to the degrading and tormenting spectacle... of human beings submerged in themselves and in things.[167]

For Ţuţea, the moral and political vacuum exposed by the collapse of Communism shows that humankind is incapable of providing its own order. His message is that people need a reorientation toward God, a rediscovery of the sacred. This clearly has significance for an age in which traditional Christianity is profoundly questioned by young people searching for personal, political, and ecological solutions at a time of global crisis.

Sacred and Profane in Relation to Deification

The Sacred and the Profane

Central to Ţuţea's thinking is the belief that all systematic inquiry, whether pertaining to sacred theology or to secular mental disciplines, deals with 'utilitarian' rather than 'true' experiences. At the same time it should be understood that both the sacred and

---

166   See Max Scheler, *Ressentiment*, trans. William W. Holdheim, introd. by Lewis A. Coser (New York: Free Press, 1961).

167   OLD AGE, pp. 129–30.

the profane are actual areas of inquiry. Țuțea believes that the truths of faith can be experienced and tested in a secular environment. In a profane context faith should be affirmed all the more boldly, with that prophetic 'violence' inherent in the sacred. Țuțea's reflections on the uncompromising confession of faith of the early Christian apologist Tertullian and on the association of primitive religions with violence relate to the ideas of René Girard. Girard, writing from an ethnological perspective, sees Christianity as the 'end of the sacred', since the Crucifixion is not a means but rather the revelatory self-offering of Christ's divinity.[168] Oswald Spengler's *The Decline of the West*,[169] describing a self-contained secular culture in its terminal stage of decadence, points to the Last Judgement, when evil is punished by the eternal Logos with sacred violence:[170]

> It is of the essence of religious thought not to be satisfied with finite temporal experiences. Paul's hierarchy of two worlds makes earthly order possible. Tertullian's 'dour style' is put to the service of this ideal order. It cannot be understood without logos, ethos and pathos. The effectiveness of transcendent truth makes choice possible. This is how we must understand decision. Tertullian affirms he is a Christian because he 'wants to be a Christian'. His choice has not been difficult, since it arose naturally from the comparison between two worlds in conflict.
>
> Cioran makes an interesting observation on style: 'Aggressiveness is a common feature of human beings and new gods'. Those in the twilight, like pagans, exercise disdain because of their exhaustion. Those who are convinced – and religion belongs to the realm of mysteries, in which convictions operate – that they are in possession of eternal truths consider all forms of violence sacred.[171]

While Țuțea recognises that secular philosophy, science, art, technology, and existential techniques no longer serve Christian faith – and are indeed often hostile to it – they nevertheless, in their own way, prepare the human psyche for the experience of the holy. This is still God's initiative. Awareness of the interplay between sacred and secular (which, not only for censorship reasons but also for theological reasons, Țuțea expressed in spiritually 'neutral' terms, as interrelationship of the eternal

---

168 René Girard, *Things hidden since the Foundation of the World*, trans. Stephen Bann and Michael Metteer (London: Athlone Press, 1987), p. 233.

169 See Oswald Spengler, *The Decline of the West*, abridged edn by Helmut Werner, trans. Charles Francis Atkinson, ed. Arthur Helps (Oxford: Oxford University Press, 1991).

170 For 'generative violence' see 'The Gods, the Dead, the Sacred and Sacrificial Substitution', in René Girard, *Violence and the Sacred*, trans. Patrick Gregory (London: Athlone Press, 1995), p. 258.

171 THEATRE, p. 190. Cf. Matt. 11:12. In the present era of terrorist violence, relating to religious fundamentalism, this issue is clearly critical. While one may assume Țuțea would not condone extremist violence (just as he explicitly condemned extreme nationalism), I know that he took to be equally serious the abuse of power by the 'great' nations, and the possibility of modern (military) technology enabling the smaller nations to assert themselves – see Chapter 10. For Țuțea's rejection of 'integral nationalism' see BGMP, p. 367.

and the transient) helps individuals to negotiate the boundary of the unknown and the experience of transcendence. Such awareness is unattainable by reason or convention; it can come only through personal enlightenment and communal ritual. In an absolutist, atheist State this was indeed subversive, since the Liturgy, celebrated 'in spirit and in truth', nourishes active Christian discipleship within the social context.

The Sacred as Deification

The twentieth century saw the final emergence of a self-desecrated humanity (using Țuțea's more 'violent' level of language). The notion of human dignity deriving from creation in the image and likeness of God was replaced by a self-centredness, dominated by consumerism and moral relativism, both material and spiritual. As a result, sacred and profane can, in Țuțea's view, no longer be in harmony, although they may sometimes have a common goal. He placed the alienation of science, art, and technology from religion within the broad cultural context in which Renaissance Christian humanism developed out of the Medieval (theocentric) 'Age of Faith'.

In the Middle Ages, morality, art, religion, music, and science were all closely related within the unifying authority of the Church (the sometimes repressive limitations of ecclesiastical authority notwithstanding). This unity was manifest in the Church's physical and political structures. In modern times, by contrast, each area of culture is independent within a secular environment 'which would look utterly bleak, were it not punctuated by churches'.[172] That sense of unity has been lost in the specialist focus of everything upon itself. Despite this, Țuțea believed that it is possible for human beings to escape the containment and inertia of these bubbles of cosmic loneliness filled with anxiety and nothingness. For, both secular and profane are ultimately contained in the triangle God–creation–humanity. Without acknowledgement of this triangle, however, secular compartmentalised culture will continue to sink into solipsism, cut off from vivifying contact with the common source (that contact with humanity's divine origins that brings liberation from the captivity of Fallen creation).

Țuțea's vision is clearly soteriological. The key to human deification is 'imitation of Christ'. God's plan from the very beginning is the deification of the entire created order. In this, human deification is crucial. Ultimately it is God's initiative, yet there is a level at which human beings can prepare and conform themselves to receive the divine offering, as I have shown. At this preparatory level, learning and human *askesis* are valid as information and means for the 'awakening of vocation', even 'in the absence of inspiration'.[173]

Imitatio Christi is not a question of copying the particular 'style' of the life of Jesus of Nazareth. Rather, it means taking up the Cross of personal circumstances, temperament, gifts, and opportunities day by day. It is the working out of individual

---

172   APHORISMS, p. 25.
173   SOPHISTRY, p. 172. Cf. OLD AGE, p. 131; Țuțea, *Philosophia Perennis*, p. 130.

vocation after the example of Jesus Christ and in obedience to His words (cf. Matt. 16:24; Mark 8:34, 10:21; Luke 23:26).

For Țuțea, human efforts to achieve perfection are doomed to failure. The imitation of Christ, ultimately depending on grace, is true *mimesis*, the only complete representation of the sacred within the created order:

> In Christianity it is essential to be sincere in one's attitudes. Faith must be demonstrated here within the confines of ordinary earthly human capacity. It is the saint who represents the purest form of religious expression, placed as he is at the summit of the scale of human values.[174]

By showing forth the will of God and reflecting Christ's glory, the saint is able, through the grace of the Holy Spirit, to demonstrate that even amid the self-glorifying achievement of Fallen humanity the 'divine mask' of humanity's true nature can be revealed.

---

174   OLD AGE, p. 127.

Chapter 8

Theatre as Seminar

From the late 1960s to 1980, in an explicit response to Eugène Ionesco's 'theatre of the absurd',[1] Țuțea developed his own complex and original view of theatre. He had planned to write a number of dialogues (*Bios, Eros, Ethos, Logos*),[2] an essay, and a play to discuss and illustrate his concept. In the end, however, he completed only two of the dialogues (*Bios* and *Eros*), the play *Întâmplări Obișnuite* (*Everyday Happenings*), and the essay *Teatrul Seminar. Prezentare*[3] (*Theatre as Seminar. A Presentation*). He finished the dialogues and play between 1968 and 1969, and the essay in 1980. *Bios* and *Everyday Happenings* both have the same introduction: *Teatrul Seminar. Prolog* (*Prologue to Theatre as Seminar*). This indicates that Țuțea saw the theoretical and the practical aspects of theatre as unified. In 1993 the *Prologue* and these four works (*Everyday Happenings, Bios, Eros*, and the *Theatre as Seminar. A Presentation*) were edited, selectively abbreviated, and published together by Mircea Coloșenco in one volume, *Lumea ca teatru. Teatrul seminar.*[4] It is this that I use in the present book, although I prefer to use Țuțea's own titles, which I edit in accord with the manuscripts in my possession.

---

1   See Aurel Ion Brumaru, in PROJECT, p. 33. In June 1958 Kenneth Tynan, the drama critic of the London *Observer*, launched an attack against Ionesco's so-called anti-realism: 'Here at last was a self-proclaimed advocate of *anti-théâtre*: explicitly anti-realist and by implication anti-reality as well. Here was a writer ready to declare that words were meaningless and that all communication between human beings was impossible.' Ionesco protested against Tynan's imputation: 'The very fact of writing and presenting plays is surely incompatible with such a view. I simply hold that it is difficult to make oneself understood, not absolutely impossible... No society has been able to abolish human sadness, no political system can deliver us from the pain of living, from our fear of death, our thirst for the absolute.' See Martin Esslin, *The Theatre of the Absurd* (London: Penguin, 1980), pp. 128–9. In Țuțea's 'realm of certainty' it is precisely this 'thirst for the absolute' that delivers people from 'fear of death and nothingness'. See PROJECT, pp. 139–41.

2   Personal conversation, Bucharest, 10 June 1985. See also Brumaru, 'Adaos 2', in PROJECT, p. 20.

3   The Romanian title defies satisfactory translation. 'Seminar' is a noun, used adjectivally to qualify 'theatre' and carrying the double meaning of 'seminar' as in English and 'seminary' (that is, a forum of priestly preparation). I offer the reader *Theatre as Seminar*, conscious that this lacks the concision and suggestiveness of the original, but hoping that it conveys at least a sense of the interplay of spectacle, learning, and personal–relational elements that Țuțea is concerned with.

4   Meaning *The World as Theatre*. *Theatre as Seminar*, a more accessible, if clichéd, title.

Let us now examine how Țuțea envisages his 'unified' approach to theatre. Knowledge is, for him, inherently a dramatic enactment of divine truth played out on a stage of cosmic celebration. *Teatrul seminar* is a written attempt to give substance to this elusive and essentially interactive understanding. At once discursive, dialogic, suggestive, polemical, and celebratory, it provides the context for the mature formulation of his thought.

Țuțea's anthropological thinking was cultural in the broadest sense. Before prison, his cultural matrix was the classic canon of European high culture. Specifically, in his exploration of the human condition (conventionally understood as tragic, meaningless, and absurd) through the idiom of theatre, it was Shakespeare and Balzac who, in both the widest and the most precise sense, offered a dramatic paradigm for his conceptual and formal vision:

> The content of my meditations on history is comprised under two famous titles: *La Comédie Humaine* (Balzac), a vast *Comedy of Errors* (Shakespeare). With these borrowings I distance myself from the absurd perspective of the tragic.[5]

Meanwhile, it was Dante who provided him with an implicit structure:

> Dante taught me that tragic constructions are banal and durable, for tragic events endlessly recur. Comedy is called to release us from their fatal chain and, in its essence, constitutes a splendid adventure of the spirit. It is *The Divine Comedy*.[6]

I will show that it is also possible to draw a parallel between Țuțea's discussion of *theatrum mundi*, or 'life as spectacle', and Hans Urs von Balthasar's 'theological aesthetics' as 'Theo-drama'. Within this frame of reference Țuțea developed his theology of the human person through the kaleidoscopic vision of comedy, tragedy, and drama which he worked out in *Teatrul Seminar*. Stressing the educational and cathartic functions of theatre, whose roots he identifies in religious ritual and liturgy, he finds the original harmony between humanity and God restored in the drama of the 'mystical union' of the human and the divine. The images of mask, rôle, and stage, to be explored in detail in Chapter 9, are used to express his understanding of divine image and likeness, personal vocation, and Eucharistic Liturgy.

Teatrul Seminar

The scientific and poetic character of 'theatre as seminar' makes it, 'like any *seminar*', 'predominantly non-dramatic'.[7] It is best read in the spirit of the Platonic dialogues, which have actors who are also spectators 'sitting in armchairs',

---

5   PROBLEMS, p. 205.
6   THEATRE, p. 171.
7   THEATRE, p. 519.

conversing without gestures on great themes, abstract or topical.[8] It is cathartic not simply in an Aristotelean sense. For Ţuţea, true purification can be effected only by liturgy and prayer. His 'theatre as seminar', having ritual and liturgical roots,[9] reflects aspects of human nature in a holistic way capable of effecting transformation. Through theatre the Communist world could be encouraged to examine itself thoughtfully and thus perhaps come to its senses.

This potential of theatre to bring about transformation was explored with particular deliberateness by the Jesuits in the early seventeenth century. The Baroque united the visual and auditory elements of art, and was used by the Catholic Church in its Counter-Reformation propaganda.[10] The eclectic style of Ţuţea's writings on theatre similarly indicates a code of interpretation. It implies a metaphysical initiation, which it in fact performs. There is a sense in which, as a subversive teacher of Christian truth, Ţuţea resembles the Baroque *hombre secreto*[11] (the man who never discloses his personal secrets, yet seeks to enter others' minds). Citing the great art historian Heinrich Wölfflin, he maintains that the Baroque can only be described, not defined; he sees it as a movement not of ideas or principles, but of artistic techniques rooted in the primordial Promethean revolt.[12] Through aphoristic discourse and a kind of spiritual dexterity, combining scholarship with insight into human nature, Ţuţea leads his audience to *astonishment* (as a pastoral technique somewhat along the lines of Baroque *meraviglia*),[13] to what he calls a spiritual 'awakening'.[14]

---

8   THEATRE, p. 9.

9   See THEATRE, p. 2.

10   This 'art of unity' was developed in Rome from 1620 within the Counter-Reformation movement to help the Catholic Church regain spiritual and temporal territory lost to Protestantism. In the sixteenth century, Ignatius of Loyola's University provided youngsters aged approximately ten to thirteen with a thorough grounding in Latin grammar, taking them through an intensive two-year programme of rhetoric, poetry, and history. Cicero's rhetoric and the Renaissance admiration for eloquence, right reason, and oratorical style (*eloquentia perfecta*) combined to make the Jesuit a formidable adversary in confrontations with the Reformers. Not surprisingly, the public nature of discourse and debate soon evolved into dramatic form, and Jesuit theatre quickly became integral to the student's practical education in the art of Latin eloquence, as well as a practical means of inculcating Catholic values into wider society in order to transform it. See Douglas Letson and Michael Higgins, *The Jesuit Mystique* (London: Fount, 1996), p. 139.

11   See 'El Discreto', in Baltasar Gracián, *Obras Completas, I*, ed. and introd. by Miguel Batllori y Ceferino Peralta (Madrid: Atlas, 1969), pp. 313–65. Cf. Edgar Papu, *Lumini Perene* (Bucharest: Eminescu, 1989), p. 229.

12   See Heinrich Wölfflin, *Renaissance and Baroque*, trans. Kathrin Simon, introd. by Peter Murray (London: Fontana, 1964). For Ţuţea's comment on Wölfflin's work see THEATRE, pp. 474–6.

13   Papu, *Lumini Perene*, p. 230. Academician Papu sees the Jesuit Baltasar Gracián's Baroque *arte de prudencia* as laying the foundations of psychology as a science. See Baltasar Gracián, *The Art of Worldly Wisdom*, trans. Joseph Jacobs (London: Shambhala, 1993).

14   'Truth can be awakened by inspiration, priests, or free dialogue', THEATRE, p. 409.

General Context

Țuțea's 'heroic Christian apologia in the face of physical and mental brutality' became well known in Romanian political prisons.[15] But not many people are aware that after his release from Aiud in 1964 he started to write and, to some extent, publish his ideas on *Theatre as Seminar*, according to a definite plan.

In 1968, a dramatic year in both Eastern and Western Europe, Ceaușescu opposed the Soviet occupation of Czechoslovakia. His policies gave some false indications of liberalisation and 'seemed to encourage innovative Marxist approaches'.[16] During the short period of relaxation which followed in Romanian domestic policy, greater freedom for publishing was allowed; thus, sections of Țuțea's two dialogues and of the play already mentioned were published in the monthly magazine *Familia* between February 1968 and March 1969.[17] At that point, Țuțea re-defined *teatrul seminar* as a means of enabling the spectator to stop living 'in ignorance, suffering as he does from what Goethe named *chronophagia*' (that is, futile consuming of time):

> I have called my play *Everyday Happenings*, precisely because my aim is to elevate everyday life to dramatic significance. Humanity itself becomes a stage performance.[18]

In one of his dialogues, when asked why he was so concerned with theatre, Țuțea insisted that deep understanding of the world can only be displayed, not conceptually expressed: 'I have never felt the need to write, but I thought that the contemporary world should be presented as it is.'[19]

Theatre was Țuțea's interactive image for revealing the truth about Romanian society under Communist rule: remaining faithful to his Christian beliefs, living under continuous surveillance, and trying to publish his work in the face of censorship, he stresses that practising Christians 'move between the possible and the impossible,

---

In other words, personal experience of God is either immediate or mediated (through sacraments, preaching, and genuine companionship).

15   Miller, *The Gift of the World*, p. 20. I quote from Fr Miller's book having enjoyed the privilege of discussing Țuțea with him in Oxford.
16   Vladimir Tismăneanu, 'Understanding national Stalinism: reflections on Ceaușescu's socialism', *Communist and Post-Communist Studies*, 32, 1999, p. 167.
17   See Bibliography. It is significant that Țuțea's works were published in Oradea, a provincial centre in the North-West of Romania – that is, with less strict surveillance than Bucharest. Censorship soon tightened again, however, and Țuțea's work was banned until after 1989. Tragically, he died before any of his *Theatre* could be presented on stage. On 20 November 1992 a dramatised production of *Theatre as Seminar* (*Prologue, Bios,* and *Eros*) had its premiere at the Odeon Theatre in Bucharest. In 1993 a group of Romanian actors directed by Dragoș Galgoțiu staged the dialogues *Bios* and *Eros* in the open air in front of the Egyptian pyramids at Giza. On his return from Cairo to Bucharest the leading actor, Dragoș Pâslaru, became a monk.
18   BGMP, p. 82.
19   Petre Țuțea, *Neliniști Metafizice* (Bucharest: Eros, 1994), p. 181. [*Metaphysical Angst.*] See also THEATRE, p. 255.

since they have access to the Absolute through faith'.[20] What appears impossible in this world (salvation, resurrection, and eternal life) becomes possible for the faithful to whom, as to St Paul (2 Cor. 4:18), two worlds have been revealed. This world represents limitation. Human beings are 'anchored in the world of phenomena', which can and should be known, since 'the Saviour urges us to be bold in order to rule this world' (Luke 16:18), while perfection is 'related to life eternal and to the other world':[21]

> When I think of the Saviour's Passion, His Glory and Resurrection, and of the value of Christian suffering in space and time, I understand 'la renonciation totale et douce, soumission totale à Jésus Christ' in Pascal's *Mémorial*, as an expression of his thirst for perfection. For Christian purity means escape from our bondage to time and space. This is eternal life as paradox (Kierkegaard).[22]

In *Teatrul Seminar* Ţuţea demonstrates both his 'oral genius' and his scholarship, in the tradition of the Roman tribune who speaks for the common people in a way that is also meaningful to the intellectuals and élite. He combines realist, classical, and 'concrete' approaches:

> I tried to avoid both flattery and denigration, and to adopt the precision of a geologist formulating his stratigraphic findings. Objective depiction of human types is a feature of realism. Indeed, it is a feature of classicism, which is static in character because governed by a harmony of form and content, and by the urge to achieve something definitive. Classical perfection implies a frozen harmony.[23]

When Ţuţea speaks here of 'precision',[24] it should be borne in mind that he rejected the culture of 'socialist realism' and the rigid stereotypes of Romania's neo-Stalinist culture, including the mythology of the 'working-class heroes' which nourished the Ceauşescu personality cult in the 1970s.[25] Rather, he uses dynamic, concrete reality in order to express 'the struggle between old and new', and 'the conflicts of interest which need to be resolved'. This 'concretism', as he calls it, is not to be confused either with 'realism'[26] (that is, socialist realism) or with the science of the Real (that is, theology).[27]

The educative function of theatre, which in a relatively short space of time can influence large audiences, becomes apparent here. 'Theatre as seminar', as I have noted, is inspired by the Platonic dialogue, whose function was both to 'awaken'

---

20   THEATRE, p. 515.
21   THEATRE, pp. 515–16.
22   THEATRE, p. 516.
23   THEATRE, p. 255.
24   See Ţuţea's distinction between human precision and God's exactness, in Chapter 6.
25   Cf. Georgescu, *Romanians*, p. 256.
26   THEATRE, p. 255.
27   PROBLEMS, p. 7.

people in the street and *agora* from passivity, and to encourage them to persevere in identifying 'inspired solutions' to contemporary problems:[28]

> Theatre is an ongoing school for the masses. It is the most appropriate means of communicating to them human truths and errors. In short, my play [*Everyday Happenings*] is a literary construction in the form of theatre-as-seminar – so called because it sets forth, in dialogue form, the fundamental problems of our time and how these are to be solved. Some of these problems are permanent, because integral to human nature, others are only transient. This dramatic construction starts from a definition of humanity as a complex 'thread-ball' of questions which cannot always be untangled.[29]

Ţuţea, in the tradition of Hellenic *paideia*, believed that education can and should affect the whole person. There is no disjunction between physical instruction and theoretical learning, because body and psyche are created as a single unity.[30] Education leads to 'the supreme human bond', spiritual and physical 'affinity' with 'The Good' ($\tau\grave{o}\ \alpha\gamma\alpha\theta\acute{o}\nu$) and ultimately with God.[31] Education then is the source of freedom. Living under an oppressive dictatorship, Ţuţea appreciated this all the more keenly. His implicit criticism of the régime is apparent when he writes:

> The soul must feel itself determined to its very depths by Truth, and not by that submission to a leader which Plato in *The Symposium* rejects as 'slavery'. There are two constant elements in the education of people who live within the confines of community and nature: first, the disciple's free, morally endowed soul and its affinity with the thing explored, and then the master with his sharp mind. Both terms meet in 'The Good' of Plato. Yet humanity, society, nature, and things accessible to the senses are sources not of Truth, but of language which, although functional, is external to the nature of things... History demonstrates how humanity lives without knowledge of Truth (as conceived by Plato), for Truth is transcendent in essence.[32]

Archetypal Theatre?

As a teacher and metaphysician, Plato distinguishes between divine and human creativity. It is God who creates things and their archetypes: human beings imitate them. However, Ţuţea is aware that what Plato 'predicates in the *Sophistes*, in order to distinguish between true and false, has nothing to do with Truth in itself which is beyond dialectics, since the Idea as essence, as Truth, is "intuitive, not discursive"'.[33]

---

28   See BGMP, p. 192.
29   THEATRE, p. 255.
30   Ţuţea saw the human person in Christian terms, as an integrated unity of body and soul. He rejected Plato's doctrine of the pre-existence and transmigration of souls (which leads to a split view of the person): REFLECTIONS, I, p. 127.
31   See REFLECTIONS, II, p. 307.
32   REFLECTIONS, II, p. 307.
33   REFLECTIONS, II, p. 278. In REFLECTIONS, I, p. 17, Ţuţea discusses *noesis* and *dianoia*. He follows the distinction made by the Fathers between *dianoia* as discursive,

Țuțea tries to establish whether there can be a Platonic Idea of theatre and, if so, whether it is reflected in what he calls 'pure' or 'archetypal theatre'. He explores the possibility of a 'theatre of Ideas' conceived as a multi-disciplinary synthesis.

The pseudo-dramatic method is influenced by the theory advanced in Plato's *Meno*, that knowledge is recollection (*anamnesis*): genuine knowledge 'is acquired, not through the senses or as information conveyed from one mind to another by teaching, but by recollection in this life of realities and truths seen and known by the soul before it was born into this world'.[34] Țuțea, too, believed that truth can be awakened in others, because it is already present. Learning is thus *anamnesis*. However, whereas Plato attributed this to the pre-existence of the soul, Țuțea's view arises out of his belief that humankind is made in the image and likeness of God, who is discovered in the way of Christ-likeness.

Notwithstanding the synthesis achieved in *Teatrul Seminar*, Țuțea concludes that archetypal theatre, as such, does not exist. For Țuțea, then, there can be no such thing as a Platonic Idea of Theatre. 'Theatre' cannot be a primordial Idea, since it derives from human beings. Theatre portrays human beings, it cannot simply portray an archetype. In *Everyday Happenings* Țuțea suggests that theatre must portray human beings in action:

My theatre observes the classical veneration of truth, clarity of expression, and romantic freedom. My play is called *Everyday Happenings*. In it I discuss theatre as seminar, not [Platonic] pure theatre. I have thought about archetypal theatre. There can be no such thing. The Platonic Idea of theatre, like any Platonic Idea, is an absolute unity. If you consistently applied pure theatre, in the sense in which we have used it, it would lead to the conclusion that historical forms of theatre are manifestations of primordial theatre. And that is not true. In the Platonic universe, the Idea of theatre must be considered alongside the Idea of the human being. The symbolism of dramatic art should develop from this principle.

In that case, what is the content of the Idea of theatre? Gods, titans, legendary and historical heroes embody Ideas that are historical components of theatre. Like any art or technique, theatre is a synthesis of various disciplines and it produces an aesthetic effect. In principle, the object of theatre is to portray human beings historically in terms of their temporal programme, or essentially in terms of their eternal significance. Ideological aspects describe human beings in their wholeness only to a partial degree. Sacrifice for the sake of a religious, moral, or political idea is also an expression of human nature.[35]

---

conceptualising, and logical reason, and *nous* as the intuitive 'eye of the soul' (St John of Damascus) which, 'when raised to the state above nature, finds the fruits of the Holy Spirit' (St Mark the Ascetic): Archim. Hierotheos Vlachos, *Orthodox Psychotherapy, The Science of the Fathers*, trans. Esther Williams (Levadia: Birth of the Theotokos Monastery, 1994), pp. 126–7. See also Kallistos Ware's foreword to Sherrard, *Christianity, Lineaments of a Sacred Tradition*, p. xxxii.

34   Francis M. Cornford, *Plato's Theory of Knowledge, The 'Theaetetus' and the 'Sophist' of Plato*, trans. with comment. (London: Routledge, 1970), p. 2.

35   THEATRE, pp. 252–3.

Țuțea thus implies that ideological definitions of humanity such as those imposed in the national curriculum under Communism are inevitably partial and distorted. As I will show in the following chapters, in place of Marxist–Leninist ideology he proposes a theology of sacrifice and a typology of human beings on a journey to deification. In terms of cognitive discipline, these are, for Țuțea, the only way of approaching the whole human person – that is, humankind created in the image and likeness of God. As a 'technique of the self', theatre as seminar is doomed to fail unless the older Christian 'technologies of the self' (for example, spiritual exercises and observance and their focused expression in monastic life) are re-appropriated from a new perspective, combining the older Christian emphasis on 'self-disclosure as self-renunciation' with the modern view of 'self-disclosure as creation of a new identity'.[36]

Țuțea's conclusion is that neither historically nor in a Platonic sense can human beings be made vehicles of truth through straight dramatic representation within the terms of 'pure theatre'. Symbolic representation reduced to itself is an artificial, obscure construction 'from below', not a product of clear vision or divine inspiration 'from above'.[37] By contrast, his theatre as seminar points to a *liturgy* (from λειτουργία, meaning etymologically *public service*) of sacred texts and rituals which, as a divine gift, fosters spiritual growth and personal transformation. This is very different from concepts of formal imitation. It points beyond 'pure concepts' defined by Țuțea as 'Kant's categories, Kantian apriorism, logical forms of the subject's supposedly pure intellect':[38]

> At the human level, 'the pure' can be expressed only by means of representations whose origin is in objects of the sensible world. What is pure can be thought of, but not represented [other than by 'impure' means], for a human being cannot have 'pure intuitions'. Rather he needs to be content with being awakened [by 'the pure'] and to reflect [on it] by means of images related to this world (of which he is an integral part).[39]

Țuțea had no hesitation in saying that, although Plato's mystical philosophy is pre-Christian, it was inspired by God. He stressed the authentic character of 'the pure

---

36 Nathan D. Mitchell, *Liturgy and the Social Sciences* (Collegeville, MN: The Liturgical Press, 1999), p. 71. On p. 66, Mitchell draws on Michel Foucault's project 'to produce a history of the "political technology of the body"', as described in Luther H. Martin, Huck Gutman, and Patrick H. Hutton (eds), *Technologies of the Self: A Seminar with Michel Foucault* (Amherst: University of Massachusetts Press, 1988).

37 Țuțea defines pure theatre as 'dramatic mime' prompted by and 'confused with a hermetic text': Petre Pandrea, *Memoriile Mandarinului Valah* (Bucharest: Albatros, 2000), p. 125. See also Kallistos Ware's foreword to Sherrard, *Christianity, Lineaments of a Sacred Tradition*, pp. xxix–xxxiv, for the distinction between two methodological principles 'from within' and 'from above' which are characteristic of both Sherrard's and Țuțea's epistemological approaches, and are decisively influenced by Plato's doctrine of Ideas.

38 ELIADE, p. 80.

39 THEATRE, p. 152.

science of non-creative human beings who by divine favour' share the inspired vision of Ideas.[40] He considered all human individuals to have a basic *bun simţ* ('good sense'),[41] which gives guidance in 'the world of mysteries'. In the pre-Christian era it was this that directed poets and sages in their reading of religious truth from nature, 'that book of God opened to the enlightened'.[42] Alluding to this grace of *bun simţ*, intrinsic to Incarnation, which mediates relational, living, knowledge of the archetypes, Ţuţea maintained that all human beings have the capacity 'to reflect on what is absolute, infinite, and eternal'; within this aspect of the economy of the Incarnation, Plato's Ideas themselves have life: 'Platonic archetypes are not simple images, perfect in their entirety, but primordial forms and forces, as Schopenhauer calls them. They are *living eternities*.'[43]

Catechetic Theatre

In Ţuţea's view *pure* knowledge, whether in art or science, is received from above and points to ultimate explanations of things:

> It has an essential character. 'Blessed are those who can know the causes of things' (Virgil, *Georgics*). Nobody throughout the whole of history has been able to answer the question: what is the ultimate purpose of things?... Reduced to ourselves, we shall not find salvation.[44]

In the introduction to the first volume of his *Treatise on Christian Anthropology* Ţuţea states that 'there is no such thing as artistic catharsis, in the Aristotelean sense, but only ritual catharsis'.[45] In *Teatrul Seminar* he suggests that true purification is achieved only in a liturgical context defined as the preparation for, and sharing in, Eucharist: 'Aristotelian catharsis is a pseudo-purifying aesthetic moment, to be distinguished from the liturgical moment which is genuinely purifying.'[46] In a society in which access to the Eucharist was often hindered, theatre as seminar could have an instructive, even catechetic function:

> I am experimenting with theatre as seminar, in the style of the religious drama adopted by the Jesuits as an educational tool to correct the heresies of the Reformation. The spectator comes to the seminar to be instructed and enlightened – not to be entertained or purified in the Aristotelian sense of catharsis.[47]

---

40 THEATRE, p. 510.
41 I have already shown that Ţuţea distinguished between *bunul simţ* ('good sense') and *simţul comun* ('common sense'). See section on 'Exactitude and Precision', in Chapter 6.
42 THEATRE, p. 511.
43 THEATRE, p. 152.
44 THEATRE, p. 515.
45 PROBLEMS, p. 7.
46 THEATRE, p. 390.
47 Interview, Bucharest, 15 March 1990. Ţuţea's idea of 'theatre as seminar' is perhaps also rooted in the vernacular mystery plays based on the Bible, which derive from ancient liturgical drama in Latin on the life, death, and resurrection of Jesus Christ.

Țuțea acknowledged his debt not only to Jesuit drama, but also to medieval Mystery and Miracle Plays, as much as Passion Plays (which influenced J.S. Bach in the eighteenth century), as a means of educating the uneducated classes and enabling participation in the Passion of Christ and in the lives of saints.[48]

Theatre as Christian Apologia

I have shown that, for Țuțea, knowledge of the Real is linked to 'a concrete experience of the impossible'; this is defined by G.K. Chesterton in terms of Christian theological paradoxes: 'to believe what is unbelievable, to hope what is hopeless, and to love what is unlovable'.[49] What Țuțea calls 'the impossible' can be equated with 'Christian purity', 'holiness', which 'penetrates the opaque meaning of existence'. For him, existence as such (without consciousness of the unity between this world and the world to come) is 'impenetrable' and reduces the universe to the strictly 'existential level' described by Heidegger and non-Christian French existentialists such as Jean-Paul Sartre and Albert Camus. He prefers Dante's medieval style, based on a mystical and mythical conception employing personification and allegory, which he contrasts with 'modern man's vulgar use of concrete reality'.[50] Therefore, 'Dante's medieval style must be adopted also by the author of theatre as seminar' for whom Christian pure science or theology, in the sense of *scientia* or knowledge, is a 'manifestation of the Real as opposed to existentialist failure and materialist darkness'; it is in this sense of Christian theology as *scientia universalis* that Țuțea addresses the fundamental question posed in his *Teatrul Seminar*: is there a *pure science* and a *pure art* (with 'the constructs of pure thought' as their ideal content)?[51] Țuțea's answer is negative because 'real unities cannot be deciphered if they are not revealed'.[52] On a strictly human level Realism is impossible. However, his 'theatre as seminar' is intended (although it can only succeed, so to speak,

---

48   Interview, Bucharest, 1 March 1990.

49   THEATRE, p. 516. I have been unable to track down this quotation. It was from Țuțea himself that I learned it (and rendered it back into English). Perhaps Țuțea paraphrased Chesterton's saying in *Orthodoxy*, Chapter VI, 'The Paradoxes of Christianity': 'Stated baldly, charity certainly means one of two things – pardoning unpardonable acts, or loving unlovable people'. See Chesterton, *Orthodoxy*, p. 137. See also Tertullian, 'De Carne Christi', 5:25 (*certum est quia impossibile*), in Ernest Evans (ed.), *Tertullian's Treatise on the Incarnation*, introd., trans., and comment. by Ernest Evans (London: SPCK, 1956), p. 18.

50   THEATRE, p. 516.

51   THEATRE, p. 516. Țuțea understands theology as the sacred science of the Real, revealed from above. Ultimate reality remains 'inaccessible' from below, 'in this world of choices'. Cf. THEATRE, p. 515. He maintains that 'in Christianity, the sacred, the pure, and the good are united in the self that reflects the Absolute One, the new Trinitarian Deity', who grants human beings loving access to knowledge of the Real in the mystery of deification: THEATRE, p. 510.

52   PROBLEMS, p. 326.

liturgically, with divine intervention) to be 'pure', that is, to mediate revealed or inspired knowledge.[53] In Țuțea's view:

> pure science and pure art are mystical. Language as a whole, which is a mystery in itself, constitutes no more than a linguistic symbolism, unless it is a vehicle for the revealed essence of things (or 'things in themselves').[54]

Mystical View of Theatre

Țuțea believes that all human types, characters, and actions can be presented in the symbolism of literary dialogue and dramatic spectacle. Theatre as seminar can thus integrate the 'types' of the saint, priest, statesman, scientist, artist, cultivated individual, or psychotic tyrant. These types are interwoven mythically, magically, rationally, and mystically, with the beliefs, prejudices, and superstitions of 'ordinary people'. What Țuțea calls 'the eternal interplay of quest and inspiration' includes lyric, epic, and dramatic elements, all embraced in the mystery of Christian existence:

> 'Theatre as seminar' must be ruled by the Christian view of life and the world. In this view, the aesthetic perspective of the contemplative, creative playwright situates the tragic, the sublime, the comic, the grotesque, the satirical, the fantastic-magical, and the rational-logical, at the level of the human vantage point. This human 'perspectivism' can only be[come] objective by a majority consensus. But it can never be *obiectic*,[55] because objecticity transcends the generally accepted point of view: the gratuitous amusement of time-consuming ('chronophagic') man devoured by his ego, by society and nature.[56]

Țuțea's view of 'objecticity' as 'the transcendence of the object contemplated'[57] was influenced by Alexius von Meinong's 'Gegenstandstheorie'.[58] For Meinong, an

---

53   PROBLEMS, p. 326.

54   THEATRE, p. 515.

55   According to Țuțea, the difference between what is subjective and what is objective is 'a matter of degree, not of nature'. If it is God-given, reality is 'objectic' (*obiectic*). If it is a product of the human mind it is 'subjective' and confined, but human language describes this on a scale that ranges between 'subjective' and 'objective': THEATRE, p. 358. See also introductory section of Chapter 3.

56   THEATRE, p. 390.

57   OLD AGE, p. 90.

58   'Meinong widened the conception of an object to include objects which were not nothing, but which nevertheless did not exist; in the same way he has added to the realm of facts a set of entities which resemble facts in every essential respect, but differ from them in so far as they are not the case, that is, in so far as they lack the kind of being which is appropriate to facts. To the whole class of entities of which some are, and others are not, the case, he has given the name of objectives... Meinong tries to prove that they are a unique and irreducible sort of entity, indispensable to our knowledge of reality and to reality itself': *Meinong's Theory of Objects and Values*, 2nd edn, trans. and ed. J.N. Findlay (Oxford: Clarendon Press, 1963), p. 60. On p. 49, Findlay shows that in his *Über Gegenstandstheorie* Meinong formulates his doctrine on pure objects: 'the pure object

object (or 'objective')[59] is 'anything that can be intellectually grasped or intended: real, possible, or indeed even impossible things'.[60]

Liberal View of Theatre

Christian societies have often condemned theatre for promoting fiction, deception, and artificiality. There are two main reasons for early Christendom's traditional hostility to theatre: first, that it is untrue, and, as fiction, encourages people to live a lie and experience the imaginary feelings of characters on stage rather than their own feelings; and second, in the late Roman empire it was associated with immorality and actresses were often high-class prostitutes.

The first of these charges remains a problem even for modern theatre, especially in film and television, in spite of the theory of catharsis in Aristotle's *Poetics*. Without denying the early Fathers, however, Ţuţea was interested in the positive function of theatre. He contrasted liturgical catharsis[61] (which effects true spiritual purification) with the Aristotelean theory that through watching drama the audience is purged of unworthy emotions, and through the pity and fear felt for imaginary characters they are able to understand their own true condition in the world. Ţuţea was also aware that, due to the alienating reverse of all values under Communism, the whole of society had become a living stage, with the reality of the spiritual world replaced by the fictions of Marxism–Leninism.

His acceptance of theatre as compatible with Christianity overcomes a view which early Christian thinkers like Tertullian held on this issue. In *De Spectaculis*, Tertullian rejects theatre and masks as expressions of pagan idolatry and hypocrisy (in the normal debased sense of the word, rather than in its original sense of the actor's rôle).[62] Ţuţea sees the same issues in his own age:

> The same psychological and moral problems are posed today. Is a reform of modern theatre possible in the sense of replacing vulgar pleasures of the senses with the pure joy of [contemplating] Ideas? Can the art of deception be replaced by the art of truth?[63]

---

stands beyond being and non-being; both alike are external to it. Whether an object is or not, makes no difference to what the object is. The pure object is said to be *außerseiend* or to have *Außersein*: it lies "outside".'

59   D.W. Hamlyn, *The Penguin History of Western Philosophy* (London: Penguin, 1987), p. 319.

60   ' *"Gegenstand"* [object] *ist alles, was intellektuell erfaßt oder gemeint werden kann: die wirklichen wie die möglichen oder auch unmöglichen Dinge*': Schmidt, *Philosophisches Wörterbuch*, p. 272.

61   PROBLEMS, p. 7.

62   'And then all this business of masks, I ask if God can be pleased with it, who forbids the likeness of anything to be made, how much more of His own image. The Author of truth loves no falsehood; all that is feigned is adultery in His sight': Tertullian, *De Spectaculis*, XXIII, in Tertullian, *Apology, De Spectaculis* and Minucius Felix, *Octavius*, trans. T.R. Glover and G.H. Rendall (London: Heinemann, 1966), p. 287.

63   THEATRE, p. 195.

He considers Tertullian's *De Spectaculis* as a 'Christian pamphlet' inspired to the level of 'lyrical excess', but also as 'a model for the way the critical spirit should be exercised'.[64] He agrees with Monseigneur Freppel's assessment of Tertullian's rejection of the theatre as 'exaggerated in itself', but understandable and excusable in view of the 'disorders produced by the spectacles of paganism'.[65] Tertullian's 'apocalyptic style' marks the ends and beginnings of historical stages:[66]

> Tertullian rejects theatre in itself, even when its lesson is the victory of virtue, since vices presented during the spectacle are more seductive than prosaic virtues. Evil is sovereign in the world of illusions and has the sophisticated skill to present 'poison wrapped in honey'.[67]

Ţuţea concludes, however, that 'it never does any harm to place a mirror in front of human beings to make them aware of their limitations'; he sees his more subtle, liberal view of theatre as perfectly compatible with Christian truth and virtue:

> The mystical vision of life and of the world springs not only from Scriptural values, from Tradition and the glorious aspects of Church history, but also from repeated recognition of the provisional character of human rational constructs.[68]

Ultimately, the supreme spectacle is not contained within nature or human creativity.[69] It is 'the Last Judgement and the glory of eternal life' which 'go beyond our imagination'.[70] Ţuţea believes that theatre can convey Christian values and 'prophetic lucidity',[71] which by definition is optimistic rather than tragic, for it always points to salvation and is inspired by belief that the impossible can be overcome through all-embracing love. However, existentialism in philosophy and the absurd in aesthetics express accurately and tragically, in his view, 'the madness of the modern European

---

64 THEATRE, p. 196.
65 See Mgr l'Abbé Freppel, *Tertullien – Cours d'éloquence sacrée fait à la Sorbonne, pendant l'année 1861–1862*, 2 vols (Paris: Ambroise Bray, 1864), I, pp. 189–209, quoted in THEATRE, p. 193.
66 THEATRE, p. 195.
67 THEATRE, p. 193.
68 THEATRE, p. 197.
69 By contrast, Fr Alexander Elchaninov, who died in 1934, gives a modern version of Tertullian's view of theatre: 'Why should priests not go to the theatre? The very principle of theatrical show is rejected by the Church, which forbids masquerading, mumming, dressing up in the clothes of the opposite sex, all this being a sham, ambiguity, falsehood. Even to be no more than a spectator means that one is in a way taking part in it all. As regards the actor, the greater his passion in performing, the greater the harm he causes to his soul, allowing confusion and untruth to take up their abode in it.' See Alexander Elchaninov, *The Diary of a Russian Priest*, trans. Helen Iswolsky, ed. Kallistos Ware, introd. by Tamara Elchaninov and a foreword by Dimitri Obolensky (London: Faber and Faber, 1967), p. 101.
70 THEATRE, p. 197.
71 PROBLEMS, p. 70.

human being'. For what point is there for an individual to engage with, or be detached from:

> a world without meaning, characterised by an overwhelming infinity, which comes out of nowhere and is going nowhere? In the theatre of the absurd the boundary between truth and error, tragedy and comedy, good and evil, beauty and ugliness, the sacred and the satanic, is obliterated and there is no question of love. God, the devil, humankind, and nature are caught up together in a grotesque whirlpool.[72]

In Țuțea's view, the aesthetics of the absurd are opposed to Dante's conception of the world in which love is the universal bond and the principle of order which prevents the total dissolution of creation.

On the Theatre of the Absurd

In a 1972 paper dictated for the thesis of Ioana Pavelescu,[73] a drama student (daughter of Țuțea's friend, the actress Corina Constantinescu) who was to become one of the leading Romanian actresses of the 1980s, Țuțea makes the following assessment of Camusian existentialism:

> Camus's *Myth of Sisyphus* is the clear and courageous representation of the human condition. It expresses the pride and contempt of the isolated individual in a hostile world, whose conscience will not permit him to give up...

> In *The Rebel*, the idea of revolt goes beyond the idea of temporal revolution and any concept of frozen order: the author depicts human beings as lively, eternally clear-minded, and innovative...

> When 'eternity wears the face of humanity', as Camus says, people direct their energy towards what Pindar calls 'exhausting the domain of the possible'... In this sense, revolt is understood as the active principle of conscience which, without denying history, seeks to affirm itself within it...

> Atheist existentialists like Camus reckon failure more important than the awakening of human consciousness, within the context of cultural decline at the conclusion of a historic cycle in Western Europe.[74]

---

72   PROJECT, p. 139.
73   Ioana Pavelescu now lives in New York. She kindly gave me permission to quote from 'her' thesis stored at the Academy of Theatre and Film in Bucharest and also to make public that Țuțea was the real author of its theoretical section. Under Communism, theory was typically of primary importance in the assessment of an artist. Ioana Pavelescu was, not surprisingly, less expert than Țuțea in the finer details of existentialist philosophy.
74   Ioana Pavelescu, 'Despre rolul Martha, din piesa *Neînțelegerea* de Albert Camus' (unpublished MA thesis, Institute of Drama and Film, Bucharest, June 1972), pp. 8–11. ['On the Rôle of Martha, in Albert Camus's Play *The Misunderstanding*'.]

This critique of *Caligula* expresses Țuțea's dissident view of Ceaușescu's tyranny. In reading his analysis of that play it is again important to remember the historical context in which he was writing. Romania was governed by a 'mad emperor' capable of extreme brutality, a man bent on destroying all traditional national culture and establishing a 'new culture' influenced by the vast publicly orchestrated displays which he had witnessed in North Korea and China in 1971. Ceaușescu's Chinese experience became for the people of Romania the starting point of a tragic drama of 'absurdity'. The theme of *Caligula* is:

> in the first place, the discovery of the absurd symbolised by that mad emperor, Master of the Roman empire, who comes to the conclusion that 'nothing lasts' and that 'men die and are not happy'. This is what the absurd is: obsession with death and the presence of death. In the second place, Caligula conceives liberation as the destruction of the existing order of established values, through the exercise of 'complete freedom' without restraint...
>
> What is Caligula's conclusion? There is no such thing as pure life in the biological sense, nor pure consciousness in the theoretical and moral sense. Human life is made up of these two things. The oppositions of good and evil, beautiful and ugly, sacred and profane, freedom and bondage, do not incapacitate the morally gifted who must struggle to find happiness here on earth, the only happiness possible to them.[75]

In an absurd universe into which humanity has been thrown, and in which it is surrounded by hostile forces, everything happens in conformity with a symbolically realised plan. Thus, in Țuțea's view, Camus wants to awaken his contemporaries to a tragic awareness of existence and to focus their attention on an authentic universe of values based on the idea of a free human being. He suggests that to interpret Camus's play *The Misunderstanding* according to the principles of 'socialist realism' is to take the symbols of the theatre of the absurd as models of totalitarian society – that is, to commit an aesthetic solecism. Although it is symbolic, dramatic action does not allow too great a departure from reality. Drama copies reality, but does not really convey it. 'Pure symbols' of the absurd cannot be expressed dramatically: 'the stage is incapable of going beyond verisimilitude'.[76] Totalitarian society is more absurd than the theatre of the absurd can ever be.

'The Problem of Being an Actor'

Țuțea links what Nietzsche calls 'the problem of being an actor' (or artist) with the vocation of being faithful to God. Nietzsche describes dramatic art as an eternal game of hide-and-seek, 'which in the case of animals is called mimicry', and which eventually becomes 'domineering, unreasonable, and intractable, an instinct that learns to lord it over other instincts, and generates the actor, "the artist" (the zany,

---

75   Pavelescu, 'On the Rôle of Martha', pp. 11–13.

76   Pavelescu, 'On the Rôle of Martha', p. 13.

the teller of lies, the buffoon, fool, clown at first, as well as the classical servant)'.[77] Nietzsche's stance against theatre is illustrated by his picture of deception with a good conscience, of 'the delight in simulation exploding as a power that pushes aside one's so-called "character"', and of 'the inner craving for a rôle and mask, for appearance'.[78]

Țuțea recognises that it is difficult to operate in a world of symbols (as the Church does) when looking for 'a model of pure humanity'; also, that it is impossible to 'escape the interplay of appearances, which includes fabricated people, those tedious "cardboard cut-outs"'.[79] However, in contrast to Nietzsche, Țuțea professes deep empathy for actors and the theatre, an empathy rooted in his warm personality, sense of civic responsibility, and irrepressible love for the other.[80] He refers to his own experience of moving from his peasant background to a cosmopolitan intellectual environment, to state the profound epistemological rôle of theatre as integral to civilised consciousness:

> The 'problem of being an actor' is not as simple [as Nietzsche claims], especially if we consider human beings as social and adaptation as necessary for the preservation of life. I must make a confession: at school I learned how to use my critical faculty and apply the rules of grammar. It was actors who taught me to speak correctly, to behave properly, and to express through my actions what was going on inside my head. 'Bedeutend wirkt ein edler Schein', as Goethe says.[81] I have left my home in a rural village and am not prepared to

---

77   Friedrich Nietzsche, *The Gay Science, with a Prelude in Rhymes and an Appendix of Songs*, trans. and comment. by Walter Kaufmann (New York: Vintage Books, 1974), pp. 316–17. Cf. THEATRE, pp. 174–5.

78   Nietzsche, *The Gay Science*, p. 316. Nietzsche does not go quite so far in condemning actors as a certain Scottish pamphleteer in the reign of King James I of England who wrote: 'It is agreed upon by sober pagans themselves that play actors are the most profligate wretches and vilest vermin that Hell ever vomited out, that they are the filth and garbage of the Earth, the scum and stain of human nature, the pests and plague of society, the debauchers of men's minds and morals, unclean beasts, idolatrist papists or atheists, and the most horrid and abandoned villains that ever the sun shone upon': quoted by Robert Powell on Richard Whiteley's 'Countdown', Channel 4, 19 February 2001.

79   THEATRE, p. 175.

80   His familiarity with the theatrical milieu is attested by his friendships begun in the 1930s with prestigious Romanian actors such as Haig Acterian, a disciple of Gordon Craig, Marietta Sadova, wife of Ion Marin Sadoveanu, Director of the National Theatre in Bucharest, Corina Constantinescu, and many others. Corina Constantinescu, interview, Bucharest, 20 April 1999. Cf. Marietta Sadova's letter of 22 July 1940 to Haig Acterian, Romanian Academy Library, inv. 223316.

81   In his dialogue *Bios*, Țuțea describes Nietzsche's critical view of acting as analysed in Ernst Bertram's classic book *Nietzsche. Versuch einer Mythologie* (Berlin: Georg Bondi, 1922). The chapter entitled 'Maske' begins with a motto from Goethe – *Bedeutend wirkt ein edler Schein* ('a noble appearance has significant effect') – and a quotation from 'Vom Probleme des Schauspielers', in Nietzsche, *Die fröhliche Wissenschaft*. See also Nietzsche, *The Gay Science*, pp. 317–18.

return there. By temperament, I dislike speaking too much to myself, especially since I am aware that I have an obligation to my fellow Romanians. Also I do not enjoy speaking to stones.[82]

Țuțea thus recognised his need of theatre and that only the actor can interpret all human types and the whole of life, 'from the sublime to the grotesque':[83]

> Creative artists and those who re-create through interpretation have the faculty of expressing any form of existence and style, whether it be classic, romantic, impressionist, expressionist, or absurd, according to the accuracy with which they present these masks. This distinguishes them from the equivocal experience of ordinary human beings who act out imperfectly the rôle of their own existence.
>
> The ordinary human being, the non-professional, does not realise that he is learning through the stage performance. In the theatre, every spectator learns, irrespective of his cultural level. He learns correct speech. He learns how to behave. He learns to distinguish virtue from vice.[84]

The actor, then, is the only one who can wear a variety of masks, and still remain true to his personal vocation of inspiring others to live lives worthy of their humanity.

A New Socrates

Țuțea had something of a reputation as a latter-day Socrates.[85] Indeed, he adopts a Socratic manner when challenging the stupidity and hypocrisy of the Communist world. Like Socrates, he had little patience with stupidity. It is reason that enables people to understand stupidity:

> The stupid person is neither good nor bad, inferior or superior, but purely and simply stupid. His satisfactions can be considered privileges. No value judgement can explain the essence of stupidity. As long as stupidity cannot be eliminated it must be reckoned an example of bad luck. Deep compassion compels us to invite stupid people to the banquet of life when they do not have the cheek to take their place at the table by themselves.[86]

Țuțea regarded his own intolerance of stupidity as a pagan element within himself. Nevertheless, it points beyond itself. Socrates's intolerance of stupidity points to the fact that the human being must become perfect, and truth be logically thought out and

---

82   THEATRE, p. 175.
83   Petre Țuțea, 'Viața ca formă a bucuriei pure', II, interview by Sanda Diaconescu, *Jurnalul Literar*, Bucharest, 22 January 1990, p. 3.
84   Țuțea, 'Viața ca formă a bucuriei pure', II, p. 3.
85   Ștefan Augustin Doinaș, 'Ultimul Socrate', *Secolul XX*, 328–30 (4–5–6, 1988), Bucharest, 1991, pp. 127–31.
86   THEATRE, p. 215. Cf. 'The eyes of the Lord are in every place, beholding the evil and the good', Prov. 15:3.

clearly proclaimed: 'This apostolate derives from the exoteric character of Socratic doctrine.'[87]

Ţuţea sees public exposition of truth as intrinsic to both Socratic and Christian morality. He suggests that the intellectual curiosity of the Athenians 'establishes a baseline of dialectical finesse', just as today the people of Bucharest 'dislike pointless theological subtleties in sermons'.[88] In this context Ţuţea explains why a mask can be useful to defend or even reveal truth. If, to begin with, Nietzsche is against masks and actors, he eventually accepts the mask of a god and the illusion which enables the masked man to imagine himself a demiurge, like the god whose mask he wears. In the end, Nietzsche sees the mask as 'the only link between the human individual and God and other human beings'.[89] Ţuţea acknowledges the view of Napoleon that 'Powerful people have no need of a mask, or rather cannot wear one because they are recognised behind any mask.'[90] However, in order to fulfil one's vocation within society it is necessary to have a mask, even though exceptional individual personality will be recognisable through any mask:

> The more spiritually outstanding a person is, the more he needs a mask to avoid being 'crucified' by political leaders. In spite of the sophistication of the mask worn by Socrates, it could not save him from the anger of the rulers of Athens, although he cultivated self-deprecation in the presence of others to protect himself from criticism and to teach others.[91]

If Socrates had not, so to speak, worn a mask, his disciples would have been inhibited by his wisdom and frightened by his dissident teaching. The same could have been said of Ţuţea. Following Ernst Bertram, the Nietzsche scholar, Ţuţea considered Socrates's careful self-deprecation at the beginning of his dialogues to be a mask. This Nietzschean earthly mask (*die listige Selbstverkleinerung*) enabled Socrates to develop his method of maieutic inquiry, bringing the interlocutor's latent ideas out into his conscious mind:

> The Socratic method did not die. History repeats itself. Human beings are anxious to know truth which, being a mystery, is enfolded by reason in an endless series of masks. 'Man is not God'. Therefore, as scholar, artist, prophet, or simple believer, we experience during our development many contradictions borne through these masks.[92]

Ţuţea's immense carnival of masks and the chromatic interplay of his 'philosophy of nuances' allow us to experience God's mystery which, embracing humanity and nature, exists beyond both. As I will show in the following section, when the mask fits a person's vocation (which is received by grace) it enables them to discover the

---

87   THEATRE, p. 183.
88   THEATRE, p. 183.
89   THEATRE, p. 215.
90   THEATRE, p. 181.
91   THEATRE, p. 181.
92   THEATRE, p. 186.

image of God in which they are made. When divine inspiration visits us in the contemplation of nuances, our minds are drawn toward God. By means of the primordial mask and inspirational nuance, truth is awakened in us as an urge for knowledge of the Divine in a *mystical union* between uncreated and created energies. This union is dependent upon divine inspiration. It also needs to be prepared for by human ascetic effort.

Aware of divine truth and of his personal vocation, Țuțea, like Socrates, realised the need of the mask with its dual function: educational proclamation of truth and protective defence against criticism (although it could not protect Socrates from trial and death or Țuțea from arrest and torture). When analysing Bertram's monograph, Țuțea takes issue with Nietzsche's discussion on prayer in *The Gay Science*. While Nietzsche considers this a poetic exercise, an apparently monological art supposedly addressed to a dead God, Țuțea argues that prayer can transcend human frailty and limitation and communicate with the uncreated One. For Țuțea, if the human spirit is cut off from its God-given roots, 'it slides into a vacuum'.[93] Left to his own devices, the so-called autonomous man will see the world as a tragic spectacle.

Satire and Comedy

Țuțea's 'theatre as seminar' presents an interweaving of sacred and secular: the sacred reflected in the liturgical[94] living out of truth received through revelation, and the secular only meaningful to the extent that it bears the sacred. The liturgical and educative functions of theatre as seminar do not exclude the entertaining and cathartic aspects of dramatic art.[95]

Țuțea's sense of humour is reflected in his apologia for satire and comedy. He was aware of the enormous impact which the refreshing spirit of comedy can have in a totalitarian régime, when the satirical playwright combines fiction with reality because he knows that everyday life often goes far beyond the fabrications of the imagination.[96] He establishes a typology of human persons related to his 'scale of human values'. In order to define the subject of satire for a playwright, 'three categories of people are necessary: those born healthy (*bine-născuții*), those born with impairments (*rău-născuții*), and those badly brought up (*rău-crescuții*)'.[97]

The first category are healthy in body and mind. Through the Church they are taught to respect Christian virtues, and civil society expects them to live in accordance with moral principles. Christianity and liberalism are compatible: the values of both can be adopted, applied, and developed by the *bine-născuții*, who in this way are well brought up. As a rule, those who are well brought up are not subject

---

93   THEATRE, p. 172.
94   See 'A Note on Țuțea's Use of Language', p. xix.
95   See THEATRE, p. 517.
96   Petre Țuțea, 'Profil: Aurel Baranga', in *Aurel Baranga, interpretat de...* (Bucharest: Eminescu, 1981), p. 259. ['Aurel Baranga. A Portrait'.]
97   Țuțea, 'Aurel Baranga. A Portrait', in *Aurel Baranga, interpretat de...*, p. 259.

to satire. They can be used as a standard by which the other two categories can be judged.

Then, to satirise the *rău-născuţii* because of their disabilities is 'pointless cruelty'. Those who are handicapped with hereditary psychosomatic disadvantages 'cannot be helped by our criticisms: they come within the purview of medicine'.[98]

By contrast, the *rău-crescuţii* mock the gifts of God and civic values. They have no respect for their calling as responsible persons, and do not value what others can do which they cannot. They are people born healthy who inherit or adopt immoral habits from their family and from society. The *rău-crescuţii* are criticised and ridiculed by the satirist, whose function is thus to educate the audience and arouse in them a sense of justice. The *rău-crescuţii* are bad insofar as they are also stupid when they choose to reject or to waste the spiritual gifts with which they are endowed. Those who are stupid are therefore blameworthy. Ţuţea insists that they must be exposed by satire on stage and punished by the law of the land.

In his conversations Ţuţea would stress that the Last Judgement applies to all, but Hell is probably full of stupid people. I have shown that 'stupid people' means to Ţuţea *homo Sovieticus*, a manifestation of *homo stultus*, the lowest category on his scale of human values. There is, thus, a larger view of God's saving activity, from which the 'stupid man' (however clever in worldly terms) excludes himself through lack of belief. Although aesthetically his theatre is intended to combine 'aristocratic and democratic styles, as in Aristotle's art of government',[99] Ţuţea is aware that 'the religious nature of truth requires moderation in words and deeds'.[100] Such moderation is a sign of Christian humility and hope.

Ţuţea would agree with the observation of the playwright Václav Havel that living in an Eastern bloc country was somehow unreal – less real or less meaningful than a stage play – because living in a totalitarian régime requires the pretence that the world is one thing when it is known to be another.[101] The Communists' immoderate falsification of history was ultimately an institutionalised challenge to God's order.

The 'drastic suppression of history' described by Havel, the 'pseudo-reality', and the totalitarian 'living within a lie' ended in Romania on that December day in 1989 when Ceauşescu tried to quieten the crowd from the balcony of the Communist Party headquarters in Bucharest.[102] He could no longer speak to them because they were no longer pretending to believe him. As Ţuţea put it, Ceauşescu proved then that 'his was not the mask of a Caesar, but of a thug'.[103] That was a peripeteia in the 'comedy' of truth for Romanian Communism.

---

98   Ţuţea, 'Aurel Baranga. A Portrait', in *Aurel Baranga, interpretat de...*, p. 259.
99   THEATRE, p. 517.
100   THEATRE, p. 521.
101   Václav Havel, *Living in Truth, Twenty-two essays published on the occasion of the award of the Erasmus Prize to Václav Havel*, ed. Jan Vladislav (London: Faber and Faber, 1990), pp. 41–5. George Orwell's *Animal Farm* also explored this grotesquely surreal aspect of socialist realism and reality.
102   Havel, *Living in Truth*, p. 33.
103   BGMP, p. 46.

Conclusion

Țuțea takes theatre as an extended analogy for creation. Theatre persists even in a Communist pseudo-culture because it enables people to experience *anything*. It can communicate profound things in a way that a written text cannot. Ironically, a world that is 'parallel' to reality can help communicate truth in a way that a direct approach to truth cannot. Repressive régimes close down theatres.[104] In Romania the Communists demolished churches, tortured Christians, and exterminated those who refused to abjure their faith. What they could not do was to abolish the presence of Christ in people's hearts. The human heart is ultimately the protagonist of *theatrum mundi*, and the authentic stage for this drama is the Eucharistic Liturgy. As I have shown, a liturgy beyond the Divine Liturgy (as normally celebrated in Church) was enacted in prison, where the holy gifts and even prayer were prohibited. For Christians detained in Communist prisons, encounter with Christ could be eucharistically celebrated anywhere, even if it was only in 'the inner chamber' (Matt. 6:6) of the heart. Whether in the splendour of the Metropolitan Cathedral or in the starkness of prison, the Eucharist is the sacred space for the drama wherein purity is recovered both symbolically and actually, and where the image of God is re-presented and human beings are rehearsed inwardly to live out their Christian rôle:

> By means of the liturgical certainties experienced in Church,[105] we can recover peace, spiritual balance, and the mask of religious dignity as divine creatures – the only real dignity.[106]

---

104 Publication of Țuțea's play, *Everyday Happenings*, in *Familia* was interrupted in 1968. It was only published in full in 1993 after his death.

105 Or in 'the chamber of the heart' when the faithful cannot gather together as the Church, in the literal sense.

106 THEATRE, p. 440. For Țuțea's criticism of Hegel's pantheistic view of human dignity see also PROBLEMS, p. 190. Following the German philosopher Johann Friedrich Herbart (1776–1841), Țuțea regards Hegel's pantheism as 'pan-satanism': THEATRE, p. 405.

Chapter 9

Masks

Under Communist rule theatre was able sometimes to reflect, albeit partially and paradoxically, spiritual reality. Țuțea's *Teatrul Seminar* was conceived as a liturgical dialogue marked by 'sacred punctuation of time and space'.[1] In his view, theatre had to rediscover its liturgical roots in order to become an image of truth, for which there was no other means of presentation. The Communist authorities disliked the theatre precisely because people could express disagreeable (unofficial) truths there. Both in his essays on theatre and in his only play, *Everyday Happenings*, Țuțea suggests that such truths could and should be conveyed indirectly through theatre in its key elements of mask, rôle, and stage.

A Theology of Masks

The concept of 'mask' is essential to Țuțea's theology. It also helps us to understand the process of unmasking that was forced on prisoners of conscience in Communist Romania. The way Țuțea builds up his Christian anthropology around the idea of mask is characteristic and distinctive. The reader must bear in mind that, on the whole, Țuțea does not use the word 'mask' to imply falsehood. The word *mask* is thought to have come into Romanian (as into English) via the French *masque*, derived from the Latin *mascus, masca*. Țuțea reinvests the word with one of its original Latin meanings, 'ghost'.[2] In English and German *ghost* and *Geist* also mean 'spirit'. A further meaning of *mascus* was 'larva', that is, life in a transitional state of being, equipped to undergo basic structural change through a complex *metamorphosis*[3] (rendered in Latin as *transfiguratio*).

---

1   THEATRE, p. 516.
2   A.M. Macdonald (ed.), *Chambers Twentieth Century Dictionary*, rev. edn, with supple-
     ment (Edinburgh: T. & A. Constable, 1977), pp. 805–6. The same association is made in
     J.A. Simpson and E.S.C. Weiner (eds), *The Oxford English Dictionary*, 2nd edn, 20 vols
     (Oxford: Clarendon Press, 1989), IX, p. 425: 'It is difficult to believe that the word
     [mask] has no connection with med. L. *mascus, masca*, which render O.E. *gríma* mask,
     spectre, in the Corpus Glossary c. 725.'
3   *Glossarium Mediae et Infimae Latinitatis, conditum a Carolo du Fresne… Editio Nova*,
     10 vols (Niort: L. Favre, 1885), V, p. 294. '*Mascha* is used c. 680 by Aldhelm in
     association with *larva*, which had the senses "mask" and "spectre"': Simpson and Weiner
     (eds), *The Oxford English Dictionary*, IX, p. 425.
        Interestingly enough, the Latin *larva* also meant *daemones aerii*, relating to Greek

215

For Țuțea, 'mask' could also be understood as referring to the original image of God in all human creatures. Yet a further element of its meaning is that Christ-likeness, made manifest in the uncreated light of the Transfiguration and into which we grow as we seek to follow the Saviour. Although Patristic writers will sometimes distinguish between image and likeness, Jesus Christ harmonises the two, embodies them both, as the Way that is at the same time Truth and Life itself. This unifying, paradigmatic, and salvific mask is the ineffaceable hallmark of the Creator upon His human creatures. Divinity indwells them from the very moment of conception, and accompanies them as they grow into Christ-likeness. Țuțea saw humanity as a potentiality fully completed in God. Realisation of human potential for likeness to God involves mind, spirit, and natural endowments, which are all gifts of the One God who will never disown humanity. No torture, cruelty, or corruption can erase God's image from the soul, or cancel His gifts. Țuțea's understanding of mask as carrying some sense of vocation implies a call for everyone to lead a life that is worthy of the divine image. For those who live unworthily, the divine mask is reduced to a 'theatrical' mask (in the pejorative sense); their lives are a pretence, and the saving Cross is a dead weight which drags them down to abysmal darkness.

The created human spirit derives from the uncreated Holy Spirit, but, as a consequence of the Fall, the human spirit takes on a distorted form. However, it preserves the *image* of God in which human beings are made, and is, at the creaturely level of response, the motivating power which enables a person to become like God. Yet, although the image and likeness in which we are created have been perfectly revealed in the Incarnation of the Word of God, they have still to be restored in each individual. Jesus Christ is the icon of true humanity. In his divine manhood, the original mask of humanity is indivisibly united to the Godhead itself.

Mask is perhaps also semantically linked to the Greek word χαρακτήρ, which originally bore the meaning, among others, of exact likeness, full expression, and imprint.[4] Thus, 'character' literally carries the sense of an impress marked upon the individual by God.[5] For Țuțea it has the incarnational sense of God's self-limitation, by which human creatures have free access to the Godhead. The Son of God takes on 'garments of skin' (Gen. 3:21) so that man in turn can exchange his earthly

---

daimonion, idolon, and *fantasia: Glossarium,* p. 32. Cf. the German *entlarven,* to unmask what is corrupt or false.

4   Following Heinrich Schmidt's *Philosophisches Wörterbuch,* pp. 64–6, Țuțea links the literal sense of the German word *Charakter* (as *das Eingeritzte, Eingegrabene, Eingravierte* – engraving) to E. Kretschmer's classic *Körperbau und Charakter* (1921). See THEATRE, p. 353.

5   One interesting use of 'character' is Hebrews 1:3 where χαρακτήρ means the exact imprint of the person, implying that Christ is the imprint of the Father. The divine seal is set upon Christ, so that seeing Christ the believer knows God (by having a 'representation of the essence of Him'), according to J.D. Douglas (ed.) *The New Greek English Inter-linear New Testament,* trans. Robert K. Brown and Philip W. Comfort (Wheaton, IL: Tyndale, 1990), p. 757.

'persona'[6] for a divine one. There is thus a kenotic dimension to Țuțea's concept of original mask. The word *kenosis* is used by the Greek Fathers to designate the Incarnation of God as His self-emptying (from the Greek verb κενόω, in Phil. 2:7). Like Maximus the Confessor,[7] to whom in this, as in other matters, he is much indebted, Țuțea speaks of the image of God in which humans are made as that which asserts the original integrity between Creator and Creation. Individuals are to be clothed with the uncreated light of Christ and to bear His heavenly image which is, so to speak, the original, divine mask of humanity put on like armour at their Christian Baptism: 'For as many of you as were baptised into Christ have put on Christ' (Gal. 3:27). Thus there is an authentic, divine mask which leads to salvation if a person lives in Christ, and there is an artificial mask which leads to passion, sin, and death, for it is conformed to the worldly-minded who are 'careless of their own salvation'.[8]

In presenting Țuțea's reflections on 'masks', I seek to respect the spirit of his theology, which is ever critical of systematisation: 'Systematic enquiry and thought are forms of demonic seduction... As an antechamber of the world to come, this world can be known, but perfection can be accomplished through grace, not through seeking.'[9] The purpose of the schematisation of his ideas is to present their inner integrity and consistency rather than a 'survey' of their 'content'.

Țuțea's concept of mask, integral to his understanding of the relationship between Creator and creature, is complex and relational rather than inorganic and statically descriptive. He employs the concept of mask, although he also refers to mankind as created in the image and likeness of God. He sees human identity in terms of a three-fold relationship of primordial, divine, and human masks. Though I ignore at my peril Țuțea's caution against systematic thinking, the distinction he makes between the three masks can be roughly organised as follows:

1   the *primordial mask* equates roughly to God's *image* in the human person; it is that by which the light of God shines in the heart of everyone (John 1:9) and which cannot be removed by the Fall, although it can be obscured or distorted. It is ultimately God's vision of humanity, which, as such, is indestructible and

---

6   'Persona' is a complex word. I write it in inverted commas to indicate that I am using it in a technical Jungian sense as the 'rôle a person takes on by virtue of the pressures of society'. See Arthur S. Reber (ed.), *The Penguin Dictionary of Psychology* (London: Penguin, 1985), p. 532. This process of development of a personal rôle through social pressure is not necessarily negative, but is part of the economy of incarnational grace. Țuțea is well aware of Jung's terminology: see, for example, PROBLEMS, p. 324; SYSTEMS, p. 195. He explicitly relates 'mask' to Jungian 'persona' when speaking of 'the mask imposed on the individual by the external world': NUANCES, p. 122. Cf. OLD AGE, p. 109.

7   See Thunberg, 'The Image of God in Man', in *Microcosm and Mediator*, pp. 113–20.

8   See Disc., XVIII, 4:70, in Symeon the New Theologian, *The Discourses*, trans. C.J. de Catanzaro, introd. by George Maloney SJ, preface by Basil Krivocheine (London: SPCK, 1980), p. 211.

9   PROBLEMS, p. 300.

218 Petre Țuțea

eternally perfect, yet which individuals either perceive 'through a glass, darkly' (1 Cor. 13:12) or wilfully deny (by blasphemy 'against the Holy Spirit');

2 the *divine mask* corresponds roughly to divine *likeness* perceivable in human beings; it is that by which individuals see each other to be 'children of God' (Phil. 2:15); this can be either destroyed through evil living, or cleansed and finally restored through deification;

3 the *human mask* points to the individual rôle or *vocation* in this life; it is that by which each person can choose either the path of perdition, following 'the spirit who now works in the sons of disobedience' (Eph. 2:2), or the path of salvation, following Christ.

This theology of masks provides the key to Țuțea's understanding of sanctity in terms of union with Christ. It is the Incarnation that makes possible the restoration of a person's mask to its original state, and, moreover, effects salvation. Through the power of the Incarnate Word and God's grace at work in humanity, sustaining individual capacity for faithful Christian discipleship, we can return to the original divine image, and indeed acquire it in ever-increasing fullness, as we receive 'grace upon grace'.[10] This turning again toward God's image in us is effected through 'participation in our personal act of salvation'[11] in our full liturgical life as members of the Church.

When public liturgical celebration is denied to Christians by Caesar, the private 'liturgy' of personal prayer and Christian living can still bring believers back into harmony with baptismal grace. However, human effort to respond to the divine call to perfection will be ineffective without participation in the Eucharist (wherever circumstances permit it). Even in prison people risked death to celebrate the Eucharist.

Primordial Purity and Powers

As I have already shown, the organic harmony of image and likeness, destroyed by the Fall, is restored in the Incarnation of Christ and the process of human deification,[12] in particular through the rite of Baptism, whereby a person shares in the death and Resurrection of Jesus Christ (Rom. 6:3–6):

---

10 The Christ-story 'provides not simply the initial impetus of Christian morality but also a perceptible form or contour for its growth': John B. Webster, 'Christology, Imitability and Ethics', *The Scottish Journal of Theology*, 39:3, August 1986, p. 311.

11 PROBLEMS, p. 258.

12 Țuțea's non-systematic reflections on human deification and God's perfection accord with Fr Stăniloae's view that, 'Deification is perfection and the full permeation of human beings by God's presence, given that they cannot otherwise attain perfection and fullness as spiritual beings'. See Dumitru Stăniloae, *Trăirea lui Dumnezeu în Ortodoxie* (Cluj-Napoca: Dacia, 1993), p. 179. Cf. PROBLEMS, pp. 46–7.

By the coming of the Saviour, of the Word made flesh, Christ the Redeemer has brought us the joy of the great mystery of God-manhood and, by His life, sacrifice and Resurrection, He has created the New Adam,[13] purified by Baptism, according to St Paul. And perhaps the idea of the New Adam can serve to explain the restoration of humanity to its *primordial purity*.[14]

For Țuțea 'primordial purity' seems at once the original state of Adam and yet something greater through incorporation in Christ. By its very nature, perhaps the primordial image is not a static absolute to which humanity can return; by virtue of the eternal procession of the Holy Spirit, the primordial state of Edenic purity is inherently dynamic, super-abundant in creative transcendence, reflecting the divine energies. The return to that state is therefore a 'return' to something more. In the domain of human history God grants 'primordial powers' to inspired scientists:

It is not correct to say that Otto Hahn[15] discovered nuclear fission by chance. While Hahn was in fact looking for something else, he was inspired to make a discovery that led to a new era in science, a discovery springing from the will of God who decided that this was necessary.

The One Above necessarily intervenes in history, endowing humanity with new powers to dominate nature, *primordial powers*, lost by humanity as a consequence of original sin and acquired again through the Redeemer...[16]

Țuțea's 'primordial powers' point towards God's original design in creating human nature, which was distorted by the Fall and is restored in Christ. Their presence in human beings illustrates the desire of God to develop to infinity his relation with the creature he has made in his own image and likeness:

The divine image of human beings – who move between earth and heaven – justifies their attempt to attain perfection and absolute freedom, whose origin is neither in humanity nor in nature. This image was restored by our Saviour.[17]

---

13   Țuțea extends the traditional image of Christ as 'Second Adam', returning to the New Testament phrase 'the New Adam' (corresponding to St Paul's 'new man', Eph. 4:24), and 'the last Adam' (which translates St Paul's expression ὁ ἔσχατος Ἀδαμ, 1 Cor. 15:45). See PROBLEMS, pp. 179, 321.

14   PROBLEMS, p. 99 (italics added). Țuțea contrasts this 'restoration of humanity to its primordial purity' with Origen's doctrine of *apokatastasis* in *De Principiis*, a teaching which he clearly rejects: 'In sacred history nostalgia for Paradise and Origen's *apokatastasis* have no place, since the Christian looks ahead', PROBLEMS, p. 335. (There is, nevertheless, scriptural reference to *apokatastasis* in Acts 3:21, which refers to the restoration of the blessings of paradise to be accomplished by the Messiah.)

15   Otto Hahn (1879–1968), German physicist. With Strassmann, he demonstrated the nuclear fission of uranium, when it is bombarded with neutrons. In 1944 he won the Nobel prize for chemistry.

16   SYSTEMS, p. 215 (italics added). Cf. note 15, Chapter 6.

17   PROBLEMS, p. 189.

Without a theological basis of belief in the creation of humanity in God's image and likeness, this human attempt to attain perfection and absolute freedom is, of course, no more than another attempt to construct the Tower of Babel. Ţuţea's talk of deification is therefore organised around the mystical theology of God's 'image' (primordial mask): 'I have a mystical interest in the real[18] human being' (and his accomplishments) 'who preserves "the image of God"'.[19]

Primordial and Divine Masks

In relation to the 'primordial mask', Ţuţea refers explicitly to the original creation of human beings in the image and likeness of God. However, in the fallen world this is no longer a harmonious unity:

> Human beings were created in the image and likeness of God. The Book of Genesis includes the story of the creation of the cosmos, the living world, the human mind, and human society, as well as of language and sin... Through original sin human beings have fallen, become mortal, and been *stripped of their divinity* while retaining only their *primordial mask*.[20]

This 'divinity' of which we have been 'stripped' may be understood as corresponding to human 'likeness' to God.[21] In Ţuţea's terms, the divine Logos assumed flesh so that once again the primordial and divine masks might coincide. This restoration of the organic oneness of the divine image and divine likeness is the fruit of co-operation between God's intervening grace and human free will. Within the limits of personal vocation, we can choose our own 'human type' or rôle. In Ţuţea's view, the mind of the believer sways between that of 'the saint and Don Juan, the two poles of existence', for 'human types wear divine masks'[22] which can save them from sin. On the other hand, working with a purely human anthropology, 'the distinction between a human being and an animal is one of degree, not of nature'.[23]

The divine mask is lost through original sin and returned to humanity through the sacrifice of the Incarnate Word (although, as has been suggested, this does not

---

18   Ţuţea equates 'real humanity' to 'all-embracing integral humanity' defined as 'mystery and God-manhood, Resurrection and salvation': PROBLEMS, p. 196.

19   PROBLEMS, p. 103.

20   PROBLEMS, pp. 86–7 (italics added). Addressing the subject of divinity in human beings, Ţuţea argues that even 'if we can speak of divine substance, it is not known to us as such, since the Incarnation is an act of God who loves mankind, reveals Himself, and redeems. In this sense we can say: Truth equals God': REFLECTIONS, I, p. 28. For a reference to Ţuţea's understanding of 'divine masks', see also ELIADE, p. 56.

21   The image of God denotes human nature as it was originally created. The likeness relates to sanctity or *theosis*, what it is possible to become as humans through God's grace with the co-operation of human freedom. See note 31 in this chapter.

22   THEATRE, p. 419.

23   THEATRE, p. 419.

exclude the need for human discipleship). Even after the Fall, however, human beings remain the crowning glory of God's creation: the primordial mask ('God's image') is retained and preserved. For Țuțea, this is the ultimate imprint of the divine. Nevertheless, he seems to imply that even the primordial mask is in a certain sense deformed. Thus, the persistence of death after the coming of the Saviour – who 'defeated death' – is a 'vestige of original sin'.[24] Wherever Țuțea speaks of this, he makes reference (albeit not always explicitly) to St Paul. His view that, as far as human effort is concerned, 'original purity is irreversibly corrupted by original sin'[25] is part of his development of a Pauline vision within the context of his own experience and times.[26]

Baptism and Eschatology

Although sinful humanity 'has been restored by the Saviour', for Țuțea 'the perfection of humanity and the world must be thought of in eschatological terms'.[27] Individuals must direct their lives forward, to the light of the Last Judgement, rather than backwards to the Garden of Eden.[28]

Țuțea worked within the prevalent view of the Greek and Latin Fathers that the sacrament of Baptism confers complete purification from sin. He seems nevertheless to follow Augustine's view that, although through Baptism all are released from guilt, inherited or actual, Baptism does not, of itself, restore us to the state of Adam before the Fall. Baptism brings full forgiveness of the stain of sin (*reatus culpae*) but leaves a weakness of the will (*infirmitas voluntatis*).[29] According to Augustine, before original sin Adam has a gift of integrity (*donum integritatis*) that is not immediately recovered by the newly-baptised.[30] Augustine teaches that this persisting consequence of the Fall can only be healed slowly, through obedience,

---

24 PROBLEMS, p. 312. Cf. PROBLEMS, p. 335.
25 PROBLEMS, p. 258.
26 Just as St Paul suffered in prison, dictated letters, and left no systematic corpus, so perhaps Țuțea can be seen as modelling a Pauline 'methodology' of mystical, preached theology. Țuțea would, however, have been the first to reject any implication that he was 'another Paul' (just as he dismissed comparison between himself and Socrates).
27 PROBLEMS, p. 324. Cf. THEATRE, pp. 416, 420.
28 I have already shown that the Christian always looks 'ahead' (see note 3 on the transformative nature of 'mask') with hope, faith, and love inspired by the Sermon on the Mount, not with nostalgia for the state of Adam before the Fall.
29 For Țuțea as for Augustine and many of the Greek Fathers, evil was not a substance, but, in essence, *privatio boni*. See PROBLEMS, p. 258. Cf. F.L. Cross and E.A. Livingstone (eds), *The Oxford Dictionary of the Christian Church*, 3rd edn (Oxford: Oxford University Press, 1997), p. 1505. Cf. Rom. 7:13–25.
30 See *Retractationes* I, xv, 2 (*Patrologia Latina* 32, 609): 'concupiscentiae reatus in Baptismate solvitur, sed infirmitas manet'; *Contra Julianum* VI, xvi, 49 (*Patrologia Latina* 44, 850–51): 'qui baptizatur... omni... peccato caret, non omni malo'.

ascetic effort, and martyrdom. All must struggle throughout life, and only when, by God's grace, an individual attains sanctity is that fatal *infirmitas* overcome.[31]

Ţuţea's position is similar to that of Augustine, but he lays more emphasis on the mystery of the *eschaton*.[32] In general, Ţuţea speaks of the 'perpetual significance and actuality' of '*felix culpa*'.[33] In particular, he shows that Augustine's 'inspired' perception of original sin as *felix culpa*, has two-fold mystical significance: first, that 'happy fault' has occasioned the coming of the Saviour, the mystery of God-manhood; and, second, in contrast to the irreversibility of the biological and historical processes of human lives and of the world, there is now the possibility of reversal – even in this world, as well as at the Day of Judgement – of the Fallen human condition.[34]

Thus human beings enter into redemption through Baptism, even though in later life they may fall away from baptismal grace. Yet 'the coming of the Saviour revealed to us... eternal life, putting an end to the anxiety produced by the prospect of the infinite and of absolute death'.[35] Therefore, 'salvation must be thought of in eschatological terms',[36] for 'biblical guilt is removed in the righteous by our Saviour'.[37] According to Genesis,[38] 'prior to' their original sin Adam and Eve had access to 'the tree of life' (Gen. 3:24) but not to 'the tree of the knowledge of good and evil' (Gen. 2:17). Following 'the Great Resurrection',[39] however, humanity has

---

31   Diadochos of Photiki holds a similar view (I quote here from *The Philokalia*, I (1979), pp. 251–96). For him, Baptism means that Satan no longer works within the depths of the heart, but only attacks from outside (Cent. 82, p. 283). However, Diadochos considers that, although Baptism frees people from the 'defilement' (*rypos*) of sin (what Augustine terms the *reatus*), there is a certain 'duality of the will' which continues after Baptism (Cent. 78, p. 280; cf. Cent. 25, p. 259; Cent. 88, p. 287). Diadochos spells this out in terms of the distinction between image and likeness. The sacrament of Baptism restores the image of God and cleanses it, but does not automatically restore the likeness of God: 'Divine grace confers on us two gifts through... baptism... one being infinitely superior to the other. The first gift is given to us at once, when grace renews us in the actual waters of baptism and cleanses... our soul, that is, the image of God in us, by washing away every stain of sin' (Cent. 89, p. 288). Likeness, for Diadochos, equals sanctity: 'All men are made in God's image; but to be in His likeness is granted only to those who through great love have brought their own freedom into subjection to God' (Cent. 4, p. 253).

32   PROBLEMS, p. 321. See also PROBLEMS, p. 109 (for Ţuţea's comment on Christian eschatology).

33   See THEATRE, p. 342; PROBLEMS, p. 7.

34   THEATRE, p. 342.

35   PROBLEMS, p. 293.

36   PROBLEMS, p. 39.

37   PROBLEMS, p. 165.

38   For Ţuţea's discussion of Genesis from the standpoint of Christian eschatology, see PROBLEMS, pp. 178–9.

39   For Ţuţea's emphasis on I Cor. 15:15–17, see PROBLEMS, pp. 179, 190.

knowledge, both responsible and actual, of good and evil and eschatological access to eternal life within the triangle God–humanity–nature:[40]

> The Saviour reopened the way to the tree of life. The right to participate in divine perfection, entrusted to human beings, confers on them the eternal life and absolute freedom to which humanity has no access in this world.[41]

A 'thirst for perfection',[42] for 'real', 'primordial purity', is innate within human nature. This thirst is in defiance of the distortion of God's image within everyone, which can never be reversed by individual effort. Țuțea looks through and beyond the Sacrament of Baptism to sacrificial discipleship, inspired by grace, which is the way to deification, 'to the measure of the stature of the fullness of Christ' (Eph. 4:13).

Masks and the Human Person

Țuțea developed the distinction between 'image' and 'likeness' through his idea of a third mask (the *human mask*), which suggests that each person has a unique path to deification, namely their human vocation. This is an extension of the universal human vocation to follow Christ's way of love.

'When the human being has a theological vocation, his reason becomes a vehicle for the unique truth.'[43] This idea of a 'human mask' accords with the essential vision of 'theatre as seminar', and reflects the etymology of the word *person*, which originally meant a masked actor.[44] Țuțea speaks of 'the divine mask falling away'.[45] For instance, the torturer loses his divine mask, the *prosopon*[46] that is integral to personhood, through actions that destroy human participation in the love of the Word Incarnate. Torturers adopt a distorted and distorting human (vocational) mask, and thereby deny their true humanity. However gifted an individual might be, unless the human mask is in accord with that person's divine vocation, it will be a pernicious simulacrum rather than the living truth of their human fulfilment. Meanwhile, the lack of exceptional gifts in what Țuțea calls 'ordinary people' (who have no individual natural vocation, but follow the path to perfection) has no profound effect on their Christian receptivity to truth. For him Nietzsche's 'pathos of distancing from God' is

---

40 See PROBLEMS, pp. 189, 288.

41 PROBLEMS, p. 190.

42 PROBLEMS, p. 49.

43 PROBLEMS, p. 43.

44 From πρόσωπον, 'face, countenance, appearance', Barclay M. Newman, Jr, *A Concise Greek–English Dictionary of the New Testament* (Stuttgart: Deutsche Bibelgesellschaft, United Bible Societies, 1971), p. 155. See also Christos Yannaras, *The Freedom of Morality*, trans. Elizabeth Briere, foreword by Kallistos Ware (Crestwood, NY: St Vladimir's Seminary Press, 1996), p. 20, n. 4.

45 PROBLEMS, p. 329.

46 Literally, his *face*.

meaningless. The Superman's pathos is 'corrected' at the religious level 'by love, as set forth in the Sermon on the Mount and at the Last Supper'.[47]

At the level of Christ's love for humanity, personal vocation[48] should be followed according to the various gifts which God confers on each individual. On the one hand, as beings made in God's image and likeness, everyone has the capacity to fulfil the universal human vocation by following Christ's call to perfection[49] (Matt. 5:48). On the other hand, everyone must live out the rôle of the human type assigned to them, in order to become fully themselves. In the words of Thomas Dalzell, commenting on Hans Urs von Balthasar, the believer is called to be, 'the person God wants one to be by participating in Christ's mission and personhood'.[50] Only the actor can interpret all human types, and 'He can also wear the mask of indifference'.[51]

When human beings neglect or ignore their human vocation (mask), falling away from baptismal grace, they cease to be creative and become destructive or even indifferent, and the divine likeness is marred if not completely lost. Thus, again, in Aiud prison, when the divine mask was stripped from the torturers by their own will, their fellow human beings could no longer recognise God's image in them, other than by the miraculous grace which was experienced at times even in that 'hell'.

Communist Romania saw the rise to power of a tyrant (with his clan) who refused 'to mirror God's religious and moral commandments' and 'to reflect them on a social, national, or global level'.[52] The Ceauşescus wanted to rule at any cost, fabricating 'super'-human masks and falsifying national and even international history:[53]

> Ceauşescu wore not the mask of a Caesar, but that of a thug on the rampage. I never imagined that an illiterate ruffian could have such a lust for luxury. In his villa at Neptun [on the Black Sea coast] everything was made of gold.[54]

Following Plato's suggestion (that the ideal Republic should be ruled by philosopher-kings elected against their will), Ţuţea warns us that, especially in politics, to pursue mere individual ambition, at the expense of personal vocation, leads inevitably to the disaster consequent upon denial of God and of human personality. In the same Platonic spirit, he affirms that, not only in Eastern Europe but in the world at large, 'metaphysical thought needs to be reshaped by a right understanding of the true,

---

47   OLD AGE, pp. 129–30.
48   See THEATRE, p. 338.
49   See PROBLEMS, pp. 116, 189. 'The Christian knows through love, which relates him to the Absolute', according to the New Law established 'by the Saviour's commandment': PROBLEMS, p. 143.
50   Thomas G. Dalzell, *The Dramatic Encounter of Divine and Human Freedom in the Theology of Hans Urs von Balthasar*, 2nd edn (Berne: Peter Lang, 2000), p. 250.
51   Ţuţea, 'Viaţa ca formă a bucuriei pure', II, p. 3.
52   THEATRE, p. 446.
53   THEATRE, p. 446. For instance, in the 1950s children in Romanian schools were taught that Newton's law of gravity had already been discovered by a Russian scientist.
54   BGMP, p. 46.

the good, and the beautiful' and by 'the spiritual imperative' (*cerinţa spirituală*)[55] to dethrone the idols of technological utilitarianism which stifle the noble ideals to which human beings aspire. Materialistic '*homo faber* is placed between infinity and nothingness', characterised by 'animalism' and 'the infantile joy of the stupid man who enjoys seeing the mask created by God falling from him'.[56] Ţuţea exhorts humanity 'back to the Christian order of perfection and salvation'.[57]

Dantean Vision of Divine Order

'Theatre as seminar is structured as a divine comedy enacted between Hell and Paradise.'[58] Ţuţea's dramatic vision perhaps reflects the different settings of the Dantean Comedy, although it is important to remember that Orthodox Christianity (unlike the Uniates, who use the Byzantine liturgy and also acknowledge the authority of the Pope) has no doctrine of Purgatory. In terms of Ţuţea's concept of masks: Paradise reflects the realm of those whose human and divine masks concur; Purgatory expresses the state of those who have lost their divine mask, yet in this life have shown true repentance and desire to love God; Hell is the condition of those who eternally deny their divine vocation at the most fundamental level, that of the primordial mask.

Deliberate destructiveness is sin against the Holy Spirit, Lord and Giver of Life, and as such is unforgivable (Matt. 12:32) since it closes the door on the possibility of repentance. To reject the possibility of repentance and change is to reject the indestructible primordial mask. Unrepentant denial of individual ultimate identity (the capacity to be – through *metanoia*, in Christ – the self-revealing and self-sufficient image of God), and deliberate conformity of the human mask to a false (insufficient) identity, confines individuals to the dimension of this world – a created, finite order – wherein they have turned their back on love.

In contrast to this *Inferno*, Ţuţea's typology of the 'saint', according to which all human types can achieve 'saintly' (Christ-like) perfection in their particular vocation, perhaps reflects the different spheres and varying brightness of the stars in the Dantean Paradise. The drama of movement and light in the *Paradiso* perhaps also provides a clue to Ţuţea's view of the relationship of sanctity to union with Christ. This brings us to the function of the divine mask which, as I have shown, can be distorted or indeed actually destroyed. Yet it may, through genuine repentance and vocational striving (that is, reforming of the human mask), be ultimately restored, albeit in a Dantesque drama of Purgatory wherein the divine initiative is most clearly discernible not as the Good or the True, but as transformative Love[59] – not a *deus*

---

55 Ţuţea, MS O, p. 34.
56 Ţuţea, MS O, p. 34.
57 THEATRE, p. 446.
58 THEATRE, p. 375.
59 'Eros', Ţuţea's dialogue on the nature of Love, actually ends with an analysis of the Dantean vision, quoting the final seven *terzine* of the *Commedia* in full. In relation to human understanding of love (and in this sense, to knowledge of divine Love as Ţuţea

ex machina who rewards repentance by an instant exercise of supernatural authority, but the eternal redemptive power of relational, creative, and joyous being.

Rôle

In Ţuţea's view, personal vocation is given rather than chosen. The Romanian word he uses is *rol* which, like its French and English counterpart *rôle*, can convey a sense of something artificially assumed. But he does not intend it in that sense. Just as 'mask' does not usually convey for him the sense of falsehood and deception, so *rol* implies nothing pejorative. 'Rôle' is not merely something enacted in external relations with others, like the assumed rôle of a character in the theatre:

> My dialogue *Bios* is not in itself a spectacle, it looks at the theatre of life (*theatrum mundi*). If we regard life as a theatre, then every human being plays out the rôle of his or her own existence as an actor, according to the maxim: *totus mundus agit histrionem*. Obviously, not all are perfect actors. The man in the street cannot, as an actor, compete with the professional. Everyone is an actor, but not necessarily a good one. It takes a Shakespeare to create true theatre.[60]

For Ţuţea the concept of rôle implies God's call for a person to fulfil their divinely given vocation. However it may be realised individually, the human vocation is ultimately to co-operate with God in the process of deification. To achieve this is to live out the reality of Baptism. Holiness reflects a perfect overlap of the primordial and divine masks. There is an analogy here between vocation and rôle or character as realised on stage at the deeper level of theatre. Ţuţea suggests that every person can choose between their God-given rôle and other rôles and vocations that attract or distract along the way. Only when personal will coincides with the will of God, when individuals rightly discern their vocation and pursue it, can fulfilment be found – that is, only then can a person live fully in the image and likeness of God. Loss of immediate awareness of true vocation is a consequence of the Fall.

Supreme actors are those who assume the original rôle of perfection to which Christ calls them. According to Ţuţea, such 'actors' are saints, gradually losing their false human mask and no longer resisting the will of God. The path of true freedom lies in this willingness to 'put on the whole armour of God' (Eph. 6:11). This might

---

conceives this) it is important to bear in mind that the Romanian language has three common words to denote love: *dragoste, iubire, amor*. In seeking to understand Ţuţea's remarkable synthesis of Eastern and Western Christian spirituality, those whose mother tongue is English need to be aware of the often untranslatable nuances of a language that is unknown to most Westerners (no doubt the spiritual nuances of Western 'Comedy' will be unknown to many Orthodox Christians – as indeed it is also to many in the West, especially in more Protestant and Catholic positivist circles).

60 Interview, Bucharest, 15 March 1990. For Ţuţea 'real theatre' is 'mystical theatre', whose values are Christian: 'Remove Scripture from Shakespeare's plays, and he becomes a tragic jester', APHORISMS, p. 24.

lead to personal martyrdom on the road to perfection or a life lived as a confessor – that is, the experience of those who have 'washed their robes and made them white in the blood of the Lamb' (Rev. 7:14).

For Țuțea prison was a place of grace, because false rôles were 'stripped away' and true vocation became discernible. God is the only one who can judge how each person has played their rôle in the drama of their life; at the same time, God, the ultimate authority of judgement, is fully involved through the Incarnation in the story line. Several years after Țuțea published fragments in 1968–69, which later formed part of *Teatrul Seminar* (first version completed in 1971), Hans Urs von Balthasar took up the same theme in his *Theodramatik*:[61]

> Christ, the Son of God, is not just *any* incarnation: he is the sole incarnation, revealing God's whole mind. God the Father, who sends him, remains in the background as the real 'spectator' before whom 'the great theatre of the world' is performed; but since Father and Son are one, this role of spectator on God's part cannot be separated from his entering into the action on the stage. And when the Spirit proceeds from the Father and the Son and is breathed into the Church of Christ, something of God himself speaks in the mouths of the actors.[62]

According to von Balthasar, the problem of a person's rôle, and how it is to be discovered, is as old as the metaphor describing human life as a theatre, and it implies all the problems suggested by this metaphor. Not only has the individual in the world theatre (*Welttheater*) to perform the particular function allotted to him:

> he also, if he is to be really himself, has to identify himself with the role he plays, in spite of the fact that at some mysterious point he is *not* identical with it. Or, after all, should he rather *not* identify himself with it, ought he to maintain a distance between himself and the role, aware that 'in principle' he could be someone else and that, to be himself, he must avoid losing himself in the role?[63]

Von Balthasar is aware that identification presupposes non-identity and a bridging of the gap between actual identity and 'the role into which society has cast all *dramatis personae*':[64]

> In the case of the mentally healthy person this may be achieved almost unconsciously and without friction, but it can prove extremely difficult with the mentally sick and unbalanced; hence the interest taken by all forms of psychotherapy in the problem of role and identification... But who can show me the role in which I can really be myself?...

---

61   See Hans Urs von Balthasar, *Theodramatik*, 5 vols (Einsiedeln: Johannes Verlag, 1973–83), I (1973).

62   Hans Urs von Balthasar, *Theo-drama, Theological Dramatic Theory*, 5 vols, trans. Graham Harrison (San Francisco: Ignatius Press, 1988–98), I (1988), p. 319.

63   See von Balthasar, *Theo-drama*, I, p. 46.

64   See von Balthasar, *Theo-drama*, I, p. 47.

Destiny can fundamentally change my social role, not only on the basis of free decisions but even more through the possibility of more and more thorough 'refunctioning' [*Umfunktionierungen*] by society, by cybernetics, biochemical means, and so forth.[65]

But destiny is not the answer. Von Balthasar suggests an answer by quoting the title of Bertolt Brecht's play *Mann ist Mann* (1927), which raises the issue of manipulation by means of technology.[66] This links up with Ṭuṭea's criticism of radical anthropocentrism that reduces human life to the status of objects of research and techniques of existence. For him, 'vocation and inspiration are in permanent opposition to questioning and seeking'.[67] Like von Balthasar, he insists that one cannot find one's rôle by psychological, sociological, or psychoanalytical means. Both self-identity and personal rôle are ultimately defined in relation to salvation, as living in God and following Christ: 'For I through the law died to the law, that I might live to God. I have been crucified with Christ; it is no longer I who live, but Christ who lives in me' (Gal. 2:19–20). Self-offering love rooted in the Incarnation is the ultimate vocation.[68]

Stage

The Stage as Sacred Space

Ṭuṭea sees the world as a stage on which all too often individuals perform for others. What he calls the Nietzschean *Übermensch*'s obsession with external signs of superiority is played out not only in the economic sphere, but also in all aspects of society. People resort to any means to fulfil their desire to dominate others, which is to deny their vocation and to make themselves a 'Sisyphus-like Prometheus'.[69] For Ṭuṭea, original temptation is 'Titanism' (that is, the human quest for divinisation by means of knowledge and curiosity): pride urges people to grasp at equality with God. In humanism this pride which seeks perfection takes another form: replacement of God with a perfectible humanity.[70]

---

65   See von Balthasar, *Theo-drama*, I, p. 47.
66   Brecht's play anticipates Heidegger's view of *techné* as 'the mode of advancing against *physis*', the end point of which is technological domination of entities: Martin Heidegger, *Gesamtausgabe, Grundfragen der Philosophie*, ed. Friedrich-Wilhelm von Herrmann, winter semester 1937–38 (Frankfurt am Main: Vittorio Klostermann, 1984), vol. 45, p. 179.
67   PROBLEMS, p. 184.
68   For von Balthasar, as for Ṭuṭea, the problem of how to find one's rôle 'emerges in all areas of sociology and psychology and overflows into the sphere of theo-drama... No other theology but Christian theology can utter the redemptive word here' (von Balthasar, *Theo-drama*, I, p. 48).
69   ELIADE, p. 486.
70   See PROBLEMS, p. 11.

The world is the stage where this usurpation takes place, but there is, as I have shown, a higher, Eucharistic stage of true drama. This is sacred space, where 'the impossible becomes possible'; it mediates purification even though, at the human level, 'purity is merely symbolic, an interplay between image and sign'.[71] 'Sisyphus-like Prometheus' seeks to ascend to heaven by using human strength to reach upwards. By contrast, the Eucharist is, through God's initiative, the place of the renewal of primordial harmony, the place where the divine image is re-stamped. Here the priest is the actor whose rôle is to mediate and also experience directly God's redeeming work in the sacrifice of Christ, though this is an experience in which the whole people of God will share. In prison, the celebration of, and participation in, the Eucharistic Liturgy could mean physical extermination. This brought its true meaning into intense focus. To be denied the Eucharist may be part of Christian martyrdom.

For Țuțea, as for von Balthasar in his *Theodramatik*, seeing is organically one with transformation, and human perception of Christ's glory is ultimately embraced and itself redeemed in God's transforming love. As the Dominican scholar Aidan Nichols puts it, 'a theory of perception cannot be advanced in this context without a doctrine of conversion, and so ultimately of sanctification'.[72] For Nichols, the function of theatre is to exhibit the dramatic aspects of existence itself and so 'to hold up a mirror to the drama of life', not only that we may understand it better, 'but also reorient ourselves within it according to whatever light the dramatic author, as interpreted by his cast and their director, can throw' on the drama.[73] Țuțea contrasts the 'world as spectacle' with the dramatic process of reconciliation between God and humanity (where Christ stands at the centre):

When I see the world as merely spectacle, my spirit strays. For the visible world in which we live is actually not a theatrical spectacle. The world is God's creation. And God does not make theatre. Only man makes theatre. God does not present Himself as a spectacle on the Shakespearean 'stage of the world'. God offers Himself on the Cross, and shares His presence in the mysteries of the Church. During the Eucharistic Liturgy, when a Christian approaches the Holy Mysteries, 'in the fear of God, with faith, and with love', God shakes him out of his present fallen condition.[74]

Since human beings are created for communion, bearing the divine image, and thus ultimately one with God and their neighbour, Țuțea uses the dictum *unus homo, nullus homo* (one man, no man) with direct reference to the Eucharistic Liturgy. It is in the Eucharist that the reality of that oneness is experienced. Through the sacraments

---

71 PROBLEMS, p. 305.
72 Aidan Nichols, OP, *No Bloodless Myth, A Guide Through Balthasar's Dramatics* (Edinburgh: T. & T. Clark, 2000), p. 3.
73 Nichols, *No Bloodless Myth*, p. 11.
74 Conversation with Țuțea, Bucharest, 1 March 1990. See also von Balthasar, *Theo-drama*, III (1992), p. 121; cf. 'Cosmic Liturgy' in Thunberg, *Microcosm and Mediator*, pp. 397–8.

humanity can participate in the life of Christ and become so imbued with Christ's spirit that others too are caught up in the divine presence:

> The genuine humanity and compassion of a Christian characterise him from the beginning as a New Man. He is, in essence, the timeless religious person whose love derives from the Christ of the Last Supper. The Christian is both chosen and placed hierarchically to serve his fellow human beings according to his divine call.[75]

On the Communist Stage

Human beings, the crown of God's creation, are endowed with rôles or personal vocations ascribed to them by God. When people seek either to replace God, or to acquire a social position that conflicts with their given rôle, they slip off 'the ladder of divine ascent' and like Adam and Eve they fall from eternity into historical time:

> Correctly understood, the historic human being is a caricature of the eternal human being... He does without doing and knows without knowing. With this grotesque mask he plays his part before our eyes.[76]

Through abuse or manipulation of the human mask, the divine mask can be distorted and even destroyed. It should be recalled, however, that the primordial mask is ultimately indestructible. Thus Hell is confinement to an order of being that denies its own ultimate identity.

Isolation, as part of the prison experience, is, to Țuțea, by definition dehumanising. So is the banning of Eucharistic celebration, although in reality the *anamnesis* continues through the Incarnation. He recognises the presence of the Holy Spirit in everybody, even in those who deny it, but establishes a radical difference between Christians and atheists, more particularly, *homo stultus* (for example, those responsible for the experiment of re-education and unmasking):[77]

> When I talk with an atheist it is as though I were addressing a brick wall. There is no communication between a believer and an unbeliever. One is spiritually dead, while the other is alive. The Christian believer is the one who is alive.[78]

Thirty-five years after Țuțea's release from prison, I interviewed the former governor of Aiud, Colonel Gheorghe Crăciun, who had been in charge of re-education in the early 1960s. Retired and facing prosecution as a Communist criminal, he had become a practising Christian.[79] He confessed to me that his experience of interrogating Țuțea

---

75   PROBLEMS, p. 139.
76   SOPHISTRY, p. 156.
77   See Țuțea's discussion of *homo stultus* in Chapter 5.
78   BGMP, p. 280.
79   Colonel Gheorghe Crăciun, interview, Bucharest, 16 October 1999. Cf. Demostene Andronescu, '"Spovedania" Colonelului Crăciun', *Puncte Cardinale*, Sibiu, February–March 1998, p. 16.

had turned him towards God. His primordial mask had always been there. The divine mask had gone. He now has to live out his vocation of discipleship through that sincerity, repentance, struggle, and hope which is the redemptive discovery of his unique human mask. Ţuţea would no doubt see Crăciun's acts as a torturer as a temporary negation of his vocation.

In my encounters with those who survived the persecution of Christians in Romania, and with their relatives and friends, I have been struck and deeply moved by the way many people who suffered nevertheless express forgiveness towards their torturers, and refuse to blame them. Ţuţea's refusal to talk about his sufferings in prison, and his determination to blame the system which led to those terrible experiences rather than the individual torturers, speak for themselves. For him prison was an infernal place, yet it gave him the opportunity to meet God. He suggests people should pray not only for the victims of persecution, but also for the persecutors. 'I must forgive although I cannot forget', he would say. For those who personally have nothing to 'forget', there is a different yet perhaps equally great mystery and spiritual struggle towards forgiveness and reconciliation.

Conclusion

Although this chapter has given a somewhat schematised account of Ţuţea's understanding of the human person, it has enabled me to convey his overriding concern for the salvation of humanity. Life is, in a deep sense, a masked carnival,[80] (from Latin *carnem levare*, to put away flesh). Fallen humans must put away the things of the flesh (Rom. 8:5) before they can discover their true selves in the image and likeness of God, through the Word made flesh. Ultimately this depends on the divine author. Creative human co-operation is, however, also necessary. The only proper exercise of God's gift of free will is for each person to act their part – to enact in their own lives the drama that is unfolded, eucharistically, in the celebration of Christ the Way, the Truth, and the Life.

Where this 'acting' is sham, half-hearted, or resentful (for human beings have a genuine choice either to reject their rôle, or else to allow God to 'direct' them), the actors destroy themselves. Moreover, they will help to destroy the stage of the 'cosmic liturgy' upon which a person's liberating rôle is performed and their persona and ultimate dignity eschatologically acknowledged (see Matt. 25:21).

For Ţuţea it became increasingly clear that God's will is for humanity to develop the 'inner man' (Eph. 3:16), able to experience God's salvific presence – not only as His unifying mark on the countless 'nuances' of the created order, but also as humanity's infinitely 'nuanced', and thus creative, response to the divine call to perfection.

---

80 Ţuţea speaks of the Carnival of Florence and quotes Antonio Alamani's burlesque *Il carro della Morte*: THEATRE, p. 410.

Chapter 10

Philosophy of Nuances

In a totalitarian society, ideology affects every aspect of life, both corporate and individual. An atheist system, which maintains that human fulfilment can be achieved within the sphere of the material world without recourse to the transcendent, epitomises what, to the spiritual person is eternal confinement and ultimately death. The society in which Țuțea lived, and with which he struggled, was such a 'system' – a kind of reverse image of the mystical Body of the Church, in which believers are 'living stones' (1 Pet. 2:5). In such a context the Christian *kerygma* of the Body, of the true Church, must be articulated with boldness and subtlety.[1] To proclaim the Body of Christ in its mystical and joyous fullness within Ceaușescu's Romania required great powers of vision and thought, as well as extraordinary courage and physical stamina if imprisonment was to be survived. For Țuțea such a witness involved his whole being – his mind, heart, body, and spirit. His philosophical vision, which I will investigate in this chapter, was formed from paradoxes, from the inexplicable, the odd, and the endlessly rich emotional content of personal experience. His essay entitled *Filosofia Nuanțelor* ('Philosophy of Nuances'),[2] finished in 1969, is relatively short, yet contains the central themes of his life's work. The significance of 'nuance' is intimately related to two of Țuțea's other works: the first volume of his *Treatise on Christian Anthropology, Problems, or the Book of Questions*,[3] and a 'Note on Philosophy of Nuances'.[4]

'Nuance' cannot be simply defined. It helps the reader to realise that everything in life has a dimension that is not immediately apparent. 'Philosophy' here has an ambivalent meaning: it does not imply a strictly rational process of thought. Rather, as a literal 'lover of wisdom' (*philosophos*) in a world conformed to mere

---

1   See PROBLEMS, p. 193.
2   The Romanian word *nuanță* is much more frequently used than the English 'nuance'. However, there is no precise English equivalent, and in the philosophical context it seems as well to use the word 'nuance' in English too. Țuțea's essay was written in 1969 and first published in 1990 in the weekly magazine *Baricada*. See Petre Țuțea's 'Filosofia Nuanțelor' ('The Philosophy of Nuances'), in his volume of collected essays, *Philosophia Perennis*, pp. 258–73. This essay was also published in NUANCES, pp. 23–40.
3   Finished in 1986.
4   Dictated in 1990 and published as 'Petre Țuțea – Notă la Filosofia Nuanțelor', with an introd. by Alexandru Prahovara [Popescu], *Cuvântul Românesc* (Hamilton, Canada, September 1990), p. 12. ['Note on Philosophy of Nuances'.]

'philosophical' constructs,[5] Țuțea invites his readers to approach a truth that cannot be encompassed by the mind – but which encompasses them and frees them to fulfil their calling. As Țuțea himself puts it, 'a reverse reading of the processes of nature, the cultivation of paradox and obscurity, a thirst for the impossible, are our only means of preserving freedom in a universe in which we live enchained'.[6]

Țuțea as a Man of Culture

Țuțea's education as well as his general background was that of a cultivated European with an extreme appetite for knowledge of all sorts. As well as appreciating music and art (he interviewed Brâncuși[7] as a young man), he loved poetry,[8] in particular Homer, Pindar, Dante, Shakespeare, and Eminescu. Particularly relevant are his references to the nineteenth-century French poet Charles Baudelaire, whom he often quotes. He was especially fond of the phrase *forêts de symboles*, from Baudelaire's sonnet *Correspondances*. Baudelaire was himself influenced by Swedenborg's theory of *synaesthesia*,[9] and *Correspondances* is a poetic exploration of this theory of interrelationship between the senses and their distant commingling in *une ténébreuse et profonde unité*.[10] Other poetic points of reference for Țuțea are Goethe (he quotes Goethe's 'theory of colours' and discusses the concept of time in *Faust*),[11] Hölderlin (the nuances of inspiration and madness), and Mallarmé (shades of subjectivisation and objectivisation vis-à-vis the Absolute).

It is particularly striking that a man of Țuțea's refinement, subjected to the violence and squalor of the re-education process, to the greyness and monotony of prison routine, and the manipulative imposition of pre-packaged ideology, should develop by way of defence not a sophisticated intellectual form of retaliation, but a philosophy of nuances – a way of thinking, indeed of being, whose power is the power of gentleness, which discerns creative multiplicity and subtlety of difference. The opposite of the satanised mask of the system, Țuțea's way of thinking points to the divine mask within everyone.

---

5   As I have shown, in Țuțea's terminology 'philosophers' stand for the fallen world – they look for certainty. 'Theologians' stand for experience of God – they proclaim certainty. In this sense 'Philosophy of Nuances' may be read as a theologian's epistle to philosophers.

6   NUANCES, p. 27.

7   See ON ART, p. 8.

8   For Țuțea, 'poetry is the mother tongue of humanity', philosophical thought is not higher than poetry. See THEATRE, p. 373.

9   Țuțea also refers to the Swedish theologian Emanuel Swedenborg (1688–1771) portrayed as mad by Kant in *Träume eines Geistersehers* (*Dreams of a Spirit-Seer*). See PROBLEMS, p. 28.

10   See for example PROBLEMS, p. 166; ELIADE, p. 29. See also Petre Țuțea, 'Viața ca formă a bucuriei pure', I, interview by Sanda Diaconescu, introd. by Marin Sorescu, *Jurnalul Literar*, Bucharest, 15 January 1990, p. 3.

11   See PROBLEMS, pp. 234–47.

In elaborating his understanding of nuance, Țuțea used disparate concepts in a truly original way. Most striking is the way in which the concept of taste (with reference to both Brillat-Savarin,[12] the great French gastronome of the Napoleonic era, and Voltaire,[13] the supreme Enlightenment philosopher) is worked in with the concept of materiality (drawing, as I have shown, not only on Origen and Thomas Reid, but also on Bonaventure).[14] Combining the superficial and the profound, the submissive and the intractable, gastronomic literalness and the savour of divine *sapientia*, nuance is concerned with nothing less than the body's way of being that is 'the stature of the fullness of Christ' (Eph. 4:13).

Etymology

The English word 'nuance' derives, via the French, from Latin *nūbēs*,[15] a cloud. This suggests something shifting and intangible, yet thoroughly real. In its colloquial sense it is used to convey a shade of meaning that, for all its subtlety, denotes a real distinction. Referring to the etymology given in Bescherelle's *Dictionnaire national*,[16] Țuțea states:

> Nuance is related to the idea of change. This is not just a simple association, in order to obtain psychological results at the level of the intellect or the senses. The word 'nuance' comes from *muto* – change. For a long time, it was pronounced *muence*. It was used as such by Montaigne and some of his contemporaries, meaning each distinct shade of a given colour, regardless of how many different shades a single colour can go through. The mixing of different colours and the separating out of a single colour, both produce an infinite variety of nuances.[17]

According to both etymologies, nuances, then, convey subtle gradations of change, through which our perception and understanding of life are determined. The word tends mostly to be associated with literary and artistic, rather than scientific, imagination. Țuțea, by contrast, applies it to all areas of experience, for in his thought

---

12 See *Physiologie du Goût ou Méditations de gastronomie transcendante*, par un Professeur (Bruxelles: J.P. Meline, 1835).

13 See Voltaire, *Le Temple du Goût*, ed. E. Carcassonne (Paris: Librairie E. Droz: 1938).

14 Bonaventure is not mentioned in Țuțea's writings. He used to refer to this saint in our conversations. See also note 83, Chapter 7.

15 Macdonald (ed.), *Chambers Twentieth Century Dictionary*, p. 902. Lesley Brown (ed.), *The New Shorter English Dictionary, on historical principles*, 2 vols (Oxford: Clarendon Press, 1993), II, p. 1951, gives the same etymology linking *nuance* with the French verb *nuer*, to show cloud-like variations in colour, f. *nue* cloud f. pop. Latin var. of Latin *nūbēs*.

16 Louis Nicolas Bescherelle, *Dictionnaire national, ou dictionnaire universel de la langue française*, 14th edn, 2 vols (Paris: Garnier Frères, 1845), II, p. 54.

17 NUANCES, p. 38.

the word stresses the unlimited material variety (gradations of colour, sound, density, and so on) of both the perceivable and the spiritual world.

Philosophical Sources

Heraclitus

Although within the Communist world Heraclitus was generally regarded as an early exponent of materialism and dialectical thinking,[18] Țuțea understands him differently, considering him to be a mystic who sees beyond the eternal flux of life.[19] In Țuțea's view, Heraclitean 'hidden harmony'[20] unifies the pairs of apparent contradictions that make up the visible world. Indeed, according to Țuțea, Heraclitus maintains that this 'hidden harmony' is superior to the 'visible harmony'[21] and regards it as a stability 'better than movement and change in the world of appearances, since the laws of reason are the only ones which bring serenity and happiness'.[22] This is an idea that permeates all Țuțea's thinking, although he, of course, has an eschatological vision of the eternal world of 'things which are not seen' (1 Cor. 4:18). He remarks on how this awareness of a mysterious harmony liberates Heraclitus from the dialectic of joy and sadness experienced when thinking focuses purely on the transient world: 'If Heraclitus had explored only the transient world, he would have reaped a huge harvest of illusory joy and sadness.'[23] However, Țuțea adds, there is always an epistemological risk, inherent in any scientific enquiry, in seeking to know the unknowable essence of God: 'You think of and seek for the Absolute under the deceptive mask of universal flux, but you cannot, without risk, go beyond the interplay of appearances.'[24] Only through humility before the mystery of God and God's loving and fruitful care for the created world can this danger be negotiated. Referring to Heraclitus's Fragment 24, Philip Wheelwright notes:

---

18   For an illustration of this unsubtle approach to Heraclitean philosophy, see Apostol, et al. (eds), *Dicționar de Filozofie*, pp. 325–6. Cf. Traian Podgoreanu, *Curs de Filosofie Marxistă*, 5th edn, 2 vols (Bucharest: University of Bucharest, 1981), I, p. 22. In fact, 'even so learned a Heraclitean scholar as Hermann Diels made the mistake, some fifty years after compiling his valuable collection of the Fragments, of putting forward an interpretation of Heraclitus as a metaphysical dualist': Philip Wheelwright, *Heraclitus* (Oxford: Oxford University Press, 1999), p. 103.

19   Wheelwright, *Heraclitus*, p. 29.

20   Wheelwright, *Heraclitus*, p. 102. See Heraclitus's Fragment 116: 'The hidden harmony is better than the obvious.'

21   Wheelwright, *Heraclitus*, p. 102; see also Wheelwright's comments in Chapter VIII, 'The Hidden Harmony', pp. 102–10.

22   NUANCES, p. 36.

23   NUANCES, p. 37.

24   NUANCES, p. 37.

A sort of intelligence displays itself in God's nature and operations, Heraclitus observes, but it is an intelligence only remotely and abstractly like anything we know on the human level, and we shall mistake it profoundly if we allow any further human associations to colour our description of it.[25]

Țuțea's reading of Heraclitus leads him to similar conclusions. He would not agree with scholars like Jonathan Barnes that, although Heraclitus was a paradoxographer whose account of the world is fundamentally inconsistent, he was not a mystical figure, standing aloof from the rationalism of Miletus.[26] Thus, Heraclitus's paradoxical statements about flux and the unity of opposites can, in Țuțea's view, *only* be discussed on a mystical plane transcending discursive reason.[27]

Like Heraclitus, Țuțea was intrigued by the fact that life and history are continuously changing and are, as processes, experienced but not fully known.[28] He takes up Heraclitus's tantalising reference to a 'hidden' ἁρμονία[29] and points to the fact that personal becoming is part of being in harmony with Christ. His anthropology stresses that we are called to become perfect through right choices and right actions, and that this involves experiencing the world around us, interpreting the nuances of its infinite variety. The worst act of inhumanity is to remove human beings from the experience of the ordinary world by imprisoning them, whether physically or through ideological or psychological manipulation.

Țuțea suggests that Heraclitus's philosophical 'obscurity' is rooted in a confusion between 'totality, i.e. the reality which needs or has to be known' and 'generality as a fruit of knowledge, a product of the enquiring mind'.[30] Țuțea proposes a nuanced statement of the mystical unity between being and knowledge, rather than the imposition of an absolute logical distinction.[31] In interpreting Heraclitus in this way, he was actually reshaping one of the very foundation blocks of Marxist ideological orthodoxy. Țuțea's approach, quite different from a straight dialectical confrontation,

---

25   Wheelwright, *Heraclitus*, p. 73.

26   Barnes, *The Presocratic Philosophers*, pp. 80–81.

27   For an affective, highly personal poetic 'redemption' of Heraclitus, see the remarkable poem 'That Nature is a Heraclitean Fire and of the Comfort of the Resurrection', by the Jesuit poet-priest Gerard Manley Hopkins (1844–89), in his *Poems and Prose*, select. and ed. W.H. Gardner (London: Penguin, 1968), pp. 65–6.

28   For Țuțea, Heraclitus's thinking cannot elucidate the riddle of human beginning, becoming, and end. Thus, he often quotes a fragment of Alcmeon of Croton, another pre-Socratic thinker: 'Men perish for this reason, that they cannot attach the beginning to the end'. See Barnes, *The Presocratic Philosophers*, p. 115.

29   About the nature of this 'hidden harmony' there appears to be no definitive agreement among Heraclitean scholars. See Wheelwright, *Heraclitus*, pp. 106–8.

30   NUANCES, p. 23. It is important to note that for Wheelwright too, 'the unity of things as Heraclitus understands it is a subtle and hidden sort of unity, not at all such as could be expressed by either a monistic or a dualistic philosophy': Wheelwright, *Heraclitus*, p. 105.

31   See PROBLEMS, p. 299.

is itself illustrative of a nuanced mind, in which something can perhaps be glimpsed of what it means to be 'wise as serpents and harmless as doves' (Matt. 10:16).

Ţuţea objects to what he calls Heraclitus's 'meaningless silence before the pseudo-mystery of nature'.[32] The true mystery is Christ the Saviour, the divine Word who, in the infinite yet altogether real nuances of 'flesh', brings perfect peace (John 14:27) and the reconciliation of humanity with God. By self-abnegation and suffering 'the loss of all things', the loss of all human certainties in the nuances of lived and living actuality, 'knowledge of Jesus Christ' can be attained (Phil. 3:8).

Georg Simmel

The title of Ţuţea's essay 'Philosophy of Nuances' is borrowed from the German *Lebensphilosoph* and neo-Kantian sociologist Georg Simmel.[33] Simmel's *Lebensphilosophie* is centred on the three concepts of human 'life', 'more-life', and 'more-than-life'. Simmel uses these three terms to describe different modes of experience, as summarised by Rudolph Weingartner:

> It is one thing to know an object, another to appreciate that it is beautiful, and still another to revere it as an object of worship. In Simmel's view, the content of what is experienced in each of the three cases may be the same, although it is not the same in experience. The objects of the three experiences differ in that the contents are given shape – are objectified – by means of three different ways of experiencing. The same contents differ in form.[34]

So Simmel's *Leben* refers to simple worldly knowledge of an object, while *Mehr-Leben* introduces a cultural and aesthetic dimension. *Mehr-als-Leben*, as the name suggests, implies moving beyond this world to the transcendent. Simmel's transcendent, however, does not refer to anything mystical or spiritual.[35] Rather, his concern is to define rationally 'the essence of society, that which is changeless and ahistorical, thus freezing history into motionless structures by his mode of perception'.[36] In *Die Probleme der Geschichtsphilosophie* (*The Problems of the Philosophy of History*), Simmel refers to 'the nuances of the principal categories'.[37]

Starting from Kant's transcendental logic, Simmel, so to speak, interposed, between the Kantian categories (quantity, quality, relation, and modality) that shape

---

32   THEATRE, p. 492.
33   'Note on Philosophy of Nuances', p. 12.
34   Rudolph H. Weingartner, entry on 'Simmel', in Paul Edwards (ed.), *The Encyclopedia of Philosophy*, 8 vols (London: Collier-Macmillan, 1967), VII–VIII, pp. 442–3.
35   Kurt H. Wolff (ed.), *The Sociology of Georg Simmel*, trans. and introd. by Kurt H. Wolff (London: Free Press, 1950), pp. xxx–xxxi.
36   See Renate Mayntz, entry on 'Simmel, Georg', in David L. Sills (ed.), *International Encyclopedia of the Social Sciences*, 17 vols (London: Free Press, 1968), XIV, p. 257.
37   Georg Simmel, *The Problems of the Philosophy of History, An Epistemological Essay*, trans., ed., and introd. by Guy Oakes (New York: Free Press, 1977), p. 208. See also Georg Simmel, *Die Probleme der Geschichtsphilosophie, Eine erkenntnistheoretische Studie*, 5th edn (Munich: Duncker & Humblot, 1923), p. 74.

all experience of contents, an infinite number of gradations or nuances (what he calls *Nuancierungen, Abstufungen*)[38] to characterise the eternal flux of life.[39] His sociological 'forms', in terms of which all human experience may be ordered,[40] correspond to Kant's a priori categories of cognition. However, they differ in two important respects: first, they 'inform not only the cognitive realm, but any and all dimensions of human experience'; and second, 'they are not fixed and immutable, but emerge, develop, and perhaps disappear over time'.[41]

Țuțea was aware that Simmel's aim in using nuances was to expand philosophical thought and to develop Kant's system of categories in order to know more-than-life (*Mehr-als-Leben*). According to Kant all human experience of contents is shaped by forms or a priori categories. Contents, however, Simmel argues, are not experienced in themselves, for they are shaped by the psyche as they are being experienced. Human experience produces cultural objects that can then be experienced as sources of other experiences. In Simmel's terms, life is not a static scheme, but a process of becoming: more-life and more-than-life.

Simmel, and Țuțea with him, criticise Kant for explaining cognitive processes exclusively in terms of objects that can be known empirically through the functions of the intellect applied to sensible matter. In their view, if a person thinks of a thing as a unity, it is artificial to distinguish between a direct perception of that thing and an indirect perception of it, that is, between intuitions and concepts.

For Simmel, if 'intuitions without concepts are blind, then concepts without intuitions are empty'.[42] Unity of apprehension comes from a synthesis of concepts and intuitions. The philosopher has 'a sense for the wholeness of things and of life' (*einen Sinn für die Gesamtheit der Dinge und des Lebens*), and an 'organ for recording and reacting to the whole' (*das aufnehmende und reagierende Organ für die Ganzheit*).[43] The capacity to translate intuitions into concepts and vice versa corresponds to what Simmel calls 'original unity', whose conventional separation into concept and intuition is not inherent in its own structure.

---

38   Țuțea quotes Simmel's original use of *Schattierungen* to express the same English word, 'nuances' (corresponding to the Romanian *nuanțe*).

39   PROBLEMS, p. 137.

40   Georg Simmel, *On Individuality and Social Forms, Selected Writings*, ed. and introd. by Donald N. Levine (Chicago: University of Chicago Press: 1971), p. 38.

41   Levine's introduction to Simmel, *On Individuality*, p. xv. According to Levine: 'for Simmel, the mind not only is active in that it brings its own categories to make cognition possible, it is involved in creating those categories and refining them and seeking new areas in which to apply them' (Simmel, *On Individuality*, p. xxxvii).

42   '*Anschauungen ohne Begriffe blind, Begriffe ohne Anschauungen leer sind*': Georg Simmel, *Rembrandt, Ein kunstphilosophischer Versuch* (Leipzig: Kurt Wolff, 1916), p. 18. Cf. Georg Simmel, *Rembrandt*, Romanian trans. and foreword by Grigore Popa, introd. by Ion Frunzetti (Bucharest: Meridiane, 1978), p. 72. Simmel's memorable dictum was often quoted by Țuțea in our conversations.

43   Georg Simmel, *Hauptprobleme der Philosophie*, 7th edn (Berlin: Walter de Gruyter, 1950), p. 11.

In contrast to Simmel, who used the concept of nuance to expand Kant's system of categories, Țuțea uses it to express a Christian vision of life in the context of an atheist society, and to launch a counter-attack on logical reductionism. His irrepressible mystical joy and non-systematic style transcend the conformism of Communist ideology (as also of consumer materialist individualism) and point to the divine mystery wherein human wholeness, wellbeing, and bliss find ultimate fulfilment.

A nuance belongs to the world of the senses, as gradation of colour, sound, and so on, while a category has a purely notional character. Both, however, are directly linked with experience. Nuances and categories alike belong to this transient world and can describe neither Simmel's *Mehr-als-Leben*[44] nor the eternal spiritual world as spoken of by Țuțea: 'Our experience remains stuck in "the ante-chamber of knowledge" (Rickert)[45] unless separated from the senses through consciousness ennobled by the truth of faith.'[46] Ennoblement 'by the truth of faith' is, of course, ennoblement precisely through the revelation of the Word made flesh – that is, through the very actuality of the economy of the Incarnation. Țuțea sees the ahistorical nature of Simmel's somewhat Romantic *Lebensphilosophie* as a mere anti-rationalist position which, being also agnostic, precludes the possibility of fruitful encounter with divine mystery. In criticising Simmel's anti-rationalism, however, Țuțea does not simply advocate rationalism. He is clear that rationalism is ultimately sterile, it 'dries up' the very 'roots of life', for 'its simplifications do not take into account the endless flux of the nuances of life'.[47]

The interplay of rationalism and anti-rationalism is itself an imprisoning dialectic that reflects the tragic state of unredeemed creation. In Țuțea's view, 'creatures need the Creator's grace'[48] to be released from their captivity to matter.[49] This is itself a nuanced option between mere rationalism and anti-rationalism, affirming both within a perspective that redefines each. Any 'act of real knowledge is a vocational mystery'.[50] In other words, the only way out of this ultimately deadening dialectic is the Mystery that is Christ – the Word Incarnate calling humanity not merely to admire or to be moved, but to 'follow' (Mark 10:21) in the gradations of lived discipleship that constitute the ladder of divine ascent.

---

44   Georg Simmel, *Brücke und Tür, Essays des Philosophen zur Geschichte, Religion, Kunst und Gesellschaft*, select. by Margarete Susman, ed. Michael Landmann (Stuttgart: K.F. Koehler, 1957), p. 24.

45   See Heinrich Rickert, *Die Philosophie des Lebens. Darstellung und Kritik der philosophischen Modeströmungen unserer Zeit*, 2nd edn (Tübingen: Mohr, 1922; 1st edn 1920). Cf. note 49, in Chapter 6.

46   PROBLEMS, p. 103.

47   THEATRE, p. 218.

48   PROBLEMS, p. 251.

49   See THEATRE, p. 399. Cf. NUANCES, p. 27.

50   PROBLEMS, p. 271.

Nuance versus Other Philosophies

Țuțea was not influenced by Heraclitus and Simmel alone. At the beginning of his 'Philosophy of Nuances', before suggesting his own theological position, he describes five different philosophical approaches:[51]

1 *Determinism* – which is based on the idea that all events including human actions and choices are predetermined by preceding events and states of affairs (theological determinism says all human actions are brought about by God).
2 *Indeterminism* – which affirms free will and maintains that behaviour is not entirely determined by motives, brain states, or anything else.
3 *Chaos Theory* – which describes disorder, not in terms of Greek mythology (as primordial Chaos transformed by gods into cosmos), but as apparently random phenomena which have underlying order.
4 *The Philosophy of Impasse* (or aporetic philosophy) – which, in neo-Kantian terms, is a method of raising problems and objections to which there are not necessarily answers.
5 *Eleatic philosophy* – which Țuțea calls 'philosophy of petrifaction' (or changelessness), based on Parmenides's negative or apophatic arguments about the nature of being.

For Țuțea none of these is satisfactory. Order and chaos are relative, since randomness can be discovered in apparently predictable systems, and chaos, to be perceivable, requires some kind of underlying order. Nuance enables Țuțea to reflect on 'a logic of nature' as part of 'a universal rational order',[52] mirroring 'divine reason' and 'divine harmony',[53] but providing no access thereto. This gives him confidence that, while the universe is more unpredictable than we have imagined, in respecting the created order as a comprehensive whole, we find it to be less threatening in its elemental aspects. In the words of Suzuki and Dressel:

> When we broke aspects of nature down into their component parts... we lost sight of the patterns of nature and the symbiosis within ecosystems, the way every part has a purpose... But science is always changing. There is a new way of thinking, a fresh view that is beginning to focus on relationships and patterns – and on the role of the most minute, as well as the greatest, creatures in the world around us.[54]

Țuțea's philosophy of nuances, written thirty years before Suzuki and Dressel's *Naked Ape to Superspecies*, is such a new 'way of thinking', highlighting the relational aspects of the world and pointing beyond the logic of becoming. As a

---

51 Summarised after NUANCES, pp. 24–7.
52 NUANCES, p. 25.
53 THEATRE, p. 448.
54 David Suzuki and Holly Dressel, *Naked Ape to Superspecies, A Personal Perspective on Humanity and the Global Ecocrisis* (St Leonards, Australia: Allen & Unwin, 1999), p. 12.

mystic, Țuțea proposes nuance as a means of preparing the believer for 'breaking the deadlock' of human captivity to nature, 'by opening a window to the real Absolute'.[55]

The world is ultimately explicable. Even creation *ex nihilo* is not in the ultimate sense a mystery, since it can be 'explained' through God's love. The ultimate 'explanation' of the universe is very God, the truly Real, the only inexhaustible mystery. Nuance, as I will show, has a sacramental function in helping to mediate this mystery.

'Trăirism' and Existentialism

Trăirism developed from the thought of Nae Ionescu, whose philosophical term *trăire* ('living-ism') became an inspiration for the younger intellectuals[56] between the two World Wars. Țuțea was influenced by this, along with Mircea Eliade and Emil Cioran. The fact that Ionescu is not universally held in high regard today should not be allowed either to obscure his historical significance, nor debar him from consideration as a thinker in his own right. Ionescu developed *trăirism* in a religious and non-materialist direction. His horror of system, especially of Marxism,[57] is shared by Țuțea, who refers to Ionescu's description of the system as a 'coffin', in contrast

---

55   NUANCES, p. 30.
56   Cave, *Mircea Eliade's Vision* , pp. 106–7. On p. 107, Cave shows that *trăire*:
       also means living life on the proper planes of reality. According to Ionescu, the three planes of reality are: 1 the scientific (which stresses induction and reason and is of the hard sciences, and of politics and economics), 2 the metaphysical (of 'essences,' logic, and ethics, and includes the aesthetic realm of art and literature; this plane is absolute only for the individual), and 3 the religious (of revealed truth which is absolute for all. This plane includes faith, and, along with the metaphysical plane, sees love as an instrument of knowledge).
       Cf. Ion Papuc's comment on *trăirism*, in DIALOGUES, p. 45.
57   Ionescu's rejection of Marxist circular causality is illustrated in the following passage:
       Historical materialism is far from being a scientific theory. It relies on two fundamental affirmations: first, that in social life everything happens by virtue of an almost mechanical causality; and second, that of all elements constitutive of social life, only those which have an economic function are decisive, since they are the cause of all the others. From this Marx concludes that, in order to understand and control the progress of social life it is enough to identify the causal chain of economic factors and to intervene as appropriate. This is where Marxist theory proves its unscientific character and its lack of authenticity. Today it is truly unscientific to proceed from causes in order to explain anything. For a long time causality has been no longer a scientific, but a metaphysical, concept, for the very simple reason that contemporary science establishes facts and does not explain anything. Science works today at best with functions and correlations (hence the extraordinary development of statistics), since the constitutive elements of life are correlated and not placed within a causal series. Thus, one can conceive of a history of mankind based on economic development. But, in the same way, one can conceive of a history of mankind based on its spiritual development.
       See Nae Ionescu, *Între ziaristică și filosofie* (Iassy: Timpul, 1996), p. 125.

to 'living thought'.[58] He quotes Ionescu's view that salvation precludes any sense of 'frozen form'.[59] This fundamental emphasis in Ionescu profoundly influenced Ţuţea's own stance against rigidly conceived and constructed systematic thought.

Eliade and especially Cioran transmuted *trăirism*, as it was originally conceived, into a form of secular existentialism which, Ţuţea claimed, was itself a system incapable of leading beyond the 'antechamber of life'.[60] Secular existentialism 'cannot accommodate holiness or heroism'.[61] Hence Camus's 'radical pessimism' and view of absurdity as the ultimate context of all experience, at the end of *The Myth of Sisyphus*: 'The struggle itself toward the heights is enough to fill a man's heart. One must imagine Sisyphus happy.'[62]

Furthermore, for Camus, Sisyphus is almost a Romantic hero or anti-hero. Ţuţea's criticism of Camus grows out of his very different experience of life – in its crudest physical and mental brutality. For Ţuţea, Sisyphus in Hades, pushing his great boulder up the mountain only to have it roll down again as he reaches the top, represents stupefying mindlessness, dehumanising emptiness, and barren stereotyping of humanity as a concept rather than joyful creative celebration of human personality in the infinite diversity and extent of its actual living 'nuances'. Ţuţea regards what Camus calls obliquely Sisyphus's 'happiness' as a form of moral suicide inseparable from the absurdity[63] of his toil. Camus's existentialism was simply concerned with existence, not life. Although Ţuţea appreciated the attempt of *trăirism* to engage with the totality of the human person, he was unable to accept the existentialist world view of Ionescu's disciples.

'Absurd indifference toward, and existential disgust for, the world are characteristics of the period in which we live.'[64] Chaos (meaninglessness) and aesthetic anarchy, in Ţuţea's view, provide no worthwhile response to, or escape from, the deadening commonplaces and clichés of existence. He rejects pursuit of the absurd, the gratuitous, and the grotesque as means of escape from existential impasse. He has no patience with Camus's declaration (at the beginning of *The Myth of Sisyphus*) that suicide is 'la question fondamentale de la philosophie'.[65] Reduced to the level of 'existential technique', secular existentialism indicates a condition of drained

---

58   NUANCES, p. 27.

59   NUANCES, p. 27. *Pace* that supreme canticle of nuanced doxology, the '*Benedicite, omnia Opera*': 'O ye dews and frosts... frost and cold... ice and snow, bless ye the Lord: praise him, and magnify him for ever' (from 'Order for Morning Prayer', in *The Book of Common Prayer*, 1662).

60   See PROBLEMS, pp. 317, 340.

61   PROBLEMS, p. 200.

62   '*La lutte elle-même vers les sommets suffit à remplir un cœur d'homme. Il faut imaginer Sisyphe heureux*': Albert Camus, *Le mythe de Sisyphe, essai sur l'absurde* (Paris: Gallimard, 1979), p. 166.

63   Maurice Friedman, *Problematic Rebel: Melville, Dostoievsky, Kafka, Camus*, rev. edn (Chicago: University of Chicago Press, 1970), p. 451.

64   Ţuţea, personal conversation, Bucharest, 21 November 1980. Cf. PROJECT, p. 141.

65   Camus, *Le mythe de Sisyphe*, p. 15.

communicativeness derived from a kind of colour-blindness in the use of nuance: 'Lack of communication leads to solipsism, for which Schopenhauer prescribes internment in the madhouse.'[66]

Within a perspective bounded absolutely by human birth and death, existential pessimism and despair are not surprising, for existence is characterised merely by the futility of change, and by circular, repetitive experience (including failed attempts at escape). Because secular existentialists like Camus live 'without hope and illusion', their happiness is 'inseparable from the absurd' in which 'Sisyphus forever shoulders anew his futile burden'.[67] Their concept of movement being limited to this world, they can know nothing of nuance in the liberating, transformative, sacramental sense which Țuțea offers.

As a Christian form of existentialism, *trăire* means, for Țuțea, 'mystical experience which releases the human being from the antechamber of life and knowledge' and which, 'through faith, makes the impossible possible in the believer's heart'.[68] It comprehends the whole of a person's being, and leads to spiritual growth: 'This is the sense of Nae Ionescu's *trăirism*. *Trăirism* should be conceived in theological rather than philosophical terms.'[69] Yet Țuțea's philosophy of nuances, as I will show later in this chapter, goes beyond the theological, into terms essentially sacramental in nature – perhaps (to suggest a different nuance of categorisation) a kind of affirmative liturgical 'philosophy'.

Nuance versus Number

Nuanced Vision under the 'Brutal Dominance of Number'[70]

It is important from the outset to remember that Țuțea is not just an apologist for humane sensitivity in a culture of mechanistic organisational ideology (although he is, of course, always that). He also argues against the materialistic corruption and politically self-serving abuse of human sensibility in the democratic capitalist world. Although in a discussion of the concept of 'nuance' the following account of Țuțea's vision of intellectual endeavour may seem over-schematic, it may nevertheless illuminate further this key concept.

---

66   PROJECT, p. 140.
67   Friedman, *Problematic Rebel*, p. 451.
68   PROBLEMS, p. 340.
69   Țuțea's view was perhaps influenced by St Gregory of Nyssa. Gregory places at the heart of his theology the contrast between stereotypical change (that leads only to meaningless repetition) and perpetual progress (that involves a positive change). See section 5, 'Progress in Sanctity', in Jean Daniélou's introduction to Herbert Musurillo (ed.), *From Glory to Glory, Texts from Gregory of Nyssa's Mystical Writings*, trans. Herbert Musurillo (Crestwood, NY: St Vladimir's Seminary Press, 1995), pp. 46–56.
70   Personal conversation, Bucharest, 10 June 1985. Țuțea also used the phrase *sub tutela numărului* ('under the tutelage of number').

Subjectivity and objectivity are merely two ends of a continuum, with 'objecticity' as 'the Real', which these (either separately as Romanticism or rationalism, mysticism, or existentialism, or together locked in dialectic) strive towards, yet are doomed never to attain. The creaturely world of flux and dialectic is essentially that of Fallen matter – or perhaps it would be more appropriate to say that, by describing the universe in such terms, Țuțea is attempting to give a philosophical[71] account of what is meant by the Fall. The 'objectic' reality of matter is, as has been indicated, signified in the word *materiality*: and within this brief schematisation, it can be said that, while matter is eternally subject to 'the brutal dominance of number', *materiality* is signified by nuance. Numbers, in Țuțea's view, are immanent (that is, constitutive of the created order, but confined to it). By the grace of its own logic – albeit, I trust, in the redemptive grace of the divine Word, not merely to 'destroy' but to 'fulfil' (Matt. 5:15) the intention it bears – nuance itself must confound any attempt to schematise it.

What, then, is this 'brutal dominance of number'? I have shown how, in Țuțea's view, the absurdity of secularised existence (and purely 'psychic' religion) is experienced not only under Communism, but also in Western consumerist societies. Selfish materialism excludes God's self-giving love from human community, and thus falsifies the divine mask. Such a world sees the mask of un-redeemed 'psychic' (1 Cor. 15:45) flesh as normal, as real – and thus pursues the Real entirely within the (mathematical) logic and scientistic vision of that mask. For Țuțea it is vital not to confuse the definable sphere of the material world (however wonderful and complex), with the sphere of absolute being – the eternal self-giving of the divine Absolute in the spiritual human being, formed in the image and likeness of God.[72] The impress of God in 'flesh' is perceivable not through statistical recording or photographic realism, but through the nuances which are experienced by people as they follow their calling of inner peace, certainty, and joy, towards Christ-like perfection. This 'vocational' dimension of being encompasses every aspect of physical, intellectual, pedagogic, and creative life, for it is reflected in the infinite multiplicity of unique individual gifts and social and historical 'styles'.

Contemplating the historical development of humanity, for instance, Țuțea looks at different nuances of time in relation to human perception: the irretrievable, frozen, and sometimes empty past, the living present, and the uncertain future. He has an optimism about the future that is at once courageous and subtle. Uncertainty is full of charm because it embraces everyone. There is, within historical processes, an almost imperceptible, but also inescapable relativism:

The servant no longer appears as his master's shadow[73]... and the great are brought down, step by step, together with their established order of domination, since they are facing the

---

71   See note 5 in this chapter.
72   THEATRE, p. 421.
73   A reference to Hegel's 'Master/Slave dialectic': G.W.F. Hegel, *Phenomenology of the Spirit*, trans. A.V. Miller, foreword and notes by J.N. Findlay (Oxford: Clarendon Press, 1977), pp. 111–19.

same dangers as everyone else. They watch and are watched... I enjoy contemplating the long sunset of the superpowers, with a profound and strange pleasure, with no trace of melancholy. I greet the fresh sunrise of a new era with the excitement of a naive soul, and the sunset with the finer perception of a contemplative who rejoices to witness the disintegration of the foolish conceit of the great. Geographical and insoluble misfortunes, caused by [the brutal dominance of] number, are slowly and steadily disappearing. And so are privileges which are the result of great systems and styles.[74]

This is far from post-modern relativism, although his style might seem in some respects to anticipate the sometimes archly non-conceptual mood of post-modernism. Ţuţea's writing has an intellectual confidence and joy (not mere bullish vigour), conveying, through nuances rather than categorical articulation, new possibilities of value. Using this mode of thought and expression Ţuţea was able to reflect not only on his own immediate situation, but also on all aspects of the human condition, in a holistic rather than specific way. For him the ultimate concern of philosophy is to prepare humanity for the proclamation of the Gospel. The philosophy of nuances is a kind of prophetic call to 'make straight the way' for the Gospel (John 1:23). It opens the way to the possibilities of freedom as opposed to the self-referential meaning of system, and to mutuality in Christ which fulfils individual uniqueness, as opposed to earthly egalitarianism which confines the individual to generality. He provides an intellectual tool which can be used to discuss vital issues that defy intellectual definition – the fundamental matter of divine revelation.

I have shown that for Ţuţea, following Hamilton, logical ideas of the infinite 'cannot replace the Absolute revealed to humanity saved by our Redeemer'.[75] 'The locus of freedom is not in mathematics, as Cantor thought,[76] but in theology, since mathematics does not transcend logical paradoxes and numerical limits.'[77] For Ţuţea, to reconcile the formal nuances of the 'exact' sciences with the certainties of the Christian faith is a cause for joy: 'How agreeable to meet a Christian mathematician, interpreter of the universe!'[78]

Nuance and Science

Nuance represents the dimension of freedom in a secular world, transcending statistical models of humanity and mathematical models of infinity. In giving an account of the human being, there is an infinite variety of gradations of data, each immeasurable yet essential.

Ţuţea's nuanced classification of intellectual disciplines is methodologically related to the now classic distinction made in Germany before the First World War

---

74   NUANCES, pp. 39–40.
75   PROBLEMS, p. 217.
76   Georg Cantor (1845–1918). Professor of Mathematics at Halle University, he provided the first formal theory of the infinite.
77   PROBLEMS, p. 217.
78   THEATRE, p. 373.

between human, cultural, social, historical, or social sciences (*Geisteswissenschaften*) and natural sciences (*Naturwissenschaften*).[79] He was also influenced by Wilhelm Windelband's idea that natural sciences employ a *nomothetic* or generalising method (seeking to discover normative and general relationships and properties), whereas social or cultural sciences use an *ideographic* or individualising procedure (seeking to identify the non-recurring events in reality and the particular or unique aspects of any phenomenon).[80] In his essay on nuances Ţuţea contrasts empirically exact and socially nuanced methods:

[*Empirical sciences*] Max Planck[81] maintains that he has no need of Kant's table of categories to construct the universe of physics, but does not recommend that it should be thrown away, because it might be of use at some stage.

[*Social sciences*] With the help of reason, the human being distinguishes truth from error, and justice from injustice, controls passions and extends his goodwill, because he makes them social and universal (Marcus Aurelius).[82]

Ţuţea maintains that human approximations are rooted in the mind (whose hypotheses cannot explain the unpredictable and uncertain principles of nature) and in the wholes which are to be found outside human experience (partially knowable, undefinable, or, more precisely, inexplicable). In his view statistical formulae – which are like images, although more abstract – illustrate but do not prove. However, he believes that spiritual thinking must be integrated with technological advancement if freedom, in the full sense of the word, is to be achieved:

An outstanding spiritual culture deprived of a sound material base saddens us because of our impotence, and makes our tyrannical regime much more difficult to bear than if we were on a lower spiritual level... The historical development of free peoples depends on the level of their theoretical and technical knowledge. This truth has to be transformed into an article of faith. Only so can it become effective.[83]

Nuance here becomes a glimpse into the humble world of the Virgin Mary, whose song[84] points the way toward a properly revolutionary world peace which cannot

---

79   Ţuţea discusses the way Wilhelm Dilthey employs this distinction in *Der Aufbau der geschichtlichen Welt in den Geisteswissenschaften* (1910) to define sciences in terms of their subject matter. See PROBLEMS, pp. 275–6. See also PROBLEMS, pp. 250–51, 256, 264, 314.
80   Marshall (ed.), *The Concise Oxford Dictionary of Sociology*, p. 196.
81   Max Planck (1858–1947), German physicist who first formulated the quantum theory (1900).
82   Marcus Aurelius Antonius, Roman emperor (AD 161–180) renowned particularly for his *Meditations*, propounding his Stoic way of life. Quotation summarised after NUANCES, p. 30.
83   NUANCES, p. 29.
84   'He has put down the mighty from their thrones, and exalted the lowly' (Luke 1:52).

be achieved by violence. In contrast to Francis Fukuyama, who sees the twentieth century (with its World Wars, the Holocaust, and the Gulag) as having turned everyone into 'historical pessimists',[85] Țuțea sees the unprecedented global development of science and technology as a source of optimism, for it can and should eventually abolish barriers between peoples. As an 'authoritarian liberal', however, he challenges any project of modern democracy founded on the essentially Marxist 'cult of labour'.[86]

Nuance and Order

Christian Nuances and Politics

Accepting that Christianity and liberalism are compatible (in the 1930s, as I have shown, Țuțea considered them incompatible), Țuțea's belief in a new and just world order 'is the principal motivation for thinking in nuance'.[87] Nuance here is a kind of diplomacy of 'whole' corporate being, helping people to 'distinguish between cunning and finesse', showing them 'the ambiguity of expressions and the emptiness of systems'.[88] Years before devolution, diversity, and subsidiarity became fashionable words in politics, Țuțea was exploring, through the concept of nuance, ways of re-envisioning world order along such lines.

He was not a pacifist, and believed that in the future even poverty-stricken nations should be able to develop more sophisticated military defences, not necessarily nuclear, which might help control the abuse of power by the strong nations.[89] More fundamentally, his nuanced vision brings into focus the moral, cultural, and spiritual aspects of international relations, through which 'military arrogance' is ultimately challenged. Humanity does not simply have to accept the imposition on smaller nations of the so-called 'historical' priorities and 'vital' interests of the most powerful nations:

> We need to re-examine past and present, and project new light onto the future. Already people and peoples have begun to see themselves differently. A new vision of universal order is coming into being, based on the value of the human mask, on the hope and encouraging data of science and technology. The concentration of great force in small areas of physical space has become possible for smaller nations. This allows us to reckon as false the position of the so-called great nations, and to take their conceit with a pinch of salt.

---

85   Francis Fukuyama, *The End of History and the Last Man* (New York: Avon Books, 1993), p. 3.
86   THEATRE, p. 478.
87   NUANCES, p. 29.
88   NUANCES, p. 39.
89   The terrorist attack on the USA on 11 September 2001 illustrates how, in practice, such military capacity breeds further violence, and can, at best, perhaps establish a universal 'cold war' solution. Cf. Petre Țuțea, 'Convorbiri cu Magistrul', ed. Marian Munteanu, *Cuvântul Studențesc*, 1:1, Brașov, 1993, p. 9. ['Conversations with the Master'.]

We have still to participate in the summits of superpowers, because their privileges remain as before, due to their scientific and technological primacy, their conquest of space, their wealth, the size of their populations, and their recent and more remote histories. Their material superiority claims 'values' that are gradually being emptied of content... Science, art, and philosophy challenge their military arrogance, which is both ethically, socially, and politically damaging and spiritually sterile.[90]

Nuance also works at the personal level in defining and strengthening the prophetic power of individual experience. Țuțea lived his own faith with genuine joy and optimism in the face of tyranny. Even amid the stereotypes of *homo stultus*, nuances of human originality and vitality could be discerned, and through carefully observed characteristics, free of imposed hypotheses, the individual and the nation could be seen in symbiosis beyond the schematic grid of ideology. In the context of Soviet cultural hegemony, his confidence in the spiritual genius of the Romanian nation expressed nuanced awareness and spiritual hope:

> I have learned that the celebrated philosopher Heidegger saw the Romanian people as having a key rôle as a Latin nation. His conviction derived from what he knew of our promising beginnings on the spiritual level, projections of a great spiritual force possessed by the Romanian people, a force whose irrepressible genius will one day, in a climate of genuine freedom, be manifest in great creativity. Nevertheless we are unable to enjoy the privileges which come from purely spiritual creativity, since people and nations still tend to go downhill in a world of international relations where brute force continues to predominate.[91]

In contrast to the decadent 'twilight' of Western civilisation described by Oswald Spengler in his *Decline of the West*,[92] Țuțea envisaged a new 'dawn' of Christian spirituality in Romania and in the world generally. In his view Christian order can be established on earth only when, 'by divine grace, the cult of force, pride, hatred, and Manichaean simplifications are eradicated'[93] from national and international affairs. The establishing of this order can only be achieved in the spirit of the Sermon on the Mount, in accord with God's way, not through military or economic coercion: 'War as *ultima ratio* belongs not to man but to God.'[94]

It is not apparent how Țuțea resolves the contradiction between Jesus's injunction to love your enemies (Matt. 5:44) and the suggestion that smaller countries might

---

90   NUANCES, p. 28.
91   NUANCES, pp. 28–9.
92   Oswald Spengler (1880–1936), German philosopher of history whose main work, *Der Untergang des Abendlandes* (2 volumes: 1918, 1922) rejects traditional unilinear accounts of history, arguing that civilisations go through natural cycles of growth and decay and that every system of thought or value, being culturally determined, is ultimately devoid of universal validity. See English trans. Spengler, *The Decline of the West*.
93   PROBLEMS, p. 192.
94   PROBLEMS, p. 193.

somehow counteract the hegemony of the nuclear powers through developing a 'concentration of great force in small areas of physical space'. Although he had an optimistic enthusiasm for technological progress, he had no programmatic views as to how Romania might effectively arm itself through innovative technology. His main emphasis was always on spiritual vitality and creativity. When talking to younger people, in particular, he always challenged defeatism, the victim syndrome, and the idea of Romania being fated to remain a client-State. His style of discourse was meant to awaken the anaesthetised hope of those brought up under Communist ideology, to make them aware of their own dignity and creative capacity. He inspired in all sorts of people a new and deeper understanding of the Good News of Christ, affirming the vocation of all to love their neighbour and to grow in discipleship into union with God who is love (1 John 4:8).

How this squares with his theories of active 'defence policy', however, remains a dilemma, which can be seen as a weakness in his overall theology from a systematic point of view.[95] In seeking to understand him better in relation to this dilemma, it may be helpful to look at the traditional imagery of spiritual warfare, familiar to him from *The Ladder of Divine Ascent*. Crucial to 'divine ascent' is watchful focus on God. To focus on the attacks of the evil one is already to have succumbed in the 'invisible warfare'. In modern times the need for a just world peace has become ever more imperative at the most practical level. Yet the traditional religious imagery of spiritual combat is that of a pre-industrial world, and this nowadays all too often encourages a historicist spiritual attitude. In response to this, Ţuţea offers a philosophy of new, loving focus upon God through inspired openness to the infinity of nuances of human imagination, feeling, sense, and thought.

Where does the universal Church stand in relation to all of this? Under Communism the Divine Liturgy could be celebrated in Romania, but the application of Gospel teaching to social order and individual lives could not be expounded without enormous risks. A natural danger for the Church in such a situation was that its understanding of spiritual warfare should become a kind of interiorised symbolism.

---

95   This dilemma is not untypical of late twentieth-century theologians. In Dietrich Bonhoeffer, *The Cost of Discipleship* (London: SCM Press, 1990), pp. 175f., Bonhoeffer advocated the practical applicability of the Sermon on the Mount, yet was involved in a plot to assassinate Hitler. See Stephen E. Fowl and L. Gregory Jones, *Reading in Communion, Scripture and Ethics in Christian Life* (London: SPCK, 1991), p. 158:

Bonhoeffer understood his participation in the resistance as an act of repentance for the guilt of his Church, his nation, and also his class. Because his Church, his nation, and his class were all complicit in helping to give rise to Hitler, they needed to act. But he also knew that there would be punishment by God. Thus by taking up the sword, Bonhoeffer also presumed that he would need to 'pray to God for the forgiveness of the sin and pray for peace'.

Cf. 'The Tragedy of Dietrich Bonhoeffer', in James William McClendon, Jr, *Systematic Theology Ethics* (Nashville, TN: Abingdon Press, 1986), pp. 205–8.

Just as the Western Reformation emphasised the importance of Scripture, and criticised the Roman Catholic Church's often venial theology and distorted focus on the Mass, so Țuțea came to a new sense of how the Gospel might be proclaimed in the Orthodox context. While he can in no sense be labelled a 'Protestant', it is worth observing that the Protestant Churches, with their focus on the Bible rather than the Liturgy, were particularly 'discouraged' in Communist Romania. Like them, Țuțea emphasised the importance of Scripture and *imitatio Christi*. He also affirmed the importance of relating the Divine Liturgy to the way Christians live and fulfil their vocation, whatever the cost. Only when the Church preaches the Gospel in its fullness will it truly engage in the spiritual warfare which is its vocation.

Țuțea's philosophy of nuance asserts the claim of the sacred not only in traditional theological terms (which always run the risk of descending into self-referential religious jargon), but also in the arena of the desacralised language and intellectual systems of the world that Christ redeems. It suggests ways of revitalising theological and spiritual language, to meet the urgent needs of the time.

Christian Hope versus Naive Optimism

Țuțea's vision of philosophy and science as the servants of theology is founded on his understanding of nuance as a threshold to the sacred. His own personal battle against the forces of evil is integral to his exposition of the Christian *kerygma*. His affirmation of the Kingdom of God, not as a grand spiritual vista of total meaning or truth, but in the nuanced light of the Sermon on the Mount with its blend of pragmatism, beauty, and the demand for perfection, is genuinely prophetic. His is a proclamation of Christian hope.

It is through the play of nuances that we acquire our images of the world and of history, which, however, can never be more than approximate. Desacralised, uprooted from their divine origin, and stripped of mystical significance, nuances drown in the world of flux. They seem to 'satisfy the pride of man who believes himself to be the architect of his universe', but this in fact separates him 'from the essence of things in a way that creates anxiety'.[96] Conceived as Heraclitean war, in terms of conflicts and contrasts between opposed categories, the world is ultimately meaningless. Only a mystical view of the eternal flux of life can bear the fruits of salvation, for it leads to acceptance of a necessary 'extra-mundane order':[97]

> It is possible to awake from the 'dogmatic sleep' (Kant) of oppressive systems and styles and to escape from the privileges claimed by those who possess them, by means of the endless interplay of nuances in modern thought. I once said that everything is psychological except eternity. But even eternity can be conceived psychologically...
>
> In the realm of rational thought – enveloped in a great unknown – space, time, and number gradually lose their import and become simple symbolic sign-posts, expressions of

---

96   NUANCES, p. 23.
97   PROBLEMS, p. 173.

theoretical, technological, and practical consciousness. But what seems more exciting, in the immense process of equalising relations between people and peoples, is the mystery which embraces the beginning and the end of all things. People become more humble when, at the same time as they lose the privileges which derive from material power, they are confronted with their inability to know the causes of things and the unique cause of creation. For these causes cannot be located within, but outside things.[98]

Țuțea takes pleasure in 'the ever actual joy of living out nuances'.[99] By making it possible to reflect on history in a mystical way, with tools other than those of dialectical and historical materialism, his philosophy of nuances is a source of Christian hope. This hope would, clearly, be naive optimism if read as a practical guide to actual living 'in the world'. The prophetic nature of his theology of hope is, in obedience to Christ's injunction to be 'in' the world but not 'of' it, an assertion of the sacred in a world that 'of' itself either denies the sacred or materialises and (idolatrously) conceptualises it:

> In the philosophy of nuances we encounter not only the gratuitous pleasures of art, but also material, ethical, and political joys. If old systems have been emptied of their content, this does not mean that new systems cannot be created. But, if systems and styles are difficult to replace, the endless play of nuances offers unlimited possibilities to the creative spirit of people and nations. Only in this way can the idea of progress be released from the sphere of naive optimism, and nations from their fear of enslavement and humiliation and the shame of being ruled by other nations.[100]

As a diplomat and economist, a religious dissident and prisoner of conscience, Țuțea was fully aware of the ways 'of' the world, at their most brutal and complex. His vision of hope, however, is an offering of sacral, intellectual vulnerability 'in' the world of self-aggrandising political and religious *Realpolitik* – a humility reflecting the spirit of that Mystery of Trinity which I explored in Chapter 6.

Holistic View of the Human Person

In the domain of art or science nuance is a fruit of the creative anxiety which humans experience in their 'thirst for the true, the good, and the beautiful, and for the new, which always makes us anxious'.[101] Țuțea sees any single nuance as 'a passing wave in Heraclitus's river', yet nevertheless resting in the transcendent mystery of the 'hidden harmony'; nuances preserve their defining chromatic-sensitive character of infinite gradation:

---

98   NUANCES, p. 31.
99   NUANCES, p. 33.
100 NUANCES, p. 40.
101 NUANCES, p. 35.

A chromatic concrete reality, regarded as the play of nuances, rescues nuances from the realm of the subjective and of nothingness, because 'a nuance is one and the same both for the eyes of the spirit and for those of the body' (Bescherelle).[102]

Personal Unity: Body and Soul

Awareness of the nuances of life in all its aspects stimulates awareness of the wholeness of things, of the human person and of the cosmos. This section will focus particularly on human wholeness, for this is, so to speak, the field of personal awareness of nuances, and reflects that image of the divine which I will consider in the next section.

In the concrete world of human biology Țuțea sees taste as perhaps the key concept, both as a sensory faculty and as intellectual 'style' and psychosomatic being:

> Taste has its roots in us and outside us. Irrational, subtle, and irritating, taste ranges from the concrete physiological to the ideal realm of spiritual values... We may observe that the proverb, *de gustibus non disputandum*, does not rank as an absolute maxim, because tastes can be 'certain', refined, bad, good, and corrupt. Thus we move from Brillat-Savarin's *Physiology of Taste* through to Voltaire's *Temple of Taste*. In Bescherelle's dictionary, we find the essential characteristics of tastes, not only sensory, but also spiritual or affective. Taste includes the styles of a particular epoch. It includes: 'common sense, tact, and genius'. When we think of lack of taste, we include stupidity.[103]

Simmel, in his classic monograph on Rembrandt, speaks of a fundamentally unifying function that constitutes body and soul as a single entity.[104] Split into separate entities, a human being can be regarded as a mechanical rather than a living whole. Țuțea takes a similar view of the unity of the human person, which can be split only at a philosophical level. He notes the proposition of the French philosopher Pierre Laromiguière (1756–1837), that the senses are 'abstracting machines' which 'allow us to perceive separately qualities which cannot exist separately in bodies or in concrete objects as we encounter them, translating them into objects of thought'.[105] Thus through nuance, which as I have shown reflects 'concrete reality as perceived by the senses',[106] thought is expanded.

Țuțea maintains that the limitations of psychosomatic dualism can be overcome only if people accept God as the agent who sustains the mysterious and thus ultimately incomprehensible union of soul and body. He rejects, with scholars such as Richard Swinburne, the idea that there is 'a deep *noumenal* feature of the world in

---

102 NUANCES, p. 35.
103 NUANCES, p. 32.
104 '*Es ist überhaupt unsinning, von Körper und Seele wie von Teilen zu sprechen, die den Menschen zusammensetzen*': Simmel, *Rembrandt, Ein kunstphilosophischer Versuch*, p. 17.
105 NUANCES, p. 23.
106 NUANCES, p. 23.

consequence of which consciousness depends necessarily on the brain'.[107] Ţuţea argues against the view that material neurophysiological processes are the origin of 'immaterial' consciousness, and sees Kant's system as an unproven synthesis connecting 'pure concepts of the intellect, transcendental categories, with sensible intuition'.[108]

Ţuţea speaks of *noumena* not as things in themselves (whose phenomenal aspects are, for Kant, the source of experience but are not in themselves knowable). Rather, he is concerned with other-worldly things or the 'extra-mundane Real (ignored by Kant in his limited, inconclusive agnosticism which has no consolation to offer)'.[109]

Ţuţea believes, with St Paul and with credal Church tradition, that not only the soul but also the body is to be resurrected at the Last Judgement, and that both are thus indispensible in the economy of salvation (1 Cor. 15:35–43). They have a common end, a unifying relationship to the Creator. All created things are material and God alone is non-material in an absolute sense.[110] Materiality signifies, in effect, createdness.

Ţuţea rejects both dualism and monism as 'abstract fictions' which 'eliminate the complexity of material and spiritual life'[111] and thus put the Incarnate Logos merely on a level with created things. 'By faith', he declares, 'one can accept a materiality to which intellect and senses have no access.'[112] It is through being alive to the nuances of sensory and inner experience (intellectual, emotional, spiritual, and aesthetic) that human consciousness can conceive of materiality.

The soul is, for Ţuţea, a given of personal uniqueness, not an arithmetical extrapolation of personality in an impersonal world. The body is a showing forth of the infinite nature of matter, our full participation in that universe of multiplicity and becoming that is God's original delight ('God saw that it was good', Gen. 1:31). To proclaim 'the resurrection of the body' is to assert the irreducible value of matter and the factual material nature of mystery. Ţuţea has an intense personal awareness of

---

107   Richard Swinburne, *The Evolution of the Soul*, rev. edn (Oxford: Clarendon Press, 1997), p. xii.

108   PROBLEMS, p. 73.

109   PROBLEMS, p. 73.

110   The idea that there must be a universal, though subtle, materiality of creation is held by some of the Greek Fathers. Some of them call angels ἀσώματοι because in comparison with human beings they are bodiless, but in comparison with God they are not entirely non-material. See G.W.H. Lampe (ed.), *A Patristic Greek Lexicon* (Oxford: Clarendon Press, 1976), pp. 254–5. This is a view one can find, for example, in Origen for whom no created being can live without a body. Cf. Origen, *On First Principles*, Book II, Chapter II, 1–2, pp. 81–2. The Macarian Homilies suggest that nothing created is altogether immaterial: Homily IV. 9, in A.J. Mason (ed.), *Fifty Spiritual Homilies of St Macarius the Egyptian* (London: SPCK, 1921), p. 25.

111   PROBLEMS, p. 189. In his speeches Ţuţea also referred to St Bonaventure who held that the human soul consisted of 'spiritual' stuff (*materia*) informed by a form. Bonaventure's view is summarised in Swinburne, *The Evolution of the Soul*, note 6, p. 327.

112   PROBLEMS, p. 189.

a world in which 'everything is enveloped in mystery'. By mystery, as I stated in Chapter 7, he does not mean vagueness, irrationality, or pantheist empathy. Rather, through living to the full, with gusto (in the original sense of the word – as taste – ranging from the crudely voracious and irrepressibly humorous, to the most sublime refinement of intellectual and artistic discipline and intuition, *gran gusto*) we define what it is to be wholly human. That is, we are liberated from mere abstract concepts of wholeness or perfection into the actual (vocational) wholeness of our unique particularity:

> Nuance deals with sound, colour, and word in endless combinations, in order to discern the mystery hidden in things, either simplifying or expanding, either through growth or through diminution of the number of signs. A readiness to think in nuances tends to bring the senses closer to reason, to lead to simultaneous understanding of unity and diversity. This signifies style, that is, unity *in* diversity. The predominantly chromatic character of nuance shows up the anxiety and dissatisfaction deriving from the nothingness of pure concepts. It is a smooth, imperceptible passing above the game of living and dying, above life and the universe.[113]

Unified View of the Human Intellect

Țuțea describes two types of humanity: the human being who knows truth ('the mystical dogmatist') and the human being who seeks truth ('the creative sceptic').[114] Through 'creative anxiety':

> we lose the privilege of certainty characteristic of the dogmatic spirit, but paradoxically we gain in precision and subtlety through the perspective opened up to us in the domain of endless experience. That which we find freezes us, the One to be found keeps us awake and alive.[115]

For Țuțea, rationalist philosophy reduces life to 'frozen' images.[116] It literally 'freezes' life, which is why, in his view, the cultural landscape of Europe must be re-animated with Romantic and mystical elements. The changing aspects of reality interweave with constants, the fabrications of the imagination with the constructs of reason. But all these are just links in the chain of causality, poles of the dialectic of appearance and disappearance.[117] Only the transcendent can make real sense of it all:

> How pleasing it would be if we knew ourselves and all phenomena in their unfolding as deriving one from another, as Thales of Miletus envisaged. We would float up the ladder of our perfecting. But the chain of causation and of the Sceptics' questioning can end only through acceptance of the principle of sufficient reason located of necessity in the mystery

---

113 NUANCES, p. 38 (italics added).
114 See NUANCES, p. 27.
115 NUANCES, p. 27.
116 See NUANCES, p. 27.
117 PROBLEMS, p. 67.

of origin. When we read the book of nature with humility, real progress is made, and we attain that inner silence of which Spinoza speaks, which comes from reconciliation with ourselves, with others, with nature, and with the Absolute understood as mystery and incomprehensibility.[118]

Just as rationalism tends to consider everything only in the categories of human capacity to conceive, and, similarly, anti-rationalism can overlook the fact that divine energies are at work in the ordered structuring of the world, so apophatic and cataphatic theology have complementary merits (and also shortcomings). Ţuţea employs nuance to address these shortcomings, fusing the philosophical and the theological in dynamic wholeness, rejoicing in the contradictions of the psyche:

> We need to experience with the utmost passion philosophical terms such as the essence and appearance of things, theoretical, practical, and technical consciousness, and to renew the ways in which we struggle for adaptation in this world. This philosophy of nuances can bring us into the presence of absolute reality, in which substance is interwoven with chance, the fabrications of the imagination with rational constructions. The tendency towards thinking in nuances is all-embracing. It cannot be reduced only to the form and to the perfecting of philosophical expression.[119]

'Philosophy of Nuances' is a celebration of materiality in a profusion of insights about the nature of the Incarnation,[120] 'the Real in its totality', wherein the uncreated essence of God, the uncreated energies, and the created are proclaimed one, the pure joy of the All-Holy, the Holy One, in Love.

---

118   NUANCES, pp. 31–2.
119   NUANCES, p. 37. For Kant 'the quality of the feeling in a pure judgement of taste' lies in its 'being devoid of all interest' to the feeling subject, 'or, more simply, disinterested': Henry Allison, *Kant's Theory of Taste* (Cambridge: Cambridge University Press, 2001), p. 85. In introducing this thesis, Kant claims that: 'Everyone must admit that a judgement about beauty in which there is mixed the least interest is very partial and not a pure judgement of taste.' Kant intends 'to resolve the faculty of taste into its elements and to unite them ultimately in the idea of a common sense'. See Immanuel Kant, *Critique of the Power of Judgement*, ed. Paul Guyer, trans. Paul Guyer and Eric Matthews (Cambridge: Cambridge University Press, 2000), (5:205), p. 91 and (5:240), p. 124. This approach would not satisfy Ţuţea. It would fall short of the 'good sense' which is always open to further refinement by 'nuances' and therefore always capable of greater purity. Cf. Chapter 4, 'Kant's Ethical Alcoholism', in Michel Onfray, *Le Ventre des Philosophes, Critique de la Raison Diététique* (Paris: Grasset & Fasquelle, 1989).
120   'I have come that they may have life, and that they may have it more abundantly' (John 10:10).

Nuances as *Therapeia*[121]

Sacramental Emphasis

In the previous section I showed how, through nuances (holistically experienced as taste), Țuțea affirms the wholeness of the human person. I will now explore the relationship of this wholeness to healing and holiness. Țuțea's style may not be to everyone's liking,[122] and there will always be those who mistake visionary hope for 'naive optimism'. Grounded in human dignity reflecting divine love, however, his thought opens new ways of conceiving and sustaining life in a world dominated by compulsive rationalism and reactive emotionalism.

I have already mentioned how the philosophy of nuances has a sacramental dimension. As an intellectual endeavour it has a sacred, liturgical dynamic, for it helps the mind to become more fully a vehicle of the Holy Spirit: 'In the world of essences, questions come to an end' and 'the energies revealed in this world of appearances are salvific'.[123] Țuțea contrasts the artist and the priest: modern artists 'by means of technique have shifted the locus of freedom to art' away from the contemplation of God, whereas it is the priest who, through the celebration of the Eucharist, 'communicates supernatural revelation and miracles to release us from the grip of natural laws'. The Eucharist is 'a modern way of revealing mystery, everlasting living reality'.[124] Nuanced being prepares us for Eucharistic encounter. It makes preparatory confession deeper and more incisive. It sharpens sensory appreciation of the liturgy, while helping to prevent the believer falling into a kind of aesthetic trance. It refines, broadens, and strengthens our love for our neighbour, by making us more intensely aware of the uniqueness of each person. Through a richer and more finely tuned sense of personal vocation, believers come to the Divine Liturgy not for a holy 'fix', but, through Communion, to know the formative, sustaining, and guiding energy of the discipleship that is their whole life. Nuances enable the mind to be released from its worldly position of dominance over the heart and body, through a vision that is polychromatic rather than black and white, receptive to the Word rather than

---

121 From θεραπεύειν, meaning 'minister to', or 'treat medically'.

122 See, for instance, 'the peripheral, although highly picturesque, Petre Țuțea, a former Antonescu minister and Nae Ionescu disciple, friend of Emil Cioran, but primarily an oral genius with no significant literary legacy... Of course, this is not to deny Țuțea's amazing versatility, fabulous memory, and real suffering in Communist jail': Vladimir Tismăneanu and Dan Pavel, 'Romania's Mystical Revolutionaries: The Generation of Angst and Adventure Revisited', *East European Politics and Societies*, 8:3, Fall 1994, pp. 418–19. Such criticisms are based on what Țuțea called 'scientific prejudice' about the nature and significance of mystical experiences and theology: THEATRE, p. 63. The literary critical approach of analysts such as Tismăneanu and Pavel is bound to miss the fundamental meaning of personal martyrdom as a crucial tool for interpreting the dissident culture which developed under Communist persecution.

123 NUANCES, p. 37.

124 NUANCES, p. 27.

analytically judgmental (as the autonomous rational mind must always be). Equally, it resists the temptation of regarding intellectual activity as somehow unholy. It offers a subtly articulated vision of the soul uncorrupted by doctrinaire spiritual prejudice against the mind. It enables the Eucharist to be indeed a 'reasonable' sacrifice (Romans 12:1). Nuance points beyond the endless processes of dialectic, yet without denying their value:[125]

> The stability of things and their mutability move both feeling and thinking between enchantment and freedom. The tedium of eternally open dialectical processes is alleviated by the joy of an illusory freedom, and by aesthetic and epistemological satisfactions produced through the endless interplay of nuances: we are mortal and we are not; the human being is a mixture of animal and god; things appear to be at times accidental, at other times necessary.[126]

This description of the economy of dialectical existence conveys Țuțea's appreciation of the nuances of everyday civilised intellectual life. As I have shown, however, he recognises the simplifying character of merely rationalist, logical epistemology – for such systems produce distorted images of the true unifying foundation of all things. Rationalism is not so much wrong or bad in itself, but wanting. Only God has the power to teach us how 'to discern the signs of the times', rather than merely read 'the face of the sky' (Matt. 16:3). Although people are free to choose to follow Christ's call to perfection, only He, in the power of the Spirit, can raise souls and minds to the higher understanding of divine reason, which can be attained in daily discipleship, step by step on the 'ladder of divine ascent', each step a sacramental nuance of actual knowledge of God. And it is in this sense that nuance is therapeutic. Through nuance understood as the living vision of wholeness of life in God, who works 'All in All' (1 Cor. 12:6), we receive the ministry of Christ and the healing power of the Real. Țuțea speaks of 'the thaumaturgical virtue of sacred representation'.[127] And Christ, 'the image of the unseen God' (Col. 1:15–20), is the definitive sacred representation, the summation of all nuances, spiritual and material, of form, tone, colour, structure, and style, both actual and (in the actuality of the *parousia*) potential.

As the sacramental redemptive medium of mystical thinking (liberating the 'mystical' from its purely psychic status), nuance becomes a kind of liturgy of the *nous*, in its engagement with Christ the Saviour, the Incarnate One, the *holy logos* (ἱερός λόγος).[128]

---

125 As captive to dialectical logic, 'even when they are defined in terms of art, Simmel's *nuances* do not enrich thought'. Țuțea insists that, at most, Simmel's use of *nuances* refines philosophical thinking. See PROBLEMS, p. 67.

126 NUANCES, pp. 37–8.

127 THEATRE, p. 437.

128 NUANCES, p. 26.

Metaphysical Pessimism and Mystical Joy

For Țuțea, 'the most important reason for thinking in nuances is the need to overcome pessimism'.[129] Nuances point to another world. They enable human beings to escape that rationalism which restricts them to the fallen world (what Nikolai Berdyaev[130] calls the 'rationalised *ténèbres*').[131] At the metaphysical level, they diminish anxieties caused by fear of death in those who accept captivity to the endless flux of this world.[132] However, for Țuțea humanity is ontically predetermined even in its original paradisal state. This predetermination (which is on the one hand a direct consequence of createdness, and on the other hand a consequence of the emergence of order out of divine reason) means that human knowledge is in proportion to creaturely capacity and divine comprehension. Irrespective of an individual's degree of social, economic, or political freedom, their capacity to know in this sense can neither diminish nor increase, however subtle or nuanced their thought. Through *hubris* people experience this as captivity to profane history. Not content with the condition of rational, mortal animals, humanity becomes metaphysically depressed:

> We must see history as the confused wanderings of human beings in their endless search for truth in nature, motivated by a thirst for perfection towards which they move asymptotically in the same way that they move towards absolute Truth.[133]

Any materialist philosopher who is both 'aware of human finitude' and also 'consistent with his metaphysical position' must, in Țuțea's view, be 'anthropologically pessimistic'.[134] Nevertheless, he distinguishes between two kinds of pessimism. If in the realm of art pessimism – which for him is the metaphysical expression of lucidity

---

129 NUANCES, p. 29.
130 Nikolai Berdyaev (1874–1948), Russian Orthodox intellectual and writer. He became Professor of Philosophy at Moscow University in 1920, but was forced by the Bolsheviks to emigrate in 1922. He spent most of the last two decades of his life in exile in France. His works were first read by Țuțea in French in Berlin in the 1930s.
131 Nikolai Berdyaev, *Împărăția Spiritului și Împărăția Cezarului*, trans. and notes by Ilie Gyurcsik (Timișoara: Amarcord, 1994), pp. 59–60. I have shown how, influenced by Meinong's *Gegenstandstheorie*, Țuțea speaks about an 'objectic' reality which transcends both objectivity and subjectivity: THEATRE, p. 434. His 'objecticity' is similar to Berdyaev's 'authentic reality, other than that of objects, a non-illusory and non-fictitious reality' which escapes 'the slavery of objectification' (or 'objectivization') whereby one treats creatures just as objects and therefore imposes mathematical formulae on human beings made in the image and likeness of God: Berdyaev, *Împărăția Spiritului*, p. 22. In Berdyaev's view there is 'a struggle against the power of objectivization, that is, against Caesar's power', which takes place within the frontiers of 'the kingdom of objectivization': Berdyaev, *Împărăția Spiritului*, p. 226. See also OLD AGE, p. 75.
132 See THEATRE, p. 393.
133 PROBLEMS, p. 17.
134 PROBLEMS, p. 189. Cf. THEATRE, p. 484.

– makes creation more subtle and smoother, in science, technology, and particularly politics, it is an 'absolute nonsense'.[135]

Lucid pessimism must be distinguished from confused melancholy, described as hopeless subjective sadness.[136] The latter is a symptom of depression, because not every inner human anxiety leads to spiritual creativity.[137] Țuțea sees nuance as deriving from an anxiety which in turn is produced by a 'thirst for God', as I have shown. This anxiety is destructive when it is met with *hubris* – that is, refusal to accept individual ontic predetermination.

'The joy of experiencing the endless dialectical processes of existence is infantile'[138] and 'illusory'.[139] True joy comes from a humility of perspective that discerns the quirks and peculiarities, the petty (or not so petty) failings and the lovable (or all too unlovable) idiosyncrasies that constitute real human being. This is why Comedy, in every nuance of genre, from slapstick to high lyricism, refreshes the spirit with a draught of reality, in contrast to the self-centred earnestness of ideological 'correctness'. Laughter has virtues that can correct the world. *Castigat ridendo mores* – Țuțea would give his characteristic guffaw of assent to that. 'Only cosmic death can extinguish laughter.'[140]

Therefore, when anxiety is confronted with humility – the humility of trust in the goodness and love of God – it becomes a creative energy. It is out of this creative energy that nuances can be perceived. Although nuances, in themselves, must be thought of in a Heraclitean sense as the waves of the eternal flux that flow on, without expanding thought beyond categories,[141] they now affirm rather than challenge the divine reason that determines and sustains human being. This affirmation, which may more properly be called doxology, is a source of great joy.

Conclusion

Nuance has two important functions: it releases us from ideological dogmatism and man-made systems and points beyond itself to a transcendent order governed by God. Nuance is the fruit of anxiety produced by thirst for God in a fallen world, but it nevertheless refines people's vision to the point at which they become capable of receiving the divine light. This is its sacramental function, within a theology that must bear the cross of tortuous paradoxes (*felix culpa*). It helps redeem theology itself by contributing to the deification of fallen humanity, by restoring perfect harmony between things which are radically opposed, and revealing Truth within what we

---

135   NUANCES, p. 29. Cf. DAYS, p. 162.
136   DAYS, p. 162.
137   See NUANCES, p. 30.
138   THEATRE, p. 404.
139   See THEATRE, p. 357.
140   Țuțea, 'Aurel Baranga. A Portrait', in *Aurel Baranga, interpretat de...*, pp. 261–2.
141   See PROBLEMS, pp. 16–17.

cannot literally or figuratively comprehend, for 'then I shall know just as I also am known' (1 Cor. 13:12).

Expressing and communicating the *correspondances* between sensory taste, aesthetic taste, spiritual discernment, intellectual joy, ontic mystery, vocational activity, scientific curiosity, and social identity – the infinite gamut of creaturely existence – nuances reflect a polychromatic splendour that in God's own time and way breaks forth in the unified light of glory. Through the mystery (with a small 'm') of the incomprehensible known in this multiplicity, we are brought to a vision of the Holy, the Great Mystery, such as it was revealed to the disciples on Mount Tabor.

However, like the disciples, we then enter 'a cloud' (Luke 9:34), and lose the vision. Such moments out of time cannot be memorialised or systematised. Nevertheless after such an experience we can no longer be content with the glory of this world. In all fields of enquiry – philosophical, scientific, technological or theological – we shall forever thirst for what we know is beyond, for the beauty and power experienced which can at best be recalled through prayer and liturgical celebration. Only through lived discipleship can we grow and abide in what has been granted us. And it is impossible to say in advance where this will lead, for 'with God all things are possible' (Matt. 19:26).

Țuțea's philosophy of nuances in this way is a paradigm for a new configuration of theological witness. It is at first glance strikingly different from the witness of his friend and fellow prisoner in Aiud, Dumitru Stăniloae, whose outstanding contribution to theology is beginning to receive the recognition it merits.

Stăniloae's work is in direct theological descent from the Fathers of the *Philokalia*. Brought up in a Romanian Orthodoxy which had been much influenced by Latin systematic theology, he started his work on Gregory Palamas before the Second World War, and began working on the *Philokalia* before the Communist takeover in Romania (see Appendix II). Although his personal experience of prison and totalitarianism did not explicitly shape his theology (nor indeed does Țuțea make explicit reference to these experiences, although they helped form his world view), the Hesychast spirit of prayer so powerfully manifested in prison, as I have shown, must surely have given him an even more profound understanding of the Philokalic tradition. So his work is not essentially different from that of Țuțea, who presents a deeply traditional Orthodoxy in an often disconcertingly secular, interdisciplinary guise.

Țuțea's intellectual expertise and cultural comprehensiveness were informed and reformed in prison by that same spirituality. In their different ways, therefore, both Stăniloae and Țuțea are traditionalists: the former revitalising tradition, and the latter extending its application. Țuțea presents a critique of the neo-Kantian position, which even today remains so dominant in its cultural outworking and so attractive in its seeming effectiveness. His critique is rooted in the Fathers, but is not limited to a restatement of their theology in the language of earlier ages. Rather, it contributes to the theological discourse of his contemporaries and to arguments of pressing relevance today. The spirit of patristic theology was in Țuțea's veins, yet the theological and philosophical language which he uses is both attentive to, and in dialogue with, aspects of modernity. Synthesising patristic theology and spirituality with modernity, the philosophy of nuances does not give an objective statement of truth or the nature of truth. Rather, it is intended to lead to a new attitude of mind, a new level of awareness, and a new posture of being.

While Țuțea's work may seem to bear little relation to Orthodox theology in the narrow sense, just as it does not fit into any single ready-made intellectual discipline, it nevertheless springs from that deeply traditional definition of the theologian as the one who prays. For some, this is a weakness. For others, prepared to engage with new and unfamiliar nuances in their own inner experience and outer intellectual understanding of faith, Țuțea offers a kind of apostolic encouragement and an invitation to 'come and see' (John 1:46).

Chapter 11

Conclusions

It will be clear from all that has been said in this book that Petre Țuțea was more than an 'oral genius' and colourful character of his time. The often quoted tag 'oral genius', together with the aphoristic nature of his writing, and the all too easily mythicised persona of the prisoner of conscience, perhaps combine to obscure the substantive content of his thought.

As I have attempted to demonstrate, the fundamental theme of his life's work, as of his life's vision, was that of deification. All ideas, experiences, references, centre on this mystery that at once sustains, is defined by, yet ever eludes and inspires both his intellectual endeavour and his simple delight in being.

With the aim of presenting an account of his life and work, I have finished with the 'Philosophy of Nuances', which, being written relatively early (during the late 1960s), deploys the map for the spiritual journey Țuțea was to undertake for the next three decades. It gives an overview of the methodological terrain, and of the goal. The journey itself was begun, but not completed. In the *Treatise on Christian Anthropology* (begun in the mid-1980s), on which Țuțea worked in his later years, the implications of a nuanced Christian vision and intellectual sensibility begin to be worked out in practice. However, the true originality and richness of his *Christian Anthropology*, and its radical implications, in themselves merit a book.

What I hope to have done here is to have stimulated awareness of, and interest in, a remarkable and engaging Christian thinker, and to have provided a basis of information and analysis upon which more detailed exploration of his work can be undertaken. Let me now conclude by summarising the major elements of his *oeuvre*.

Țuțea's Contribution to Tradition

The circumstances of Țuțea's life were such that his faith became truly grounded in the reality of lived experience. As a result, his work is particularly important for those seeking the 'Way' in an age when, at least in Western societies, traditional doctrinal language (sin, salvation, heaven, the holy, and so on) is widely considered to have little relevance, or, even worse, to be an ecclesiastical impediment to true spiritual understanding. Through the 'confession' of his very flesh and blood, not merely of his mind, heart, and soul, Țuțea's theology earths eternal Christianity in life as we know it. Eucharist, for him, was not only a liturgical experience – a vital experience forbidden in prison – it was something he lived. Christ's Lordship was integral to his whole being, not only spiritually and intellectually, but also physically in the most profound sense. This is what, in the end, enabled him to survive imprisonment.

While to base theological thinking on experience might, to some, imply subjectivity or neglect of doctrine, Ţuţea's whole mode of thought was in fact shaped by the Orthodox tradition in which he had been nurtured, and which was essential to him. At the same time, however, he expanded the boundaries that unnecessarily restrict that tradition, and opened a way for many who might otherwise have been excluded. Traditional Christian denominations often appear to non-adherents as inward-looking: organisations that recreate the world in their own image and likeness. Secular liberalism meanwhile has still not completely abandoned its dream of building the New Jerusalem here on earth, while socialist utopias, whether National Socialist or Communist, have horrifically failed to live up to their promise. But Christ came into this world not to bring clinical doctrinal purity, uniform perfection, or maximum comfort with minimum inconvenience, but to bring life and life in abundance (John 10:10). For Ţuţea, humanity and the world are givens 'whose roots are transcendent', as he insists, and whose fulfilment depends on human acknowledgement of dependence on God's creative will:

> Even when man imagines himself to be autonomous, he makes use of things from the created world which exist according to predetermined laws. When he is aware of his dependence on the Creator, as a receiver blessed by God, he has a charismatic nature. Within the triangle God–humanity–nature, man knows that his knowledge or creativity comes from above, that nothing is new under the sun; he does not consider what is received to be the fruit of his own seeking. Those who lack inspiration and faith live in peace or anxiety within the bounds of this world. They limit their life to their existence between birth and death. They do not extend their hope to the other world where ignorance is drawn to an end in the contemplation of Truth.[1]

Ultimate freedom and equality are the fruits of a faith that proclaims the common origin and eternal goal of all human beings.[2]

Self-Giving Solidarity

For Ţuţea the Bible is not a book of doctrine. Through its record of the relationship of humanity with God, it provides, so to speak, the fundamental data, memory, and format for the development of doctrine. The Gospels are written to show and convince humanity that Jesus is the fulfilment of this relationship (Matt. 5:17), the Messiah.

At one level the Scriptures can teach little about living in the modern world. They of course show us the need to live in love with God and with our neighbour, but how individuals are to do this in their own place and time remains a question of active participation – involving all of their heart, soul, mind, and strength (Luke 10:27) – in this eternal relationship of the human and the divine. Biblical teaching cannot simply

---

1   THEATRE, p. 484.
2   See THEATRE, p. 484.

be applied as if cultural and social change were not part of the world of the 'flesh' which the Word has embraced in the Incarnation.

Țuțea's thought represents a two-fold challenge for the contemporary Church. First, to accept that human beings do not have answers – God alone *is* the answer, ultimate and mysterious – and as dependent rather than independent beings they proclaim this Truth. Second, human beings are also *inter*dependent and have a mutual responsibility of loving engagement and interaction (of body, mind, and heart) towards each other. This interdependence reflects something of the Trinitarian nature of God in whose image we are made. These defining aspects of faith co-inhere in Christ, who both reveals God and points to the sacrificial demand and redemptive power of love. The universal Church represents the solidarity of the people of God, vulnerable but unconquerable. In Țuțea's view, individuals are free and peaceful only in church. In prison, they can also experience freedom and peace by being one with the witnessing Church, by keeping alive within themselves the liturgical spirit and the presence of Christ represented by His priest.[3]

The self-transcendence experienced when participating in the eternal, universal, *koinonia* of the Church, even in prison, led Țuțea to recognise that individuals are truly equal *only* in the sight of God.[4] It is the vision of God that defines true equality, which has no other legitimate (real) form.

Eucharistic Presence

Țuțea's life and work are founded on the traditional understanding that through the Eucharistic presence God feeds humanity. Nourishing each person individually, He makes of all one body, one in Christ. At the same time, Eucharist is sustenance for a journey: partakers are one in the 'Way' who is 'Truth and Life' (John 14:6).

In seeking to live this 'Way', however, individuals may falter and lose direction. Thus, for instance, it is possible to come to approach communion in an almost utilitarian spirit, as a means of feeding a sense of personal self-worth, as recognition for good behaviour, as routine, or for merely aesthetically cathartic religious stimulation. For Țuțea, communion is 'daily bread', sustaining humanity for the Day to come, strengthening us to know and live according to the truth (John 8:32). Goodness is not reducible to a moral code, however sophisticated. Moralism, he would say, is the arch-enemy of religion, 'for religion requires worship of God rather than of human morality'.[5] 'Autonomous morality in itself is more dangerous to religion than atheism'.[6] For Țuțea, 'non-religious morality' is 'insignificant'.[7] While

---

3   DAYS, p. 143.
4   APHORISMS, p. 45.
5   INTERVIEW, p. 3.
6   APHORISMS, p. 73.
7   PROBLEMS, p. 92.

he would apply this with direct reference to certain forms of Protestant philosophy,[8] he found it applicable also to religious bodies. Moreover, he regarded secular discussion of human rights as ultimately leading to a question of belief in, or rejection of, God. In this respect he contrasts *homo faber* (defined by the Communist Manifesto) with *homo religiosus* (defined in terms of the Sermon on the Mount):

> In nature and society conceived in a natural way *homo faber* rules. He freely decides to set up an order on a hierarchical basis, which dialectical and historical materialists wish to correct in a tyrannical political way... In the Christian order (which includes the family, private property, and social and civil hierarchy) *homo religiosus* rules. His attitude is determined by love, which acts in the natural order to temper the harshness of the world. For those with power possess no rights, only the duty to help the weak.[9]

What Ţuţea valued in Orthodoxy was not just its elaborate ritual, but the way in which it draws upon the simple Eucharistic elements and their primary symbolism, offered to humanity in the 'upper room' (Mark 14:15), and valid for all time. As the early Christians sought to proclaim the majesty of God in ever grander buildings, liturgical celebration similarly became more and more elaborate. Parallel to this, the tradition of Hesychast prayer developed in the solitude and harshness of the desert, as part of the spiritual battle to preserve the essential integrity of the Church (in the sense of the mystical Body). Centuries later this same tradition sustained Christians like Ţuţea, imprisoned for their beliefs, in the desert of Communist confinement where, deprived of the opportunity for ritualised liturgy, they were forced back on the bare essentials – bread and wine acquired at huge cost and consecrated at the risk of their lives.

At one level, for all the complexity of his thought and the densely-woven texture of his language, Ţuţea's faith remains extremely simple: love of God and love of neighbour, human mutuality and recognition that human beings do not have ultimate answers. All his thinking flows from this acknowledgement of creaturely dependence upon the God of love. He wrestles with the question (and invites and challenges all who might chance upon his words to wrestle with it too) of how organised structural Christianity can show forth the Mystery of Christ in the world – a world which

---

8   For example, Ţuţea rejects Max Scheler's 'phenomenology of values' and his 'phenomenology of emotive life'; see Scheler, *Formalism*, p. 64. So-called non-formal (that is, non-logical) values cannot give content to Kant's 'sterile formalism' because, Ţuţea says, 'the world of values' remains ultimately 'related to our feelings', which cannot 'melt' into individual intellect: THEATRE, p. 324. Cf. PROBLEMS, p. 274. In Ţuţea's view the human being cannot be reduced to what Scheler calls 'the totality of spirit' (*des Geistes*) which includes 'feeling, preferring and rejecting, loving and hating': Scheler, *Formalism*, p. 65. For Ţuţea 'the autonomy of values is illusory and so is their reality in this transient world': THEATRE, p. 351. *Die materiale Wertethik* (which Ţuţea translates as *axiologie materială* or 'material axiology') leads to an unsurpassable split between human and divine knowledge. I have shown that, for him, supreme 'values' are not of this world, since they express God's divine love. 'Only the saint's love is pure in this world, for it is related to the transcendent Heaven': THEATRE, p. 352.

9   THEATRE, pp. 424–5.

continues to live by the quantitative pseudo-mystery of 'numbers', despite the horrors of Communism and of exploitation in the modern global economy. The confession of faith that he offers is, simply, his life – his personal witness to the crucified and risen Messiah – a realised icon of Christian vision and hope prayed, enacted, drawn out, and invested with subtle and radiant colour through a living martyrdom leading not to Stoic severity but to joy.

Bridging East and West

Against suggestions such as those of the historians Samuel Huntington and Norman Davies that European civilisation ends where Orthodoxy begins,[10] Țuțea has an optimistic view of the compatibility of Orthodox Christianity and liberal European civilisation. His life and work demonstrate that a creative and harmonious union of these different outlooks is possible.

Essentially experiential, yet informed by an exceptional range of reading and personal sympathy, Țuțea's witness has direct bearing on ecumenical dialogue. It is on such a basis, at once personal and universal, that points of unity can be discerned, which focus on the unsearchable riches of Christ poured out upon all people, rather than on differences of emphasis and interpretation which serve only to separate and estrange.

Țuțea's early life had brought him into contact with the world of cosmopolitan Western and Central Europe, a far cry from that of the Orthodox priest's son brought up in a rural village in Romania. Yet, rather than reject one or other of these cultures, he pursued in all aspects of his experience and person that quest for the universal and the true which is fulfilled in God alone. He never accepted received opinions without subjecting them to analysis by his powerful and dauntingly well-informed mind which was always attentive to the Mystery of liberating, self-giving Love within the depths of the human heart. His Orthodoxy was filled with love as well as 'salted' with criticism. It was grounded in faith, understood with the objectivity acquired during and after his student days, and rediscovered as it was tested and transformed in the 'refiner's fire' of oppression (Mal. 3:2). Aware that God alone enabled him to survive in prison, he used his Western learning not only to confound his captors (whose system of belief was of course the product of the same Western cultural tradition), but also to find, from within a profoundly Orthodox spirituality and Trinitarian frame of reference, a distinctive 'voice' that could open the opportunity for others to discover the universal Gospel unencumbered by denominational restrictions.

---

10   Samuel P. Huntington, *The Clash of Civilizations and the Remaking of World Order* (London: Touchstone, 1998), p. 158. Cf. Norman Davies, *Europe, A History* (London: Pimlico, 1997), pp. 7–31.

Spiritual Presence

To judge by the number of his books on people's shelves in Romania, Țuțea has a huge following. However, it is unlikely that, given their uncompromisingly abstract and often abstruse content, these books in themselves have widespread appeal. His real impact was made through his appearances on television beginning in the Spring of 1990, when he came before the Romanian public, weak and aged, but with an energy and conviction in his voice, as he spoke about freedom and God, that roused his audience. The public saw him as a sage, a martyr, a phenomenon, while his ideas and mode of thought were beyond most people's grasp. Yet this 'humble prophet of the poor in the Balkans'[11] was able to communicate simply by his presence, because he manifested within his own person the presence of God.

To the younger generation of Romanians in 1990 this man was a symbol of life rising from the ruins of a system that for more than four decades had sought to contain people in death. His voice was one of youth and hope. His vision was one of love – the only foundation upon which a future can be built.

---

11   DIALOGUES, p. 23.

Chapter 12

Envoi

It is vital for Christians in the affluent West to hear and appreciate the testimony of those who, like Țuțea, lived and continued to confess Christ throughout the periods of Nazi and Communist rule, which together lasted almost fifty years. The West has not had to endure the experience of totalitarianism. Yet technologically advanced nations are threatened by an ideology of consumerism that denies the spiritual and is all the more disastrous for being at once half-heartedly tempered (by, for instance, ecological concern) and aggressively re-asserted. Western theologians and thinkers have crucial lessons to learn from those in other parts of the world who, even when brutally silenced, have affirmed spiritual freedom and the dignity of creation. Confronted with suffering and evil on a scale that seems incompatible with the existence of an all-powerful, loving God, religious faith is tried and purified. Out of his experience of testing, Țuțea offers a theological vision rooted not in logical justification, but in prayer and a life lived in fellowship with the communion of saints.

His friend and colleague Mircea Vulcănescu (1904–52), a former Secretary of State in the Romanian Ministry of Finance,[1] died at Aiud prison, 28 October 1952, from pneumonia which he contracted after he had lain on the floor of his cell to allow a critically ill young man to rest on his body, there being no furniture.[2] The young man miraculously survived. Vulcănescu's dying words to his fellow prisoners were: *Să nu ne răzbunați!*[3] ('Let no one take revenge on our behalf!').

Petre Țuțea never expressed any desire for revenge – nor even, indeed, regret at what he had experienced. Yet his was not the serenity of a philosopher, nor the charitable spirit of a theologian, but rather an obstinate boldness in living the 'pure joy'[4] of abundant life: life in Christ.

---

1   Vulcănescu was described in 1933 by Thomas Masaryk, then President of Czechoslovakia, as 'ce Prince de l'Esprit': see Ștefan J. Fay, *Sokrateion, Mărturie despre Mircea Vulcănescu*, 2nd edn (Bucharest: Humanitas, 1998), p. 9.

2   Fay, *Sokrateion*, pp. 129–30.

3   Fay, *Sokrateion*, p. 142. See also Mircea Vulcănescu, *Ultimul Cuvânt și Alte Texte*, ed. with notes and a chronology by Măriuca Vulcănescu, annex with a letter from Emil Cioran and a portrait by Mircea Eliade (Bucharest: Crater, 2000), p. 18. In Țuțea's terms, Vulcănescu was 'a saint, not a hero'; see Petre Țuțea, 'Sunt un om politic înfrânt', interview by Dan Arsenie, *Vatra*, Târgu Mureș, April 1990, pp. 9, 27. ['I Am a Defeated Politician'.]

4   Țuțea, 'Viața ca formă a bucuriei pure', I, p. 3. See PROJECT, p. 147: 'The keys of bliss and suffering, of happiness and sadness, are in the hand of the Creator.' Cf. Rev. 1:18.

A decision has to be made, for or against God as revealed in the person of Jesus Christ. This decision is a matter of life or death, but one which a person must make freely. To decide against God, whether as an individual or as a nation, is spiritual suicide. To choose God is to choose life – a life that indeed entails sacrifice, but one which, through sacrifice, reveals a purpose, a grace, and a joy beyond anything conceivable in human ideals and aspirations. The life and work of Petre Ţuţea presents the world with this choice.

ὃς γὰρ ἐὰν θέλῃ τὴν ψυχὴν αὐτοῦ σῶσαι ἀπολέσει αὐτήν· ὃς δ᾽ ἂν ἀπολέσῃ τὴν ψυχὴν αὐτοῦ ἕνεκεν ἐμοῦ εὑρήσει αὐτήν (Ματθ. 16:25).

For whoever desires to save his life will lose it, but whoever loses his life for My sake will find it (Matt. 16:25).

Că cine va voi să-şi scape sufletul şi-l va pierde; iar cine îşi va pierde sufletul pentru Mine îl va afla (Matei 16:25).

Appendix I

The Emergence of Modern Romania

During the Middle Ages Romania, as it now exists, consisted of three separate principalities: Wallachia, Moldavia, and Transylvania. Transylvania came under Hungarian rule in the eleventh century, becoming part of the Habsburg Empire in 1699. Wallachia and Moldavia lived within the Bulgar and Byzantine sphere of influence until 1417, and then for three centuries under Turkish suzerainty. The three principalities were briefly united in 1600 by Michael the Brave (1593–1601). Thus, when the idea of Romania as an independent State in its present form started to take shape, Romanians took their inspiration from a projected future, not (as the Bulgarians and Serbs did) from a historic medieval unified State.

Romanian nationalism before 1800 found expression through a cultural regeneration in all three principalities. In Transylvania, for example, Romanians were the majority ethnic group, but were predominantly peasants, thus forming the lowest stratum of society. They had virtually no political rights. Their nationalism was inspired by the discovery of a distinguished cultural and linguistic heritage. Scholarly arguments about the history of the Romanians found their way into political works such as *Supplex Libellus Valachorum* of 1791, the petition of the representatives of the Romanian people of Transylvania to the Habsburg Emperor Leopold II, in which they claimed equality of rights with the other privileged 'nations' and representation in the Diet in direct relation to the number of taxpayers.

In the aftermath of the Crimean War an independent Romanian State had been an attractive prospect to Britain and France because it could become a 'useful buffer between Russia, Austria and Turkey and between Russia and the Dardanelles'.[1] Following the Paris Convention, the United Principalities of Moldavia and Wallachia were established in 1859.

Nationalist ideas born in the nineteenth century dominated the Romanian political scene by the turn of the century, although by 1914 political leaders could not agree on a clear direction for such nationalist aspirations. In 1916 Romania entered the First World War on the side of the Entente by declaring war on the Austro-Hungarian Empire. Initially its participation led to disaster on the Danube when the Romanian army was defeated at Turtucaia on 6 September. This was the first of many defeats, which between September 1916 and January 1917 reduced Romania drastically in size. By 3 December 1916 the Romanian government was forced to flee from Bucharest and establish itself on the north-eastern frontier at Iassy, in Moldavia.

---

1   Felipe Fernández-Armesto, *The Times Guide to the Peoples of Europe* (London: Times Books, 1994), p. 264.

Between January and June 1917 the Romanian army, including the Corps of Transylvanian Volunteers, converged in the Putna Valley, about a hundred miles from Iassy, where they established a new front and defeated a strong German–Austro-Hungarian offensive under the command of Marshal August von Mackensen at Mărăşti, Mărăşeşti, and Oituz. Though inferior in military terms, the Romanian army was highly motivated, and the enemy was prevented from conquering the remaining Romanian territory in Moldavia.

In December 1917 the imperial Russian army, which had been protecting the northern Romanian flank, collapsed following the Bolshevik Revolution, and the Russian commander in Moldavia began to negotiate an armistice with Germany. There was fighting between Romanians and Bolsheviks until January 1918, by which time the Bolsheviks were expelled from Moldavia. In January the Soviet government officially broke off diplomatic relations with Romania in protest at what they claimed to be the invasion of Bessarabia by Romania. In March 1918 with the Treaty of Brest-Litovsk which allowed Germany to occupy Ukraine, Moldavia found itself surrounded, and the Romanian government was forced to accept the harsh conditions of the Treaty of Bucharest, by which Romania lost the southern region of Dobrudja on the Black Sea and a large part of the Carpathians. The return of Bessarabia in March 1918 was Romania's only initial gain from the First World War.

The military situation on the western front changed radically when Marshal Foch's counter-offensive broke through on the Somme. At the same time, the allied armies in the Balkans advanced through the Bulgarian front towards Sofia and Constantinople. The pro-German puppet government in Bucharest fell in November 1918. The newly elected Romanian government demanded that the German occupying force leave Romanian territory, and sent Romanian troops into Transylvania, where Romanians and Hungarians had been fighting for control since the collapse of the Austro-Hungarian dual monarchy in October. The same month, at a meeting in Oradea, near the north-western border with Hungary, the Romanian National Party of Transylvania unanimously adopted a declaration of self-determination for the Romanian majority in Transylvania. In the same month in Budapest, the Romanian National Party representative in the Hungarian Parliament declared Transylvania's independence and, on 1 December 1918, the historic Grand National Assembly of Alba Iulia voted to unite Transylvania with Romania. A few days earlier, in November, the Romanian National Council in Bukovina had also voted for union with Romania. In December 1918, the principalities of Wallachia, Moldavia, and Transylvania united as Greater Romania. Thus, the long-felt aspirations to a unitary State were at last fulfilled.

The most highly populated country in the Balkans, Romania sought to protect its new-found political identity against Bolshevik expansionism. In 1919 Romanian troops invaded the newly established Hungarian Soviet Republic led by Comintern agent Bela Kun, and occupied Budapest. The following year, after their withdrawal, Admiral Nicholas Horthy (often regarded as Europe's first Fascist) instituted a dictatorship there which was to last for twenty-four years.

By contrast, under King Ferdinand, Romania enjoyed a period of liberalism during the 1920s, with agrarian and electoral reforms and a new Constitution, based on the Belgian model, adopted in 1923. By 1926 the Liberal Party was at the height of its power. However, 1926 also saw the formation of the National Peasant Party.[2] This party had come into being following the political crisis precipitated by Crown Prince Carol's renunciation (for the second time) of his succession to the throne.[3] At this stage the Communist Party created in 1921 was as yet insignificant, with a small membership, following a pro-Soviet line. The formation of the Social Democratic Party in 1927 united the Socialists on the Romanian political scene.

Romania was politically stable until the late 1920s, when, with the death of King Ferdinand in 1927, and coincidentally also the deaths of the three leading Liberal politicians of the day, there ensued a period of vacillation and dissension. The National Peasant Party was divided, and with the accession of Carol II, non-liberal policies became dominant, with corruption rampant. In 1934 censorship was reintroduced.

It was in this period that the Legionary Movement emerged. This movement, officially founded in 1927 as the Legion of the Archangel Michael, had its beginnings between 1922 and 1923, when Corneliu Zelea Codreanu formed the Association of Christian Students and then, with Alexandru C. Cuza, the National Christian Defence League. After 1930 the Legionary Movement was also called the Iron Guard. It initially had no links with the Nazis or the Italian Fascists, 'nor did it borrow from their ideologies'.[4] It did, however, undoubtedly receive impetus from other countries' rightward shift.

The Iron Guard was banned from acting as a political organisation in 1931, but reappeared in 1935, more influential than ever. In the election of 1937 no single party received a majority sufficient to lead the government. The Liberals (divided into two parties) had polled about 40 per cent of the vote, the National Peasant Party about 20 per cent, and the Legionary Movement (under the name 'All for the Country' or 'Iron Guard') 16 per cent. Carol II, however, stepped in to take control of the country, trying to legitimise his action by appointing the National Christian Party, which had polled only 9 per cent, to form his new government: 'fearing a consolidation of right-wing elements, [he] dissolved parliament, suppressed political parties, and imposed a royal dictatorship (10 February 1938)'.[5]

---

2   The National Peasant Party was created through the union of the National Party of Transylvania and the Peasant Party, founded in 1918 in the Old Kingdom of Wallachia and Moldavia. Cf. Georgescu, *Romanians*, p. 192.

3   In August 1918 the Prince had left his regiment and gone to Odessa to marry Zizi Lambrino. The marriage was declared unconstitutional and illegal, and he renounced the throne. He later married Princess Helen of Greece, who bore him a son and heir, Prince Mihai, but the marriage was annulled on 21 June 1928. In November 1925, after attending the funeral of Queen Alexandra, the widow of King Edward VII, he went to Paris where he joined his mistress Madame Lupescu. In a letter to his father, King Ferdinand, he then renounced the throne once more. See Tilea, *Envoy Extraordinary*, p. 95.

4   See Georgescu, *Romanians*, pp. 194–5.

5   Georgescu, *Romanians*, pp. 196–7.

In April 1938 the Legionary leader Corneliu Zelea Codreanu was arrested. In November 1938, 'by order of the King and under the supervision of Prime Minister Armand Călinescu' he was assassinated, while in detention, along with thirteen other Legionary leaders.[6] Other Legionaries, as well as many sympathisers, were detained in concentration camps. Through the night of 21 September 1939, following the retaliatory assassination of Călinescu by a Legionary group, hundreds of Legionaries were killed in prison camps and military hospitals.[7] Relations between the monarch and the Iron Guard continued to be tense, with further outbreaks of violence, during the months prior to the start of the Second World War, despite a general move to the right and pro-German policies.

Initially Romania remained neutral during the Second World War. In June 1940, however, almost a third of its territory was lost by the annexation of Bessarabia and Bukovina by the USSR following the secret Ribbentrop–Molotov agreement (concluded on 23 August 1939). Tens of thousands of Romanians were deported from Bessarabia and Bukovina to Siberia following the annexation. Transylvania was then ceded to Hungary with the Vienna Diktat in August 1940, thus giving Germany easy access to the rich oil fields of Ploieşti, about forty miles north-east of Bucharest.

In this situation a state of political hysteria developed. On 13 September, with the backing of the Iron Guard, the Commander-in-Chief of the army, Marshal Ion Antonescu, seized power, and established the National Legionary State. The king and his mistress were guaranteed a safe passage out of the country. Carol took with him a trainload of national treasures. At the border near Timişoara, Legionaries attempted to prevent the train from leaving the country, but Antonescu had authorised the train not to stop. The main democratic parties, the National Liberal Party and the National Peasant Party, refused to co-operate with Antonescu's dictatorial régime. In October 1940 Antonescu permitted German troops to enter Romania. Meanwhile Carol's 19-year old son Mihai had remained in Romania (to become instrumental in Antonescu's eventual overthrow in August 1944).

Tension between Antonescu and the Legionary government increased, leading to the open conflict that was subsequently labelled the *Rebeliunea Legionară*. On 23 January 1941 the Iron Guard was outlawed.[8] On 27 January, with German help, the National Legionary State was formally replaced by Antonescu's military dictatorship.

---

6   Codrescu, *În căutarea Legiunii pierdute*, p. 108. Codrescu's book gives a rare critical account of Legionary history based on written and archival information and on testimonies of former political dissidents under Communism.

7   Also, between two and four prominent Legionaries in every county were executed and their corpses publicly exposed: Dinu C. Giurescu, *România în al Doilea Război Mondial* (Bucharest: All, 1999), pp. 9–10. For a list of Legionaries who were killed on that night, see Nae Tudorică, *Mărturisiri în Duhul Adevărului, Mişcarea Legionară şi Căpitanul aşa cum au fost* (Bacău: Plumb, 1993), pp. 285–9.

8   The German Intelligence Service secretly helped the Iron Guard leaders escape from Romania to Germany: Georgescu, *Romanians*, p. 458. This was for potential leverage against Antonescu, rather than an expression of solidarity between the Legion and the Third Reich.

By June 1941 Antonescu had liberated Bessarabia and northern Bukovina, from where, along with the German army, he continued his advance beyond the Dniester into the USSR against the wishes of the young King Mihai. By October 1941 the Romanian army had captured Odessa and was involved in fighting at Stalingrad, in the Caucasus, Kuban, and Crimea. In 1943 the Soviet victory and counter-offensive at Stalingrad led to a dramatic change in the Allies' fortunes. The Romanian army, along with the Germans, was pushed back towards the Carpathians. By 1944 the democratic forces in Romania, with the support of King Mihai, decided to change sides. On 23 August there was a royal coup. Antonescu was arrested and extradited to Russia. Romania joined the Allies in the struggle against Germany.

The democratically elected parties (the National Liberal Party and the National Peasant Party) joined forces with the Socialists and Communists to form a Democratic Parties Block. Tragically, the National Peasant Party, which might have provided strong popular leadership, was not sufficiently prepared to accept the king's offer of power in August 1944. This opened the door to the Communist Party which, by September 1944, had firmly established its presence within the government (Soviet influence having become even stronger since earlier that year). With the Soviet-backed installation of Dr Petru Groza's government in February 1946, the Communist hold over Romania was complete. Antonescu was tried in May 1946 and executed in June the same year. Rigged elections were held in November 1946. On 30 December 1947 King Mihai, aged twenty-six, was forced to abdicate by Groza. That same day, Romania was proclaimed a People's Republic and the so-called dictatorship of the proletariat was installed along Stalinist lines.

The Soviet-engineered establishment of a Republic was the first step towards the creation of a totalitarian State. The second step was the consolidation of the Romanian Workers' Party created in 1948 when Gheorghe Gheorghiu-Dej was elected Secretary General. Even before the Soviet takeover, Gheorghiu-Dej had murdered party comrades who blocked his rise to power. With the help of the *Securitate*, created in 1948, he started to construct a police State by launching a reign of terror in which pre-war politicians, prominent intellectuals, businessmen, religious leaders, students, and suspected dissidents were imprisoned, interned in labour camps, or sent to special psychiatric hospitals.

In June 1948 nationalisation of industry, banks, transport, insurance, and mining companies not only introduced centralised planning, but destroyed the economic basis of those labelled 'class enemies'.[9] Determined to outdo capitalism, the new Stalinist régime collectivised agriculture between 1949 and 1962. This involved 'total expropriation' in the name of the 'struggle against bourgeois *kulaks*'.[10] Peasants who opposed collectivisation were tried publicly, imprisoned, and subjected to 're-education' in prisons such as Piteşti, Aiud, Gherla, and Ocnele Mari. Organised

---

9   Dennis Deletant, *Romania under Communist Rule*, rev. 2nd edn (Oxford: The Centre for Romanian Studies in co-operation with the Civic Academy Foundation, 1999), p. 60.

10   See Popescu, '"The Peasant Chats over the Fence with God"', *Humanitas*, pp. 63–6.

armed resistance in the mountains, and spontaneous resistance to collectivisation, continued over a decade, but were in the end powerless to reverse the situation.

Repression of the Church was an essential element in the imposition of a Soviet model on Romania. The Romanian Orthodox Church and the Greek Catholic Church in Transylvania had been instrumental in the creation of a sense of national cohesion and identity before the formation of Greater Romania in 1918, and millions of Romanians belonged to these denominations.[11] The Romanian Orthodox Church and the State have never existed entirely separate from each other. The institutions of Orthodoxy in Romania were themselves used by the police State to undermine opposition: the Law on Religious Confessions of August 1948 established State control over episcopal appointments, ensured strong Communist Party representation in the Holy Synod, and imposed a new statute on the Romanian Orthodox Church (the principal confession with some ten and a half million members) which centralised its administration under the Patriarch. All Church property was nationalised and the Greek Catholic Church was forcibly united with the Orthodox Church by Decree no. 358/1948. The spiritual leaders of the Jewish and Muslim communities and of various Protestant churches were imprisoned or exiled, while Orthodox and Greek-Catholic priests and bishops who refused to collaborate became one of the largest groups of political prisoners. By Decree no. 410/1959 Orthodox monasteries and monastic seminaries were closed, and most monks and nuns aged fifty-six or younger were forced to leave their monasteries and to find secular jobs.[12]

After the death of Stalin in 1953, Gheorghiu-Dej tried to distance himself from the Soviet Union, albeit giving Nikita Khrushchev vital support in his quelling of the Hungarian uprising in 1956. His rift with Moscow and the withdrawal of the Red Army from Romania in 1958 gained him domestic support. However, a new period of terror began in 1958 when Decree no. 318/1958, defining new crimes punishable by death, was passed to prevent any similar uprising in Romania.

After Gheorghiu-Dej's sudden death in 1965, Nicolae Ceaușescu emerged as the First Secretary of the Romanian Communist Party, and the period of terror came to an end. Ceaușescu soon gained international respect when he recognised the state of Israel and refused to support the Soviet invasion of Czechoslovakia in 1968. Following his visits to North Korea and China in 1971, however, he embarked upon a neo-Stalinist personality cult and a new brand of nepotistic despotism. During his *Epoca de Aur* ('Golden Age') in the 1980s, with the Soviet bloc starting to disintegrate, the Romanian countryside was devastated by a policy of village 'systematisation'.[13]

---

11   Deletant, *Romania under Communist Rule*, p. 61.
12   Fr Ioan Dură, *Monahismul Românesc în anii 1948–1989, Mărturii ale românilor și considerații privitoare la acestea* (Bucharest: Harisma, 1994), pp. 7–8.
13   In the early 1970s *sistematizare* had been defined as: a) destruction of the traditional urban built area almost in its entirety and its replacement by tenement apartment buildings; and b) resettlement of the entire rural population of more than eleven million people from privately owned, one-family houses into apartment buildings where they became tenants. See Dinu C. Giurescu, *The Razing of Romania's Past* (Washington, DC: The Preservation Press & World Monuments Fund, 1992), p. 67.

Known also as the rural resettlement plan, it used an authoritarian, centralised system of coercion. Like other Soviet bloc countries Romania harnessed its internal resources – its 'labour potential' who in the 1970s mostly worked the land – and exploited them by exporting their produce and that of newly-created agricultural industries.

Systematisation was also an urban policy: like Mussolini and Hitler before him, Ceauşescu expressed his totalitarian vision through architecture.[14] About a third of Bucharest was demolished to make way for a grandiose civic centre and architectural backdrop to power. Before systematisation Bucharest was known as the 'little Paris' of Eastern Europe: a city of charm and individuality with haphazardly winding streets, *Belle époque* buildings, and brick and stucco architecture of the seventeenth and eighteenth centuries. After the partial fulfilment of a plan to erase all that was not 'modern' in the Romanian capital, a vast area of the city now confronts the passer-by with concrete rectangular blocks along rectilinear streets. More than a decade after the precipitate trial which led, on Christmas Day 1989, to the execution of Ceauşescu and his wife, the pompous symmetry and dull grandiosity of the *Bulevardul Victoria Socialismului* ('Victory of Socialism Boulevard') provide the set upon which the institutions of the emergent 'free market' proclaim the victory of a different kind of internationalism. It is ironic that *Casa Poporului* (the 'People's House' – needless to say, under 'the best loved son of the Romanian people', the people of Romania were strictly barred from this monstrous palace) is now Bucharest's major tourist attraction.

---

14   See Deletant, *Ceauşescu and the Securitate*, pp. 294–5.

Appendix II

Short History of Hesychasm in Romania[1]

'Stillness of soul is the accurate knowledge of one's thoughts, an unassailable mind... The cell of a Hesychast is the body that surrounds him, and within him is the dwelling place of knowledge.'[2] Hesychasm, broadly understood, is the quest for God through inner silence achieved by constant prayer (1 Thess. 5:17). The most common form of words in the Hesychast tradition is the so-called Jesus Prayer: 'Lord Jesus Christ, Son of God, have mercy on me, a sinner'. This prayer is simply repeated over and over again. In early monastic sources *hesychia* (ἡσυχία) refers to the outwardly visible way of life of the hermit monk. It is closely associated with the monk's cell. 'The cell, understood in this way as the outward framework of *hesychia*, is envisaged above all as a workshop of unceasing prayer.'[3] However, the quotation above from St John Climacus indicates the deeper spiritual meaning of *hesychia*.

Hesychasm transcended national borders and became a pan-Orthodox movement. According to Aurel Jivi, its international character was first discernable on Mount Athos, 'whose monastic population, though not directly proportional, represented the entire Orthodox spectrum'.[4] It was here that many monks, from various countries, discovered Hesychasm and later took it to their home monasteries. Hesychasm, while primarily a monastic movement, also influenced ordinary lay people during and after the fourteenth century. It was during the fourteenth century that it became fully developed, when St Gregory Palamas (1296–1359) successfully defended the Hesychast method of prayer against Barlaam the Calabrian (c. 1290–1348), a Greek neo-Platonist philosopher from South Italy[5] who had attacked it. A younger contemporary of St Gregory of Sinai (1255–1345), the leading exponent of

---

1   This subject is studied in detail by Dumitru Stăniloae in his magisterial *Din Istoria Isihasmului în Ortodoxia Română* (Bucharest: Scripta, 1992), 172 pp., selected from vol. 8 of Stăniloae's trans. of the *Philokalia*, published in 1979. My analysis focuses on 'neo-Hesychasm' as experienced in Romanian political prisons, a subject not covered by Stăniloae.

2   Climacus, *The Ladder of Divine Ascent*, p. 262.

3   Ware, *The Inner Kingdom*, p. 91; see also pp. 89–110 for Ware's detailed interpretation of *hesychia*.

4   Aurel Jivi, *Orthodox, Catholics, and Protestants: Studies in Romanian Ecclesiastical Relations* (Cluj-Napoca: Cluj University Press, 1999), pp. 7–8. The quote from Jivi's book is from the first chapter, 'Romanian Perspectives on St Gregory Palamas and Hesychasm', pp. 7–24.

5   John Meyendorff, *St Gregory Palamas and Orthodox Spirituality*, trans. Adele Fiske (Crestwood, NY: St Vladimir's Seminary Press, 1998), p. 102.

Hesychasm, Palamas distinguished between God's *uncreated divine essence* (unknowable to the human mind) and God's *uncreated energies* (accessible to those who, through deification, attain mystical union with God).[6] Laying itself open to accusations of encouraging delusion (πλάνη), doctrinal deviance, and even mental unbalance, Palamas's apophatic theology declares that:

> we cannot know God in his essence; we can, however, know him in his energies. The distinction he makes between essence and energies, already found in an undeveloped form among the Cappadocians, does not imply any division in God; rather, it is because God is personal that his existence is not limited to his essence, but is revealed to us through his energies.[7]

Acceptance of this form of mystical practice and visionary experience at the Third Palamite Council in 1351 prepared the way for Palamas's canonisation in 1368.

The Hesychast tradition in Romania is often considered to have begun with St Nikodimos of Tismana (c. 1320–1406).[8] However, scholars such as Metropolitan Tit Simedrea,[9] with the backing of archaeological research,[10] show that when Nikodimos, with a group of Romanian monks,[11] crossed the Danube from Serbia to settle in the Romanian principalities between 1364[12] and 1368,[13] there already existed a very ancient monastic tradition of prayer which he revitalised. Nikodimos's work was part of the first flowering of Hesychast spirituality in the Balkans. His arrival in

---

6   For Palamas's doctrine about the distinction between essence and energies in God, see John Meyendorff, 'An Existential Theology: Essence and Energy', in *A Study of Gregory Palamas*, trans. from French by George Lawrence (New York: The Faith Press, St Vladimir's Seminary Press, 1974), pp. 202–27.
7   Ken Parry, et al. (eds), *The Blackwell Dictionary of Eastern Christianity*, foreword by Kallistos Ware (Oxford: Blackwell, 1999), p. 225.
8   Not to be confused with St Nikodimos of the Holy Mountain (c. 1749–1809) who published the Greek *Philokalia* in collaboration with Makarios Notaras of Corinth. St Nikodimos of Tismana was 'a Hesychast missionary in the spirit of St Gregory of Sinai, whom he had known in his youth': Bishop Seraphim Joantă, *Romania: Its Hesychast Tradition and Culture* (Wildwood, CA: St Xenia Skete, 1992), p. 48. St Nikodimos of Tismana 'had been trained by the disciples of Sts Gregory of Sinai and Euthymios of Tirnovo': *Elder Basil of Poiana Mărului (1692–1767), His Life and Writings*, trans. into English with introd. and notes by a Monk of the Brotherhood of Prophet Elias Skete, Mount Athos (Liberty, TN: St John of Kronstadt Press, 1996), p. 12.
9   Tit Simedrea, 'Viața mănăstirească în Țara Românească înainte de anul 1370', *Biserica Ortodoxă Română*, 80:7–8, 1962, pp. 673–87.
10   Victor Brătulescu, 'Sfântul Nicodim', *Mitropolia Olteniei, 600 Ani de la Întemeiere*, nr. 5–6, Craiova, 1970, p. 591.
11   Jivi, *Orthodox, Catholics, and Protestants*, p. 11.
12   *Viața, Acatistul și Paraclisul Sfântului Nicodim cel Sfințit* (Tismana: Tismana Monastery, 2000), p. 4.
13   Brătulescu, 'Sfântul Nicodim', p. 597. According to other scholars, Nikodimos came to Wallachia between 1370 and 1371: Jivi, *Orthodox, Catholics, and Protestants*, p. 11.

Wallachia was preceded by a long stay on Athos and a period of time spent in Serbia. In 1369, with the support of the Wallachian *voivode* Vlaicu Vodă (1364–77), he built Vodiţa, the first Romanian monastery linked to his name. Archaeological evidence indicates that he established this monastery on the site of an older one.

Over the following centuries, the Hesychast tradition in Romania continued, in mountain caves and around monasteries such as Tismana (where Nikodimos is buried), Cozia in Wallachia, and Prislop in Transylvania (all of them founded or refounded by Nikodimos); it also continued in the caves and hermitages of the Buzău Mountains (Aluniş, Bozioru, and Colţi)[14] and the Carpathian regions of Muscel-Argeş (Cotmeana, Tutana, Corbi, and Nămăeşti – near Boteni, Petre Ţuţea's birthplace).[15]

Between the fifteenth and sixteenth centuries the practice of *hesychia* developed, especially in Moldavia, and in particular in the monasteries, *schituri*[16] and caves of Mount Ceahlău ('the Athos of Romania'). The most famous of the fifteenth-century Romanian Hesychast monks was perhaps Daniil Sihastrul[17] (Daniel the Hesychast) who was consulted before battle by the *voivode* of Moldavia, Stephen the Great (1457–1504).[18] In the eighteenth century, the Romanian principalities became the centre of a second flowering of Hesychasm. Monks aspiring to the Hesychast life such as Elder Basil of Poiana Mărului settled in small hermitages in the Buzău Mountains. Basil[19] was the 'spiritual father' of St Paisy Velichkovsky (1722–1794), who collected Hesychast writings and translated them from Greek into Slavonic at the monastery of Neamţ, in Moldavia. Known as the *Philokalia* (*Dobrotolyubie*), this famous collection of texts had a decisive influence on nineteenth-century Russian spirituality and literature.[20] Paisy's influential work thus flowed out of the Hesychast spirituality of Moldavia and Wallachia. Forced to leave his native Ukraine by the anti-Orthodox attitudes of both the local Uniate Church and Polish Catholicism, and the 'enlightened' policies of Peter the Great and Catherine II in Russia, Paisy had

---

14   Archimandrite Ioanichie Bălan, *Vetre de Sihăstrie Românească*, sec. IV–XX (Bucharest: Editura Institutului Biblic şi de Misiune al Bisericii Ortodoxe Române, 1982), p. 184.

15   Bălan, *Vetre de Sihăstrie Românească*, pp. 243–4.

16   The Romanian word *schit* (plural, *schituri*) is probably less familiar to most readers than the Greek *skete*. 'The chief centres of Hesychast prayer have been the lesser *sketes*, the hermitages housing only a handful of brothers and sisters, living as a small and closely integrated monastic family hidden from the world': Ware, *The Inner Kingdom*, p. 106.

17   The word *sihastru* is still used in modern Romanian for the Greek *hesychast*. See Stăniloae, *Din Istoria Isihasmului*, pp. 10–13.

18   Stephen scored brilliant victories against the Ottomans, helping to block their advance on Europe after the fall of Constantinople.

19   Elder Basil 'collected a significant patristic library of both manuscripts and printed books in his newly-founded *skete* of Poiana Mărului': *Elder Basil of Poiana Mărului, His Life and Writings*, p. 26.

20   Dan Zamfirescu, *A Fundamental Book of European Culture* (Bucharest: Roza Vânturilor, 1991), pp. 1–3. Zamfirescu's study accompanies the anastatic reproduction of the sole complete copy of Paisy Velichkovsky, *Dobrotolyubie* (Moscow: 1793; Romanian Academy Library, MS III 603560).

found in the Romanian lands the spiritual milieu in which he could fulfil his vocation. He was the first to achieve that synthesis of Byzantine and Russian spirituality that is so characteristic of Romanian Orthodoxy.

Paisy's teaching was also spread by Romanian disciples such as St Calinic of Cernica near Bucharest, who added the dimension of secular work to the discipline of monastic prayer.[21] The tradition of Cernica and Paisy continues to the present day, in particular through disciples of the twentieth-century spiritual fathers Hieromonk Arsenie Boca (1910–89)[22] in Transylvania, and Archimandrite Ilie Cleopa (1912–98)[23] in Moldavia. The lives of these two great men of prayer illustrate both the continuity of Hesychasm in the Carpathian mountains and the spiritual resistance of monasticism in Communist Romania. Boca instructed both monastics and lay people (for example, local peasants, students, and university lecturers) in the practice of the Jesus Prayer, and inspired a powerful spiritual movement at Brâncoveanu Monastery, Sâmbăta de Sus.[24] He was imprisoned in a labour camp in the early 1950s.

Cleopa was forced to live in hiding in the mountains, under sentence of death, following Decree no. 410/1959, when the Romanian Orthodox hierarchs were compelled by the government to close hundreds of monasteries and to forbid people from entering the monastic life. Managing to evade capture, he settled at Sihăstria Monastery in 1964, the year of political amnesty. Here he remained until his death, the sheer power of his spiritual presence challenging the Communist system, drawing hundreds of people to the monastery every day.

Meanwhile the Romanian Hesychast tradition was further revitalised by the 'Burning Bush' movement. Archimandrite Ivan Kulygin[25] (1885–c. 1947, deported

---

21   Dragoş Seuleanu and Carmen Dumitriu (eds), *Amintirile Mitropolitului Antonie Plămădeală* (Bucharest: Cum, 1999), p. 121.

22   Fr Arsenie Boca studied the fine arts at Bucharest and theology at Sibiu. A disciple of Nichifor Crainic (see chapter 2, section 'Prison and Prayer'), he travelled to Mount Athos in 1939. In 1946 he started to write *Cărarea Împărăţiei* (*The Road to the Kingdom*), a book of Hesychast teaching for contemporary Christians. See Hieromonk Arsenie Boca, *Cărarea Împărăţiei*, ed. Fr Simion Todoran and Nun Zamfira Constantinescu (Sibiu: Editura Episcopiei Ortodoxe Române a Aradului, 1995).

23   Alexandru Popescu, 'Archimandrite Cleopa Ilie, The good shepherd: Obituary' *Guardian*, London, 8 December 1998, p. 18. See Archimandrite Ioanichie Bălan, *Shepherd of Souls, The Life and Teachings of Elder Cleopa, Master of Inner Prayer and Spiritual Father of Romania (1912–1998)* (Platina, CA: St Herman of Alaska Brotherhood, 2000), pp. 102–40.

24   Dumitru Stăniloae, in the introduction to his seminal translation of the Greek *Philokalia*, described Fr Arsenie as having 'revived the spirit of the *Philokalia* in the religious life of the Romanian people': *Filocalia sfintelor nevoinţe ale desăvârşirii sau culegere din scrierile sfinţilor Părinţi care arată cum se poate omul curăţi, lumina şi desăvârşi*, 2nd edn, trans., introd., and notes by Dumitru Stăniloae, 12 vols (Bucharest: Humanitas, 1999–), III (1999), p. 8. Cf. Boca, *Cărarea Împărăţiei*, p. 336.

25   Fr Ivan's Hesychast formation had been in the Optina Hermitage and the Kiev Monastery of the Caves. In the Caucasus Mountains, he had received spiritual direction from Hieromonk Hilarion. Hilarion was perhaps a spiritual leader of the *Imyaslavtsy* ('name

to Siberia in 1947) was a co-founder, together with Romanian monks and intellectuals, of the Burning Bush movement at the monastery of St Antim Ivireanul in Bucharest.[26] Between 1945 and 1958 these men sought a deeper knowledge of the Prayer of the Heart and a sharper intellectual apprehension of the Jesus Prayer as practised by the monks of Cernica.

One of these monks, Archimandrite Roman Braga, at that time a student at the Theological Institute of Bucharest, received a special blessing from Kulygin to begin the Prayer of the Heart (a 'little ordination'). He remembers:

> I was caught between two worlds: one was the world of the Burning Bush with the Russian method of St Paisy Velichkovsky, a kind of democratisation of Hesychasm which said this Prayer should be for all; and the other world, less spectacular, but I think more profound – the attitude of the Cernica monks... The intellectuals of the Burning Bush started to develop a whole theology around the Prayer of the Heart, which without doubt has its own place; otherwise the *Philokalia* would not have been written, nor would any writings of the Holy Fathers have been left to us in this generation. But monks in the monastery are practical people; they condensed the whole theology into the practice of prayer.[27]

The Burning Bush movement included scholars such as Archimandrite Vasile Vasilachi[28] and Dumitru Stăniloae.[29] There were also monks and lay intellectuals,

---

worshippers') monks from the North Caucasus region who, shortly before the First World War, following Athonite teaching, believed that Jesus Christ's Holy Name should be the object of special veneration. See Archimandrite Sofian Boghiu, 'Rugul Aprins şi Temniţa', *Solia/The Herald* (Jackson, MI: July 1999), p. 20. Cf. Dinu Cruga, *Trepte Duhovniceşti: Interviu cu Părintele Roman Braga* (Alba Iulia: Tipografia Arhiepiscopiei Ortodoxe Alba Iulia, 1998), p. 37; Gheorghe Vasilescu (ed.), *Cuviosul Ioan cel Străin (Din Arhiva Rugului Aprins)*, afterword by Fr Sofian Boghiu (Bucharest: Anastasia, 1999), p. 37. For the implications of *Imyaslavtsy* doctrine see also Rowan Williams (ed.), in *Sergii Bulgakov, Towards a Russian Political Theology*, with comment. by Rowan Williams (Edinburgh: T. & T. Clark, 1999), pp. 9–13; Prof. Vladimir Shchelkashchyov, interview, Moscow, 5 May 2001.

26   'The Burning Bush celebration on 6 September, according to Fr Ivan, constitutes, in silence, the moment and place of reunion in the Holy Spirit of all those blessed with the gift of Hesychast experience and knowledge': André Scrima, *Timpul Rugului Aprins, Maestrul Spiritual în Tradiţia Răsăriteană*, foreword by Andrei Pleşu, ed. Anca Manolescu (Bucharest: Humanitas, 1996), p. 170. For a factual history of the Burning Bush movement, see Seuleanu and Dumitriu (eds), *Amintirile Mitropolitului Antonie Plămădeală*, pp. 86–120. Cf. Antonie Plămădeală, *Rugul Aprins* (Sibiu: Tipografia Eparhială Sibiu, 2000), pp. 101–14.

27   Roman Braga, *Exploring the Inner Universe, Joy – the Mystery of Life* (Rives Junction, MI: HDM Press, 1996), pp. 33–4, 36.

28   See Hieromonk Vasile Vasilachi, *Predica în Evul Mediu* (Iassy: Institutul de Arte Grafice 'Albina Românească', 1938). This doctoral dissertation in 1938, *Medieval Preaching*, devoted a significant part to St Gregory Palamas.

29   In 1946, following the initiative, and with the help, of Arsenie Boca, Stăniloae had started to publish the second Romanian translation of the Greek *Philokalia* – the first, though not

many of whom were to become political prisoners for alleged membership of the right-wing Legionary Movement. During the nights of 13 June and 4 August 1958, members of the Burning Bush group were arrested in Bucharest, and accused of 'conspiracy against the Communist State'.[30] Braga, then archdeacon for the Metropolitan Bishop of Iassy, was arrested in 1959 for discussing the works of St Basil the Great, St John Climacus, and St Gregory of Nyssa, which were held to be 'inimical to the régime'.[31]

Under Communism, Hesychasm flowered anew in the political prisons,[32] where prisoners schooled in the Romanian Athonite–Serbian tradition encountered other prisoners brought up in the Russian–Ukrainian tradition (itself of course stemming from Paisy's work).[33]

---

published, being that of Paisy's disciples. See Zamfirescu, *A Fundamental Book*, p. 13. Stăniloae had also published *The Life and Teaching of St Gregory Palamas*, with translations of four *Triads*: Dumitru Stăniloae, *Viața și Învățătura Sfântului Grigorie Palama, cu patru tratate traduse*, 2nd rev. edn (Bucharest: Scripta, 1993; 1st edn 1938).

30   Florentin Popescu, *Detenția și Sfârșitul lui V. Voiculescu* (Bucharest: Vestala, 2000), p. 121.

31   Braga, *Exploring the Inner Universe*, p. 51.

32   Hieromonk Daniil (Sandu Tudor) Theodorescu (1899–c. 1963, Aiud prison), founder of this spiritual movement, named it after the Burning Bush (*Exodus* 3:2–5), which he regarded as a biblical symbol of the unceasing Prayer of the Heart (Archimandrite Sofian Boghiu, interview, Antim Monastery, Bucharest, 29 September 1999). Cf. Gheorghe Vasilescu, *Benedict Ghiuș, Duhovnicul Inimii*, foreword by Archimandrite Sofian Boghiu, Starets of Antim Monastery (Bucharest: România Creștină, 1998), p. 6.

33   This convergence had in fact begun in 1943, when Archbishop Nicolai III of Rostov (1860–1944) and his spiritual father Archimandrite Ivan Kulygin were given protection by the Romanian army on its retreat from the Battle of Stalingrad. Soon after the Germans and their Romanian allies captured Rostov-on-Don in July 1942, eight churches were opened whereas at the beginning of the war only one was functioning. According to local accounts, people began to restore the Church of All Saints which had been bombed. Soon afterwards Archbishop Nicolai, deported five times by the Soviet régime and discovered by the German Army in 1941 in Azov doing hard physical labour, set up a diocesan administration and church structure (*blagochinie*) and began energetically to ordain priests. The German secret service reported that after the Don region was captured, churches which had been closed under the pre-war Stalinist régime began to be opened on local initiative in all areas under German occupation. A total of 243 churches were opened. When the Red Army re-established control of Rostov-on-Don, Archbishop Nicolai, accused of having links with the Nazis, found refuge in Romania under the protection of Patriarch Nicodim of the Romanian Orthodox Church in 1943. Archbishop Nicolai, already ill, was granted permission to settle as a monk at the monastery of Cernica, where he died the following year. See 'Rasstrelyannyi Arkhipastyr', *Tserkovnyi vestnik Rostovskoi eparkhii*, nr. 5 (68), Rostov-on-Don, May 1999, p. 5; Hieromonk Amvrosy Vinnik, interview, Rostov-on-Don, 4 May 2001. See also V. Vorobiev (ed.), *Za Khrista postradavshie, goneniya na Russkuyu Pravoslavnuyu Tserkov, 1917–1956, II, L-Ya* (Moscow: St Tikhon Orthodox Theological Institute, 1997), p. 193.

Between 1946 and 1948,[34] before the final stages of the Soviet takeover, some of the Legionaries imprisoned in Aiud under Ion Antonescu received, as a gift from Arsenie Boca,[35] the first three volumes of Stăniloae's new translation of the *Philokalia*. According to Virgil Maxim, political prisoner and author of Hesychast poetry,

> Christ was not only an external ideal to whom we wanted to arrive sometime. He Himself was our daily life, at every moment, the desire to be part of Him, as a permanent way of being... The *Paterikon* or the *Philokalia* were lived again, put to the test as possibilities to be realised by political prisoners, not only intellectually but in practical living. The chief characteristic of the new prison saints was humility.[36]

Although not directly connected either with the Sâmbăta de Sus or the Burning Bush movements, they began to follow the Hesychast way of prayer. This sustained them through the Soviet experiment of re-education:

> To experience torture was a kind of insane pleasure. At that time they were putting me in the so-called 'fixed position' which aimed to induce a nervous breakdown. We sat with our legs stretched out and with our hands on our knees, staring at a light bulb or at our toes without blinking. The Prayer of the Heart alone had the power to keep us sane in all these torments.[37]

Petre Ţuţea was influenced by these prisoners' Hesychast spirituality. In political prisons, where so many experienced martyrdom, many also experienced an extraordinary discovery of freedom. It may be argued that theirs was a charismatic neo-Hesychasm.[38]

---

34   Before 6 November 1944 the prison regulations stipulated the prisoners' right to pray according to their faith and denomination (Article 12), and to receive weekly visits (Article 19): Ion Bălan, *Regimul Concentraţionar din România, 1945–1964* (Bucharest: Fundaţia Academia Civică, 2000), p. 53.

35   Maxim, *Imn*, I, p. 135. See also Zamfira Constantinescu, 'Post-scriptum la o lucrare de istorie a isihasmului românesc', *Gândirea*, Sibiu, January–March 1998, p. 96.

36   Maxim, *Imn*, I, p. 182.

37   Maxim, *Imn*, II, p. 82. Cf. Maxim, *Imn*, I, pp. 110–16.

38   For a discussion on neo-Hesychasm, see Archimandrite Teofil Părăian, 'Neoisihasmul, "O Bucurie"', *Altarul Banatului*, Timişoara, April–June 1998, pp. 136–40.

Bibliography

Primary Sources

Unpublished Works of Petre Ţuţea

Manuscripts and Typescripts[1]

MS O (Bucharest: undated), 45 pp. numbered 1–45, typescript.
'Triumful Aparent al Sofisticii în Lumea Modernă, sau Caricatura Utilă a Realului' (Bucharest: undated), 29 pp. numbered 155–83. ['The Apparent Triumph of Sophistry in the Modern World, or the Utilitarian Caricature of the Real' (typescript).]
'Reflecţii Religioase asupra Cunoaşterii', part II (Bucharest: 1977), 149 pp. numbered 162–310. ['Religious Reflections on Human Knowledge' (manuscript).]
MS Chirilă, 'Teatrul Seminar. Prezentare' (Bucharest: 1980), 244 pp. numbered 1–244. ['A Presentation of Theatre as Seminar' (typescript).]
MS 1982 (Bucharest: 1982), 41 pp. numbered 23–9; 64–97, dictated manuscript.
MS 1983 (Bucharest: 1983), 22 pp. numbered 101–20 and pp. 308, 309, dictated manuscript.
'Stilurile, sau Cartea Unităţilor Cultural Istorice şi a Modalităţilor Estetice ale Artelor, sau Omul Estetic', 2 parts (Bucharest: December, 1988). Part I, pp. 1–134 and part II, pp. 135–274. ['Styles, or the Book of Historical Cultural Unities and of the Aesthetic Forms of the Arts, or Aesthetic Humanity', I and II (typescript).]
'Omul, IV, Dogmele sau Primirea Certitudinii' (Bucharest: 15 May 1989), 108 pp. numbered 1–108. ['Dogmas, or the Reception of Certainty' (typescript).]

Letters

18 September 1929 from Săpânţa, Maramureş, to V.V. Tilea in Cluj-Napoca.
26 November 1929 from Pui, Hunedoara, to V.V. Tilea in Cluj-Napoca.
28 October 1934 from Berlin to V.V. Tilea in Bucharest.
11 August 1935 from Săpânţa, Maramureş, to V.V. Tilea in Bucharest.
7 November 1939 from Bucharest to V.V. Tilea in London.

Records of Reflections and Conversations

Philosophical reflections on French existentialism dictated by Ţuţea to Ioana Pavelescu in her 'Despre rolul Martha, din piesa *Neînţelegerea* de Albert Camus' (unpublished MA thesis, Institute of Drama and Film, Bucharest, June 1972). ['On the Rôle of Martha, in Albert Camus's Play *The Misunderstanding*'.]

---

1   Ţuţea's unpublished works quoted here are in my private archive.

Personal conversations:
Municipal Hospital, Bucharest, 21 November 1980
Cișmigiu Park, Bucharest, 10 June 1985
Țuțea's flat, Bucharest, 1 March 1990
Emergency Hospital, Bucharest, 26 April 1990

Interviews recorded on audio cassettes, Bucharest:
28 January 1990
11 February 1990
21 February 1990
1 March 1990
15 March 1990
25 March 1990
26 April 1990
23 May 1990
3 June 1990
25 June 1990
19 November 1990

Conversation with Prof. Dumitru Mazilu, Palatul Victoria, Bucharest, 1 January 1990.

Published Works of Petre Țuțea

This bibliography contains all books and some of the small number of essays published 1968–69, 1972–73, and 1985–19, in addition to the most important interviews of Țuțea published after 1990, listed in chronological order, and quoted in this study. Before the Second World War he contributed articles to *Patria* and *Chemarea Tinerimei Române* (1929–32) in Cluj-Napoca, *Stânga* (1932–1933) and *Cuvântul* (1938; 1940) in Bucharest, from which we include only works quoted in the biographical chapter.

'Discuții în jurul problemei Universității', *Patria*, Cluj-Napoca, 31 March 1929, p. 11. ['On the Problem of University Education'.]
'Bacalaureatul', Patria, Cluj-Napoca, 20 April 1929, p. 3. ['The Baccalaureate'.]
'Democrație și forță', *Patria*, Cluj-Napoca, 8 August 1929, p. 3. ['Democracy and Force'.]
'"Cocoșii" consiliilor de administrație de pe Valea Jiului', *Chemarea*, Cluj-Napoca, 11 August 1929, p. 1. ['The Administrative "Turkeys" of the Jiu Valley'.]
'Democrație național-țărănistă', *Patria*, Cluj-Napoca, 15 August 1929, p. 3. ['National Peasant Democracy'.]
'Judecătoria din Pui sau grajdul d-lui jude Bogdan', *Chemarea*, Cluj-Napoca, 24 November 1929, p. 3. ['Pui Court or Judge Bogdan's Pigsty'.]
'Câinele bătrân nu piere', *Chemarea*, Cluj-Napoca, 15 December 1929, p. 4. ['The Old Dog Never Dies'.]
'Procesul Chemării: Un proces politic sau lupta între două lumi', *Chemarea*, Cluj-Napoca, 2 November 1930, p. 1. ['The Trial of "Chemarea": A Political Trial on the Conflict between Two Worlds'.]
'Regulile jocului democratic', *Stânga*, Bucharest, 13 November 1932, p. 1. ['The Rules of the Democratic Game'.]
Manifestul Revoluției Naționale, in collaboration with Sorin Pavel, Ioan Crăciunel, Gheorghe Tite, Nicolae Tatu, and Petre Ercuță (Sighișoara: Tipografia Miron Neagu,

1935); re-edited by Marin Diaconu (Bucharest: Crater, 1998). [*The National Revolution Manifesto*.]

'Ieftinirea vieţii: ix. Economie înapoiată', *Cuvântul*, Bucharest, 27 February 1938, p. 8. ['Reducing the Price of Human Subsistence: ix. Underdeveloped Economy'.]

'Negociatorul legionar', *Cuvântul*, Bucharest, 30 October 1940, p. 6; reprinted in Constantin Petculescu and Alexandru Florian (eds), *Ideea care ucide, Dimensiunile ideologiei legionare* (Bucharest: Institutul de Teorie Socială al Academiei Române, Editura Noua Alternativă, 1994), pp. 327–9. ['The Legionary Negotiator'.]

'Întreprinzătorul în regimul legionar', *Cuvântul*, Bucharest, 4 November 1940, p. 6; reprinted in Petculescu and Florian (eds), *Ideea care ucide*, pp. 332–5. ['The Entrepreneur in a Legionary Regime'.]

'Ştiinţă şi putere', *Cuvântul*, Bucharest, 9 November 1940, p. 22; reprinted in Petculescu and Florian (eds), *Ideea care ucide*, pp. 336–8. ['Science and Power'.]

'Teatrul. Bios', I–VI, *Familia*, Oradea, February 1968 (I), pp. 18–19; March 1968 (II), pp. 20–21; April 1968 (III), p. 10; May 1968 (IV), p. 15; June 1968 (V), p. 18; July 1968 (VI), p. 9. ['Theatre. Bios', fragments of dialogue.]

'Întâmplări Obişnuite. Piesă în trei acte şi prolog', *Familia*, Oradea, September 1968, pp. 7 and 22; October 1968, p. 16; November 1968, pp. 20–21; December 1968, pp. 14–15; January 1969, pp. 16–17. ['Everyday Happenings. Play in three Acts with a Prologue', published serially in the monthly periodical *Familia*, Oradea, September 1968 – January 1969. Authorship of the first Act at first attributed jointly to Ţuţea and his friend Gheorghe Lăpuşneanu. In the December and January issues, Ţuţea is acknowledged as the sole author.]

'Teatrul. Eros', *Familia*, Oradea, March 1969, pp. 20–21. ['Theatre. Eros', fragments of dialogue.]

'Profil: Aurel Baranga', *Tribuna*, Cluj-Napoca, 16 March 1972, p. 12; reprinted in *Aurel Baranga, interpretat de...* (Bucharest: Eminescu, 1981), pp. 258–62. ['Aurel Baranga. A portrait'.]

'Petre Vancea', *Tribuna*, Cluj-Napoca, 2 August 1973, p. 12. [Reminiscences on the eye surgeon Prof. Petre Vancea (1902–87).]

'Petre Ţuţea', in Barbu Brezianu, 'Comemorări Constantin Brâncuşi (1876–1957), două mărturii', *Arta*, 34:5, Bucharest, 1987, pp. 5–6. [Ţuţea's reminiscences on Brâncuşi; first published under pseudonym, Petre Boteanu, as 'O întâlnire cu Brâncuşi' ('A Meeting with Brâncuşi'), *'Viaţa Românească' Almanac*, Bucharest, 1985, pp. 99–100.]

'Sistemele – întreguri logice', *'Viaţa Românească' Almanac*, Bucharest, 1988, pp. 94–5. ['Systems – Logical Wholes', published under pseudonym, Petre Boteanu.]

'Viaţa ca formă a bucuriei pure', I, interview by Sanda Diaconescu, introd. by Marin Sorescu, *Jurnalul Literar*, Bucharest, 15 January 1990, p. 3. ['Life as a Form of Pure Joy'.]

'Viaţa ca formă a bucuriei pure', II, interview by Sanda Diaconescu, *Jurnalul Literar*, Bucharest, 22 January 1990, p. 3.

'Viaţa ca formă a bucuriei pure', III, interview by Sanda Diaconescu, *Jurnalul Literar*, Bucharest, 29 January 1990, p. 3.

'Firimituri de la un festin interzis', interview by M. Bădiţescu, *Altfel, Curier Literar de Târgovişte*, Târgovişte, February 1990, p. 4. ['Crumbs from a Forbidden Banquet'.]

'Mircea Eliade', I–VIII, *Familia*, Oradea, February 1990 (I), pp. 10–11; March 1990 (II), p. 10; April 1990 (III), pp. 10–11; May 1990 (IV), p. 10; June 1990(V), pp. 12, 18; July 1990 (VI), pp. 10–11; August 1990 (VII), pp. 10–11; September 1990 (VIII), pp. 8 and 18. ['Mircea Eliade', fragments of essay.]

'Restaurarea ordinei naturale, De vorbă cu Petre Ţuţea', interview by Ion Coriolan Maliţa and

Alexandru Prahovara [Popescu], *Timpul*, Iassy, 17 March 1990, p. 4. ['The Restoration of the Natural Order, Conversation with Petre Țuțea' (transcript revised by Țuțea before publication).]

'Filosofia Nuanțelor', I–V, *Baricada*, Bucharest, 27 March 1990 (I), p. 6; 3 April 1990 (II), p. 6; 10 April 1990 (III), p. 6; 17 April 1990 (IV), p. 6; 1 May 1990 (V), p. 6.

'Sunt un om politic înfrânt', interview by Dan Arsenie, *Vatra*, Târgu Mureș, April 1990, pp. 9, 27. ['I Am a Defeated Politician'.]

'Intra-viu pe masa de operație', introd. by Alexandru Prahovara [Popescu], *Viața Medicală*, Bucharest, 6 April 1990, p. 3. ['Interview on the Operating Table' (transcript revised by Țuțea before publication).] Republished in *Baricada*, Bucharest, 22 May 1990, p. 6.

'Masele pot fi înșelate în istorie, O declarație a domnului Petre Țuțea', recorded and introduced by Alexandru Prahovara [Popescu], România Liberă, Bucharest, 10 June 1990, p. 2. ['The Masses Can Be Deceived in History, A Declaration by Petre Țuțea'.]

'Oaspete la Petre Țuțea', interview by Theodor Redlow, *Alternative*, Bucharest, June 1990, p. 1. ['A Visit to Țuțea'.]

'Sentimentul dureros al neîmplinirii, Declarație a domnului Petre Țuțea comunicată domnului Gabriel Liiceanu', *Revista '22'*, Bucharest, 15 June 1990, p. 3. ['The Painful Sense of Unfulfilment. Petre Țuțea's Declaration to Gabriel Liiceanu' (dictated to and ed. Alexandru Popescu, 4 June 1990).]

'Toți ne călăresc pe deșelate, De vorbă cu Petre Țuțea', interview by Petru Bejan, *Timpul*, Iassy, July 1990, p. 4. ['Everyone is Sucking this Country Dry, Conversation with Petre Țuțea'.]

'Petre Țuțea: "de meserie român"', fragments of interviews recorded by Sanda Diaconescu, *Jurnalul Literar*, Bucharest, 13 August 1990, pp. 1, 4. ['Petre Țuțea: "Romanian by Profession"'.]

'Cu Petre Țuțea despre Emil Cioran', I, conversation recorded by Marcel Petrișor and Ion Coja, *Jurnalul Literar*, Bucharest, 20 August 1990, pp. 1; 2. ['Petre Țuțea on Emil Cioran'.]

'Cu Petre Țuțea despre Emil Cioran', II, conversation recorded by Marcel Petrișor and Ion Coja, *Jurnalul Literar*, Bucharest, 27 August 1990, p. 3.

'Petre Țuțea – Notă la Filosofia Nuanțelor', with an introd. by Alexandru Prahovara [Popescu], *Cuvântul Românesc*, Hamilton, Canada, September 1990, p. 12. ['Note on Philosophy of Nuances'.]

'Omul este un animal care poate fi mișcat din loc de iluzie', interview by Marius Costineanu, *Tinerama*, Bucharest, 16–23 November 1990, p. 16. ['Man is an Animal Who Can Be Swayed by Illusion'.]

'Petre Țuțea despre Emil Cioran', conversations with Marcel Petrișor, *Secolul XX*, 328–30 (4–5–6, 1988), Bucharest, 1991, pp. 133–6. ['Țuțea on Cioran'.]

'Eu sunt un om neîmplinit', fragments of interviews by Liliana Stoicescu and Delia Verdeș, *România Liberă*, Bucharest, 7–8 December 1991, pp. 1–2. ['I am an Unfulfilled Man'.]

Bătrânețea și Alte Texte Filosofice, afterword by Ion Papuc (Bucharest: Viitorul Românesc, 1992). [*Old Age and Other Philosophical Texts*.]

'Convorbire cu Petre Țuțea', interview, in Dorin Popa, *Convorbiri Euharistice* (Iassy: Institutul European, 1992), pp. 9–45. ['Conversation with Petre Țuțea'.]

Între Dumnezeu și Neamul Meu, ed. Gabriel Klimowicz, foreword and afterword by Marian Munteanu (Bucharest: Anastasia, Arta Grafică, 1992). [*Between God and My People* (interviews, essays, letters).]

Jurnal cu Petre Țuțea, ed. with comment. by Radu Preda, preface by Gabriel Liiceanu (Bucharest: Humanitas, 1992). 2nd edn, with a preface by Radu Preda (Sibiu: Deisis, 2002). [*Days with Petre Țuțea* (includes transcripts of tape recorded interviews with Țuțea).] The references in the present book are from the 1st edn.

Mircea Eliade (eseu), foreword by Crăciun Bejan, afterword and interview by Dumitru Chirilă, ed. Ioan Moldovan (Oradea: Biblioteca Revistei Familia, 1992). [*Mircea Eliade. An Essay.*]

Omul, Tratat de Antropologie Creştină, vol. 1, Problemele sau Cartea Întrebărilor, afterword and ed. Cassian Maria Spiridon (Iassy: Timpul, 1992). [*The Human Being, Treatise on Christian Anthropology, vol. 1, Problems, or the Book of Questions.*]

Philosophia Perennis, essays ed. Horia Niculescu, afterword by Matei Albastru (Bucharest: Icar and Horia Niculescu, 1992).

Proiectul de Tratat. Eros, foreword and ed. Aurel Ion Brumaru (Braşov and Chişinău: Pronto and Editura Uniunii Scriitorilor, 1992). [*Project for a Treatise. Eros.*]

Reflecţii Religioase asupra Cunoaşterii, part I, introd. and afterword by Ion Aurel Brumaru (Bucharest: Nemira, 1992). [*Religious Reflections on Human Knowledge.*]

'Convorbiri cu Magistrul', ed. Marian Munteanu, *Cuvântul Studenţesc*, 1:1, Braşov, 1993, p. 9. ['Conversations with the Master'.]

'Convorbiri cu Petre Ţuţea', ed. Marian Munteanu, *Cuvântul Studenţesc*, 1:2, Braşov, 1993, pp. 8–9. ['Conversations with Petre Ţuţea'.]

Lumea ca Teatru. Teatrul Seminar, text established, ed., and annotated with a foreword by Mircea Coloşenco (Bucharest: Vestala and Alutus, 1993). [*The World as Theatre. Theatre as Seminar.*]

Omul, Tratat de Antropologie Creştină, vol. 2, Sistemele sau Cartea Întregurilor Logice, Autonom-Matematice, Paralele cu Întregurile Ontice, afterword and ed. Cassian Maria Spiridon, obituary by Viorel Ţuţea (Iassy: Timpul, 1993). [*The Human Being, Treatise on Christian Anthropology, vol. 2, Systems, or the Book of Logical Wholes, Mathematically Autonomous, Parallel to Ontic Wholes.*]

'Petre Ţuţea', television interviews, in Vartan Arachelian, *Cuvântul care Zideşte* (Bucharest: Roza Vânturilor, 1993), pp. 64–83.

321 de vorbe memorabile ale lui Petre Ţuţea, foreword and ed. Gabriel Liiceanu (Bucharest: Humanitas, 1993); *322 de vorbe memorabile ale lui Petre Ţuţea*, 2nd edn, foreword and ed. Gabriel Liiceanu (Bucharest: Humanitas, 1997). [*321/322 Aphorisms of Petre Ţuţea.*] The references in the present book are from the 1st edn.

Nelinişti Metafizice, foreword and ed. Petre Anghel (Bucharest: Eros, 1994). [*Metaphysical Angst* (essays).]

Filosofia Nuanţelor (Eseuri. Profiluri. Corespondenţă), anthology, preface, and notes by Mircea Coloşenco, ed. Sergiu Coloşenco, afterword by Sorin Pavel (Iassy: Timpul, 1995). [*Philosophy of Nuances. Essays, portraits, letters.*]

'Constantin Brâncuşi and Petre Ţuţea: On the Power and Limits of Art', ed., annotated, and introd. by Alexandru Popescu, *Sourozh*, nr. 69, Oxford, August 1997, pp. 8–16. [The English translation of the complete text of this dialogue (published in *Deisis*, Regensburg, 5–6/1997, pp. 45–8) includes censored fragments signed by Ţuţea and dictated to the author in 1983.]

Ieftinirea Vieţii, Medalioane de antropologie economică, preface and text established by Mircea Coloşenco (Bucharest: Elion, 2000). [*Reducing the Price of Human Subsistence, Essays on Economic Anthropology.*]

Omul, Tratat de Antropologie Creştină (ultima parte), Dogmele sau Primirea Certitudinii, foreword and ed. Cassian Maria Spiridon (Iassy: Timpul, 2000). [*The Human Being, Treatise on Christian Anthropology (final part), Dogmas, or the Reception of Certainty.*]

Ultimile Dialoguri cu Petre Ţuţea, with an unpublished letter to Emil Cioran and a literary portrait by Ion Papuc, foreword and ed. Gabriel Stănescu (Norcross, GA: Criterion Publishing, 2000). [*Last Dialogues with Petre Ţuţea.*]

'Mistica', ed. with a note by Cassian Maria Spiridon, *Origini-Romanian Roots*, Norcross, GA, May–June 2001, pp. i, iv. ['Mysticism'.]

Omul, Tratat de Antropologie Creştină, Addenda: Filosofie şi Teologie, foreword and ed. Cassian Maria Spiridon (Iassy: Timpul, 2001). [*The Human Being, Treatise on Christian Anthropology, Addenda: Philosophy and Theology.*]

Reformă Naţională şi Cooperare, in collaboration with Sorin Pavel, et al., texts established and preface by Mircea Coloşenco, afterword by Mihail Şora (Bucharest: Elion, 2001). [*National Reform and Cooperation.*]

'Viziunea economică a lui Petre Țuțea', fragments selected by Răzvan Codrescu, *Puncte Cardinale*, Sibiu, December 2001, p. 7. ['Petre Țuțea's Vision of Economics'.]

Anarhie şi Disciplina Forţei, preface, notes and ed. Mircea Coloşenco (Bucharest: Elion, 2002). [*Anarchy and the Discipline of Force.*]

'Despre filosofi şi filosofie', *Puncte Cardinale*, Sibiu, December 2002, p. 6. ['On Philosophers and Philosophy'.]

Archival Sources[2]

Unpublished Letters

Letter to Werner Sombart from Sergii Bulgakov, Moscow, 6/18 April 1896.[3]
Letter to Țuțea from V.V. Tilea, Cluj-Napoca, 1 December 1929.
Letter to Nicolae Tatu from Sorin Pavel, Brăila, 18 June 1936.
Letter to Nicolae Tatu from Sorin Pavel, Iassy, 28 July 1936.
Letter to Haig Acterian from Marietta Sadova, Bucharest, 22 July 1940.[4]
Letter to Țuțea from Emil Cioran, Paris, 22 February 1990.
Letter to Alexandru Popescu from Simone Boué, Paris, 21 August 1997.
Humboldt-Universitätsarchiv, Berlin, Rektorat 125 (18.10.1934–7.6.1935), matriculation nr. 2044.

Typescripts

Grigore Gafencu, 'Jurnal (1 Iunie – 13 Decembrie 1940)', typescript ed. and annotated by Ion Ardeleanu and Vasile Arimia, Bucharest, pp. 445, 466–7.

Bazil Gruia, 'Tinereţea lui Petre Țuțea: Studii şi debut publicistic la Cluj', typescript, Cluj-Napoca, 1994.

Simion Ghinea, 'Cuşca cu şobolani', typescript, Bucharest, 1994.

Records and Files

Arhiva Primăriei Boteni, Argeş, Registrul Stării Civile 1/1902, Naşteri, nr. 72.
Arhiva Ministerului Afacerilor Externe, Bucharest: Telegram of 13 November 1940, Fond 71, 1920–1944, URSS, Telegrame Moscova 1940, vol. 3, MAE; Telegram of 28 February 1941, Fond 71, 1920–1944, URSS, Telegrame Moscova 1941–1944, vol. 4, MAE.

---

2   Unless otherwise specified, these unpublished sources are in my private archive.
3   Geheimes Staatsarchiv Preußischer Kulturbesitz, Berlin-Dahlem, I. HA, Rep. 92 Sombart, Nr. 10a, Bd.1, fol. 182.
4   Romanian Academy Library, inv. 223316.

Arhivele Naţionale ale României, Direcţia Arhivelor Centrale, Bucharest, Ministerul Industriei
  şi Comerţului, Direcţiunea Comerţului Interior, Dosar 130/1933, f. 15; Dosar 131/1933, f.
  276; Dosar 74/1936; Ministerul Economiei Naţionale, Oficiul de Studii, Dosar 3/1943, f. 32.
Arhiva Sistemului Român de Informaţii, Dosar nr. 105531/6, Dosar nr. 501/1956 (Petre Ţuţea's
  personal file) and fols 125, 128–30 (from his case file); Dosar 25375/23: fols 274, 295–7;
  Dosar 25375/25: fols 69, 90, 119.
Arhiva Parohiei Sf Paraschiva, Boteni, Argeş: Ţuţea's letter of 26 January 1970 to Fr Stanca
  Sisoe, parish priest; Ţuţea's letter of 20 March 1991 to the parish council.
Ministerul de Interne, Direcţia Secretariat, letter to Ţuţea, nr. 77011, 10.05.1991.
Dumitru Stăniloae's autograph dedication to Ţuţea, inscribed on the front page of Stăniloae's
  book *Spiritualitate şi Comuniune în Liturghia Ortodoxă*, Bucharest, 9 May 1990.

Interviews

Virgil Mateiaş, Washington, DC, 12 August 1990
Fr Gheorghe Calciu, Washington, DC, 12–13 August 1990
Octavian Voinea, Toronto, 1 September 1990
Emil Cioran, Paris, 15–17 August 1992
Wendy Muston-Noica, Tolleshunt Knights, Essex, 24 August 1992
Christinel Eliade, Chicago, 25 October 1993
Nicolae Tatu, Bucharest, 16 March 1994
Simion Ghinea, Bucharest, 29 August 1994
Dr Mihai Neagu, Freiburg im Breisgau, 15 September 1995
Dr Nicolaus Sombart, London, 25 December 1995; Berlin, 20 September 1996
Ion Larian Postolache, Bucharest, 29 December, 1995
Dr Maria Cortez, Bucharest, 14 April 1996
Ioan Alexandru, Bonn, 6 September 1996
Marie-France Ionesco, Paris, 19 September 1997
Archbishop Bartolomeu Anania, Cluj-Napoca, 4 November 1998
Dr Horia Stanca, Bucharest, 3 September 1997; 18 October 1999
Prof. Walter Biemel, Aachen, 7 October 1997
Victor Ţuţea (Ţuţea's brother), Boteni, Muscel, 12 April 1999
Angela Chirilă (Ţuţea's sister), Bucharest, 19 April 1999
Corina Constantinescu, Bucharest, 20 April 1999
Dumitru Bordeianu, Melbourne, 17 June 1999; Aiud, 14 September 2001
Archimandrite Roman Braga, Rives Junction, Michigan, 9 July 1999
Mihai Cârciog, London, 19 July 1999; 8 April 2001
Archimandrite Sofian Boghiu, Antim Monastery, Bucharest, 29 September 1999
Colonel Gheorghe Crăciun, Bucharest, 16 October 1999
Ioana Pavelescu, New York, 12 March 2000
N.P., Ocnele Mari, 3 July 2000
Cornel Deneşeanu, Sâmbăta de Sus, Sibiu, 23 July 2000
Dragoş Galgoţiu, Bucharest, 24 July 2000
Traian Popescu, Bucharest, 24 July 2000
Lieutenant-Colonel Aurel Langu, Aiud, 18 August 2000
Cornel Tican, Boteni, 23 August 2000
Gheorghe Măruţă, Bucharest-Tg. Jiu, 24–25 August 2000
Fr Iustin Pârvu, Petru Vodă Monastery, Neamţ, Moldavia, 2 September 2000
Mircea Nicolau, Bucharest, 4 September 2000

Ion Halmaghi, Sibiu, 13 September 2000; 13 September 2001
Aristide Ionescu, Bucharest, 23 September 2000
Hieromonk Amvrosy Vinnik, Rostov-on-Don, 4 May 2001
Prof. Vladimir Shchelkashchyov, Moscow, 5 May 2001
Chiriachiţa Popescu, Madrid, 1 September 2001
Prof. Hugh Trevor-Roper, Didcot, 19 March 2002

Works and Testimonies about Ţuţea: 1936–2002[5]

Cioran, Emil, 'Patru scrisori către Nicolae Tatu', *Apostrof*, 6:3/4, Cluj-Napoca, 1995, p. 3. [Four letters to Tatu from Cioran, Germany, 1933–34.]

Şerbulescu, Andrei, 'Ofensiva "culturală" a fascismului românesc',[6] *Era Nouă*, nr. 3, Bucharest, April 1936, p. 98.

Almanach de Gotha, Annuaire Généalogique, Diplomatique et Statistique 1944 (Gotha: Justus Perthes, 1944), p. 1081.

Pandrea, Petre, (interview), in *Lumea de Mâine, II*, ed. Ion Biberi (Bucharest: Forum, [1946]), pp. 206–26; reprinted as 'Prolog' in Petre Pandrea, *Eseuri (Portrete şi controverse; Germania hitleristă; Pomul vieţii)*, ed. Gh. Stroia, preface by George Ivaşcu (Bucharest: Minerva, 1971), pp. 1–24.

Lavu, Ştefan, 'Confuzie', *Familia*, Oradea, December 1968, p. 23.

Oprişan, I., *Lucian Blaga printre Contemporani, Dialoguri adnotate* (Bucharest: Minerva, 1987), p. 21.

Stanca, Horia, *Fragmentarium Clujean* (Cluj-Napoca: Dacia, 1987), p. 263.

Lăzărescu, Dan A., 'Patriarhul Liberalismului Românesc',[7] *Liberalul*, Bucharest, 15–22 June 1990, p. 1.

Stanca, Horia, 'Efigia lui Socrate', *Apostrof*, 1:2, Cluj-Napoca, 1990, pp. 22–3.

Acterian, Jeni, *Jurnalul unei fiinţe greu de mulţumit* (Bucharest: Humanitas, 1991), pp. 243, 271.

Ciomâzgă, Cornel, 'O, genii întristate care mor...', *Tinerama*, Bucharest, 6–12 December 1991, p. 16.

Cipariu, Dan Mircea, 'Petre Ţuţea îngrijit de biserică', *Tineretul Liber*, Bucharest, 26 September 1991, p. 5.

Doinaş, Ştefan Augustin, 'Ultimul Socrate', *Secolul XX*, 328–30 (4–5–6, 1988), Bucharest, 1991, pp. 127–31.

Dumitrescu, Sorin, 'Dom' Profesor', *România Liberă*, Bucharest, 5 December 1991, p. 1.

Ionescu, Liana, 'Ultimul Socrate şi scepticul de serviciu', *România Liberă*, Bucharest, 18 December 1991, p. 4.

Mateiaş, Virgil, 'Anii de groază din România Comunistă', printed typescript, Făgăraş, 21 March 1991, pp. 4, 52.

---

5   This select bibliography is arranged in chronological order.

6   Following the publication of *Manifestul Revoluţiei Naţionale*, Ţuţea was listed among the ideologues of Romanian Fascism by Comintern agent Andrei Şerbulescu (real name Herbert Silber).

7   Shortly after the first 'post-Communist' elections of 20 May 1990 and the arrival of some ten thousand miners in Bucharest's University Square on 13 June 1990, Ţuţea was portrayed as 'Patriarch of Romanian Liberalism' on the front page of the National Liberal Party's newspaper.

Mărgineanu, Nicolae, *Amfiteatre şi Închisori (Mărturii asupra unui veac zbuciumat)*, ed. and introd. by Voicu Lăscuş (Cluj-Napoca: Dacia, 1991), pp. 257–8.

'Petre Ţuţea: Obituary', *Independent*, London, 20 December 1991, p. 27.

'Petre Ţuţea: Romania's White Monk, Symbol of Resistance and Renaissance', *Guardian*, London, 31 December 1991, p. 17.

Sorescu, Constantin, 'În memoria lui Petre Ţuţea', statement made in the Romanian Parliament, *Buletinul Oficial*, II, Bucharest, December 1991.

Acterian, Arşavir, *Jurnalul unui pseudo-filosof* (Bucharest: Cartea Românească, 1992), pp. 138, 198, 247–8.

Boeru, Adrian, 'Schiţă de portret', *Revista de Filosofie*, 39:3, Bucharest, May–June 1992, pp. 331–4.

Chioreanu, Nistor, *Morminte Vii*, ed. with notes by Marius Cristian (Iassy: Institutul European, 1992), pp. 9, 207, 294–6, 320, 339.

Chişu, Lucian, 'Fluxul şi refluxul memoriei', *Literatorul*, Bucharest, 24 April 1992, p. 4.

Dimitriu, Paul, *Exerciţii de memorie* (Bucharest: Editura Fundaţiei Culturale Române, Colecţia Biblioteca Memoriei, 1992), pp. 87–8.

Gheorghe, Gabriel, 'In memoriam Petre Ţuţea', *Getica*, 1:1–2, Bucharest, 1992, pp. 111–14.

Izverna, Pan, 'La trecerea lui Petre Ţuţea', *Revista de Filosofie*, 39:3, Bucharest, May–June 1992, pp. 328–31.

Liiceanu, Gabriel, 'Prefaţă la un film despre Cioran', in *Apel către Lichele* (Bucharest: Humanitas, 1992), pp. 52–60.

Spiridon, Cassian Maria, 'Petre Ţuţea – Un om care nu s-a plictisit', *România Liberă*, Bucharest, 6 October 1992, p. 6.

Stanca, Horia, 'Petre Ţuţea între extreme', *Apostrof*, 3:12, Cluj-Napoca, 1992, p. 12.

Trancă, Dumitru, *Clubul Pensionarilor, File din Dosarul Petre Ţuţea, Roman* (Bucharest: Edimpex and Speranţa, 1992).

Ţuţea, Viorel, 'Dr Petre Ţuţea. Date bio-bibliografice', *Revista de Filosofie*, 39:3, Bucharest, May–June 1992, pp. 325–8.

Ultimul Socrate: Petre Ţuţea, Încercare de portret, Festschrift in honour of Petre Ţuţea (Bucharest: Academia Universitară Athenaeum, 1992).

Andriţoiu, Alexandru, 'Pantheon: Amintiri despre Petre Ţuţea', *Dimineaţa*, Bucharest, 29–30 May 1993, p. 2.

Chişu, Lucian, 'Un proiect de antropologie creştină: Petre Ţuţea, "Reflecţii religioase asupra cunoaşterii"', *Literatorul*, Bucharest, 23 July 1993, p. 4.

Codreanu, Theodor, 'Petre Ţuţea şi "Noua Dreaptă"', I, *Vremea*, Bucharest, 8 January 1993, pp. 1; 3.

Codreanu, Theodor, 'Petre Ţuţea şi "Noua Dreaptă"', II, *Vremea*, Bucharest, 9 January 1993, p. 2.

Codreanu, Theodor, 'Petre Ţuţea şi "Noua Dreaptă"', III, *Vremea*, Bucharest, 12 January 1993, p. 2.

Coloşenco, Mircea, 'Un portret al lui Petre Bădescu, tatăl lui Petre Ţuţea', *Literatorul*, Bucharest, 24 September – 1 October 1993, p. 10.

Constantinescu, Cornel, 'Ţuţocalia sau Căţăratul pe statui', *Adevărul*, Bucharest, 5 July 1993, p. 3.

Eliade, Mircea, *Jurnal, vol. I (1941–1969)*, ed. Mircea Handoca (Bucharest: Humanitas, 1993), pp. 18, 458.

Hurezean, Gabriela, 'Petre Ţuţea: "Lumea ca teatru. Teatrul seminar"', *Tineretul Liber*, Bucharest, 21 December 1993, p. 4.

Miu, Monica, 'Mișcarea Pentru România, un real pericol pentru tineret', *România Mare*, Bucharest, 30 July 1993, p. 5.

Ornea, Zigu, 'Nevroza Țuțea', *România Literară*, Bucharest, 26 January – 3 February 1993, p. 11.

Paleologu, Alexandru, in Vartan Arachelian, *Cuvântul care zidește* (Bucharest: Roza Vânturilor, 1993), pp. 226, 228–9.

Stanca, Dan, 'Țuțea despre democrație', *Tineretul Liber*, Bucharest, 6 July 1993, p. 3.

Ulici, Laurențiu, 'Pe marginea unui Tratat', *România Literară*, Bucharest, 30–31 January 1993, p. 2.

Arșavir, Acterian, *Jurnal în căutarea lui Dumnezeu* (Iassy: Institutul European, 1994), pp. 31, 168–9, 233.

Ciachir, Dan, 'O nuanță a credinței'; 'O carte de Petre Țuțea', in *Gânduri despre Nae Ionescu* (Iassy: Institutul European, 1994), pp. 110–13, 114–17.

Cristea, Valeriu, 'M-am fâțâit așa, un pic, în epocă...', *Caiete Critice*, 4–5 (77–8), Bucharest, 1994, pp. 8–12.

Ghinea, Simion, 'Foamea rusească de spațiu și ruga lui Petre Țuțea pe rangă', in *Silogismul Slav (Contribuții la o nouă istorie a relațiilor româno-ruse)* (Bucharest: Fundația Buna Vestire, c. 1994), pp. 34–40.

Neagu, Mihai, 'Amurgul lui Petre Țuțea', *Vatra*, 44:194, Freiburg im Breisgau, June 1994, pp. 5–8.

Popescu, Alexandru, 'Petre Țuțea', *Sobornost* incorporating *Eastern Churches Review*, 16:2, Oxford, 1994, pp. 47–9.

Stanca, Horia, *Așa a fost să fie* (Cluj-Napoca: Dacia, 1994), pp. 113, 279–88.

Tismăneanu, Vladimir, and Dan Pavel, 'Romania's Mystical Revolutionaries: The Generation of Angst and Adventure Revisited', *East European Politics and Societies*, 8:3, Fall 1994, pp. 402–38 (pp. 428–31).

Brumaru, Aurel Ioan, *Pariul cu Legenda, sau Viața lui Petre Țuțea așa cum a fost ea* (Bucharest: Athena, 1995).

Coja, Ion, et al., 'Actualitate: Petre Țuțea', *Renașterea*, Cluj-Napoca, December 1995, pp. 4–5.

Liiceanu, Gabriel, *Itinerariile unei vieți: E.M. Cioran, Apocalipsa după Cioran, Trei zile de convorbiri – 1990* (Bucharest: Humanitas, 1995), pp. 26–7, 82–4, 116; French trans. Alexandra Laignel-Lavastine: *Itinéraires d'une vie: E.M. Cioran, suivi de Les Continents de l'insomnie, entretien avec E.M. Cioran* (Paris: Michalon, 1995), pp. 30, 97–9, 129–30.

Paleologu, Alexandru, 'Statornicit pe veci', *Renașterea*, Cluj-Napoca, December 1995, p. 6.

Popescu, Alexandru, 'Petre Țuțea (1902–1991): The Urban Hermit of Romanian Spirituality', *Religion, State, & Society*, 23:4, Oxford, 1995, pp. 319–41.

Ciachir, Dan, 'Despărțirea de Țuțea', in *Luciditate și Nostalgie* (Iassy: Institutul European, 1996), pp. 128–31.

Coposu, Corneliu, *Confesiuni, Dialoguri cu Doina Alexandru* (Bucharest: Anastasia, 1996), pp. 144–8.

Lovinescu, Monica, *Insula Șerpilor, Unde scurte VI* (Bucharest: Humanitas, 1996), pp. 292–3.

Patapievici, Horia-Roman, *Cerul văzut prin lentilă*, 2nd edn, foreword by Virgil Ierunca (Bucharest: Humanitas, 1996), pp. 106, 204.

Pleșu, Andrei, 'Idolatrie' and 'Petre Țuțea – un țăran imperial', in *Chipuri și măști ale tranziției* (Bucharest: Humanitas, 1996), pp. 320–22, 323.

Popescu, Alexandru, 'Alexander Webster: "The Price of Prophecy: Orthodox churches on peace, freedom and security"', book review, *Studies in Christian Ethics*, 9:2, 1996, pp. 123–6 (125).

Preda, Radu, 'Petre Țuțea', *Deisis*, Regensburg, March–April 1996, p. 64.

Prigoana: Documente ale Procesului C. Noica, C. Pillat, N. Steinhardt, Al. Paleologu, A. Acterian, S. Al-George, Al. O. Teodoreanu etc. (Bucharest: Vremea, 1996), pp. 137–42, 145, 310–11, 361, 478–80.

Sebastian, Mihail, *Jurnal 1935–1944*, ed. Gabriela Omăt, foreword and notes by Leon Volovici (Bucharest: Humanitas, 1996), p. 516.

Zamfirescu, Dan, 'Sunt filolog și securist', interview by Constantin Stănescu and Lelia Munteanu, in Constantin Stănescu, *Interviuri din tranziție* (Bucharest: Editura Fundației Culturale Române, 1996), pp. 217–19.

Codrescu, Răzvan, 'Eșecul "omului autonom" (La un simpozion "Petre Țuțea")', in *Spiritul Dreptei* (Bucharest: Anastasia, 1997), pp. 28–38; reprinted in Răzvan Codrescu, *De la Eminescu la Petre Țuțea* (Bucharest: Anastasia, 2000), pp. 213–24.

Eliade, Mircea, *Memorii, 1907–1960*, 2nd edn (Bucharest: Humanitas, 1997), pp. 323–4.

Petrișor, Marcel, *La capăt de drum* (Iassy: Institutul European, 1997), pp. 125, 134–7, 157–61, 185–7.

Roncea, George, 'Petre Țuțea a fost reabilitat de Curtea Supremă de Justiție', *Ziua*, Bucharest, 21 October 1997, p. 12.

Stănescu, Gheorghe, *Jurnal din Prigoană, 1952–1955*, 3rd edn (Bucharest: Venus, c. 1997), p. 198–9.

Ghinea Vrancea, Simion, *Mircea Eliade și Emil Cioran* (Bucharest: Elisavaros, 1998), pp. 60, 97, 121–4, 128, 151, 161, 195–7, 199, 225, 232–4, 240.

Halmaghi, Ion, 'Un moment cu Petre Țuțea la Aiud', *Permanențe*, Bucharest, 3 March 1998, p. 15.

Pârvu, Iuliu, *Barițiștii, Zări întrerupte* (Cluj-Napoca: Napoca Star, 1998), pp. 35–8.

Stoica, Victor, *Memorii, Petre Țuțea la verticală* (Iassy: Fides, 1998), pp. 63, 86–92.

Țuțea, Viorel, 'Petre Țuțea știa să facă să râdă în hohote un copil de câțiva ani', interview by Roxana Iordache, *România Liberă*, Bucharest, 28 March 1998, p. 14.

Furdui, Dumitru, *Teatrul în Comunism*, 2 vols (Alba Iulia and Paris: Fronde, Librairie Roumaine Antitotalitaire, 1999), II, pp. 228, 232, 262–4.

Sorescu, Marin, 'Un anume Țuțea', in *Jurnal: Romanul Călătoriilor* (Bucharest: Editura Fundației 'Marin Sorescu', 1999), pp. 248–53.

Sorescu, Radu, *Viața și Opera lui Petre Țuțea* (Bucharest: Scripta Press, 1999).

Coja, Ion, *Salonul de Reanimare* (Bucharest: Alfa, 2000).

Ierunca, Virgil, *Trecut-au anii... Fragmente de jurnal. Întâmpinări și accente. Scrisori nepierdute* (Bucharest: Humanitas, 2000), pp. 387–9.

Pandrea, Petre, *Memoriile Mandarinului Valah*, with a chronological table by Ion Nistor (Bucharest: Albatros, 2000), pp. 29, 44–5, 63, 105, 120, 125, 146, 151, 237, 257, 277–8, 294–6, 299, 300–301, 315, 424–5, 431–7, 470, 498, 504, 543.

Pandrea, Petre, *Reeducarea de la Aiud*, ed. Nadia Marcu-Pandrea (Bucharest: Vremea, 2000), pp. 35, 129, 180, 235, 253, 256, 258–9, 266, 268–9, 354–7, 487–8.

Ștefănescu, Alex., 'Gândirea exclamativă, Un autor care a renunțat la birocrația scrisului', *România Literară*, Bucharest, 23–29 February 2000, www.romlit.ro, pp. 1–3.

Aronescu, Constantin, 'Istoria are un cod moral', *Origini–Romanian Roots*, Norcross, GA, May–June 2001, p. ii–iii.

Groza, Horia Ion, 'Ultimele Dialoguri', *Origini–Romanian Roots*, Norcross, GA, May–June 2001, p. i.

Opriș, Ioan, *Cercuri Culturale Disidente* (Bucharest: Univers Enciclopedic, 2001), pp. 281–300.

Pandrea, Petre, *Crugul Mandarinului, Jurnal intim (1952–1958)*, ed. Nadia Marcu-Pandrea, preface by Ștefan Dimitriu (Bucharest: Vremea, 2001), pp. 105–6, 156–7, 226–8, 313.

Pandrea, Petre, *Garda de Fier. Jurnal de filosofie politică. Memorii penitenciare*, ed. Nadia Marcu-Pandrea (Bucharest: Vremea, 2001), pp. 307, 393–420.

Pandrea, Petre, *Helvetizarea României (Jurnal intim 1947)*, ed. Nadia Marcu-Pandrea (Bucharest: Vremea, 2001), p. 323.

Hossu, Andrei-Iustin, *Tăinuind cu Petre Ţuţea* (Norcross, GA: Criterion Publishing, 2002).

Lovinescu, Monica, *Jurnal 1981–1984* (Bucharest: Humanitas, 2002), p. 270.

Petrescu, Radu, *Prizonier al Provizoratului, Jurnal 1957–1970*, ed. Ruxandra Mihăilă, chronology by Adela Petrescu (Ploieşti: Paralela 45, 2002), p. 408.

Popescu, Alexandru, ' "The Peasant Chats over the Fence with God": A Christian Sense of the Land with Reference to the Thought of the Romanian Dissident Petre Ţuţea', *Humanitas*, 4:1, Birmingham, 2002, pp. 59–88.

Tiberian, Florea, 'De la mistică la gnoză (pe marginea unui text al lui Petre Ţuţea)', *Puncte Cardinale*, Sibiu, December 2002, p. 7.

Vosganian, Varujan, 'La Centenarul lui Petre Ţuţea (1902–2002)', *Puncte Cardinale*, Sibiu, October 2002, p. 16.

Ciachir, Dan, *Când Moare o Epocă* (Bucharest: Anastasia, 2003), pp. 35–44.

Lovinescu, Monica, *Jurnal 1985–1988* (Bucharest: Humanitas, 2003), pp. 146, 157.

Ştefănescu, Alex., 'Petre Ţuţea la o nouă lectură', *România Literară*, Bucharest, 8–14 October 2003, pp. 10–11.

Secondary Sources

Aioanei, Constantin, and Cristian Troncotă, 'Modelul reeducării prin autoanaliză: Aiud şi Gherla 1960–1964', *Arhivele Totalitarismului*, 2:1–2, Bucharest, 1994, pp. 60–73.

Allison, Henry, *Kant's Theory of Taste* (Cambridge: Cambridge University Press, 2001).

Almanach de Gotha, Annuaire Généalogique, Diplomatique et Statistique 1944 (Gotha: Justus Perthes, 1944).

Andreyev, Leonid, *Juda Iscarioth şi alte povestiri*, trans. George B. Rareş (Bucharest: Editura Traducătorului, 1925).

Andronescu, Demostene, 'Reeducarea de la Aiud', I–IV, *Puncte Cardinale*, Sibiu, August–September 1993, p. 6 (I); October 1993, p. 6 (II); November 1993, p. 6 (III); December 1993, p. 6 (IV).

Andronescu, Demostene, '"Spovedania" Colonelului Crăciun', *Puncte Cardinale*, Sibiu, February–March 1998, p. 16.

Andronescu, Demostene, 'Avocatul Diavolului: Petre Pandrea, "Garda de Fier. Jurnal de filosofie politică. Memorii penitenciare"', *Puncte Cardinale*, Sibiu, March 2002, p. 6.

Apostol, Pavel, et al. (eds), *Dicţionar de Filozofie* (Bucharest: Editura Politică, 1978).

Appel, Michael, *Werner Sombart: Theoretiker und Historiker des modernen Kapitalismus* (Marburg: Metropolis, 1992).

Aquinas, Thomas, *Summa Theologiae, A Concise Translation*, ed. Timothy McDermott (Chicago: Christian Classics, 1991).

Ardeleanu, George, *Nicolae Steinhardt, Monografie* (Braşov: Aula, 2000).

Aristotle, *De Anima (On the Soul)*, trans. with introd. and notes by Hugh Lawson-Tancred (London: Penguin, 1986).

Augustine, *Four Anti-Pelagian Writings*, trans. John A. Mourant and William J. Collinge, introd. and notes by W.J. Collinge (Washington, DC: The Catholic University of America Press, 1992).

Bacu, Dumitru, 'Cred în destinul acestui neam', interview by Marcel Petrişor, *Puncte Cardinale*, Sibiu, December 1991, p. 8.

Bacu, Dumitru, *Piteşti, Centru de Reeducare Studenţească*, 2nd edn, foreword by Fr Gheorghe Calciu (Bucharest: Atlantida, 1991); English trans., *The Anti-Humans, Student 'Re-education' in Romanian Prisons*, introd. by Warren B. Heath (Englewood, CO: Soldiers of the Cross, 1971; 1st edn 1963).

Bădescu, Ilie, and Dan Dungaciu, 'Experimente totalitare. Modelul reeducării: Piteşti, Gherla, Canal, 1949–1952', *Arhivele Totalitarismului*, 2:3, Bucharest, 1994, pp. 7–16.

Bâgu, Gheorghe, *Mărturisiri din Întuneric* (Bucharest: Editura Tehnică, 1993).

Bălan, Archimandrite Ioanichie, *Vetre de Sihăstrie Românească, sec. IV–XX* (Bucharest: Editura Institutului Biblic şi de Misiune al Bisericii Ortodoxe Române, 1982).

Bălan, Archimandrite Ioanichie, *Shepherd of Souls, The Life and Teachings of Elder Cleopa, Master of Inner Prayer and Spiritual Father of Romania (1912–1998)* (Platina, CA: St Herman of Alaska Brotherhood, 2000).

Bălan, Ion, *Regimul Concentraţionar din România, 1945–1964* (Bucharest: Fundaţia Academia Civică, 2000).

Barnes, Jonathan, *The Presocratic Philosophers* (London: Routledge & Kegan Paul, 1982).

Barthes, Roland, 'Un raport secret', *Memoria*, 34, January 2001, pp. 82–6.

Baudelaire, Charles, *Les Fleurs du Mal*, afterword and notes by Antoine Compagnon (Paris: Seuil, 1993).

Berdyaev, Nikolai, *The Meaning of History*, trans. George Reavey (London: Centenary Press, 1936).

Berdyaev, Nikolai, *Împărăția Spiritului și Împărăția Cezarului*, trans. and notes by Ilie Gyurcsik (Timișoara: Amarcord, 1994).

Bertram, Ernst, *Nietzsche. Versuch einer Mythologie* (Berlin: Georg Bondi, 1922).

Bescherelle, Louis Nicolas, *Dictionnaire national, ou dictionnaire universel de la langue française*, 14th edn, 2 vols (Paris: Garnier Frères, 1845).

Bethell, Nicholas, *The Last Secret, Forcible Repatriation to Russia: 1944–1947*, introd. by Hugh Trevor-Roper (London: Penguin, 1995).

Bettelheim, Bruno, *Freud and Man's Soul* (London: Hogarth Press, 1983).

Blaga, Lucian, *Orizont și Stil* (Bucharest: Fundația pentru Literatură și Artă 'Regele Carol II', 1936).

Blaga, Lucian, *Geneza Metaforei și Sensul Culturii* (Bucharest: Fundația pentru Literatură și Artă 'Regele Carol II', 1937).

Bleuler, Eugen, *Dementia Praecox or the Group of Schizophrenias*, English trans. Hoseph Zinkin (New York: International Universities Press, 1950; 1st German edn 1911).

Bloch, Sidney, and Paul Chodoff (eds), *Etică Psihiatrică*, trans. R. Țuculescu, A. Popescu, N. Bizamcer, and L. Cosma, ed. Valerian Țuculescu (Bucharest: The Association of Romanian Free Psychiatrists, Geneva Initiative on Psychiatry, 2000).

Blumenthal, H.J., 'Nous Pathêtikos in Later Greek Philosophy', *Oxford Studies in Ancient Philosophy*, supplement, 1991, pp. 191–206.

Boca, Fr Arsenie, *Cărarea Împărăției*, ed. Fr Simion Todoran and Nun Zamfira Constantinescu (Sibiu: Editura Episcopiei Ortodoxe Române a Aradului, 1995).

Bociurkiw, Bohdan R., 'Lenin and Religion', in Leonard Schapiro and Peter Reddaway (eds), *Lenin: The Man, the Theorist, the Leader* (London: Pall Mall Press, 1967), pp. 107–34.

Boghiu, Archimandrite Sofian, 'Rugul Aprins și Temnița', *Solia/The Herald* (Jackson, MI: July 1999), p. 20.

Boia, Lucian, *Istorie și Mit in Conștiința Românească*, 2nd edn (Bucharest: Humanitas, 1997).

Bonaventura, St, *Quaestiones (...) super primo libro sentencia[rum]* [Strassbourg: pr. of Henricus Ariminensis, c. 1474/77].

Bonhoeffer, Dietrich, *The Cost of Discipleship* (London: SCM Press, 1990).

Bordeianu, Dumitru, *Mărturisiri din Mlaștina Disperării*, 2nd edn (Bucharest: Scara, 1993).

Borisov, Vadim, 'Personality and National Awareness', in Alexander Solzhenitsyn, et al. (eds), *From under the Rubble*, trans. Michael Scammell (London: Fontana, 1975), pp. 194–228.

Bottomore, Tom, et al. (eds), *A Dictionary of Marxist Thought* (Oxford: Blackwell, 1983).

Bousquet, G.H., *Vilfredo Pareto: Sa Vie at Son Oeuvre* (Paris: Payot, 1928).

Bouyer, Louis, *Mystery and Mysticism*, ed. A. Plé and Louis Bouyer, et al. (New York: The Philosophical Library, 1956), pp. 18–32, 119–37.

Braga, Archimandrite Roman, *Exploring the Inner Universe, Joy – the Mystery of Life* (Rives Junction, MI: HDM Press, 1996).

Brătulescu, Victor, 'Sfântul Nicodim', *Mitropolia Olteniei, 600 Ani de la Întemeiere*, nr. 5–6, Craiova, 1970, pp. 587–98.

Brooke, John Hedley, *Science and Religion: Some Historical Perspectives* (Cambridge: Cambridge University Press, 1998).

Brown, J.A.C., *Freud and the Post-Freudians* (London: Penguin, 1961).

Brown, Lesley (ed.), *The New Shorter English Dictionary, on historical principles*, 2 vols (Oxford: Clarendon Press, 1993).

Brown, Peter, *The Body and Society: Men, Women, and Sexual Renunciation in Early Christianity* (New York: Columbia University Press, 1988).

Bukovsky, Vladimir, *To Build a Castle, My Life as a Dissenter* (London: André Deutsch, 1978).

Burnyeat, Myles, *The Theaetetus of Plato*, with a trans. of Plato's *Theaetetus* by M.J. Levett, rev. by Myles Burnyeat (Cambridge: Hackett, 1990).

Cabasilas, Nicholas, *The Life in Christ*, trans. Carmino J. de Catanzaro, introd. by Boris Bobrinskoy (New York: St Vladimir's Seminary Press, 1982).

Caillois, Roger, *Omul si Sacrul*, trans. Dan Petrescu (Bucharest: Nemira, 1997).

Calciu, Fr George, *Christ Is Calling You! A Course in Catacomb Pastorship* (Platina, CA: St Herman of Alaska Brotherhood, St Paisius Missionary School, 1997).

Călinescu, Nicolae, 'Procesele de Brainwashing', *Permanenţe*, Bucharest, February 1998, pp. 12–13.

Călinescu, Nicolae, *Sisteme şi Procese de Brainwashing în România Comunistă* (Bucharest: Gama, 1998).

Camus, Albert, *Le mythe de Sisyphe, essai sur l'absurde* (Paris: Gallimard, 1979).

Cavanaugh, William T., *Torture and Eucharist, Theology, Politics, and the Body of Christ* (Oxford: Blackwell, 1998).

Cave, David, *Mircea Eliade's Vision for a New Humanism* (Oxford: Oxford University Press, 1993).

Caygill, Howard, *A Kant Dictionary* (Oxford: Blackwell, 1995).

Chesterton, G.K., *Orthodoxy*, foreword by Philip Yancey (London: Hodder & Stoughton, 1996).

Cioran, E.M., *Oeuvres* (Paris: Gallimard, 1995).

Clark, Maudemarie, *Nietzsche on Truth and Philosophy* (Cambridge: Cambridge University Press, 1995).

Climacus, St John, *The Ladder of Divine Ascent*, trans. Colm Luibheid and Norman Russell, notes by Norman Russell, introd. by Kallistos Ware, preface by Colm Luibheid (London: SPCK, 1982).

Codrescu, Răzvan, *În căutarea Legiunii pierdute* (Bucharest: Vremea, 2001).

Constantinescu, Ştefan, et al. (eds), *Archive of Pain/Arhiva Durerii*, trans. Adrian Solomon, Allen Poole, and Joan Tate (Bucharest: Fundaţia Academia Civică, 2000).

Constantinescu, Zamfira, 'Post-scriptum la o lucrare de istorie a isihasmului românesc', *Gândirea*, Sibiu, January–March 1998, pp. 95–6.

Coposu, Corneliu, *Confesiuni, Dialoguri cu Doina Alexandru* (Bucharest: Anastasia, 1996).

Corban, Camelia, 'Părintele Iustin Pârvu – isvor al demnităţii româncşti', *Permanenţe*, Bucharest, March 2001, pp. 3–4.

Cornford, Francis M., *Plato's Theory of Knowledge, The 'Theaetetus' and the 'Sophist' of Plato*, trans. with comment. (London: Routledge, 1970).

Courtois, Stéphane, et al. (eds), *Le Livre Noir du Communisme, Crimes, terreur et répression* (Paris: Robert Laffont, 1997); Romanian trans. Maria Ivănescu, et al., *Cartea Neagră a Comunismului, Crime, teroare, represiune* (Bucharest: Humanitas, 1998), with an Addenda about Communist Romania.

Crainic, Nichifor, *Sfinţenia – Împlinirea Umanului, Curs de Teologie Mistică (1935–1936)*, ed. Hierodeacon Teodosie Paraschiv (Iassy: Editura Mitropoliei Moldovei şi Bucovinei, 1993).

Crainic, Nichifor, *Ortodoxie şi Etnocraţie, cu anexa: Programul Statului Etnocratic*, introd., notes, and ed. Constantin Schifirneţ (Bucharest: Albatros, 1997).

Crainic, Nichifor, *Dostoievski şi Creştinismul Rus*, foreword by Archbishop Bartolomeu Anania, afterword by Răzvan Codrescu (Cluj-Napoca, Bucharest: Arhidiecezana Cluj, Anastasia, 1998).

Cristi, Renato, *Carl Schmitt and Authoritarian Liberalism: Strong State, Free Economy* (Cardiff: University of Wales Press, 1998).

Cross, F.L. and E.A. Livingstone (eds), *The Oxford Dictionary of the Christian Church*, 3rd edn (Oxford: Oxford University Press, 1997).

Crouzel, Henri, *Origen*, trans. A.S. Worall (Edinburgh: T. & T. Clark, 1989).

Cruga, Dinu, *Trepte Duhovniceşti: Interviu cu Părintele Roman Braga* (Alba Iulia: Tipografia Arhiepiscopiei Ortodoxe Alba Iulia, 1998).

Cusa, Nicholas of, *Selected Spiritual Writings*, trans. and introd. by H. Lawrence Bond, preface by Morimichi Watanabe (New York: Paulist Press, 1997).

Dalzell, Thomas G., *The Dramatic Encounter of Divine and Human Freedom in the Theology of Hans Urs von Balthasar*, 2nd edn (Berne: Peter Lang, 2000).

Davies, Norman, *Europe, A History* (London: Pimlico, 1997).

de Chardin, Teilhard, *Le Milieu Divin, An Essay on the Interior Life* (London: Fontana, 1975).

Deletant, Dennis, *Ceauşescu and the Securitate, Coercion and Dissent in Romania, 1965–1989* (London: Hurst, 1995).

Deletant, Dennis, *România sub Regimul Comunist* (Bucharest: Fundaţia Academia Civică, 1997); English trans., *Romania under Communist Rule*, rev. 2nd edn (Oxford: The Centre for Romanian Studies in co-operation with the Civic Academy Foundation, 1999).

de Maistre, Joseph, *Les soirées de Saint-Pétersbourg, ou entretiens sur le gouvernement temporel de la Providence*, introd. by L. Arnould de Grémilly, notes by Pierre Mariel (Paris: La Colombe, 1960).

de Ruggiero, Guido, *The History of European Liberalism*, preface and trans. R.G. Collingwood (Boston: Beacon Press, 1959).

Dobre, Florica, and Alesandru Duţu, *Distrugerea Elitei Militare sub Regimul Ocupaţiei Sovietice în România, vol. 1, 1944–1946* (Bucharest: Academia Română, Institutul Naţional pentru Studiul Totalitarismului, 2000).

Douglas, J.D. (ed.), *The New Greek English Interlinear New Testament*, trans. Robert K. Brown and Philip W. Comfort (Wheaton, IL: Tyndale, 1990).

Dubovsky, Steven L., *Clinical Psychiatry* (Washington, DC: American Psychiatric Press, 1988).

Dumitrescu, G., *Demascarea* (Bucharest: Jon Dumitru & Mediana, 1996).

Dură, Fr Ioan, *Monahismul Românesc în anii 1948–1989, Mărturii ale românilor şi consideraţii privitoare la acestea* (Bucharest: Harisma, 1994).

Eagleton, Terry, 'Qui s'accuse, s'excuse', *London Review of Books*, London, 1 June 2000, pp. 34–5.

Edwards, Paul (ed.), *The Encyclopedia of Philosophy*, 8 vols (London: Collier-Macmillan, 1967), VII–VIII.

Eisler, Rudolf, *Kant-Lexikon*, ed. Anne-Dominique Balmès and Pierre Osmo (Paris: Gallimard, 1994).

Elchaninov, Fr Alexander, *The Diary of a Russian Priest*, trans. Helen Iswolsky, ed. Kallistos Ware, introd. by Tamara Elchaninov, foreword by Dimitri Obolensky (London: Faber and Faber, 1967).

Elder Basil of Poiana Mărului (1692–1767), His Life and Writings, trans. into English with introd. and notes by a Monk of the Brotherhood of Prophet Elias Skete, Mount Athos (Liberty, TN: St John of Kronstadt Press, 1996).

Eliade, Mircea, *A History of Religious Ideas*, trans. Willard R. Trusk, 3 vols (London: Chicago University Press, 1978–85).

Eliade, Mircea, *The Sacred and the Profane, The Nature of Religion*, trans. Willard R. Trask (London: Harcourt Brace, 1987).

Eliade, Mircea, *Patterns in Comparative Religion*, trans. Rosemary Sheed, introd. by John Clifford Holt (London: University of Nebraska Press, 1996).

Ellis, Jane, *The Russian Orthodox Church: Triumphalism and Defensiveness* (London: Macmillan, in assoc. with St Antony's College, Oxford, 1996).

Eminescu, Mihai, *Poesii*, ed. Titu Maiorescu (Bucharest: Socec, 1884).

Eminescu, Mihai, *Lecturi Kantiene, Traduceri din Critica Rațiunii Pure*, ed. C. Noica and Al. Surdu, fragments trans. Titu Maiorescu (Bucharest: Univers, 1975).

Eminescu, Mihai, *Opere Politice*, 3 vols (Iassy: Timpul, 1997–99), II (1998).

Erasmus of Rotterdam, *Praise of Folly and Letter to Maarten Van Dorp*, trans. Betty Radice, introd. and notes by A.H.T. Levi (London: Penguin, 1993).

Esslin, Martin, *The Theatre of the Absurd* (London: Penguin, 1980).

Evans, Ernest (ed.), *Tertullian's Treatise on the Incarnation*, introd., trans., and comment. by Ernest Evans (London: SPCK, 1956).

Evans, G.R., *Augustine on Evil* (Cambridge: Cambridge University Press, 1982).

Fackenheim, Emil L., *The Religious Dimension in Hegel's Thought* (Chicago: University of Chicago Press, 1967).

Fay, Ștefan J., *Sokrateion, Mărturie despre Mircea Vulcănescu*, 2nd edn (Bucharest: Humanitas, 1998).

Fernández-Armesto, Felipe, *The Times Guide to the Peoples of Europe* (London: Times Books, 1994).

Filocalia sfintelor nevoințe ale desăvârșirii sau culegere din scrierile sfinților Părinți care arată cum se poate omul curăți, lumina și desăvârși, 2nd edn, trans., introd., and notes by Fr D. Stăniloae, 12 vols (Bucharest: Humanitas, 1999–).

Foucault, Michel, *Surveiller et punir: Naissance de la prison* (Paris: Gallimard, 1975).

Fowl, Stephen E., and L. Gregory Jones, *Reading in Communion, Scripture and Ethics in Christian Life* (London: SPCK, 1991).

Frankl, Viktor E., *Man's Search for Meaning* (New York: Washington Square Press, 1985).

Freeden, Michael, 'Is Nationalism a Distinct Ideology?', *Political Studies*, XLVI, 1988, pp. 748–65.

Freppel, Mgr l'Abbé Charles Emile, *Tertullien – Cours d'éloquence sacrée fait à la Sorbonne, pendant l'année 1861–1862*, 2 vols (Paris: Ambroise Bray, 1864).

Freud, Sigmund, *Case Histories II, The 'Rat Man', Schreber, The 'Wolf Man', A Case of Female Homosexuality*, trans. under the general editorship of James Strachey, compiled and ed. Angela Richards (London: Penguin, 1979).

Freud, Sigmund, *Art and Literature: Jensen's Gradiva, Leonardo da Vinci and other works*, trans. under the general editorship of James Strachey, ed. Albert Dickson (London: Penguin, 1985).

Friedman, Maurice, *Problematic Rebel: Melville, Dostoievsky, Kafka, Camus*, rev. edn (Chicago: University of Chicago Press, 1970).

Fukuyama, Francis, *The End of History and the Last Man* (New York: Avon Books, 1993).

Gafencu, Grigore, *The Last Days of Europe* (London: F. Muller, 1947).

Gavrilă-Ogoranu, Ion, *Brazii se frâng, dar nu se îndoiesc*, 2 vols (Timișoara: Marineasa, 1993; 1995).

Georgescu, Vlad, *The Romanians: A History* (Columbus: Ohio State University Press, 1991).

Gerth, H.H., and C. Wright Mills, (eds), *From Max Weber: Essays in Sociology*, trans. H.H. Gerth and C. Wright Mills (London: Routledge, 1991).

Gheorghiță, Viorel, *Et Ego: Sărata–Pitești–Gherla–Aiud, Scurtă istorie a devenirii mele* (Timișoara: Marineasa, 1994).

Girard, René, *Things Hidden since the Foundation of the World*, trans. Stephen Bann and Michael Metteer (London: Athlone Press, 1987).

Girard, René, *Violence and the Sacred*, trans. Patrick Gregory (London: Athlone Press, 1995).

Giuran, Mihail, 'Crimele lui Andrei Coler', *Buletin de Informaţii al Românilor din Exil (BIRE)*, nr. 775, Paris, 16 May 1983, pp. 7–8.

Giurescu, Constantin G., et al. (eds), *Chronological History of Romania* (Bucharest: Editura Enciclopedică Română, 1972).

Giurescu, Dinu C., *The Razing of Romania's Past* (Washington, DC: The Preservation Press & World Monuments Fund, 1992).

Giurescu, Dinu C., *România în al Doilea Război Mondial* (Bucharest: All, 1999).

Gleason SJ, Robert W. (ed.), *The Essential Pascal*, trans. G.F. Pullen (London: Mentor-Omega, 1966).

Glossarium Mediae et Infimae Latinitatis, conditum a Carolo du Fresne... Editio Nova, 10 vols (Niort: L. Favre, 1885), V.

Gluzman, Dr Semyon, *On Soviet Totalitarian Psychiatry* (Amsterdam: International Association on the Political Use of Psychiatry, 1989).

Goblot, Edmond, *Vocabulaire philosophique* (Paris: Armand Colin, 1938).

Gozman, Leonid, and Alexander Etkind, *The Psychology of Post-Totalitarianism in Russia*, trans. Roger Clarke, preface by Charles Janson (London: CRCE, 1992).

Gracián, Baltasar, *Obras Completas, I*, ed. and introd. by Miguel Batllori y Ceferino Peralta (Madrid: Atlas, 1969).

Gracián, Baltasar, *The Art of Worldly Wisdom*, trans. Joseph Jacobs (London: Shambhala, 1993).

Graham, George, and G. Lynn Stephens, *Philosophical Psychopathology* (London: MIT Press, 1994).

Haag, John J., 'Othmar Spann and the Politics of "Totality": Corporatism in Theory and Practice' (unpublished D.Phil. thesis, Rice University, Houston, Texas, May 1969).

Hamilton, Malcolm, *The Sociology of Religion, Theoretical and Comparative Perspectives* (London: Routledge, 1995).

Hamilton, William, *Discussions on Philosophy and Literature, Education and University Reform*, 3rd edn (London: Blackwood, 1866).

Hamlyn, D.W., *The Penguin History of Western Philosophy* (London: Penguin, 1987).

Hare, R.M., *Plato* (Oxford: Oxford University Press, 1982).

Hausherr, Irénée, *Spiritual Direction in the Early Christian East*, trans. Anthony P. Gythiel, foreword by Kallistos Ware (Kalamazoo, MI: Cistercian Publications, 1990).

Havel, Václav, *Living in Truth, Twenty-two essays published on the occasion of the award of the Erasmus Prize to Václav Havel*, ed. Jan Vladislav (London: Faber and Faber, 1990).

Hegel, G.W.F., *Aesthetics, Lectures on Fine Art*, trans. T.M. Knox, 2 vols (Oxford: Clarendon Press, 1975).

Hegel, G.W.F, *Phenomenology of the Spirit*, trans. A.V. Miller, analysis of the text and foreword by J.N. Findlay (Oxford: Clarendon Press, 1977).

Heidegger, Martin, *Gesamtausgabe, Grundfragen der Philosophie*, ed. Friedrich-Wilhelm von Herrmann, winter semester 1937–38 (Frankfurt am Main: Vittorio Klostermann, 1984), vol. 45.

Henegaru, Nicolae, and Silvia Colfescu (eds), *Memorialul Ororii, Documente ale Procesului Reeducării din închisorile Piteşti, Gherla* (Bucharest: Vremea, 1995).

Hierotheos, Metropolitan of Nafpaktos, *The Mind of the Orthodox Church* trans. Esther Williams (Levadia-Hellas: Birth of the Theotokos Monastery, 1998).

Hierotheos, Metropolitan of Nafpaktos, *The Person in the Orthodox Tradition*, trans. Esther Williams (Levadia-Hellas: Birth of the Theotokos Monastery, 1998).

Hopkins, Gerard Manley, *Poems and Prose*, select. and ed. W.H. Gardner (London: Penguin, 1968).

Huntington, Samuel P., *The Clash of Civilizations and the Remaking of World Order* (London: Touchstone, 1998).

Ijsseling, Samuel, *Mimesis: On Appearing and Being*, trans. Hester Ijsseling and Jeffrey Bloechl (GA Kampen: Pharos, 1997).

Iliescu, Victor, *Fenomenologia Diabolicului* (Bucharest: Eminescu, 1995).

Iliescu, Victor, *Cele Trei Alibiuri şi Condiţia Noastră Umană Posttotalitară* (Bucharest: Vitruviu, 1999).

'Înalt Decret Regal', nr. 870/1938, *Monitorul Oficial*, nr. 39, 17 February 1938.

Ionescu, Aristide, *Dacă vine ora H, pe cine putem conta? File de jurnal*, 2nd rev. edn (Timişoara: Gordian, 1998).

Ionescu, Nae, *Între ziaristică şi filosofie* (Iassy: Timpul, 1996).

Iovan, Fr Ioan, *Memorialul durerii* (Tg. Mureş: Recea Monastery, no date).

Jela, Doina, *Lexiconul Negru, Unelte ale represiunii comuniste* (Bucharest: Humanitas, 2001).

Jivi, Aurel, *Orthodox, Catholics, and Protestants: Studies in Romanian Ecclesiastical Relations* (Cluj-Napoca: Cluj University Press, 1999).

Joantă, Père Romul, *Roumanie: Tradition et culture hésychastes*, foreword by Olivier Clément (Bégrolles-en-Mauges: Abbaye de Bellefontaine, 1987); English trans., *Romania: Its Hesychast Tradition and Culture* (Wildwood, CA: St Xenia Skete, 1992).

Jones, Cheslyn, Geoffrey Wainwright, Edward Yarnold SJ (eds), *The Study of Spirituality* (London: SPCK, 1986).

Jung, C.G., *The Undiscovered Self*, trans. R.F.C. Hull (London: Routledge & Kegan Paul, 1958).

Jung, C.G., *Jung: Selected Writings*, select. and introd. by Anthony Storr (London: Fontana, 1983).

Kant, Immanuel, *Critica raţiunii practice*, trans. Cristian Amzăr and Raul Vişan, with two introductions by C. Rădulescu-Motru and Nae Ionescu (Bucharest: Editura Institutului Social Român, undated).

Kant, Immanuel, *Prolegomena to Any Future Metaphysics That Will Be Able To Come Forward As Science*, the Paul Carus trans., newly rev. by James W. Ellington (Cambridge: Hackett, 1974).

Kant, Immanuel, *Der einzig mögliche Beweisgrund/The One Possible Basis for a Demonstration of God*, trans. and introd. by Gordon Treash (London: University of Nebraska Press, 1994).

Kant, Immanuel, *Critique of Pure Reason*, trans. Werner S. Pluhar, introd. by Patricia W. Kitcher (Cambridge: Hackett, 1996).

Kant, Immanuel, *Religion and Rational Theology*, trans. and ed. Allen W. Wood and George di Giovanni (Cambridge: Cambridge University Press, 1996).

Kant, Immanuel, *Critique of Practical Reason*, trans. H.W. Cassirer, ed. G. Heath King and Ronald Weitzman, with an introd. by D.M. MacKinnon (Milwaukee: Marquette University Press, 1998).

Kant, Immanuel, *Critique of the Power of Judgement*, ed. Paul Guyer, trans. Paul Guyer and Eric Matthews (Cambridge: Cambridge University Press, 2000).

Kaufmann, Walter (ed.), *The Portable Nietzsche*, trans. Walter Kaufmann (New York: Penguin, 1954).

Kautsky, Karl, *Terrorism and Communism: A Contribution to the Natural History of Revolution*, trans. W.H. Kerridge (London: National Labour Press, 1920).

Kearney, Richard, *Heidegger's Three Gods, with a response by Martin Warner* (University of Warwick: Centre for Research in Philosophy and Literature, 1992).

Kempis, Thomas à, *The Imitation of Christ*, trans. Betty I. Knott (Glasgow: Collins, Fount, 1990).

Kligman, Gail, *The Politics of Duplicity, Controlling Reproduction in Ceauşescu's Romania* (Los Angeles: University of California Press, 1998).

Lalande, André, *Vocabulaire technique et critique de la philosophie*, 6th edn, 2 vols (Paris: Presses Universitaires de France, 1988).

Lampe, G.W.H. (ed.), *A Patristic Greek Lexicon* (Oxford: Clarendon Press, 1976).

Laplanche, Jean, and J.-B. Pontalis, *Vocabulaire de la Psychanalyse* (Paris: Presses Universitaires de France, 1990).

Larchet, Jean-Claude, *Thérapeutique des maladies spirituelles. Une introduction à la tradition ascétique de l'Église orthodoxe*, 3rd rev. edn (Paris: Éd. du Cerf, 1997).

Lebovics, Herman, *Social Conservatism and the Middle Class Germany, 1914–1933* (Princeton, NJ: Princeton University Press, 1969).

Lehmann, Hartmut, *Max Webers 'Protestantische Ethik'* (Goetingen: Vandenhoeck & Ruprecht, 1996).

Lenger, Friedrich, *Werner Sombart, 1863–1941, Eine Biographie* (München: C.H. Beck, 1994).

Letson, Douglas, and Michael Higgins, *The Jesuit Mystique* (London: Fount, 1996).

Lossky, Vladimir, *The Mystical Theology of the Eastern Church* (Cambridge: James Clarke, 1973).

Louth, Andrew, *The Origins of the Christian Mystical Tradition* (Oxford: Clarendon Press, 1981).

Lüder, Elsa, 'Corina Leon Sombart (Iaşi–Berlin–Heidelberg)', *Dacia Literară*, 5:13, nr. 2, Iassy, 1994, pp. 29–30.

Macdonald, A.M. (ed.), *Chambers Twentieth Century Dictionary*, rev. edn, with supplement (Edinburgh: T. & A. Constable, 1977).

Mailleux, Paul, *Exarch Leonid Feodorov: Bridgebuilder between Moscow and Rome* (New York: P.J. Kennedy and Sons, 1964).

Makarenko, Anton S., *Problems of Soviet School Education*, compiled by V. Aransky and A. Piskunov, trans. O. Shartse (Moscow: Progress Publishers, 1965).

Makarenko, Anton S., *The Road to Life (An Epic of Education), Book One*, trans. Ivy and Tatiana Litvinov (Moscow: Progress Publishers, 1973).

Manolescu, Nicolae, 'Mircea Eliade', *România Literară*, Bucharest, 19–25 March 1997, p. 1.

Manolescu, Nicolae, 'Declaraţie', *România Literară*, Bucharest, 11–17 November 1998, p. 1.

Mantzaridis, Georgios I., *The Deification of Man: St Gregory Palamas and the Orthodox Tradition*, trans. Liadain Sherrard, foreword by Kallistos Ware (Crestwood, NY: St Vladimir's Seminary Press, 1984).

Marcel, Gabriel, *The Mystery of Being*, trans. René Hague, 2 vols (London: Harvill Press, 1951).

Mărculescu, Radu, *Pătimiri şi Iluminări din Captivitatea Sovietică* (Bucharest: Albatros, 2000).

Marshall, Gordon (ed.), *The Concise Oxford Dictionary of Sociology* (Oxford: Oxford University Press, 1994).

Martin, Luther H., Huck Gutman, and Patrick H. Hutton (eds), *Technologies of the Self: A Seminar with Michel Foucault* (Amherst: University of Massachusetts Press, 1988).

Mason, A.J., (ed.), *Fifty Spiritual Homilies of St Macarius the Egyptian* (London: SPCK, 1921).

Maxim, Virgil, *Nuntaşul Cerului (Isihas), Poeme creştine cu teme isihaste* (Zalău: [n. pub.], 1992).

Maxim, Virgil, *Imn pentru Crucea Purtată*, 2 vols (Timişoara: Gordian, 1997).

Maximus the Confessor, St, *Ambigua*, trans., introd., and notes by D. Stăniloae (Bucharest: Editura Institutului Biblic şi de Misiune al Bisericii Ortodoxe Române, 1983).

Mazilu, Dumitru, *Revoluția Furată, Memoriu pentru Țara mea* (Bucharest: Cozia, 1991).

McClendon, Jr, James William, *Systematic Theology Ethics* (Nashville, TN: Abingdon Press, 1986).

McCutcheon, Russell T. (ed.), *The Insider/Outsider Problem in the Study of Religion, A Reader* (London: Cassell, 1999).

McGinn, Bernard, *The Foundations of Mysticism, Origins of the Fifth Century* (London: SCM Press, 1992).

McPherran, Mark L., *The Religion of Socrates* (University Park, PA: Pennsylvania University Press, 1996).

Mehring, Reinhard, *Carl Schmitt zur Einführung* (Hamburg: Junius, 2000).

Meinong's Theory of Objects and Values, 2nd edn, trans. and ed. J.N. Findlay (Oxford: Clarendon Press, 1963).

Meyendorff, John, *A Study of Gregory Palamas*, trans. George Lawrence (New York: The Faith Press, St Vladimir's Seminary Press, 1974).

Meyendorff, John, *Christ in Eastern Christian Thought* (Crestwood, NY: St Vladimir's Seminary Press, 1975).

Meyendorff, John, *St Gregory Palamas and Orthodox Spirituality*, trans. Adele Fiske (Crestwood, NY: St Vladimir's Seminary Press, 1998).

Migne, J.P., (ed.), *Patrologia Cursus Completus: Series Latina*, 221 vols (Paris: Ateliers Catholiques, 1844–64).

Migne, J.P., (ed.), *Patrologia Cursus Completus: Series Graeca*, 162 vols (Paris: Ateliers Catholiques, 1857–66).

Miller, Charles, *The Gift of the World, An Introduction to the Theology of Dumitru Stăniloae* (Edinburgh: T. & T. Clark, 2000).

Mitchell, Nathan D., *Liturgy and the Social Sciences* (Collegeville, MN: Liturgical Press, 1999).

Miu, Constantin, *Vasile Voiculescu – Poet Isihast* (Bucharest: Florile Dalbe, 1997).

Mladenatz, Gromoslav, *Socialismul și Cooperația* (Bucharest: Independența Economică, 1946).

Mourelatos, Alexander P.D. (ed.), *The Pre-Socratics, A Collection of Critical Essays* (Princeton, NJ: Princeton University Press, 1993).

Musurillo SJ, Herbert (ed), *From Glory to Glory, Texts from Gregory of Nyssa's Mystical Writings*, trans. Herbert Musurillo SJ, and introd. by Jean Daniélou (Crestwood, NY: St Vladimir's Seminary Press, 1995).

Nandriș-Cudla, Anița, *Twenty Years in Siberia*, trans. Mabel Nandriș, afterword by Gheorghe Nandriș (Bucharest: Editura Fundației Culturale Române, 1998).

Năstase, Puiu (Petre Grigore C. Anastasis), *Înfruntarea: Reeducările de la Gherla* (Bucharest: Ramida, 1997).

Neagoe, Stelian, *Istoria Guvernelor României, de la începuturi – 1859 până în zilele noastre – 1995* (Bucharest: Machiavelli, 1995).

Nellas, Panayiotis, *Deification in Christ, Orthodox Perspectives on the Nature of the Human Person*, trans. Norman Russell (Crestwood, NY: St Vladimir's Seminary Press, 1987).

Neoplatonic Saints, The Lives of Plotinus and Proclus by their Students, trans. and introd. by Mark Edwards (Liverpool: Liverpool University Press, 2000).

Newman, Jr, Barclay M., *A Concise Greek–English Dictionary of the New Testament* (Stuttgart: Deutsche Bibelgesellschaft, United Bible Societies, 1971).

Nicholl, Donald, *The Beatitude of Truth, Reflections of a Lifetime*, ed. Adrian Hastings (London: Darton, Longman and Todd, 1997).

Nichols OP, Aidan, *No Bloodless Myth, A Guide Through Balthasar's Dramatics* (Edinburgh: T. & T. Clark, 2000).

Nietzsche, Friedrich, *The Birth of Tragedy and the Case of Wagner*, trans. and comment. by
    Walter Kaufmann (New York: Vintage Books, 1967).
Nietzsche, Friedrich, *The Gay Science, with a Prelude in Rhymes and an Appendix of Songs*,
    trans. and comment. by Walter Kaufmann (New York: Vintage Books, 1974).
Nietzsche, Friedrich, *Human, All Too Human, A book for free spirits*, trans. R.J. Hollingdale,
    introd. by Erich Heller (Cambridge: Cambridge University Press, 1986).
Noica, Constantin, *Mathesis sau Bucuriile Simple* (Bucharest: Humanitas, 1992).
Noica, Constantin, *Şase Maladii ale Spiritului Contemporan* (Bucharest: Humanitas, 1997).
North, Gary, *Marx's Religion of Revolution, Regeneration Through Chaos* (Fort Worth, TX:
    Institute for Christian Economics, 1989).
O'Donovan, Oliver, *The Desire of the Nations: Rediscovering the Roots of Political Theology*
    (Cambridge: Cambridge University Press, 1996).
Onfray, Michel, *Le Ventre des Philosophes, Critique de la Raison Diététique* (Paris: Grasset &
    Fasquelle, 1989).
Oprişan, Constantin, and Ştefan Vlădoianu, *Doi Poeţi Damnaţi, Versuri memorate în
    închisoare de Gheorghe Calciu, Iosif V. Iosif si Marcel Petrişor* (Bucharest: Majadahonda,
    Fundaţia 'Profesor George Manu', 1995).
Origen, *On First Principles*, being Koetschau's text of the *De Principiis*, trans., introd., and ed.
    George W. Butterworth (London: SPCK, 1936).
The Orthodox Study Bible, New Testament and Psalms (Nashville, TN: Thomas Nelson, 1993).
Osipova, Irina, *Se il mondo vi odia...: Martiri per la fede nel regime sovietico* (Milano: R.C.
    Edizioni La Casa di Matriona, 1987).
Otto, Rudolf, *The Idea of the Holy, An Inquiry into the non-rational factor in the idea of the
    divine and its relation to the rational*, 2nd edn, English trans. John W. Harvey (Oxford:
    Oxford University Press, 1950).
Pals, Daniel L., *Seven Theories of Religion* (Oxford: Oxford University Press, 1996).
Pană, Zahu (ed.), *Poezii din închisori* (Hamilton, Canada: Editura 'Cuvântul Românesc', 1982).
Pandrea, Petre, *Beiträge zu Montesquieus deutschen Rechtsquellen, Eine Untersuchung der
    hinterlassenen Manuskripte* (Bucharest: Cartea Românească, 1934).
Pandrea, Petre, *Brâncuşi, Amintiri şi Exegeze* (Bucharest: Meridiane, 1976).
Papu, Edgar, *Lumini Perene* (Bucharest: Eminescu, 1989).
Părăian, Archimandrite Teofil, 'Neoisihasmul, "O Bucurie"', *Altarul Banatului*, Timişoara,
    April–June 1998, pp. 136–40.
Parry, Ken, et al. (eds), *The Blackwell Dictionary of Eastern Christianity*, foreword by Kallistos
    Ware (Oxford: Blackwell, 1999).
Partington, Angela (ed.), *The Oxford Dictionary of Quotations*, 4th edn (London: Oxford
    University Press, 1992).
Pegis, Anton C. (ed.), *The Basic Writings of Saint Thomas Aquinas*, with introd. and notes,
    2 vols (Cambridge: Hackett, 1997).
Petculescu, Constantin, and Alexandru Florian (eds), *Ideea care ucide, Dimensiunile
    ideologiei legionare* (Bucharest: Institutul de Teorie Socială al Academiei Române, Editura
    Noua Alternativă, 1994).
Petrescu, Aspazia Oţel, *Strigat-am către Tine, Doamne...* (Bucharest: Fundaţia Culturală Buna
    Vestire, 2000).
*The Philokalia. The Complete Text Compiled by St Nikodimos of the Holy Mountain and St
    Makarios of Corinth*, trans. G.E.H. Palmer, Philip Sherrard, and Kallistos Ware, 4 vols
    (London: Faber and Faber, 1979–95).
Physical and Mental Consequences of Imprisonment and Torture, Lectures Presented at the
    Conference at Lysebu near Oslo, 5–7 October 1973 (London: Amnesty International, 1973).

Physiologie du Goût ou Méditations de gastronomie transcendante, par un Professeur (Bruxelles: J.P. Meline, 1835).

Piccone, Paul, 'Ostracizing Carl Schmitt: Letters to "The New York Review of Books"', *Telos*, nr. 109, Fall 1996, pp. 87–91.

Pichler, J. Hanns (ed.), *Othmar Spann, oder: Die Welt als Ganzes* (Wien: Böhlau, c. 1988).

Pickstock, Catherine, *After Writing, On the Liturgical Consummation of Philosophy* (Oxford: Blackwell, 1998).

Plămădeală, Antonie, *Rugul Aprins* (Sibiu: Tipografia Eparhială Sibiu, 2000).

Plato, *Protagoras and Meno*, trans. W.K.C. Guthrie (London: Penguin, 1956).

Plato, *Phaedrus and Letters VII and VIII*, trans. Walter Hamilton (London: Penguin, 1973).

Plato, *Phaedrus*, with trans. and comment. by C.J. Rowe (Warminster, Wiltshire: Aris & Phillips, 1986).

Plato, *The Republic*, 2nd edn, trans. and introd. by Desmond Lee (London: Penguin, 1987).

Plato, *Phaidon*, Romanian trans. Petru Creția, introd. and notes by Manuela Tecușan (Bucharest: Humanitas, 1994).

Platon, *Scrisori (1–13)*, trans., foreword, and notes by Adelina Piatkowski (Bucharest: Humanitas, 1997).

Podgoreanu, Traian, *Curs de Filosofie Marxistă*, 5th edn, 2 vols (Bucharest: University of Bucharest, 1981).

Polanyi, Michael, *Personal Knowledge, Towards a Post-Critical Philosophy* (London: Routledge, 1998).

Popescu, Alexandru, 'Psychiatric Abuse in Romania Today', communication to Jubilee Campaign/Parliamentary Human Rights Group, Parliamentary Briefing Session: *Romania's Psychiatric Prison Hospitals* (London: The House of Commons, 7 November 1991).

Popescu, Alexandru, 'Archimandrite Cleopa Ilie, The good shepherd: Obituary', *Guardian*, London, 8 December 1998, p. 18.

Popescu, Alexandru, 'Tradition as the Transfigured Cross', *Fairacres Chronicle*, 34:1, Oxford, Spring 2001, pp. 14–22.

Popescu, Emilian, *Christianitas Daco-Romana* (Bucharest: Editura Academiei Române, 1994).

Popescu, Florentin, *Detenția și Sfârșitul lui V. Voiculescu* (Bucharest: Vestala, 2000).

Popescu, Traian, *Experimentul Pitești, Terorismul din închisorile Pitești, Gherla, Canal, Tg. Ocna, Atacul brutalității asupra conștiinței* (Bucharest: Crater, 2000).

Potts, Timothy C., *Conscience in Medieval Philosophy* (Cambridge: Cambridge University Press, 1980).

Putnam, Hilary, *Reason, Truth, and History* (Cambridge: Cambridge University Press, 1981).

Quick reference to Diagnostic Criteria from DSM–IV^{TM} (Washington, DC: American Psychiatric Association, 1994).

Rădulescu, Mihai, *Casa Lacrimilor Neplânse. Martor al Acuzării în Procesul 'Reeducatorilor'* (Bucharest: Ramida, 1993).

Rădulescu-Motru, Constantin, *Revizuiri și Adăugiri, vol. 6, 1948*, ed. Rodica Bichis (Bucharest: Floarea Darurilor, 2000).

Rahner, Karl, and Herbert Vorgrimler, *Concise Theological Dictionary*, ed. Cornelius Ernst, OP, trans. Richard Strachan (London: Burns & Oates, 1968).

'Rasstrelyannyi Arkhipastyr', *Tserkovnyi vestnik Rostovskoi eparkhii*, nr. 5 (68), Rostov-on-Don, May 1999, p. 5.

Rawls, John, *A Theory of Justice* (Oxford: Oxford University Press, 1973).

Reber, Arthur S. (ed.), *The Penguin Dictionary of Psychology* (London: Penguin, 1985).

Reid, Thomas, *An Inquiry into the Human Mind*, ed. and introd. by Timothy Duggan (Chicago: University of Chicago Press, 1970).

Rennie, Bryan S., *Reconstructing Eliade, Making Sense of Religion*, foreword by Mac Linscott Rickets (New York: State University of New York Press, 1996).

Rickert, Heinrich, *Die Grenzen der naturwissenschaftlichen Begriffsbildung: Eine logische Einleitung in die historischen Wissenschaften*, 4th edn (Tübingen: Mohr, 1921; 1st edn 1902).

Rickert, Heinrich, *Die Philosophie des Lebens. Darstellung und Kritik der philosophischen Modeströmungen unserer Zeit*, 2nd edn (Tübingen: Mohr, 1922; 1st edn 1920).

Rickert, Heinrich, *Die Gegenstand der Erkenntnis*, 6th edn (Tübingen: Mohr, 1928; 1st edn 1892).

Rickert, Heinrich, *Science and History: A Critique of Positivist Epistemology*, trans. George Reisman, ed. Arthur Goddard (London: D. Van Nostrand, 1962).

Rist, J.M., *Plotinus, The Road to Reality* (Cambridge: Cambridge University Press, 1967).

Robul 1036 (Traian Trifan), *Mărturisesc* (Bucharest: Scara, 1998).

Rusan, Romulus (ed.), *Analele Sighet 9, Anii 1961–1972: Țările Europei de Est, între speranțele reformei și realitatea stagnării* (Bucharest: Fundația Academia Civică, 2001).

Russell, Norman, 'The Concept of Deification in the Early Greek Fathers' (unpublished D.Phil. dissertation, The University of Oxford, Trinity 1988).

Russkie Monastyri, Tsentralnaya Chast' Rossii (Moscow: Ocharovannyi strannik, 1995).

Samuels, Andrew, Bani Shorter, and Fred Plaut, *A Critical Dictionary of Jungian Analysis* (London: Routledge, 1991).

Schapiro, Leonard, *The Communist Party of the Soviet Union* (London: Methuen, 1963).

Schapiro, Leonard, and Peter Reddaway (eds), *Lenin: The Man, the Theorist, the Leader* (London: Pall Mall Press, 1967).

Schapiro, Leonard, *Totalitarianism* (London: Pall Mall, 1972).

Scheler, Max, *Ressentiment*, trans. William W. Holdheim, introd. by Lewis A. Coser (New York: Free Press, 1961).

Scheler, Max, *Der Formalismus in der Ethik und die materiale Wertethik*, 5th edn, ed. Maria Scheler (Bern: Francke, 1966); English trans. Manfred S. Frings and Roger L. Funck *Formalism in Ethics and Non-Formal Ethics of Values, A New Attempt toward the Foundation of an Ethical Personalism* (Evanston, IL: Northwestern University Press, 1973).

Scheler, Max, *On Feeling, Knowing, and Valuing*, ed. and introd. by Harold J. Bershady (Chicago: Chicago University Press, 1992).

Schmemann, Alexander, *For the Life of the World, Sacraments and Orthodoxy* (Crestwood, NY: St Vladimir's Seminary Press, 1968).

Schmidt, Heinrich, *Philosophisches Wörterbuch*, 9th edn (Leipzig: Alfred Kröner, 1934).

Schmitt, Carl, *Political Theology, Four Chapters on the Concept of Sovereignty*, trans. and introd. George Schwab (Cambridge, MA: MIT Press, 1985).

Schmitt, Carl, *The Crisis of Parliamentary Democracy*, trans. Ellen Kennedy (London: MIT Press, 1988).

Schmitt, Carl, *The Concept of the Political*, trans. and introd. by George Schwab, new foreword by Tracy B. Strong (London: Chicago University Press, 1996).

Scholem, Gershom, *On the Kabbalah and Its Symbolism*, trans. Ralph Manheim, foreword by Bernard McGinn (New York: Schocken Books, 1996).

Schopenhauer, Arthur, *Philosophical Writings*, ed. Wolfgang Schirmacher, trans. E.F.J. Paine (New York: Continuum, 1998).

Scobie, Alex, *Hitler's State Architecture, The Impact of Classical Antiquity* (London: The Pennsylvania State University Press, 1990).

Scrima, André, *Timpul Rugului Aprins, Maestrul Spiritual în Tradiția Răsăriteană*, foreword by Andrei Pleșu, ed. Anca Manolescu (Bucharest: Humanitas, 1996).

Scruton, Roger, *Kant* (Oxford: Oxford University Press, 1996).

Sertillanges, A.D., *Dieu ou rien?*, 2 vols (Paris: Flammarion, 1933).

Seuleanu, Dragoş, and Carmen Dumitriu (eds), *Amintirile Mitropolitului Antonie Plămădeală* (Bucharest: Cum, 1999).

Shaw, Fr Gilbert, 'Recovery' (unpublished address to the Community of the Sisters of the Love of God, Oxford, 1962).

Sherrard, Philip, *The Sacred in Life and Art* (Ipswich: Golgonooza, 1990).

Sherrard, Philip, *Christianity, Lineaments of a Sacred Tradition*, foreword by Kallistos Ware (Edinburgh: T. & T. Clark, 1998).

Sills, David L. (ed.), *International Encyclopedia of the Social Sciences*, 17 vols (London: Free Press, 1968), XXIV.

Simedrea, Tit, 'Viaţa mănăstirească în Ţara Românească înainte de anul 1370', *Biserica Ortodoxă Română*, 80:7–8, 1962, pp. 673–87.

Simmel, Georg, *Die Probleme der Geschichtsphilosophie, Eine erkenntnistheoretische Studie*, 5th edn (Munich: Duncker & Humblot, 1923).

Simmel, Georg, *Hauptprobleme der Philosophie*, 7th edn (Berlin: Walter de Gruyter, 1950).

Simmel, Georg, *Brücke und Tür, Essays des Philosophen zur Geschichte, Religion, Kunst und Gesellschaft*, select. by Margarete Susman, ed. Michael Landmann (Stuttgart: K.F. Koehler, 1957).

Simmel, Georg, *On Individuality and Social Forms, Selected Writings*, ed. and introd. by Donald N. Levine (Chicago: University of Chicago Press: 1971).

Simmel, Georg, *The Problems of the Philosophy of History, An Epistemological Essay*, trans., ed., and introd. by Guy Oakes (New York: Free Press, 1977).

Simmel, Georg, *Rembrandt, Ein kunstphilosophischer Versuch* (Leipzig: Kurt Wolff, 1916); Romanian trans. and foreword by Grigore Popa, *Rembrandt*, introd. by Ion Frunzetti (Bucharest: Meridiane, 1978).

Simon, Ulrich, *A Theology of Auschwitz* (London: SPCK, 1978).

Simpson, J.A., and E.S.C. Weiner (eds), *The Oxford English Dictionary*, 2nd edn, 20 vols (Oxford: Clarendon Press, 1989), IX.

Skvorecky, Josef, *The Cowards*, trans. Jeanne Němková (London: Penguin, 1980).

Snyder, Louis L., *Encyclopedia of the Third Reich* (Ware, Hertfordshire: Wordsworth, 1998).

Solacolu, Barbu, *Sombart, în marginea omului şi a operei* (Bucharest: Analele Economice şi Statistice, 1930).

Solzhenitsyn, Aleksandr I., *The Gulag Archipelago, 1918–1956, An Experiment in Literary Investigation, I–II*, trans. Th.P. Whitney (London: Harper & Row, 1974).

Sombart, Nicolaus, *Jugend in Berlin, 1933–1943. Ein Bericht* (Frankfurt am Main: Fischer Taschenbuch, 1994).

Sombart, Werner, *Das Lebenswerk von Karl Marx* (Jena: Gustav Fischer, 1909).

Sombart, Werner, *Die Juden und das Wirtschaftsleben* (Leipzig: Duncker & Humblot, 1920; 1st edn 1911); English trans. M. Epstein, *The Jews and Modern Capitalism* (London: T.F. Unwin, 1913).

Sombart, Werner, *Le Bourgeois, Contribution à l'histoire morale et intellectuelle de l'homme économique moderne*, trans. Dr S. Jankélévitch (Paris: Payot, 1926).

Sombart, Werner, *Vom Menschen. Versuch einer geisteswissenschaftlichen Anthropologie*, 2nd edn (Berlin: Duncker & Humblot, 1956; 1st edn 1938).

Spann, Othmar, *Der wahre Staat, Vorlesungen über Abbruch und Neubau der Gesellschaft*, rev. edn (Leipzig: Quelle & Meyer, 1923; 1st edn 1921).

Spann, Othmar, *Kategorienlehre* (Jena: Gustav Fischer, 1924).

Speake, Jennifer, Antony Flew, et al. (eds), *A Dictionary of Philosophy* (London: Macmillan, 1984).

Spengler, Oswald, *The Decline of the West*, abridged edn by Helmut Werner, trans. Charles Francis Atkinson, ed. Arthur Helps (Oxford: Oxford University Press, 1991).

Spranger, Eduard, *Lebensformen, Geisteswissenschaftliche Psychologie und Ethik der Persönlichkeit*, 5th rev. edn (Halle: Max Niemeyer, 1925); English trans. Paul J.W. Pigors, *Types of Men, The Psychology and Ethics of Personality* (Halle: Max Niemeyer, 1928).

Stănescu, Flori, and Dragoş Zamfirescu, *Ocupaţia Sovietică în România, Documente 1944–1946* (Bucharest: Vremea, 1998).

Stănescu, Mircea, 'Istorie, memorie şi practică în editarea lui Petre Pandrea', *Memoria*, 34, January 2001, pp. 106–20.

Stăniloae, Dumitru, *Ortodoxie şi Românism* (Sibiu: Tiparul Tipografiei Arhidiecezane, 1939).

Stăniloae, Dumitru, 'The Orthodox Conception of Tradition and the Development of Doctrine', *Sobornost*, 5:9, Summer 1969, pp. 652–62.

Stăniloae, Dumitru, *Din Istoria Isihasmului în Ortodoxia Română* (Bucharest: Scripta, 1992).

Stăniloae, Dumitru, *Iisus Hristos sau Restaurarea Omului* (Craiova: Omniscop, 1993).

Stăniloae, Dumitru, *Trăirea lui Dumnezeu în Ortodoxie* (Cluj-Napoca: Dacia, 1993).

Stăniloae, Dumitru, *Viaţa şi Învăţătura Sfântului Grigorie Palama, cu patru tratate traduse*, 2nd rev. edn (Bucharest: Scripta, 1993; 1st edn 1938).

Stăniloae, Dumitru, *The Experience of God* (Brookline: Holy Cross, 1994), p. 45.

Steinhardt, Nicolae, *Jurnalul Fericirii* (Cluj-Napoca: Dacia, 1991).

Stenzel, Julius, *Platon der Erzieher*, introd. by Konrad Gaiser (Hamburg: Felix Meiner, 1928; repr. 1961).

Stoica, Victor, *Soldaţii de Plumb* (Iassy: Polirom, 1996).

Suzuki, David, and Holly Dressel, *Naked Ape to Superspecies, A Personal Perspective on Humanity and the Global Ecocrisis* (St Leonards, Australia: Allen & Unwin, 1999).

Swedberg, Richard, *Max Weber and the Idea of Economic Sociology* (Princeton, NJ: Princeton University Press, 1998).

Swinburne, Richard, *The Evolution of the Soul*, rev. edn (Oxford: Clarendon Press, 1997).

Symeon the New Theologian, St, *The Discourses*, trans. C.J. de Catanzaro, introd. by George Maloney S.J., preface by Basil Krivocheine (London: SPCK, 1980).

Symeon the New Theologian, St, *On the Mystical Life, The Ethical Discourses*, trans. Alexander Golitzin, 3 vols (Crestwood, NY: St Vladimir's Seminary Press, 1995–97), III: *Life, Times and Theology* (1997).

Talaban, Iréna, *Terreur communiste et résistance culturelle: Les arracheurs de masques* (Paris: Presses Universitaires de France, 2000).

Témoin de Dieu chez les sans-Dieu: Journal de prison de Mgr Boleslas Sloskans (Paris: Aide à l'Eglise en Détresse, 1986).

Tertullian, *Apology, De Spectaculis* and Minucius Felix, *Octavius*, trans. T.R. Glover and G.H. Rendall (London: Heinemann, 1966).

Thau, C., and A. Popescu, 'Romanian Psychiatry in Turmoil', *Bulletin of Medical Ethics*, 78, May 1992, pp. 13–19.

Thunberg, Lars, *Man and the Cosmos, The Vision of St Maximus the Confessor* (Crestwood, NY: St Vladimir's Seminary Press, 1985).

Thunberg, Lars, *Microcosm and Mediator, The Theological Anthropology of Maximus the Confessor*, 2nd edn, foreword by A.M. Allchin (Chicago: Open Court, 1995).

Tilea, Ileana (ed.), *Envoy Extraordinary, Memoirs of a Romanian Diplomat: Viorel Virgil Tilea* (London: Haggerston, 1998).

Timaru, Mihai, 'Mecanismele terorii', *Memoria*, 33, April 2000, pp. 102–7.

Tismăneanu, Vladimir, 'Understanding national Stalinism: reflections on Ceauşescu's socialism', *Communist and Post-Communist Studies*, 32, 1999, pp. 155–73.

Trethowan, Illtyd, *Mysticism and Theology, An Essay in Christian Metaphysics* (London: Geoffrey Chapman, 1975).

Trifoiu, Nicolae (ed.), *Studentul Valeriu Gafencu, Sfântul închisorilor din România* (Cluj-Napoca: Napoca Star, 1998).

Tserkovnyi vestnik Rostovskoi eparkhii, nr. 5 (68), Rostov-on-Don, May 1999.

Tucker, Robert C. (ed.), *The Marx–Engels Reader*, 2nd edn (London: Norton, 1978).

Tudorică, Nae, *Mărturisiri în Duhul Adevărului, Mişcarea Legionară şi Căpitanul aşa cum au fost* (Bacău: Plumb, 1993).

Turner, Denys, *The Darkness of God, Negativity in Christian Mysticism* (Cambridge: Cambridge University Press, 1998).

Vaihinger, Hans, *Die Philosophie des Als Ob: System der theoretischen, praktischen und religiösen Fiktionen der Menschheit auf Grund eines idealistischen Positivismus*, 3rd rev. edn (Leipzig: Felix Meiner, 1918; 1st edn 1911); English trans. C.K. Ogden *The Philosophy of 'As if', A System of the Theoretical, Practical and Religious Fictions of Mankind*, 6th edn, (London: Kegan Paul, 1924).

Vălenaş, Liviu, *Convorbiri cu Mircea Dimitriu: Mişcarea Legionară, între adevăr şi mistificare* (Timişoara: Marineasa, 2000).

Vanhoozer, Kevin, 'Human being, individual and social', in Colin Gunton (ed.), *The Cambridge Companion to Christian Doctrine* (Cambridge: Cambridge University Press, 1997), pp. 158–88.

Vasilachi, Hieromonk Vasile, *Predica în Evul Mediu* (Iassy: Institutul de Arte Grafice 'Albina Românească', 1938).

Vasilachi, Fr Dr Vasile, *Another World, Memories from Communist Prisons* (New York: [n. pub.], 1987).

Vasilescu, Gheorghe, *Benedict Ghiuş, Duhovnicul Inimii*, foreword by Archimandrite Sofian Boghiu, *starets* of Antim Monastery (Bucharest: România Creştină, 1998).

Vasilescu, Gheorghe (ed.), *Cuviosul Ioan cel Străin (Din Arhiva Rugului Aprins)*, afterword by Archimandrite Sofian Boghiu (Bucharest: Anastasia, 1999).

Velichkovsky, St Paisy, *Dobrotolyubie* (Moscow: 1793; Romanian Academy Library, MS III 603560); anastatic reproduction, ed. with an introd. by Dan Zamfirescu (Bucharest: Roza Vânturilor, 1990).

Viaţa, Acatistul şi Paraclisul Sfântului Nicodim cel Sfinţit (Tismana: Tismana Monastery, 2000).

Vlachos, Archimandrite Hierotheos, *Orthodox Psychotherapy, The Science of the Fathers*, trans. Esther Williams (Levadia: Birth of the Theotokos Monastery, 1994).

Voicescu, Fr Constantin, 'Cuvânt la slujba de înmormântare a martirilor de la Târgu Ocna', *Din Documentele Rezistenţei*, nr. 5, Arhiva Asociaţiei Foştilor Deţinuti Politici din România, Bucharest, 1992, pp. 269–83.

Voinea, Octavian, *Masacrarea Studenţimii Române în închisorile de la Piteşti, Gherla şi Aiud, Mărturii*, ed. Gheorghe Andreica (Bucharest: Majadahonda, 1996).

Voix de l'effroi, La Roumanie sous le communisme, Récits et Témoignages, trans. Luc Verly (Bucharest and Versailles: Editura M.C. and Association Europe Chrétienne, 2000).

Voltaire, *Le Temple du Goût*, ed. E. Carcassonne (Paris: Librairie E. Droz, 1938).

von Balthasar, Hans Urs, *Theodramatik*, 5 vols (Einsiedeln: Johannes Verlag, 1973–83); trans. Graham Harrison, *Theo-Drama, Theological Dramatic Theory*, 5 vols (San Francisco: Ignatius Press, 1988–98).

Vorobiev, V. (ed.), *Za Khrista postradavshie, goneniya na Russkuyu Pravoslavnuyu Tserkov, 1917–1956, II, L-Ya* (Moscow: St Tikhon Orthodox Theological Institute, 1997).

Vulcănescu, Mircea, *Ultimul Cuvânt şi Alte Texte*, ed., notes, and a chronology by Măriuca Vulcănescu, annex with a letter from Emil Cioran and a portrait by Mircea Eliade (Bucharest: Crater, 2000).

Walsh, David, *After Ideology: Recovering the Spiritual Foundations of Freedom* (New York: HarperCollins, 1990).

Ward, Benedicta (ed.), *The Wisdom of the Desert Fathers: Apophthegmata Patrum* (The Anonymous Series), trans. with an introd. by Sister Benedicta Ward, SLG, foreword by Archbishop Anthony Bloom (Oxford: SLG Press, 1975).

Ware, Kallistos, 'Tradition and Personal Experience in Later Byzantine Theology', *Eastern Church Review*, 3:2, Autumn 1970, pp. 131–41.

Ware, Kallistos, 'The Debate about Palamism', *Eastern Churches Review*, 9:1–2, 1977, pp. 45–63.

Ware, Kallistos, 'The Orthodox Experience of Repentance', *Sobornost* 2:1, 1980, pp. 18–28.

Ware, Kallistos, 'What is a Martyr?', *Sobornost*, 5:1, 1983, pp. 7–18.

Ware, Kallistos, 'The Hesychasts: Gregory of Sinai, Gregory Palamas, Nicolas Cabasilas', in Cheslyn Jones, et al., *The Study of Sprituality* (London: SPCK, 1986), pp. 242–55.

Ware, Kallistos, 'The Understanding of Salvation in the Orthodox Tradition', in *For Us and Our Salvation: Seven Perspectives on Christian Soteriology*, ed. Rienk Lanooy (Utrecht-Leiden: Interuniversitair Instituut voor Missiologie en Oecumenica, 1994), pp. 107–31.

Ware, Kallistos, *The Inner Kingdom* (Crestwood, NY: St Vladimir's Seminary Press, 2000).

Weber, Max, *The Protestant Ethic and the Spirit of Capitalism*, trans. Talcott Parsons, introd. by Anthony Giddens (London: Routledge, 1996).

Webster, John B., 'The Imitation of Christ', *The Tyndale Biblical Theological Lecture*, 1985, pp. 95–120.

Webster, John B., 'Christology, Imitability and Ethics', *Scottish Journal of Theology*, 39:3, August 1986, pp. 309–26.

Wheelwright, Philip, *Heraclitus* (Oxford: Oxford University Press, 1999).

Williams, Rowan (ed.), *Sergii Bulgakov, Towards a Russian Political Theology*, with comment. by Rowan Williams (Edinburgh: T. & T. Clark, 1999).

Wolff, Kurt H., *The Sociology of Georg Simmel*, trans., and introd. Kurt H. Wolff (London: Free Press, 1950).

Wölfflin, Heinrich, *Renaissance and Baroque*, trans. Kathrin Simon, introd. by Peter Murray (London: Fontana, 1964).

World Health Organisation, 'Constitution of the World Health Organisation', *Official Record of the World Health Organisation*, nr. 2, 1946, p. 100.

Wurmbrand, Richard, *In God's Underground*, ed. Charles Foley (London: W.H. Allen, 1968).

Yannaras, Christos, *The Freedom of Morality*, trans. Elizabeth Briere, foreword by Kallistos Ware (Crestwood, NY: St Vladimir's Seminary Press, 1996).

Zaehner, Robert C., *Mysticism: Sacred and Profane* (Oxford: Clarendon Press, 1957).

Zamfirescu, Dan, *A Fundamental Book of European Culture* (Bucharest: Roza Vânturilor, 1991).

Zugravu, Nelu, *Geneza Creştinismului Popular al Românilor* (Bucharest: Ministerul Educaţiei, Institutul Român de Tracologie, Bibliotheca Thracologica, XVIII, 1997).

Index

McGinn, Bernard 132
madness, *see* mental illness
magician 183–4
maieutics 3 n3
Makarenko, Anton 68
Mallarmé, Stéphane 234
Marcel, Gabriel 112
Mărculescu, Radu 62–3, 64
Marcus Aurelius 247
Marx, Karl xiii, 11, 37, 64, 88, 89, 104, 105,
    140, 163, 188
Marxism 36, 143, 237, 242
    co-operative principle and 89
    critique of religion 89, 104
    see also labour theory of value
masks 215–31
    Communist stage 230–31
    divine mask 218, 220–21
    human mask 218, 223–5
    primordial mask 217–18, 220–21
    rôle and 226–8
    stage as sacred space 228–30
    theology of 215–26
    unmasking as part of re-education 24, 67,
        71, 79, 85–6
Mateiaş, Virgil 68 n22
materialism 88–9 n87, 236
    dialectical materialism 64, 127, 163
materiality 90, 245, 256
    as createdness 254
    and nuance 245
    of the human psyche 107
matter 102, 107–8 n95, 172, 173, 245, 254
Maxim, Virgil 285
Maximus the Confessor, Saint 125, 161, 217
Mazilu, Dumitru 27
Meinong, Alexius von 203
mental illness 117–18, 122–7
    nebun 127 n200
    spiritual foolishness and 123–4
metaphysical autism 121–2, 187
metaphysical pessimism 259–60
Michael the Brave 271
Mihai I, King 21, 22, 64, 274, 275
mimesis 112–13, 191
miracle 14, 169
Mircea Eliade (Ţuţea) 160
monarchy 16
    Romanian 19, 21, 64, 272–5

monastic tradition, *see* Hesychasm
monism 254
Montaigne, Michel de 235
Munteanu, Marian 28
mystagogy 111, 174
mystery 51, 103, 112, 122, 135, 154, 261,
    266
    of God 100
    mysterium tremendum et fascinans 185
    sacred language as 184–6
    system and 135–44
    Ţuţea's understanding of 154
mysticism 50
    definition of 51 n18
    mystical knowledge 51, 134, 143–4, 180
    mystical triangles 139–41, 162, 178
    mystical union 178–82, 211, 280
    mystical view of theatre 203–4
    Platonic 51, 175
    see also health
myths 103, 154, 176

Nandriş-Cudla, Aniţa 62 n6
Napoleon I Bonaparte 210
Năstase, Puiu 70
National Christian Party 273
National Liberal Party 31, 42, 45, 273, 275
National Peasant Party 9, 273, 275
National Revolution Manifesto (1935) 16–18
National Socialism 16
national sovereignty 14, 40
nationalism
    Romanian 8, 16, 29–35, 271
    Russian 119
    Ţuţea and 29–35, 44
nature 104, 234
    and culture 162
    environment 36, 37
    see also mystical triangles
Neagu, Mihai 129 n1
Nellas, Panayiotis 102
neurosis 106–7
Newton, Isaac 134–5
Nicholas Cabasilas, Saint xx
Nicholas of Cusa 166, 168
Nicholl, Donald xii
Nichols, Aidan 229
Nietzsche, Friedrich 92, 93, 94, 161, 163,
    188, 207–8, 210, 211, 223